MARY BERRY'S
COMPLETE
COOKBOOK

MARY BERRY'S
COMPLETE COOKBOOK

DK

LONDON, NEW YORK, MELBOURNE, MUNICH, AND DELHI

ORIGINAL 1995 EDITION: Editorial consultant Jeni Wright,
Art editor Bill Mason, **Design development** Grade Design
Consultants, **Managing editor** Gillian Roberts, **Managing art
editor** Karen Sawyer, **Category publisher** Mary-Clare Jerram
REVISED 2003 EDITION: Photographer Edward Allwright,
Food stylist Vicki Smallwood, **Stylist** Rosie Hopper

UPDATED 2012 EDITION
Editorial consultant Jeni Wright
Senior art editor Sara Robin
Senior editor Laura Nickoll
Senior jackets creative Nicola Powling
Managing editor Dawn Henderson
Managing art editor Christine Keilty
Production editors Siu Yin Chan, Clare McLean
Creative Technical Support Sonia Charbonnier
Photographer William Shaw
Food stylists Jane Lawrie, Emma Jane Frost, Fergal Connolly,
Laura Fyfe, Vicki Smallwood
Editorial assistance Andrew Roff, David Fentiman

DK INDIA
Senior art editor Neha Ahuja
Senior editor Chitra Subramanyam
Editors Aditi Batra, Ligi John
Art editors Simran Kaur, Mansi Nagdev, Divya PR, Aastha Tiwari
Managing editor Glenda Fernandes
Managing art editor Navidita Thapa
CTS manager Sunil Sharma
Senior DTP designer Tarun Sharma
Production manager Pankaj Sharma
DTP designers Neeraj Bhatia, Arjinder Singh

First published in Great Britain in 1995
This updated edition published in 2012
by Dorling Kindersley Limited
80 Strand, London WC2R 0RL
Penguin Group (UK)
   4 6 8 10 9 7 5
007 – 181952 – Feb/12

A CIP catalogue record for this book is available
from The British Library

ISBN 978 1 4053 7095 0

Colour reproduction by Media Development & Printing Ltd, UK
Printed and bound in Italy by L.E.G.O. S.p.A.

Discover more at **www.dk.com**

Contents

Special Menu Index

The index on pages 6–11 is an easy-to-use reference and visual guide to choosing a special dish, whether you are cooking for a celebration, planning a party, or simply looking to expand your culinary repertoire. Some of the menus present a complete main course – Christmas Roast Turkey, for example. Others – as in Fresh Ways with Salmon Fillets – show how to ring the changes on old favourites. There is inspiration from Italy, India, and Japan as well as indulgent treats to satisfy the sweetest tooth. Whichever dish takes your fancy, I hope you will have as much fun choosing as making and eating it.

First Courses

Tapas   **60**

Vegetables with garlic dips Boiled or grilled vegetables with spicy or garlic mayonnaises.

Chick pea and red pepper salad An earthy salad of contrasting textures.

Andalucian mushrooms Serrano ham brings the taste of Southern Spain to this dish.

Tuna tostados Toasted garlic breads topped with tuna, tomato, and melting cheese.

Prepare-Ahead First Courses   **68**

Asparagus and quails' egg salad An extremely simple starter that always impresses.

Double salmon tian Individual fresh salmon and soft-cheese rounds on peppery salad leaves, topped with luxurious smoked salmon.

Smoked salmon terrine The richness of the salmon is tempered by low-fat cheese and the snap of creamed horseradish.

Poultry and Game

Chicken and Turkey Salads   **160**

Tarragon chicken with avocado A classic combination enlivened with anchovies, and garnished with peppery watercress.

Vietnamese turkey salad With fish sauce, chilli, mint, and crunchy white cabbage.

Red pepper herbed chicken salad A low-fat and colourful salad with a mouthwatering dressing that includes basil and parsley.

Marinated Barbecued Chicken   **170**

Fruity coriander barbecued chicken Aromatic chicken drumsticks with a fresh mango salsa.

Yogurt and mint barbecued chicken A couscous salad with pine nuts complements the Middle Eastern flavours of this dish.

Orange and rosemary barbecued chicken Tangy chicken with a colourful and spicy salsa.

Fish and Shellfish

Simple Fish Sushi 118

Nigiri sushi Bite-sized mouthfuls of prawn, delicious sticky rice, and fiery wasabi (Japanese horseradish) paste.

Sushi squares with smoked salmon A modern interpretation of sushi, topped with palate-cleansing pickled ginger slices.

Hoso maki Rolls of seaweed with vinegared sushi rice, crabmeat, and cucumber.

Classic Buffet Party Salmon 126

Whole poached salmon A perfect centrepiece for a summer celebration. The fish is poached with black peppercorns, bay leaves, and other aromatics for added flavour, then served cold, with jumbo prawns to garnish, and the traditional accompaniment, fresh dill mayonnaise. Impressive, yet easily made at home.

Fresh Ways with Salmon Fillets 136

Herb roasted salmon A breadcrumb, parsley, and cheese topping keeps the fish moist.

Thai chilli salmon Spicy salmon fillets with chilli, lime, and a coriander garnish.

Griddled salmon tranches Served with a crème fraîche and dill sauce.

Warm honeyed salmon salad Served with a herbed yogurt dressing.

Poultry and Game

Meat Dishes

Christmas Roast Turkey 176

Golden roast turkey A festive feast with all the traditional trimmings – a chestnut, bacon, and pork sausagemeat stuffing, rich gravy, bread sauce flavoured with onion, cloves, bay leaf, and black peppercorns, fruity cranberry sauce, crispy bacon rolls, and chipolata sausages.

Chicken and Turkey Stir-Fries 184

Lacquered duck A new take on a classic dish, sticky, sweet, and satisfying.

Chinese chicken with mango Marinated chicken stir-fried with cashew nuts, peppers, pak choi, mushrooms, and mango.

Turkey to go A serve-yourself combination of spiced turkey and red pepper to wrap in warm, soft tortillas – appetizing, and fun to eat as well.

Mexican Buffet Party 216

Chargrilled steaks with red vegetables Juicy steaks, onions, and peppers served with the Mexican classic, refried beans.

Vegetarian enchiladas Crispy tortillas oozing with cheese, beans, and spicy tomato sauce served with guacamole.

Mexican bean salad Nutritious and tasty, this combination of beans in a herby dressing makes an ideal buffet party dish.

Meat Dishes

The Best Burgers   226

Thai beef burgers Top quality beef, lightly spiced and formed into burgers, ideal with a crunchy salad or raw vegetables strips alongside.

Lamb burgers Served in warm pitta bread with a cool cucumber and mint yogurt.

Veggie burgers Meatless but protein-packed, made with beans, cheese, carrots, pine nuts, and dried apricots.

Kebabs on the Barbecue   240

Beef and red onion kebabs Classic steak and onions with all the flavour of food cooked on the grill.

Curried lamb kebabs Chunks of lamb in a spicy yogurt marinade with coriander and mint.

Oriental pork kebabs Pork and pineapple combine to make this a dish with a difference.

Sausage and sesame kebabs Served with a side dish of grilled vegetables.

Pasta, Rice, and Noodles

Easy Pasta Supper Dishes   300

Fusilli with double tomatoes Pasta spirals tossed with asparagus, mushrooms, fresh cherry tomatoes, and sun-dried tomatoes.

Red hot ragù A lively pasta dish of pork sausagemeat, chillies, and a spicy tomato sauce.

Rigatoni with mushrooms and rocket Wilted rocket leaves add pep to this dish of pasta, mushrooms, and a creamy pesto sauce.

Vegetarian Dishes

Vegetable Casseroles   270

Roasted vegetable medley Cauliflower, butter beans, carrots, and other tasty vegetables caramelized in a hot oven and dressed with herbs.

Mushroom Stroganoff A vegetable twist on the classic (beef) dish – artichoke hearts, peppers, and mushrooms in a creamy wine sauce.

Spicy pumpkin casserole Sweet-tasting parsnips, pumpkin, potatoes, and onions, lightly curried. Garnished with chopped fresh coriander.

Vegetarian Bakes   276

Majorcan tumbet casserole Layers of vegetables in a tomato sauce flavoured with garlic and rosemary.

Kilkerry pie Potatoes and leeks in a tangy cheese sauce topped with crisp filo pastry.

Tuscan cannelloni Beans, sun-dried tomatoes, and a creamy blue cheese make up the filling in this Italian pasta dish.

Vegetarian Curries   280

Niramish Vegetables, including red peppers and green beans, in a rich coconut milk sauce.

Sag aloo Spinach (sag) and potato (aloo) with mustard and cumin seeds, onion, garlic, fresh root ginger, and other spices. Served with a dollop of cooling yogurt.

Dhal A hearty and nutritious lentil dish flavoured with cinnamon, coriander seed, and cumin – the perfect accompaniment to any curry.

Ravioli 306

Chicken and prosciutto ravioli Parcels of Italian cured ham and chicken in a tomato and basil sauce.

Ricotta and spinach ravioli A familiar flavour combination, best simply served with butter, Parmesan, and freshly ground black pepper.

Crab and prawn ravioli Seafood parcels that melt in the mouth, in a fragrant coriander sauce.

Oriental Noodle Dishes 312

Singapore noodles A simple dish with complex flavours, made with pork and vegetables.

Szechuan noodles with water chestnuts Strong contrasts of taste and texture define this favourite Chinese dish.

Pad Thai with tiger prawns Chicken and prawns transform a traditional Thai side-dish into a heavy yet fragrant main course.

Nasi Goreng 318

Quick nasi goreng Fried rice with bean sprouts, mushrooms, and succulent prawns.

Vegetarian nasi goreng Thinly sliced white cabbage, peppers, and tomatoes in a spicy stir-fry with rice, and a garnish of omelette strips.

Chicken nasi goreng A highly seasoned rice dish with chickens, prawns, bacon, and the crunch of toasted almonds.

Oriental Vegetarian Suppers 286

Peking tofu with plum sauce Fried tofu replaces the duck in this classic Chinese dish.

Japanese noodle soup Delicately spiced, with tofu and spring onions – a meal in a bowl.

Firecracker stir-fry Pak choi, sugarsnap peas, peppers, and mushroom in a fiery stir-fry.

Thai curry The heat of the curry is tempered by the coconut milk. Served with jasmine rice.

Chargrilled Vegetable Platter 342

For barbeque or grill An assortment of fresh vegetables – aubergines, courgettes, red and yellow peppers, red onion, asparagus, pattypan, squash, and mushrooms – brushed with good olive oil, then grilled until sweet and tender, and lightly charred. Serve hot as a side dish with any meat or firm fish, or cold as an unusual salad.

Fresh and Light Salads 352

Italian pesto salad Broccoli, cauliflower, and black olives with the classic Italian basil sauce.

Puy lentil salad A simple salad dressed with a sharp-sweet balsamic vinegar and olive oil.

Tabbouleh Nutritious, nutty bulgur wheat, lifted by the refreshing taste of mint and lemon.

Herb salad with orange and mustard dressing A tangy orange and mustard dressing is tossed with fine asparagus, sun-dried tomatoes, and leaves including lamb's lettuce.

Yeast Cookery

Thin-Crust Pizzas   372

Mini pizzas Perfect for snacks, with goat's cheese, black olives, artichokes, and Parma ham.

Four seasons pizza Salami and oregano, mozzarella and mushrooms, anchovies and black olives, and sweet red peppers top each of the four quarters.

Napoletana pizza Anchovies are the definitive ingredient in this typical Italian pizza.

Tuna and caper pizza An easy, quickly made pizza, using ingredients from the storecupboard.

Danish Pastries   376

Crescents Filled with pure almond paste – the connoisseur's choice for breakfast, or at any time.

Kites A double-almond delight, pastry filled with almond paste and topped with toasted almonds.

Pinwheels Filled with almond paste and topped with a cherry.

Envelopes Almond paste and apricots, drizzled with a sweet white icing.

Chilled Desserts

Red Fruit Desserts   424

Port and claret jelly For adults only. Served with seasonal fresh berries or currants.

Raspberry passion Fresh raspberries topped with a mixture of crème fraîche, yogurt, and passion fruit, and a sprinkling of brown sugar.

Cranberry and vodka sparkle Clear and jewel-like, another jelly just for the grown-ups.

Jubilee trifle Sponge cake, jam, cherries, and pears topped with custard and whipped cream.

Pies, Tarts, and Hot Desserts

Dessert Fondues   394

Dark chocolate fondue A velvety-textured fondue with a subtle hint of orange.

White chocolate fondue Sumptuous and rich, for dipping fresh fruits or crisp biscuits.

Chocolate fudge fondue A really special treat for those indulgent moments – two favourite flavours blended and enriched with butter, syrup, and cream.

The Apple Collection   406

Classic apple crumble Tart cooking apples, flavoured with sugar and lemon zest, then topped with a sweet crumble and baked until golden brown. Traditionally served with custard.

Apple tarte au citron A light lemon and apple filling that is both sweet and sharp, baked in a butter-rich shortcrust pastry shell.

Blackberry and apple cobbler Warming and comforting, with a scone topping.

Fruit Tartlets   414

Raspberry tartlets Slightly sharp berries with sweetened mascarpone in a light pastry shell.

Tropical tartlets Delicate almond pastry shells, filled with creamy custard, and topped with mandarin oranges, apricots, and toasted almonds.

Blueberry puffs Layers of puff pastry, cream, and blueberries, with additional fruitiness coming from sliced peaches or nectarines.

Chilled Desserts

Meringues   432

Fresh fruit baskets Berries of your choice, cream, and meringue served with raspberry sauce.

Mocha meringue mille-feuilles Thin discs of meringue and almonds layered with sweetened coffee cream.

Chocolate meringue shells Crisp, light meringue shells, drizzled with melted plain chocolate, then sandwiched together with a rich chocolate cream.

Fresh Fruit Salads   438

Fruits of the forest salad Balsamic vinegar and green peppercorns add zip to fresh berries.

Spiced fruit salad A mix of succulent dried fruits, with vanilla and star anise.

Orange passion salad Just fruit: oranges, papaya, passionfruit, and lime juice, with no added sugar.

Tropical island fruit salad Physalis and Asian pears star in this unusual salad.

Sorbets   446

Lime, apricot, raspberry, and pear and ginger So easy to make, from a basic mixture of sugar, water, and egg white, sorbets capture the vivid colours and pure flavours of your favourite fruits in a light, low-fat refreshing mouthful. The perfect ending to a rich meal or (for a special occasion) try offering a small serving between courses as a palate cleanser.

Cakes and Teabreads

Small Chocolate Cakes   460

Best-ever brownies Soft, moist squares of chocolate with the added crunch of walnuts.

Chocolate cup cakes Enjoy a whole chocolate cake all to yourself, embellished with smooth chocolate icing.

Double-chocolate muffins Bitter cocoa powder and best-quality dark chocolate chips, enhanced with a little strong coffee, for a deeply chocolatey experience.

Christmas Cakes   468

Candied fruit cake A traditional rich fruit cake with a spectacular topping of apricot jam, nuts, and candied fruit and peel. Finished with a colourful ribbon.

Snow white cake Fairytale icing hides a delicious secret – a moist cake packed with dried fruits, nuts, and candied citrus peel, covered with a layer of home-made marzipan. Decorated with fresh cranberries and silver dragees, or as you wish.

Choux Pastries   478

Coffee éclairs Oozing with whipped cream and topped with a silky coffee icing.

Religieuses Fresh from the patisserie: tiny cream-filled choux buns sitting atop larger ones, crowned with a decadent chocolate icing.

Chocolate profiteroles Golden choux pastry baked until light as air, then split, filled with whipped cream, and drizzled with a creamy warm chocolate sauce. Who could resist?

Foreword

Mary Berry's Complete Cookbook has been the reliable, trusted companion of home cooks for many years. But much has changed since it was first published. We lead busier lives, fulfilling greater dreams. We entertain less formally than in the past, but so much more comfortably, often in the warmth of a cosy kitchen where guests can chat with the cook and enjoy the fun of preparing a meal together. Travel has broadened our horizons, and given us a taste for different foods.

Now, we know what it means to eat well in the modern sense, downplaying butter and sugar and rich sauces, preparing healthier meals using natural ingredients, and letting their flavour and freshness shine through. Fortunately, there's an abundance of good foods available – seasonal fruits and vegetables; fresh fish and lean meat; locally produced cheeses and interesting artisan breads not mass produced but lovingly formed by hand and baked in the traditional way. Supermarkets as well as small neighbourhood shops have responded to our more adventurous tastes – acquired during holidays to exotic destinations – and provide us with all manner of unusual ingredients, including the herbs, spices, and flavourings that enhance the appeal of simple ingredients.

This new edition of the book takes account of all these changes while retaining the features that made the original one so special – the visual recipe choosers at the beginning of each chapter, the ease of use, and the knowledge that each one of the tried-and-tested recipes can be made with absolute confidence of a great result. In preparing the book, I've been enormously helped by my assistant, Lucy Young, who helped to develop the new recipes and lent her youthful view to the enterprise, and my editor, Jeni Wright, who suggested many good changes. My grateful thanks to them both.

Mary Berry

Penn, Buckinghamshire

Useful Information

Equipment

Good equipment makes cooking easy. With top-quality knives, pots and pans, and other utensils, you will be able to cook efficiently and with pleasure. If you are equipping your first kitchen, the bare minimum is all that is required – there is no need for fancy utensils to turn out delicious meals. As your experience grows, you can gradually add to your collection, buying more specialist and unusual items as your skills increase.

Always buy the best equipment you can afford – it is false economy to save money, because cheap equipment simply will not last. Using a thin pan in which food always sticks and burns, or trying to chop vegetables with a flimsy knife, will soon turn cooking into a chore.

Measuring equipment

Even experienced cooks need accurate measuring tools to ensure ingredients are in correct proportion to one another – vital when baking – or the right size, or at the optimum temperature.

▪ **Kitchen scales** may be balance, electronic, or spring-operated. Balance scales give the most accurate results, especially for small amounts. Being strong and simple in construction, with no complicated mechanism to wear out, they will last a lifetime. Electronic scales, which run on batteries, are not very accurate with amounts under 30 g (1 oz), but have the advantage that many can be returned to zero when weighing more than one ingredient in the bowl at the same time.

▪ **Measuring jugs** made of toughened glass are very useful – those made from clear plastic are usually cheaper but will not withstand the heat of boiling liquid. Buy the biggest measuring jug you can store (it can be used for mixing too), and with both metric and imperial calibrations marked on the outside. New and ingenious is an angled measuring jug that allows you to check the accuracy of measurements either from the side or by looking straight down into it.

▪ **Measuring cups**, as used in American recipes, are normally sold in sets of four: 1 cup (which holds 250 ml or 8 fl oz), ½ cup, ⅓ cup, and ¼ cup. In the US, and in other countries such as Canada and Australia, both dry ingredients and liquids are measured by volume in standard cups (dry ingredients levelled across the top).

▪ **Measuring spoons,** for accurate dispensing of small amounts, usually come in nesting sets of four as follows: 15 ml (1 tablespoon), 5 ml (1 teaspoon), 2.5 ml (½ teaspoon), and 1.25 ml (¼ teaspoon). Unless a recipe specifies a heaped spoon of a dry ingredient, it should be levelled off with a knife.

▪ **A meat thermometer**, to measure the internal temperature of meat and poultry during cooking, takes the guesswork out of roasting, and ensures thorough, safe cooking. The most common type is inserted into the meat or poultry before cooking begins, whereas instant-read thermometers and thermo forks are used as a spot check during cooking or at the end of the cooking time (these types are very useful when grilling and barbecuing).

▪ **A deep-frying thermometer** checks the temperature of the oil to be sure of the best and crispiest fried results, but the safest way to deep-fry is to use an electric deep-fat fryer that has its own built-in thermometer.

▪ **A sugar thermometer** performs the same function as a deep-frying thermometer, but for sugar syrups.

▪ **A tape measure** and/or a ruler will enable you to roll or cut pastry and pasta to the correct dimensions, and also check that pans and tins are the required size.

▪ **An automatic timer** helps avoid overcooking disasters when you are busy and forget to watch the clock.

Pots and pans

On the hob, pans need to be heavy enough to sit securely without tipping, yet not so heavy that you have trouble lifting them. A heavy base is important for gentle, even heat distribution. Pots and pans also need to have lids that fit tightly and sturdy handles that stay cool. Ovenproof handles make it easy to transfer pots and pans from the hob to the oven, when necessary.

- **Saucepans with straight sides** have a multitude of uses, from sauces and vegetables to soups and stews. You need a minimum of three in different sizes, starting with one about 1.5 litres (2½ pints) in capacity. Two handles on larger pans make for easier lifting, and if the handles are short and made of metal the pan can also double up as a casserole in the oven.

- **A small milk pan**, about 1 litre (1¾ pints) in capacity, should have a non-stick coating (milk and cream sauces tend to stick) and pouring lips on both sides.

- **A pasta pan** is tall and fairly narrow, with a perforated inner basket that lifts out for draining; some have an additional insert for steaming. A pasta pan can also be used for steaming puddings, and for making stock and large quantities of soup.

- **A steamer** at its simplest is a collapsible basket that fits inside a large saucepan. Special steamer pans have steamer compartments with perforated bases, which stack on top of each other. Chinese stacking bamboo steamers that fit inside a wok are an alternative.

- **A wok** with one long handle is easier to use than a wok with two small handles, and one with a flat base is most stable on both gas and electric hobs. The cheapest Chinese woks are made from unseasoned carbon steel; if pre-seasoned or non-stick, the wok will be easier to clean. A large wok (35 cm/14 in across the top) is the most versatile. Many come complete with lids (very useful) and cooking tools.

- **A sauté pan** is more versatile than a frying pan because it has deeper sides. Choose from stainless steel or non-stick (the most useful size is 23–28 cm/9–11 in). Non-stick pans with titanium coatings are the best, because they can be used with metal utensils.

- **An omelette pan**, shallow with curved sides, is often made of cast iron or stainless steel; a non-stick finish is easier to use. A 16 cm (5½ in) pan is the right size for a 2-egg French omelette, a 23 cm (9 in) pan for a thick, flat Spanish or Italian omelette. A shallower crêpe or pancake pan is an optional extra.

- **The chargrill pan** is traditionally made of ridged cast iron, but non-stick pans are equally good, especially ones with deep sides that allow for making a sauce in the pan. For low-fat cooking, deep ridges will lift the food out of the fat, and give a "barbecued" finish.

Materials for cookware

- **Copper** (an excellent heat conductor) reacts chemically with food, air, and liquid, so copper pans must be lined. Stainless steel has replaced tin and silver as the most common lining. Lined copper pans are truly the best, preferred by many professional chefs, but they are expensive and heavy.

- **Stainless steel** is lightweight and durable but not a very good heat conductor, so the bases of stainless steel pans for use on the hob are usually "sandwiched" with aluminium, copper, or a copper and silver alloy. Pans with such heavy-gauge bases are expensive but should last a lifetime. Ovenware is usually limited to roasting tins.

- **Cast iron** can be heated to a high temperature, so cast-iron pans, such as chargrills, are perfect for cooking food quickly and evenly. It also retains and transmits low heat well so is appropriate for long, slow cooking too. Cast-iron pans need to be "seasoned" before use, so food does not stick, and must be thoroughly dried after washing to prevent rusting. Enamelled cast iron will not rust, and is good for flameproof casseroles as it makes very strong, sturdy (though heavy) vessels.

- **Aluminium** (another efficient heat conductor) scratches easily and can react with acidic foods, giving them a metallic taste. It is usually covered with another material, such as stainless steel or a non-stick coating.

- **Glass** is not as good a conductor of heat as metal, so pastry baked in thick, ovenproof glass will never be as crisp as that baked in a metal tin, but it is very useful for baking dishes, and for taking straight from oven to table.

- **Porcelain, stoneware, and glazed earthenware** are quite tough and sturdy materials for ovenware (take care not to chip or crack them), and most can double as serving dishes.

- **Non-stick** coatings make pans and tins quick and easy to clean. Some coatings are readily scratched and wear off with time; other, newer versions, such as titanium, are more durable and can be used with metal utensils.

Ovenware

Cooking in the oven requires sturdy vessels that conduct and retain heat efficiently. For convenience, choose oven-to-table dishes that are attractive enough for serving too. The choice of metal or ceramic, non-stick or uncoated, depends largely on the job you want the tins or dishes to do. Whatever you buy, look after it to avoid rusting and scratching.

- **A roasting tin** needs to be deep, strong, and rigid. If possible, have two in different sizes, one of them as big as your oven will take. Too small a tin makes it difficult to baste the meat or poultry properly; roasting in a tin that is too large will cause juices to evaporate and burn. With a lip or spout on the edge of the tin you can pour off juices; a rack that fits inside the tin enables meat to be roasted free of its fat. Hinged racks can be folded to cradle a bird.

- **Baking sheets** have many uses – to bake biscuits, meringues, small pastries, pizzas – and to provide a heat-conducting base for pastry cases; you'll need at least two. Buy the largest that will fit comfortably in your oven, and be sure they are heavy-duty, inflexible, and completely flat. Good-quality non-stick coatings are a boon when it comes to cleaning.

- **Loaf tins** with deep sides are used for baking breads and cakes, and for pâtés and terrines. Two different sizes are needed: one 500 g (1 lb) and the other 1 kg (2 lb). Some have hinged drop-down sides.

- **A deep loose-bottomed cake tin**, round or square and 20 or 23 cm (8 or 9 in) in diameter, is used mainly for rich fruit cakes.

- **A springform cake tin** is ideal for delicate cakes, cheesecakes, and layered mousse cakes – it has a clasp on the side to open the tin and release the base, so the cake can be removed easily. Tins with a removable central tube and fluted base can double as a tube tin.

- **Sandwich or sponge tins** are round and shallow. For making layered cakes, you will need two. The most useful size is 20 cm (8 in) in diameter.

- **The shallow Swiss roll tin** usually measures 23 x 33 cm (9 x 13 in). It is used for both sweet and savoury sponge mixtures and roulades; a non-stick coating makes unmoulding these very simple. The tin can also double as a small baking tray.

- **A traybake tin** is similar to a Swiss roll tin in size, but it is deeper. It is used for baking cake mixtures that are cut into squares or rectangles for serving.

- **A muffin or bun tin/sheet** will bake American muffins and fruit buns as well as cup cakes and individual Yorkshire puddings. Tins may have 6 or 12 holes or cups, and the width and depth of the holes varies according to what is to be baked.

- **A pie tin** has plain, sloping sides and a lip for the pie edging. A good all-purpose size is 23 cm (9 in) measured across the top.

- **An oval pie dish** with a wide lip is traditional for deep-dish sweet and savoury pies.

- **A shallow fluted tin** 20 or 23 cm (8 or 9 in) in diameter is best for making quiches and sweet and savoury tarts, as the fluted edge helps to strengthen the fragile pastry case. For easy serving, choose a metal tin with a loose bottom: lift the quiche or tart from the side of the tin and serve it on the tin base. Or bake in a fluted ceramic dish and serve from it.

- **A straight-sided, deep soufflé dish**, 1.4 litres (2¼ pints) in capacity, can double as a baking dish for crumbles and other puddings. Small soufflé dishes and ramekins are used for individual soufflés, and baked puddings such as crème caramel, baked eggs, and mousses. Average capacity is 150 ml (¼ pint). Both soufflé dishes and ramekins can be brought straight from the oven to the table.

- **Gratin and baking dishes** come in many different shapes and sizes, and are very versatile. They are used for making vegetable and other gratins, baked pasta dishes, shepherd's pie, and moussaka, and for baking fish and puddings of all kinds; also for roasting. Most gratin and baking dishes will resist very high temperatures, which means they can be put under the grill as well as into a hot oven.

- **A range of casseroles** in various sizes, and with tight-fitting lids, is also useful. Choose ones that are described as "flameproof", which means they can be used on the hob as well as in the oven.

- **Re-usable baking mats** or cooking liners spread out in a baking sheet or tin will prevent sticking. These are non-stick, and are good for low-fat cooking as usually no added fat or oil is needed. They are re-usable, and save on washing-up as they can be wiped clean.

Electric equipment

There is an ever-increasing choice of electric appliances to help you in the kitchen. Equipping yourself with the full range is costly and wastes storage space, so when buying, think carefully about what you cook and how often you are likely to use the appliance.

- **Electric mixers** work much faster than whisking and mixing by hand. They may be compact and hand-held or large and heavy-duty, standing on the worktop. The hand-held mixer is good for whisking egg whites and whipping cream, and can be used in a pan over the heat. Choose a powerful one with at least three speeds, and check that the beaters are easy to remove for cleaning. To mix cake batters and bread doughs efficiently, choose a large mixer with a stand and bowl. Most have a dough hook attachment for kneading and some come with a separate blender, mincer, juice extractor, pasta maker, potato peeler, and a shredder and slicer. Of course, mixers like this are expensive and take up space.

- **Blenders**, also called liquidizers, make smooth soups, sauces, vegetable purées, dips, batters, and drinks. Look for a model with a large container, and blades set low to cope with small quantities. **A hand-held blender**, a less expensive and more portable version, will purée soup directly in a pan or small quantities in a beaker or deep bowl. It is easier to wash up than the free-standing blender and takes up less storage space.

- **A food processor** almost eliminates the need for a free-standing blender. Different blades chop, grate, slice, or purée all kinds of ingredients, or mix pastry and bread doughs. The more expensive the processor, the more sophisticated the jobs it will do. Some come with a mini bowl for processing small quantities, which is particularly useful for herbs, spices, and nuts.

- **Electric grinders** will quickly produce freshly ground coffee or spices, and can also be used for grinding nuts and breadcrumbs.

- **An ice-cream maker, bread machine, pasta machine, rice cooker, slow cooker, contact grill, and thermostatically controlled deep-fryer** are nice items to have if space and budget permit.

Cutting tools

A set of sturdy, well-made, and sharpened knives is vital for efficient food preparation. Make sure they are comfortable to hold: the best balanced have the metal of the blade running through the handle, which should be securely riveted, or the knife may be made from a whole piece of metal. Keep knives on a magnetic strip, or in a knife block, rather than in a drawer where they will not keep so sharp but will be dangerous to fingers.

- **A small knife**, with a rigid, pointed 7 or 10 cm (3 or 4 in) blade makes trimming fruit and vegetables easy.

- **A paring knife** is similar in shape to the small knife but slightly larger – its blade is 12 or 15 cm (5 or 6 in) long. Use it for fine work, such as peeling (paring) and cutting cores from apple quarters and peppers.

- **A small serrated knife**, with a thin, flexible blade, is ideal for slicing lemons, tomatoes, and other fruits and vegetables with tough or slippery skins.

- **The chef's or cook's knife**, with a rigid, heavy, wide blade 19 or 20 cm (about 8 in) long that tapers to a pointed tip, is the all-purpose cutting tool, unbeatable for slicing and chopping vegetables and fruit into dice, and for chopping herbs.

- **A bread knife** has a long, thin, firm blade with a serrated edge to cut through bread crusts cleanly. Serrated knifes cannot be sharpened.

- **A carving knife** is long, thin, and flexible, with a blade that has a straight, sharp edge curving upwards towards the tip. To hold the meat firmly, use with a two-pronged carving fork that has a safety prong to prevent the knife blade from slipping towards you.

- **A cleaver** with a wide, heavy blade is the tool for tough chopping jobs.

- **The mezzaluna** has a crescent-shaped single or double blade and two handles. It works by being rocked over the food to be chopped, and is especially efficient for large quanities of tender-leafed herbs.

- **Knife sharpeners** are available in manual or electric models, or you can have your knives sharpened professionally once or twice a year. At home, sharpen them every few days – blunt knives cause accidents.

- **Cutting boards** are indispensable. Have at least two, either wooden or polypropylene/polyethylene. One should be kept for raw meat and poultry, to ensure that they do not contaminate cooked food or fruits and vegetables to be eaten raw. Always clean boards thoroughly with hot, soapy water, and dry well.

Utensils

It is essential to use the right tool for the job – a cliché but a concept that is very important in the kitchen. The wrong tools will only cause frustration and waste valuable time.

▪ **A set of mixing bowls** in varying sizes is essential. Have at least four, and choose ones that fit inside each other so that they do not take up all your storage space. Toughened glass is heatproof and versatile, and gives you an all-round view of what you are mixing.

▪ **Flexible rubber or plastic spatulas**, either flat or spoon-shaped, will scrape bowls clean so nothing is wasted, and they are good for folding mixtures too. Have at least two, one for savoury and the other for sweet mixtures.

▪ **Wooden spoons and spatulas**, in varying sizes, are useful for all kinds of tasks, both in preparation and cooking. Wooden spoons will mix and beat; with long handles they are good for stirring mixtures on the hob (they won't scratch a pan). A spoon with a corner will reach right to the edges or the bottom corner of the pan. The flat-sided spatula can be used for folding mixtures together. It doubles up as a lifter and turner too.

▪ **A slotted (or perforated) spoon** is invaluable when removing food from liquids for serving or testing for doneness, and for skimming fat or scum off the surface of stocks and soups. It is also essential for draining fat or oil from food you have fried, either before further cooking or serving.

▪ **A fish slice** is used for any solid food that needs turning in the pan or lifting carefully from pan to plate. It is especially useful for delicate foods like fish (hence its name) that have a tendency to break up.

▪ **Tongs** are also useful for turning and moving pieces of hot food, such as when chargrilling, and for moving long pasta like spaghetti and tagliatelle from pan to plate. They grasp the food without piercing it, as a fork would do.

▪ **A palette knife** has a flat, blunt, flexible blade. Despite its name, it is used for spreading, not cutting, and for turning and lifting foods. It is useful to have two: one with a blade 23-25 cm (9-10 in) long and the other much shorter, about 13 cm (5 in). An angled or cranked metal spatula (also called an offset spatula) looks like a bent palette knife. Use it to remove slices of tart or cake from rimmed tins.

▪ **A long-handled ladle** scoops out hot liquids such as soups, stews, and pasta sauces for serving, so that they don't have to be poured from heavy pans. It can also be used for pouring batter into a pancake pan.

▪ **Whisks** incorporate air into egg whites to produce a snowy foam and into cream to thicken it. To make light work of these tasks, choose a balloon whisk with a comfortable handle and a large balloon of springy wire. A flat coil whisk is ideal for whisking a sauce over the heat or gravy in a roasting tin to produce smooth, well-blended results.

▪ **Graters** come in many guises. The most familiar are box or conical graters, which have a different grating surface on each face. Flat graters – like the individual faces on box graters – are less convenient to use as they will not stand up on their own. New style **flat graters** with handles come in a variety of ultra-sharp surfaces: fine for rapid zesting, grating, or puréeing; coarse for cheese and chocolate; ribbon graters for hard cheeses; and slicers for shavings of chocolate, Parmesan, or root ginger. Also useful are a **hand-operated rotary grater** and a **nutmeg grater**.

▪ **Vegetable peelers** either have a fixed blade, for peeling potatoes and other round fruits and vegetables, or a swivel blade for straight-sided vegetables such as carrots. Some peelers have a pointed end for digging out "eyes" from potatoes.

▪ **A garlic press** will crush garlic without fuss, although the aroma and taste will be stronger than if the garlic were chopped by hand. Be sure to choose a press with a detachable grille to make cleaning easy.

▪ **A citrus zester** has a row of small holes in its wide, flat end that remove the zest (the coloured, oil-rich part of the peel) from citrus fruits in tiny strips. The zest can then be chopped finely if wanted. To take slightly thicker strips of zest, a canelle knife is used.

▪ **Scissors** (kept solely for kitchen use) are perfect for trimming rind off bacon, snipping herbs, and a myriad other small tasks. Stainless steel ones are easy to keep clean.

▪ **Sturdy poultry shears** work like garden secateurs, making light work of jointing chicken and other birds.

▪ **A lemon squeezer** will juice halved citrus fruits of all kinds very quickly. Choose one with a well-fitting strainer to catch the pips. The traditional reamer is an attractive alternative, and it extracts a lot of juice, but you will need to strain out the pips afterwards.

▪ Buy the biggest **pestle and mortar** you can store – apart from grinding herbs, spices, and garlic it is the traditional vessel for making pounded sauces such as pesto. Porcelain is a good choice as it has the weight of marble without the prohibitive cost.

- **Sieves** sift dry ingredients and strain wet ones, and can also purée cooked fruit and vegetables. It is handy to have two, large and small, and the best material for a sieve is stainless steel because it will not rust over time.

- **A potato masher** needs to be strong and with a comfortable handle so that it can mash and purée cooked potatoes and other root vegetables efficiently. For the lightest, dry, and fluffy results, use a ricer; a dishwasher-proof model is easiest to clean.

- **A sturdy colander**, with legs or a base so it is freestanding, will ensure safe draining of hot cooked vegetables, pasta, and pulses.

- **A salad spinner** operated by a handle or pulley uses centrifugal force to remove water from salad leaves without bruising them.

- **A gravy separator** enables you to pour fat-free gravies and sauces. The jug either has two spouts, one shallow and one coming up from near the bottom, or just one deep spout. Fat, being light, will float to the surface of the gravy and can be poured off through the shallow spout (or the gravy can just be poured from beneath the fat using the deep spout).

- **A long, heavy rolling pin** is needed for pastry, hand-rolled pasta, and sweets. One that is 5–7 cm (2–3 in) in diameter is the best choice. Wooden pins are fine, although marble ones stay cooler for rolling pastry and chocolate.

- **A pastry scraper** is a small oblong of flexible plastic that resembles the tool used for smoothing plaster. It is invaluable for scraping up rich doughs that are made directly on the work surface.

- **Pastry cutters** are used for stamping out biscuits, scones, and tartlet cases. They may be plain or fluted, as well as in a wide range of shapes and sizes.

- **A pastry brush** is the best tool for glazing and sealing pastry, greasing cake tins, and basting meat. The flat, paintbrush type is easier to use than a round brush.

- **A wire rack** allows air to circulate around cakes, biscuits, and breads as they cool.

- **A piping bag and nozzles** are handy for piping cream and icings, and for shaping meringues and choux pastry.

- **A cherry stoner, apple corer, and cutlet beater** are inexpensive but useful items that don't take up space.

And don't forget...

- paper towels
- foil
- cling film
- greaseproof paper
- baking parchment
- fine white (undyed) string for trussing and tying
- cocktail sticks
- can opener
- corkscrew and bottle opener (a bottle stopper too for leftovers)
- salt and pepper mills
- small skewers for testing cakes, meat, and poultry; long metal skewers and bamboo ones for kebabs and satay
- ice-cube trays

Freezing

A freezer offers one of the most natural and economical methods of food preservation, and is invaluable in a busy household: most of the fresh food needed for a week, or even a month, can be bought in just one shopping trip and then frozen until it is needed.

Equipment needs to be airtight and moisture-proof so the food does not spoil or develop "freezer burn" – dry, grey patches on the surface of the food that are not dangerous but spoil the appearance and texture.

- **Use rigid** polythene or foil containers with lids, or freezer bags.
- **Freezer-quality** cling film, wrap, and foil are good and convenient for interleaving and wrapping.
- **Freezer tape** will seal packages securely; ordinary sticky tape peels off.

What freezes well?

- **Fruit** frozen raw will always be slightly softer after thawing, but is still good. More successful are fruits poached in syrup or juice, puréed or cut in chunks for pies and other puddings. Storage: 12 months
- **Vegetables** – most need to be blanched first (see below), or they can be frozen in cooked dishes such as soups and casseroles. Storage: 12 months
- **Meat, poultry, game birds, and fish** must be very fresh; smaller pieces are best. (Shellfish such as crabs, lobsters, and prawns are better bought frozen.) Storage: beef 8 months; lamb, veal, and pork 6 months; bacon and sausages 1 month; game birds 12 months; poultry 8 months; white fish 3 months; oily fish and shellfish 2 months

- **Fresh pasta,** both filled and unfilled. Pasta in sauces tends to turn soft when thawed, although made-up pasta dishes work well. Storage: 3 months
- **Dairy products** – the higher the fat content the better – full-fat hard cheeses freeze best. Storage: hard cheese 6 months; full-fat soft cheese 6 weeks; butter 3 months; homogenized milk and full-fat yogurt 1 month
- **Breads, pastries, and cakes** – both cooked and uncooked pastry freezes well; quiche fillings should be made with cream, not milk. Cakes are best frozen before filling or icing. Storage: most bread 6 months; crusty bread: 3 weeks; cakes and pastries 3 months

Thawing and reheating

For some foods, thawing before cooking or reheating is not necessary, but others must be thoroughly thawed before cooking. Cook thawed food immediately, to kill any bacteria, and never refreeze foods already thawed unless you cook them first.

- **Vegetables and pasta** – add directly to boiling water.
- **Fish fillets and shellfish** – cook from frozen.
- **Sauces and soups** – heat gently until thawed.
- **Thicker pieces of meat** – thaw before cooking.
- **Poultry** – unwrap, cover loosely, and thaw completely on a lipped plate in the refrigerator (bacteria multiply at room temperature).

Ways to freeze

A few simple techniques will keep frozen items at their freshest and best.

Liquids
Pour liquids into rigid containers, leaving 1 cm (½ in) headroom. Freeze until solid, then remove and re-wrap in freezer bags.

Interleaving
Separate individual items like chops and steaks so they do not stick together when frozen, then pack them in a freezer bag.

Tray freezing
Arrange delicate items like berries and meringues on trays so they freeze separately, then pack in freezer bags once solid.

Blanching
Blanch vegetables in boiling water then plunge into iced water and drain well before freezing. This helps retain colour and texture.

Microwaving

The microwave has revolutionized cooking for people with busy lifestyles. It can cook fish and many vegetables and fruit to perfection, retaining vitamins, colour, and texture, and it thaws frozen food quickly and successfully. It also performs myriad other tasks that speed preparation in the kitchen.

Special equipment is not essential for cooking in a microwave, as many containers and implements used for conventional cooking are suitable. For convenience, use the dish you want to eat from.

- **Round or oval dishes** with straight sides are the most efficient for even heat distribution.
- **Ovenproof glass** and ceramic dishes are excellent as are plastics specially made for the microwave (other plastic containers may soften and distort, or even melt and collapse). Metal tins should not be used.
- **Use large containers** for liquids, and keep stirring to avoid a build up of hot spots and prevent liquids from boiling over.

Tips for success

Arranging food properly (see below) will ensure even cooking. Just remember that microwaves penetrate food from the outside towards the middle. Covering food with a lid or cling film (not foil) prevents it from drying out during cooking and traps steam, which helps to heat the food.

- **Most microwaves** contain a turntable, which rotates the food and exposes it evenly to the microwaves.

Arranging foods

Simple, but clever, techniques will help you microwave food as quickly and efficiently as possible.

Arrange unevenly shaped food in a circle with the densest parts – for example, the thick stalks of broccoli or the meaty parts of chicken drumsticks – facing outwards in the dish.

Position foods of the same size and shape, or small individual dishes, in a circle, with space between them, so that the microwaves can penetrate and reach the food from all sides.

- **If cooking** in a dish that does not have a lid, cover it securely with cling film, or put the food directly in a roasting bag and fasten with a plastic (not metal) tie.
- **Paper towels** are useful for soaking up moisture and covering foods loosely to prevent spattering (do not use recycled paper, which may contain tiny fragments of metal). You can also use greaseproof paper.
- **For thorough, even cooking**, stir foods halfway, or regularly, during microwaving. The microwaves will continue to produce heat inside the food after it has come out of the oven, so food should always stand for a few minutes to finish cooking before serving.

Thawing know-how

Thawing must be done slowly and gently, so that the outside does not begin to cook before the inside is thawed. For this reason always use the Defrost setting.

- **Break up** and stir stews, soups, and sauces as they thaw.
- **Set frozen bread**, pastry, and cakes on paper towels so that moisture will be absorbed as they thaw.
- **Be sure** meat and poultry are completely thawed before cooking.
- **Cook food** as soon as possible once it is thawed.

Use a microwave to...

- soften cold butter
- toast nuts
- warm bread, rolls, croissants, bagels, and the like
- cook bacon rashers perfectly crisp (snip rind to prevent curling)
- make deliciously creamy scrambled eggs
- soften chopped onions
- cook rice perfectly
- make breakfast porridge
- cook corn on the cob (set it on paper towels)
- melt chocolate (stir halfway)
- soften crystallized honey (take lid off jar) and ice cream
- warm citrus fruit so it yields more juice

The well-provisioned kitchen

With a supply of useful ingredients always to hand, you should never be short of ideas for an impromptu meal or interesting flavourings to add zest to your cooking, or the basics for a cake, a loaf of bread, or a favourite pudding. Everyone will have a different list of essential staples, according to what they prefer to cook and eat, but most of our storecupboards, refrigerators, and freezers will contain many of the same basic elements.

The storecupboard

Gone are the days when every home had a larder or pantry, a dry, sometimes dark, cold room in which to keep essential ingredients like vegetables and fruit that would otherwise quickly deteriorate in the warmth of the kitchen.

Nowadays most of us have to manage with a cupboard in the kitchen, using the refrigerator for storage more than we used to, if only because it is the only cold place we have. You will find advice on storing different foods in the Know-How pages of individual chapters, but here are some general tips:

- **Choose a cupboard** in the coolest part of your kitchen – not next to the radiator, boiler, or oven – and make sure it is dry.

- **Pack the shelves** logically – bags of flour together, alongside packets of sugar or of rice and pasta, for example – with the things that you use most often arranged at the front.

- **Regularly check** use-by dates on packets, bottles, and cans, and on bought chilled and frozen food. Also check if foods need to be refrigerated once opened.

Dry goods

Grains, pasta, and pulses form the backbone of the storecupboard – combined with fresh foods they will provide an infinite variety of nutritious meals. Other dry staples to keep on hand are sugars and flours, as well as nuts and seeds, dried fruits (those labelled "ready to eat" are best because they do not need soaking), spices and dried herbs, crispbreads and other savoury biscuits, and breakfast cereals. If you like to bake cakes and biscuits or breads, baking powder, bicarbonate of soda and dried yeast are a must. You might also want to stock cream of tartar, gelatine (leaves and/or powder) and cocoa powder, plus stock cubes or bouillon powder. Not forgetting salt and pepper, and coffee and tea.

Rice is so versatile – it can be served as an accompaniment or used as an ingredient in both savoury and sweet dishes. Many types are available, varying in size and shape of grain, colour, and texture, whether wholegrain or polished (white). Wholegrain rice has had only the outer, inedible husk removed, which makes it more nutritious than white rice. Here is a selection of different rices worth keeping in your storecupboard.

- **Long-grain rices**, which stay in separate grains once cooked, include flavourful basmati, red rice (which is a wholegrain rice), Thai fragrant rice, also called jasmine rice, and long-grain (patna or Carolina) rice. Parboiled or converted rice is a very nutritious white long-grain rice; easy-cook rice has grains that never stick together.

- **Medium- and short-grain rices** have starchy grains that tend to cling together after cooking. Types include risotto rice with plump oval grains (sometimes labelled as arborio or carnaroli rice) and a similar paella rice, the best of which is said to come from Valencia; pudding rice, which looks very like risotto rice but is sweeter; sticky rice (also called glutinous rice – a misnomer because it contains no gluten); and Japanese sushi rice.

Other grains offer interesting and tasty alternatives to rice, as well as meals or flours, and flakes for muesli and porridge. They include:

- **Bulgur**, which is part-cooked, cracked, and crushed wheat grains, is very easy to prepare – it needs only soaking or a few minutes cooking. It is popular in the Mediterranean and Middle East. **Cracked** or **Kibbled Wheat** is similar but takes longer to cook.

- **Couscous** is not a true grain but a type of pasta made from semolina flour. It is used much like rice as an accompaniment or as part of a salad or other dish.

- **Oatmeal**, in varying degrees of coarseness, can be used in bread, biscuits, and oatcakes.

- **Pearl barley**, and its wholegrain form pot barley, are most often used in soups and casseroles but can also be cooked like rice for side dishes and pilafs.

- **Polenta** (sometimes called cornmeal) is a yellow, granular meal ground from maize or corn; cooked with water or stock until it thickens, it makes the northern Italian dish of the same name. Polenta can also be used to make bread, cakes, and biscuits.

- **Dried pasta** is available in very many shapes and sizes – the majority of which are interchangeable in recipes. Italian pasta is made from wheat, sometimes enriched with egg, whereas **Oriental and Non-wheat Pastas** can be made from ground mung beans (cellophane or transparent noodles), rice (Chinese vermicelli and rice sticks), buckwheat flour (Japanese soba), corn, barley, and soya beans. **Spaghetti, Tagliatelle, Penne, and Fusilli** are the most useful basic pasta shapes to keep in your storecupboard, plus some Oriental noodles to partner quick stir-fries or add to soups.

- **Pulses – dried beans, peas, and lentils** – are easy to prepare, although (with the exception of lentils) they need to be soaked before cooking. To save time, use canned pulses, which are just as nutritious as dried.

Unusual grains to try

- **Kasha**, roasted whole or cracked buckwheat grains, tends to break down when cooked so it is good if used in risotto-type dishes.

- **Quinoa** (pronounced "keenwa") is a very nutritious and ancient grain from South America. It contains more protein than any other grain, and is also higher in unsaturated fats and lower in carbohydrates than most – all of which make it a useful addition to a healthy diet. Quinoa is quite bland, with a flavour similar to that of couscous. It can be cooked in the same ways as rice.

- **Whole grains** of oat, rye, and wheat, also known as kernels, groats, and berries, make an unusual substitute for brown rice.

Pulses

Dried beans, peas, and lentils make up the family of pulses. All but lentils require soaking for at least 8 hours, and 10 minutes' hard boiling at the beginning of cooking.

Red kidney beans
Popular in Mexican cooking, especially in chilli con carne, their bright red skins add colour to many different salads and stews.

Cannellini beans
These are a good general-purpose bean to use in soups, salads, stews, especially in Italian dishes. French dried white haricots are similar.

Black beans
Traditional in Caribbean, Mexican, Chinese, and Brazilian dishes, these slightly sweet beans go well with rice and spicy sauces.

Borlotti beans
Creamy in consistency, borlotti are a favourite with Italians in soups, salads, casseroles, and dips. They are slightly bittersweet in flavour.

Aduki beans
Tender-textured beans with a strong flavour, aduki are used in Chinese and Japanese rice dishes and soups, and in red bean paste.

Chickpeas
Most famous in hummus, felafel, and other Middle Eastern dishes, chickpeas are also used in Indian and Spanish cooking.

Split peas
Yellow and green are available, and interchangeable in soups, purées, and bakes. Green split peas are used for "mushy peas".

Lentils
Red and orange lentils cook quickly and become mushy, while green, brown, and Puy lentils retain their shape.

Sauces, preserves, syrups, oils and vinegars

For use at the table and as quick-and-easy instant flavourings.

▪ **Tabasco, horseradish, chilli, and Moroccan harissa** are hot and spicy sauces that will give a kick to any bland food. The green version of Tabasco is less fiery than the usual red kind but still packs a punch.

▪ **Worcestershire** has a piquant salty flavour, good in sauces and marinades.

▪ **Pesto, tapenade (black olive paste), and sun-dried tomato paste** can be stirred into pasta, rice, and dips.

▪ **Mayonnaise** can be used in sandwiches and salad dressings as well as dips. Reduced-fat and flavoured versions are available.

▪ **Tomato ketchup** is good for mixing into sauces, dressings, and relishes as well as stews. A spoonful or two of **Tomato purée or paste** will add flavour and colour to sauces, soups, and stews, while tomato **Passata** (sieved crushed tomatoes) can form the basis of a pasta sauce or soup.

▪ **Chinese and Japanese sauces** – soy, oyster, chilli, hoisin, teriyaki, and bean, plus miso, sesame, and wasabi pastes – are traditional in Oriental dishes and add exciting flavours to Western ones. For South-east Asian cooking, you might want to keep fish sauce (also called nam pla), tamarind paste, and creamed coconut. Coconut products are high in saturated fat, so look also for reduced-fat coconut milk.

▪ **Curry pastes** come in varying strengths, and are ideal for quickly spicing curries as well as soups and dressings.

▪ **Preserves**, such as mango chutney, redcurrant jelly, and marmalade, add fruity sweetness to a dish, other chutneys offer hot and spicy flavours, while pickles may be sweet or tangy, according to your preference.

▪ **Mustard** appears in many different flavours, colours, and textures, and all types can be used in cooking or as a condiment. It is useful to stock the three basics: strong Dijon mustard, coarse-grain mustard, and very hot and pungent English mustard.

▪ **Oils** are used for frying, brushing, and basting, as well as in marinades and dressings. Two types – a neutral flavoured general purpose oil such as sunflower and a more flavourful olive oil – are the basics to keep in stock. In addition, you might want to add walnut, hazelnut, or toasted sesame oils, or an oil or two flavoured with your favourite herbs or spices.

▪ **Vinegars** add pep to dressings and sauces as well as being essential in pickles and chutneys. Red or white wine vinegar is a must, with cider, sherry, and balsamic vinegars being optional choices. The cheaper balsamics are satisfactory for cooking, the more expensive varieties are best kept for drizzling on food before serving or at the table.

▪ **Syrups** – honey, maple, and golden – make instant sweet sauces for ice-cream and hot puddings.

Tomatoes

These three tomato-based products are useful in the storecupboard for boosting the flavour of fresh tomatoes when they are lacking in taste of their own.

Sun-dried tomatoes in oil
Sold loose at the delicatessen or in jars and tubs, these pieces or halves of tomato can be used as they are or chopped. Sun-blushed tomatoes are similar, but sweeter and softer.

Tomato concentrate
Called tomato purée or paste, this is very strong, useful for adding depth of colour and flavour to cooked dishes. Sun-dried tomato versions are milder and sweeter.

Passata
Tomatoes that have been crushed and then sieved to make a smooth liquid. Sold in bottles and cans, it is useful in sauces, soups, and stews that are better without bits.

Canned goods

Storecupboard shelves laden with a variety of canned foods are a boon for a busy cook. If you keep a basic stock of canned fish, vegetables, and fruits, you will be able to whip up a meal at a moment's notice.

- **Fish**, such as salmon, tuna, sardines, pilchards, herring, and anchovies, are available in many different forms packed in various oils or in water or brine, or in flavourful sauces. Use your favourites in fish pies, as sandwich fillings, on pizzas, and in salads and pasta sauces.

- **Tomatoes** come whole or chopped, in natural juice or purée, plain or flavoured with herbs and garlic. Fresh tomatoes are always available, but often lack flavour; canned tomatoes taste good year round. They are also wonderfully convenient, needing no peeling or deseeding before using in soups, sauces, and stews.

- **Pulses in cans** – chickpeas, kidney, and haricot beans, and so on – are a quick alternative to their dried form, as they only have to be drained and rinsed well, and just as nutritious. They are excellent in salads and to make dips such as hummus as well as in all kinds of hot dishes, from chilli con carne to pasta with beans.

- **Oriental vegetables**, such as bamboo shoots and water chestnuts, will add crunch to stir-fries and other Chinese dishes.

- **Canned fruits** – in natural juice for the best and truest flavour – are great standbys for quick puddings. You can also use them to bulk up a stir-fry or a fresh fruit salad.

- **Custard** in cans (or refrigerated cartons) is excellent in fools and trifles.

The cold store

The refrigerator and freezer are natural extensions of the storecupboard, the places where more perishable standbys can be kept safely on hand. Stocking a good selection of chilled and frozen foods means you can have the makings of all kinds of quickly prepared meals.

- **Dairy products** – milk and the foods based on it such as butter, cheese, cream, and yogurt – are found in most people's refrigerator. There is such an amazing choice of types of milk and cream, varieties of cheese, and flavours of yogurt, that what you stock is up to you, but two very useful staples are: a piece of Parmesan to grate as needed, and plain or Greek yogurt to serve with and/or in sweet and savoury dishes, or to blend with fruit to make healthy smoothies. In the freezer, you can keep milk, butter, cream, and full-fat yogurt for emergencies, and grated cheese to add frozen to sauces or as a topping. For instant desserts, ice cream and frozen yogurt are a must in the freezer.

- **Eggs** are another essential standby. They can make simple, nutritious meals by themselves, or be added to countless other dishes, both sweet and savoury.

- **Vegetables**, bought ready-prepared in bags for refrigerator storage or frozen, are a real time-saver. Chilled prepared vegetables range from trimmed whole mangetout, green beans, and baby corn, to shelled fresh peas, cut-up root vegetables for soups and stews, and ready-washed spinach and salad leaves. Frozen vegetables, which are often more nutritious than fresh, are usually best cooked from frozen, which makes them the ultimate convenience food.

- **Fruit** such as apples stay deliciously crisp in the refrigerator, ideal for snacks or adding to fruit salads, and citrus fruits also store well in the fridge. Soft fruits – raspberries, red and black currants, loganberries, gooseberries, cranberries, and so on – are very useful to have in the freezer for quick puddings, as are grated citrus zest, apple or other fruit purée or chunks for pie fillings, and fruit juice (decant bought juice into rigid containers).

- **Bread** is a top freezer standby. With a sliced loaf, you can take out slices as you need them – they can be toasted from frozen, as can pitta bread. If you prefer unsliced bread, cut loaves into halves or quarters and freeze in separate bags so you can take them out when you need them – this way you will always have fresh bread. Most part-baked bread can be baked from frozen. Also handy are croûtons and breadcrumbs, good ways to use up the last of a staling loaf.

- **Seafood** such as fish fillets, raw and cooked prawns, crab, and other shellfish bought ready-frozen does not need to be thawed before cooking.

- **Other foods** useful in the freezer are chicken fillets and sausages (both must be thoroughly thawed before cooking), fresh pasta (drop it frozen into a big pot of boiling water), herbs, unsalted nuts (they stay fresher in the freezer than in the storecupboard) and coffee.

Flavouring food

Herbs, spices, and the essential seasonings, salt and pepper, enhance the flavours of the food we eat, and also often add enticing aromas and vibrant colours. It is hard to imagine cooking without them.

Herbs

With their wonderful flavours, scents, and colours, herbs can transform even the simplest dish into something very special. Most savoury dishes benefit from the inclusion of one or more herbs to add flavour during cooking, or as a garnish to be sprinkled over the top of a dish just before serving. Sweet dishes, too, can be perfumed with herbs such as mint and lemon balm, and decorated with delicate herb flowers such as borage. Herbs are also used to make drinks known as infusions or tisanes.

Preserving herbs

Preserve fresh herbs by freezing them. This is a much better method of preserving most herbs than drying because a fresher flavour is retained. Herbs that freeze well include parsley, tarragon, chives, dill, and fennel. Chop or pull off leaves or small sprigs, then mix with water in ice-cube trays or freeze in small plastic bags.

Herbs that can be dried successfully at home include bay leaves, sage, and rosemary. Hang them in a warm place, such as above the boiler, until dry, then pull or rub off the leaves from the stalks. Pack whole bay leaves into jars; chop or crumble sage and rosemary first.

Storing herbs

Buy or gather fresh herbs only when they are needed. If you have to store them for a day or so, keep them in a cool place or in the refrigerator. If they have stalks, stand them in a jug of water, like cut flowers, and cover with a plastic bag.

Dried herbs must be stored correctly or they will quickly lose their flavour. Dark glass jars or earthenware pots with airtight lids are the best for storage, but if you only have clear glass jars, keep them in a dark cupboard or drawer because light causes dried herbs to deteriorate. Make sure they are kept in a cool dry place, away from kitchen heat and steam.

Dried herbs will not keep for ever, even if they are stored correctly. Herbs you have dried yourself will keep for 1 year, shop-bought herbs much less, so it is best to buy in small quantities from a shop that has a rapid turnover, checking the label for the best-before date.

Using herbs

Always try to use fresh herbs, particularly in salads and sauces, as they always taste better than dried or frozen. Bunches and packets of a wide variety of fresh herbs are available now, so there is usually no need to use dried.

Fresh herbs are often chopped or shredded before being added to a dish, and this is best done at the last possible moment. The volatile oils in herbs are released by heat or oxidation, so unless the herbs are used as soon as they are prepared, they will quickly lose their flavour and they may start to discolour (this is especially true of basil). If whole herb sprigs or leaves are used to flavour a dish, lift them out before serving. For easy removal, tie with string or wrap in muslin, as in a bouquet garni (see opposite).

Herbs that dry well include sage, oregano and marjoram, bay, and dill, and these are good used in dishes that require long cooking. When buying dried herbs, look for those that are freeze-dried as they have the best flavour, colour, and aroma.

Another option you might want to try are the preserved herbs packed in squeezy tubes or bottled in oil – they are very convenient, and useful to keep in the refrigerator for those times when you run out of fresh herbs at the last moment and there is no chance of getting any more.

Dried herbs are more pungent than fresh, so a smaller quantity is required. Use $1/2$ teaspoon finely powdered dried herb or 1 teaspoon crumbled dried herb in place of 1 tablespoon chopped fresh herb.

Herb flavours

The range of herbs in the shops is exciting for adventurous cooks, and even more varieties can be grown at home. These are the most commonly used.

- **Fresh-tasting herbs**: parsley (used both as a flavouring and garnish; flat-leaf has a more pronounced, spicier flavour than curly) and chives (a delicate taste of onion with a crunchy texture).

- **Sweet herbs**: basil (spicy and aromatic; many varieties in addition to sweet basil, such as opal or purple basil and anise-flavoured Thai basil), bay leaves (with a pungent, resinous aroma), mint (including cool and mellow spearmint or garden mint, pungent peppermint, spicy Moroccan mint, and fruity apple mint), and oregano and marjoram (marjoram is subtly spicy while oregano has a more peppery or lemony bite; they can be used interchangeably).

Anise-flavoured herbs: chervil (delicate taste and pretty leaves), tarragon (pungent), dill (fragrant and tangy; seeds are used as a spice) and fennel (mild and slightly sweet; seeds are used as a spice).

Pungent herbs: rosemary (aroma and flavour are not reduced by long cooking), sage (spicy, often slightly musky), thyme (pleasantly strong and slightly peppery), coriander (spicy citrus aroma and taste) and garlic (whole cloves roasted or simmered are mellow, crushed and sautéed much stronger); new "wet" garlic is milder in flavour than dried garlic.

Herb mixtures

There are classic combinations of herbs, most of them from France, that are often used in cooking, especially in dishes like stews and casseroles that need long, slow simmering or cooking in the oven.

Dried mixed herbs, which can be used in most savoury dishes, is usually a mixture of marjoram, oregano, rosemary, summer savory, and thyme, but brands vary according to manufacturer.

A bouquet garni is used in many long-cooked dishes. For a fresh bouquet garni, the basic combination is parsley, thyme, and bay, but this may be varied according to the dish being flavoured (see box, below). Only tie the string around the stalks of the herbs or you will strangle their flavours. If using dried herbs, wrap them in a muslin bag. Remember to remove the bouquet garni before serving (if you use a long piece of string, this can be tied to the pan handle for easy removal after cooking).

- **Herbes de Provence**, an aromatic mixture of sage, basil, savory, thyme, rosemary, and marjoram, is another popular combination. Good in stews, it should be used sparingly. If you do not have any, use dried mixed herbs (left) instead.

- **Fines herbes** combines equal quantities of tarragon, chervil, parsley, and chives. It works well in omelettes and with fish and poultry.

Growing your own herbs

The range of fresh herbs available in shops and supermarkets is extensive, but buying them is much more expensive than using those you grow yourself, especially if you use large amounts. Also, growing your own gives you the chance to try more unusual varieties of herbs. Cultivation, indoors or out, is simple and satisfying. Herbs can be grown in the garden, in pots on a paved terrace or patio, in a hanging basket or in a window box. Indoors, they will flourish in a box or in pots on a sunny windowsill.

Preparing herbs

Rinse the herbs well under cold running water, then dry with paper towels. Then remove the leaves or sprigs from the stalks.

Chopping
Gather the leaves or sprigs into a compact pile on a chopping board. Chop the leaves with a sharp knife, rocking the blade back and forth, until the herbs are as fine as you want them. A mezzaluna (see page 17) is useful for chopping a large quantity.

Snipping
A pair of sharp scissors is best for snipping chives. Hold the stalks in one hand and snip into short lengths, either into a bowl or directly into the dish you are flavouring. This technique is also good for finely shredding large leaved herbs such as sage.

Making a bouquet garni
Hold 2–3 sprigs each of thyme or marjoram and parsley with 1–2 bay leaves. Wrap in two pieces of pared orange zest (or two pieces of celery) if you like, then tie in a bouquet with undyed string. Orange and celery go well in beef and pork casseroles.

Spices

In the past spices were often used to mask the taste of less-than-perfect food, and at one time were so precious and expensive that they would be locked away in special spice boxes or cupboards. Today, spices are no longer a luxury seasoning, and modern cooks use them to enhance flavours rather than to disguise them.

Buying and storing spices

If they are whole, spices do not deteriorate as quickly as herbs (which is why it is best to buy whole spices and grind them as you need them). Store in tightly sealed containers in a cool, dark, dry place. Whole spices will keep for 1 year, ground spices for about 6 months.

Using spices

Because spices need time to release their aromas and flavours, they are usually added near the start of cooking. If the cooking process is prolonged, whole, cracked, or bruised spices are normally used rather than ground spices, which may become bitter.

Toasting or warming whole or ground spices before use brings out their flavours, and is a good thing to do if the spices are to be added to a dish that is cooked for only a short time. When toasting, use a heavy frying pan over a low heat because the spices can scorch easily; if toasting ground spices add a little oil to the pan. Warm the spices just until they smell aromatic.

Salt

Salt is the essential seasoning, both for cooking and as a table condiment. It enhances the natural flavours of all savoury foods and some sweet ones, and is important in baking and in the preservation of food. There are two types: rock salt, which is mined from underground, and sea salt which is evaporated from sea water. Both rock and sea salts are available coarse (in large or medium-size crystals) or as table salt (refined to very small grains, with anti-caking agents added to keep it free-flowing).

Monosodium glutamate (MSG) is used in a similar way to salt, to accentuate flavours.

Spice flavours

Spices come in many shapes and sizes, with subtly differing flavours and fragrances. They can be as exotic as rosebuds and liquorice root or as familiar as cinnamon and cloves. Here are some of the most commonly used.

- **Hot spices** stimulate the palate and sharpen the appetite as well as encouraging the body to produce perspiration – an excellent means of cooling down in a hot climate. The best known hot spice is chilli, which is available as whole chillies (fresh or dried), crushed dried chillies (also called chilli flakes), and ground into chilli powder (usually a blend of ground chillies and other spices), very hot cayenne pepper and paprika (may be mild or hot). In addition there are chilli sauces and pastes, oils, and jam. Just as the hundreds of different varieties of chilli vary from pleasantly warm through to burning hot, so do the spices and mixtures derived from them.

Preparing spices

The way in which spices are prepared depends on the recipe in which they are used and the depth of flavour required.

Whole spices
Whole spices (and herbs) that are to be removed before serving are best tied in a piece of muslin, which allows them to be lifted out of the dish all at once.

Toasting spices
Heat a heavy frying pan until hot. Add the spices and cook over a low heat for 1–2 minutes, stirring occasionally, until the aromas are released. Leave to cool, then grind.

Grinding spices
Put the whole spices into a mortar; crush them with a pestle to the required consistency. Or, grind in a small electric mill kept especially for grinding spices.

Soaking saffron
Put threads into a small bowl. Add hot water (usually an amount in the recipe). Soak for 10 minutes. Use the liquid only, or the threads as well, according to the recipe.

Pepper is an aromatic hot spice. Black, white, green, and red or pink peppercorns are available, each different in taste and fragrance. Freshly ground black pepper is used in almost every savoury dish plus a few sweet ones and is an essential table condiment. There are also two Asian peppers: fragrant Sichuan pepper and Japanese sansho.

Other hot spices are the familiar mustard, root ginger, and galangal. Mustard is available as whole seeds, powder, or ready-made paste; and in blended mixtures that include herbs, other spices, or even fruit flavours – the French *moutarde au cassis*, for example, contains crème de cassis (blackcurrant) liqueur for a rich taste and vibrant red colour. Root ginger and the less familiar galangal are similar in appearance and in taste; they are actually knobbly rhizomes, not roots. Both are available fresh (try oriental shops or a large supermarket), as powder, and in dried slices which need to be soaked in water before using (they are good to flavour soups and stews, but take care to remove the slices before serving).

Warm, fragrant spices provide a sweet note. They are usually added at the beginning of cooking so that their flavour and aroma can permeate the dish, be it sweet or savoury. Warm spices include allspice (a single spice that is like a peppery mixture of cloves and cinnamon), green cardamom (pods contain tiny, sticky black seeds), cinnamon, cloves, coriander seed, pretty star anise and anise seed (both liquorice-like), nutmeg and mace (nutmeg is the seed and mace – usually available only ground – its wrapping), and vanilla (use pods or pure essence or extract).

Nutty spices include poppyseeds and sesame seeds.

Pungent spices are assertive in taste so should be used judiciously. They include juniper berries (slightly sweet and resinous), cumin (warm and a bit sharp), and caraway.

Fruity spices may be sweet or refreshingly tart. They range from sourish tamarind (available as dried pulp in a block, paste, or concentrate) to lemon grass stalks and kaffir lime leaves.

Colouring spices will tint and flavour a dish. Saffron is expensive but only a pinch is needed to colour a dish yellow (and add a warm, musky taste). Turmeric gives a richer, yellow-ochre hue, and is slightly more bitter. The dark red colour of goulash and chorizo sausages comes from paprika (ground chilli).

Spice mixtures

Although there is nothing like the thrill of inventing and grinding your own mixtures from whole spices, ready-

The pepper family

The different powders derived from dried chillies can be confusing. Some are much hotter than others, so it is wise to know which is which.

Paprika
The mildest of the pepper family, paprika is available in three forms – sweet (mild), sharp (hot), and smoked (musky).

Cayenne
A searingly hot powder made from one of the hottest varieties of chilli with nothing added. Use with caution.

Chilli powder
A blend of chillies with herbs and other spices, usually oregano and cumin, plus garlic. Strength varies according to brand.

made blends of ground spices do save time for the busy cook. Mixtures vary according to individual manufacturers and brands; try different brands to find which you prefer. These are the most common.

- **Curry powder** may be perfumed and mild or hot, according to the blend of spices (usually turmeric, fenugreek, coriander, cumin, cardamom, chilli, cinnamon, and paprika). It gives curries an authentic flavour, which is often difficult to achieve yourself.

- **Garam masala**, an aromatic curry spice, is usually a mixture of cumin, coriander, cardamom, cinnamon, pepper, cloves, turmeric, and ginger, sometimes with mace and bay. It is best added to a dish towards the end of the cooking time to preserve its fine aroma.

- **Mixed spice** is a traditional English mixture of six sweet spices: usually allspice, cinnamon, cloves, coriander, mace, and nutmeg.

- **Five-spice powder** is a Chinese blend of five flavours (salty, sour, bitter, pungent, and sweet) – hence its name. It is a mixture of ground star anise, fennel, cloves, cinnamon and Sichuan pepper. Dried ginger, cardamom, or liquorice can be added to the mixture, although commercial ones rarely include these.

Safe and healthy cooking

It is important to handle and store perishable foods with care, so they remain at their best, and to help prevent food poisoning. The common-sense food safety guidelines are easy to follow and will ensure that you can enjoy what you eat without worries.

Dairy products

Eggs should be stored in the refrigerator. It is best to leave them in their box so you can keep an eye on the date stamp. The "best before" date is a better indicator of age than the packing date, which could be several days after laying.

Even among eggs from free-range hens, it is known that some can harbour the salmonella bacterium, which can cause food poisoning. Health guidelines therefore recommend that it may be safest to avoid eating raw eggs (such as in home-made mayonnaise, mousses, and the like) altogether. Vulnerable groups (pregnant women, babies and young children, the very old, the sick and people with damaged immune systems) should definitely eat only thoroughly cooked eggs (hard boiled rather than soft boiled, for example).

Soft cheeses ripened using moulds (such as Brie and Camembert) and soft blue cheeses (whether made from pasteurized or unpasteurized milk) may harbour the listeria bacterium, which can cause an illness similar to flu. Listeria is of no concern to adults in normal health, but it is recommended that vulnerable groups (as listed above) should avoid these sorts of soft cheeses.

Meat and poultry

Raw meat can contain bacteria that cause food poisoning, so it must be handled safely. Keep it in the refrigerator, in its original wrapping or transferred to fresh wrapping or a covered dish.

Poultry such as chicken and turkey can also harbour food-poisoning bacteria, commonly salmonella and campylobacter. So, as with meat, keep poultry in the fridge (in its original wrapping if you are going to cook it within a few hours, otherwise in fresh, loose wrapping). Thorough cooking will kill any bacteria that might be present. To ensure this, it is recommended that the body cavity not be stuffed (this could pevent heat penetrating to the centre of the bird). If you do want to stuff the body cavity, fill it loosely and only two-thirds full, and stuff no more than 3 hours before cooking. Then at the end of the cooking time test the temperature of the bird and of the stuffing with an instant-read thermometer: the thigh meat and the stuffing should be at least 75°C (170°F) and the breast meat 71°C (160°F).

With leftovers, cool them as quickly as possible (no more than 2 hours at room temperature) and then wrap and store in the refrigerator or freezer.

Seafood

Mussels, clams, and oysters bought live are very perishable. Store, covered with a damp cloth, in the coldest part of the refrigerator, and use the same day. When preparing mussels for cooking, discard any that have broken shells or with open shells that do not close when sharply tapped (these are not safe to eat). After cooking, discard any that have not opened.

Crab, prawns, and lobster, must also be very fresh; they become poisonous when stale. If they smell of ammonia or at all unpleasant, do not buy them.

Fish bought as fresh may previously have been frozen, and this is not always clearly labelled. If it was previously frozen it must not be frozen again (unless it is first used to make a cooked dish such as fish pie).

Grains and pulses

Leftover cooked rice should always be cooled quickly and stored in a covered container in the refrigerator (for no longer than a day or so) or in the freezer – if not kept cool it could develop food-poisoning toxins. Be sure to reheat cooked rice until it is very hot.

Most pulses contain toxic proteins that can cause severe food poisoning symptoms. To destroy the toxins, give all pulses (except chickpeas, lentils, and split peas) a 10–15 minute period of fast boiling at the start of cooking.

A note about organic produce

It is often thought that fruit and vegetables produced organically are free of pesticide and herbicide residues, but this is not always the case as much organic produce is imported from countries where regulations are not strictly followed. If in doubt, wash fruit and vegetables thoroughly under running cold water, scrubbing if necessary, and peel before cooking or eating.

Hot and Chilled Soups

Under 45 minutes

ECONOMICAL

DINNER PARTY

Watercress soup
Smooth and creamy: blended onions, potatoes, watercress, stock, and milk, lightly flavoured with a bay leaf. Can be served hot or cold.
SERVES 6   140 CALS PER SERVING
Takes 25 minutes   Page 39

Curried parsnip soup
Smooth and spicy: parsnips blended with mild curry powder, onion, garlic, and stock, and enriched with single cream.
SERVES 6–8   197–147 CALS PER SERVING
Takes 35 minutes   Page 37

Tzatziki soup
Cool and refreshing: yogurt, cucumber, and garlic blended with olive oil, white wine vinegar, and mint, and served chilled.
SERVES 4–6   138–92 CALS PER SERVING
Takes 15 minutes, **plus chilling**   Page 50

45–60 minutes

FAMILY CHOICE

Winter vegetable soup
Assortment of seasonal vegetables simmered with stock, seasoned with dill and turmeric, and coloured with spinach.
SERVES 6   153 CALS PER SERVING
Takes 55 minutes   Page 46

AMERICAN CLASSIC

Clam chowder
Fresh clams cooked in fish stock, then simmered with milk, onion, and potatoes, and flavoured with bacon and bay leaf.
SERVES 4   497 CALS PER SERVING
Takes 50 minutes   Page 43

Blue Stilton and onion soup
Creamy and rich: finely sliced onions combined with stock, blue Stilton cheese, bay leaves, and nutmeg make a tasty soup.
SERVES 8   255 CALS PER SERVING
Takes 50 minutes   Page 43

Game soup
Rich and aromatic: bacon and mushrooms simmered in game stock, flavoured with a citrus and herb bouquet and redcurrant jelly.
SERVES 4   223 CALS PER SERVING
Takes 50 minutes   Page 49

Vichyssoise
Leeks, onion, and potatoes blended with chicken stock, chilled, then combined with cream, result in this renowned velvety soup.
SERVES 4–6   251–167 CALS PER SERVING
Takes 45 minutes, **plus chilling**   Page 50

Over 60 minutes

Chicken noodle soup
Rich and warming: simmered chicken, carrots, and stock, flavoured with garlic, parsley, and dill, and served over noodles.
SERVES 6   261 CALS PER SERVING
Takes 2½ hours   Page 51

FRENCH CLASSIC

French onion soup
Thinly sliced caramelized onions simmered in beef stock and topped with a traditional Gruyère croûte.
SERVES 8   353 CALS PER SERVING
Takes 1¼ hours   Page 38

Butternut squash soup
Fresh butternut squash roasted in olive oil, simmered in vegetable stock, and puréed to form a thick, rich soup. Served hot with crusty bread.
SERVES 6   197 CALS PER SERVING
Takes 1½ hours   Page 47

Goulash soup
Rich and wholesome: beef, roasted red peppers, onions, potatoes, and tomatoes cooked in stock, and flavoured with paprika.
SERVES 6   363 CALS PER SERVING
Takes 2¼ hours   Page 48

Split pea and gammon soup
Green split peas and flavoursome gammon, simmered with onion, celery, potatoes, and leeks, make a substantial meal.
SERVES 8   338 CALS PER SERVING
Takes 3¾ hours, **plus soaking**   Page 42

Creamy carrot and orange soup
Smooth and tangy: carrots and stock mixed with crème fraîche, orange zest and juice, and flavoured with fresh chives.
SERVES 6–8   308–231 CALS PER SERVING
Takes 1¼ hours   Page 36

Vegetable minestrone
Hearty soup: dried beans cooked and added to a tomato soup with stock, leeks, cabbage, and arborio rice.
SERVES 4–6   250–167 CALS PER SERVING
Takes 1¾ hours, **plus soaking**   Page 39

Borscht
Beetroot, cabbage, potatoes, and tomatoes simmered with stock, vinegar, sugar, and dill for a rich sweet-sour flavour.
SERVES 4   244 CALS PER SERVING
Takes 1¼ hours   Page 40

DINNER PARTY

Lobster bisque
Rich-tasting and luxurious: lobster tails, shallots, brandy, wine, stock, and spices combined with cream (optional) and lemon juice.
SERVES 6   192 CALS PER SERVING
Takes 1½ hours   Page 44

Bouillabaisse
Mediterranean favourite: assorted white fish and shellfish simmered in stock with vegetables, orange zest, and Provençal herbs.
SERVES 8   337 CALS PER SERVING
Takes 1¼ hours   Page 45

Soups know-how

A batch of soup in the fridge is one of the best convenience foods ever, highly nutritious and wonderfully versatile. On a cold day, a bowl of soup is warming and sustaining, and with a sandwich or just some bread it can make a well-balanced lunch or supper. Soup is great for entertaining too, the ideal prepare-ahead starter. And soup is comforting at bedtime or, indeed, at any time of day.

There are all kinds of soups: light and delicate or rich and hearty; simple and quick to prepare or cooked long and slow to extract maximum flavour from the ingredients; velvety smooth in texture or full of delicious pieces of meat, vegetables, pulses, or pasta. Soups may be served hot or chilled, in a mug, a bowl, or a soup plate, plain or attractively garnished. There are even sweet and fruity soups that can double up as desserts.

Stocks

A well-flavoured stock forms the base of many soups, and nothing tastes as good as home-made stock. Stock is economical to make because it is based on meat, poultry, or fish bones and trimmings, and vegetables. Although it usually takes time to make stock – several hours of gentle simmering for meat and poultry stocks – it is easy to prepare, and can be made well in advance and in large quantities. It can then be frozen until needed. Recipes for stocks can be found on pages 107, 146, 202, and 266. If you don't have any home-made stock, there are fresh stocks available in the chilled cabinets in supermarkets, or you can use stock made from bouillon powder or a cube. Remember, though, that stock cubes are often strong and salty, so go easy on the salt. Another quick alternative is to use canned consommé.

Clarifying stock

Skimming will make a stock quite clear, but for crystal-clear results it needs to be clarified. When cold pour into a large pan. For each 600 ml (1 pint) add an egg white and crushed egg shell. Heat slowly, whisking. When frothy and starting to rise up, stop whisking and remove from the heat to subside. The crust that forms will act as a filter, collecting all the impurities. Repeat the rising up and subsiding 2 or 3 times, then simmer gently for 45 minutes. Strain through a muslin-lined sieve, holding back the crust.

Skimming soups

As a soup is brought to the boil, foam or scum may form on the surface. This is most likely with soups that contain meat or poultry, particularly on the bone, or root vegetables and pulses. This foam, which contains impurities, should be removed as it forms.

Use a large metal spoon or skimmer (slotted if there are herbs and whole spices in the soup) to skim off the foam.

If there is a lot of fat on the surface of a soup, skim it off with a large metal spoon, or blot it with paper towels, before serving.

Thickening soups

Many soups can be slightly thickened simply by being puréed to a smooth consistency. Puréed soups that contain starchy ingredients such as rice, pasta, and potatoes will be even thicker.

In some soup recipes, flour is used as a thickener. Normally it is added to the softened vegetables, to bind the fat and juices together. The mixture is then cooked to remove the raw flour taste before the stock is stirred in. Flour can also be added to puréed soups at the end of cooking if they are not thick enough: blend the flour with cold stock, whisk in and simmer until thickened.

Adding cream and yogurt

Double and whipping cream and full-fat crème fraîche can be added to a hot soup and heated further, with no danger of curdling.

Single cream, soured cream, and yogurt will curdle if overheated, so add them just before serving and warm through over a low heat. For chilled soups, add cream or yogurt once the soup has been chilled, before serving.

Garnishes

An attractive garnish can lift a soup, adding a contrast in colour, texture, and flavour. Here are some ideas.
- Fresh herbs, either chopped or as whole leaves – mint, chives, thyme, parsley, basil, tarragon, and coriander are all popular. Choose a herb that complements or mirrors any herbs in the soup, and add at the last minute so that it retains its freshness.
- Grated or crumbled cheese
- Chopped hard-boiled egg
- Fine shreds of citrus zest or whole berries
- Crisp pieces of bacon; diced meat or poultry
- Toasted nuts; sunflower seeds
- Croûtons

Garnishing with cream

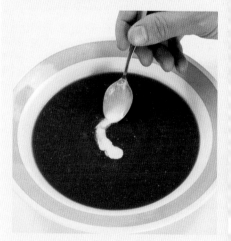

With a teaspoon, quickly swirl single or whipping cream in a spiral on each serving.

Chopped, diced, sliced, or grated vegetables such as spring onions, cucumber, carrots, peppers, and fennel
A spoonful of a sauce such as pesto
A blob or decorative swirl of cream or yogurt (see box, below left)

Freezing

Soups taste best if freshly made, but most can be frozen without impairing flavour or texture. Avoid freezing soups containing ingredients such as pasta, potatoes, and rice as they become mushy. It is always best to underseason, as further seasoning can be added when reheating. Add any cream, eggs, and milk at the reheating stage, as freezing could cause separation or curdling.

To thaw a soup to be served hot, heat from frozen in a heavy saucepan over low heat, stirring occasionally. If the soup appears to be separating, whisk briskly until smooth or work in a blender or food processor, or with a hand-held blender, for a few seconds. Thaw soup to be served cold in its freezer container, in the refrigerator.

Microwaving

For many soups, a microwave cannot give the same results as conventional long, slow cooking, but it can produce light vegetable soups in minutes. And it is useful for thawing frozen stocks and soups, and for reheating soups. The most efficient way of heating soup in the microwave is to transfer the soup to individual bowls or mugs, because soup in larger containers will take longer to heat up than it would in a pan on top of the stove. For cooking soup in the microwave, use a container that is large enough to allow the soup to rise up slightly. Stir once or twice during cooking or heating, and just before serving, as the soup at the edge will be hot and bubbling long before that in the centre. Add single cream, soured cream, or yogurt and any garnish just before serving.

Puréeing soups

Soups are often puréed to give them a velvety-smooth texture. This also gives them a thicker texture. Starchy vegetables and a little flour will help to thicken them even more.

Blender or food processor
Either of these can be used to process the cooked ingredients in batches. Scrape the sides of the container once or twice to ensure there are no solid pieces left unprocessed.

Hand-held blender
Use this to purée directly in the saucepan (which should be deep to prevent splashes). It's not useful for large quantities, but is ideal for blending in a final addition of cream or yogurt.

Sieve
To make a puréed soup ultra smooth, and remove any fibres, seeds, or skins, work it through a fine sieve with a wooden spoon. This is much easier to do if the soup is first puréed in a blender or food processor.

Somerset mushroom soup

⊘ **SERVES 4–6**   109–73 CALS PER SERVING

30 g (1 oz) butter

1 small onion, finely chopped

1 garlic clove, crushed

500 g (1 lb) mushrooms, sliced

1.25 litres (2 pints) vegetable or chicken stock

150 ml (¼ pint) dry white wine

2 tsp chopped fresh oregano

1 tsp chopped fresh thyme

salt and black pepper

1 Melt the butter in a large saucepan, add the onion and garlic, and cook gently, stirring occasionally, for a few minutes until soft but not coloured. Add the mushrooms and cook, stirring from time to time, for 10 minutes.

2 Pour in the stock and wine, then add the oregano and half of the thyme, and season with salt and pepper. Bring to a boil, cover, and simmer gently for 10 minutes or until the mushrooms are tender.

3 Taste for seasoning and serve hot, sprinkled with the remaining fresh thyme.

French pea soup

⊘ **SERVES 4–6**   179–119 CALS PER SERVING

30 g (1 oz) butter

1 large onion, coarsely chopped

1 tbsp plain flour

500 g (1 lb) frozen peas

1.25 litres (2 pints) vegetable chicken or stock

½ tsp caster sugar

2 large mint sprigs

salt and black pepper

shredded fresh mint to garnish

1 Melt the butter in a large saucepan, add the chopped onion, and cook very gently, stirring occasionally, for about 10 minutes until soft but not coloured.

2 Sprinkle in the flour and stir for a further 1–2 minutes, then add the frozen peas, stock, caster sugar, and sprigs of mint.

3 Bring to a boil, cover, and simmer gently, stirring occasionally, for 5 minutes or until the peas are soft. Do not simmer any longer than this or the peas will lose their fresh green colour.

4 Remove the mint sprigs and discard. Purée the soup in a food processor or blender until smooth.

5 Return the soup to the rinsed-out pan, reheat, and add salt and pepper to taste. Serve hot, garnished with shredded fresh mint.

Roasted tomato and garlic soup

This soup is light in consistency but full of flavour, making it perfect for late summer when tomatoes are at their ripest and best. Charring the tomatoes in the oven gives the soup a wonderful smoky flavour.

⊘ **SERVES 4**   127 CALS PER SERVING

1 kg (2 lb) ripe tomatoes

2 tbsp olive oil

1 onion, chopped

3 garlic cloves, coarsely chopped

1.5 litres (2½ pints) chicken or vegetable stock

salt and black pepper

ready-made pesto to serve

1 Cut the tomatoes in half and arrange them, cut-side down, in a roasting tin. Roast in a preheated oven at 220°C (200°C fan, Gas 7) for 15 minutes or until the skins are charred.

2 Remove the tomatoes from the oven and leave until they are cool enough to handle, then peel off the skins and discard them. Chop the flesh coarsely, retaining the juice.

3 Heat the oil in a large saucepan, add the onion and garlic, and cook gently, stirring occasionally, for a few minutes until soft but not coloured.

4 Add the stock and the tomato flesh and juices, and bring to a boil. Lower the heat and simmer for 5 minutes, then add salt and pepper to taste.

5 Serve the soup hot, with a bowl of pesto so everyone can stir in a spoonful before they eat.

Creamy carrot and orange soup

⊘ **SERVES 6–8**   308–231 CALS PER SERVING

30 g (1 oz) butter

1 onion, coarsely chopped

1 kg (2 lb) carrots, thickly sliced

1.5 litres (2½ pints) vegetable stock

grated zest of ½ orange

300 ml (½ pint) orange juice (squeezed fresh or from a carton)

salt and black pepper

300 ml (½ pint) full-fat crème fraîche

3 tbsp snipped fresh chives

1 Melt the butter in a large saucepan, add the onion, and cook gently, stirring occasionally, for a few minutes until soft but not coloured. Add the carrots, cover, and cook gently, stirring from time to time, for 10 minutes.

2 Add the stock and bring to a boil. Cover and simmer, stirring from time to time, for 30–40 minutes until the carrots are soft.

3 Purée the soup in a food processor or blender until smooth. Return the soup to the rinsed-out pan, add the orange zest and juice, and salt and pepper to taste. Stir in the crème fraîche and then gently reheat the soup.

4 Stir in half of the snipped chives, and garnish individual servings with the remaining chives.

♡ **Healthy note**

The crème fraîche makes this soup rich and creamy for a dinner-party first course, but for an everyday soup full of zest and vitality, you can omit it and increase the stock by 300 ml (½ pint) in step 2. Another healthy option is to cook the onion in step 1 in 1 tbsp each olive oil and water rather than using butter.

Curried parsnip soup

🍽 SERVES 6–8   197–147 CALS PER SERVING

30 g (1 oz) butter

750 g (1½ lb) parsnips, coarsely chopped

1 large onion, chopped

1 large garlic clove, crushed

2 tsp mild curry powder

1.8 litres (3 pints) vegetable or chicken stock

salt and black pepper

200 ml (7 fl oz) single cream

snipped fresh chives to garnish

1 Melt the butter in a large saucepan, add the chopped parsnips, onion, and crushed garlic, and cook gently, stirring occasionally, for 5 minutes or until the onion is softened but not coloured.

2 Stir in the curry powder, and cook for 1 minute, then blend in the stock, and season with salt and pepper. Bring to a boil, stirring, then cover, and simmer gently for 20 minutes or until the parsnips are tender.

3 Purée the soup in a food processor or blender until smooth. Return the soup to the rinsed-out pan, heat gently to warm through, stirring constantly, then taste for seasoning.

4 Stir in the single cream and reheat gently. Serve at once, garnished with fresh chives.

💙 **Healthy note**

If you are concerned about the fat content, omit the cream and use stock or water instead.

French onion soup

🍴 **SERVES 8**   **353 CALS PER SERVING**

45 g (1½ oz) butter

1 tbsp sunflower oil

1 kg (2 lb) large white onions, thinly sliced

2 tsp caster sugar

30 g (1 oz) plain flour

1.8 litres (3 pints) vegetable, chicken, or beef stock

salt and black pepper

8 Gruyère croûtes (page 44)

1 Melt the butter with the oil in a large saucepan, and caramelize the onions with the sugar (see box, right). Sprinkle the flour into the pan and cook, stirring constantly, for 1–2 minutes.

2 Gradually stir in the stock and bring to a boil. Season with salt and pepper, then cover and simmer, stirring from time to time, for 35 minutes.

3 Taste the soup for seasoning, then ladle into warmed bowls. Float a Gruyère croûte in each bowl and serve at once.

Caramelizing onions

Cook the onions in the butter and oil for a few minutes until soft. Add the sugar and continue cooking over a low heat, stirring occasionally, for 20 minutes or until the onions are golden brown.

Vegetable minestrone

 SERVES 4–6   250–167 CALS PER SERVING

2 tbsp olive oil

1 onion, chopped

2 celery stalks, chopped

2 carrots, finely diced

1 x 400 g can chopped Italian plum tomatoes

1 tbsp tomato purée

1 garlic clove, crushed

salt and black pepper

1.5 litres (2½ pints) chicken or vegetable stock

1 x 400 g can cannellini or red kidney beans, drained

250 g (8 oz) leeks, trimmed and finely sliced

125 g (4 oz) Savoy cabbage, finely shredded

2 tbsp arborio (risotto) rice

grated Parmesan cheese to serve

1 Heat the oil in a large saucepan, add the onion, celery, and carrots, and cook gently, stirring, for 5 minutes.

2 Add the tomatoes, tomato purée, and garlic, and season with salt and pepper. Stir, then pour in the stock and bring to a boil over a high heat.

3 Cover the pan and lower the heat so the soup is gently simmering. Cook for 15 minutes, stirring occasionally.

4 Add the beans, leeks, cabbage, and rice, and simmer for a further 20 minutes. Taste for seasoning.

5 Serve hot, with a bowl of grated Parmesan cheese for everyone to help themselves.

Cook's know-how

If you haven't got arborio or any other type of risotto rice, use broken spaghetti instead. You will need 30 g (1 oz).

Asparagus soup

 SERVES 6   96 CALS PER SERVING

250 g (8 oz) potatoes, chopped

1.5 litres (2½ pints) vegetable or chicken stock

500 g (1 lb) asparagus

2 garlic cloves, crushed

2 tbsp chopped fresh basil (optional)

salt and black pepper

30 g (1 oz) butter (optional)

1 Put the potatoes into a large saucepan, add the stock, and bring to a boil. Cover and simmer for 15 minutes or until the potatoes are tender.

2 Meanwhile, cut any woody ends off the asparagus and discard. Cut off the tips and chop the stalks into chunks.

3 Add the asparagus and garlic to the pan, and cook for 5 minutes, stirring from time to time, until the asparagus is tender. Remove 9 tips; reserve for the garnish.

4 Purée the soup in a food processor or blender until smooth.

5 Return the soup to the rinsed-out pan and reheat. Add the basil, if using, and salt and pepper to taste. Slice the reserved asparagus tips lengthways in half. Serve the soup hot, garnished with the asparagus tips, and small nuggets of butter, if wished.

Artichoke soup

Use 1 x 400 g can artichoke hearts or bottoms, drained and diced, instead of the asparagus, and garnish with basil.

Healthy note

This is a soup for a special occasion, and the butter garnish makes it an absolute classic – melted butter is traditional with asparagus. If you are concerned about the fat content, you can garnish with torn basil instead.

Watercress soup

 SERVES 6   140 CALS PER SERVING

30 g (1 oz) butter

1 onion, finely chopped

2 potatoes, coarsely chopped

125 g (4 oz) watercress, tough stalks removed

900 ml (1½ pints) vegetable or chicken stock

300 ml (½ pint) milk

1 bay leaf

salt and black pepper

single cream to garnish (optional)

1 Melt the butter in a large saucepan, add the onion, and cook gently, stirring from time to time, for a few minutes until soft but not coloured.

2 Add the potatoes and the watercress to the saucepan and cook for about 5 minutes until the watercress is wilted.

3 Pour in the chicken or vegetable stock and milk, add the bay leaf, and season with salt and pepper.

4 Bring the mixture to a boil, cover, and simmer very gently for 15 minutes or until the potatoes are tender.

5 Remove the bay leaf and discard. Purée the soup in a food processor or blender until smooth. Return the soup to the rinsed-out pan, reheat, then taste for seasoning.

6 Serve hot, garnishing each bowl with a little single cream if you like.

Tomato soup

SERVES 6–8   134–101 CALS PER SERVING

30 g (1 oz) butter

2 onions, coarsely chopped

1 garlic clove, crushed

1 tbsp plain flour

1.25 litres (2 pints) vegetable or chicken stock

2 x 400 g cans tomatoes

1 bay leaf

salt and black pepper

4 tbsp ready-made pesto

single cream (optional) and fresh basil leaves to garnish

1 Melt the butter in a large saucepan, add the onions and garlic, and cook gently, stirring from time to time, for a few minutes until soft but not coloured.

2 Add the flour to the pan and cook, stirring constantly, for 1 minute.

3 Pour in the stock, then add the tomatoes and their juice and the bay leaf. Season with salt and pepper. Bring to a boil, cover the pan, and simmer gently for 20 minutes.

4 Remove the bay leaf and discard. Purée the soup in a food processor or blender until smooth.

5 Return the soup to the rinsed-out pan, add the pesto, and heat through. Taste for seasoning.

6 Serve at once, garnished with cream (if you like) and fresh basil leaves.

Quick tomato soup

Passata, Italian sieved tomatoes, makes a beautiful, deep red soup. Substitute 750 ml (1¼ pints) of bottled or canned passata for the canned tomatoes and then cook as directed.

♥ Healthy note

For a really healthy version of this soup, omit the butter, flour, and pesto and simply simmer the onions and garlic with the stock, tomatoes, and bay leaf. Cook for 30-40 minutes to develop the flavours before puréeing, then serve topped with torn basil.

Borscht

SERVES 4   244 CALS PER SERVING

175 g (6 oz) white cabbage, coarsely shredded

200 g (7 oz) waxy potatoes, peeled and diced

1 x 225 g can chopped tomatoes

1 small carrot, chopped

1 small onion, chopped

1.5 litres (2½ pints) vegetable or chicken stock, more if needed

500 g (1 lb) cooked beetroot, peeled and diced

3–4 dill sprigs, chopped

30 g (1 oz) sugar

2 tbsp wine vinegar

salt and black pepper

soured cream and dill sprigs to garnish

1 Put the cabbage, potatoes, tomatoes, carrot, and onion into a large pan with the stock.

2 Bring to a boil, then simmer for 30–40 minutes until the vegetables are very tender. Add extra stock if necessary.

3 Add the diced beetroot, dill, sugar, and vinegar, and simmer for 10 minutes to let the sweet–sour flavours develop. Add salt and pepper to taste, and more sugar and vinegar if necessary.

4 Serve at once, garnished with spoonfuls of soured cream and sprigs of dill.

Winter vegetable soup

SERVES 6   153 CALS PER SERVING

45 g (1½ oz) butter

1 leek, trimmed and diced

1 onion, chopped

1 celery stalk, diced

1 small potato, peeled and diced

1 turnip, diced

1 small carrot, diced

3 garlic cloves, crushed

1.5 litres (2½ pints) vegetable or chicken stock

250 g (8 oz) spinach, coarsely shredded (see box, below)

3 spring onions, thinly sliced

salt and black pepper

1 Melt the butter in a large saucepan, add the leek, and cook gently, stirring occasionally, for 5 minutes or until softened. Add the onion, celery, potato, turnip, carrot, and garlic, and cook for 8 minutes.

2 Pour in the stock, and bring to a boil. Cover and simmer, stirring occasionally, for 25 minutes or until the vegetables are tender.

3 Add the spinach and spring onions, and cook for just 3 minutes until the spinach is wilted and still bright green. Season well, and serve hot.

Shredding spinach

Remove the stalks and stack several spinach leaves. Roll up tightly, and cut crosswise into shreds.

Opposite: Winter vegetable soup.

Split pea and gammon soup

🍴 SERVES 8   338 CALS PER SERVING

500 g (1 lb) green split peas

500 g (1 lb) gammon knuckle

2.5 litres (4 pints) water

1 large onion, finely chopped

4 celery stalks, finely chopped

3 potatoes, peeled and diced

3 leeks, trimmed and sliced

3 tbsp chopped parsley (optional)

salt and black pepper

1 Put the green split peas and the gammon knuckle into separate large bowls and cover generously with cold water. Leave to soak overnight.

2 Drain the split peas and gammon knuckle, then put them both into a large saucepan with the measured water. Bring to a boil, then simmer, uncovered, for about 1 hour.

3 Add the onion, celery, potatoes, and leeks to the pan, cover, and simmer gently for 2½ hours until the gammon is tender and the peas are cooked. Add more water, if needed, during cooking.

4 Skim the surface if necessary. Remove the gammon knuckle from the

saucepan and let it cool slightly. Pull the meat away from the knuckle bone, discarding any skin and fat.

5 Coarsely chop the meat and return it to the saucepan. Add the parsley, if using, and salt and pepper to taste, then heat gently to warm the meat through. Serve hot.

🔍 Cook's know-how

Gammon knuckles are meaty, yet inexpensive. Your butcher will have them, if you can't get one at the supermarket.

Spiced autumn soup

SERVES 8 171 CALS PER SERVING

60 g (2 oz) butter

2 large onions, coarsely chopped

2 potatoes, coarsely chopped

2 carrots, coarsely chopped

3 garlic cloves, crushed

pared zest and juice of 1 orange

2 tsp mild curry powder

1.8 litres (3 pints) vegetable or chicken stock

2 x 400 g cans chopped tomatoes

2 eating apples, peeled and chopped

salt and black pepper

herb croûtes (page 44) to serve

1 Melt the butter in a large saucepan, add the onions, potatoes, carrots, garlic, and orange zest, and cook gently, stirring from time to time, for about 5 minutes.

2 Add the curry powder, and cook, stirring constantly, for 1–2 minutes.

3 Add the stock, orange juice, tomatoes, and apples, and season with salt and pepper. Bring to a boil, cover, and simmer gently for 30 minutes or until the vegetables are tender. Discard the orange zest.

4 Purée the soup in a food processor or blender until smooth. Return to the rinsed-out pan, reheat, and taste for seasoning. Serve hot, with herb croûtes.

Paring orange zest

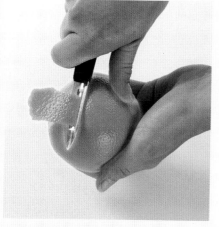

With a vegetable peeler, remove strips of zest, excluding the bitter white pith.

Blue Stilton and onion soup

SERVES 8 255 CALS PER SERVING

600 ml (1 pint) milk

2 bay leaves

¼ tsp grated nutmeg

90 g (3 oz) butter

2 large onions, finely sliced

75 g (2½ oz) plain flour

1.5 litres (2½ pints) vegetable or chicken stock

salt and black pepper

150 g (5 oz) blue Stilton cheese, crumbled

single cream to serve (optional)

1 Pour the milk into a saucepan, add the bay leaves and nutmeg, and bring almost to a boil. Remove from the heat, cover, and leave to infuse for 20 minutes.

2 Meanwhile, melt the butter in a large pan, add the onions, and cook very gently, stirring occasionally, for about 10 minutes or until they are soft but not coloured.

3 Add the flour, and cook, stirring, for 2 minutes. Strain the milk and gradually blend it into the onion and flour. Add the stock, and season with salt and pepper. Bring to a boil and simmer, half covered, for 10 minutes.

4 Add the cheese and stir over a very low heat until it melts (do not boil or the cheese will be stringy). Taste for seasoning, and stir in a little cream if you wish. Serve hot.

♡ Healthy note

There are ways of making this soup lighter if you are concerned about the fat content. Use semi-skimmed milk in step 1, only 30 g (1 oz) butter in step 2, and omit the flour in step 3. At the end, whisk the flour to a paste with a little cold stock or water, then whisk into the soup and boil, whisking, until thickened. Add only 60-90 g (2-3 oz) cheese in step 4.

Clam chowder

SERVES 4 497 CALS PER SERVING

500 g (1 lb) fresh clams in their shells, cleaned (page 107)

250 ml (8 fl oz) fish stock

45 g (1½ oz) butter

1 onion, chopped

3 unsmoked bacon rashers, rinds removed, diced

2 tbsp plain flour

2 potatoes, peeled and diced

750 ml (1¼ pints) milk

1 bay leaf

salt and black pepper

1 Put the clams into a large saucepan, add the fish stock, and bring to a boil. Lower the heat, cover, and cook over a medium heat for 5–8 minutes until the clam shells open.

2 Discard any clams that have not opened. Set aside 12 clams in their shells for garnish and keep warm. Remove the remaining clams from their shells. Discard the shells and strain the cooking juices.

3 Melt the butter in a large pan, add the onion, and cook gently for a few minutes until soft but not coloured. Add the bacon and the flour, and cook, stirring, for 1–2 minutes.

4 Add the potatoes, milk, strained clam juices, and bay leaf to the pan. Bring to a boil, then lower the heat and simmer for 15 minutes. Add the shelled clams, and heat gently for about 5 minutes. Remove the bay leaf and discard.

5 Add salt and pepper to taste. Serve hot, garnished with the reserved clams in their shells.

Lobster bisque

A bisque is a purée flavoured with brandy, white wine, and cream, prepared by a complex process that brings out the maximum flavour. When made with lobster, it is perfect for a special occasion. This lighter and healthier version of the traditional recipe is just as delicious.

 SERVES 6   **192 CALS PER SERVING**

30 g (1 oz) butter

6 shallots, coarsely chopped

½ carrot, finely chopped

1 cooked large lobster

pinch of cayenne pepper

½ tsp paprika

juice of 1 small lemon

4 tbsp brandy

300 ml (½ pint) dry white wine

1.5 litre (2½ pints) fish stock

60 g (2 oz) long-grain rice

about 3 tbsp single cream (optional)

1 Melt the butter in a large saucepan, add the shallots and carrot, and cook gently for about 5 minutes until softened.

2 Using a mallet or wooden rolling pin, crack the lobster shells, remove the cooked meat (page 109), and set aside. Reserve a single large piece of the shell to add to the bisque, and discard the rest.

3 Slice the meat from the large claws and tail of the lobster, reserving a few pieces for garnish.

4 Add the cayenne, paprika, lemon juice, and brandy to the shallots and carrot in the pan, and reduce over a high heat to about 2 tablespoons.

5 Add the wine, fish stock, rice, and reserved lobster shell to the pan, and cook for about 15 minutes until the rice is tender. Remove the lobster shell, and discard.

6 Add the lobster meat (except the garnish) to the pan, and season lightly with salt and pepper. Cook the soup over a low heat just until the lobster is heated through, about 5 minutes.

7 Purée the soup in a food processor or blender until smooth. Pour the purée through a sieve to remove any tiny pieces of lobster shell.

8 Return the purée to the pan, and add the cream if using. Taste for seasoning, and adjust if necessary.

9 Serve the soup at once, garnished with the reserved lobster slices.

Croûtes and croûtons

These need not be reserved for special occasions. They can turn the most basic of everyday soups into a complete meal.

Herb croûtes
Trim the crusts from slices of bread. Cut each slice into a square or decorative shape. Heat a very thin film of oil in a non-stick frying pan, add the bread, and brown on both sides. Finely chop some parsley or separate into small sprigs. Drain the croûtes on paper towels. Roll the edges of the croûtes in the parsley or put a leaf on top of each one.

Garlic croûtons
Trim the crusts from slices of bread and cut into 1 cm (½ in) cubes. Heat a very thin film of oil in a non-stick frying pan. Peel and crush 1 garlic clove and cook for 1 minute. Add the bread cubes and cook, stirring occasionally, until brown all over. Remove, and drain on paper towels.

Gruyère croûtes
Cut slices from a baguette and toast on one side under a hot grill. Remove from the heat and turn the slices over. Grate Gruyère cheese evenly over the untoasted sides of the bread slices. Return to the grill and cook until the cheese has melted and is gently bubbling.

Bouillabaisse

Bouillabaisse, the classic fish soup–stew with the authentic flavours of Provence, is one of the most satisfying and delectable dishes you can bring to your table. In France it is traditionally served with thick slices of toasted bread spread with rouille, a chilli-flavoured mayonnaise.

 SERVES 8   **337 CALS PER SERVING**

2 tbsp olive oil

1 large onion, chopped

1 small fennel bulb, sliced

4 garlic cloves, crushed

1 tbsp chopped parsley

1 bay leaf

1 litre (1¾ pints) water

600 ml (1 pint) fish stock

500 g (1 lb) ripe tomatoes, finely chopped

a strip of orange zest

¼ tsp fennel seeds (optional)

2–3 potatoes, cut into chunks

500 g (1 lb) assorted fish, cut into bite-sized pieces

500 g (1 lb) assorted shellfish, shelled

pinch of saffron threads

salt and black pepper

8 toasted baguette slices, to serve

ROUILLE

3 garlic cloves

125 ml (4 fl oz) mayonnaise

2 tsp paprika

1 tsp mild chilli powder

3 tbsp olive oil

1 small fresh red chilli, halved, seeded, and finely chopped

1 tbsp lemon juice

salt

1 Heat the olive oil in a large, heavy saucepan. Add the onion, fennel, garlic, parsley, and bay leaf, and cook, stirring occasionally, for 5 minutes.

2 Add the water, stock, tomatoes, orange zest, and fennel seeds (if using). Bring to a boil, cover, and simmer for 30 minutes.

3 Meanwhile, make the rouille (see box, right). Chill until needed.

4 Add the potatoes to the soup, cover, and simmer for 10 minutes. Do not stir or the potatoes will break up.

5 Add the fish, shellfish, and saffron, and season with salt and pepper. Cover and cook for a few minutes, just until the fish turns opaque.

6 Remove the bay leaf and orange zest, and discard. Serve the bouillabaisse with slices of toasted baguette spread with the rouille.

Making rouille

Use a knife blade to crush the garlic to a paste. Mix in a bowl with the mayonnaise, paprika, and chilli powder.

Pour in the olive oil, drop by drop, whisking constantly as the oil is absorbed into the spicy mayonnaise.

Add the red chilli and lemon juice to the sauce; add salt to taste, and stir well to combine.

Butternut squash soup

🍴 SERVES 6 197 CALS PER SERVING

3 small butternut squash, about 1.7 kg (3½ lb) total weight

2 tbsp olive oil

grated nutmeg

salt and black pepper

30 g (1 oz) butter

1 large onion, roughly chopped

2 large carrots, roughly chopped

2 large celery stalks, roughly chopped

1.2–1.3 litres (2–2¼ pints) vegetable stock

crusty bread to serve

1 Cut each squash lengthways in half, then scoop out and discard the seeds and stringy fibres. Arrange the squash halves cut-side up in a roasting tin just large enough to hold them in a single layer. Drizzle the olive oil over the flesh of the squash, and season with nutmeg, salt, and pepper. Pour 150 ml (¼ pint) cold water into the tin around the squash. Roast in a preheated oven at 200°C (180°C fan, Gas 6) for about 1 hour until tender. Remove from the oven, and set aside until cool enough to handle.

2 Meanwhile, melt the butter in a large saucepan, and add the chopped vegetables. Cook over a high heat for a few minutes until lightly coloured, stirring constantly. Pour in the stock, season with salt and pepper, and bring to a boil. Cover, and simmer gently for 20 minutes or until the vegetables are tender. Remove from the heat.

3 Scoop the flesh from the squash skins into the soup in the pan, then purée in a food processor or blender until smooth. (If using a food processor, purée the vegetables with a little of the liquid first, then add the remaining liquid and purée again.) Return the soup to the rinsed-out pan, reheat, and taste for seasoning. Serve hot, with crusty bread.

Pumpkin soup

🍴 SERVES 6 329 CALS PER SERVING

1.5 kg (3 lb) pumpkin

150 g (5 oz) butter

2 leeks, trimmed and sliced

1 litre (1¾ pints) chicken or vegetable stock

¼ tsp grated nutmeg

salt and black pepper

30 g (1 oz) petits pois

250 g (8 oz) spinach leaves, finely chopped

300 ml (½ pint) single cream

1 Cut out the flesh from the pumpkin, discarding the seeds and fibres. Cut the flesh into 2 cm (¾ in) chunks.

2 Melt 100 g (3½ oz) of the butter in a large saucepan. Add the leeks, and cook very gently, covered, for 10 minutes or until soft.

3 Add the stock, pumpkin chunks, and nutmeg, and season with salt and pepper. Bring to a boil, cover, and simmer for 30 minutes or until the vegetables are very soft.

4 Meanwhile, cook the petits pois in boiling salted water for 5 minutes. Drain thoroughly.

5 Melt the remaining butter in a saucepan. Add the spinach, cover, and cook gently for 3 minutes until wilted.

6 Purée the soup in a food processor or blender until smooth, in batches if necessary. Return to the pan and stir in the cream. Stir the petits pois and spinach into the soup, heat through, and serve hot.

🔍 Cook's know-how

You can serve the soup in small hollowed-out pumpkins, scalloping the edges. Other possibilities include leaving the soup chunky rather than puréeing it, using double the amount of spinach and omitting the peas, and halving the butter and cream to reduce the fat content.

Hot and sour soup

🍴 SERVES 4–6 249–166 CALS PER SERVING

2 dried Chinese mushrooms

¼ head Chinese leaves, sliced

1.5 litres (2½ pints) chicken or vegetable stock

60 g (2 oz) Chinese noodles, such as rice sticks

salt

125 g (4 oz) firm tofu, diced

90 g (3 oz) drained canned bamboo shoots, sliced

90 g (3 oz) cooked lean boneless, skinless chicken, diced

30 g (1 oz) bean sprouts

3 tbsp cornflour mixed with 3 tbsp cold water

2 eggs, lightly beaten

2 tbsp white wine vinegar

1 tbsp dark soy sauce

¼ tsp cayenne pepper

TO SERVE

2 tsp sesame oil

2 spring onions, thinly sliced coriander sprigs

1 Put the mushrooms into a bowl, cover with hot water, and leave to soak for about 30 minutes.

2 Meanwhile, put the sliced Chinese leaves into a large saucepan, add the stock, and bring to a boil. Simmer for 15 minutes. Set aside.

3 Break the noodles into pieces. Simmer in boiling salted water for 3–4 minutes until just tender. Drain.

4 Drain the mushrooms, reserving the soaking liquid. Squeeze the mushrooms dry, then cut them into thin strips.

5 Add the tofu, bamboo shoots, chicken, bean sprouts, noodles, and the mushrooms and their liquid to the Chinese leaves and stock. Heat until almost boiling, then stir in the cornflour mixture. Simmer until the soup thickens slightly, then drizzle in the beaten eggs to form strands.

6 Combine the vinegar, soy sauce, and cayenne pepper, and pour into the soup. Taste for seasoning. Drizzle a little sesame oil over each serving, and garnish with spring onion slices and coriander sprigs.

Opposite: Butternut squash soup.

Goulash soup

 SERVES 6   363 CALS PER SERVING

2 red peppers

2 tbsp sunflower oil

500 g (1 lb) stewing beef, trimmed and cut into 3.5 cm (1½ in) pieces

2 large onions, thickly sliced

1 tbsp plain flour

2 tsp paprika

1.5 litres (2½ pints) beef stock

1 x 400 g can chopped tomatoes

2 tbsp tomato purée

1 tbsp red wine vinegar

1 garlic clove, crushed

1 bay leaf

salt and black pepper

750 g (1½ lb) potatoes, peeled and diced

dash of Tabasco sauce

soured cream and snipped fresh chives to garnish (optional)

1 Roast and peel the red peppers (page 345). Cut the flesh into chunks.

2 Heat the oil in a large pan. Add the beef and brown all over. Add the onions, peppers, flour, and paprika, and stir over a high heat for 1–2 minutes.

3 Add the stock, tomatoes, tomato purée, vinegar, garlic, and bay leaf, and season with salt and pepper. Bring to a boil, cover tightly, and simmer for 1½ hours.

4 Add the potatoes and cook for 30 minutes or until the beef and potatoes are tender. Remove the bay leaf and discard.

5 Add a little Tabasco sauce and taste for seasoning. Serve hot, garnished with soured cream and snipped chives if you like.

Cook's know-how

To save time, use about 4 pieces of bottled roasted red pepper instead of roasting your own. They can be preserved in oil or brine, whichever you prefer.

Game soup

🍴 SERVES 4   223 CALS PER SERVING

30 g (1 oz) butter

125 g (4 oz) smoked streaky bacon rashers, rinds removed, diced

1 onion, sliced

125 g (4 oz) chestnut mushrooms, sliced

1 tbsp plain flour

1.25 litres (2 pints) game stock (page 146)

salt and black pepper

1 tbsp redcurrant jelly

ORANGE–HERB BOUQUET

6 parsley stalks

pared zest of 1 orange

1 bay leaf

1 large thyme or marjoram sprig

1 Make the orange-herb bouquet (see box, below) and set aside.

2 Melt the butter in a large saucepan, add the bacon, and cook over a high heat, stirring occasionally, for 5–7 minutes until crisp.

3 Lower the heat, add the onion to the pan, and cook gently, stirring from time to time, for a few minutes until softened but not coloured.

4 Add the mushrooms to the pan, and cook for about 5 minutes, then add the flour and cook, stirring constantly, for 1 minute. Add the stock and the orange-herb bouquet, season with salt and pepper, and bring to a boil. Cover and simmer for 30 minutes.

5 Discard the bouquet, then stir in the redcurrant jelly. Taste for seasoning before serving.

Orange-herb bouquet

Tie the parsley, orange zest, bay leaf, and thyme or marjoram with a piece of white string. Leave a length of string to tie to the saucepan handle, so that the orange and herb bouquet can be easily lifted from the pan at the end of cooking.

Lentil and bacon soup

🍴 SERVES 4–6   301–201 CALS PER SERVING

30 g (1 oz) butter

1 onion, chopped

1 carrot, diced

1 celery stalk, diced

3 garlic cloves, crushed

2–3 lean back bacon rashers, rinds removed, diced

175 g (6 oz) red lentils

about 125 g (4 oz) potatoes, swede or turnip, peeled and diced

2 bay leaves

2 litres (3½ pints) vegetable or chicken stock

salt and black pepper

chopped parsley to garnish

1 Melt the butter in a large saucepan, add the onion, carrot, celery, and garlic, and cook, stirring, for 5–6 minutes until soft and lightly coloured.

2 Add the bacon, lentils, potato, swede or turnip and bay leaves. Cook for 15 minutes.

3 Pour in the stock and bring to a boil, then simmer gently, uncovered, for about 20 minutes or until the lentils and vegetables are tender. Add salt and pepper to taste.

4 Remove the bay leaves and discard. Serve hot, sprinkled with chopped parsley.

Lentil and frankfurter soup

For a hearty main meal soup, add 250 g (8 oz) frankfurters. Chop them into 1 cm (½ in) pieces and add to the soup about 5 minutes before the end of the cooking time, so that they warm through but do not overcook. Smoked sausages can also be used.

Chinese crab and sweetcorn soup

🍴 SERVES 4   216 CALS PER SERVING

375 g (12 oz) frozen sweetcorn kernels

1 litre (1¾ pints) hot chicken stock

3 spring onions, thinly sliced

1 cm (½ in) piece of fresh root ginger, peeled and grated

1 garlic clove, crushed

1 tbsp light soy sauce

250 g (8 oz) cooked crabmeat

1 tbsp cornflour mixed with 2 tbsp cold water

salt and black pepper

sesame oil and coriander sprigs to serve

1 Purée the sweetcorn with one-quarter of the hot stock in a food processor or blender until smooth.

2 Pour the remaining stock into a pan, and add the spring onions, ginger, garlic, and soy sauce. Heat until bubbles form at the edge.

3 Add the crabmeat and the sweetcorn purée, and continue to heat until bubbles form again. Blend the cornflour mixture into the soup, and cook, stirring occasionally, for 10 minutes or until it thickens slightly. Season to taste with salt and pepper.

4 Pour the soup into bowls, drizzle a little sesame oil over each serving, and garnish with coriander. Serve hot.

Use fresh corn if it is in season. Remove husks, boil the cob for 6-8 minutes, and cut the kernels from the cob with a sharp knife. You would need at least 2-3 cobs to get 375 g (12 oz) kernels.

Tzatziki soup

SERVES 4–6   138–92 CALS PER SERVING

600 g (1 lb 3 oz) plain yogurt

250 ml (8 fl oz) water

1 cucumber, seeded (see box, below) and diced

4 garlic cloves, coarsely chopped

1 tbsp olive oil

1 tsp white wine vinegar

1 tsp chopped fresh mint

salt and black pepper

2–3 tbsp chopped fresh mint and 3 spring onions, thinly sliced, to garnish

1 Purée the yogurt, measured water, one-quarter of the diced cucumber, the garlic, oil, vinegar, and mint in a food processor or blender until smooth. Season well with salt and add pepper to taste.

2 Transfer the soup to a large bowl and stir in the remaining cucumber. Cover and chill for at least 1 hour.

3 Taste for seasoning. Sprinkle the soup with chopped fresh mint and spring onions before serving.

Seeding a cucumber

Trim the cucumber with a small knife, then cut it in half, lengthways. With a teaspoon, scoop out and discard the seeds from each cucumber half.

Thai spiced soup

SERVES 4   238 CALS PER SERVING

90 g (3 oz) thin egg noodles

salt and black pepper

500 ml (16 fl oz) chicken stock

1 x 400 g can coconut milk

1 small carrot, coarsely chopped

30 g (1 oz) French beans, cut into 1 cm (½ in) pieces

3 spring onions, thinly sliced

250 g (8 oz) cooked lean boneless and skinless chicken, shredded

125 g (4 oz) mixed green leaves, such as spinach and pak choi, shredded

30 g (1 oz) bean sprouts

2 tbsp fish sauce

2 tsp Thai curry paste (green or red)

¼ cucumber, cut into matchstick-thin strips, and coriander sprigs to garnish

1 Cook the noodles in boiling salted water for 2–3 minutes, or according to package instructions, until just tender. Drain and rinse in cold water. Set aside while preparing the soup.

2 Put the stock, coconut milk, carrot, French beans, and spring onions into a large saucepan; bring to a boil.

3 Lower the heat, add the chicken, green leaves, bean sprouts, fish sauce, and spice paste, and cook for 2 minutes or until the green leaves are just wilted. Season to taste with salt and pepper.

4 To serve, divide the cooked noodles among warmed bowls. Ladle the hot soup over the noodles, and garnish with cucumber strips and coriander sprigs.

Cook's know-how

For a vegetarian version, omit the cooked chicken and use a vegetable stock instead of the chicken stock. You can also vary the vegetables, but their cooking times may be different. Try shredded white cabbage instead of the green leaves and mangetout instead of French beans. Shredded Swiss chard would also be good in this soup, as would a small quantity of sweetcorn kernels or peas, and even a little diced aubergine.

Vichyssoise

SERVES 4–6   251–167 CALS PER SERVING

60 g (2 oz) butter

3 large leeks, trimmed and sliced

1 small onion, chopped

2 potatoes, peeled and coarsely chopped

1.25 litres (2 pints) chicken stock

salt and black pepper

TO SERVE

150 ml (¼ pint) single cream

milk (optional)

2 tbsp fresh snipped chives

1 Melt the butter in a large saucepan, add the leeks and onion, and cook very gently, stirring occasionally, for 10–15 minutes until soft but not coloured.

2 Add the potatoes, stock, and salt and pepper to taste, and bring to a boil. Cover and simmer gently for 15–20 minutes until the potatoes are tender.

3 Purée the soup in a food processor or blender until smooth. Pour into a large bowl or pass through a sieve for a smoother finish. Cover and chill for at least 3 hours.

4 To serve, stir in the cream. If the soup is too thick, add a little milk. Taste for seasoning. Garnish with snipped chives before serving.

Chicken noodle soup

SERVES 6　　261 CALS PER SERVING

0 g (1 lb) chicken thighs

0 g (1 lb) carrots, sliced

head celery, chopped

small onion, peeled but left whole

3 garlic cloves, coarsely chopped

few parsley sprigs

75 litres (3 pints) chicken stock

lt and black pepper

5 g (4 oz) thin noodles

opped fresh dill to garnish

1 Put the chicken thighs into a large saucepan with the carrots, celery, onion, garlic, and parsley. Pour in the stock and bring to a boil. Using a slotted spoon, skim off the foam that rises to the top of the pan.

2 Lower the heat and season with salt and pepper. Cover and simmer gently for 30 minutes.

3 Skim any fat from the surface of the soup. With a slotted spoon, lift out the parsley, onion, and chicken. Discard the parsley. Chop the onion, and shred the chicken meat, discarding the skin and bones. Set aside.

4 Break the noodles into 5 cm (2 in) pieces and drop them into the soup. Bring to a boil, cover, and simmer for about 10 minutes or until tender.

5 Return the onion and chicken to the soup, heat through, and taste for seasoning. Serve hot, garnished with dill.

Healthy note

To reduce the fat content of the soup, strip the skin off the chicken thighs before cooking. Chicken meat is low in fat and calories; the fatty part is in the skin and just underneath it.

Gazpacho

SERVES 4–6   249–166 CALS PER SERVING

1 kg (2 lb) tomatoes, peeled (see box, below), quartered, and seeded

1 large Spanish onion

1 x 200 g jar roasted peppers (in oil or brine), drained

2 large garlic cloves

600 ml (1 pint) cold vegetable or chicken stock

75 ml (2½ fl oz) olive oil

4 tbsp red wine vinegar

juice of ½ lemon

salt and black pepper

TO GARNISH

½ cucumber, diced

1 small green pepper, halved, seeded, and diced

garlic croûtons (page 44)

1 Coarsely chop the tomatoes, onion, peppers, and garlic. Purée in a food processor or blender with the stock, oil, and vinegar until smooth.

2 Turn the mixture into a bowl and add the lemon juice, and salt and pepper to taste. Cover and chill for at least 1 hour.

3 Serve the soup well chilled in bowls, each one garnished with spoonfuls of diced cucumber, green pepper, and garlic croûtons.

Peeling tomatoes

Cut the cores from the tomatoes and score an "x" on the base. Immerse the tomatoes in boiling water for 8–15 seconds until their skins start to split. Transfer at once to cold water. When the tomatoes are cool enough to handle, peel off the skin with a small knife.

Chilled curried apple and mint soup

SERVES 6   110 CALS PER SERVING

30 g (1 oz) butter

1 onion, coarsely chopped

1 tbsp mild curry powder

900 ml (1½ pints) vegetable stock

750 g (1½ lb) cooking apples, peeled, cored, and coarsely chopped

2 tbsp mango chutney

juice of ½ lemon

7–8 fresh mint sprigs

salt and black pepper

100 g (3½ oz) plain yogurt

a little milk, if needed

1 Melt the butter in a large saucepan, add the onion, and cook gently, stirring occasionally, for a few minutes until soft but not coloured. Add the curry powder and cook, stirring constantly, for 1–2 minutes.

2 Add the stock and chopped apples and bring to a boil, stirring. Cover and simmer for 15 minutes or until the apples are tender.

3 Purée the apple mixture, mango chutney, and lemon juice in a food processor or blender until very smooth.

4 Strip the mint leaves from the stalks, reserving 6 small sprigs for garnish. Finely chop the mint leaves.

5 Pour the soup into a large bowl, stir in the chopped mint, and add salt and pepper to taste. Cover and chill in the refrigerator for at least 3 hours.

6 Whisk in the yogurt, then taste for seasoning. If the soup is too thick, add a little milk. Garnish with the reserved mint before serving.

Cook's know-how

This soup is equally delicious served hot. After puréeing, return the soup to the rinsed-out pan and reheat it gently, stirring occasionally. Stir in the chopped mint, then remove from the heat and swirl in the yogurt. Serve at once.

Chilled strawberry soup

SERVES 4   169 CALS PER SERVING

250 ml (8 fl oz) dry white wine

90 g (3 oz) caster sugar

1 very small piece of pared lime zest (optional)

250 g (8 oz) strawberries

250 ml (8 fl oz) orange juice (squeezed fresh or from a carton)

4 mint sprigs to garnish

1 Put the wine and sugar into a saucepan and bring to a boil. Continue boiling for 5 minutes, then remove the pan from the heat and add the lime zest, if using. Leave to cool.

2 Remove and discard the lime zest, if used. Hull and chop the strawberries, reserving 4 for garnish.

3 Purée the wine syrup and strawberries in a food processor or blender until very smooth.

4 Turn the purée into a large bowl and stir in the orange juice. Cover and chill for at least 3 hours.

5 Serve well chilled and garnished with the reserved strawberries and mint sprigs.

Strawberry and Champagne soup

Omit the white wine and lime zest. Purée the strawberries, reserving a few for garnish, with the sugar and orange juice. Divide the mixture among chilled glass serving bowls, and top with chilled Champagne or dry sparkling wine. Garnish and serve.

Strawberry and watermelon soup

Remove the seeds from a 1 kg (2 lb) piece of watermelon. Cut up the flesh and purée until smooth, then combine with the wine syrup, strawberries, and a little lime juice. Omit the orange juice.

First Courses

Under 45 minutes

Avocado with tomatoes and mint
Light and refreshing: chopped tomatoes
combined with mint and vinaigrette
dressing, and piled into avocado halves.
SERVES 4   232 CALS PER SERVING
Takes 15 minutes   Page 79

Salmon quenelles
Little dumplings of salmon, egg whites, and
cream, shaped and poached, and served with
a luxurious asparagus sauce.
SERVES 6   511 CALS PER SERVING
Takes 30 minutes, **plus chilling**   Page 71

PREPARE AHEAD

Gravadlax
Scandinavian speciality: fresh salmon fillets
pickled in sugar, sea salt, dill, and black
pepper, sandwiched together, and chilled.
Served in slices, with a rice sauce.
SERVES 16   395 CALS PER SERVING
Takes 30 minutes, **plus chilling**   Page 72

PREPARE AHEAD

Three fish terrine
Layers of smoked fish pâtés - trout, salmon,
and mackerel - wrapped in smoked salmon
slices.
SERVES 10   424 CALS PER SERVING
Takes 40 minutes, **plus chilling**   Page 65

Spicy meatballs
Tiny warm meatballs seasoned with garlic,
onion, paprika, fresh coriander, and tomato
purée. Served with a sesame dip.
SERVES 6   481 CALS PER SERVING
Takes 25 minutes   Page 58

Chèvre croûtes
Goat's cheese and pesto, on toasted baguette
slices and sprinkled with olive oil, give a tang
flavour to this inviting appetizer.
SERVES 4   450 CALS PER SERVING
Takes 20 minutes   Page 5

QUICK AND EASY

Hummus
Smooth and summery: cannellini beans
blended with rosemary, olive oil, and lemon
juice, and richly flavoured with garlic.
SERVES 6   150 CALS PER SERVING
Takes 10 minutes   Page 67

Canapés
Lightly tossed bread served with a selection
of toppings: anchovy and prawn, cheese and
spring onion, salami, and asparagus.
SERVES 4   251 CALS PER SERVING
Takes 40 minutes   Page 56

**Beef carpaccio with vegetables and
mustard dressing**
Beef fillets encrusted with herbs and lightly
fried in olive oil. Served with asparagus and
carrots and drizzled with a mustard dressing
SERVES 6   302 CALS PER SERVING
Takes 25 minutes   Page 7

45-60 minutes

PREPARE AHEAD

Salmon and prawn filo purses
Bite-sized pieces of salmon combined with prawns in light-textured filo pastry purses. Served with a wine, cream, and dill sauce.

MAKES 8   448 CALS EACH
Takes 55 minutes   Page 63

Smoked salmon roulade
Savoury spinach roulade layered with smoked salmon, a mixture of soft cheese, yogurt, spring onions, and tomatoes.

SERVES 4–6   407–271 CALS PER SERVING
Takes 45 minutes, **plus chilling**   Page 77

MEXICAN CLASSIC

Nachos grande
Spicy and nourishing: refried beans, tomatoes, chilli, onion, garlic, and green pepper, enclosed in tortilla chips. Topped with cheese.

SERVES 6   396 CALS PER SERVING
Takes 45 minutes   Page 62

Baked figs with Camembert
Large ripe figs stuffed with Camembert cheese, wrapped in ham slices, and baked. Served on salad leaves tossed in mustard and honey dressing.

SERVES 6   180 CALS PER SERVING
Takes 55 minutes   Page 74

Smoked haddock mousse
Tender smoked fish blended with soft cheese, mayonnaise, and vibrant turmeric for a rich colour and flavour.

SERVES 6   217 CALS PER SERVING
Takes 45 minutes, **plus chilling**   Page 66

Over 60 minutes

Herbed mini sausage rolls
Pork sausagemeat flavoured with parsley and thyme, wrapped in puff pastry to create tiny rolls, and then baked. Best when served warm.

MAKES 36   83 CALS EACH
Takes 1¼ hours   Page 62

Brandied chicken liver pâté
Chicken livers blended with bread, bacon, thyme, egg, and nutmeg, and flavoured with brandy. Baked, then chilled.

SERVES 8   268 CALS PER SERVING
Takes 1¼ hours, **plus chilling**   Page 66

Smoked chicken tart
Strips of smoked chicken mixed with onion, mushrooms, and spinach, in a light pastry shell, and baked with an egg and crème fraîche topping.

SERVES 6   290 CALS PER SERVING
Takes 1¼ hours, **plus chilling**   Page 66

Canapés

Home-made canapés are an excellent accompaniment for drinks, or they can be served as an appetizer before dinner. These use toasted bread as a base, but if you prefer, fry the bread in a mixture of oil and butter instead.

SERVES 4   **251 CALS PER SERVING**

4 slices of white bread, crusts removed

ANCHOVY TOPPING

1 tbsp mayonnaise

1 or 2 spring onion tops

8 anchovy fillets, drained

4 prawns, cooked and peeled

CHEESE TOPPING

30 g (1 oz) full-fat soft cheese

2 spring onion tops, very finely sliced

4 capers

SALAMI TOPPING

15 g (½ oz) butter

2 slices of salami

4 slices of gherkin

ASPARAGUS TOPPING

1 tbsp mayonnaise

6 asparagus tips, cooked and drained

2 slices of radish

a few parsley leaves to garnish

1 Make the canapé bases: toast the white bread lightly on both sides. Leave to cool.

2 Make the anchovy topping: spread 1 piece of toast with mayonnaise and cut into 4 squares. Cut the spring onion tops into 4 pieces, then make vertical cuts to separate each piece into strands. Cut the anchovies in half and arrange in a lattice pattern on each square. Place a prawn on top, and garnish with the spring onions.

3 Make the cheese topping: spread 1 piece of toast with soft cheese and cut into 4 squares. Arrange the spring onion slices diagonally across the cream cheese. Place a caper on each square.

4 Make the salami topping: butter 1 piece of toast and cut into 4 rounds with a pastry cutter.

5 Cut each slice of salami in half to make 2 half-moon-shaped pieces. Roll each piece to form a point at the straight end so that a cornet shape is made. Put 1 cornet and 1 piece of gherkin on each canapé.

6 Make the asparagus topping: spread 1 piece of toast with mayonnaise and cut into 4 squares. Halve the asparagus tips lengthways. Halve the radish slices and cut away the centres to form 4 crescents. Put 3 halved asparagus tips on each square, arrange the radish on top, and garnish.

Cook's know-how

Ring the changes with different types of salami. The Danish salami used here is mild in flavour, but you may prefer spicier Italian salami, such as salame di Milano or salame di Napoli.

Above: Chevre croûtes.

Chevre croûtes

SERVES 4   450 CALS PER SERVING

½ baguette

about 2 tbsp ready-made pesto

1 log-shaped goat's cheese

olive oil for sprinkling

black pepper

radicchio and frisée leaves to serve

chervil sprigs to garnish

1 Cut the baguette into 8 slices, 1 cm (½ in) thick, and toast under a hot grill on one side only. Lightly spread the untoasted sides of the baguette slices with the ready-made pesto.

2 Cut the goat's cheese into 8 slices, 1 cm (½ in) thick, and arrange on top of the pesto. Toast the topped croûtes under the hot grill, 7 cm (3 in) from the heat, for 2 minutes or until the cheese just begins to soften. Remove the grill pan from the heat.

3 Lightly sprinkle a little olive oil and grind a little pepper over each cheese croûte. Return the croûtes to the hot grill, close to the heat, for 3 minutes or until the cheese begins to bubble and is just tinged golden brown.

4 Line a serving platter with radicchio and frisée leaves, arrange the croûtes on top, and garnish with chervil sprigs. Serve at once.

Italian bruschetta with goat's cheese

Substitute 8 slices of Italian ciabatta for the baguette. After toasting the topped croûtes in step 3, sprinkle chopped pitted black olives over them and drizzle with extra virgin olive oil. Serve sprinkled with fresh basil leaves.

Cheese aigrettes

SERVES 10–12   238–198 CALS PER SERVING

300 ml (½ pint) water

60 g (2 oz) butter

125 g (4 oz) self-raising flour

2 egg yolks

2 eggs

125 g (4 oz) mature Cheddar cheese, grated

salt and black pepper

vegetable oil for deep-frying

1 Put the water and butter into a saucepan and bring to a boil. Remove from the heat, and add the flour. Beat well until the mixture is smooth and glossy and leaves the side of the pan clean. Leave to cool slightly.

2 In a bowl, lightly mix the yolks and eggs, then beat into the flour mixture a little at a time. Stir in the cheese. Add salt and pepper to taste.

3 Heat the oil to 190°C (375°F). Lower the mixture a teaspoonful at a time into the oil, and cook very gently until golden brown. Lift out and drain on paper towels. Serve warm.

🔍 Cook's know-how

These little deep-fried French savouries made from choux pastry are traditionally cheese-flavoured, but chopped anchovies are sometimes added for extra piquancy.

Cheese and olive bites

SERVES 4   317 CALS PER SERVING

175 g (6 oz) mature Cheddar cheese, grated

90 g (3 oz) plain flour

15 g (½ oz) butter, plus extra for greasing

1 tsp paprika

½ tsp mustard powder

20 pimiento-stuffed green olives

cayenne pepper and parsley sprigs to garnish

1 Work the cheese, flour, butter, paprika, and mustard powder in a food processor until the mixture resembles fine breadcrumbs.

2 Flatten the dough mixture, and wrap around the olives (see box, below).

3 Butter a baking tray. Add the wrapped olives and bake in a preheated oven at 200°C (180°C fan, Gas 6) for 15 minutes until the pastry is golden.

4 Remove the cheese and olive bites from the baking tray and leave to cool slightly.

5 Serve warm or cold, sprinkled with cayenne pepper and garnished with parsley sprigs.

Wrapping the olives in the dough

Take a thumb-sized piece of the dough mixture and flatten on a work surface. Place an olive in the middle of the dough. Wrap the dough around the olive, pressing to make it stick. If the pastry is too crumbly and will not stick, add a little water. Repeat with the remaining dough and olives.

Poor man's caviar

SERVES 4   179 CALS PER SERVING

750 g (1½ lb) aubergines

salt and black pepper

2 shallots, halved

1–2 garlic cloves

4 tbsp lemon juice

4 tbsp olive oil

4 tbsp chopped parsley

2 tbsp tahini paste

1 Cut the aubergines in half lengthways. Score the flesh in a lattice pattern, sprinkle with salt, and leave to stand for 30 minutes.

2 Rinse the aubergine halves with cold water, and pat dry with paper towels. Place on a baking tray and bake in a preheated oven at 200°C (180°C fan, Gas 6) for 20 minutes.

3 Add the shallots and garlic to the baking tray, and bake for 15 minutes.

4 Purée the aubergines, shallots, and garlic with the lemon juice, oil, parsley, tahini paste, and salt and pepper to taste in a food processor until smooth.

5 Turn the dip into a bowl. Cover and chill for at least 1 hour before serving.

Taramasalata

SERVES 4   714 CALS PER SERVING

500 g (1 lb) smoked cod's roe, skinned and coarsely chopped

4 small slices of white bread, crusts removed

4 tbsp lemon juice

1 large garlic clove, coarsely chopped

250 ml (8 fl oz) olive oil

salt and black pepper

1 Purée the cod's roe in a food processor or blender until smooth. Break the bread into a bowl, add the lemon juice, and let the bread soak for 1 minute. Add to the cod's roe with the garlic, and purée until smooth.

2 Pour the oil into the mixture, a little at a time, and purée until all the oil has been absorbed. Add salt and pepper to taste. Turn the taramasalata into a bowl. Cover and chill for at least 1 hour before serving.

Bagna cauda

SERVES 4   327 CALS PER SERVING

150 ml (¼ pint) good-quality olive oil

2 garlic cloves, crushed

1 x 60 g can anchovy fillets, drained and chopped

black pepper

1 Heat the oil in a frying pan, add the garlic, and cook gently, stirring occasionally, for a few minutes until soft but not coloured. Add the anchovies and cook over a very low heat until they dissolve in the oil. Season with black pepper.

2 To serve, carefully pour the bagna cauda into an earthenware pot (or a fondue pot) and place over a candle heater to keep warm.

Classic olive tapenade

SERVES 4   188 CALS PER SERVING

1 garlic clove, roughly chopped

juice of 1 lemon

3 tbsp capers, drained and chopped

6 anchovy fillets in olive oil, drained and chopped

250 g (8 oz) black olives, pitted

20 g (¾ oz) fresh flat-leaf parsley, roughly chopped

about 3 tbsp olive oil

salt and black pepper

1 Put the garlic, lemon juice, capers, and anchovies into a food processor or blender, and purée for about 10 seconds until quite smooth.

2 Add the olives and parsley, and purée again. With the machine running, add enough olive oil to make a paste. Taste the tapenade, and season with salt and pepper if necessary.

3 Serve at once, or refrigerate in a covered container for up to 3 days and allow to come to room temperature before serving.

Spicy meatballs

SERVES 8   481 CALS PER SERVING

1 kg (2 lb) lean minced beef

1 small onion, grated

2 garlic cloves, crushed

1 egg, beaten

90 g (3 oz) fresh breadcrumbs

2 tbsp tomato purée

2 tbsp paprika

2 tbsp chopped fresh coriander

salt and black pepper

3 tbsp olive oil for frying

chopped parsley to garnish

crudités to serve

SESAME DIP

2 tbsp soy sauce

2 tbsp sesame oil

1 tbsp rice wine or sherry

1 spring onion, thinly sliced

1 tbsp sesame seeds, toasted

1 Make the sesame dip: whisk all the ingredients together and set aside.

2 Combine the meatball ingredients in a bowl. Using your hands, roll the mixture into little balls.

3 Heat the oil in a frying pan, and cook the meatballs, in batches, over a medium heat for 5 minutes or until browned, firm, and cooked through. Garnish, and serve warm with the sesame dip and crudités.

Opposite: Spicy meatba

Vegetables with garlic dips

🍴 SERVES 4   240 CALS PER SERVING

750 g (1½ lb) small new potatoes

2 aubergines, cut into chunky wedges

olive oil for brushing

2 red peppers, roasted and peeled (page 345)

TO SERVE

small bunch of watercress

rouille and aïoli (pages 45 and 70)

1 Boil the potatoes for 10–15 minutes until just tender. Drain and leave to cool, or keep warm, as desired.

2 Arrange the aubergine wedges in a grill pan and brush with olive oil. Cook under a hot grill, 10 cm (4 in) from the heat, for 10 minutes or until tender and lightly browned, turning occasionally. Cut the roasted peppers into chunks.

3 Arrange the vegetables on a serving plate, garnish with the watercress, and serve with rouille and aïoli.

Chick pea and red pepper salad

🍴 SERVES 4   158 CALS PER SERVING

1 x 400 g can chick peas, drained

½ red onion or 3 spring onions, chopped

3 garlic cloves, crushed

3 tbsp olive oil

2 tbsp white wine vinegar

salt and black pepper

a bunch of flat-leaf parsley

1 red pepper, roasted and peeled (page 345)

about 12 pimiento-stuffed olives

1 Combine the chick peas with the onion, garlic, oil, vinegar, and salt and pepper to taste. Remove the parsley leaves from the stems, chop them roughly and stir in.

2 Cut the red pepper into small chunks and chop the olives if you like. Stir into the chick pea mixture until evenly mixed.

Andalucian mushrooms

🍴 SERVES 4   92 CALS PER SERVING

250 g (8 oz) button mushrooms

2 tbsp olive oil

6 shallots, chopped

3 garlic cloves, crushed

30 g (1 oz) serrano ham, cut into strips

¼ tsp mild chilli powder

¼ tsp paprika (preferably sweet smoked)

1 tsp lemon juice

90 ml (3 fl oz) dry red wine

4 tbsp chopped flat-leaf parsley to garnish

1 Pull the mushroom stems from the caps. Heat the olive oil in a frying pan until hot, add the shallots and half of the garlic, and cook, stirring, for about 5 minutes until soft but not coloured. Add the mushroom caps and stems, and cook, stirring, for 3 minutes until lightly browned.

2 Add the serrano ham, chilli powder, and paprika, and cook, stirring constantly, for 1 minute.

3 Add the lemon juice, and cook over a high heat for a few minutes until the liquid has almost evaporated and the mushrooms are just tender.

4 Add the red wine and continue to cook over a high heat until the liquid is reduced and flavourful. Stir in the remaining garlic, sprinkle with the chopped parsley, and serve at once.

Tuna tostados

🍴 SERVES 4   316 CALS PER SERVING

½ baguette, sliced on the diagonal

1 garlic clove, crushed

3 tbsp olive oil

2 ripe tomatoes, thinly sliced

100 g can tuna, drained

100 g (4 oz) manchego or Cheddar cheese, grated or thinly sliced

1 Lightly toast the bread on both sides under a hot grill. Meanwhile, combine the garlic with the olive oil.

2 Brush each slice of toasted bread with a little of the garlic oil, then top with a thin slice of tomato. Place a little tuna on each, then top with cheese.

3 Return to the grill and cook, about 10 cm (4 in) from the heat, for 2–3 minutes, until the cheese has melted. Serve piping hot.

Traditional tapas

An appetizing selection of tapas does not have to involve a lot of work. In addition to the dishes on this page, serve some of the following - they require little or no preparation.

- pan-fried and salted almonds
- black or green olives
- slices or chunks of manchego cheese
- squares of Spanish omelette (page 88)
- slices of chorizo (spicy sausage)
- chunks of crusty bread
- jumbo prawns (good with aïoli)

Opposite, clockwise from top: Vegetabl with garlic dips (rouille and aïol Chick pea and red pepper sala Andalucian mushrooms, Tuna tostado

Above: Nachos grande.

Nachos grande

🍴 SERVES 6   396 CALS PER SERVING

2 tbsp sunflower oil

1 onion, finely chopped

½ green pepper, chopped

3 garlic cloves, crushed

1 x 225 g can chopped tomatoes

½–1 fresh green chilli, halved, seeded, and finely chopped

½ tsp chilli powder

½ tsp paprika

1 x 400 g can refried beans

75 ml (2½ fl oz) water

1 x 75 g packet tortilla chips

¼ tsp ground cumin

175 g (6 oz) Cheddar cheese, grated

extra paprika to garnish

1 Heat the oil in a frying pan, add the onion, green pepper, and garlic, and cook gently, stirring occasionally, for 5 minutes or until softened.

2 Add the tomatoes and chilli, and cook over a medium heat for a further 5 minutes, or until most of the liquid has evaporated.

3 Stir in the chilli powder and paprika, and cook for 3 minutes, then add the refried beans, breaking them up with a fork. Add the measured water and cook, stirring from time to time, for 8–10 minutes, until the mixture thickens.

4 Spoon the beans into a baking dish, arrange the tortilla chips around the edge, and sprinkle with cumin. Sprinkle the cheese over the beans and tortilla chips.

5 Bake in a preheated oven at 200°C (180°C fan, Gas 6) for 15–20 minutes until the cheese has melted. Sprinkle paprika in a lattice pattern on top.

Spicy chicken wings

🍴 SERVES 4–6   206–137 CALS PER SERVING

500 g (1 lb) chicken wings

2 tbsp sunflower oil

1 tsp lemon juice

1 tbsp paprika

1 tsp ground cumin

½ tsp oregano

½ tsp mild chilli powder

black pepper

parsley sprigs and cress to garnish

TO SERVE

½ red pepper, cut into strips

½ celery head, cut into sticks, plus leaves

blue cheese dressing (page 329)

1 Cut the chicken wings in half and put the pieces in a shallow dish.

2 In a large bowl, combine the oil, lemon juice, paprika, cumin, oregano, chilli powder, and black pepper. Brush the mixture over the chicken, cover, and leave to marinate at room temperature for at least 1 hour.

3 Line a large baking tray with foil and place a rack on top. Lay the chicken wings in a single layer on the rack, and cook in a preheated oven at 200°C (180°C fan, Gas 6) for 40 minutes, or until browned, sizzling, and crispy.

4 Remove the chicken from the rack and drain on paper towels. Serve with red pepper strips, celery sticks, and blue cheese dressing, and garnish with parsley and cress.

Herbed mini sausage rolls

🍴 MAKES 36   83 CALS EACH

knob of butter

1 large onion, finely chopped

500 g (1 lb) pork sausagemeat

finely grated zest and juice of ½ lemon

2 tbsp chopped parsley

1 tsp chopped fresh thyme

salt and black pepper

375 g (12 oz) ready-made puff pastry

2 tsp sun-dried tomato paste

beaten egg to seal and glaze

1 Melt the butter in a frying pan, and fry the onion gently for about 8 minutes until soft. Set aside to cool.

2 Put the sausagemeat, lemon zest and juice, and herbs into a bowl. Add the onion, season with salt and pepper, and mix with your hands until thoroughly combined.

3 Cut the pastry in half, and roll out each piece on a lightly floured surface to a 25 x 30 cm (10 x 12 in) rectangle. Cut each rectangle lengthways into 3 strips – so you have 6 long strips.

4 Spread a little tomato paste along the middle of each strip. Divide the sausagemeat mixture into sixths, then spread one-sixth over each line of tomato paste to cover it completely from one end to the other. Brush the pastry around the filling with beaten egg, fold over the pastry lengthways to enclose the filling, and seal the long edges by pressing with a fork. Lay the strips on 2 baking trays lined with baking parchment, and chill for 30 minutes.

5 Slice each strip crosswise into 6 pieces to make 36 sausage rolls, and separate the pieces a little. Brush with beaten egg, and make 3 small slashes in the top of each piece. Bake in a preheated oven at 200°C (180°C fan, Gas 6) for 25–30 minutes until golden. Serve warm.

Salmon and prawn filo purses

These crisp, golden purses and their creamy sauce are ideal for a party as they can be prepared up to 24 hours ahead, kept covered with a damp tea towel in the refrigerator, and cooked at the last minute. For a really special occasion, use scallops instead of prawns.

🥘 MAKES 8   448 CALS EACH

500 g (1 lb) tail end of salmon, boned, skinned, and cut into bite-sized pieces

250 g (8 oz) cooked peeled prawns

lemon juice for sprinkling

salt and black pepper

x 250 g packet filo pastry

0 g (2 oz) butter, melted

butter for greasing

lemon slices and dill sprigs to garnish

WHITE WINE SAUCE

00 ml (3½ fl oz) dry white wine

00 ml (½ pint) double cream

tsp chopped fresh dill

Combine the salmon pieces and prawns. Sprinkle with lemon juice, and add salt and pepper to taste. Set aside.

2 Cut the filo into sixteen 18 cm (7 in) squares. Brush 2 squares with a little of the melted butter, covering the remaining squares with a damp tea towel. Make a filo purse (see box, right). Repeat to make 8 purses.

3 Butter a baking tray. Add the filo purses, lightly brush with the remaining melted butter, and bake in a preheated oven at 190°C (170°C fan, Gas 5) for 15–20 minutes, until crisp and golden.

4 Meanwhile, make the sauce: pour the wine into a saucepan, and boil rapidly until it has reduced to about 3 tbsp. Add the cream and simmer until it reaches a light coating consistency. Remove from the heat and add the dill, and salt and pepper to taste.

5 Pour the sauce into a bowl. Garnish the purses with the lemon slices and dill sprigs and serve with the warm sauce.

♡ Healthy note

You can use about 2 tbsp olive oil to brush the filo rather than melted butter, and serve the purses with lemon halves for squeezing rather than the creamy sauce.

Making a filo purse

Place one-eighth of the salmon and prawn mixture in the middle of one buttered filo pastry square.

Fold 2 sides of filo pastry over the mixture to form a rectangle. Take the 2 open ends and fold one over the filling and the other underneath.

Place this parcel on the second buttered pastry square and draw up the edges. Squeeze and twist the pastry close to the filling.

Sardine pâté

 SERVES 8   **197 CALS PER SERVING**

2 x 125 g cans sardines in oil, drained, bones removed

125 g (4 oz) butter, softened

125 g (4 oz) low-fat soft cheese

3 tbsp lemon juice

black pepper

lemon twists and parsley sprigs to garnish

1 Purée the sardines, butter, cheese, and lemon juice in a food processor until almost smooth. Add pepper and more lemon juice to taste.

2 Divide the sardine mixture among 8 small ramekins (or put into 1 large bowl) and level the surface. Cover and chill in the refrigerator for at least 30 minutes.

3 Serve chilled, garnished with lemon twists and parsley sprigs.

Prawn pâté

Substitute 250 g (8 oz) cooked peeled prawns for the sardines.

Individual fish pâtés

Rich in flavour, these little pâté parcels make an ideal starter for a special occasion. With the gelatine, they are firm enough to be unmoulded. For softer pâtés, omit the gelatine and wine and serve in ramekins.

SERVES 8   **217 CALS PER SERVING**

250 g (8 oz) haddock fillets

150 ml (¼ pint) milk

20 g (¾ oz) butter

20 g (¾ oz) plain flour

1 tsp powdered gelatine

4 tbsp dry white wine

250 g (8 oz) smoked salmon pieces

2 tbsp mayonnaise

4 tbsp double cream

dash of lemon juice

black pepper

oil for greasing

smoked salmon, lemon slices, and dill sprigs to garnish

1 Put the haddock into a saucepan, and add the milk. Bring almost to a boil, then simmer gently for 10 minutes or until the fish is opaque and flakes easily.

2 Lift the haddock out of the pan, remove the skin and bones, and discard. Flake the fish and leave to cool. Reserve the cooking liquid.

3 Melt the butter in a small pan, add the flour, and cook, stirring, for 1 minute. Gradually blend in the reserved cooking liquid, and bring to a boil, stirring constantly, until the mixture thickens. Place a piece of damp greaseproof paper over the surface of the sauce to prevent a skin forming, and leave to stand until cold.

4 Sprinkle the gelatine evenly over the wine in a small bowl. Leave to stand for about 3 minutes or until the gelatine becomes spongy.

5 Put the bowl into a saucepan of gently simmering water for about 3 minutes or until the gelatine has dissolved. Leave to cool slightly.

6 Purée the haddock, cold white sauce, smoked salmon, and mayonnaise in a food processor or blender until almost smooth. Gradually add the gelatine mixture, pulsing between each addition. Add the cream and lemon juice, season with pepper, and pulse again.

7 Grease 8 small moulds. Spoon the pâté into the moulds, cover, and chill for at least 2 hours.

8 To serve, unmould each pâté and garnish with smoked salmon, lemon slices, and dill sprigs.

♡ Healthy note

Sardines are an oily fish, rich in omega-3 fatty acids, which can help to discourage heart disease and blood clots. They also provide vitamin D and, if you eat the bones as you do in this pâté, they are an important source of calcium.

Three fish terrine

Three kinds of smoked fish – trout, salmon, and mackerel – are blended with soft cheese, arranged in layers, then wrapped in smoked salmon for a subtle variety of flavours. The finished terrine can be frozen for up to 1 month.

🕐 **SERVES 10**   **424 CALS PER SERVING**

sunflower oil for greasing

175–250 g (6–8 oz) smoked salmon slices

salt and black pepper

watercress to garnish

TROUT PATE

175 g (6 oz) smoked trout

90 g (3 oz) butter

90 g (3 oz) full-fat soft cheese

1½ tbsp lemon juice

SALMON PATE

125 g (4 oz) smoked salmon pieces

60 g (2 oz) butter

60 g (2 oz) full-fat soft cheese

½ tbsp lemon juice

1 tbsp tomato purée

1 tbsp chopped fresh dill

MACKEREL PATE

175 g (6 oz) smoked mackerel

90 g (3 oz) butter

90 g (3 oz) full-fat soft cheese

1½ tbsp lemon juice

1.2 litre (2 pint) loaf tin or terrine

1 Make the trout pâté: remove the skin and bones from the trout and purée with the butter, cheese, lemon juice, and salt and pepper to taste in a food processor until smooth and well blended. Turn into a bowl, cover, and chill.

2 Make the salmon pâté: purée the smoked salmon pieces, butter, cheese, lemon juice, tomato purée, dill, and salt and pepper to taste in a food processor until smooth and well blended. Turn into a bowl, cover, and chill.

3 Make the mackerel pâté: remove the skin and bones from the mackerel and purée with the butter, cheese, lemon juice, and salt and pepper to taste in a food processor until smooth and well blended. Turn into a bowl, cover, and chill.

4 Assemble the terrine (see box, right). Cover and chill overnight.

5 To serve, carefully turn out the terrine, cut into thick slices, and arrange on individual serving plates with a watercress garnish.

Assembling the terrine

Oil the loaf tin and line with overlapping slices of smoked salmon. Arrange them crosswise and allow 3.5–5 cm (1½–2 in) to overhang the sides of the tin.

Turn the trout pâté into the loaf tin and spread it evenly with a palette knife, levelling the surface. If necessary, wet the knife to prevent sticking. Add the salmon pâté in the same way, and then top with the mackerel pâté.

Fold the smoked salmon over the mackerel pâté, tucking in the ends.

Smoked haddock mousse

🍴 SERVES 6   217 CALS PER SERVING

250 g (8 oz) smoked haddock, skinned

juice of ½ lemon

salt and black pepper

250 g (8 oz) full-fat soft cheese

2 tbsp reduced-calorie mayonnaise

1 tbsp turmeric

6 small bowls

1 Line a baking sheet with a long, wide piece of foil, and place the haddock on it. Sprinkle the fish with the lemon juice, and season with pepper. Bring the long edges of the foil together, and fold to seal. Bring each of the short edges together, and fold to seal, forming a parcel.

2 Bake the fish in a preheated oven at 160°C (140°C fan, Gas 3) for 7–10 minutes, or until the fish is just cooked and flakes easily with a fork. Set aside in the foil parcel until cold.

3 Flake the fish, removing any bones. Place in a food processor or blender, adding any juices that are left on the foil. Add the cheese, mayonnaise, and turmeric. Season lightly with salt.

4 Process or blend the mixture until smooth, then check and adjust the seasoning if necessary.

5 Lightly oil the bowls and spoon in the fish mixture. Cover and chill for at least 3 hours, when the mixture will be set to a soft mousse.

6 Serve with thin slices of plain wholemeal toast (the cheese adds richness to the mousse, so no butter is needed).

Brandied chicken liver pâté

🍴 SERVES 8   268 CALS PER SERVING

125 g (4 oz) bread, crusts removed

1 garlic clove, coarsely chopped

125 g (4 oz) streaky bacon rashers, rinds removed, coarsely chopped

2 tsp chopped fresh thyme

500 g (1 lb) chicken livers, trimmed

1 egg

4 tbsp brandy

½ tsp grated nutmeg

salt and black pepper

60 g (2 oz) butter, melted

1 kg (2 lb) loaf tin or terrine

1 Line the loaf tin with foil, leaving 5 cm (2 in) foil overhanging on each side.

2 Cut the bread into thick chunks, and work them with the garlic in a food processor to form fine breadcrumbs. Add the bacon and thyme, and work until finely chopped.

3 Add the chicken livers, egg, brandy, and nutmeg, season with salt and pepper, and purée until smooth. Add the butter and purée again.

4 Put the pâté mixture into the prepared loaf tin, level the surface, and fold the foil over the top. Place in a roasting tin, pour in boiling water to come about halfway up the side of the loaf tin, and bake in a preheated oven at 160°C (140°C fan, Gas 3) for 1 hour.

5 Test the pâté for doneness (see box, below). Leave the pâté to cool completely, then cover, and leave to chill in the refrigerator overnight. To serve, cut the pâté into slices.

Is it cooked?

Insert a skewer into the middle of the pâté. If it comes out hot and clean, the pâté is cooked.

Smoked chicken tart

🍴 SERVES 6   290 CALS PER SERVING

250 g (8 oz) ready-made shortcrust pastry

15 g (½ oz) butter

½ small onion, finely chopped

60 g (2 oz) mushrooms, thinly sliced

60 g (2 oz) baby spinach, washed

salt and black pepper

200 ml (7 fl oz) full-fat crème fraîche

2 large eggs

2 tbsp chopped parsley

90 g (3 oz) cooked smoked chicken, sliced into thin strips

30 g (1 oz) Cheddar cheese, grated

18 cm (7 in) flan dish or tin

1 Roll out the pastry, and use to line the flan dish or tin. Prick the bottom of the pastry with a fork. Line the pastry shell with foil or greaseproof paper, and fill with baking beans, rice, or pasta.

2 Place the dish or tin on a heated baking tray, and bake in a preheated oven at 220°C (200°C fan, Gas 7) for about 15 minutes, removing the foil and beans for the final 5 minutes. Remove from the oven and turn the temperature down to 180°C (160°C fan, Gas 4).

3 Melt the butter in a frying pan, add the onion, cover, and cook gently for 10–15 minutes until soft. Remove the lid, increase the heat, add the mushrooms, and cook for 1–2 minutes. Add the spinach and cook until just wilted, then season and leave to cool.

4 Mix the crème fraîche, eggs, and parsley in a bowl, and season with salt and pepper. Mix the chicken with the cold spinach, spread over the pastry base, and top with the grated cheese. Pour the egg mixture over the top and bake for 25–30 minutes until golden brown and set. Serve warm.

Shaping and wrapping the pâtés

Mould the pâté mixture into 8 equal-sized oval shapes, using your hands.

Lay a bacon rasher flat, put a pâté oval at one end and roll the bacon around it.

Twist the rasher around the ends to enclose the pâté, then tuck it in underneath to secure. Repeat with the remaining bacon rashers and pâté.

Pan-fried pâté

These little bacon-wrapped chicken liver and spinach pâtés are easy to make, and they are at their most delicious when served with a tangy salad of sliced tomatoes and chopped onions in a herb vinaigrette dressing.

 SERVES 4   392 CALS PER SERVING

30 g (1 oz) butter

125 g (4 oz) chicken livers, trimmed

5 shallots, coarsely chopped

125 g (4 oz) lean bacon rashers, rinds removed, coarsely chopped

60 g (2 oz) spinach leaves, shredded

2 tbsp chopped parsley

1 tsp chopped fresh thyme leaves

1 garlic clove, crushed

salt and black pepper

8 streaky bacon rashers, rinds removed

1 Melt half of the butter in a frying pan, add the chicken livers, and cook gently, stirring occasionally, for 3 minutes or until they are browned on the outside but still pink inside.

2 Purée the chicken livers in a food processor until smooth. Turn into a large bowl and set aside.

3 Melt the remaining butter in the frying pan, add the shallots, and cook gently, stirring occasionally, for a few minutes until soft but not coloured.

4 Add the shallots to the chicken livers with the chopped bacon, spinach, parsley, thyme, and garlic. Season with salt and pepper. Purée half of this mixture until smooth, then stir it into the remaining mixture in the bowl.

5 Shape and wrap the chicken liver pâtés (see box, left).

6 Heat a frying pan, add the pâtés, and cook them gently until browned all over. Lower the heat, cover, and cook over a very gentle heat for 35–40 minutes.

7 Serve the pan-fried pâtés either warm or at room temperature.

 Cook's know-how

To trim the chicken livers, use kitchen scissors to cut away any membranes.

Hummus

 **SERVES 6   150 CALS PER SERVING**

2 x 400 g cans chick peas, drained

2–3 garlic cloves, coarsely chopped

1 tbsp tahini paste, or to taste

3 tbsp olive oil, or to taste

juice of 1 lemon, or to taste

salt and black pepper

1 Purée the chick peas, garlic, tahini paste, oil, and lemon juice in a food processor or blender until smooth.

2 Add salt and pepper to taste, and more oil, tahini, and lemon juice if you think it needs it, then purée again.

3 Spoon into dishes and level the surface. If you like, garnish with rosemary, red pepper, and olives.

Asparagus and quails' egg salad

SERVES 6   222 CALS PER SERVING

12 quails' eggs

18 asparagus spears

1 x 340 g jar roasted artichoke hearts in oil

TO SERVE

1 tbsp balsamic vinegar

salt and black pepper

about 30 g (1 oz) Parmesan shavings

1 Put the eggs in a pan of cold water, bring to a boil, and boil for 3 minutes (start timing as soon as the water comes to a boil). Drain and rinse under cold running water, then peel immediately. The shells come off very easily when the eggs are just cooked.

2 Peel the asparagus stems with a potato or vegetable peeler if they are woody, then cut the asparagus into 5 cm (2 in) lengths. Cook in boiling salted water for about 2 minutes until only just tender. Drain into a sieve and rinse thoroughly under cold running water, then pat dry with kitchen paper.

3 Drain the artichoke hearts, reserving the oil. Cut the artichokes and eggs lengthways in half. Divide the artichokes and asparagus among 6 plates, and top each serving with four egg halves.

4 Make a dressing by mixing 3 tbsp of the reserved oil from the artichoke jar with the balsamic vinegar, and season with salt and pepper.

5 To serve, drizzle the dressing over the salad, top with Parmesan shavings, and serve with crusty rolls.

Asparagus spears are vitamin-rich and tender when young and fresh. Keep them loosely wrapped or in a paper bag in the refrigerator.

Double salmon tian

SERVES 6   232 CALS PER SERVING

650 g (1 lb 5 oz) fresh salmon fillet, skinned

200 g (7 oz) full-fat soft cheese

4 tbsp chopped fresh dill

salt and black pepper

TO SERVE

50–60 g (1½–2 oz) fresh mizuna leaves, or any other peppery leaves such as rocket

6 small slices of smoked salmon, total weight about 200 g (7 oz)

6 lemon wedges to serve

6 x 7.5 cm (3 in) metal rings or 150 ml (5 fl oz) ramekins

1 Wrap the fresh salmon tightly in foil, and bake in a preheated oven at 190°C (170°C fan, Gas 5) for 15–20 minutes or until just cooked. Leave to cool in the foil.

2 Mix the cheese and dill in a large bowl until smooth. Flake the cooled salmon into the bowl, including any fish juices and jelly, but discarding any bones. Season well with salt and pepper, and fold gently together.

3 Put the metal rings on a flat plate or baking tray (if using ramekins, line them with cling film). Divide the salmon and cheese mixture among them, smoothing the surface with the back of a metal spoon. Cover and refrigerate for at least 2 hours, overnight if possible.

4 To serve, divide the salad leaves among 6 plates. Lift a ring filled with salmon on to the leaves using a fish slice, then carefully ease off the ring. (If using ramekins, invert the salmon on to the leaves and gently remove the cling film.) Top each tian with a loosely curled piece of smoked salmon and serve with wedges of lemon for squeezing.

Smoked salmon terrine

SERVES 8   186 CALS PER SERVING

275 g (9 oz) thinly sliced smoked salmon

black pepper

250 g (8 oz) low-fat soft cheese

125 g (4 oz) unsalted butter, softened

2 tbsp creamed horseradish

4 canned anchovy fillets (more if you wish)

1–2 tbsp chopped fresh parsley or dill, or a mixture of the two

TO SERVE

salad leaves, tossed in your favourite dressing

lime or lemon wedges

500 g (1 lb) loaf tin

1 Dampen the loaf tin and line with cling film, letting it overhang the sides. Divide the smoked salmon into four equal piles. Cover the base of the tin with a quarter of the salmon and sprinkle with black pepper.

2 Put the soft cheese, butter, horseradish, anchovies, and parsley or dill into a blender or food processor, season with black pepper, and work to a very smooth paste. Do not add salt. (If you haven't got a blender or food processor, beat the mixture vigorously with a wooden spoon.)

3 Spread a third of the paste over the salmon in the tin and cover with a second layer of salmon. Continue alternating the layers, finishing with salmon Tightly pull the cling film over the top and press down firmly. Refrigerate for at least 6 hours, preferably overnight.

4 To serve, put the terrine in the freezer for 30 minutes (this will make it easy to slice). Turn it out of its tin and discard the cling film, then cut into 16 thin slices. Serve 2 slices on each plate, on a bed of dressed salad leaves, with lime or lemon wedges for squeezing.

Opposite, clockwise from top: Smoked salmon terrine, Asparagus and quails' egg salad, Double salmon tian

Jumbo prawns with aïoli

SERVES 4   482 CALS PER SERVING

2 tbsp olive oil

12 uncooked jumbo prawns in their shells

1 tbsp chopped parsley

lemon wedges and flat-leaf parsley sprigs to garnish

AIOLI

2 garlic cloves, coarsely chopped

salt and black pepper

1 egg yolk

1 tsp mustard powder

150 ml (¼ pint) olive oil

1 tbsp lemon juice

1 Make the aïoli: in a small bowl, crush the garlic with a pinch of salt until it forms a smooth paste. Add the egg yolk and mustard powder, and beat well. Beat in the oil, drop by drop, whisking constantly until the mixture is thick and smooth, and all the oil has been absorbed. Beat in the lemon juice, and add pepper to taste.

2 Heat the oil in a large frying pan, add the prawns, and toss over a high heat for 3–4 minutes, just until the shells turn bright pink. Remove the prawns from the frying pan and drain on paper towels.

3 To serve, arrange the prawns on warmed plates, sprinkle with chopped parsley, and garnish with lemon wedges and parsley sprigs. Serve with individual bowls of aïoli.

Cook's know-how

Uncooked, or raw, prawns are usually grey in colour – it is only when they are cooked that they turn into the pink prawns we are more familiar with. The golden rule when cooking prawns is never to overcook them, so remove them from the heat as soon as they turn pink. Overcooked prawns are rubbery, chewy, and tasteless.

Moules marinière

SERVES 6   302 CALS PER SERVING

90 g (3 oz) butter

1 small onion, finely chopped

1 garlic clove, crushed

3 kg (6 lb) mussels, cleaned (page 107)

450 ml (¾ pint) dry white wine

6 parsley sprigs

3 thyme sprigs

1 bay leaf

salt and black pepper

1 tbsp plain flour

3 tbsp chopped parsley to garnish

1 Melt two-thirds of the butter in a large saucepan, add the onion and garlic, and cook gently, stirring occasionally, for a few minutes until soft but not coloured.

2 Add the mussels, wine, parsley, thyme, and bay leaf, and season with salt and pepper. Cover the saucepan tightly and bring to a boil.

3 Cook, shaking the saucepan frequently, for 5–6 minutes or until the mussels open.

4 Throw away any mussels that are not open. Transfer the open mussels to a warmed tureen or large serving bowl.

5 Strain the cooking juices into a small pan and boil until reduced by one-third.

6 Mix the remaining butter and the flour on a plate to make a paste (beurre manié).

7 Whisk the beurre manié into the cooking liquid, and bring to a boil, stirring constantly. Taste for seasoning, and pour over the mussels. Garnish and serve at once.

Healthy note

This classic recipe is made with a butter-and-flour beurre manié, which thickens the sauce. For a healthier option, cook the onion and garlic in 2 tbsp olive oil rather than butter, and omit the beurre manié. To compensate for the lack of thickening, boil the cooking juices in step 5 until reduced by about half.

Scallops with cheese sauce

SERVES 4   297 CALS PER SERVING

8 scallops, with 4 shells if possible

150 ml (¼ pint) water

4 tbsp medium dry white wine

1 bay leaf

salt and black pepper

lemon wedges and bay leaves to garnish

MORNAY SAUCE

45 g (1½ oz) butter

3 tbsp plain flour

4 tbsp single cream

60 g (2 oz) Gruyère cheese, grated

1 Cut each scallop into 2–3 pieces. Put the measured water, wine, and bay leaf into a small pan, and season with salt and pepper. Bring to a boil, then lower the heat and add the scallops.

2 Poach for 1 minute or until the scallops are just tender when tested with the tip of a knife. Lift out the scallops with a slotted spoon, strain the cooking liquid, and reserve.

3 Make the Mornay sauce: melt the butter in a saucepan, add the flour, and cook, stirring, for 1 minute. Gradually stir in the reserved cooking liquid, and bring to a boil, stirring constantly, until the mixture thickens. Simmer gently for about 5 minutes. Lower the heat, and stir in the cream and half of the grated cheese. Taste for seasoning.

4 Stir the scallops into the sauce, divide among the shells, and sprinkle with the remaining cheese.

5 Place the filled shells under a hot grill, 7 cm (3 in) from the heat, for 5 minutes or until the cheese has melted and the sauce is golden and bubbling. Garnish with lemon wedges and bay leaves.

Salmon quenelles

uenelles are delicate little dumplings,
aditionally oval but sometimes round, which
n be made with fish, meat, or chicken. The
ame comes from Knödel, the German word
r dumpling. They are simple to make, and yet
ey look elegant and impressive as if they
quire professional skills.

SERVES 6   511 CALS PER SERVING

0 g (1 lb) salmon fillet, skinned, boned,
d cut into chunks

gg whites

t and white pepper

0 ml (¼ pint) double cream

non slices and flat-leaf parsley sprigs to garnish

PARAGUS SAUCE

ml (3 fl oz) dry white wine

g (9 oz) young asparagus, trimmed, woody parts
noved

ml (½ pint) double cream

Make the quenelles: purée the salmon, egg
whites, and salt and pepper to taste in a food
cessor until completely smooth.

With the machine still running, pour in the
cream in a steady stream until it is thoroughly
nded. Turn the mixture into a large bowl, cover,
d chill for about 2 hours.

3 Bring a saucepan of salted water to a
simmer. Shape and cook the quenelles
(see box, right). Keep the quenelles warm while
you make the sauce.

4 Make the asparagus sauce: pour the wine
into a saucepan and boil rapidly for about
2 minutes until it is reduced to a thin syrup.

5 Cook the asparagus in a pan of boiling
salted water for 3–5 minutes until tender.
Drain, then cut off the asparagus tips, and
reserve them for garnish.

6 Purée the reduced wine and the asparagus
stalks until very smooth.

7 Boil the cream in a saucepan for 4 minutes
or until it is thick enough to coat the back
of a metal spoon. Stir in the purée, and taste
for seasoning.

8 Pour the sauce on to warmed plates,
arrange the quenelles on top, and garnish
with the reserved asparagus tips, and the lemon
slices and parsley sprigs.

🔍 Cook's know-how

Take care not to overprocess the purée when
blending the quenelle mixture. If you work it too
hard, this could cause the cream to curdle.

Shaping and cooking the quenelles

Dip a dessertspoon into the simmering
water, then take a spoonful of the
chilled quenelle mixture. Using a
second warm, wetted dessertspoon
or your fingers, mould into an oval.
Repeat with the remaining mixture.

Lower some quenelles into the
simmering water and cook for 6–10
minutes until they are firm when
pressed with a finger. Do not put too
many into the pan at one time.

Remove the quenelles with a slotted
spoon, drain well, and keep them
warm while you cook the remainder.

Gravadlax

You can buy this Scandinavian "pickled" salmon, but it is easy (and less expensive) to make it yourself – and your guests will be very impressed. Serve it with thin slices of dark rye bread. You will find the gravadlax easier to slice if it has been frozen for about 4 hours beforehand.

 SERVES 16   **395 CALS PER SERVING**

2.25 kg (4½ lb) whole fresh salmon, boned, and cut lengthways in half into 2 fillets (ask your fishmonger)

dill sprigs and lemon segments to garnish

PICKLING MIXTURE

75 g (2½ oz) granulated sugar

4 tbsp coarse sea salt

4 tbsp chopped fresh dill

salt and black pepper

MUSTARD DILL SAUCE

3 tbsp Dijon mustard

2 tbsp caster sugar

1 tbsp white wine vinegar

1 egg yolk

150 ml (¼ pint) sunflower oil

2 tbsp chopped fresh dill

1 Make the pickling mixture: put the granulated sugar, sea salt, and chopped fresh dill into a small bowl, season generously with black pepper, and stir well to mix.

2 Sandwich the salmon fillets together (see box, right).

3 Wrap the fillets in a double thickness of foil and place in a large dish. Weigh down with kitchen weights or heavy cans, and keep in the refrigerator for 24 hours. Halfway through this time, turn the salmon over.

4 Make the mustard dill sauce: in a medium bowl, whisk together the mustard, sugar, vinegar, and egg yolk, then whisk in the oil a little at a time. The sauce should have the consistency of mayonnaise. Add salt and pepper to taste, and stir in the chopped dill.

5 Unwrap the gravadlax. A lot of sticky, salty liquid will drain from the fish when it has been pickled: this is quite normal. Remove the fish from the pickling liquid, and dry well. Separate the 2 salmon fillets.

6 To serve, slice each fillet on the slant, cutting the flesh away from the skin. The slices should be a little thicker than for smoked salmon and each one should have a fringe of dill. Garnish with dill sprigs and lemon segments, and serve with the mustard dill sauce.

Prawn cocktail

🍴 SERVES 4   338 CALS PER SERVING

150 ml (¼ pint) mayonnaise

2 tbsp creamed horseradish

1 tbsp lemon juice

1 tsp Worcestershire sauce

1 tsp tomato purée

¼ tsp caster sugar

a few drops of Tabasco sauce

black pepper

250 g (8 oz) cooked peeled prawns

salad leaves to serve

thin lemon wedges, parsley sprigs, and 4 large cooked prawns in their shells to garnish

1 Make the dressing: in a medium bowl, combine the mayonnaise, creamed horseradish, lemon juice, Worcestershire sauce, tomato purée, caster sugar, and Tabasco sauce, and season well with a little black pepper.

2 Add the peeled cooked prawns and stir to coat with the dressing.

3 Line 4 individual glass serving bowls with the salad leaves and top with the prawn mixture. Garnish each serving with a thin lemon wedge, a parsley sprig, and a large prawn.

Mimosa fish salad

🍴 SERVES 4   213 CALS PER SERVING

2 hard-boiled eggs

300 g (10 oz) firm white fish fillets, cooked, skinned, and flaked

3 tbsp soured cream

3 tbsp mayonnaise

1 tbsp chopped parsley

1 tsp chopped fresh dill

a few drops of Tabasco sauce

salt and black pepper

4 large tomatoes, halved

lemon twists, flat-leaf parsley sprigs, and celery leaves to garnish

1 Remove the yolk from one egg and reserve. Chop the white and the remaining egg.

2 Mix the fish with the chopped egg, soured cream, mayonnaise, parsley, dill, and Tabasco. Add salt and pepper.

3 Top the tomatoes with the fish mixture. Sieve the egg yolk, sprinkle it over the mixture, and garnish with lemon, parsley, and celery.

Sardines with coriander

🍴 SERVES 4   511 CALS PER SERVING

12–16 large sardines

olive oil for brushing

salt and black pepper

lime wedges and flat-leaf parsley sprigs to garnish

CORIANDER LIME BUTTER

1 tsp ground coriander

60 g (2 oz) unsalted butter, at room temperature

1½ tsp lime juice

1 shallot, finely chopped

¼ tsp finely grated lime zest

1 Scale the sardines with the back of a kitchen knife. With a sharp knife, cut the stomachs open, and scrape out the contents, particularly any dark blood.

2 Rinse the sardines inside and out, and pat dry. Brush all over with oil, and sprinkle with salt and pepper.

3 Prepare the coriander lime butter: heat a heavy pan, add the coriander, and toast lightly. Transfer the coriander to a bowl and leave to cool slightly.

4 Add the butter and lime juice to the coriander and whisk until thick. Stir in the shallot and lime zest, and salt and pepper to taste.

5 Place the sardines under a hot grill, 10 cm (4 in) from the heat, and grill for 1½–2 minutes on each side until they begin to feel firm.

6 Transfer the sardines to a platter, and spread a little coriander lime butter on each one. Garnish with lime wedges and flat-leaf parsley sprigs, and serve at once.

Ground coriander forms the base of many curry powders and spice mixes. Its woody, spicy fragrance lends itself well to rich, oily fish.

Sandwiching the salmon fillets

...ut 1 salmon fillet skin-side down on ... board, cover the surface with the ...ickling mixture, and place the ...econd fillet on top, skin-side up.

Above: Baked figs with Camembert.

Baked figs with Camembert

⏱ SERVES 6   180 CALS PER SERVING

175 g (6 oz) Camembert cheese

6 just-ripe large figs

12 slices of Parma ham

TO SERVE

6 tbsp olive oil

3 tbsp white wine vinegar

1 tsp Dijon mustard

2 tsp clear honey

salt and black pepper

125 g (4 oz) mixed green salad leaves

1 Put the Camembert into the freezer, and freeze for about 30 minutes until hard – this will make it easier to cut the cheese into neat slices.

2 Sit the figs on a board, remove their stalks, and cut a cross in the stalk end of each one to come about halfway down the fruit. Cut the cheese into 6 thin slices, and push 1 slice into each cross so that the cheese sits inside the fig.

3 Wrap each fig in 2 slices of ham, and scrunch the ham at the top to make a ruffle. Place the figs on a baking tray.

4 Bake in a preheated oven at 200°C (180°C fan, Gas 6) for 10–12 minutes or until the ham is crisp and the cheese just beginning to melt.

5 Meanwhile, whisk the olive oil and vinegar in a salad bowl with the mustard and honey, and season with salt and pepper. Add the salad leaves, and toss until they are coated in the dressing.

6 Divide the salad leaves among 6 plates, and sit a fig in the middle of each pile of leaves. Serve immediately.

Sun-dried tomato crostini

⏱ SERVES 8   165 CALS PER SERVING

1 baguette

2 garlic cloves, crushed

about 3 tbsp olive oil

4 sun-dried tomatoes in oil

30 g (1 oz) butter

salt and black pepper

12 pitted black olives, chopped

¼ tsp fresh rosemary, chopped

1 Cut the baguette into 24 thin slices and arrange them on 2 baking trays. Add the garlic to the olive oil, then brush

about half of the mixture on to the slices of bread. Bake in a preheated oven at 180°C (160°C fan, Gas 4) for 10 minutes.

2 Remove the baking trays from the oven, turn the slices of bread over, brush with a little more garlic oil, and bake for a further 10 minutes or until crisp and golden. Leave to cool.

3 Dry the sun-dried tomatoes with a paper towel and cut them into pieces. Put the tomato and butter in the small bowl of a food processor and work until finely chopped (or pound them with a mortar and pestle). Season with salt and pepper to taste.

4 Spread the sun-dried tomato purée over the crostini, arrange the chopped olive on top, and sprinkle with rosemary.

Mozzarella, tomato and basil salad

⏱ SERVES 8   147 CALS PER SERVING

4 slicing or beefsteak tomatoes

250 g (8 oz) mozzarella cheese

4 tbsp shredded fresh basil

4 tbsp olive oil

1 tbsp balsamic vinegar or wine vinegar

salt and black pepper

basil sprig to garnish

1 Peel the tomatoes: cut out the cores and score an "x" on the base of each one, then immerse in boiling water until the skins start to split. Transfer at once to cold water; when cool, peel off the skin. Thinly slice the tomatoes.

2 Slice the mozzarella and arrange with the tomato slices alternately on a plate overlapping one another.

3 Just before serving, sprinkle with the basil, olive oil, and vinegar, and salt and pepper to taste. Garnish with a basil sprig.

🔎 Cook's know-how

As well as the salad and crostini, make up a platter of sliced Parma ham, mortadella, bresaola, and salami. Another good choice for antipasti is a seafood salad of prawns, mussels, and squid, which you can buy at supermarkets and delicatessens.

Beef carpaccio with vegetables and mustard dressing

🍽 SERVES 6   302 CALS PER SERVING

500 g (1 lb) beef fillet cut from the centre, trimmed

2 tbsp olive oil

1 tbsp chopped fresh rosemary

1 tbsp chopped fresh thyme

salt and black pepper

4 large carrots, cut into very thin matchstick strips

125 g (4 oz) fine asparagus tips

1 red pepper, halved, seeded, and cut into very thin matchstick strips

MUSTARD DRESSING

3 tbsp olive oil

2 tbsp white wine vinegar

1 tbsp Dijon mustard

½ tsp caster sugar

TO SERVE

60–90 g (2–3 oz) wild rocket leaves

crusty bread

1 Place the fillet on a board, and rub the olive oil all over the meat. Scatter the herbs and salt and pepper on the board, and roll the fillet in the herbs and seasoning until coated on all sides.

2 Heat a frying pan over a high heat until very hot, and quickly fry the fillet for a few minutes just until browned on all sides. Transfer to a baking tray, and roast in a preheated oven at 220°C (200°C fan, Gas 7) for 10 minutes. Set aside to rest and cool.

3 Bring a large saucepan of salted water to a boil. Add the carrots, and bring the water back to a boil, then add the asparagus and simmer for 2 minutes. Drain and rinse under cold running water, pat dry, and tip into a large bowl. Toss in the red pepper.

4 Put the dressing ingredients into a small bowl, season with salt and pepper, and whisk until thoroughly combined. Pour half of the dressing over the vegetables, and toss to mix.

5 Carve the cold beef into 18 very thin slices. Place 3 slices of beef on each plate, drizzle with a little of the remaining dressing, and arrange a bundle of vegetables and a handful of rocket alongside. Serve at room temperature, with crusty bread.

🔍 Cook's know how

Traditionally, carpaccio is made with raw beef, but this version made with rare beef is for those who prefer not to eat raw meat. Encrusted with herbs it loses nothing by being briefly cooked, and has an excellent flavour with the dressing and vegetables.

Seafood blini

Blini are small Russian pancakes made with yeast and buckwheat flour. Buckwheat flour is available from health food shops but if you cannot find any, use wholemeal flour instead. This mixture makes about 24 blini.

 SERVES 6–8   369–227 CALS PER SERVING

BLINI

125 g (4 oz) plain flour

125 g (4 oz) buckwheat flour

½ tsp salt

½ tsp fast-action dried yeast

450 ml (¾ pint) milk, warmed

1 egg, separated

sunflower oil for frying

TO SERVE

2 x 75 g jars lumpfish roe (1 red, 1 black)

125 g (4 oz) cooked peeled prawns

125 ml (4 fl oz) crème fraîche

lemon segments and fresh chives to garnish

1 Put both types of flour into a large bowl. Add the salt and yeast, then stir together until evenly mixed.

2 Gradually beat in the warm milk to make a smooth batter. Cover the bowl and leave in a warm place for about 40 minutes until the mixture is frothy and has doubled in volume.

3 Beat the egg yolk into the flour and yeast mixture. Put the egg white into a clean bowl and whisk until stiff but not dry, then fold into the mixture.

4 Heat a large non-stick frying pan or griddle, brush with oil, and heat until the oil is hot. Spoon about 2 tbsp batter into the pan for each blini (you should be able to cook 3 or 4 at a time), cover, and cook over a moderate heat for 2–3 minutes, or until bubbles rise to the surface and burst.

5 Turn the blini over with a palette knife and cook for a further 2–3 minutes until golden on the other side. Wrap the cooked blini in a tea towel and keep them warm.

6 Cook the remaining batter in batches until all the batter is used up, lightly oiling the pan between each batch.

7 To serve, arrange the blini on warmed plates, with spoonfuls of red and black lumpfish roe, prawns, and crème fraîche. Garnish with lemon segments and snipped fresh chives.

Cook's know-how

If you buy ready-made blini, they will need to be gently warmed through.

Smoked salmon roulade

[Th]e richness of the cheese and smoked-salmon [la]yers is offset by a thin layer of tomatoes that [pr]ovides a fresh and tangy contrast. Here the [ro]ulade is served in slices, but you could serve [it] whole, with just a few slices cut at one end.

SERVES 4–6   407–271 CALS PER SERVING

[15] g (½ oz) butter

[1] garlic clove, crushed

[15]0 g (5 oz) spinach leaves, cooked, squeezed dry, [an]d chopped

[4] eggs, separated

[1 tb]sp chopped fresh rosemary

[pin]ch of grated nutmeg

[sal]t and black pepper

[sal]ad leaves and lemon slices to garnish

[FIL]LING

[20]0 g (7 oz) full-fat soft cheese

[1 tb]sp Greek yogurt or 2 tbsp milk

[3 sp]ring onions, thinly sliced

[125] g (4 oz) thinly sliced smoked salmon

[4 ri]pe tomatoes, thinly sliced

[23 x] 33 cm (9 x 13 in) Swiss roll tin

1 Make the roulade: line the Swiss roll tin with [a] sheet of baking parchment, cutting the [co]rners of the paper so that it fits snugly into [the] tin.

2 Put the butter into a saucepan, add the garlic, and cook gently until the butter [me]lts. Remove from the heat. Stir in the spinach.

3 Add the egg yolks, rosemary, and nutmeg, season to taste, and beat into the spinach mixture.

4 In another bowl, whisk the egg whites until firm but not dry. Fold 2–3 spoonfuls into the spinach mixture, then fold in the remainder.

5 Spread the mixture in the Swiss roll tin, and bake in a preheated oven at 190°C (170°C fan, Gas 5) for 10–12 minutes until the mixture feels firm. Remove from the oven, cover with a damp tea towel, and leave to cool.

6 Meanwhile, make the filling: beat the cheese and yogurt or milk together until smooth, then stir in the onions.

7 Turn out the cooled roulade and peel off the paper. Fill and roll the roulade (see box, right).

8 Wrap the roulade in foil, then overwrap with a damp tea towel, and chill overnight.

9 To serve, trim off the hard edges of the roulade, cut into thick slices, and arrange on a serving platter. Garnish with salad leaves and lemon slices.

Parma ham roulade

Substitute 125 g (4 oz) thinly sliced Parma ham for the smoked salmon.

🔍 Cook's know-how

This roulade can be prepared up to the end of step 8 up to 2 days ahead, making it ideal for a dinner party or other special occasion.

Filling and rolling the roulade

Arrange the slices of smoked salmon on top of the roulade, leaving a 2.5 cm (1 in) border on each side.

Spread the cheese filling over the salmon, using a palette knife. Arrange the tomato slices over half of the cheese filling, looking at it widthways.

Roll up the roulade, starting from the end where the tomato slices have been placed.

Brioches with wild mushrooms and watercress

🍴 SERVES 6   295 CALS PER SERVING

30 g (1 oz) butter

250 g (8 oz) wild mushrooms, trimmed and sliced

60 g (2 oz) watercress, finely chopped

4 tbsp double cream

squeeze of lemon juice

salt and black pepper

6 brioches (page 375)

watercress sprigs to garnish

1 Melt the butter in a large frying pan, add the mushrooms, and cook over a high heat, stirring from time to time, for 3 minutes or until all the liquid has evaporated. Add the watercress, cream, lemon juice, and salt and pepper to taste, and cook until the watercress is just wilted.

2 Hollow out the brioches (see box, below). Spoon in some of the mixture.

3 To serve, transfer the brioches to warmed serving plates and replace the brioche tops. Spoon the remaining mushroom and watercress mixture on to the plates beside the brioches, and garnish with watercress sprigs.

Preparing brioches

Remove brioche top and set aside. Using your fingers, pull out the soft inside, leaving a 5 mm (¼ in) crust. Repeat with the remaining brioches.

Asparagus with quick hollandaise

🍴 SERVES 4   384 CALS PER SERVING

625 g (1¼ lb) asparagus

salt and black pepper

lemon twists to garnish

QUICK HOLLANDAISE

1 tbsp lemon juice

1 tbsp white wine vinegar

4 egg yolks, at room temperature

150 g (5 oz) unsalted butter, melted

1 Cut any woody ends off the asparagus and discard. Lay the spears flat in salted boiling water in a shallow pan (a sauté pan or frying pan is ideal), and simmer gently for 3–4 minutes until the asparagus is tender but still firm.

2 Meanwhile, make the quick hollandaise: three-quarters fill a food processor or blender with hot water from the kettle and pulse or process briefly, to warm the bowl. Pour the water away and dry the bowl.

3 Put the lemon juice and vinegar into the warm bowl of the food processor or blender, add the egg yolks, and pulse or process briefly.

4 With the machine running, gradually pour in the melted butter, and work until thick and creamy. Season to taste.

5 To serve, drain the asparagus. Ladle the hollandaise sauce on to warmed plates, arrange the asparagus on top, and garnish with lemon twists.

💙 Healthy note

An alternative way to cook asparagus, and one that gives it lots of flavour, is to chargrill it. Heat a ridged non-stick or cast-iron chargrill pan until very hot. While it is heating up, roll the asparagus spears in a little olive oil, sea salt, and freshly ground black pepper. As soon as the pan is hot but not smoking, lay the spears across the ridges and cook for 3–4 minutes, turning them with tongs so they become evenly charred on all sides. Instead of serving with a buttery Hollandaise, sprinkle with a little extra-virgin olive oil and grated Parmesan cheese.

Caponata

🍴 SERVES 4–6   297–198 CALS PER SERVING

about 4 tbsp olive oil

1 large aubergine, cut into 1 cm (½ in) chunks

½ head celery, diced

2 onions, thinly sliced

125 g (4 oz) tomato purée

60 g (2 oz) sugar

125–175 ml (4–6 fl oz) red wine vinegar

125 g (4 oz) pitted green olives

30 g (1 oz) capers (optional)

1–2 garlic cloves, crushed

30 g (1 oz) parsley, chopped

salt and black pepper

1 Heat 3 tbsp of the oil in a large saucepan, add the aubergine, and cook gently, stirring, for 8 minutes or until tender. Remove the aubergine from the pan with a slotted spoon.

2 Heat the remaining oil in the pan, add the celery, and cook gently, stirring occasionally, for 7 minutes or until browned.

3 Return the aubergine to the pan with the onions, tomato purée, sugar, and vinegar. Cook over a medium heat for 10 minutes to reduce the harshness of the vinegar. Add a little water if the mixture becomes too thick and starts sticking to the pan.

4 Remove from the heat, and add the green olives, capers, if using, garlic, and half of the parsley. Add salt and pepper to taste. Cover and leave to cool. To serve, transfer to serving plates and sprinkle with the remaining parsley.

Summer melons

SERVES 4   282 CALS PER SERVING

2 x 750 g (1½ lb) ripe melons with different coloured flesh (see box, below)

500 g (1 lb) tomatoes

1 tbsp chopped fresh mint

mint sprigs to garnish

DRESSING

90 ml (3 fl oz) sunflower oil

2 tbsp white wine vinegar

¼ tsp caster sugar

salt and black pepper

1 Cut the melons in half, and remove and discard the seeds. Using a melon baller or a knife, cut balls or neat cubes of flesh into a bowl.

2 Peel the tomatoes: cut out the cores and score an "x" on the base of each one, then immerse in a bowl of boiling water until the skins start to split. Transfer at once to a bowl of cold water. Peel and seed the tomatoes, then cut the flesh into long strips. Add the strips to the melon.

3 Make the dressing: in a small bowl, whisk together the sunflower oil and vinegar, then add the caster sugar, and salt and pepper to taste. Pour the dressing over the melon and tomato mixture. Cover and chill for at least 1 hour.

4 To serve, stir the chopped mint into the melon and tomato mixture, spoon the salad into chilled bowls, and garnish each serving with a mint sprig.

Cook's know-how

Choose two or three varieties of melon to make an attractive colour combination. Honeydew has pale greenish yellow flesh, cantaloupe has either pale green or orange flesh, Ogen and Galia have pale yellow or green flesh, while Charentais melons have deep orange flesh.

Avocado with tomatoes and mint

SERVES 4   232 CALS PER SERVING

4 small firm tomatoes

2 ripe avocados

1 tbsp chopped fresh mint

mint sprigs to garnish

DRESSING

2 tsp white wine vinegar

1 tsp Dijon mustard

2 tbsp olive oil

¼ tsp caster sugar

salt and black pepper

1 Peel the tomatoes: cut out the cores and score an "x" on the base of each one, then immerse in a bowl of boiling hot water until the skins start to split. Transfer at once to a bowl of cold water. Peel, seed, and then coarsely chop the tomato flesh.

2 Make the dressing: in a small bowl, whisk together the vinegar and mustard. Gradually whisk in the oil, then add the caster sugar, and salt and pepper to taste.

3 Halve and stone the avocados. Brush the flesh with a little dressing to prevent discoloration.

4 Combine the tomatoes, chopped mint, and dressing. Pile the tomato mixture into the avocado halves, garnish with mint sprigs, and serve at once.

Healthy note

Avocados are full of heart-healthy nutrients, such as vitamin E, folate, potassium, and monounsaturated fats, but they are also quite calorific: a large avocado may contain up to 400 calories.

Ceviche with tomato and avocado salsa

SERVES 6   328 CALS PER SERVING

3 large scallops (with or without corals according to taste), sliced horizontally in half

200 g (7 oz) cleaned squid, cut into thin strips

125 g (4 oz) skinless salmon fillet, cut across the grain into wafer-thin strips

juice of 2 limes

SALSA

3 tomatoes, peeled, seeded, and cut into thin strips

3 spring onions, finely chopped (including a little of the green leaves)

1 fresh green chilli, halved, seeded, and finely chopped

1 large avocado, halved, stoned, peeled, and finely chopped

salt and black pepper

125 ml (4 fl oz) olive oil

juice of 1 lime

2 tbsp chopped parsley

1 Put the scallops, squid, and salmon into a bowl. Add the lime juice, and stir gently until the fish is coated in juice. Cover, and chill for 4–5 hours until the fish is opaque.

2 Meanwhile, make the salsa: put the tomatoes, spring onions, chilli, and avocado into a bowl, and season with salt and pepper. Add the olive oil and lime juice, and stir gently to mix. Cover, and chill with the ceviche.

3 To serve, drain the juice from the fish, and mix the juice gently into the salsa with the chopped parsley. Arrange the fish on 6 plates, and spoon the salsa on top.

Cook's know-how

It is essential to use very fresh fish for ceviche, because the fish is marinated and served raw, not cooked. Really fresh raw scallops are translucent and creamy grey in colour, not as white as they appear when cooked. Do not leave the ceviche to marinate for any longer than the recipe states or it will begin to lose its texture and colour, and always serve chilled, straight from the refrigerator.

Smoked chicken salad with walnuts

SERVES 6   472 CALS PER SERVING

1 smoked chicken, weighing about 1.25 kg (2½ lb)

100 ml (3½ fl oz) sunflower oil

2 tbsp walnut oil

75 ml (2½ fl oz) orange juice

¼ tsp ground coriander

¼ tsp caster sugar

salt and black pepper

375 g (12 oz) mixed salad leaves

4 oranges, peeled and segmented

60 g (2 oz) walnut pieces

1 Remove the meat from the chicken carcass, and discard all of the skin and any gristle. Cut the meat into thin, neat slices. Put the chicken into a shallow non-metallic dish.

2 In a small bowl, combine the sunflower and walnut oils, orange juice, ground coriander, and sugar. Season with salt and pepper. Pour the mixture over the chicken slices and toss them gently until evenly coated.

3 Arrange the salad leaves, orange segments, and chicken slices on individual serving plates, scatter the walnut pieces over the top, and serve immediately.

Warm duck salad

Substitute 375 g (12 oz) smoked duck or turkey breast for the chicken. Gently heat the poultry slices in the dressing, and add warm garlic croûtons (page 44) to the salad.

Warm salad with bacon and scallops

SERVES 4   276 CALS PER SERVING

375 g (12 oz) mixed salad leaves, such as radicchio, lamb's lettuce, frisée, and rocket

8 shallots, finely chopped

1 tbsp sunflower oil

250 g (8 oz) lean unsmoked bacon rashers, rinds removed, diced

12 scallops, halved

3 tbsp white wine vinegar

2 tbsp walnut oil

salt and black pepper

1 Put the salad leaves into a large bowl and sprinkle with half of the shallots.

2 Heat the oil in a frying pan, add the bacon, and cook quickly, stirring occasionally, for 5 minutes or until crisp. Add the scallops and cook quickly for 1–2 minutes until just opaque. Remove from the pan and keep warm.

3 Add the remaining shallots and cook for 1 minute. Add the vinegar and boil rapidly, stirring to incorporate the pan juices.

4 Sprinkle the walnut oil over the salad leaves and toss together until the leaves are evenly coated and shiny. Add the bacon and scallops, hot vinegar and shallots, and season to taste.

Cook's know-how

Stirring vinegar into the frying pan loosens and dissolves the flavoursome juices on the bottom of the pan so they are not wasted. This is called deglazing.

Eggs and Cheese

Under 45 minutes

Spinach and mushroom frittata
Firm and chunky Italian omelette enclosing bacon, mushrooms, and spinach, sprinkled with Parmesan, and browned under the grill.
SERVES 3   449 CALS PER SERVING
Takes 25 minutes   Page 88

Raclette
Boiled new potatoes topped with Swiss raclette cheese, and heated in oven until sizzling. Served with gherkins and onions.
SERVES 4   446 CALS PER SERVING
Takes 25 minutes   Page 96

Oeufs en cocotte
Warm creamy snack: whole eggs in ramekins, topped with double cream and parsley, and steamed or baked.
SERVES 4   176 CALS PER SERVING
Takes 25 minutes   Page 100

Eggs Benedict
Hearty snack: poached eggs and bacon rashers on toasted muffins, topped with lemon-flavoured hollandaise sauce.
SERVES 4   602 CALS PER SERVING
Takes 25 minutes   Page 100

Croque señor
Sandwich of Cheddar cheese and ham given a Mexican flavour with a salsa of tomatoes, chilli, and red pepper. Cooked until golden.
SERVES 4   413 CALS PER SERVING
Takes 30 minutes   Page 98

Eggs Florentine
Nutritious and creamy: spinach mixed with spring onions and double cream, topped with a poached egg and Parmesan cheese sauce.
SERVES 4   475 CALS PER SERVING
Takes 30 minutes   Page 100

45-60 minutes

Pizza tartlets
Rich and tangy: tomatoes, black olives, and Fontina or mozzarella cheese, with garlic and oregano, set in shortcrust pastry tartlet shells spread with pesto and sprinkled with cheese.
MAKES 12   198 CALS EACH
Takes 55 minutes   Page 9

Spinach, leek, and Gruyère tart
Nourishing and creamy: leek and spinach in shortcrust pastry shell with a mixture of eggs milk, cream, and Gruyère cheese.
SERVES 6   480 CALS PER SERVING
Takes 60 minutes, **plus chilling**   Page 9

FRENCH CLASSIC

Quiche Lorraine
Classic savoury tart: shortcrust pastry sprea with lightly cooked onion and crispy streaky bacon. Sprinkled with Gruyère cheese, filled with an egg and cream mixture, and baked until golden brown. Served warm or cold.
SERVES 6   504 CALS PER SERVING
Takes 60 minutes, **plus chilling**   Page

SWISS CLASSIC

Cheese fondue
Gruyère and Emmental cheeses melted in a fondue pot with wine, garlic, and kirsch. Serve with bread and apple for dipping.
SERVES 6   813 CALS PER SERVING
Takes 30 minutes   Page 99

FAMILY CHOICE

Strata with cheese and pesto
Savoury custard of eggs, crème fraîche, and milk, poured over slices of bread and pesto. Sprinkled with Italian cheeses.

SERVES 4   600 CALS PER SERVING

Takes 50 minutes   Page 93

DINNER PARTY

Garlic and goat's cheese soufflé
Tangy soufflés combining garlic-flavoured milk with butter, flour, goat's cheese, egg yolks, and whisked egg whites.

SERVES 6   267 CALS PER SERVING

Takes 55 minutes   Page 98

Mexican omelette
Classic omelette with a substantial filling of onion and garlic cooked with green pepper, tomatoes, mushrooms, and Tabasco.

MAKES 2   547 CALS PER SERVING

Takes 50 minutes   Page 87

Soufflé pancakes with broccoli and cheese
Pancakes with a soufflé filling combining tiny broccoli florets, Cheddar cheese, and mustard.

MAKES 8   200 CALS EACH

Takes 45 minutes, **plus standing**   Page 93

Creamy seafood crêpes
Pieces of cod fillet cooked with onion, garlic, tomatoes, fresh dill, cream, and prawns, and flavoured with fresh basil.

SERVES 6   308 CALS PER SERVING

Takes 50 minutes, **plus standing**   Page 95

Over 60 minutes

TRADITIONAL

Classic cheese soufflé
Delicate and light: milk flavoured with bay leaf, parsley, and onion, combined with butter, flour, eggs, and Cheddar cheese.

SERVES 4   363 CALS PER SERVING

Takes 1¼ hours   Page 94

VEGETARIAN

Swiss double cheese soufflés
Rich and creamy: individual soufflés flavoured with Gruyère cheese and chives. Twice-baked and topped with double cream and cheese.

SERVES 6   465 CALS PER SERVING

Takes 1 hour 5 minutes   Page 96

Smoked salmon and asparagus quiche
Salmon and asparagus set in a shortcrust pastry shell with a savoury custard of Greek yogurt, eggs, and dill.

SERVES 6–8   321–241 CALS PER SERVING

Takes 1¼ hours, **plus chilling**   Page 89

Eggs and cheese know-how

Eggs are one of the most useful foods in a cook's repertoire. They can be cooked in many delicious ways, from simple boiling, poaching, and scrambling to omelettes and soufflés that require a little more skill. Eggs are also used to enrich pastries and doughs, give volume and moistness to cakes and many puddings, thicken sauces and custards, bind mixtures ranging from burgers to pâtés, and provide a coating for foods to be fried.

Cheese has countless culinary uses. Apart from its everyday use as a sandwich filling, it is found in sauces, fondues, and pizza toppings; it flavours savoury pastries, doughs, and quiche fillings; it is essential in many pasta dishes; and it is popular in puddings such as cheesecake and tiramisu.

Buying and storing

Most of the eggs we eat are hen's eggs, although there are also tiny quail's eggs, large duck eggs, and even larger goose eggs. Hen's eggs are usually described according to the farming method used – for example, "free-range", "barn", "from caged hens" (ie the battery system), and "organic" – and these descriptions guarantee that the eggs have been produced according to certain rules. Labels such as "farm fresh" and "country" are meaningless. Whichever you buy, choose the ones with the longest "use-by" date, and check that none is damaged or cracked. Store eggs in their box in the refrigerator (away from strong foods so that they do not absorb flavours and odours through their shells).
If you place them pointed end down, the yolk will remain centred in the white. Always use them by their use-by date.

Cheese deteriorates once cut, so do not buy it in a large piece unless you know it will be used up quickly. Keep all cheeses well wrapped in the refrigerator or in a cool larder (soft cheeses must be stored in the refrigerator and used within a few days).

Freezing

Shelled raw eggs freeze very successfully, and can be stored for up to 6 months. If whole, whisk gently to mix the yolk and white; add a little salt to whole eggs and egg yolks for use in savoury foods or sugar for use in sweet dishes (nothing needs to be added to whites). Thaw at room temperature. Egg-based dishes such as quiches, custards, and mousses can also be frozen.

Hard and firm cheeses freeze well, as do soft ripened cheeses such as Brie. Store them for up to 1 month. Thaw in the refrigerator before use. Note that the texture of hard cheeses may change after freezing, becoming more crumbly, making the cheeses suitable only for cooking. Soft fresh cheeses and soft blue-veined cheeses do not freeze well.

Microwaving

Never microwave an egg that is still in its shell as it will burst. Even out of its shell, a whole egg may burst, so always pierce the membrane on the yolk with a toothpick before cooking. The yolk cooks more quickly than the white, so standing time should be allowed to let the white continue cooking. Where yolks and whites are combined, as for scrambled eggs, the mixture will appear undercooked but will firm up during standing time.

Cheeses melt quickly in the microwave, so take care not to overcook or burn them. Hard or firm mature cheeses and processed cheeses are the best. Frozen soft ripened cheeses can be softened and brought to room temperature in the microwave before serving.

All about eggs

Hen's eggs are graded by weight. Those weighing 73 g and over are classified as "very large"; eggs weighing 63-73 g are "large"; eggs weighing 53-63 g are "medium"; and eggs below 53 g are "small".

The shell - usually brown or white, but now also blue, green, pink, or speckled - is a result of the breed of hen.

The colour of the yolk depends on the hen's diet and added natural or artificial colourants.

Separating eggs

For best results, take eggs straight from the fridge so they are well chilled.

1 Holding an egg over a bowl, break open the shell. Carefully transfer the yolk from one half shell to the other, letting the egg white run into the bowl. Repeat several times.

2 Put the yolk in another bowl. Remove any yolk from the white with the tip of a spoon (the white will not whisk if there is any trace of yolk).

Cooking eggs

Eggs are one of the cheapest sources of protein and could not be easier to cook. Once you have mastered the basic techniques you will be able to produce a wide range of nutritious meals in minutes.

Boiling

Use eggs at room temperature (the shells are less likely to crack). Put the eggs into a pan of simmering water. Bring back to a boil, then simmer gently. Cooking times are calculated from the time the water comes back to a boil, and can vary according to individual taste and on the size and freshness of the eggs. For soft-boiled eggs, simmer gently for 4–5 minutes; for hard-boiled eggs, allow 8–10 minutes. After cooking hard-boiled eggs, lift them out of the water and crack the shell to allow steam to escape, then plunge the eggs into iced water. Peel when cool enough to handle. (An unsightly black line may form round the yolk if you cook them too long, or keep them in the shell.) Use straight away or keep in a bowl of cold water in the refrigerator for up to 24 hours.

Hard boiled eggs

Soft boiled eggs

Cooking with cheese

Cheese needs to be cooked with care as heat can spoil its texture, making it rubbery or stringy. Hard and firm cheeses can withstand heat best, melting and blending smoothly. When adding cheese to a sauce, do this at the end of cooking and melt gently; do not boil. If grilling a cheese topping, cook as briefly as possible.

Frying

Fresh eggs are essential for successful frying because they keep their shape during cooking. Fry the eggs in your favourite oil, adding a knob of butter for extra flavour if you like.

1 Heat a thin layer of oil in a non-stick frying pan. When the oil is very hot and starting to sizzle, slip in an egg and cook over a medium heat.

2 Spoon the oil over once or twice to give a white top. Remove and serve, or turn over and cook for a few seconds, to set the yolk a little more.

Scrambling

Scrambled eggs can be served plain, or flavoured with herbs, cheese, ham, or smoked salmon. Allow 2 eggs per person.

1 Lightly beat the eggs with salt and pepper to taste and a little milk, if you like. Melt a knob of butter in a pan. Add the eggs.

2 Cook over a medium heat, stirring constantly with a wooden spatula or spoon, until almost set – they will continue to cook after they have been removed from the heat. Serve at once.

Poaching

The classic method for poaching eggs is in a pan of simmering water. Use the freshest eggs possible, as they will keep a neat shape.

1 Bring a wide pan of water to the boil. Lower the heat so that the water is simmering, and slide in an egg. Swirl the water round the egg to give it a neat shape. Simmer for 3–4 minutes until the egg is cooked to your taste.

2 Lift out the egg with a slotted spoon and drain briefly on paper towels. To keep them warm, or to reheat them if they have been prepared ahead, immerse them in a bowl of hot water (they will take 1 minute to reheat).

Making an omelette

Omelettes are best made in a special pan kept solely for the purpose, then they are less likely to stick. If you do not have one, use a small frying pan, no more than 20 cm (8 in) in diameter.

Making pancakes

The quantities given here will make enough batter for about 12 thin pancakes (the kind that the French call crêpes), using an 18-20 cm (7-8 in) pan. Do not worry if the first pancake or two is a failure: it acts as a test for the consistency of the batter and the heat of the pan, and if you are new to pancake making you may prefer to make them slightly thicker, to be on the safe side, in which case you may only make 8 pancakes. Any uneaten pancakes will keep in a stack for 24 hours, or they can be frozen.

1 Beat 2–3 eggs with salt and pepper, plus chopped fresh herbs if you like. Heat the pan, then add a knob of butter. When the butter is foaming, tilt the pan to coat the bottom. Pour in the eggs.

1 Sift 125 g (4 oz) plain flour into a bowl and make a well in the middle. Whisk together 1 egg, 1 egg yolk, and a little milk taken from 300 ml (½ pint), then pour into the well. Whisk with a little of the flour.

2 Gradually whisk in half of the remaining milk, drawing in the rest of the flour a little at a time, to make a smooth batter. Stir in the remaining milk. Cover and leave to stand for about 30 minutes.

2 Cook over a medium heat. As the eggs begin to set, lift and pull back the edge of the omelette towards the middle, and tilt the pan so the liquid egg runs underneath.

3 Heat the frying pan and brush with a little oil. Ladle 2–3 tbsp batter into the pan and tilt the pan so that the batter spreads out evenly over the bottom.

4 Cook the pancake over a medium–high heat for 45–60 seconds until small holes appear on the surface, the underside is lightly browned, and the edge has started to curl. Loosen the pancake and turn it over by tossing or flipping it with a palette knife. Cook the other side for about 30 seconds until golden.

3 Continue cooking until the omelette is just set and the underside is golden. Tilt the pan, loosen the edge of the omelette and flip over in half, to fold it. Slide on to a plate to serve.

5 Slide the pancake out of the pan. Heat and lightly grease the pan again before making the next pancake. Serve the pancakes as they are made, or stack them on a plate and reheat before serving. (If the pancakes are hot when you stack them they will not stick together; there is no need to interleave them with greaseproof paper.)

Omelette know-how

Gently stir to combine the yolks with the whites: vigorous beating will make the omelette rubbery. Make sure the pan is hot and the butter foaming when you add the eggs. The omelette will continue to cook after you remove it from the heat, so the middle should still be a little moist.

Mushroom omelette with ciabatta

SERVES 2   **673 CALS PER SERVING**

4 eggs

salt and black pepper

30 g (1 oz) butter

50 g (2 oz) shiitake mushrooms, sliced

1 tbsp snipped fresh chives

1 loaf of ciabatta bread, warmed and split lengthways

1 Break the eggs into a small bowl, season with salt and black pepper, and beat with a fork.

2 Melt half of the butter in a small frying pan, add the mushrooms, and cook over a high heat for 3–5 minutes until all the liquid has evaporated. Remove from the heat, stir in the chives, season with salt and pepper, and keep hot.

3 Heat an omelette pan or small frying pan until very hot. Add the remaining butter and swirl the pan to evenly coat the base and sides. When the butter is foaming, pour in the seasoned egg mixture.

4 Cook the omelette over a medium heat, pulling back the edge as the eggs set, and tilting the pan to allow the uncooked egg to run to the side of the pan. Continue until the omelette is lightly set and the underside is golden brown. Remove from the heat.

5 Scatter the mushrooms over half of the omelette, then flip the uncovered half over them. Fill the warmed split ciabatta with the omelette, cut the ciabatta in half crosswise, and serve at once.

Savoury soufflé omelette

MAKES 2   **479 CALS EACH**

4 eggs, separated

30 g (1 oz) butter

FILLING

2 tbsp olive oil

½ onion, thinly sliced

1 garlic clove, crushed

1 courgette, sliced

1 red pepper, halved, seeded, and sliced

1 x 200 g can chopped tomatoes

1 tbsp chopped fresh thyme leaves

salt and black pepper

1 Make the filling: heat the oil in a frying pan, add the onion and garlic, and cook gently for 5 minutes or until softened. Add the courgette and red pepper, and cook for about 2 minutes. Add the tomatoes and thyme, season with salt and pepper, and simmer for about 20 minutes.

2 Whisk together the egg yolks and salt and pepper. Whisk the egg whites until stiff, then fold into the yolks.

3 Melt half of the butter in an omelette pan. When it foams, add half of the egg mixture, and cook over a gentle heat for 3 minutes. Add half of the filling, fold the omelette in half, and serve. Repeat with the remaining eggs and filling.

Mexican omelette

An omelette is one of the most useful of all egg dishes, quick and easy to make, and nutritious either plain or with a filling. This recipe combines a classic French omelette with a piquant filling, but you can add whatever filling you like.

MAKES 2   **547 CALS EACH**

6 eggs

30 g (1 oz) butter

chopped parsley to garnish

FILLING

2 tbsp olive oil

1 onion, finely chopped

1 garlic clove, crushed

1 green pepper, halved, seeded, and finely chopped

2 ripe tomatoes, finely chopped

125 g (4 oz) button mushrooms, thinly sliced

¼ tsp Worcestershire sauce

a few drops of Tabasco sauce

salt and black pepper

1 Make the filling: heat the oil in a frying pan, add the onion and garlic, and cook for 5 minutes or until softened. Add the pepper, and cook, stirring, for 5 minutes.

2 Add the tomatoes and mushrooms, and cook, stirring, for 10 minutes. Add the Worcestershire and Tabasco sauces, season with salt and pepper, and simmer for about 5 minutes. Keep warm.

3 Beat 3 of the eggs in a bowl with salt and pepper. Heat an omelette pan or small frying pan and add half of the butter.

4 When the butter is foaming, add the eggs, and cook over a medium heat, pulling back the edge as the eggs set, and tilting the pan so the liquid egg runs underneath. Continue until lightly set and golden.

5 Spoon half of the filling on to the half of the omelette farthest from the pan handle. With a palette knife, lift the uncovered half of the omelette and flip it over the filling.

6 Slide the omelette on to a warmed plate, and garnish with chopped parsley. Make the second omelette in the same way, reheating the pan before adding the butter.

Mushroom omelette

Substitute 175 g (6 oz) sliced button mushrooms for the filling. Cook in a little melted butter, and season with salt and pepper.

Smoked chicken omelette

Substitute 125 g (4 oz) diced smoked chicken and 1 tbsp snipped fresh chives for the filling.

Tomato omelette

Substitute 5 finely chopped ripe tomatoes for the filling. Cook the tomatoes in a little butter for 2–3 minutes. Season well, and stir in a few snipped fresh chives.

Courgette and Parma ham frittata

SERVES 4   270 CALS PER SERVING

2 tbsp olive oil

625 g (1¼ lb) small courgettes, thinly sliced on the diagonal

6 eggs

salt and black pepper

60 g (2 oz) Parma ham, diced

shredded fresh basil or chopped flat-leaf parsley to garnish

1 Heat the olive oil in a large frying pan. Add the courgettes and cook gently for 5 minutes or until just tender.

2 Break the eggs into a bowl, season with salt and pepper, and beat with a fork.

3 Add the ham to the courgettes in the frying pan, then pour in the eggs.

4 Cook over a medium heat for about 10 minutes. As the eggs set, lift the frittata with a spatula and tilt the pan to allow the uncooked egg to run underneath. Continue until almost set and the underside is golden brown.

5 Place the frying pan under a hot grill, 10 cm (4 in) from the heat, for 1–2 minutes until the top is a light golden brown colour and the egg is cooked through and quite firm when pressed.

6 Cut the frittata into wedges, and lightly garnish with shredded fresh basil or chopped parsley. Serve hot or cold.

Spanish omelette

SERVES 4   389 CALS PER SERVING

3 tbsp olive oil

2 large potatoes, diced

2 large onions, chopped

6 eggs

salt and black pepper

1 tbsp chopped parsley

1 Heat the oil in a frying pan, add the potatoes and onions, and stir until coated with the oil. Cook gently for about 10 minutes until golden brown. Pour the excess oil from the pan.

2 Break the eggs into a bowl, season with salt and pepper, and beat with a fork.

3 Pour the eggs into the pan, and mix with the vegetables. Cook for about 10 minutes until the eggs are almost set, then brown the top of the omelette under a hot grill for 1–2 minutes.

4 Slide the omelette on to a warmed plate, and cut into quarters. Sprinkle with chopped parsley and serve warm or cold.

Mixed bean omelette

Lightly cook 60 g (2 oz) French beans and 125 g (4 oz) shelled broad beans. Add to the pan in step 3, when mixing the potatoes and onions with the eggs.

Spinach and mushroom frittata

SERVES 3   449 CALS PER SERVING

3 tbsp olive oil

60 g (2 oz) thick-cut smoked bacon rashers, rinds removed, diced

250 g (8 oz) chestnut mushrooms, quartered

125 g (4 oz) spinach leaves, coarsely chopped

6 eggs

salt and black pepper

2 tbsp grated Parmesan cheese

1 Heat the oil in a large frying pan. Add the bacon and mushrooms and cook over a high heat, stirring, for about 7 minutes or until the bacon is crisp. Add the spinach and turn it in the oil for 1–2 minutes. Do not allow the spinach to wilt. Lower the heat.

2 Break the eggs into a bowl, season with salt and pepper, and beat with a fork.

3 Pour the eggs over the mushrooms and spinach and cook over a medium heat for 10 minutes. As the eggs set, lift the frittata with a spatula and tilt the pan so the uncooked egg runs underneath.

4 When the eggs are set, sprinkle with grated Parmesan, and place the pan under a hot grill, 10 cm (4 in) from the heat, for 1–2 minutes or until the top is golden brown and firm when pressed. Serve at once.

Courgettes have a mild flavour and soft texture that works well with salty Parma ham. Choose the smallest, youngest courgettes you can find.

♡ Healthy note

You can omit the bacon to lower the fat content of this frittata (and make it vegetarian too). To compensate for the lack of flavour, add a splash of soy sauce in step 2. Always add soy sauce sparingly, because it has a high salt content.

moked salmon
nd asparagus
uiche

SERVES 6–8   **321–241 CALS PER SERVING**

g (4 oz) fine asparagus, cooked, drained, and
into 3.5 cm (1½ in) lengths

(3 oz) smoked salmon, cut into strips

g (10 oz) Greek yogurt or full-fat crème fraîche

gs

sp chopped fresh dill

k pepper

SHORTCRUST PASTRY

175 g (6 oz) plain flour

90 g (3 oz) butter

about 2 tbsp cold water

23 cm (9 in) loose-bottomed fluted flan tin

baking beans

1 Make the pastry: tip the flour into a bowl, rub in the butter with your fingertips, then add enough water to bind to a soft dough. Wrap in cling film and chill for 30 minutes.

2 Roll out the pastry, and use to line the tin. Prick the pastry with a fork. Line the pastry shell with foil or greaseproof paper, and fill with baking beans (or rice or pasta if you have no beans).

3 Place the tin on a heated baking tray and bake in a preheated oven at 220°C (200°C fan, Gas 7) for 15–20 minutes, removing the foil and beans for the final 10 minutes.

4 Arrange the asparagus and half of the salmon in the pastry shell. Mix the yogurt or crème fraîche, eggs, dill, and plenty of pepper, and pour into the shell. Arrange the remaining salmon on top.

5 Reduce the oven temperature to 180°C (160°C fan, Gas 4), and bake for 35 minutes or until golden and set. Serve warm or cold.

Quiche Lorraine

This most famous of all quiches is named after the area from which it comes – Alsace-Lorraine in north-eastern France – where it was traditionally served on May Day, following a dish of roast suckling pig.

 SERVES 6   504 CALS PER SERVING

30 g (1 oz) butter

1 onion, chopped

175 g (6 oz) unsmoked streaky bacon rashers, rinds removed, diced

125 g (4 oz) Gruyère cheese, grated

250 ml (8 fl oz) single cream or milk

2 eggs, beaten

salt and black pepper

SHORTCRUST PASTRY

125 g (4 oz) plain flour

60 g (2 oz) butter

about 1 tbsp cold water

20 cm (8 in) loose-bottomed fluted flan tin

baking beans

1 Make the pastry with the flour, butter, and water (see box, right). Wrap in cling film and chill for 30 minutes.

2 Roll out the pastry on a lightly floured work surface, and use to line the flan tin. Prick the bottom of the pastry shell with a fork.

3 Line the pastry shell with a sheet of foil or greaseproof paper, and fill with baking beans (or rice or pasta if you have no beans). Place the flan tin on a heated baking tray and bake the shell in a preheated oven at 220°C (200°C fan, Gas 7) for 15–20 minutes, removing the foil and beans for the final 10 minutes.

4 Meanwhile, make the filling: melt the butter in a frying pan, add the onion and bacon, and cook gently, stirring occasionally, for 10 minutes or until the onion is golden brown and the bacon is crisp.

5 Spoon the onion and bacon into the pastry shell, and sprinkle the cheese on top. Mix the cream and eggs in a jug, season with salt and pepper, and pour into the pastry shell.

6 Reduce the oven temperature to 180°C (160°C fan, Gas 4), and bake the quiche for 25–30 minutes until the filling is golden and set. Serve warm or cold.

Making shortcrust pastry

Tip the flour into a bowl and rub in the butter lightly with your fingertips until the mixture looks like fine breadcrumbs.

Add the water and mix with a round-bladed knife to form a soft but not sticky dough.

Roquefort quiche

SERVES 6   336 CALS PER SERVING

90 g (3 oz) Roquefort or other blue
cheese, crumbled

175 g (6 oz) full-fat soft cheese

2 eggs, beaten

150 ml (¼ pint) full-fat crème fraîche

1 tbsp snipped fresh chives

salt and black pepper

SHORTCRUST PASTRY

125 g (4 oz) plain flour

60 g (2 oz) butter

about 1 tbsp cold water

20 cm (8 in) loose-bottomed fluted flan tin

baking beans

1 Make the pastry: tip the flour into a bowl
and rub in the butter with your fingertips.
Add enough water to bind to a soft dough.
Wrap in cling film and chill for 30 minutes.

2 Roll out the shortcrust pastry, and use to
line the flan tin. Prick the bottom of the
pastry shell with a fork.

3 Line the pastry shell with foil or greaseproof paper, and fill with baking beans
(or rice or pasta if you have no beans).
Place the tin on a heated baking tray, and
bake in a preheated oven at 220°C (200°C
fan, Gas 7) for 15–20 minutes, removing the
foil and beans for the final
10 minutes.

4 Meanwhile, make the filling: mix the
Roquefort and full-fat cheese in a bowl,
then beat in the eggs, crème fraîche, and
chives, and season with salt and pepper.
Take care not to add too much salt as
blue cheese is quite salty.

5 Pour the mixture into the pastry shell,
reduce the oven temperature to
180°C (160°C fan, Gas 4), and bake the
quiche for about 30 minutes until golden
and set. Serve warm or cold.

Spinach, leek, and Gruyère tart

SERVES 6   480 CALS PER SERVING

30 g (1 oz) butter

175 g (6 oz) leeks, trimmed and finely sliced

250 g (8 oz) young spinach leaves,
coarsely chopped

2 eggs, beaten

150 ml (¼ pint) each double cream and milk,
or 300 ml (½ pint) milk

90 g (3 oz) Gruyère cheese, grated

salt and black pepper

SHORTCRUST PASTRY

175 g (6 oz) plain flour

90 g (3 oz) butter

about 2 tbsp cold water

23 cm (9 in) loose-bottomed fluted flan tin

baking beans

1 Make the pastry: tip the flour into a bowl
and rub in the butter with your fingertips.
Add enough water to bind to a soft dough.
Wrap in cling film and chill for 30 minutes.

2 Roll out the pastry on a lightly floured
work surface, and use to line the flan
tin. Prick the bottom of the pastry shell with
a fork.

3 Line the pastry shell with foil or greaseproof paper, and fill with baking beans
(or rice or pasta if you have no beans). Put
the tin on a heated baking tray, and bake
in a preheated oven at 220°C (200°C fan,
Gas 7) for 15–20 minutes, removing the foil
and beans for the final 10 minutes.

4 Meanwhile, make the filling: melt the
butter in a frying pan, add the leeks,
and cook over a high heat for 5 minutes
or until just beginning to turn golden brown.
Add the spinach and cook for about
2 minutes until it just begins to wilt. Spoon
the filling into the pastry shell.

5 Mix together the eggs, milk, cream, and
Gruyère cheese in a jug, season with salt
and pepper, and pour into the pastry shell.

6 Reduce the oven temperature to 180°C
(160°C fan, Gas 4), and bake for 25
minutes or until the filling is golden and set.
Serve warm or cold.

Pizza tartlets

These tartlets, with their traditional pizza flavours, will serve 4 people as a light lunch or supper dish, accompanied by a crisp, green salad. They also make a tasty appetizer to serve with pre-dinner drinks. They taste just as good cold as warm, so they can be prepared well in advance.

MAKES 12   198 CALS EACH

90 g (3 oz) ready-made red or green pesto

250 g (8 oz) ripe tomatoes, finely chopped

2–3 garlic cloves, crushed

9 black olives, pitted and quartered

125 g (4 oz) Fontina or mozzarella cheese, grated

2–3 tbsp grated Parmesan cheese

1 tsp dried oregano

SHORTCRUST PASTRY

175 g (6 oz) plain flour

90 g (3 oz) butter

about 2 tbsp cold water

1 Make the pastry: tip the flour into a bowl and rub in the butter with your fingertips. Add enough water to bind to a soft dough. Wrap in cling film and chill for 30 minutes.

2 Make the tartlet shells (see box, right).

3 Spread the pesto in the tartlet shells, then fill the shells with the tomatoes, garlic, black olives, and Fontina cheese.

4 Sprinkle the grated Parmesan cheese over the tartlets, covering the pastry edges as well as the filling. Sprinkle the dried oregano on top.

5 Bake the tartlets in a preheated oven at 200°C (180°C fan, Gas 6) for 20–30 minutes until the edges are a golden brown colour and the cheese topping has melted and become crispy. Serve the tartlets warm or cold.

Goat's cheese tartlets

Cut a log of goat's cheese into 12 slices and use instead of the grated Fontina or mozzarella.

Making tartlet shells

Sprinkle the work surface with flour, then roll out the shortcrust pastry until 3–5 mm (⅛–¼ in) thick.

Cut out 12 rounds from the pastry, using a 10 cm (4 in) pastry cutter or the rim of a glass or saucer.

Fold up the edges of the rounds to form rims; put the rounds on a baking tray.

Strata with cheese and pesto

🍴 SERVES 4   600 CALS PER SERVING

~6 thick slices of stale bread

0–90 g (2–3 oz) ready-made pesto

 eggs, lightly beaten

25 ml (4 fl oz) crème fraîche

25 ml (4 fl oz) milk

75 g (6 oz) Fontina or mature Cheddar heese, grated

0 g (2 oz) mozzarella cheese, grated

0 g (1 oz) Parmesan cheese, grated

Cut off and discard the crusts from the bread. Spread the slices with pesto, hen arrange them in a single layer in baking dish.

In a bowl, combine the eggs with the crème fraîche and milk, then pour over he bread. Sprinkle with the grated cheeses.

Bake the strata in a preheated oven at 200°C (180°C fan, Gas 6) for 35–40 inutes until golden brown. It will puff up ghtly as it bakes but, unlike a soufflé, can be safely left to stand for about minutes before serving.

🔍 Cook's know-how

You need stale bread to make a good, moist strata (a Californian recipe for using up leftover bread). If the bread is fresh, the strata will be soggy.

Soufflé pancakes with broccoli and cheese

🍴 MAKES 8   200 CALS EACH

8 pancakes (page 95)

butter for greasing

2 tbsp grated Parmesan cheese

FILLING

125 g (4 oz) tiny broccoli florets

salt and black pepper

45 g (1½ oz) butter

45 g (1½ oz) plain flour

300 ml (½ pint) milk

½ tsp Dijon mustard

125 g (4 oz) mature Cheddar cheese, grated

4 eggs, separated

1 Make the filling: blanch the broccoli florets in boiling salted water for 1 minute. Drain, rinse under cold running water, and drain again.

2 Melt the butter in a small saucepan, add the flour, and cook, stirring occasionally, for about 1 minute.

3 Remove the pan from the heat, and gradually blend in the milk. Bring to a boil, stirring until thickened. Remove from the heat, add the mustard and cheese, and season with salt and pepper. Stir, then leave to cool slightly.

4 Beat the egg yolks into the sauce. In a large bowl, whisk the egg whites until soft peaks form, then fold into the cheese sauce with the broccoli.

5 Lay the pancakes on two lightly buttered baking trays. Divide the soufflé mixture among the pancakes, arranging it down the middle of each one. Fold the sides of each pancake loosely over the top of the filling, and sprinkle with grated Parmesan cheese.

6 Bake in a preheated oven at 200°C (180°C fan, Gas 6) for 15–20 minutes, until the soufflé mixture has risen and the pancakes are crisp.

Chicken pancakes florentine

🍴 MAKES 8   360 CALS EACH

500 g (1 lb) spinach leaves, coarsely chopped

30 g (1 oz) butter

pinch of grated nutmeg

8 pancakes (page 95)

125 g (4 oz) Gruyère cheese, grated

FILLING

60 g (2 oz) butter

375 g (12 oz) chestnut mushrooms, quartered

45 g (1½ oz) plain flour

300 ml (½ pint) chicken stock

375 g (12 oz) boneless and skinless cooked chicken, cut into bite-sized pieces

1 tbsp chopped fresh tarragon

salt and black pepper

1 Make the filling: melt the butter in a heavy pan, add the mushrooms, and cook, stirring often, for 2–3 minutes.

2 Add the flour, and cook, stirring, for 1 minute. Remove the pan from the heat, and gradually blend in the stock. Bring to a boil, stirring, and simmer for 2–3 minutes. Add the chicken and tarragon, and season with salt and pepper.

3 Rinse the spinach and put into a saucepan with only the water that clings to the leaves. Cook for 2 minutes or until tender. Drain well, squeezing to extract any excess water, then stir in the butter and nutmeg. Spoon into a shallow ovenproof dish.

4 Divide the chicken and mushroom mixture among the 8 pancakes. Roll up the pancakes, and place them in a single layer on top of the spinach.

5 Sprinkle with the cheese, and bake in a preheated oven at 190°C (170°C fan, Gas 5) for about 25 minutes until golden. Serve hot.

♡ Healthy note

There are several ways in which you can cut the amount of fat and calories in this dish. For the filling, halve the butter and cook the mushrooms in a non-stick pan, then halve the amount of chicken and shred it finely. The Gruyère cheese can also be halved, or you could use a reduced-fat Cheddar instead.

Classic cheese soufflé

🕐 **SERVES 4**   **363 CALS PER SERVING**

300 ml (½ pint) milk

1 bay leaf

a few parsley stalks

½ onion, peeled

pinch of cayenne pepper

salt and black pepper

45 g (1½ oz) butter, plus extra for greasing

45 g (1½ oz) plain flour

3 eggs, separated

1 tbsp Dijon mustard

125 g (4 oz) mature Cheddar cheese, grated

1.25 litre (2 pint) soufflé dish

1 Bring the milk to a boil in a saucepan with the bay leaf, parsley stalks, and onion half. Remove from the heat, cover, and leave to infuse for about 20 minutes. Strain, then add the cayenne and season with salt and pepper.

2 Melt the butter in a large pan, add the flour, and cook, stirring, for 1 minute. Remove from the heat, slowly blend in the milk, then bring to a boil. Simmer for 2–3 minutes, stirring, until thickened, then remove from the heat. Leave to cool for about 10 minutes.

3 Beat the egg yolks in a bowl. Stir them into the cooled white sauce, then stir in the mustard and all but 15 g (½ oz) of the Cheddar.

4 Whisk the egg whites until they form firm but not dry peaks. Fold 1–2 tbsp egg whites into the cheese mixture until evenly combined, then fold in the remaining egg whites.

5 Lightly butter the soufflé dish, pour in the soufflé mixture, and sprinkle with the remaining cheese.

6 Bake on a preheated baking sheet in the top half of a preheated oven at 180°C (160°C fan, Gas 4) for about 25 minutes, or until just set in the middle. Serve at once.

Bacon and Gruyère galette

SERVES 6   472 CALS PER SERVING

00 g (7 oz) smoked streaky bacon rashers, nds removed, chopped

onions, roughly chopped

75 g (12 oz) ready-made puff pastry

x 290 g jar roasted peppers, drained nd thinly sliced

tomatoes, thinly sliced

lt and black pepper

50 g (5 oz) Gruyère cheese, grated

Fry the bacon in a frying pan over a high heat for a few minutes until the t runs, then add the onions and fry for further minute. Turn the heat down to low, over, and cook for 15 minutes or until the nions are soft. Remove the lid, increase e heat to high, and fry for a few minutes evaporate any liquid, stirring frequently. t aside to cool.

Put a large baking tray in the oven, and preheat the oven to 220°C (200°C fan, as 7).

Roll out the pastry on a lightly floured surface until about 5 mm (¼ in) thick. ut out a 28 cm (11 in) round, using a nner plate or frying pan as a guide. Place e pastry round on a sheet of baking rchment, and prick all over with a fork.

Spread the bacon and onions over the pastry, and top with the peppers d tomatoes. Season with salt and pper, and sprinkle with the cheese.

Carefully lift the galette on the paper, and place it on the hot baking tray. ke for 20–25 minutes until the cheese d pastry are golden brown. Slice into edges, and serve hot or warm.

Creamy seafood crêpes

The succulent filling of prawns and white fish in a herby cream sauce makes these crêpes really rich and special – ideal for a weekend lunch served with a crisp green salad. You could also serve them as a dinner party first course, allowing just one per person. The unfilled crêpes can be made in advance and stored in the freezer for up to 1 month.

SERVES 6   308 CALS PER SERVING

FILLING

250 g (8 oz) cod fillet, skinned

375 g (12 oz) cooked prawns in their shells

2 tbsp olive oil

1 small onion, finely chopped

1 garlic clove, crushed

4 tomatoes, finely chopped

1 tbsp chopped fresh dill

salt and black pepper

3 tbsp single cream

2 tbsp chopped fresh basil

basil and lemon to garnish

PANCAKES

125 g (4 oz) plain flour

1 egg, plus 1 egg yolk

300 ml (½ pint) milk

sunflower oil for frying

1 Make the pancake batter: sift the flour into a large bowl, and make a well in the middle. Add the egg, extra egg yolk, and a little of the milk.

2 Gradually blend in the flour, beating until smooth. Add the remaining milk to make a thin, creamy batter. Leave to stand while you make the filling.

3 Cut the cod fillet into 1 cm (½ in) pieces. Reserve 12 prawns for the garnish, and peel the remainder.

4 Heat the oil in a medium saucepan, add the onion and garlic, and cook very gently, stirring occasionally, for about 10 minutes until soft but not coloured.

5 Add the cod, tomatoes, and dill, and season with salt and pepper. Cook over a medium heat, stirring, for 10 minutes or until thick.

6 Stir in the cream and prawns and heat gently. Remove from the heat and stir in the basil. Keep warm.

7 Make the pancakes. Heat a small frying pan, and brush with a little oil. Stir the batter, ladle about 3 tbsp into the pan, and cook for 1 minute until the underside is golden. Turn and cook the second side, then slide out of the pan and keep hot. Repeat to make 12 pancakes.

8 Fill the pancakes with the seafood mixture, and fold (see box, below). Garnish with basil and lemon, and the reserved prawns.

Filling and folding the crêpes

Put a pancake on a serving plate. Put 2–3 spoonfuls of the seafood filling on to one half and spread it to within 5 mm (¼ in) of the edge.

Fold the unfilled half of the pancake over the seafood filling to enclose it.

Fold the pancake in half again, to form a triangle. Transfer to a serving plate and keep warm. Repeat with the remaining pancakes and filling.

Raclette

SERVES 4   **446 CALS PER SERVING**

1 kg (2 lb) new potatoes, halved

salt

250 g (8 oz) Swiss raclette cheese, cut into 16 thin slices

1 red onion, thinly sliced

12 small gherkins

12 cocktail pickled onions

1 Cook the potatoes in boiling salted water for 12–15 minutes until just tender. Drain, and keep the potatoes warm.

2 Put 4 heavy, ovenproof serving plates into a preheated oven at 240°C (220°C fan, Gas 9) to warm for 3–5 minutes.

3 Divide the potatoes among the plates, and arrange 4 slices of raclette cheese on top of each serving. Return the plates to the oven for 1–2 minutes until the cheese is melted and sizzling.

4 Divide the red onion slices, gherkins, and pickled onions among the plates, and serve at once.

Swiss raclette cheese is a semi-soft, washed-rind variety that has a smooth texture and a rich, fruit-savoury flavour.

Broccoli soufflés

SERVES 4   **499 CALS PER SERVING**

45 g (1½ oz) butter, plus extra for greasing

45 g (1½ oz) plain flour

250 ml (8 fl oz) milk

pinch of grated nutmeg

salt and cayenne pepper

375 g (12 oz) broccoli florets

3–4 shallots, finely chopped

2 tbsp grated Parmesan cheese

4 egg yolks

175 g (6 oz) blue cheese, crumbled

6 egg whites

4 x 250 ml (8 fl oz) soufflé dishes

1 Melt 30 g (1 oz) butter in a large pan, add the flour, and cook, stirring, for 1 minute. Remove from the heat, gradually blend in the milk, then bring to a boil, stirring, until thickened. Add the nutmeg, season with salt, and stir in a pinch of cayenne pepper. Cool for 10 minutes.

2 Steam the broccoli for 2–3 minutes until just tender. Rinse under cold running water, then chop coarsely.

3 Heat the remaining butter in a pan, add the shallots, and cook gently for 3 minutes or until soft.

4 Prepare the soufflé dishes (see box, below).

5 Beat the egg yolks and add to the cooled sauce with the broccoli, shallots, and blue cheese.

6 Whisk the egg whites until they form firm but not dry peaks. Fold 1–2 tbsp of the egg whites into the broccoli mixture, then fold in the remaining egg whites.

7 Pour the mixture into the soufflé dishes. Bake the soufflés in the top half of a preheated oven at 180°C (160°C fan, Gas 4) for 30 minutes. Serve at once.

Preparing the soufflé dishes

Butter the bottoms and sides of the soufflé dishes. Sprinkle with a thin layer of grated Parmesan cheese.

Swiss double cheese soufflés

SERVES 6   **465 CALS PER SERVING**

45 g (1½ oz) butter, plus extra for greasing

45 g (1½ oz) plain flour

300 ml (½ pint) milk

60 g (2 oz) Gruyère cheese, grated

2 tbsp snipped fresh chives

salt and black pepper

3 eggs, separated

60 g (2 oz) Parmesan cheese, grated

300 ml (½ pint) double cream

snipped fresh chives to garnish

1 Melt the butter in a large saucepan, add the flour, and cook, stirring, for 1 minute. Remove from the heat and gradually blend in the milk. Return to the heat and bring to a boil, stirring until the mixture thickens.

2 Remove the pan from the heat and beat in the Gruyère cheese and chives. Season with salt and pepper, and stir in the egg yolks.

3 Whisk the egg whites until stiff but not dry. Stir 1 tbsp into the mixture, then fold in the rest.

4 Generously butter 6 small ramekins, and divide the mixture equally among them. Place the ramekins in a small roasting tin, and pour boiling water into the tin to come halfway up the sides of the ramekins.

5 Bake the soufflés in a preheated oven at 220°C (200°C fan, Gas 7) for 15–20 minutes until golden and springy to the touch. Leave the soufflés to stand for 5–10 minutes; they will shrink by about one-third.

6 Butter a large shallow gratin dish. Sprinkle half of the Parmesan cheese over the bottom. Run a palette knife around the edge of each soufflé, unmould carefully and arrange on top of the Parmesan in the gratin dish.

7 Season the cream with salt and pepper and pour over the soufflés. Sprinkle the remaining Parmesan over the top, and return to the oven for 15–20 minutes until golden. Garnish with snipped chives.

Opposite: Swiss double cheese soufflé

Garlic and goat's cheese soufflés

🍴 SERVES 6   267 CALS PER SERVING

1 head of garlic

250 ml (8 fl oz) milk

125 ml (4 fl oz) water

45 g (1½ oz) butter, plus extra for greasing

45 g (1½ oz) plain flour

150 g (5 oz) goat's cheese, diced

6 eggs, separated

salt and black pepper

fresh chives to garnish

6 x 150 ml (¼ pint) soufflé dishes

1 Separate and peel the garlic cloves. Put the milk, measured water, and all but one of the garlic cloves into a saucepan. Bring to a boil, then simmer for 15–20 minutes until the garlic is tender and the liquid has reduced to 250 ml (8 fl oz). Leave to cool. Lightly mash the garlic in the milk.

2 Melt the butter in a saucepan, add the flour, and cook, stirring, for 1 minute. Remove from the heat, and gradually blend in the garlic milk.

3 Return to the heat and bring to a boil, stirring constantly, until the mixture thickens. Simmer for 2–3 minutes. Transfer to a large bowl and leave to cool for about 10 minutes. Chop the remaining garlic clove.

4 Add the chopped garlic, diced goat's cheese, and egg yolks to the cooled sauce. Season with salt and pepper.

5 In a large bowl, whisk the egg whites until stiff but not dry. Stir 1 tbsp of the egg whites into the garlic and cheese mixture, then fold in the remaining egg whites.

6 Lightly butter the soufflé dishes, pour in the soufflé mixture, and bake in a preheated oven at 180°C (160°C fan, Gas 4) for 15–20 minutes. Serve at once, garnished with chives.

Croque señor

🍴 SERVES 4   413 CALS PER SERVING

8 slices of white bread

4 slices of mature Cheddar cheese

4 slices of ham

30 g (1 oz) butter, softened

lemon wedges and coriander sprigs to serve

SPICY TOMATO SALSA

3 ripe but firm tomatoes, finely chopped

1 red pepper, halved, seeded, roasted, and peeled (page 345), finely chopped

1 garlic clove, crushed

2 spring onions, thinly sliced

1 fresh green chilli, halved, seeded, and chopped

1 tbsp red wine vinegar

salt

1 Make the salsa: combine the tomatoes, red pepper, garlic, spring onions, chilli, and vinegar in a bowl. Season with salt and set aside.

2 Put 4 slices of bread on to a board, and arrange the cheese slices, then the ham slices, on top. Spoon the salsa over the ham.

3 Lightly spread the butter over one side of the remaining slices of bread and pu them, butter-side up, on top of the salsa.

4 Heat a heavy frying pan, and cook each sandwich, butter-side down, over a medium–high heat until the cheese begins to melt and the bread becomes golden. Lightly spread the second side of each sandwich with butter. Turn over and cook the other side until golden.

5 Garnish with lemon wedges, coriander sprigs, and any remaining spicy tomato salsa. Serve hot.

Swiss cheese and tomato rarebit

SERVES 4   640 CALS PER SERVING

garlic cloves

g (1 oz) butter, plus extra for spreading

g (1 oz) plain flour

0 g (8 oz) ripe tomatoes, finely chopped

5 ml (4 fl oz) dry white wine

5 g (12 oz) Gruyère cheese, grated

5 g (4 oz) mushrooms, chopped

bsp chopped fresh tarragon

t and black pepper

lices of bread, crusts removed

opped parsley to garnish

Crush 2 of the garlic cloves. Melt the
butter in a saucepan, add the crushed
rlic, and cook gently, stirring, for
2 minutes. Add the flour, and cook,
ring, for 1 minute. Add the chopped
matoes and cook for 2 minutes.

Pour in the wine, and cook, stirring, for
5 minutes or until the mixture thickens.
d the Gruyère cheese, a little at a time,
d stir until it has melted. Add the
opped mushrooms and tarragon, season
h salt and pepper, and cook for 3
utes or until the mushrooms are tender.

Cut the remaining garlic clove in half.
Toast the bread on both sides under a
grill. Rub one side of the toast with the
sides of the garlic.

Spread the garlic side of the toast with
butter, place on warmed plates, and
with the cheese mixture. Serve at once,
nkled with chopped parsley.

Cheese fondue

SERVES 6   813 CALS PER SERVING

1 large loaf of crusty bread, crusts left on, cut
into 2.5 cm (1 in) triangles

250 g (8 oz) Gruyère cheese, coarsely grated

250 g (8 oz) Emmental cheese, coarsely grated

30 g (1 oz) cornflour

500 ml (16 fl oz) dry white wine

1 garlic clove, lightly crushed

2 tbsp kirsch

pinch of grated nutmeg

salt and black pepper

TO SERVE (OPTIONAL)

2 eating apples, quartered and sliced

60 g (2 oz) sesame seeds, toasted

30 g (1 oz) cumin seeds, toasted

1 fondue set

1 Place the pieces of bread on a large
baking tray and put into a preheated
oven at 160°C (140°C fan, Gas 3) for 3–5
minutes until dried out slightly.

2 Put the Gruyère and Emmental cheeses
into a medium bowl, and toss with
the cornflour.

3 Put the wine and garlic into a fondue
pot and boil for 2 minutes, then lower
the heat so that the mixture is barely
simmering. Add the cheese mixture,
a spoonful at a time, stirring constantly
with a fork and letting each spoonful melt
before adding the next.

4 When the fondue is creamy and
smooth, stir in the kirsch, nutmeg,
and salt and pepper to taste.

5 Stand the fondue pot over the burner,
with the heat low so the mixture barely
simmers. Offer the baked bread round for
dipping into the fondue, with apple slices,
sesame seeds and cumin seeds if you like.

atoes are rich in vitamin C and antioxidants,
ng this dish healthier than a classic rarebit.

Eggs florentine

SERVES 4   475 CALS PER SERVING

250 g (8 oz) spinach leaves

3 spring onions, thinly sliced

2 tbsp double cream

4 eggs

3 tbsp grated Parmesan cheese

CHEESE SAUCE

30 g (1 oz) butter

30 g (1 oz) plain flour

250 ml (8 fl oz) milk

175 g (6 oz) mature Cheddar cheese, grated

pinch each of cayenne pepper and grated nutmeg

salt and black pepper

1 Rinse the spinach, and put into a medium saucepan with only the water that clings to the leaves. Cook for about 2 minutes until tender. Drain, and set aside.

2 Make the cheese sauce: melt the butter in a saucepan, add the flour, and cook, stirring, for 1 minute. Remove from the heat and gradually blend in the milk. Bring to a boil, stirring constantly until the mixture thickens. Simmer for 2–3 minutes.

3 Stir in the Cheddar cheese, add the cayenne pepper and nutmeg, and season with salt and pepper. Keep warm.

4 Combine the spinach in a bowl with the spring onions and cream, and season with salt and pepper. Set aside.

5 Poach the eggs: bring a large pan of water to a boil. Lower the heat so that the water is simmering, and slide in the eggs, one at a time. Swirl the water round the eggs to make neat shapes. Lift out with a slotted spoon.

6 Divide the spinach and spring onion mixture among 4 warmed flameproof dishes. Arrange the poached eggs on the spinach, and spoon the cheese sauce over the eggs.

7 Sprinkle the grated Parmesan cheese over the sauce, then place the dishes under a hot grill, 7 cm (3 in) from the heat, until the cheese has melted and is lightly browned, and the whole dish is heated through. Serve hot.

Eggs Benedict

SERVES 4   602 CALS PER SERVING

8 lean back bacon rashers, rinds removed

2 muffins, halved

4 eggs

butter for spreading

fresh flat-leaf parsley to garnish

HOLLANDAISE SAUCE

2 tsp lemon juice

2 tsp white wine vinegar

3 egg yolks, at room temperature

125 g (4 oz) unsalted butter, melted

salt and black pepper

1 Cook the bacon under a hot grill, 7 cm (3 in) from the heat, for 5–7 minutes until crisp. Keep the bacon warm.

2 Toast the cut sides of the muffin halves under the grill. Keep warm.

3 Make the hollandaise sauce: put the lemon juice and wine vinegar into a small bowl, add the egg yolks, and whisk with a balloon whisk until light and frothy.

4 Place the bowl over a pan of simmering water and whisk until the mixture thickens. Gradually add the melted butter, whisking constantly until thick. Season. Keep warm.

5 Poach the eggs: bring a large pan of water to the boil. Lower the heat so that the water is simmering, and slide in the eggs. Swirl the water round the eggs to make neat shapes. Simmer for about 4 minutes. Lift out with a slotted spoon.

6 Butter the muffin halves and put on to warmed plates. Put 2 bacon rashers and an egg on each one, and top with the sauce. Serve at once, garnished with parsley.

Spicy lime hollandaise

Substitute 2 tsp lime juice for the lemon juice in the hollandaise sauce, and add ½ tsp each of paprika and mild chilli powder.

Oeufs en cocotte

SERVES 4   176 CALS PER SERVING

15 g (½ oz) butter

4 eggs

salt and black pepper

4 tbsp double cream

1 tbsp chopped parsley

4 small ramekins

1 Melt the butter, and pour a little into each ramekin.

2 Break each egg into a saucer, then slid into a prepared ramekin. Sprinkle with salt and pepper, and top each egg with 1 tbsp cream.

3 Place the ramekins in a roasting tin and pour in boiling water to come halfway up the sides of the ramekins. Cover with fo

4 Bake in a preheated oven at 200°C (180°C fan, Gas 6) for 10 minutes or unti the whites are opaque and firm but the yo still soft. Or, put the ramekins into a large frying pan, add boiling water to come halfway up the sides, cover, and cook over a medium heat for 10 minutes, letting the water boil and gently steam the eggs.

5 Sprinkle a little parsley over each baked egg 1–2 minutes before the end of cooking time.

Feta cheese cocottes

After pouring the butter into the ramekins, divide 125 g (4 oz) diced feta cheese, marinated in chopped fresh herbs and diced fresh red chilli, among the ramekins. Proceed as directed, substituting 2–3 thinly sliced sprin onions for the parsley.

Fish and Shellfish

Under 45 minutes

LOW FAT

Grilled trout with cucumber and dill
Trout with a stuffing of lightly cooked cucumber, dill, and lemon juice.

SERVES 4   435 CALS PER SERVING

Takes 25 minutes   Page 122

Tuna with fennel and tomato relish
Tuna marinated in oil, lemon juice, garlic, and herbs, grilled, and topped with relish.

SERVES 4   467 CALS PER SERVING

Takes 25 minutes, **plus marinating**   Page 123

Herrings with mustard sauce
Baked herrings served with a classic sauce made from mustard powder, sugar, and white wine vinegar.

SERVES 4   479 CALS PER SERVING

Takes 25 minutes   Page 12

Prawn tacos
Crispy and hot: taco shells with a spicy filling of prawns, coriander, tomatoes, onion, garlic, green pepper, and paprika.

SERVES 4   414 CALS PER SERVING

Takes 25 minutes   Page 1

Scallops with asparagus and lemon
Fresh and aromatic: scallops cooked with asparagus and garlic, with a parsley, lemon, and tarragon sauce.

SERVES 6   159 CALS PER SERVING

Takes 20 minutes   Page 1

Tuna teriyaki
Light and simple: tuna steaks marinated in garlic, ginger, soy sauce, and sesame oil. Grilled, and sprinkled with spring onion.

SERVES 4   339 CALS PER SERVING

Takes 15 minutes, **plus marinating**   Page 1

Monkfish with ginger-orange sauce
Monkfish fillets cooked with orange, ginger, onion, and stock; served with a sauce spiked with lime.

SERVES 4   221 CALS PER SERVING

Takes 40 minutes   Page

Oriental fish parcels
White fish fillets with ginger, spring onion, sauce, and rice wine, baked in a parcel.

SERVES 4   312 CALS PER SERVING

Takes 35 minutes   Page

Fillets of sole meunière
Fresh and summery: lemon sole fillets light floured and cooked in butter, then served w parsley and lemon-flavoured butter.

SERVES 4   274 CALS PER SERVING

Takes 20 minutes   Page

Mediterranean stuffed squid
Tender squid pouches filled with breadcrumbs, onion, garlic, chopped squid, parsley, and dill, and pan-fried in butter.

SERVES 4   224 CALS PER SERVING

Takes 40 minutes   Page 111

ea bass with lemon butter sauce
Vhole sea bass baked in foil with tarragon,
emon, and wine. Served with a creamy sauce.
ERVES 4   363 CALS PER SERVING
akes 40 minutes   Page 135

Seafood and avocado salad
Poached monkfish with crabmeat and prawns
on a bed of salad leaves, avocado, and
tomatoes, dressed with crème fraîche.
SERVES 4   396 CALS PER SERVING
Takes 35 minutes, **plus cooling**   Page 112

Mussels with potatoes and chorizo
Mussels cooked with potatoes, spicy chorizo
sausage, garlic, stock, sherry, and cumin seeds.
SERVES 6   523 CALS PER SERVING
Takes 40 minutes   Page 117

FAMILY FARE

est-ever fried fish
ispy and nourishing: plaice fillets coated in
ur, beaten egg, and fresh breadcrumbs.
oked until golden and served with lemon.
VES 4   298 CALS PER SERVING
kes 25 minutes   Page 132

shroom-stuffed sole fillets
e fillets rolled and stuffed with onion and
shrooms. Baked with tarragon and wine,
ch form the base for a cream sauce.
VES 4   568 CALS PER SERVING
es 35 minutes   Page 130

Lobster with black bean salsa
Lobster tails spread with garlic and oregano-flavoured
butter and grilled. Served with black bean salsa.
SERVES 4   531 CALS PER SERVING
Takes 35 minutes   Page 113

Under 45 minutes

DINNER PARTY

Cod steaks with anchovy and fennel
Cod steaks baked with a topping of anchovies, fennel, parsley, and breadcrumbs.

SERVES 4 429 CALS PER SERVING

Takes 40 minutes   Page 139

Cajun-spiced red snapper
Red snapper fillets marinated in a piquant mixture of garlic, paprika, cumin, and chilli powder. Topped with coriander butter.

SERVES 4 258 CALS PER SERVING

Takes 15 minutes, **plus marinating**   Page 134

Severn salmon
Baked salmon flavoured with pepper, in a pool of sauce made from cream, watercress, lemon juice, butter, and egg yolk.

SERVES 6 414 CALS PER SERVING

Takes 25 minutes   Page 129

45-60 minutes

Spicy clams with coriander pesto
Clams richly flavoured with tomatoes, stock, garlic, and chilli. Served with coriander pesto

SERVES 4-6 349-233 CALS PER SERVING

Takes 45 minutes   Page 11

Baked trout with orange
Fresh and hearty dish: trout stuffed with mushrooms, shallots, orange zest and juice, white wine vinegar, thyme, and parsley.

SERVES 4 378 CALS PER SERVING

Takes 45 minutes, **plus chilling**   Page 1

Roast monkfish niçoise
Richly flavoured monkfish cooked with roasted garlic, lemon, wine, artichoke hearts herbs, olives, and sun-dried tomatoes.

SERVES 4 448 CALS PER SERVING

Takes 50 minutes   Page 1

Spiced fish with coconut
Sweet and spicy: monkfish pieces lightly coated in flour, cooked with coconut milk, onion, coriander, cumin, and turmeric.

SERVES 4 389 CALS PER SERVING

Takes 45 minutes   Page 1

Black bream niçoise
Baked black bream on a bed of fennel, onio and garlic, sprinkled with lemon juice, olive and chopped parsley.

SERVES 4 356 CALS PER SERVING

Takes 50 minutes   Page

Golden fish cakes
Cod or haddock simmered in milk flavoure with bay leaf and peppercorns. Mixed with potato and coated in fresh breadcrumbs.

SERVES 4 613 CALS PER SERVING

Takes 50 minutes   Page

Crispy-topped seafood pie
Cod poached in milk, then baked with praw leeks, and broccoli. Topped with white sauc Gruyère, and crispy pastry.

SERVES 4 575 CALS PER SERVING

Takes 55 minutes   Page

Over 60 minutes

DINNER PARTY

almon en croûte
almon fillets marinated in dill and lemon zest and juice, baked
puff pastry with spinach, spring onions, and soft cheese.
RVES 8 745 CALS PER SERVING
kes 1½ hours, **plus marinating**

Page 128

Halibut in filo parcels
Delicate and moist: leek and carrot strips
cooked with wine, stock, and saffron, form
a bed for halibut wrapped in filo pastry.
SERVES 4 564 CALS PER SERVING
Takes 1 hour 5 minutes

Page 138

libiac
ed salmon mixed with rice, onion, tomatoes, parsley, and
on. Wrapped in puff pastry and decorated with a pastry plait.
ES 8–10 518–414 CALS PER SERVING
s 1¼ hours

Page 125

Fish and shellfish know-how

Seafood is delicious, versatile, and quick to cook. Compared with other protein foods it is excellent value for money as there is usually little wastage. In addition, it is very nutritious: all fish and shellfish are good sources of essential vitamins and minerals, but oily fish are particularly rich in vitamins A and D and also provide beneficial omega-3 fatty acids.

Seafood is divided into two broad categories: fish and shellfish. Fish may be white (its oil is found mainly in the liver) or oily (the oil is distributed in the flesh); white fish are further sub-divided according to body shape (round or flat). Of the shellfish, crustaceans (crab, prawns) have shells and legs; molluscs (mussels, scallops) just have shells. Squid is a mollusc with an internal "shell".

Cleaning and boning round fish

Round fish such as trout, mackerel, herring, and salmon are often cooked whole, and boning makes them easier to serve and eat. When boned they can also be stuffed. Fishmongers will prepare the fish for you, but if you want to do it yourself, here's how.

1 To clean the fish, first snip off the fins. Cut along the belly, from the vent end to just below the head. Remove the innards, scraping away any dark blood. Lift the gill covering and remove the concertina-shaped gills. Rinse well.

2 To bone, extend the belly opening so that it goes all the way to the tail. Hold the belly open and carefully run the knife between the flesh and the bones along one side, from tail to head, to cut the flesh from the ribcage.

3 Turn the fish around and cut the flesh from the ribcage on the other side. Snip through the backbone at each end and gently pull it away from the flesh, removing it with the ribcage in one piece.

4 If the head and tail have been cut off, open out the fish and lay it skin-side up. Press along the backbone to loosen the bones. Turn over and lift or cut out the ribcage and backbone. The fish is now "butterflied".

Buying and storing

When buying fish and shellfish, aroma and appearance are your guides. Seafood should have the clean smell of the sea. If it has an unpleasantly "fishy" or ammonia-like odour it is not fresh.

Whole fresh fish should have clean, red gills, the scales should be firmly attached and it should be covered in a clear slime; the flesh should feel firm and springy. The flesh of fillets and steaks should be firm, moist, and lustrous. If at all possible ask for steaks to be cut while you wait. If buying pre-packaged fish, check the colour of any liquid that has accumulated in the pack: it should not be cloudy or off-white.

Shellfish is sold both in the shell and shelled, raw and cooked. The shells of crabs, lobsters, and prawns become pink or red when cooked. Live shellfish, such as mussels, clams, and oysters, should have tightly closed shells. If any shells are open they should close if lightly tapped; if they do not, the shellfish is dead and should be discarded. Shelled oysters, scallops, and clams should be plump; scallops should smell slightly sweet. Prawns should also smell faintly sweet, and feel firm.

Keep the fish or shellfish cool until you get home, then unwrap it, cover with a wet cloth or wet paper towels, and store in the coldest part of the refrigerator. Use oily fish and shellfish the same day; keep white fish no more than 24 hours.

Freezing

It's best to buy fish ready-frozen, as it will have been processed and frozen at very low temperatures immediately after being caught – while still at sea – to prevent there being any deterioration.

If you have fish to freeze yourself, clean it and wrap tightly. For the best flavour, store white fish for no longer than 3 months.

...ily fish and shellfish for 2 months. (When buying, be aware that some seafood sold as "fresh" may have been frozen and then thawed, so it should not be frozen again at home.)

Fish fillets and some shellfish can be cooked very successfully from frozen, but if you need to thaw seafood before cooking, do so slowly in the refrigerator or quickly in the microwave.

Microwaving

One of the best uses for a microwave is for cooking fish and shellfish: they retain their texture and all of their flavourful juices. However, care must be taken not to overcook the delicate flesh. Whether cooking or thawing, arrange pieces of fish so that the thicker areas are at the outside of the dish; overlap thin areas or fold them under. With whole fish, shield delicate areas, such as the tail and head, with smooth strips of foil. If thawing seafood, again protect thin, delicate areas by shielding them with smooth strips of foil. Except when doing this never put metal or metal containers in microwave ovens (see also page 21).

Scaling

Unless skinning a fish before cooking, the scales should be removed. Dip your fingers in salt to ensure a firm grip and grasp the fish tail. Using the blunt side of a knife, with firm strokes scrape off the scales, from tail to head. Rinse well. Or ask your fishmonger to do this.

Fish stock

Ask your fishmonger for heads, bones, and trimmings from lean white fish (not oily fish, which make a bitter-tasting stock).

Rinse 750 g (1½ lb) bones and trimmings and put them into a large pan. Add 1 litre (1¾ pints) water and 250 ml (8 fl oz) dry white wine. Bring to a boil, skimming the surface.

Add 1 sliced onion, 1 sliced carrot, 1 chopped celery stalk, 1 bay leaf, a few parsley sprigs, and a few black peppercorns. Simmer for 20-25 minutes. Strain. Use immediately, or cool, cover, and refrigerate to use within 2 days. It can also be frozen for up to 3 months.

Filleting flat fish

Either 2 wide or 4 narrow fillets can be cut from a small flat fish. Larger flat fish will yield 4 good-sized fillets. Keep the bones for making stock.

1 Make a shallow cut through the skin around the edge of the fish, where the fin bones meet the body. Cut across the tail and make a curved cut around the head. Then cut down the centre of the fish, cutting through the flesh to the bone.

2 Insert the knife between the flesh and the bones on one side at the head end. Keeping the knife almost parallel to the fish, cut close to the bones, loosening the flesh to detach the fillet in one piece.

3 Repeat to remove the second fillet on the same side. Then turn the fish over and remove both of the fillets from the other side. Check the fillets for any stray bones, pulling them out with tweezers.

4 To skin, lay each fillet skin-side down and hold the tail with salted fingers to ensure a firm grip. Cut through the flesh at the tail end, then holding the knife at an angle and cut the flesh from the skin.

Preparing mussels and clams

Most mussels and clams are sold live and are cooked by steaming in their shells. They must be scrubbed before cooking. The anchoring threads found on mussels, known as beards, must also be removed.

1 To clean the shells of mussels and clams, hold under cold running water and scrub with a small stiff brush. Use a small knife to scrape off any barnacles.

2 To remove the beard from a mussel, hold the beard firmly between your thumb and the blade of a small knife and pull the beard away from the shell.

Preparing oysters

To shuck oysters, use an oyster knife or small, sturdy knife.

Hold oyster round-side down, and insert the knife near the hinge. Lever the shells apart. Slide in the knife to sever the top muscle. Lift off the shell. Run the knife under the oyster to loosen it.

Preparing prawns

Both raw and cooked prawns can be used successfully in a variety of tasty dishes. When buying, take into account that prawns lose at least half of their weight when the heads and shells are removed.

1 Gently pull off the head and then the legs. Peel the shell from the body, leaving on the last tail section of shell if you like.

2 Make a shallow cut along the centre of the back of the prawn. Lift out the black intestinal vein and rinse the prawn under cold running water.

Preparing a cooked crab

The meat inside a crab is of two types – a soft, rich, brown meat and a flaky, sweet, white meat. When a crab is "dressed", the meat is removed from the shell, with the two types being kept separate, and then arranged back in the shell for serving.

1 Put the crab on its back and twist off the legs and claws, close to the body.

2 Using nutcrackers, a small hammer, or a rolling pin, crack the shells of the claws without crushing them. Break open the shells and carefully remove the meat, using a small fork or skewer.

3 Press your thumbs along the "perforation" to crack the central section of the shell and prise it apart. Remove and discard the "apron" flap from the underside of the body.

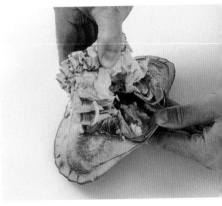

4 Pull the central body section up and away from the shell. Scoop the creamy-textured brown meat out of the shell and put it into a bowl (keeping it entirely separate from the white claw and leg meat). Scoop out any roe. Discard the stomach sac, which is located between the eyes.

5 Pull the spongy gills (known as "dead man's fingers") from the body and discard them.

6 Cut the body in half with a large knife and pick out all the white meat from the crevices. Add to the white meat from the claws.

Preparing a cooked lobster

Ready-cooked lobster meat can be added to cooked dishes for a brief heating, or it can be served cold with mayonnaise (most attractively in the shell) or in a salad.

To remove the meat

1 Twist off the large claws. Using a sturdy nutcracker, small hammer, or rolling pin, crack the shells of the claws without crushing them. Pick out the meat, in 1 or 2 large pieces. If the shell is not to be used for serving, pull apart the body and tail. Twist off the small legs, crack them, and remove the meat with a skewer or lobster pick.

2 Lift off the top of the body shell. Scoop out the grey-green liver (tomalley) and any coral-coloured roe, both of which are edible, and reserve. Discard the stomach and spongy gills ("dead man's fingers").

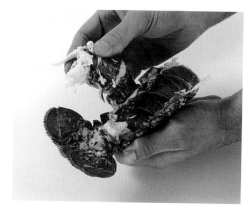

3 With scissors or a sharp knife, cut along the soft underside of the tail.

4 Bend back the flaps and carefully remove the tail meat, keeping it in 1 piece. Remove and discard the intestinal tract that runs through the centre of the tail meat. Slice the tail meat, or prepare as required, and serve with the claw and leg meat.

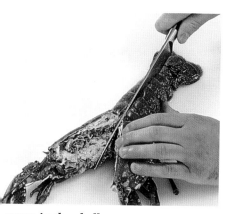

To serve in the shell

1 Use a sharp, heavy knife to split the lobster in half lengthways, cutting from the head to the tail. Pull the halves apart.

2 Scoop out the liver and roe, and discard the intestine. Twist off the legs and claws (remove the meat). Loosen the meat in the shell.

Preparing a squid

Once cleaned, fresh squid yields a tube-like body, which can be stuffed or sliced, and separate tentacles. You can buy it already cleaned or do this yourself as shown here.

1 Pull the head and tentacles away from the body (the innards will come away with the head as will the long, narrow ink sac if it is present). Cut off the tentacles, just in front of the eyes.

2 Squeeze the tentacles near the cut end so that the hard beak can be removed. Discard it. Rinse the tentacles well and set aside. Discard the head and innards (and the ink sac unless using it in a sauce).

3 Peel the skin from the body. Pull the long piece of cartilage (quill) out of the body and discard. Rinse the body thoroughly, inside and out, and pull off the two flaps (slice these for cooking).

Prawn tacos

SERVES 4   414 CALS PER SERVING

2 tbsp sunflower oil

2 onions, chopped

3 garlic cloves, crushed

1 green pepper, halved, seeded, and diced

1 tbsp paprika

2 tsp mild chilli powder

½ tsp ground cumin

4 ripe firm tomatoes, chopped

500 g (1 lb) cooked peeled prawns

2 tbsp chopped fresh coriander

salt and black pepper

12 taco shells

1 round lettuce, shredded

sliced pickled chillies, large cooked peeled prawns, and coriander leaves to garnish

1 Heat the oil in a large frying pan, add the onions, and cook gently, stirring occasionally, for 3–5 minutes until softened but not coloured. Add the garlic and diced green pepper, and cook, stirring occasionally, for 3 minutes or until the pepper is soft.

2 Stir in the paprika, chilli powder, and cumin, and cook, stirring, for 1 minute. Add the tomatoes and cook for 3–5 minutes until soft.

3 Lower the heat and stir in the prawns and chopped coriander, and season with salt and pepper.

4 Meanwhile, heat the taco shells in a preheated oven at 180°C (160°C fan, Gas 4) for 3 minutes or according to packet instructions.

5 Spoon the prawn mixture into the taco shells, top with the shredded lettuce, and garnish with chillies, prawns, and coriander. Serve at once.

♥ Healthy note

Prawns, like most shellfish, are a healthy food low in calories and fat. They are rich in the antioxidant selenium, which is linked to a healthy heart and circulation, and they are also a good source of iodine, zinc, and calcium.

Tiger prawns with tarragon sauce

SERVES 4   252 CALS PER SERVING

12 uncooked tiger prawns in their shells

olive oil for brushing

300 ml (½ pint) dry white wine

1 garlic clove, crushed

4 tbsp chopped fresh parsley

lemon and tarragon to garnish

TARRAGON SAUCE

150 ml (¼ pint) soured cream

4 tbsp chopped fresh tarragon

1 tsp Dijon mustard

squeeze of lemon juice

salt and black pepper

1 Make the tarragon sauce: combine the soured cream, tarragon, mustard, and lemon juice, and season with salt and pepper.

2 Heat a heavy frying pan. Brush the prawns with oil, add to the pan, and cook the prawns over a high heat for 2 minutes or until pink.

3 Keeping the heat high, add 150 ml (¼ pint) of the wine and the garlic. Boil rapidly for 2–3 minutes, then stir in 2 tbsp of the parsley.

4 When the wine has reduced slightly, lower the heat, and add the remaining wine, and season with salt and pepper. Simmer for 5 minutes or until the prawns have released their juices into the wine.

5 Spoon the cooking juices over the prawns, sprinkle with the remaining parsley, and garnish with lemon and sprigs of fresh tarragon. Serve hot, with the tarragon sauce.

Thai prawn stir-fry

SERVES 4   522 CALS PER SERVING

250 g (8 oz) rice noodles

salt

3 tbsp sunflower oil

1 red pepper, halved, seeded, and cut into thin strips

1 carrot, cut into thin strips

1 fresh green chilli, halved, seeded, and cut into thin strips

2.5 cm (1 in) piece of fresh root ginger, peeled and cut into thin strips

1 garlic clove, crushed

8 spring onions, sliced

2 lemon grass stalks, trimmed and sliced

500 g (1 lb) cooked peeled tiger prawns

2 tbsp white wine vinegar

2 tbsp soy sauce

juice of ½ lime

1 tbsp sesame oil

3 tbsp chopped fresh coriander to garnish

1 Put the rice noodles into a large saucepan of boiling salted water and stir to separate the noodles. Turn off the heat, cover, and leave to stand for 4 minutes. Drain well and set aside.

2 Heat 1 tbsp of the sunflower oil in a wok or large frying pan. Add the red pepper, carrot, chilli, ginger, garlic, spring onions, and lemon grass, and stir-fry over a high heat for 2 minutes.

3 Add the prawns, and stir-fry for 1 minute, then stir in the noodles.

4 Add the remaining sunflower oil, the vinegar, soy sauce, lime juice, and sesame oil, and stir-fry for 1 minute.

5 Sprinkle with the chopped fresh coriander and serve at once.

Scallop stir-fry

Substitute 500 g (1 lb) shelled scallops for the tiger prawns, cutting each scallop into two or three pieces if they are large. Stir-fry for about 2 minutes, then add the red pepper, carrot, chilli, fresh root ginger, garlic, spring onions, and lemon grass, and stir-fry for a further 2 minutes. Add the soaked and drained noodles, then continue with the recipe from the beginning of step 4.

Mediterranean stuffed squid

SERVES 4   224 CALS PER SERVING

small whole squid, cleaned (page 109)

g (1 oz) butter, plus a little extra for frying

arge onion, finely chopped

garlic cloves, crushed

g (2 oz) fine fresh breadcrumbs

bsp chopped fresh dill

bsp chopped parsley

t and black pepper

mon slices and chopped fresh parsley to serve

1 Chop the squid tentacles roughly and set aside.

2 Make the stuffing: melt the butter in a frying pan, add the onion and garlic, cover and sauté over a low heat for about 15–20 minutes until very soft.

3 Add the chopped squid tentacles, breadcrumbs, dill, and parsley to the onion and garlic, and fry over a high heat for 2–3 minutes. Season with salt and pepper, and leave to cool.

4 Fill the squid bodies with the cold stuffing, and secure the tops (see box, right).

5 Heat a little butter in a clean frying pan, and fry the stuffed squid for about 4–5 minutes until golden brown all over and firm to the touch, and the filling is heated through.

6 Garnish the squid with the lemon slices and parsley, and serve at once.

Securing the squid

Thread a cocktail stick through the top of each stuffed squid to secure the opening.

Seafood and avocado salad

 SERVES 4   396 CALS PER SERVING

500 g (1 lb) monkfish, trimmed and skinned

150 ml (¼ pint) fish stock

1 slice of onion

6 black peppercorns

squeeze of lemon juice

1 bay leaf

mixed salad leaves, such as frisée, radicchio, and rocket

2 avocados

lemon juice for brushing

2 large tomatoes, peeled (page 52), seeded, and cut into strips

125 g (4 oz) cooked peeled prawns

90 g (3 oz) white crabmeat

flat-leaf parsley to garnish

CRÈME FRAÎCHE DRESSING

125 ml (4 fl oz) crème fraîche

3 tbsp lemon juice

salt and black pepper

1 Put the monkfish into a saucepan with the stock, onion, peppercorns, lemon juice, and bay leaf. Bring to a gentle simmer, cover, and poach very gently, turning once, for 10 minutes until opaque throughout and firm.

2 Remove the pan from the heat and leave the fish to cool in the liquid, then lift it out and cut into bite-sized pieces.

3 Make the crème fraîche dressing: put the crème fraîche and lemon juice into a bowl, add salt and pepper to taste, and stir to mix.

4 To serve, arrange the salad leaves on individual plates. Halve, stone (page 327), and peel the avocados, and brush with lemon juice. Slice lengthways and arrange in a fan shape on the leaves. Add the strips of tomato, the monkfish, prawns, and crabmeat. Spoon the crème fraîche dressing over the salad, garnish with the parsley, and serve at once.

Healthy note

You can use low-fat crème fraîche for the cold dressing because it holds its shape well. It is only when you heat crème fraîche that it becomes runny and thin.

Devilled crab

 SERVES 4   502 CALS PER SERVING

75 g (2½ oz) butter

1½ tbsp plain flour

175 ml (6 fl oz) milk

¼ tsp mustard powder

¼ tsp grated nutmeg

1 egg yolk

1½ tbsp dry sherry

1 tsp Worcestershire sauce

2–3 dashes of Tabasco sauce

4 small dressed crabs with their claws (page 108), or 500 g (1 lb) white and dark crabmeat

1 spring onion, thinly sliced

salt and black pepper

125 g (4 oz) fresh breadcrumbs

paprika and finely chopped spring onions to garnish

1 Melt 45 g (1½ oz) of the butter in a saucepan, add the flour, and cook, stirring for 1 minute. Remove from the heat, and gradually blend in the milk. Bring to a boil, stirring constantly until the mixture thickens. Simmer for 2–3 minutes. Remove from the heat, and stir in the mustard and nutmeg.

2 Put the egg yolk into a small bowl, and whisk in a little of the sauce. Stir this mixture back into the sauce.

3 Add the dry sherry, Worcestershire sauce, Tabasco sauce, crabmeat, spring onion, and salt and pepper to taste, and stir to mix. Spoon the mixture into the crab shells, or into ramekins, and stand them on a baking sheet.

4 Melt the remaining butter in a saucepan, add the breadcrumbs, and cook, stirring for 5 minutes or until golden brown.

5 Spoon the breadcrumbs over the crabmeat mixture, replace the claws if you have them, and bake in a preheated oven at 200°C (180°C fan, Gas 6) for 10 minutes or until the tops are browned and bubbling. Sprinkle with paprika and chopped spring onions before serving.

Lobster tails with mango and lime

🍴 SERVES 4   442 CALS PER SERVING

4 cooked lobster tails

90 ml (3 fl oz) dry white wine

250 ml (8 fl oz) double cream

1 small mango, peeled, stoned, and cut into cubes (page 420)

grated zest and juice of 1 lime

30 g (1 oz) Parmesan cheese, grated

1 Remove the flesh from the lobster tails (see box, below), then cut each piece of lobster flesh in half lengthways. Arrange the pieces of lobster flesh, cut side-side up, in a large, shallow ovenproof dish.

2 Pour the white wine into a small saucepan and boil rapidly until it has reduced to about 2 tbsp.

3 Add the cream to the saucepan and boil until the mixture has reduced to a coating consistency. Stir in the mango cubes and grated lime zest and juice.

4 Spoon the mixture over the lobster in the dish. Sprinkle with the Parmesan cheese and bake in a preheated oven at 220°C (200°C fan, Gas 7) for about 20 minutes, until hot and bubbling. Serve hot.

Removing the flesh from a lobster tail

Hold the tail in 1 hand. With a pair of scissors, cut along both sides of the underside of the shell, towards the end, without damaging the flesh.

Pull back the underside of the shell, and lift out the lobster flesh, making sure it is all in 1 piece.

Lobster tails with black bean salsa

🍴 SERVES 4   531 CALS PER SERVING

4 cooked lobster tails

lime twists and coriander sprigs to garnish

BLACK BEAN SALSA

4 ripe but firm tomatoes, finely chopped

1 small onion, chopped

1 garlic clove, crushed

2 tbsp chopped fresh coriander

1 mild fresh green chilli, halved, seeded, and chopped

1 x 375 g can black beans, drained

salt and black pepper

GARLIC BUTTER

150 g (5 oz) butter

5 garlic cloves, crushed

2 tsp finely chopped fresh oregano

1 Make the black bean salsa: in a bowl, combine the tomatoes, onion, garlic, coriander, and chilli. Add the beans, and salt and pepper to taste.

2 With a sharp knife, cut each lobster tail in half lengthways and loosen the flesh, keeping it in the shell.

3 Make the garlic butter: cream the butter in a bowl, add the garlic, oregano, and salt and pepper to taste, and mix well. Spread half of the butter mixture over the lobster flesh.

4 Place the lobster under a hot grill, 10 cm (4 in) from the heat, and grill for 5 minutes or until slightly browned in patches and heated through.

5 Spread the lobster with the remaining garlic butter, and then garnish with lime twists and coriander sprigs. Serve hot, with the black bean salsa.

Scallops with asparagus and lemon

SERVES 6　　159 CALS PER SERVING

500 g (1 lb) fresh asparagus tips, chopped into 2 cm (1 in) lengths

60 g (2 oz) butter

500 g (1 lb) queen scallops

3 garlic cloves, crushed

juice of 1 lemon

2 tbsp finely chopped fresh parsley

1 tbsp chopped fresh tarragon

salt and black pepper

1 Blanch the asparagus in boiling salted water for about 2 minutes, then drain and refresh in cold water to stop the cooking and set the bright green colour.

2 Melt half the butter in a frying pan, and fry the scallops for about 30 seconds on each side until just opaque and firm to the touch (you may need to do this in batches). Remove the scallops with a slotted spoon, and keep warm.

3 Heat the remaining butter in the frying pan. Add the garlic, lemon juice, parsley, and tarragon, and season with salt and pepper.

4 Return the scallops and asparagus to the pan and heat them through very gently, shaking the pan to coat them in the sauce. Serve hot.

Queen scallops are sweet and succulent to taste. Care must be taken as they can easily overcook and become rubbery and tough.

Scallops with spicy cashew sauce

SERVES 6　　276 CALS PER SERVING

100 g (3½ oz) toasted, salted cashew nuts

3 tbsp sunflower oil

3 garlic cloves, crushed

500 g (1 lb) scallops

1 onion, chopped

1 green pepper, halved, seeded, and cut into thin strips

1 fresh red chilli, halved, seeded, and finely chopped

½ tsp turmeric

250 ml (8 fl oz) fish stock

1 tsp coarse-grain mustard

salt and black pepper

1 Grind the cashew nuts in a food processor or nut grinder until smooth.

2 Heat the oil in a large frying pan, add the garlic and scallops, and stir-fry for 2 minutes or just until the scallops turn opaque. Remove with a slotted spoon.

3 Add the onion, green pepper, and chilli to the frying pan, and cook gently, stirring occasionally, for 3–5 minutes until the onion is soft but not coloured. Add the turmeric and cook, stirring, for 1 minute.

4 Add the ground cashew nuts and stock to the mixture in the frying pan, bring to a boil, and simmer for 5–10 minutes until the sauce thickens.

5 Stir the scallops into the sauce, add the mustard and salt and pepper to taste, and gently warm through. Serve hot.

Cook's know-how

If you are short of time, use 2 heaped tablespoons of cashew nut butter or peanut butter (smooth or crunchy) instead of grinding the cashews in step 1.

Mussel gratin

SERVES 4　　448 CALS PER SERVING

150 ml (¼ pint) dry white wine

1 shallot, finely chopped

1 garlic clove, crushed

3 kg (6 lb) large mussels, cleaned (page 107)

300 ml (½ pint) single cream

3 tbsp chopped parsley

salt and black pepper

30 g (1 oz) fresh white breadcrumbs

30 g (1 oz) butter, melted

1 Pour the wine into a large saucepan, add the chopped shallot and crushed garlic, and bring to a boil. Simmer for 2 minutes.

2 Add the mussels, cover tightly, and return to a boil. Cook, shaking the pan frequently, for 5–6 minutes until the mussels open.

3 Using a slotted spoon, transfer the mussels to a large bowl. Discard any that have not opened; do not try to force them open.

4 Strain the cooking liquid into a saucepan bring to a boil, and simmer until reduced to about 3 tbsp. Add the cream and heat through. Stir in half of the parsley, and season with salt and pepper.

5 Remove the top shell of each mussel and discard. Arrange the mussels, in their bottom shells, on a large flameproof serving dish.

6 Spoon the sauce over the mussels, and sprinkle with the breadcrumbs and melted butter. Cook under a hot grill, 10 cm (4 in) from the heat, for 3–5 minutes until golden. Garnish with the remaining parsley and serve at once.

Cook's know-how

Mussels are often sold by volume: 900 ml (1½ pints) is equivalent to 750 g (1½ lb), which will yield about 375 g (12 oz) shelled mussels.

Opposite: Mussel gra

Classic steamed clams with parsley

🍴 SERVES 4   207 CALS PER SERVING

about 3 dozen clams, cleaned (page 107)
15 g (½ oz) butter
2 onions, coarsely chopped
2 garlic cloves, crushed
300 ml (½ pint) dry white wine
150 ml (¼ pint) water
30 g (1 oz) butter
about 6 tbsp chopped fresh parsley

1 Melt the butter in a large, deep saucepan. Add the onions and garlic, and fry for 2–3 minutes.

2 Pour in the wine and water, and add 2 tbsp of the parsley. Add the clams, cover the pan, and bring to a boil. Cook, shaking the pan, for about 12 minutes until the clams open. Discard any that have not opened; do not try to force them open.

3 Using a slotted spoon, transfer the clams to a warmed bowl or serving dish.

4 Bring the sauce to a boil, and whisk in the remaining butter and parsley.

5 Pour the sauce over the clams, and serve immediately.

Spicy clams with coriander pesto

🍴 SERVES 4–6   349–233 CALS PER SERVING

4 tbsp olive oil
6 ripe firm tomatoes, diced
4 garlic cloves, crushed
1 tbsp mild chilli powder
about 4 dozen baby clams, cleaned (page 107)
600 ml (1 pint) fish stock, or 300 ml (½ pint) each dry white wine and fish stock
juice of ½ lime
CORIANDER PESTO
12 coriander sprigs
2 tbsp olive oil
1 large garlic clove, roughly chopped
1 mild fresh green chilli, halved, seeded, and roughly chopped
salt and black pepper

1 Make the coriander pesto: strip the coriander leaves from the stalks. Purée the coriander leaves, olive oil, garlic, and green chilli in a food processor or blender until smooth. Season with salt and pepper, and set aside.

2 Heat the oil in a large saucepan, add the tomatoes, garlic, and chilli powder, and cook gently, stirring occasionally, for 8 minutes or until slightly thickened.

3 Add the clams and stir for about 1 minute, then pour in the stock. Cover the pan tightly, and cook the clams over a medium heat, shaking the pan frequently, for about 5–8 minutes until the clams open. Discard any that have not opened; do not try to force them open.

4 Using a slotted spoon, transfer the clams to a warmed bowl.

5 Pour the cooking juices into a small pan, and boil until reduced by about half. Add the lime juice, and season to taste, then pour the sauce over the clams.

6 Serve the clams at once, topped with the coriander pesto.

🔍 Cook's know-how

Hard-shell clams come in different sizes. The smallest are called littlenecks, the next size up are known as cherrystones, and the largest are chowder clams, although they may not be given these names at the fishmonger. Buy whatever you can get for this recipe, bearing in mind that the smaller they are the more fiddly they will be to prepare and eat. If clams are not available, you can use mussels instead

Mussels with potatoes and chorizo

🌀 SERVES 6   523 CALS PER SERVING

2 tbsp olive oil

2 large potatoes, diced

375 g (12 oz) chorizo sausage, diced

2 garlic cloves, crushed

125 ml (4 fl oz) fish stock

4 tbsp dry sherry or white wine

about 2 dozen large mussels, cleaned (page 107)

salt and black pepper

chopped flat-leaf parsley to garnish

1 Heat the olive oil in a large saucepan, add the potatoes, and cook gently, stirring from time to time, for 12–15 minutes until golden and softened. Add the chorizo sausage and garlic, and cook, stirring constantly, for about 2 minutes.

2 Add the fish stock, sherry or wine, and mussels, and season with salt and pepper. Cover the pan tightly, and bring to a boil. Cook, shaking the pan frequently, for 5–8 minutes or until the mussels have opened.

3 Discard any mussels that have not opened; do not try to force them open.

4 Transfer the mussel, potato, and chorizo mixture to a large serving dish, and pour over the cooking juices. Serve hot, garnished with parsley.

❤ Healthy note

Mussels, potatoes, and chorizo make a delicious combination, popular in traditional Spanish cooking. Chorizo gives this dish its characteristic russet colour, but it is a fatty sausage so you may prefer to use less – just 125 g (4 oz) will give some colour, and you could make up the remaining weight by adding frozen broad beans in step 2.

Below: Mussels with potatoes and chorizo.

Chinese-style oysters

🌀 SERVES 4   248 CALS PER SERVING

8 streaky bacon rashers, rinds removed, cut in half

1 x 100 g can smoked oysters, drained

1 small green pepper, halved, seeded, and cut into bite-sized pieces

1 garlic clove, crushed

250 g (8 oz) canned water chestnuts, drained

1 spring onion, thinly sliced

lemon wedges and Tabasco sauce to serve

1 Wrap half a bacon rasher around each oyster, and fasten securely with wooden cocktail sticks.

2 Heat a frying pan, add the bacon-wrapped oysters, and cook gently for 6–8 minutes until browned and crisp. Add the green pepper, garlic, and water chestnuts, and stir-fry over a high heat for 2 minutes.

3 Sprinkle with the spring onion slices, and serve with lemon wedges and Tabasco.

Nigiri sushi

 MAKES 10   182 CALS EACH

10 raw tiger prawns, shells and tails on

salt

a little wasabi (Japanese horseradish paste)

a bowl of vinegar water (see box, below)

prepared Simple Sushi Rice (see recipe, next column)

10 small metal skewers

1 Push a skewer lengthways through each prawn so the prawn becomes straight. Boil for 1–2 minutes in salted water until pink and cooked, drain, and cool. Remove the skewers and gently shell the prawns, leaving the tails intact.

2 Make a slit down the length of the belly of each prawn (without cutting right through), and gently open the prawn out. Remove the black vein from the back.

3 Using your finger, spread a little wasabi along the middle of the slit in the belly. Dip your hand in vinegar water and take a small amount of rice, about the size of a small walnut. Shape the rice with your hand (it will be very sticky) so that it fills the slit on top of the wasabi, then reshape the prawn around the rice by squeezing it. Turn the right way up to serve.

Cook's know-how

The secret of good sushi is to make a good sticky rice, which is very simple. Instructions are usually on the packet, but the recipe here includes a little rice wine for sweetness, and a little salt. To stop the rice sticking to your hand you will need a bowl of vinegar water (water with a little vinegar added). Always use sushi rice on the day it is made. After you have made all the sushi, you can refrigerate them for up to 24 hours until ready to serve.

Sushi squares with smoked salmon

 MAKES 40   49 CALS EACH

a bowl of vinegar water (see box, previous column)

prepared Simple Sushi Rice (see recipe, below)

4 thin slices of smoked salmon

a few strips of sushi pickled ginger (gari), from a jar

32.5 x 23 cm (13 x 9 in) Swiss roll tin

1 Line the Swiss roll tin with cling film (if you don't have a tin, cover a chopping board with cling film). Dip your hand in vinegar water, take a handful of the sushi rice, and press it into the tin, patting it level with your hand. Repeat with more handfuls of rice until the tin is full. Refrigerate for about 15 minutes until firm.

2 Turn the tin upside down on to a board and remove the cling film. Cut into about 40 small squares with a very sharp, wet knife. Cut the smoked salmon into little strips to fit on each square and top with a little pickled ginger.

Simple sushi rice

 SERVES 6   280 CALS PER SERVING

500 g (1 lb) sushi rice

4 tbsp rice wine vinegar

50 ml (2 fl oz) Japanese rice wine (mirin or sake)

¼ tsp salt

1 Put the rice into a sieve and rinse under cold running water, then tip it into a saucepan and pour in 750 ml (1¼ pints) cold water. Bring to a boil, lower the heat, and simmer, covered, for 15 minutes or until all the water has been absorbed.

2 Remove the pan from the heat and cover it immediately with a tea towel and lid (this is to make sure no steam can escape). Leave for about 10 minutes.

3 Mix together the vinegar, rice wine, and salt in a small bowl and fold gently into the rice. Continue to cut and fold through the rice while cooling with a fan or a firm piece of card (it is important to cool the rice down quickly so that it remains sticky).

Hoso maki

 MAKES 20   94 CALS EACH

2 sheets of nori (dried Japanese seaweed)

a bowl of vinegar water (see box, in first column)

prepared Simple Sushi Rice (see recipe, previous column)

a little wasabi

175 g (6 oz) canned white crabmeat, drained and flaked

½ cucumber, halved lengthways, seeded, and cut into long thin strips

bamboo rolling mat

1 Lay the rolling mat on a flat surface with one of the longest edges facing towards you. Lay one sheet of nori shiny side down on the mat.

2 Dip your hand in vinegar water, take a handful of the sushi rice, and spread it over the nori, leaving a 2.5 cm (1 in) gap along the edge furthest away from you.

3 Spread a thin layer of wasabi – about 1 cm (½ in) wide – lengthways along the middle of the rice (from left to right). Cover the wasabi with half the crab, then put a strip of cucumber on either side of the crab.

4 Moisten the uncovered edge of the nori with a little cold water. Using the mat and starting from the edge nearest to you roll the rice in the nori, squeezing it to make a tight roll. Seal the moistened edge around the roll, then wrap in cling film. Now make a second roll in the same way.

5 To serve, unwrap the rolls and cut each one into 10 pieces with a very sharp knife that has been dipped in cold water (trim off the ends first so you get neat slices).

Opposite, clockwise from top: Nigiri sushi, Sushi squares with smoked salmon, Hoso maki

Hot and sour mackerel

SERVES 4   539 CALS PER SERVING

2 carrots

1 red pepper, cored and seeded

1 fresh green chilli, halved and seeded

6 garlic cloves

8 spring onions

2 tbsp sunflower oil

1 lemon grass stalk, slit lengthways and bruised

4 x 175 g (6 oz) mackerel fillets

coriander sprigs to garnish

HOT AND SOUR SAUCE

4 tbsp Thai fish sauce or light soy sauce

4 tbsp cider vinegar, white wine vinegar, or rice vinegar

2 tbsp lime juice

2 tbsp sugar

1 Make the hot and sour sauce: in a small bowl, combine the fish sauce or soy sauce, vinegar, lime juice, and sugar.

2 Cut the carrots, red pepper, green chilli, and garlic into matchstick-thin strips. Slice the spring onions.

3 Line a grill pan with foil. Arrange the mackerel on the foil, and cook under a hot grill, 10 cm (4 in) from the heat, for 3 minutes on each side. Continue to grill until the fish is opaque and the flesh flakes easily. Meanwhile, stir-fry the vegetables.

4 Heat the sunflower oil in a wok or large frying pan. Add the carrots, red pepper, chilli, garlic, spring onions, and lemon grass, and stir-fry over a high heat for 3 minutes or until the vegetables are just tender.

5 Remove and discard the lemon grass. Arrange the vegetable mixture on top of the fish, pour the sauce over, garnish with the coriander sprigs, and serve at once.

Mackerel with gooseberry sauce

SERVES 4   489 CALS PER SERVING

4 x 250 g (8 oz) mackerel, cleaned, with heads removed (page 106)

salt and black pepper

GOOSEBERRY SAUCE

375 g (12 oz) gooseberries

2 tbsp water

30 g (1 oz) caster sugar, more if needed

30 g (1 oz) butter

½ tsp ground ginger

1 Cut the fins off the mackerel, and make 3–4 diagonal cuts on both sides of each fish. Season the mackerel inside and out with salt and pepper.

2 Make the gooseberry sauce: top and tail the gooseberries, and put them into a pan with the water and sugar. Cover tightly and simmer very gently, shaking the pan occasionally, for 5 minutes or until tender.

3 Reserve 12 of the cooked gooseberries for garnish, then work the remainder through a nylon sieve. Beat in the butter and ginger, and add more sugar if necessary. Return the sauce to the pan and keep warm.

4 Cook the mackerel under a hot grill, 10 cm (4 in) from the heat, for 7–8 minutes on each side until the fish is opaque and the flesh flakes easily.

5 Serve the mackerel hot, garnished with the reserved gooseberries. Hand the sauce separately.

Mackerel with cranberry sauce

Substitute 375 g (12 oz) cranberries for the gooseberries. You can use frozen cranberries, but they will take slightly longer to cook – simmer them until they pop open.

Herrings with oatmeal

SERVES 4   461 CALS PER SERVING

125 g (4 oz) medium oatmeal

2 tsp mustard powder

salt and black pepper

4 x 175–250 g (6–8 oz) herrings, cleaned (page 106), heads removed, and filleted

8 parsley sprigs

parsley and lemon wedges to garnish

1 In a shallow dish, combine the oatmeal and mustard powder, and season with salt and pepper.

2 Open out the herrings and press them into the oatmeal mixture to coat well on both sides.

3 Grill the herrings under a hot grill, 10 cm (4 in) from the heat, for about 4 minutes on each side or until the fish is opaque and the flesh flakes easily.

4 Arrange the grilled herrings on a warmed serving platter, and garnish with parsley and lemon wedges.

♥ Healthy note

Herrings are an inexpensive oily fish, and eating oily fish regularly (once a week) is one of the best ways to eat for good health. This is because they contain omega-3 fatty acids, which help discourage heart disease and blood clots. Herrings also provide vitamin D, which is good for healthy bones, teeth, nerves and muscles.

errings with ustard sauce

SERVES 4   479 CALS PER SERVING

175–250 g (6–8 oz) herrings, cleaned
ge 106), heads removed, and filleted

and black pepper

er for greasing

n wedges and parsley sprigs to garnish

TARD SAUCE

(1 oz) butter

(1 oz) plain flour

nl (½ pint) milk

mustard powder

caster sugar

white wine vinegar

1 Season the herrings inside and out with salt and black pepper, fold the fish over, and place in a single layer in a buttered ovenproof dish.

2 Cover and bake in a preheated oven at 200°C (180°C fan, Gas 6) for 12 minutes or until the fish is opaque and the flesh flakes easily.

3 Meanwhile, make the mustard sauce: melt the butter in a saucepan, add the flour, and cook, stirring, for 1 minute. Remove from the heat and gradually blend in the milk. Bring to a boil, stirring constantly until the mixture thickens. Simmer for 2–3 minutes. Add the mustard powder, sugar, and vinegar, season with salt and pepper, and cook for a further minute.

4 To serve, garnish the herrings with lemon wedges and parsley sprigs, and hand the mustard sauce separately.

⊙ Healthy note

Instead of the mustard sauce, make a quick "dip" by mixing a teaspoonful or two of Dijon mustard and a squeeze of lemon juice into your favourite reduced-calorie mayonnaise or low-fat crème fraîche.

Grilled trout with cucumber and dill

🍴 SERVES 4   435 CALS PER SERVING

1 cucumber, peeled

30 g (1 oz) butter

small bunch of fresh dill, chopped

salt and black pepper

juice of 1 lemon

4 x 375–425 g (12–14 oz) trout, cleaned (page 106)

dill sprigs and fresh chives to garnish

dill cream sauce (page 132) to serve

1 Cut the cucumber in half lengthways and scoop out the seeds, then cut the flesh across into 5 mm (¼ in) slices. Melt the butter in a saucepan, add the cucumber, and cook gently for 2 minutes.

2 In a bowl, combine two-thirds of the cooked cucumber with the chopped dill, season with salt and pepper, and sprinkle with the lemon juice. Stuff the trout with the mixture.

3 Line a grill pan with foil. Arrange the trout on the foil, and put the remaining cucumber around them.

4 Grill the trout under a hot grill, 10 cm (4 in) from the heat, for 4–7 minutes on each side until the flesh flakes easily.

5 Garnish the trout with dill sprigs and fresh chives, and serve at once, with dill cream sauce handed separately.

Trout with almonds

Dip the trout in seasoned flour. Melt 60 g (2 oz) butter in a large frying pan, and cook the trout, in batches if necessary, for 6–8 minutes on each side until the fish is opaque and the flesh flakes easily. Drain on paper towels, and keep warm. Wipe the pan, melt 15 g (½ oz) butter, and fry 60 g (2 oz) flaked almonds until lightly browned. Add a squeeze of lemon juice, then pour the lemon and almond mixture over the trout. Serve at once.

Baked trout with orange

🍴 SERVES 4   378 CALS PER SERVING

4 x 375–425 g (12–14 oz) trout, cleaned (page 106)

4 large thyme sprigs

4 large parsley sprigs

125 g (4 oz) button mushrooms, sliced

2 shallots, chopped

4 tbsp white wine vinegar

grated zest and juice of 1 orange

salt and black pepper

orange and thyme to garnish

1 With a sharp knife, make 2 diagonal cuts through the skin and into the flesh on both sides of each trout.

2 Strip the thyme and parsley leaves from their stalks. In a bowl, combine the mushrooms, shallots, white wine vinegar, orange zest and juice, thyme and parsley leaves, and salt and pepper to taste.

3 Reserve one-quarter of the mushroom and herb mixture to spoon over the stuffed trout.

4 Stuff the trout with the remaining mushroom and herb mixture (see box, below).

5 Arrange the trout in a non-metallic baking dish and spoon over the reserved mushroom mixture. Cover and marinate in the refrigerator for up to 4 hours.

6 Bake in a preheated oven at 180°C (160°C fan, Gas 4) for 20–25 minutes until the fish is opaque and the flesh flakes easily. Garnish with orange and thyme before serving.

Stuffing the trout

Hold the fish open, spoon in one-quarter of the mushroom and herb mixture, then press firmly to close.

Tuna teriyaki

🍴 SERVES 4   339 CALS PER SERVING

4 x 175 g (6 oz) tuna steaks, about 2.5 cm (1 in) thick

2 spring onions, thinly sliced, to garnish

MARINADE

3 tbsp dark soy sauce

2 tbsp sesame oil

1 tbsp Japanese rice wine or sweet sherry

3 garlic cloves, chopped

1 tbsp caster sugar

1 cm (½ in) piece of fresh root ginger, peeled and grated

1 Make the marinade: put the soy sauce, sesame oil, rice wine or sherry, garlic, sugar, and ginger into a non-metallic dish. Add the tuna steaks to the marinade and turn to coat. Cover the dish and marinate in the refrigerator for up to 4 hours.

2 Reserve the marinade. Cook the steaks under a hot grill, 7 cm (3 in) from the heat, brushing with the marinade, for 3–4 minutes on each side. Serve at once, garnished with spring onions.

Barbecued salmon teriyaki

Cut 4 salmon fillets into 2.5 cm (1 in) cubes and marinate in the refrigerator for up to 4 hours, as in step 1, then thread on to kebab skewers. Cook over a hot barbecue, turning and brushing frequently with the marinade, for 6–8 minutes.

💚 **Healthy note**

Fresh root ginger, a key ingredient in Asian cooking, is known to have healing properties. It helps stimulate the circulation, fights coughs and colds, and relieves indigestion. It may also relieve rheumatism.

Tuna with fennel and tomato relish

🍽 SERVES 4   467 CALS PER SERVING

tbsp olive oil

ice of ½ lemon

garlic cloves, crushed

x 175 g (6 oz) tuna steaks, about 2.5 cm
in) thick

lt and black pepper

ne wedges and fennel tops to garnish

NNEL AND TOMATO RELISH

small fennel bulb, chopped

ripe but firm tomatoes, finely chopped

bsp olive oil

bsp lemon juice

bsp tapenade (see box, right)

garlic clove, chopped

1 Combine the olive oil, lemon juice, and garlic in a large non-metallic dish. Add the tuna steaks and turn to coat. Cover dish and leave to marinate in the refrigerator, turning occasionally, for about 1 hour.

2 Meanwhile, make the relish: put the fennel, tomatoes, olive oil, lemon juice, tapenade, and garlic into a bowl, and stir well to combine.

3 Remove the tuna from the marinade, reserving the marinade. Cook the tuna under a hot grill, 7 cm (3 in) from the heat, basting once or twice with the reserved marinade, for 3–4 minutes on each side.

4 Season the tuna with salt and pepper, and top with the fennel and tomato relish. Garnish with lime wedges and fennel tops before serving.

🔍 Cook's know-how

Tapenade comes from Provence in the south of France. It is a tangy paste made of typical Provençal ingredients - black olives, anchovies, capers, and fruity olive oil. It is sold in tubes, jars, and tubs at supermarkets.

Shark with tropical salsa

🍴 SERVES 4   534 CALS PER SERVING

4 x 175 g (6 oz) shark steaks

MARINADE

125 ml (4 fl oz) olive oil

juice of ½ lemon

3 garlic cloves, crushed

1 tbsp chopped fresh coriander

1 tsp ground cumin

pinch of cayenne pepper

salt and black pepper

TROPICAL SALSA

1 x 275 g can pineapple pieces in natural juices, drained

1 small ripe papaya or mango, peeled, seeded or stoned, and diced

1 small red pepper, halved, seeded, and diced

1 mild fresh red or green chilli, halved, seeded, and diced

2 tbsp chopped fresh coriander

1 tbsp white wine vinegar

sugar (optional)

1 Make the marinade: in a non-metallic dish, combine the oil, lemon juice, garlic, coriander, cumin, and cayenne. Season with salt and pepper.

2 Turn the shark steaks in the marinade, cover, and marinate in the refrigerator for about 1 hour.

3 Make the tropical salsa: in a large bowl, combine the pineapple, papaya or mango, red pepper, chilli, coriander, and vinegar. Season with salt and pepper. If the fruit is sour, add a little sugar.

4 Remove the steaks from the marinade, reserving the marinade. Place the steaks under a hot grill, 7 cm (3 in) from the heat, basting once or twice with the marinade, for 3–4 minutes on each side until the flesh is opaque and flakes easily. Serve hot, with the salsa.

🔍 Cook's know-how

Try this cranberry and orange salsa instead of the tropical salsa. Peel, segment, and finely chop 1 orange. Mix with 250 g (8 oz) chopped cranberries and 125 g (4 oz) sugar. Serve chilled, with the hot fish.

Swordfish with orange relish

🍴 SERVES 4   429 CALS PER SERVING

4 x 175 g (6 oz) swordfish steaks

MARINADE

3 tbsp olive oil

juice of 1 orange

juice of 1 lemon

3 garlic cloves, crushed

salt and black pepper

ORANGE RELISH

2 oranges, peeled, separated into segments, and diced

3 tbsp olive oil

2 tbsp chopped fresh basil

1 Make the marinade: in a shallow non-metallic dish, combine the olive oil, orange and lemon juices, and garlic, and season with salt and pepper. Turn the swordfish steaks in the marinade, cover, and leave to marinate in the refrigerator for about 1 hour.

2 Make the orange relish: in a bowl, combine the oranges, olive oil, basil, and season with salt and pepper to taste.

3 Remove the swordfish from the marinade, reserving the marinade. Place the steaks under a hot grill, 7 cm (3 in) from the heat, and grill, basting once or twice with the marinade, for 5 minutes on each side or until the flesh is opaque and flakes easily. Serve hot, with the relish.

Tuna with orange relish

Substitute tuna steaks for the swordfish steaks, and fresh coriander for the basil.

🔍 Cook's know-how

When marinating fish, leave it for no more than 4 hours. After this time the acid in the marinade will start to seep deep into the fish, which will make it dry when it is cooked.

Salmon with avocado

🍴 SERVES 4   543 CALS PER SERVING

30 g (1 oz) butter, melted

4 x 175 g (6 oz) salmon steaks

salt and black pepper

4 tarragon sprigs

4 slices of lime

AVOCADO SAUCE

2 avocados, halved, stoned (page 327), and peeled

150 ml (¼ pint) plain yogurt

grated zest and juice of 1 lime

1 Brush 4 large squares of foil with melted butter. Put a salmon steak on each square, season, and top with a tarragon sprig and a slice of lime. Wrap the foil around the salmon. Put on a baking tray, and bake in a preheated oven at 150°C (130°C fan, Gas 2) for 25 minutes or until the fish is opaque and the flesh flakes easily.

2 Meanwhile, make the avocado sauce: put the flesh of 1 avocado into a food processor with the yogurt, and lime zest and juice. Season with salt and pepper and purée until smooth. Transfer to a serving bowl. Dice the remaining avocado, and stir into the sauce.

3 Unwrap the salmon, transfer to warmed serving plates, and serve with the avocado sauce.

Koulibiac

This is a type of salmon kedgeree enclosed in crisp puff pastry, which makes an impressive dish for a dinner party or other special occasion. In Russia, its country of origin, there is a saying, "Houses make a fine street, pies make a fine table".

SERVES 8–10   **518–414 CALS PER SERVING**

5 g (2½ oz) long grain rice

salt and black pepper

0 g (2 oz) butter, plus extra for greasing

large onion, chopped

x 400 g can chopped tomatoes, drained

00 g (1 lb) fresh salmon fillets, cooked and flaked

tbsp chopped parsley

rated zest and juice of 1 lemon

00 g (1 lb) puff pastry

egg, beaten

0 g (2 oz) butter, melted, and juice of
lemon to serve

mon twists and watercress sprigs to garnish

1 Cook the rice in boiling salted water for 12 minutes or until just tender.

2 Meanwhile, melt the butter in a saucepan, add the onion, and cook very gently for about 10 minutes until soft but not coloured. Add the tomatoes and cook for 15 minutes. Leave to cool.

3 Drain the rice thoroughly, and combine with the onion and tomato mixture, the flaked salmon, parsley, and lemon zest and juice. Season with salt and pepper.

4 Roll out 425 g (14 oz) of the puff pastry into a 28 x 40 cm (11 x 16 in) rectangle.

5 Arrange the salmon mixture down the middle of the rectangle, leaving a 7 cm (3 in) border on each side. Brush the border with a little of the beaten egg, and wrap and decorate the koulibiac (see box, right).

6 Bake the koulibiac in a preheated oven at 220°C (200°C fan, Gas 7) for 30–45 minutes until golden.

7 Transfer to a warmed serving dish, and pour the melted butter and lemon juice into the cuts. Serve in thick slices, garnished with lemon twists and watercress.

Wrapping and decorating the koulibiac

Fold the shortest ends of pastry over the salmon filling and brush the top of the folded pastry with beaten egg.

Fold the longest sides over the filling to make a long parcel. Turn the parcel over and place on a lightly buttered baking tray. Brush all over with beaten egg.

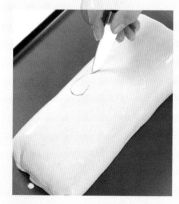

Make 2 decorative cuts in the top of the pastry. Roll the remaining pastry into a 5 x 30 cm (2 x 12 in) piece, trim, then cut into 3 equal strips. Press the ends together and plait the strips. Lay the plait down the middle of the parcel, and glaze with beaten egg.

Classic buffet party salmon

This is the perfect dish for a buffet party. The salmon is gently poached, with the skin and head for added flavour, and left to cool in the cooking liquid to keep it moist. Fish kettles can be hired from some fishmongers or the fish counters of some supermarkets.

🕐 SERVES 10   410 CALS PER SERVING

2.75 kg (5½ lb) salmon, cleaned (page 106)
salt and black peppercorns
4 bay leaves
1 onion, sliced
4 tbsp white wine vinegar
3 tbsp chopped fresh dill
about 200 ml (7 fl oz) mayonnaise (page 329)

TO GARNISH

about 14 cooked jumbo prawns, tail shells taken off but heads left on
1–2 bunches of fresh dill
lemon wedges or slices
fish kettle

1 Lift out the rack from the fish kettle and set aside. Half fill the kettle with cold water and add 2 tbsp salt, 12 black peppercorns, the bay leaves, onion, and vinegar.

2 Put the salmon on to the rack, and lower into the kettle. Bring to a boil, then simmer for 1 minute only. Remove from the heat, cover, and leave to stand for about 2 hours, until the fish is just warm.

3 Lift the rack and salmon out of the fish kettle. Strain the cooking liquid and reserve. Cover the salmon with a large piece of cling film and flip the fish over on to the cling film. Bone and skin the salmon (see box, below). Cover and chill in the refrigerator for at least 1 hour.

4 Mix the dill into the mayonnaise, then taste for seasoning. Spoon into a serving bowl, and chill until ready to serve.

5 Arrange the prawns in a line along the middle of the salmon so that the heads are facing in opposite directions (this will hide the line where the backbone was). The number of prawns will depend on the length of your salmon, so buy extra just in case – you can always use any leftover prawns around the edge of the plate as an extra garnish.

6 Arrange dill sprigs around the edge of the salmon and on the plate, together with lemon slices or wedges. Serve with the dill mayonnaise.

Boning and skinning a salmon

1 Using a chef's knife, neatly remove the head from the salmon.

2 Run the knife along the backbone of the fish to loosen the top fillet.

3 Flip the top fillet over and remove the bones from the fish.

4 Use the cling film to flip the bottom fillet back on to the top and remove the skin and any dark flesh.

5 Use the cling film to flip the fish on to a large serving plate, and remove the remaining skin.

6 With a small knife, gently scrape away the brownish flesh, leaving behind only the pink flesh.

Salmon en croûte

 **SERVES 8**   **745 CALS PER SERVING**

1.7–2 kg (3½–4 lb) salmon, cleaned and filleted
(page 106), then cut lengthways in half
and skinned

1 tbsp chopped fresh dill

grated zest and juice of 1 lemon

salt and black pepper

30 g (1 oz) butter

8 spring onions, sliced

250 g (8 oz) spinach leaves, coarsely shredded

250 g (8 oz) low-fat soft cheese

plain flour for dusting

750 g (1½ lb) puff pastry

1 egg, beaten

lemon slices, cherry tomatoes, and parsley
sprigs to garnish

1 Put the 2 pieces of salmon into a
shallow non-metallic dish and sprinkle
with the dill, lemon zest and juice, and salt
and pepper. Cover and leave to marinate
in the refrigerator for about 1 hour.

2 Melt the butter in a small pan, add the
onions, and cook gently for 2–3 minutes
until soft but not coloured. Remove from
the heat.

3 Add the spinach, toss in the butter, then
leave to cool. Drain any excess water
from the pan. Stir in the cheese, and season
with salt and pepper.

4 Roll out half of the pastry on a lightly
floured surface to a 20 x 38 cm (8 x 15 in)
rectangle. Put the pastry on a baking tray,
and place 1 salmon fillet, skinned side
down, on top. Spread with the spinach

mixture, then put the second salmon fillet
on top, skinned side up. Brush the pastry
border with a little beaten egg.

5 Roll out the remaining pastry to
a slightly larger rectangle, cover
the salmon completely, then trim and
seal the edges. Make "scales" on the
top with the edge of a spoon, then
make 2 small holes to let steam escape
during baking.

6 Brush with beaten egg and bake in
a preheated oven at 200°C (180°C fan
Gas 6) for 40–45 minutes until the pastry
is risen and golden brown. Serve hot,
garnished with lemon, tomatoes,
and parsley.

Severn salmon

🍴 SERVES 6   414 CALS PER SERVING

x 175 g (6 oz) salmon fillets or steaks

utter for greasing

alt and black pepper

atercress sprigs to garnish

ATERCRESS SAUCE

0 ml (½ pint) single cream

0 g (2 oz) watercress, trimmed

g (3 oz) butter, melted

tsp plain flour

ice of I lemon

egg yolk

Arrange the salmon fillets or steaks in a single layer in a buttered roasting tin, nd sprinkle with black pepper.

Cover tightly with foil, and bake in a preheated oven at 180°C (160°C fan, as 4) for 15 minutes or until the fish is paque and flakes easily.

Meanwhile, make the watercress sauce: put the cream, watercress, butter, flour, mon juice, and egg yolk into a food ocessor, season with salt and pepper, nd purée until smooth.

4 Transfer the cream and watercress mixture to a small saucepan, and cook over a gentle heat, stirring, until the sauce thickens. Taste for seasoning.

5 Serve the salmon hot on a pool of watercress sauce, garnished with fresh sprigs of watercress.

Salmon with spinach

🍴 SERVES 4   454 CALS PER SERVING

4 x 175 g (6 oz) salmon steaks

salt and black pepper

15 g (½ oz) butter

lemon twists to garnish

SPINACH SALSA

2 tbsp olive oil

8 spring onions, finely sliced

1 garlic clove, crushed

4 tbsp lemon juice

1 tsp wholegrain mustard

500 g (1 lb) spinach leaves, finely chopped

1 Season the salmon steaks with black pepper and dot with the butter.

2 Cook the salmon steaks under a hot grill, 7 cm (3 in) from the heat, for 2–3 minutes on each side until the fish is opaque and the flesh flakes easily. Leave to rest.

3 Make the spinach salsa: heat the oil in a frying pan, add the spring onions and garlic, and cook, stirring, for about 1 minute. Stir in the lemon juice, mustard, and spinach, and cook, stirring, for about 2 minutes. Transfer to a bowl, and season with salt and pepper.

4 Garnish the salmon with lemon twists and serve at once, with the salsa.

♡ Healthy note

Spinach is not as rich in iron as was previously thought, although it does contain a useful source. One of its main benefits to good health is that it contains a phytochemical called lutein, an antioxidant that can help protect against age-related degeneration of eyesight.

low: Severn salmon.

Mushroom-stuffed sole fillets

🍴 **SERVES 4**   **568 CALS PER SERVING**

60 g (2 oz) butter

1 onion, finely chopped

375 g (12 oz) mushrooms, finely chopped

2 large lemon sole, each cut into 4 fillets and skinned (page 107)

250 ml (8 fl oz) dry white wine

2 tsp chopped fresh tarragon

salt and black pepper

250 ml (8 fl oz) double cream

squeeze of lemon juice

1 Melt half of the butter in a saucepan, add the onion and mushrooms, and cook gently for 5 minutes.

2 Roll the fillets (see box, right), with the skinned sides facing inwards. Stand them in a shallow baking dish, and fill with the mushrooms and onion.

3 Add the wine, tarragon, and salt and pepper to taste. Cover and bake in a preheated oven at 180°C (160°C fan, Gas 4) for 15 minutes or until the fish is opaque and flakes easily.

4 Remove the fish from the dish and keep warm. Pour the juices into a saucepan and boil for 3 minutes or until reduced by half. Stir in the cream and lemon juice, heat through gently, and taste for seasoning before serving.

Rolling the fillets

Bring round the 2 ends of each fillet to form a circle, with the smaller tail end on the outside.

Thread a wooden cocktail stick through both ends of each fillet, to secure.

Hot lemon bread

Beat the grated zest of ½ lemon into 125 g (4 oz) softened butter, using a fork. Work in the juice of ½ lemon, and salt and pepper to taste.

Cut 1 baguette into 1 cm (½ in) slices, leaving the slices attached underneath.

Spread the butter in between the slices, and a little on top. Wrap in foil and bake in a preheated oven at 200°C (180°C fan, Gas 6) for 10 minutes, opening the foil for the last 5 minutes to crisp the top.

Fillets of sole meunière

🍴 SERVES 4   274 CALS PER SERVING

60 g (2 oz) plain flour

salt and black pepper

4 small lemon sole, each cut into 4 fillets and skinned (page 107)

60 g (2 oz) butter

1 tbsp chopped parsley

juice of ½ lemon

lemon slices and parsley sprigs to garnish

1 Sprinkle the flour on to a plate and season with salt and pepper. Dip the 16 fillets into the seasoned flour and shake off any excess.

2 Melt half of the butter in a large frying pan. When it is foaming, add the fillets, and cook for 2 minutes on each side or until the flesh is opaque and flakes easily. Transfer to warmed serving plates and keep warm.

3 Wipe the pan with paper towels. Melt the remaining butter and heat quickly until golden. Stir in the parsley and lemon juice, then pour over the fillets. Serve hot, garnished with lemon slices and parsley sprigs.

Lemon sole florentine

Fillets of lemon sole are topped with a cheese sauce and baked on a bed of spinach, so they stay moist while cooking. Slices of hot lemon bread – an interesting variation of garlic bread – make an unusual accompaniment.

🍴 SERVES 4   422 CALS PER SERVING

4 large lemon sole, each cut into 4 fillets and skinned (page 107)

juice of ½ lemon

salt and black pepper

45 g (1½ oz) butter

45 g (1½ oz) plain flour

450 ml (¾ pint) milk

750 g (1½ lb) spinach leaves

30 g (1 oz) Parmesan cheese, grated

hot lemon bread to serve (see box, left)

1 Sprinkle the lemon sole fillets with the lemon juice and salt and pepper. Fold the fillets in half widthways, and set aside.

2 Melt the butter in a saucepan, add the flour, and cook, stirring, for 1 minute. Remove from the heat and gradually blend in the milk. Bring to a boil, stirring constantly until the white sauce mixture thickens. Simmer for 2–3 minutes, then add salt and pepper to taste.

3 Wash the spinach and put into a pan with only the water remaining on the leaves. Cook for 2 minutes or until wilted. Drain well.

4 Stir half of the sauce into the cooked spinach and spoon into a shallow ovenproof dish. Arrange the sole on top. Pour the remaining sauce over the top and sprinkle with the cheese. Bake in a preheated oven at 200°C (180°C fan, Gas 6) for 30 minutes. Serve hot, with hot lemon bread.

Gingered plaice

🍴 SERVES 4   247 CALS PER SERVING

4 large plaice fillets

spring onions to garnish (optional)

GINGER MARINADE

2.5 cm (1 in) piece of fresh root ginger, peeled and finely sliced

1 large garlic clove, sliced

2 tbsp sunflower oil

1 tbsp sesame oil

1 tbsp dry sherry

1 tbsp sherry vinegar

2 tsp light soy sauce

1 Put the plaice fillets into a shallow non-metallic dish.

2 Make the marinade: combine the ginger, garlic, sunflower and sesame oils, sherry, sherry vinegar, and soy sauce, and pour over the fish.

3 Cover the fish and leave to marinate in the refrigerator, turning once, for 30 minutes.

4 Grill the fillets, skin-side down, under a hot grill, 7 cm (3 in) from the heat, for 4–5 minutes, until the fish is opaque and flakes easily. Serve hot, garnished with spring onions if you like.

Coating a fish fillet

Dip the fillet into the seasoned flour, to coat. Shake off any excess.

Dip the floured fillet into the beaten egg, letting any excess drain off.

Dip the fillet into the breadcrumbs, making sure it is evenly coated.

Best-ever fried fish

These plaice fillets are shallow-fried in a crisp coating of fresh breadcrumbs. This is far superior to a batter coating in both flavour and texture, and it protects the fish from the heat of the fat and keeps it moist, in the same way as batter.

 SERVES 4   298 CALS PER SERVING

3 tbsp plain flour

salt and black pepper

1 large egg, beaten

30 g (1 oz) fresh white breadcrumbs

4 large plaice fillets, skinned

2 tbsp sunflower oil

lemon wedges to garnish

1 Sprinkle the flour into a shallow dish and season with salt and pepper. Pour the beaten egg into another dish, and sprinkle the breadcrumbs into a third.

2 Lightly coat the fish fillets with breadcrumbs (see box, right).

3 Heat the oil in a large frying pan, add the coated fillets, in 2 batches if necessary, and fry over a high heat for 2–3 minutes on each side until they are crisp, golden, and juicy inside.

4 Lift the fillets out of the frying pan with a fish slice and then leave to drain briefly on paper towels. Serve the fish at once, garnished with the lemon wedges.

Sauces for fish

Dill cream sauce

Purée 300 ml (½ pint) single cream, 90 g (3 oz) butter, 1 egg yolk, the juice of 1 lemon, and 1 tsp plain flour in a food processor until smooth. Transfer the mixture to a small saucepan and heat very gently, stirring constantly, until the sauce has thickened and will coat the back of a spoon. Add salt and pepper to taste, then stir in 2 tbsp chopped fresh dill and 1 tbsp snipped fresh chives.

Tartare sauce

Purée 1 egg, 1½ tsp sugar, ½ tsp mustard powder, and salt and pepper to taste in a food processor or blender until smooth. Add 300 ml (½ pint) sunflower oil, pouring in a steady stream, and purée until the mixture is very thick and all of the oil has been incorporated. Add the juice of 1 lemon, and purée. Transfer to a bowl, and stir in 1 tbsp each chopped gherkins, capers, and parsley, and 2 tbsp chopped fresh tarragon. Cover and leave to stand for at least 1 hour to allow the flavours to blend.

Haddock with mushrooms and cream

SERVES 4–6   429–286 CALS PER SERVING

300 ml (½ pint) milk

1 slice of onion

6 black peppercorns

1 bay leaf

50 g (2 oz) butter, plus extra for greasing

750 g (1½ lb) haddock fillet, skinned

salt and black pepper

squeeze of lemon juice

250 g (8 oz) button mushrooms, sliced

25 g (1 oz) plain flour

2 tbsp single cream (optional)

25 g (1 oz) fresh white breadcrumbs

25 g (1 oz) Parmesan cheese, grated

chopped parsley to garnish

1 Put the milk into a small saucepan with the onion, peppercorns, and bay leaf, and bring just to a boil. Remove from the heat, cover, and leave to infuse for 10 minutes. Lightly butter a shallow ovenproof dish.

2 Cut the haddock into 7 cm (3 in) pieces, and place in a single layer in the dish. Sprinkle with salt and pepper.

3 Melt half of the butter in a saucepan, add the lemon juice and mushrooms, and season with salt and pepper. Cook gently, stirring occasionally, for 3 minutes until just tender. Remove the mushrooms with a slotted spoon and put them on top of the fish.

4 Strain the infused milk and set aside. Melt the remaining butter in a saucepan, add the flour, and cook, stirring, for 1 minute. Remove from the heat and gradually blend in the infused milk. Bring to a boil, stirring until the mixture thickens. Simmer for 2–3 minutes. Stir in the cream, if using, and season with salt and pepper.

5 Pour the sauce over the fish and mushrooms, then sprinkle with the breadcrumbs and Parmesan. Bake in a preheated oven at 190°C (170°C fan, Gas 5) for 25–30 minutes until the fish is cooked and the top is golden and bubbling. Garnish with parsley, and serve at once.

Roast monkfish niçoise

SERVES 4   448 CALS PER SERVING

3 tbsp olive oil

1 head of garlic, separated

1 lemon, thickly sliced

500 g (1 lb) monkfish fillets, skinned and cut into chunky pieces

1 tbsp mixed chopped fresh thyme and parsley, and snipped chives

250 ml (8 fl oz) dry white wine

125 ml (4 fl oz) fish stock

1 x 400 g can artichoke hearts, drained and rinsed

15 pitted black olives

10 sun-dried tomatoes in oil, drained

squeeze of lemon juice

salt and black pepper

lemon wedges and thyme sprigs to garnish

1 Put 1 tbsp of the oil into an ovenproof dish, add the garlic cloves, and roast in a preheated oven at 190°C (170°C fan, Gas 5) for about 10 minutes until softened.

2 Arrange the lemon slices in the dish, and put the garlic and monkfish on top.

3 Sprinkle with the remaining oil and the herbs, and pour in the wine and stock. Return to the oven for 10 minutes.

4 Add the artichoke hearts, olives, and sun-dried tomatoes, and cook for 5 minutes to heat through.

5 Transfer the fish and vegetables to a serving dish, discarding the lemon slices. Keep warm.

6 Pour the cooking juices into a small saucepan, and boil for about 8 minutes until reduced to about 125 ml (4 fl oz). Add the lemon juice, season with salt and pepper, and pour over the fish. Garnish with lemon and thyme, and serve at once.

Roast monkfish basquaise

Instead of the artichokes, use 2 peppers (1 red and 1 yellow), halved, seeded, and cut into strips, and roast with the garlic cloves.

Monkfish with ginger-orange sauce

SERVES 4   221 CALS PER SERVING

1 orange, washed and thinly sliced

1 onion, chopped

1 cm (½ in) piece of fresh root ginger, peeled and grated

500 g (1 lb) monkfish fillets, skinned

250 ml (8 fl oz) fish stock

grated zest of ½ lime

75 ml (2½ fl oz) lime juice

salt and cayenne pepper

60 g (2 oz) unsalted butter, chilled and cubed

sugar or honey to taste (optional)

orange and snipped chives to garnish

1 Put the orange slices, onion, and ginger into a pan. Add the monkfish, spring onions, and stock. Bring to a boil, and simmer, without stirring, for 10 minutes or until the fish is firm. With a slotted spoon, transfer the fish to a serving dish. Keep hot.

2 Put a sieve over a bowl, tip in the remaining contents of the pan and press hard with the back of a spoon to extract all the juices.

3 Pour the juices into a small saucepan and boil rapidly, uncovered, for about 12 minutes until the liquid has reduced to about 2 tbsp.

4 Add the lime zest and juice, season with salt and cayenne, and heat gently, stirring, until warm. Remove from the heat and finish the sauce (see box, below).

5 Pour the sauce over the fish, garnish, and serve at once.

Finishing the sauce

Add the cubes of butter one at a time, whisking between each addition until the butter melts. The sauce will become glossy at the end. Taste, and add a little sugar or honey if you like.

Cheese-topped baked bream

SERVES 4   401 CALS PER SERVING

2 x 560 g (1 lb 2 oz) black bream, filleted and skinned

grated zest and juice of ½ lemon

salt and black pepper

150 ml (¼ pint) water

butter for greasing

30 g (1 oz) mature Cheddar cheese, grated

lemon zest and parsley sprigs to garnish

WHITE SAUCE

30 g (1 oz) butter

1 tbsp plain flour

150 ml (¼ pint) milk

1 Cut the black bream fillets in half lengthways, and arrange them in a single layer in a large ovenproof dish.

2 Sprinkle the fish evenly with the grated lemon zest and season with salt and pepper. Pour the lemon juice and measured water over the fish fillets. Cover the dish with buttered greaseproof paper.

3 Bake in a preheated oven at 160°C (140°C fan, Gas 3) for about 20 minutes until the flesh flakes easily.

4 Transfer the bream to a warmed flameproof platter, cover, and keep hot. Strain the cooking liquid and reserve. Increase the oven temperature to 220°C (200°C fan, Gas 7).

5 Make the white sauce: melt the butter in a small saucepan, add the flour, and cook, stirring, for 1 minute. Remove from the heat, and gradually blend in the milk and the reserved cooking liquid. Bring to a boil, stirring constantly until the mixture thickens. Simmer for 2–3 minutes. Taste for seasoning.

6 Pour the white sauce over the fish, sprinkle with the cheese, and bake in the oven for 3–5 minutes until bubbling and golden. Serve hot, garnished with lemon zest and parsley sprigs.

Cajun-spiced red snapper

SERVES 4   258 CALS PER SERVING

4 x 150–175 g (5–6 oz) red snapper fillets

30 g (1 oz) butter

coriander butter (page 212) and watercress sprigs to serve

CAJUN SPICE MIXTURE

30 g (1 oz) plain flour

1 garlic clove, crushed

1 tbsp paprika

1 tsp ground cumin

1 tsp hot chilli powder

1 Make the Cajun spice mixture: combine the flour, garlic, paprika, cumin, and chilli powder.

2 Rub over the red snapper fillets, cover, and leave to marinate in the refrigerator for about 30 minutes.

3 Melt the butter in a large frying pan, add the fillets, and cook gently for 2–3 minutes on each side until the fish is opaque and the flesh flakes easily.

4 Top the fillets with pats of coriander butter, garnish with watercress, and serve hot.

Cook's know-how

You can buy ready mixed Cajun seasoning, but it tends to include dried garlic and onion salt, both of which overpower the spices in the mix. This simple version uses chilli powder, which is not just ground dried chillies as its name suggests, but a special fiery mixture of chilli with herbs and spices. Check the label before buying.

Black bream niçoise

🍴 SERVES 4   356 CALS PER SERVING

x 560 g (1 lb 2 oz) black bream, cleaned
page 106), with heads removed

lt and black pepper

tbsp olive oil

large onion, sliced

small fennel bulb, sliced

garlic clove, crushed

2 pitted black olives

tbsp chopped parsley

ice of 1 lemon

mon segments and parsley sprigs to garnish

Prepare the bream (see box, below).

Heat 2 tbsp of the oil in a frying pan, add
the onion, fennel, and garlic, and cook
ently, stirring occasionally, for 5–8 minutes
til the vegetables are soft but not coloured.

Spoon the vegetables into an ovenproof
dish, and place the bream on top Scatter
e olives and parsley over the fish, sprinkle
th the lemon juice, and drizzle with the
maining olive oil.

Cover the fish loosely with foil, and bake
in a preheated oven at 200°C (180°C
n, Gas 6) for 15 minutes.

Remove the foil and bake for 10 minutes
or until the fish is cooked. Garnish with
non segments and parsley sprigs before
ving.

Preparing the bream

lake 2 deep diagonal cuts in the flesh on
oth sides of each bream, using a sharp knife.
ut salt and pepper into a bowl and combine.
rinkle on the inside and outside of the bream.

Sea bass with lemon butter sauce

🍴 SERVES 4   363 CALS PER SERVING

sunflower oil for greasing

1.1 kg (2¼ lb) sea bass, cleaned and
filleted (page 106)

4 tarragon sprigs

1 lemon, sliced

salt and black pepper

2 tbsp dry white wine

LEMON BUTTER SAUCE

150 ml (¼ pint) single cream

juice of ½ lemon

45 g (1½ oz) butter, melted

1 egg yolk

1 tsp plain flour

white pepper

1 tsp chopped fresh tarragon

1 Put a large piece of foil on to a baking
tray and brush lightly with oil. Put the
sea bass on to the foil, tuck 3 of the
tarragon sprigs and all but 1–2 of the lemon
slices inside the cavity, and sprinkle with salt
and black pepper.

2 Season the outside of the fish, and lift
up the sides of the foil. Pour the wine
over the fish, then seal the foil into a loose
parcel. Bake in a preheated oven at 200°C
(180°C fan, Gas 6) for 30 minutes or until the
flesh is opaque and flakes easily.

3 Meanwhile, make the sauce: whisk the
cream in a pan with the lemon juice,
butter, egg yolk, and flour until mixed. Heat
very gently, stirring constantly, until the
mixture is thick enough to coat the back of
a spoon. Season with salt and white pepper,
and stir in the tarragon. Keep warm.

4 Remove the sea bass from the foil and
arrange on a warmed serving dish. Pour
over the cooking juices. Garnish with the
remaining lemon slices and tarragon sprig,
and serve at once. Serve the warm lemon
butter sauce separately.

Herb roasted salmon

 SERVES 4   396 CALS PER SERVING

4 x 150 g (5 oz) salmon tail fillets, skinned

salt and black pepper

a little vegetable oil

125 g (4 oz) low-fat garlic and herb soft cheese

TOPPING

30 g (1 oz) fresh white breadcrumbs

30 g (1 oz) mature Cheddar cheese, grated

2 tbsp chopped fresh flat-leaf parsley

finely grated zest of 1 lime

TO SERVE

lemon wedges

flat-leaf parsley sprigs

1 Season the salmon on both sides with salt and pepper. Place on lightly oiled foil on a baking sheet and spread with the soft cheese, not going quite to the edges.

2 Mix the topping ingredients together, adding seasoning to taste, then sprinkle over the salmon. (You can prepare ahead to this stage, cover the salmon, and keep it in the refrigerator for up to 12 hours.)

3 Cook in a preheated oven at 220°C (200°C fan, Gas 7) for 15 minutes or until the salmon is opaque and the flesh flakes easily. Garnish with lemon and parsley.

Thai chilli salmon

 SERVES 4   274 CALS PER SERVING

4 x 150–175 g (5–6 oz) middle-cut salmon fillets, skinned

MARINADE

2 tbsp fish sauce (nam pla)

finely grated zest and juice of 1 lime

1 large fresh red chilli, halved, seeded, and finely chopped

2.5 cm (1 in) piece of fresh root ginger, peeled and finely grated

a few fresh coriander stems, finely chopped

TO SERVE

fresh coriander leaves

1 lime, cut into wedges

1 Put the salmon fillets in a single layer in a shallow non-metallic dish, add the marinade ingredients and turn to coat. Cover and marinate in the refrigerator for 2–3 hours, turning the salmon once.

2 Lift the salmon from the marinade and cook under a preheated hot grill, 7.5 cm (3 in) away from the heat, for 5–6 minutes on each side until the salmon is opaque and the flesh flakes easily. Serve hot, with coriander and lime.

Griddled salmon tranches

 SERVES 4   367 CALS PER SERVING

a little olive oil

4 x 150–175 g (5–6 oz) middle-cut salmon fillets, skinned

salt and black pepper

SAUCE

200 ml (7 fl oz) low-fat crème fraîche

about 5 cm (2 in) cucumber, peeled, seeded, and finely diced

4 tbsp chopped fresh dill

pinch of caster sugar

1 tbsp capers

a good squeeze of lemon juice

1 Heat a griddle pan until piping hot, and lightly oil a sheet of foil on a baking sheet. Lightly oil and season the salmon.

2 Cook the salmon in the hot pan on one side only for 1½ minutes until golden underneath. Transfer, cooked side up, to the foil and finish cooking in a preheated oven at 190°C (170°C fan, Gas 5) for about 10 minutes or until the salmon is opaque and the flesh flakes easily. Leave to cool.

3 Mix the sauce ingredients in a bowl with salt and pepper to taste. Cover and refrigerate. When the salmon is cold, cover and refrigerate too – for up to 12 hours.

4 To serve, let the salmon come to room temperature and serve with the chilled sauce spooned alongside.

Warm honeyed salmon salad

 SERVES 4   455 CALS PER SERVING

4 x 150–175 g (5–6 oz) middle-cut salmon fillets, skinned

3 tbsp clear honey

1 tbsp olive oil

juice of 1 lemon

about 2 tbsp chopped fresh thyme

new potatoes, to serve

FOR THE SALAD

1 fennel bulb, thinly sliced

6 spring onions, thinly sliced

3 tbsp extra virgin olive oil

1 tbsp lemon juice

1 tbsp clear honey

4 tbsp Greek yogurt

salt and black pepper

1 Romaine lettuce, shredded

2 tbsp chopped parsley

2 tbsp snipped fresh chives

1 Make the salad. Mix the fennel and spring onions in a bowl with the olive oil, lemon juice, honey, yogurt and seasoning. Toss the lettuce in a separate large salad bowl with the chopped fresh herbs and seasoning. Cover both bowls and refrigerate for about 1 hour.

2 Cut each salmon fillet into four lengthways – they will look like flat sausages. Toss in the honey and season well. Heat the oil in a large non-stick frying pan and pan-fry the salmon over a high heat for 2–3 minutes on each side or until just opaque. Take care when turning the salmon as it breaks up quite easily. Add the lemon juice and thyme to the pan and heat until bubbling.

3 Toss the fennel salad through the lettuce, then spoon the honeyed salmon on top. Serve warm.

Opposite, clockwise from top: Griddled salmon tranches, Warm honeyed salmon salad, Herb roasted salmon, Thai chilli salmon

Halibut in filo parcels

Halibut is a very fine fish with a delicate flavour and firm texture. Enclosing the halibut steaks in filo parcels with matchstick-thin vegetables keeps the fish moist and seals in all the flavours, while the pastry trimmings on top provide an attractive, crunchy finish.

 SERVES 4   564 CALS PER SERVING

2 x 375 g (12 oz) halibut steaks, skinned and boned
1 carrot
1 leek, trimmed
150 ml (¼ pint) fish stock
2 tbsp dry white wine
2 tsp lemon juice
3 strands of saffron or ¼ tsp turmeric
salt and black pepper
8 large sheets of filo pastry
60 g (2 oz) butter, melted
lemon slices and dill sprigs to garnish

1 Cut the halibut steaks crossways so you have 4 equal-sized pieces. Cut the carrot and leek into matchstick-thin strips.

2 Put the vegetables into a pan with the stock, wine, lemon juice, and saffron.

3 Bring to a boil, and cook, uncovered, for 5 minutes or until the vegetables are just tender. Drain, and then season with salt and pepper.

4 Cut the filo pastry into eight 25 cm (10 in) squares, and reserve the trimmings. Brush 1 square with a little melted butter, put a second square on top, and brush with more melted butter. Make a filo parcel (see box, right). Repeat to make 4 filo parcels.

5 Place the filo parcels on a baking tray, and bake in a preheated oven at 200°C (180°C fan, Gas 6) for 20 minutes or until golden and crispy. Garnish with lemon slices and dill sprigs, and serve at once.

Salmon in filo parcels

Substitute skinned salmon fillets for the halibut, and 1 courgette and 4 spring onions, both cut into matchstick-thin strips, for the carrot and leek.

🔍 Cook's know-how

Sheets of filo pastry are usually sold in a roll, fresh or frozen. The size of the sheets may vary with different brands, so don't worry if they are slightly smaller than 25 cm (10 in) wide - just be sure there is sufficient pastry to cover the filling.

Making a filo parcel

Spoon one-quarter of the vegetable mixture into the middle of the pastry square. Put 1 piece of halibut on top of the vegetable mixture.

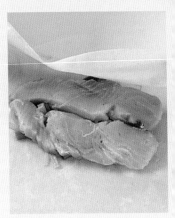

Fold 2 sides of the filo pastry over the halibut and vegetables, and tuck the remaining 2 ends underneath to form a neat parcel. Brush the top of the parcel with a little melted butter.

Crumple some of the reserved filo trimmings, and arrange them on top of the filo parcel. Brush with melted butter.

Spiced fish with coconut

SERVES 4   389 CALS PER SERVING

750 g (1½ lb) monkfish fillets, skinned

30 g (1 oz) plain flour

salt and black pepper

2 tbsp sunflower oil

1 onion, finely sliced

1 garlic clove, crushed

1 tsp ground coriander

1 tsp ground cumin

½ tsp turmeric

150 ml (¼ pint) canned coconut milk

1 x 400 g can chopped tomatoes

2 tbsp chopped fresh coriander

coriander sprigs to garnish

1 Cut the monkfish into 5 cm (2 in) pieces. Season the flour with salt and pepper. Lightly coat the monkfish with the flour.

2 Heat the oil in a large frying pan, add the onion, garlic, coriander, cumin, and turmeric, and cook gently, stirring from time to time, for 3 minutes or until the onion begins to soften.

3 Pour in the coconut milk and tomatoes, stir well, and bring to a boil. Simmer for about 5 minutes.

4 Add the monkfish, cover, and cook gently, stirring occasionally, for 10 minutes or until the fish is opaque and the flesh flakes easily. Add the chopped coriander, and taste for seasoning. Serve hot, garnished with coriander sprigs.

Cod steaks with anchovy and fennel

SERVES 4   429 CALS PER SERVING

1 x 60 g can anchovy fillets

30 g (1 oz) butter, plus extra for greasing

1 small onion, finely chopped

1 small fennel bulb, finely chopped

30 g (1 oz) parsley, chopped

125 g (4 oz) fresh white breadcrumbs

salt and black pepper

4 x 250 g (8 oz) cod steaks

dill sprigs, lemon wedges, and watercress sprigs to garnish

1 Drain the anchovy fillets, reserving the oil. Cut the anchovies into small pieces and set aside.

2 Melt the butter in a pan, add the onion and fennel, and cook over a medium heat, stirring, for 5 minutes or until soft but not browned. Remove from the heat, stir in the anchovies, parsley, and breadcrumbs. Season with salt and pepper.

3 Put the cod steaks into a buttered ovenproof dish and top each one with the anchovy and fennel mixture, pressing it down firmly with your hand.

4 Drizzle a little of the reserved anchovy oil over each steak. Bake the steaks in a preheated oven at 200°C (180°C fan, Gas 6) for 10–15 minutes until the cod is opaque and the flesh flakes easily from the bone.

5 Transfer to a warmed serving plate. Garnish the cod steaks with dill sprigs, lemon wedges, and watercress sprigs, and serve at once.

Cod steaks with sun-dried tomatoes

Omit the anchovies, fennel, parsley, and breadcrumbs. Chop 4 ripe but firm tomatoes. Drain 30 g (1 oz) sun-dried tomatoes in oil, and snip them into small pieces. Add both types of tomato to the softened onion in step 2, with 12 pitted and chopped black olives. Season with salt and pepper. Drizzle the cod steaks with 1 tbsp olive oil, top with the tomato mixture, and bake as in step 4.

Oriental fish parcels

SERVES 4   312 CALS PER SERVING

45 g (1½ oz) butter

4 x 250 g (8 oz) white fish fillets, such as sole or plaice, skinned

2 cm (¾ in) piece of fresh root ginger, peeled and thinly sliced

3 spring onions, thinly sliced

2–3 garlic cloves, crushed

2 tbsp dark soy sauce

1 tbsp rice wine or dry sherry

½ tsp sugar

non-stick baking parchment

1 Cut 8 sheets of baking parchment into oval shapes, each one measuring about 30 x 37 cm (12 x 15 in). Put the ovals together in pairs to make a double thickness.

2 Melt 30 g (1 oz) of the butter. Brush the butter over the top oval of each pair, and over 2 large baking trays.

3 Place a fish fillet on the buttered side of one of the oval pairs, positioning it on one side. Top with ginger, spring onions, and garlic, and dot with one-quarter of the remaining butter.

4 Whisk together the soy sauce, rice wine or sherry, and sugar, and drizzle one-quarter of this mixture over the fish. Fold the paper over the fish, and fold and pleat the edges together like a Cornish pasty to seal in the fish and juices. Repeat to make 4 parcels altogether.

5 Put the paper cases on to the prepared baking trays and bake the fish in a preheated oven at 230°C (210°C fan, Gas 8) for 8–10 minutes until the paper has turned brown and the cases have puffed up. Serve at once, on individual plates.

Golden fish cakes

SERVES 4   613 CALS PER SERVING

500 g (1 lb) potatoes, cut into chunks

salt and black pepper

500 g (1 lb) cod, haddock or salmon fillets (or a mixture of white fish and salmon)

300 ml (½ pint) milk

1 bay leaf

9 black peppercorns

60 g (2 oz) butter

4 tbsp chopped parsley

finely grated zest of 1 lemon

a dash of Tabasco (optional)

1 egg, beaten

175 g (6 oz) fresh breadcrumbs

sunflower oil for frying

tartare sauce (page 132) to serve

1 Cook the potatoes in boiling salted water for 15–20 minutes until tender.

2 Meanwhile, put the fish into a pan with the milk, bay leaf, and peppercorns. Bring slowly to a boil, and simmer for 10 minutes or until the fish is just opaque.

3 Drain the fish, reserving the liquid. Cool the fish, then flake the flesh, discarding the skin and bones.

4 Drain the potatoes, put them in a bowl, and mash with the butter and 3 tbsp of the fish cooking liquid. Add the fish, parsley, lemon zest, Tabasco if using, and salt and pepper to taste, and mix well.

5 Shape the mixture into 8 flat cakes, 7 cm (3 in) in diameter. Coat with beaten egg, then with breadcrumbs.

6 Heat a little oil in a frying pan and fry the fish cakes, a few at a time, for 5 minutes on each side or until golden. Serve hot, with the tartare sauce.

Crispy-topped seafood pie

SERVES 4   575 CALS PER SERVING

500 g (1 lb) cod fillet

300 ml (½ pint) milk

1 bay leaf

2 leeks, trimmed and sliced

175 g (6 oz) broccoli, cut into florets

175 g (6 oz) cooked peeled prawns

15 g (½ oz) butter

15 g (½ oz) plain flour

salt and black pepper

250 g (8 oz) ready-made shortcrust pastry, well chilled

30 g (1 oz) Gruyère cheese, grated

1 Put the cod into a saucepan with the milk and bay leaf, bring slowly to a boil, and poach gently for about 10 minutes until the fish flakes easily.

2 Meanwhile, blanch the leeks and broccoli for 3 minutes in a saucepan of boiling salted water. Drain.

3 Lift out the fish, remove and discard the skin and bones, and flake the fish. Strain and reserve the milk.

4 Put the blanched leeks and broccoli into a 2.4 litre (4 pint) pie dish, and add the cod and prawns.

5 Melt the butter in a small saucepan, add the flour, and cook, stirring, for 1 minute. Remove from the heat and gradually blend in the reserved milk. Bring to a boil, stirring constantly until thickened. Simmer for 2–3 minutes. Season to taste and pour over the pie filling.

6 Grate the pastry, and sprinkle over the sauce. Sprinkle with the grated cheese. Bake in a preheated oven at 200°C (180°C fan, Gas 6) for 25–30 minutes. Serve at once.

Poultry and Game

Under 45 minutes

Warm chicken salad with mango and avocado
Marinated chicken with mango and avocado, and rum-flavoured cooking juices.

SERVES 4   411 CALS PER SERVING

Takes 25 minutes   Page 175

Coronation chicken
Bite-sized pieces of chicken in a sauce made from spring onions, curry paste, wine, lemon, apricot jam, mayonnaise, and yogurt.

SERVES 6   580 CALS PER SERVING

Takes 15 minutes, **plus cooling**   Page 173

Chicken satay
Pieces of chicken, marinated in soy sauce, lemon juice, garlic, and spring onions. Serve with a peanut and coconut sauce.

SERVES 4   815 CALS PER SERVING

Takes 25 minutes, **plus marinating**   Page 1

Tex-Mex chicken
Chicken breasts marinated in oil, orange juice, and cumin, then grilled. Served with sliced avocado, and a tomato and lime salsa.

SERVES 4   659 CALS PER SERVING

Takes 30 minutes, **plus marinating**   Page 1

Saffron chicken
Chicken breasts marinated in saffron, ginger, lemon, cardamom, coriander, and cinnamon then roasted. Served with crème fraîche sauc

SERVES 6   527 CALS PER SERVING

Takes 40 minutes, **plus marinating**   Page 1

Lemon and herb drumsticks
Fresh and easy to make: chicken drumstick marinated in olive oil, lemon juice and zest onion, garlic, and parsley, then grilled.

MAKES 12   200 CALS EACH

Takes 25 minutes, **plus marinating**   Page 1

Greek chicken salad
Creamy and intensely flavoured with herbs pieces of cooked chicken coated in yogurt, crème fraîche, spring onions, and herbs.

SERVES 6   264 CALS PER SERVING

Takes 15 minutes   Page

Chicken tikka
Chicken marinated in yogurt, tomato purée garlic, tamarind paste, paprika, and ginger. Served with cucumber raita.

SERVES 4–6   266–177 CALS PER SERVING

Takes 20 minutes, **plus marinating**   Page

Turkey schnitzel
Turkey breast escalopes coated in seasoned flour, beaten egg, and fresh breadcrumbs, decorated with a criss-cross pattern.

SERVES 4   394 CALS PER SERVING

Takes 25 minutes, **plus chilling**   Page

Chicken with sage and orange
Fresh and tangy: chicken breasts marinated in orange juice, soy sauce, sage, and ginger. Served with a sage and orange sauce.

SERVES 6   435 CALS PER SERVING

Takes 40 minutes, **plus marinating**   Page 169

weet and sour Chinese chicken
ieces of chicken marinated in soy sauce and
ce wine. Stir-fried with peppers, celery,
nion, ketchup, pineapple, and lychees.
RVES 4–6   458–305 CALS PER SERVING
kes 30 minutes, **plus marinating**   Page 165

uck breasts with red wine sauce
ck marinated in garlic, balsamic, and
semary, then cooked, sliced, and served
a wine sauce.
VES 4   906 CALS PER SERVING
kes 40 minutes, **plus chilling**   Page 189

LOW FAT

key and lemon stir-fry
key breast strips marinated in white wine
l lemon zest and juice, stir-fried with
rgettes, green pepper, and baby sweetcorn.
ES 4   342 CALS PER SERVING
es 20 minutes, **plus marinating**   Page 179

45-60 minutes

Oriental poussins
Tangy and succulent: poussins brushed with
soy and hoisin sauces, sherry, garlic, and
ginger, and baked.
SERVES 4   395 CALS PER SERVING
Takes 50 minutes   Page 154

Chicken cordon bleu
Golden and tender: pounded chicken breasts
filled with ham and Gruyère cheese, and
folded. Coated with egg and breadcrumbs.
SERVES 4   602 CALS PER SERVING
Takes 45 minutes, **plus chilling**   Page 168

Turkey mole
Hot and spicy: turkey pieces cooked with
a blended sauce of tomatoes, almonds,
chocolate, chilli, cinnamon, and cloves.
SERVES 6   334 CALS PER SERVING
Takes 55 minutes   Page 180

Duck breasts with raspberry sauce
Rich and fruity: slices of grilled duck breast
served with a sauce of raspberries, port, and
orange juice.
SERVES 4   975 CALS PER SERVING
Takes 45 minutes   Page 188

Fragrant chicken curry with almonds
Chicken breasts cooked in an authentic blend of Indian spices,
including ground cinnamon, cardamom seeds, cloves, cumin
seeds, ginger, and garam masala, with a creamy yogurt sauce.
Served with a sprinkling of sultanas and toasted almonds.
SERVES 4   527 CALS PER SERVING
Takes 45 minutes   Page 162

Over 60 minutes

Chicken casserole
Popular wholesome meal: chicken quarters cooked with bacon, carrots, celery, onion, stock, bay leaf, thyme, and parsley.

SERVES 4   659 CALS PER SERVING

Takes 1¾ hours

Ballotine of chicken
Boned chicken pounded and stuffed with pork, liver, bacon, brandy, ham, and pistachio nuts. Rolled, cooked, chilled, and sliced.

SERVES 10   494 CALS PER SERVING

Takes 2¾ hours, **plus chilling**

Turkey salad with mango and grapes
Turkey breast poached with peppercorns, coated in lemon mayonnaise. Served with walnuts and fruits.

SERVES 4   734 CALS PER SERVING

Takes 1½ hours, **plus cooling**

TRADITIONAL

Braised rabbit with mushrooms and cider
Rabbit cooked with shallots, mushrooms, cider, herbs, and enriched with cream.

SERVES 4   506 CALS PER SERVING

Takes 2 hours

TRADITIONA

PREPARE AHEAD

Rather special game pie
A selection of meats marinated in port. Baked in a pastry case filled with jellied stock, then chilled.

SERVES 20   507 CALS PER SERVING

Takes 6 hours, **plus marinating**

Christmas roast goose
Succulent and fruity: goose stuffed with pork sausagemeat, sage, and apple, and roasted. Served with wine-flavoured gravy, enriched with goose stock, and baked apples with a stuffing of Calvados, ground cinnamon, ground allspice, and prunes.

SERVES 6–8   1228–921 CALS PER SERVING

Takes 5¼ hours, **plus cooling**

LOW FAT

oast turkey with garlic and tarragon
rkey joint marinated in lemon, tarragon,
yme, and garlic, roasted with the marinade.

RVES 4   296 CALS PER SERVING

kes 1³/4 hours, **plus marinating**   Page 178

FRENCH CLASSIC

Coq au vin
Rich and nourishing: chicken pieces cooked
with bacon, shallots, mushrooms, red wine,
stock, and a medley of fresh herbs.

SERVES 4   531 CALS PER SERVING

Takes 1¹/2 hours   Page 158

ITALIAN CLASSIC

Chicken cacciatore
Pieces of chicken sprinkled with thyme, and
cooked with bacon, onion, green pepper,
garlic, mushrooms, wine, tomatoes, and sage.

SERVES 4   540 CALS PER SERVING

Takes 1³/4 hours   Page 155

inea fowl Madeira
ces of guinea fowl cooked with shallots,
ck, wine, and Madeira, enriched with
ble cream and green grapes.

VES 6   613 CALS PER SERVING

es 1³/4 hours   Page 193

Roast duck with cranberries
Duck with a stuffing of onion, fresh brown
breadcrumbs, and cranberries, roasted until
crisp-skinned. Served with cranberry sauce.

SERVES 4   580 CALS PER SERVING

Takes 2¹/2 hours, **plus cooling**   Page 187

Mushroom-stuffed quail
Whole boned quail stuffed with shallots,
mushrooms, and breadcrumbs, and served
with a lime and crème fraîche sauce.

SERVES 6   651 CALS PER SERVING

Takes 1¹/4 hours   Page 190

ison casserole
n stew: cubes of venison marinated in
e, parsley, and allspice, and cooked with
ry, mushrooms, and carrots.

ES 6   466 CALS PER SERVING

es 2¹/4 hours, **plus marinating**   Page 196

ORIENTAL CLASSIC

Peking duck
Oriental speciality: whole duck brushed before
cooking with sherry, honey, and soy sauce.
Served with Chinese pancakes.

SERVES 6   848 CALS PER SERVING

Takes 2¹/2 hours   Page 186

Sunday roast chicken
Traditional English Sunday lunch: chicken
flavoured with parsley and thyme, and cooked
with an apple, lemon, and herb stuffing.

SERVES 4   534 CALS PER SERVING

Takes 2 hours, **plus cooling**   Page 152

Poultry and game know-how

Poultry is the term for all domesticated birds reared for the table – the most familiar being chicken, turkey, goose, and duck – but the classification "poultry" can also be applied to game birds that once lived in the wild and are now farmed, such as guinea fowl, pigeon, and quail. Pheasant and partridge are also often intensively reared, to be released into the so-called "wild" for the shooting season. Truly wild game birds taste quite different from their farmed or semi-wild counterparts; they are left to hang to enhance their "gamey" flavour and tenderize their flesh.

Buying and storing

There is a great variety of poultry available, produced by different farming methods. Free-range birds, which have been allowed access to the open air, cost more than intensively reared birds but they tend to have a superior flavour as they are slaughtered when they are older. Corn-fed chickens, which may or may not be free-range, are another option. Their diet does include maize (corn), but it is an artificial dye in their food that gives their flesh its yellow colour. The more expensive organically reared birds are not routinely given antibiotics nor artificial growth-promoting hormones in their feed.

Poultry can be bought fresh or frozen as whole birds – ranging in size from tiny quail and poussins to huge turkeys – as well as in pieces. Game birds are generally sold whole. Poultry and game birds should have a plump breast and moist, unblemished skin, and poultry should smell fresh and sweet, never "off".

All poultry and game birds are very perishable so they must be kept cool. As soon as you can, remove any tight plastic wrapping and giblets, then put the bird on a plate to collect any drips, cover it loosely, and store in the refrigerator. Check the use-by date – most poultry should be cooked within 2 days of purchase.

Types of birds

Poussins are small single-serving-size chickens; spring chickens or poulets are a little bigger. Roasters are the most widely available, either whole or in joints. The largest chickens are boiling fowl, which are old laying hens, and capons, which are neutered male birds. Turkey is sold whole as well as in escalopes, breast steaks, and large thigh, leg, or breast joints, boned or on the bone. Duck is sold whole and in legs or boneless breasts.

Other poultry (eg goose, guinea fowl, pigeon, and quail) and game birds (eg wild duck such as mallard, widgeon and teal, grouse, partridge, and pheasant) are sold whole, sometimes boned.

Freezing

Frozen poultry and game, particularly "fresh-frozen" (quickly air-cooled before freezing), is very good and a useful standby. When buying frozen poultry and game, check it is completely frozen and get it home as quickly as possible. Chicken, turkey, and wild game birds can be stored for up to 6 months; duck, goose, and guinea fowl for 4 months.

Poultry and game must be thoroughly thawed before cooking. This can take time – a 4.5 kg (10 lb) turkey needs 22–24 hours. Unwrap the bird, cover loosely with fresh wrapping, and set on a plate to thaw in the refrigerator. Remove any giblets as soon as possible. Raw poultry or game should never be re-frozen once thawed.

Microwaving

Casseroles and stews made with poultry and game can be cooked quite easily in the microwave oven. They are quick to prepare and the meat stays tender and juicy. You may choose to brown the poultry or game and any vegetables on the hob first, then transfer to a dish to finish cooking in the microwave. Be sure to transfer the flavoursome pan drippings to the microwave dish as well.

The microwave is also really good for reheating cooked poultry and game dishes, particularly when the meat is off the bone.

For roasting poultry and game, a conventional oven gives better results than the microwave.

Poultry or game stock

To make 2.5 litres (4 pints) stock, use 1.5 kg (3 lb) raw poultry or game pieces or bones, or the carcass and trimmings from a roast bird. Don't mix raw and cooked bones.

1 Crush or break up bones and carcasses. Put the bones (or pieces) into a stockpot or larg pan. Add 2 or 3 halved, unpeeled onions and cook until browned.

2 Add 4 litres (7 pints) water. Bring to a boil, skimming off any scum from the surface. Add 3 chopped carrots, 3 chopped celery stalks, 1 large bouquet garni, and a few black peppercorns.

3 Half cover the pan and simmer for 2½–3 ho Strain the stock into a bowl. Leave to cool, then remove the solidified fat from the surface and discard. Cover and keep in the refrigerate for up to 3 days, or freeze for 3 months. (You c keep raw or cooked bones in the freezer too, making stock at a later date.)

Giblet stock

Giblets are not often found in birds, but they make a really good stock.

Put the giblets (the neck, heart, and gizzard but not the liver) in a stockpot or large saucepan and cook until lightly browned. Stir in 1 litre (1¾ pints) water (or previously made stock). Bring to a boil, skimming off any scum that forms on the surface.

Add 1–2 quartered, unpeeled onions, 1 chopped celery stalk, 1 chopped carrot, a bouquet garni, and a few black peppercorns. Simmer for about 1 hour. Strain, then cool, cover, and keep in the refrigerator for up to 3 days, or freeze for 3 months.

Thorough cooking

Cook poultry thoroughly to kill any bacteria.

To test a whole roasted bird, lift it on a long fork – the juices that run out should be clear. For joints, insert a skewer into the thickest part of the meat and check the colour of the juices. Alternatively, use an instant-read thermometer: the thigh meat should register 75°C (170°F), breast 70°C (160°F).

Jellied stock

This stock is used in cold dishes such as Rather Special Game Pie (page 194), where it forms a jelly around the meat. Make it in the same way as other stocks, but use bones only, because they contain a high level of gelatine. Crack the bones before adding them to the pot. The stock will set when cool.

Stock know-how

If you do not have a carcass from a whole bird, chicken wings make a good base for a stock.

Peppercorns, instead of ground black pepper, are used in stock: prolonged cooking can turn ground black pepper bitter.

Skim off fat with a large spoon, soak it up with paper towels, or cool and lift it off.

Jointing a bird

Chicken portions are widely available, but cutting a bird into 4 or 8 serving pieces is not at all difficult to do yourself, and it can be done before or after cooking. A pair of special poultry shears makes the job particularly easy, otherwise use good, strong scissors or a sharp chef's knife.

1 Cut through to the joint between one of the legs and the body. Twist the leg out and away from the body to pop the ball and socket joint, then cut through the joint to remove the leg. Remove the other leg.

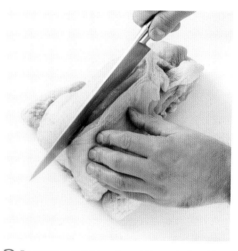

2 To remove the breasts, cut through the skin and flesh along both sides of the breastbone. Cut through the bones of the ribcage where it joins the sides of the breastbone, then remove the breastbone.

3 Turn over and cut along the backbone, to give 2 breasts with wings attached. For 8 pieces, cut each breast diagonally in two: the wing half should be slightly smaller. Cut each leg through the joint into thigh and drumstick.

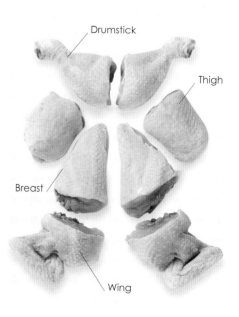

Drumstick

Thigh

Breast

Wing

Boning a whole chicken

Although boning a chicken requires a little time and effort, the result is impressive. Stuffed and rolled into a ballotine, it is ideal for entertaining because it is so easy to carve. Other birds can be boned in the same way.

Boning a quail

For a special occasion, tiny quail can be boned but left whole. It is then quite simple to fill them with a savoury stuffing and secure with a cocktail stick ready for roasting. Make sure you use a very small knife and be careful not to pierce the skin.

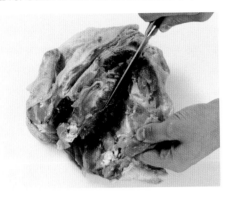

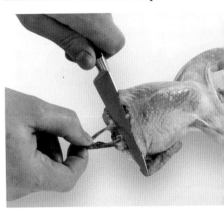

1 Set the bird breast-side down and slit the skin along the backbone. Remove the wishbone (see box, opposite). Slide the knife into the cut and gently pull and scrape the flesh away from the ribcage. Continue cutting away the flesh until you reach the leg and wing joints. Repeat on the other side.

2 Scrape away the flesh from the ribcage, working on one side at a time. Take care not to make any holes in the skin as you are doing this. Cut through the ball and socket joints connecting the legs to the carcass (they will still be attached to the skin).

1 With your fingers, carefully loosen the skin of the neck of the quail, and push it back to reveal the wishbone. With a small, sharp knife cut the flesh from around the wishbone and remove it.

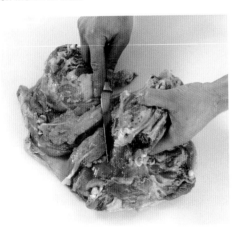

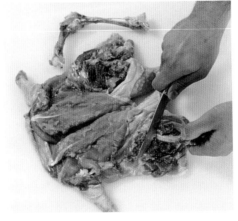

3 Keep cutting the flesh from the bone on both sides until you reach the ridge of the breastbone in the middle. Cut the breastbone free, without cutting through the skin, and lift it away with the carcass.

4 Cut through the tendons in the legs that join the flesh to the bone. Scrape back the flesh until the bones of each leg have been exposed, then pull out the bones, cutting them free of the skin.

2 Loosen 1 wing by carefully cutting through the tendon at the base. Repeat with the other wing.

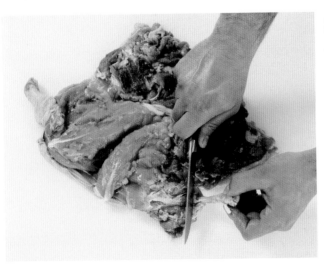

5 Bone the wings in the same way as the legs. Push the legs and wings skin-side out. The chicken is now ready for stuffing and rolling. Keep the carcass and bones for making chicken stock.

3 Insert the knife between the ribcage and the flesh and, working all around the bird, scrape the flesh from the bones, pushing it back as you go. Remove the ribcage. The bird is now ready to stuff.

patchcocking

is method of splitting and flattening a
rd makes it quicker to cook and suitable
r grilling or cooking over a barbecue.
ussins, chickens, guinea fowl, and game
rds can all be spatchcocked.

With poultry shears or a knife, cut along both
sides of the backbone and discard. Cut off
e wing tips and the ends of the legs. Remove
e wishbone.

Turn the bird over. Put your hands on top
of the breast and press down firmly with the
ls of your hands to break the breastbone
d flatten the bird.

hread a long metal skewer through the bird
t the neck end, passing through the wings.
d another skewer below the breast, passing
ugh the legs. If small birds are spatchcocked,
3 can be threaded on the same skewers.

Preparing poultry for roasting

Tying or skewering a bird before roasting holds it together so that it keeps a neat shape
during cooking. It will also prevent any stuffing from falling out. To be sure that heat can
penetrate into the centre of the bird and cook it thoroughly, it is best to put stuffing into
the neck end and not into the large body cavity.

Trussing with string

1 Thread a trussing needle with string. Put the
bird breast-side up. Push the legs back and
down. Insert the needle into a knee joint. Pass
through the bird and then out through the
other knee.

2 Pull the neck skin over the end of the bird and
tuck the wing tips over it. Push the needle
through both sections of one wing, through the
neck skin and beneath the backbone, and out
the other wing.

3 With the bird on its side, pull the string tightly,
tie the ends together, and trim. Tuck the tail
into the cavity and fold the top skin over it.

4 Push the needle through the top skin. Loop
the string around one of the drumsticks, under
the breastbone, and then around the other
drumstick. Pull the string tight and tie the ends.

Simple trussing

1 Put the bird breast-side up and push the legs
back and down. Holding the legs with one
hand, insert a skewer below the knee joint and
push it through the bird.

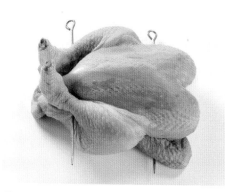

2 Turn the bird over. Pull the neck skin over
the end and tuck the wing tips over it. Push
a skewer through 1 wing, the neck skin, and out
through the other wing.

Removing the wishbone

A bird is easier to carve if the wishbone is
removed before cooking.

With your fingers, loosen the skin from the
flesh at the neck end. Fold back the skin to
expose the breastbone. Use a small, sharp
knife to cut the wishbone free, taking any
fat with it.

Roasting know-how

To calculate roasting time, weigh the bird after you have added any stuffing.

Cover large birds loosely with foil if the skin is becoming too browned.

Place fatty birds, such as duck and goose, on a rack, to allow the fat to drain away and keep the skin crisp.

Roasting times

These times are a guide only; always test a bird to make sure it is thoroughly cooked (page 147).

Bird	Oven temperature	Time
Poussin	190°C (170°C fan, Gas 5)	40-45 minutes total cooking, depending on size
Chicken	190°C (170°C fan, Gas 5)	20 minutes per 500 g (1 lb) plus 20 minutes
Duck	200°C (180°C fan, Gas 6)	25 minutes per 500 g (1 lb) for "just cooked"
Goose	180°C (160°C fan, Gas 4)	20 minutes per 500 g (1 lb) plus 20 minutes
Pheasant	200°C (180°C fan, Gas 6)	50 minutes total cooking
Turkey		
3.5-4.5 kg (7-9 lb)	190°C (170°C fan, Gas 5)	2½-3 hours total cooking
5-6 kg (10-12 lb)	190°C (170°C fan, Gas 5)	3½-4 hours total cooking
6.5-8.5 kg (13-17 lb)	190°C (170°C fan, Gas 5)	4½-5 hours total cooking

Carving ducks and geese

Once cooked, small ducks need simply to be cut into quarters or even halves for serving. Larger ducks and geese can be carved as for other poultry (right).

1 Remove trussing. Cut through the joints between legs and body to remove the legs. (Cook them further if necessary.) Cut off the wings in the same way.

2 Slit the skin along both sides of the breastbone. Slide the knife blade into the cut on one side to free the breast meat in a single piece. Repeat on the other side.

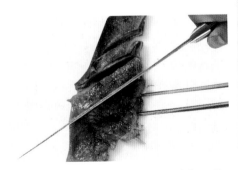

3 Carve the breast meat in diagonal slices. For a larger bird, carve the breast meat without removing it first, as for a chicken (right).

Carving poultry

After roasting, wrap bird in foil and leave to rest before carving - at least 15 minutes and up to 45 minutes for a large bird - to allow the juices to settle. Remove any trussing first.

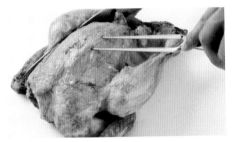

1 Put the bird breast-side up on a carving board (ideally one with a well to catch all the juices). Insert a carving fork into one breast to keep the bird steady, then cut into the joint between the far leg and body.

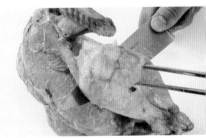

2 Turn the bird on its side and cut away the meat close to the backbone, cutting around the "oyster" meat on the back so that it remains attached to the thigh. Turn the bird over.

3 Twist the leg outwards to break the joint, then cut it to remove the leg. If preferred, divide into thigh and drumstick, cutting through the ball and socket joint. Remove the other leg.

4 Make a horizontal cut into the breast above the wing joint on one side, cutting all the way to the bone. Carve neat slices from the breast, holding the knife blade parallel to the ribcage. Repeat on the other side.

Roast chicken with orange and peppers

SERVES 4   411 CALS PER SERVING

oranges

few parsley sprigs

head of garlic, separated into cloves

7–2 kg (3½–4 lb) chicken

lt and black pepper

sp paprika

ch of cayenne pepper

g (½ oz) butter, softened

ed pepper, halved, seeded, and diced

ml (3 fl oz) orange juice

ml (2½ fl oz) brandy

opped fresh basil to garnish

Cut 2 of the oranges lengthways into quarters, leaving them unpeeled. Peel e remaining orange, and separate into gments, without the tough membranes.

Put the parsley, orange quarters, and half of the garlic cloves into the cavity the chicken.

Weigh the chicken, and calculate the roasting time at 20 minutes per 500 g b), plus an extra 20 minutes.

Rub the chicken with salt and pepper, and the paprika, cayenne, and butter. ce the chicken, breast-side down, in oasting tin. Add the red pepper and remaining garlic cloves.

Roast in a preheated oven at 190°C (170°C fan, Gas 5) for the calculated e, turning the chicken breast-side up fway through cooking.

Check that the chicken is done (page 147), then remove it from the tin with the pepper and garlic. Carve the chicken, d arrange on a warmed serving platter the red pepper and garlic. Keep hot.

poon off all but 1 tbsp fat from the oasting tin, leaving behind the cooking es. Add the orange juice and brandy boil on the hob until reduced. Add the nge segments and heat through.

poon the orange segments and sauce ver the chicken, sprinkle with the basil, serve at once.

Provençal-style roast chicken

SERVES 6   547 CALS PER SERVING

1 large onion, cut into wedges

2 large carrots, peeled and sliced

125 g (4 oz) whole button mushrooms

3 garlic cloves, peeled

250 ml (8 fl oz) dry white wine

375 ml (12 fl oz) chicken stock

1.7 kg (3½ lb) chicken, with any giblets removed

1 x 400 g can chopped tomatoes

1 tbsp tomato purée

salt and black pepper

chopped parsley to garnish

1 Arrange the onion wedges, carrot slices, whole mushrooms and garlic cloves in a single layer in a roasting tin, and pour over the wine and stock.

2 Place the chicken breast-side up on a small roasting rack, and place in the middle of the roasting tin on top of the vegetables. Roast in a preheated oven at 200°C (180°C fan, Gas 6) for 1½ hours or until the chicken is tender and done (page 147).

3 Remove the chicken from the tin, transfer to a large warmed serving dish, and keep warm.

4 Make the sauce: add the chopped tomatoes and tomato purée to the vegetables in the tin, stir well, and return to the oven for 5 minutes or until hot.

5 Carefully pour the contents of the tin into a food processor or blender, and purée until smooth. Season with salt and pepper.

6 Pour the sauce over the roast chicken, garnish with chopped parsley, and serve at once.

Sunday roast chicken

Traditional roast chicken is very much a family favourite at weekends. With its crisp skin, light, juicy stuffing of onion, apple, herbs, and lemon zest, and accompaniment of rich gravy, it is hard to beat.

 SERVES 4   **534 CALS PER SERVING**

a few parsley and thyme sprigs
1.7–2 kg (3½–4 lb) chicken
½ lemon, sliced
½ onion, sliced
60 g (2 oz) butter, softened
APPLE AND HERB STUFFING
30 g (1 oz) butter
1 small onion, finely chopped
1 cooking apple, peeled, cored, and grated
60 g (2 oz) fresh white breadcrumbs
1 small egg, beaten
1 tbsp chopped parsley
1 tbsp chopped fresh thyme
grated zest of 1 lemon
salt and black pepper
GRAVY
2 tsp plain flour
300 ml (½ pint) chicken stock or giblet stock (page 147)
splash of red wine or sherry and a spoonful of redcurrant jelly or cranberry sauce (optional)

1 Make the apple and herb stuffing: melt the butter in a saucepan, add the onion, and cook gently for a few minutes until softened. Remove from the heat, cool slightly, then stir in the apple, breadcrumbs, egg, parsley, thyme, and lemon zest. Season with salt and pepper, then leave until cold.

2 Put the parsley and thyme sprigs into the cavity of the chicken, add the lemon and onion, and season well with black pepper. Tie the legs together with string.

3 Spoon the stuffing into the neck end of the chicken, secure the skin flap over the stuffing with a small skewer, and pat into a rounded shape. Put any remaining stuffing into a baking dish.

4 Weigh the stuffed chicken, and calculate the roasting time at 20 minutes per 500 g (1 lb), plus an extra 20 minutes. Rub the butter over the breast, and season with salt and pepper.

5 Place the chicken, breast-side down, in a roasting tin. Roast in a preheated oven at 190°C (170°C fan, Gas 5) for the calculated time, turning the bird over when lightly browned and basting it every 20 minutes. Put any stuffing in the oven for the last 40 minutes.

6 Check that the chicken is done (page 1467), then transfer to a warmed serving platter, and cover with foil. Make the gravy (see box, right).

7 Carve the chicken (page 150). Remove the stuffing from the neck cavity and transfer to a serving dish with any other stuffing. Serve hot, with the gravy.

Making gravy

Tilt the roasting tin, and spoon off all but 1 tbsp of the fat that is on the surface, leaving behind the cooking juices and sediment. Put the roasting tin on the hob.

Add the flour, and cook over a medium heat for 1–2 minutes, stirring constantly with a whisk or metal spoon to dissolve any sediment from the bottom of the tin.

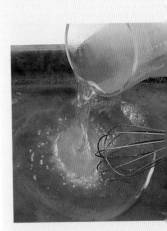

Pour in the stock, and bring to a boil, stirring. Simmer for 2 minutes, then add wine or sherry, redcurrant jelly or cranberry sauce, and salt and pepper to taste. Strain.

French roast chicken

Chicken roasted in the traditional French style is particularly moist and succulent because of the stock added to the roasting [tin]. In France, the chicken liver is often cooked in a little butter, then sliced and added to the gravy, but this is optional.

SERVES 4   **433 CALS PER SERVING**

small bunch of tarragon or rosemary

[9]0 g (3 oz) butter, softened, plus extra for greasing

[1.]7–2 kg (3½–4 lb) chicken

[sal]t and black pepper

[30]0 ml (½ pint) chicken stock or giblet stock [(p]age 147)

[4 h]eads of roast garlic (see box, below) to serve

[a] good splash of red or white wine

[1] Put the bunch of herbs and 30 g (1 oz) of the butter into the cavity of the [ch]icken. Tie the legs together with string. [W]eigh the chicken and calculate the [roa]sting time at 20 minutes per 500 g (1 lb), [pl]us an extra 20 minutes.

[2] Rub the remaining butter all over the chicken and sprinkle with salt and [pe]pper.

[3] Put the chicken, breast-side down, into a small roasting tin. Pour the stock [in]to the bottom of the tin, and cover the [chi]cken with buttered greaseproof paper [or f]oil. Roast in a preheated oven at 190°C [(17]0°C fan, Gas 5) for the calculated time. [At] regular intervals, baste the chicken and [tur]n it first on to one side, then on to the [oth]er, and finally on to its back.

[4] Check that the chicken is done (page [146]), then transfer to a warmed serving [pla]tter, and cover with foil.

[5] Leave the chicken to rest for about 15 minutes, then carve and serve with [the] cooking juices, boiled in the roasting tin [with] some red or white wine.

Roasting garlic

Cut the stalk ends off 4 heads of garlic, arrange in an oiled baking dish, and drizzle a little olive oil over the tops. Cook in a preheated oven at 190°C (170°C fan, Gas 5) for 45–60 minutes. To eat, squeeze the soft cloves of garlic from the papery skins.

Lemon poussins with artichoke hearts

SERVES 4   **555 CALS PER SERVING**

4 x 375 g (12 oz) poussins

salt and black pepper

4 garlic cloves

1 lemon, cut into quarters lengthwise

4 rosemary sprigs

60 g (2 oz) butter, softened

1 x 300 g jar artichoke hearts in oil

175 ml (6 fl oz) dry white wine

fresh rosemary and lemon wedges to garnish

1 Season the poussins inside and out, and put a garlic clove, lemon quarter, and rosemary sprig into each one. Tie the legs together with string, then rub the birds with the softened butter.

2 Put the poussins upside down on a rack in a roasting tin. Roast in a preheated oven at 190°C (170°C fan, Gas 5) for 40–45 minutes, turning them the right way up halfway through.

3 While the poussins are roasting, drain the artichoke hearts, reserving 2–3 tbsp of the oil, and cut each artichoke heart in half.

4 Check the poussins are done by pricking with a fork – the juices should run clear, not pink or red. Remove them from the tin, and keep warm. Spoon off all but 1 tbsp fat from the tin, leaving behind the cooking juices.

5 Add the wine to the tin, mix with the juices, then boil on the hob until reduced to about 90 ml (3 fl oz).

6 Stir in the artichokes and the reserved oil, and heat through gently. Serve the poussins with the artichokes and sauce, garnished with rosemary and lemon wedges.

Poussins with romesco sauce

SERVES 2   **845 CALS PER SERVING**

2 x 375 g (12 oz) poussins, spatchcocked (page 149)

8 spring onions, trimmed (optional)

coriander sprigs to garnish

MARINADE

2 tbsp olive oil

1 tbsp balsamic vinegar

4 garlic cloves, crushed

½ tsp ground cinnamon

salt and black pepper

ROMESCO SAUCE

1 x 225 g can chopped tomatoes

90 g (3 oz) blanched almonds

1 slice of stale bread, broken into pieces

2 tbsp olive oil

1 tbsp balsamic vinegar

1 garlic clove

1 small dried red chilli, crumbled

a few parsley sprigs

½ tsp ground cinnamon

1 Make the marinade: combine the oil, vinegar, garlic, and cinnamon, and season with salt and pepper. Brush over the poussins and spring onions (if using), cover, and marinate in the refrigerator for 1 hour, or overnight.

2 Place the poussins skin-side down under a hot grill, 15 cm (6 in) from the heat, and grill for 15–20 minutes on each side. Grill the spring onions, if using, close to the heat for 5–8 minutes on each side until the onions are slightly charred.

3 Meanwhile, make the romesco sauce: put all the ingredients in a food processor with a pinch of salt and purée until smooth.

4 Check the poussins are done by pricking with a fork – the juices should run clear, not pink or red. Serve hot, with the romesco sauce and the spring onions (if used). Garnish each serving with a coriander sprig.

Moroccan poussins

SERVES 2   467 CALS PER SERVING

2 x 375 g (12 oz) poussins, spatchcocked
(page 149)

MARINADE

3 tbsp olive oil

grated zest of 1 lime and juice of 2 limes

1 small onion, finely chopped

2–3 garlic cloves, crushed

2 tbsp chopped fresh coriander

1 tbsp paprika

2 tsp curry powder

pinch of cayenne pepper

salt

1 Mix all the marinade ingredients, except the salt, in a non-metallic dish. Turn the poussins in the marinade, cover, and marinate in the refrigerator for at least 3 hours (or overnight), turning occasionally.

2 When ready to cook, preheat the grill to hot, and sprinkle the poussins with a little salt.

3 Put the poussins, skin-side down, on a rack under the grill, 15 cm (6 in) from the heat, and grill for 15–20 minutes on each side, turning once and brushing with the marinade. Check the poussins are done by pricking with a fork – the juices should run clear, not pink or red. Serve hot or cold.

Oriental poussins

SERVES 4   395 CALS PER SERVING

2 x 625 g (1¼ lb) poussins

4 tbsp dark soy sauce

3 tbsp dry sherry

3 tbsp hoisin sauce

3 tbsp sunflower oil

3 garlic cloves, crushed

2 tbsp brown sugar

1 tsp five-spice powder

2.5 cm (1 in) piece of fresh root ginger,
peeled and grated

spring onions to garnish

1 Halve the poussins, and remove the backbones (see box, below).

2 Combine the soy sauce, sherry, hoisin sauce, oil, garlic, sugar, five-spice powder, and ginger. Brush this mixture on both sides of the poussins.

3 Put the poussins, skin-side up, into a roasting tin, and roast in a preheated oven at 190°C (170°C fan, Gas 5) for 30 minutes. Check the poussins are done by pricking with a fork – the juices should run clear, not pink or red.

4 With a sharp knife, finely shred the green tops of the spring onions, working on the diagonal. Serve the poussins hot, garnished with the spring onion slices.

Halving a poussin

Cut along the middle of the breast with poultry shears or sturdy kitchen scissors. Take the 2 sides and open out slightly.

Turn the poussin over and cut in half, along one side of the backbone. Remove and discard the backbone.

🔍 Cook's know-how

It is quick and easy to spatchcock poussins, but you can buy them ready spatchcocked at most supermarkets, especially during the barbecue season.

Herb grilled chicken

SERVES 8   297 CALS PER SERVING

chicken portions (legs or breasts)

HERB BUTTER

g (3 oz) butter, softened

tbsp chopped parsley

tbsp snipped fresh chives

garlic cloves, crushed (optional)

lt and black pepper

Mix the butter with the parsley, chives, and garlic, if using, and a good pinch ach of salt and pepper.

Spread the chicken with the butter, and put, skin-side down over a hot barbecue, skin-side up under a hot grill, 10 cm (4 in) om the heat. Cook for 10 minutes on each de or until the juices run clear when the icken is pierced.

ot paprika chicken

bstitute 2 tsp paprika and 2 tsp mustard wder for the parsley and chives.

maican chicken

bstitute ½ tsp crushed peppercorns (red, een, and black), 1 tsp chopped fresh thyme, d 3 chopped spring onions for the parsley d chives.

ai coriander chicken

bstitute 1–2 tbsp chopped fresh coriander d 2 tbsp Thai green curry paste for the rsley and chives.

Healthy note

utter makes the chicken luscious and golden own, but it is high in saturated fat and lories. You can reduce this by using half the nount of butter or 2 tbsp olive oil. Skinning e chicken before cooking is another option.

Chicken cacciatore

SERVES 4   540 CALS PER SERVING

8 small chicken portions (4 legs and 4 breasts or 8 thighs)

plain flour for dusting

salt and black pepper

3–4 tbsp olive oil

90 g (3 oz) streaky bacon or pancetta, cut into strips

1 large onion, chopped

1 small green pepper, halved, seeded, and diced

2 garlic cloves, crushed

250 g (8 oz) mushrooms, quartered

125 ml (4 fl oz) red or white wine

1 x 400 g can chopped tomatoes

75 ml (2½ fl oz) tomato purée

2 tsp chopped fresh sage

4 tbsp chopped parsley

grated zest of 1 lemon

2 tbsp capers, chopped

fresh sage leaves to garnish

1 Lightly dust the chicken pieces with flour seasoned with salt and pepper, and shake off any excess.

2 Heat half of the oil in a large frying pan, add the bacon or pancetta and chicken, and cook for 10–12 minutes until browned all over. Transfer to a casserole with a slotted spoon, then pour off the fat from the frying pan.

3 Heat the remaining oil in the frying pan, add the onion, green pepper, and half of the garlic, and cook gently, stirring, for 5 minutes until soft but not coloured. Transfer to the casserole with a slotted spoon. Add the mushrooms, and cook for 2 minutes. Add to the casserole.

4 Pour the wine into the frying pan, and boil until reduced to about 4 tbsp. Add to the casserole with the tomatoes, tomato purée, and the sage. Cover and cook in a preheated oven at 180°C (160°C fan, Gas 4) for 45 minutes or until the chicken is tender when pierced with a fork.

5 Combine the remaining garlic with the chopped parsley, lemon zest, and capers. Stir into the casserole, and taste for seasoning. Serve hot, garnished with sage leaves.

Filling, covering, and decorating the pie

Invert the pie dish on to the pastry, and use a small knife to cut around the edge, keeping the blade close to the dish. Reserve all trimmings. Transfer the cold filling to the pie dish, and top with the pastry.

Press the pastry with your fingertips on to the rim of the pie dish. Crimp the edge of the pastry with a fork. Brush the pastry with the beaten egg yolk, making a lattice pattern.

Cut decorative shapes from the reserved pastry trimmings with a pastry cutter. Arrange on top of the pie, and glaze the shapes with the beaten egg yolk.

Chicken pot pie

This recipe makes a great family dish, packed with tender chicken and colourful vegetables. You can vary the vegetables according to season and availability. The pie will be a great success any time of the year.

SERVES 6   508 CALS PER SERVING

1 kg (2 lb) chicken

1.25 litres (2 pints) chicken stock

1 onion, quartered

1 celery stalk, thickly sliced

pared zest and juice of 1 lemon

2 carrots

2 waxy potatoes, peeled and cut into quarters

45 g (1½ oz) butter

45 g (1½ oz) plain flour, plus extra for dusting

salt and black pepper

125 g (4 oz) frozen peas

175 g (6 oz) shortcrust pastry

beaten egg yolk for glazing

2 litre (3½ pint) pie dish

1 Put the chicken, stock, onion, celery, and lemon zest into a large saucepan. Bring to a boil, cover, and simmer for 30 minutes.

2 Add the carrots and potatoes, cover, and simmer for about 20 minutes or until the vegetables are cooked and the chicken is just tender. Remove the vegetables from the liquid and set aside. Leave the chicken to cool in the liquid.

3 Remove the meat from the chicken, and cut into bite-sized pieces, discarding the skin and bones. Dice the vegetables.

4 Skim the fat from the cooking liquid, then bring 600 ml (1 pint) to a boil. Melt the butter in another pan, add the flour, and cook, stirring occasionally, for 1 minute. Stir in the hot stock, whisking until it comes to a boil and thickens. Add the lemon juice and season with salt and pepper.

5 Stir the chicken, diced vegetables, and peas into the sauce, then leave to cool.

6 On a lightly floured work surface, roll out the pastry, then cut out the lid, and fill, cover, and decorate the pie (see box, left).

7 Bake in a preheated oven at 190°C (170°C fan, Gas 5) for 30 minutes or until the top is crisp and golden brown. Serve hot.

Chicken casserole

SERVES 4   659 CALS PER SERVING

2 tbsp sunflower oil

4 chicken portions (legs or thighs)

125 g (4 oz) streaky bacon rashers, cut into strips

250 g (8 oz) carrots, thickly sliced

2 celery stalks, thickly sliced

1 large onion, sliced

30 g (1 oz) plain flour

600 ml (1 pint) chicken stock

1 bouquet garni

salt and black pepper

4 potatoes, peeled and cut into large chunks

chopped parsley to garnish

1 Heat the oil in a large flameproof casserole. Add the chicken, skin-side down, and cook for 10–12 minutes until browned all over. Lift out and drain on paper towels. Add the bacon, carrots, celery, and onion, and cook over a high heat, stirring, until golden. Lift out with a slotted spoon, and drain on paper towels.

2 Spoon off all but 1 tbsp fat from the casserole. Add the flour, and cook, stirring constantly, for 3–5 minutes until lightly browned. Gradually pour in the chicken stock, stirring until smooth. Add the bouquet garni, and season with salt and pepper.

3 Return the chicken, bacon, carrots, celery, and onion to the casserole, add the potato and bring to a boil. Cover and cook in a preheated oven at 160°C (140°C fan, Gas 3) for 1–1¼ hours or until the chicken is tender when pierced with a fork. Serve hot, garnished with parsley.

Italian chicken casserole

Substitute 250 g (8 oz) sliced courgettes for the carrots, and 1 x 400 g can chopped tomatoes and 1 tbsp tomato purée for the chicken stock. If the mixture is too thick, add a splash of water, chicken stock, or wine.

Opposite: Chicken casserole

Coq au vin

🍴 **SERVES 4**　　**531 CALS PER SERVING**

30 g (1 oz) butter

1 tbsp sunflower oil

1.5 kg (3 lb) chicken, cut into 8 serving pieces (page 147)

125 g (4 oz) streaky bacon rashers, cut into strips

8 small shallots or pickling onions

250 g (8 oz) button mushrooms

30 g (1 oz) plain flour

300 ml (½ pint) chicken stock

600 ml (1 pint) red wine

1 bouquet garni

1 large garlic clove, crushed

salt and black pepper

2 tbsp chopped parsley to garnish

1 Melt the butter with the oil in a large flameproof casserole. Add the chicken, and cook for 10–12 minutes until browned all over. Lift out and leave to drain on paper towels.

2 Spoon off any excess fat, then add the bacon, shallots or onions, and mushrooms, and cook over a high heat, stirring, until golden brown.

3 Lift the mixture out of the pan with a slotted spoon and leave to drain thoroughly on paper towels.

4 Add the flour to the pan, and cook for 3–5 minutes, stirring constantly until lightly browned. Reduce the wine in a separate pan until it reduces to 300 ml (½ pint). Gradually pour in the stock, then the wine, stirring until smooth.

5 Return the chicken, bacon, shallots or onions, and mushrooms to the casserole,

and add the bouquet garni, and garlic. Season with salt and pepper. Bring to a boil, cover, and cook in a preheated oven at 180°C (160°C fan, Gas 4) for 45 minutes or until the chicken is tender when pierced with a fork.

6 Sprinkle the chicken with the chopped parsley, and serve hot.

💛 **Healthy note**

To reduce the fat content of this classic dish, skin the chicken before cooking, use 2 tbsp oil and no butter, and half the amount of bacon (or omit it altogether).

Chicken Marengo

SERVES 4   479 CALS PER SERVING

0 g (1 oz) butter

tbsp sunflower oil

.5 kg (3 lb) chicken, cut into 8 serving pieces
page 147)

small shallots or pickling onions

0 g (1 oz) plain flour

00 ml (½ pint) dry white wine

50 ml (¼ pint) chicken stock

x 400 g can chopped tomatoes

50 g (8 oz) button mushrooms

tbsp tomato purée

garlic cloves, crushed

bouquet garni

lt and black pepper

50 g (8 oz) cooked peeled prawns

hopped parsley to garnish

Melt the butter with the oil in a large
flameproof casserole. Add the chicken
eces, and cook for 10–12 minutes until
owned all over. Lift out and leave to
ain on paper towels.

Add the shallots or onions, and cook
over a high heat for about 8 minutes
until golden brown.

Lift out the shallots or onions and leave
to drain on paper towels. Spoon off
but 1 tbsp of the fat from the casserole,
d the flour, and cook, stirring, for 3–5
nutes until lightly browned.

Lower the heat and stir in the wine, and
stock until combined. Add the tomatoes,
ushrooms, tomato purée, garlic, and
uquet garni. Season with salt and pepper.

Return the shallots or onions and the
chicken to the casserole, and bring to
oil. Cover and cook in a preheated
en at 180°C (160°C fan, Gas 4) for 35
nutes or until the chicken is almost tender.
in the prawns, and return to the oven
another 10 minutes or until the chicken
ender when pierced with a fork. Garnish
ch serving with chopped parsley before
ving.

Tex-mex chicken

SERVES 4   659 CALS PER SERVING

4 skinless, boneless chicken breasts

2 avocados

2 tbsp lime juice

1 red onion, finely chopped

MARINADE

4 tbsp olive oil

4 tbsp orange juice

1 tsp ground cumin

SALSA

500 g (1 lb) tomatoes, chopped

1 small red onion, finely chopped

3 tbsp olive oil

2 tbsp lime juice

3 tbsp chopped fresh coriander

2 garlic cloves, crushed

1 fresh green chilli, halved, seeded, and chopped

salt

1 Make several diagonal slashes in each
chicken breast, then put the chicken
in a non-metallic dish. Mix the marinade
ingredients together, and pour over the
chicken. Cover and marinate in the
refrigerator for at least 30 minutes, or
overnight.

2 Make the salsa: combine the tomatoes,
onion, oil, lime juice, coriander, garlic,
chilli, and salt to taste. Cover and chill until
ready to serve.

3 Remove the chicken from the marinade,
and put under a hot grill, 10 cm (4 in)
from the heat. Grill for 3–5 minutes on each
side, depending on the size of the chicken,
until the juices run clear when the chicken is
pierced.

4 Meanwhile, halve, stone (page 327),
and peel the avocados. Slice
lengthways, and brush with lime juice.

5 Thinly slice the chicken breasts, following
the slashes made before marinating.
Arrange the avocado and chicken slices on
plates, and sprinkle the chopped red onion
around the edges. Spoon a little of the salsa
into the middle of each serving, and hand
the remainder separately.

Jerk chicken

SERVES 4   304 CALS PER SERVING

4 chicken legs or drumsticks

JERK PASTE

3 tbsp lime juice

2 tbsp dark rum

2 tbsp sunflower oil

4 spring onions, roughly chopped

1–2 fresh green chillies, halved, seeded, and
roughly chopped

2 garlic cloves, roughly chopped

1 tbsp ground allspice

2 tsp fresh thyme leaves

salt and black pepper

TO SERVE

chopped fresh thyme

grilled pineapple rings (optional)

1 Make the jerk paste: purée the ingredients
in a food processor with a pinch each of
salt and pepper.

2 Put the chicken pieces in a non-metallic
dish and brush them all over with the jerk
paste. Cover and marinate in the refrigerator
for at least 30 minutes, or overnight.

3 Put the chicken over a hot barbecue,
or under a hot grill, 10 cm (4 in) from
the heat. Cook for 10 minutes on each
side or until the juices run clear when the
chicken is pierced.

4 Serve the chicken hot or cold, sprinkled
with thyme, and accompanied by
grilled pineapple rings, if you like.

Garlic is an essential ingredient in classic Jerk
paste and you can use as many as 6–8 cloves if
you like. The purple-skinned varieties have the
best flavour.

Tarragon chicken with avocado

🍴 SERVES 6   382 CALS PER SERVING

500 g (1 lb) skinless, boneless cooked chicken

3 spring onions, finely sliced

SAUCE

5 tbsp sunflower oil

3 tbsp white wine vinegar

2 tsp Dijon mustard

2–3 tsp caster sugar, to taste

2 canned anchovy fillets, finely chopped

200 ml (7 fl oz) half-fat crème fraîche

1 tbsp chopped fresh tarragon

1 tbsp chopped parsley

salt and black pepper

TO SERVE

2 perfectly ripe avocados

juice of ½ lemon

1 bunch of watercress

2 spring onions, trimmed and cut lengthways into fine slices

1 Cut the chicken into bite-sized pieces and mix with the spring onions in a bowl. Whisk all the sauce ingredients together in another bowl, adding salt and pepper to taste. Mix the sauce with the chicken, cover, and marinate in the refrigerator for at least 2 hours, overnight if possible.

2 Just before serving, halve, stone, and peel the avocados, slice the flesh into 1 cm (½ in) strips, and toss in the lemon juice. The lemon juice stops it from discolouring. Gently mix the avocado into the salad, and spoon into a serving dish. Garnish with watercress and spring onions, and serve.

Vietnamese turkey salad

🍴 SERVES 4   199 CALS PER SERVING

4 tbsp fish sauce (nam pla)

500 g (1 lb) turkey breast steaks

4 tbsp lime juice

1 tbsp sugar, or more to taste

¼ tsp ground black pepper

1 small fresh red chilli, halved, seeded, and finely chopped

250 g (8 oz) hard white cabbage, finely shredded

2 medium carrots, finely shredded

1 small onion, finely sliced

1 large bunch of fresh mint

1 Half fill a medium wok or deep frying pan with water, sprinkle in half the fish sauce and bring to a boil. Turn the heat down to a simmer, lower in the turkey breast steaks, and cover the pan with a lid. Simmer for 10 minutes or until the turkey is cooked through. Lift the turkey out of the water, and leave until cool enough to handle.

2 Meanwhile, mix the remaining fish sauce in a large bowl with the lime juice, 1 tbsp sugar, the black pepper and chilli. Add the cabbage, carrots, and onion, and mix well.

3 Cut the turkey into bite-sized strips and roughly chop 2 tbsp mint. Toss the turkey and chopped mint into the salad, and mix again. Cover and marinate in the refrigerator for 2–4 hours.

4 To serve, toss the salad again, then taste for seasoning and add more sugar if you like. Serve on a bed of the remaining mint leaves.

Red pepper herbed chicken salad

🍴 SERVES 6   224 CALS PER SERVING

500 g (1 lb) skinless, boneless cooked chicken

SAUCE

1 bunch of fresh parsley

1 bunch of fresh basil

60 g (2 oz) red pepper in oil or brine (from a jar), drained

juice of 1 small lemon

2 tsp caster sugar, plus extra to taste

90 g (3 oz) low-fat Greek yogurt

4 tbsp low-fat mayonnaise

90 g (3 oz) half-fat soft cheese

salt and black pepper

TO SERVE

fresh basil

strips of red pepper

tossed salad leaves

1 Make the sauce. Put the parsley, basil, red pepper, lemon juice, and 2 tsp sugar in a food processor and pulse for about 30 seconds until quite coarsely chopped. Add the yogurt, mayonnaise, soft cheese, and seasoning and pulse again for about 30 seconds. The sauce should be mixed but not finely chopped – it should have texture and flecks of herbs. Taste and add more sugar and seasoning if you like. (If you haven't got a food processor, coarsely chop the parsley, basil, and red pepper. Mix the other ingredients together, then mix in the chopped herbs and red pepper.)

2 Cut the chicken into strips, mix into the sauce, and turn into a shallow serving dish. Cover and leave in the refrigerator for at least 4 hours, or overnight, for the flavour to infuse.

3 Before serving, check the seasoning, and garnish with basil and strips of red pepper. Serve on a bed of tossed salad.

Avocado adds a nutty flavour to salads, and its creamy flesh is rich in nutrients.

Opposite, clockwise from top: Tarragon chicken with avocado, Red pepper herbed chicken salad, Vietnamese turkey salad

Almonds

Blanch the almonds and loosen the skins: immerse in a bowl of boiling water. When cool enough to handle, squeeze the almonds between your fingers to slide and pull off the skins.

Slice the almonds in half lengthways. Cut the halves into shreds.

Place the shredded almonds on a baking tray, and toast in a preheated oven at 180°C (160°C fan, Gas 4), stirring the almonds occasionally to ensure that they colour evenly, for 8–10 minutes until lightly browned.

Fragrant chicken curry with almonds

The spices in this recipe are among those used in ready-made curry powders, but using your own individual blend of spices gives a truly authentic flavour to a curry. This is a creamy, mild dish – not too hot or spicy.

 SERVES 4   **527 CALS PER SERVING**

2 cloves

2 tsp cumin seeds

seeds of 4 cardamom pods

1 tsp garam masala

pinch of cayenne pepper

2 tbsp sunflower oil

4 skinless, boneless chicken breasts

1 large onion, finely chopped

2 garlic cloves, crushed

2.5 cm (1 in) piece of fresh root ginger, peeled and finely grated

salt and black pepper

300 ml (½ pint) chicken stock

150 ml (¼ pint) single cream

1 x 150 g carton full-fat yogurt

sultanas and whole almonds, blanched, shredded, and toasted (see box, right) to garnish

1 Crush the cloves in a mortar and pestle with the cumin and cardamom seeds. Mix in the garam masala and cayenne.

2 Heat the oil in a flameproof casserole. Add the chicken breasts, and cook for 2–3 minutes on each side until golden. Remove with a slotted spoon and leave to drain on paper towels.

3 Add the onion, garlic, and ginger to the pan, and cook gently, stirring occasionally, for a few minutes until just beginning to soften. Add the spice mixture, and season with salt and pepper, then stir over a high heat for 1 minute.

4 Return the chicken to the casserole. Pour in the stock, and bring to a boil. Cover and simmer gently for 15 minutes or until the chicken is tender.

5 Stir in the cream and yogurt, heat through very gently, then taste for seasoning.

6 Spoon the curry into a serving dish, and sprinkle with the sultanas and toasted shredded almonds. Serve hot.

Saffron chicken

SERVES 6   **527 CALS PER SERVING**

boneless chicken breasts, with the skin left on

tbsp vegetable oil

00 ml (7 fl oz) full-fat crème fraîche

lt and black pepper

hopped coriander to garnish

MARINADE

pinches of saffron threads

5 cm (1 in) piece of fresh root ginger, peeled nd grated

ice of 1 lemon

tsp ground cardamom

tsp ground coriander

tsp ground cinnamon

Make the marinade: put the saffron and the ginger into a mortar and grind with pestle. Add the lemon juice, cardamom, oriander, and cinnamon, and mix well.

Put the chicken into a non-metallic dish, and brush the marinade over it. Cover nd marinate in the refrigerator for at least minutes.

Pour the oil into a small roasting tin. Turn the chicken breasts in the oil, and put em, skin-side up, in the roasting tin. Cook a preheated oven at 190°C (170°C fan, as 5) for 15–20 minutes or until the juices clear when the chicken is pierced with ork. Remove from the tin and keep warm.

Put the tin on the hob, pour in the crème fraîche, and stir to combine with the es. Season with salt and pepper, and at through.

Divide the sauce among 6 warmed plates. Place the chicken breasts on , and sprinkle with chopped coriander ore serving.

Thai chicken with water chestnuts

SERVES 4   **272 CALS PER SERVING**

4 skinless, boneless chicken breasts, cut into 2.5 cm (1 in) pieces

3 tbsp sunflower oil

2 garlic cloves, crushed

2.5 cm (1 in) piece of fresh root ginger, peeled and grated

½–1 fresh green chilli, halved, seeded, and chopped

1 tsp light soy sauce, or more to taste

½ tsp sugar

salt and black pepper

600 ml (1 pint) chicken stock

1 stem of lemon grass, bruised

grated zest of 1 lime

1 x 200 g can water chestnuts, drained, rinsed, and sliced

1 small bunch of fresh coriander, coarsely chopped

lime wedges, sliced spring onions, and peanuts to garnish

1 Put the chicken into a dish, and add the oil, garlic, ginger, chilli, soy sauce, and sugar. Season with black pepper, stir well, then leave to stand for a few minutes.

2 Heat a non-stick wok or frying pan, add the chicken mixture, in batches if necessary, and stir-fry for 2–3 minutes or until lightly browned.

3 Pour in the stock, add any marinade left in the dish, then add the lemon grass, lime zest, water chestnuts, and coriander. Continue stir-frying for a few minutes more until the chicken is tender.

4 Taste the stir-fry and add more soy sauce, if you like. Serve at once, garnished with lime wedges, spring onion slices, and peanuts.

Chicken tikka

SERVES 4–6   **266–177 CALS PER SERVING**

750 g (1½ lb) skinless, boneless chicken breasts, cut into 2.5 cm (1 in) cubes

cucumber raita (see box, below) to serve

MARINADE

2 tbsp full-fat yogurt

2 tbsp tomato purée

1 small onion, finely chopped

2.5 cm (1 in) piece of fresh root ginger, peeled and grated

3 garlic cloves, crushed

1 tbsp tamarind paste (optional)

1 tbsp paprika

1 tsp ground cumin

large pinch of cayenne pepper

4–6 metal skewers

1 Make the marinade: in a large bowl, combine the yogurt, tomato purée, onion, ginger, garlic, tamarind paste (if using), paprika, cumin, and cayenne pepper.

2 Toss the chicken in the marinade. Cover and marinate in the refrigerator for at least 2 hours (or overnight), stirring occasionally.

3 Thread the chicken on to skewers, put under a hot grill, 10 cm (4 in) from the heat, and grill for 3–5 minutes on each side or until cooked through. Serve hot, with raita.

Cucumber raita

Cut half a cucumber in half lengthways. Scoop out the seeds, then coarsely grate the flesh into a sieve set over a bowl. Sprinkle with salt, and leave to drain for 10 minutes. Press hard to extract the juices.

Tip the cucumber into a bowl and add 1 x 150 g carton plain yogurt, 3 thinly sliced spring onions, 3 heaped tbsp chopped fresh mint, and pepper to taste. Stir well to combine. Serve chilled.

Stir-fried chicken with crisp vegetables

🍽 SERVES 4   405 CALS PER SERVING

4 skinless, boneless chicken breasts, cut diagonally into 5 mm (¼ in) strips

2 tbsp mild curry powder

black pepper

8 spring onions

250 g (8 oz) carrots

3 tbsp sunflower oil

175 g (6 oz) baby sweetcorn

175 g (6 oz) sugar snap peas, strings removed

2–3 tbsp lemon juice

2 tbsp clear honey

2.5 cm (1 in) piece of fresh root ginger, peeled and finely grated

salt

125 g (4 oz) bean sprouts

noodles to serve

1 Put the chicken strips in a bowl with the curry powder and season with black pepper. Toss until the chicken is coated, then set aside while you prepare the vegetables.

2 Finely slice the white parts of the spring onions, reserving the green tops to garnish the finished dish.

3 Peel the carrots and cut them into matchstick-thin strips.

4 Heat 2 tbsp of the oil in a wok or large frying pan. Add the chicken strips and stir-fry over a high heat for 3–4 minutes until golden brown.

5 Add the sliced spring onions, the carrot matchsticks, the whole baby sweetcorn, and the sugar snap peas, then add the lemon juice, honey, ginger, and a pinch of salt. Stir-fry over a high heat for 4 minutes or until the vegetables are tender-crisp and the chicken is cooked through.

6 Toss in the bean sprouts, and stir-fry over a high heat for 1–2 minutes until heated through. Taste for seasoning. Serve on a bed of noodles, and garnish with the reserved green spring onions.

Chicken kebabs

🍽 SERVES 6   441 CALS PER SERVING

4 skinless, boneless chicken breasts, cut into 2.5 cm (1 in) pieces

2 green peppers, halved, seeded, and cut into 2.5 cm (1 in) pieces

500 g (1 lb) cherry tomatoes

375 g (12 oz) button mushrooms

MARINADE

175 ml (6 fl oz) olive oil

125 ml (4 fl oz) dark soy sauce

4 tbsp red wine vinegar

freshly ground black pepper

12 skewers

1 Make the marinade: in a large bowl, combine the oil, soy sauce, and wine vinegar. Season with pepper, add the chicken, and mix well. Cover and marinate for 5–10 minutes.

2 Lift the chicken out of the marinade, reserving the marinade. Thread the skewers, alternating green peppers, tomatoes, chicken, and mushrooms.

3 Place the kebabs under a hot grill, 10 cm (4 in) from the heat. Grill the kebabs, basting with the marinade, for 3–5 minutes on each side or until the chicken is tender and cooked through. Serve hot.

Chicken stir-fry

🍽 SERVES 4   381 CALS PER SERVING

3 tbsp sunflower oil

4 spring onions, sliced

2.5 cm (1 in) piece of fresh root ginger, peeled and grated

1 tsp Chinese five-spice powder

½ tsp crushed dried red chillies

3 carrots, thinly sliced

2 peppers (red and yellow), halved, seeded, and cut into thin strips

4 tbsp dark soy sauce

2 tbsp dry sherry mixed with 2 tsp cornflour

4 skinless, boneless chicken breasts, cut into 1 cm (½ in) strips

1 Heat 1 tbsp of the oil in a wok or large frying pan, add the spring onions, ginger, five-spice powder, and chillies, and stir-fry for 1 minute.

2 Add the remaining oil, then add the carrots and peppers, and stir-fry over a high heat for 2–3 minutes. Add the soy sauce, sherry mixture, and chicken strips, and stir-fry for 3–4 minutes.

3 Add 125 ml (4 fl oz) water and stir-fry for 1–2 minutes until the liquid boils and thickens slightly. Serve at once.

Mustard chicken

🍽 SERVES 4   380 CALS PER SERVING

1 tbsp olive oil

4 skinless, boneless chicken breasts, cut diagonally into 2.5 cm (1 in) strips

1 garlic clove, crushed

250 ml (8 fl oz) single cream

1 tbsp plain flour

1 tbsp coarse-grain mustard

salt and black pepper

flat-leaf parsley sprigs to garnish

1 Heat the oil in a frying pan until hot. Add the chicken strips and garlic, in batches if necessary, and cook over a moderate heat, stirring frequently, for 3–4 minutes.

2 With a slotted spoon, lift the chicken and garlic out of the frying pan, and keep them warm.

3 In a small bowl, mix a little of the cream with the flour to make a smooth paste, then mix in the remaining cream.

4 Lower the heat and pour the cream into the pan. Cook gently for 2 minutes stirring constantly until the sauce has thickened. Stir in the mustard and heat through gently, then season with salt and pepper.

5 Return the chicken to the pan, coat with the sauce, and cook gently for a few minutes more until the chicken is tender when pierced with a fork. Serve hot, garnished with parsley sprigs.

🔍 Cook's know-how

Do not let the sauce boil once you have added the mustard or it may taste bitter. Coarse-grain mustard gives an interesting texture to this dish, but if you prefer a smooth sauce, use Dijon mustard.

weet and sour
hinese chicken

SERVES 4–6   **458–305 CALS PER SERVING**

g (1 lb) skinless, boneless chicken breasts, cut
2.5 cm (1 in) pieces

sp dark soy sauce

sp Chinese rice wine or dry sherry

250 g can pineapple chunks in natural juice,
ned and juice reserved

sp cornflour

sp sunflower oil

en pepper, halved, seeded, and cut into
sized pieces

pepper, halved, seeded, and cut into
sized pieces

ery stalk, thickly sliced

on, cut into bite-sized chunks

4 tbsp tomato ketchup

250 g (8 oz) canned lychees, drained and
juice reserved

salt and black pepper

chopped fresh coriander to garnish (optional)

1 Toss the chicken pieces in a large bowl
with the soy sauce and rice wine or
sherry. Cover, and marinate in the
refrigerator for at least 30 minutes.

2 Meanwhile, make the reserved pineapple
juice up to 250 ml (8 fl oz) with water and
blend with the cornflour. Set aside.

3 Heat the oil in a wok or large frying pan,
add the chicken, in batches if necessary,
and stir-fry for 3–4 minutes until golden all
over. Lift out with a slotted spoon.

4 Add the green and red peppers, celery,
and onion to the wok, and stir-fry for
about 5 minutes.

5 Add the cornflour and pineapple
juice mixture, ketchup, and reserved
lychee juice to the wok, and cook for
3–5 minutes until thickened.

6 Return the chicken to the wok with
the lychees and pineapple chunks,
and heat through. Season with salt and
pepper, and serve at once.

Chicken satay

In this traditional Indonesian speciality, the rich satay sauce made from peanuts and coconut complements the pieces of chicken tenderized by a tangy marinade. Serve as a starter or a buffet party dish.

 **SERVES 4**   **815 CALS PER SERVING**

4 skinless, boneless chicken breasts, cut into 2 cm (¾ in) pieces

chopped flat-leaf parsley and coarsely chopped peanuts to garnish

MARINADE

90 ml (3 fl oz) dark soy sauce

juice of 1 lemon

3 tbsp sunflower oil

2 tbsp dark brown sugar

3 garlic cloves, crushed

3 spring onions, thinly sliced

SATAY SAUCE

250 g (8 oz) peanut butter

2 garlic cloves, crushed

175 ml (6 fl oz) water

30 g (1 oz) creamed coconut, coarsely chopped

1 tbsp dark soy sauce

1 tbsp dark brown sugar

1 cm (½ in) piece of fresh root ginger, peeled and grated

1 tbsp lemon juice

cayenne pepper

salt and black pepper

12 bamboo skewers

1 Make the marinade: in a bowl, combine the soy sauce, lemon juice, oil, sugar, garlic, and spring onions.

2 Toss the chicken in the marinade. Cover and leave to marinate in the refrigerator for 30 minutes.

3 Soak the skewers in warm water for 30 minutes.

4 Make the satay sauce: heat the peanut butter with half of the garlic for 2 minutes. Add the water, creamed coconut, soy sauce, sugar, and ginger, and cook, stirring, for about 2 minutes or until the sauce is smooth.

5 Add the lemon juice and remaining garlic, and season with cayenne pepper, salt, and black pepper. Keep warm.

6 Thread the chicken pieces on to the skewers. Place under a hot grill, 10 cm (4 in) from the heat, and grill for 2–3 minut on each side until cooked through.

7 Serve the chicken satay at once, garnishing the sauce with chopped parsley and peanuts.

♡ Healthy note

Peanut butter is high in fat and calories, so you may wish to reduce the amount used here. Make the sauce with half the amount of ingredients, except for the lemon juice an ginger, and simmer it for longer in step 4 until it becomes thick.

Chicken thighs Normande

🕐 SERVES 4   599 CALS PER SERVING

leeks, trimmed and thinly sliced

lean back bacon rashers, rinds removed, diced

garlic cloves, crushed

50 ml (12 fl oz) strong dry cider

chicken thighs, with the bone in and skin left on

tsp chopped fresh thyme

salt and black pepper

25 ml (4 fl oz) crème fraîche

1 Put the leeks, bacon, and garlic into a roasting tin. Pour in the cider, and put the chicken on top. Sprinkle with the thyme, and season.

2 Roast in a preheated oven at 190°C (170°C fan, Gas 5) for 20–25 minutes until the chicken is tender and cooked through. Remove the chicken thighs, bacon, and vegetables, and keep warm.

3 Spoon off any excess fat from the roasting tin. Put the tin on the hob, and boil the cooking juices until reduced by half. Stir in the crème fraîche, and heat gently. Pour the sauce on to serving plates, arrange the bacon, vegetables, and chicken on top, and serve hot.

Lemon and herb drumsticks

🕐 MAKES 12   200 CALS EACH

chicken drumsticks

MARINADE

ml (¼ pint) olive oil

grated zest and juice of 1 lemon

large parsley sprigs, chopped

onion, thinly sliced

large garlic cloves, crushed

salt and black pepper

1 Make the marinade: in a bowl, combine the olive oil, lemon zest and juice, parsley sprigs, onion, and garlic. Season with salt and pepper.

2 Turn the drumsticks in the marinade. Cover and leave to marinate in the refrigerator for at least 30 minutes.

3 Place the drumsticks under a hot grill, 10 cm (4 in) from the heat, and grill, turning frequently and basting with the marinade, for 20 minutes until crisp, brown, and cooked through. Serve the drumsticks hot or cold.

Sticky honeyed drumsticks

Use a different marinade: combine 250 g (8 oz) plain yogurt, 2 tbsp clear honey, and 1 tsp ground coriander, and season with salt and black pepper.

Cheese and garlic stuffed chicken

🕐 SERVES 6   628 CALS PER SERVING

6 boneless chicken breasts, with the skin on

melted butter for brushing

STUFFING

30 g (1 oz) butter

1 onion, finely chopped

2 large garlic cloves, crushed

250 g (8 oz) full-fat soft cheese

1 tbsp chopped fresh tarragon

1 egg yolk

pinch of grated nutmeg

salt and black pepper

1 Make the stuffing: melt the butter in a small saucepan, add the onion and garlic, and cook gently, stirring occasionally, for a few minutes until soft but not coloured. Turn the onion mixture into a bowl, and leave to cool slightly.

2 Add the soft cheese to the onion mixture with the tarragon, egg yolk, and nutmeg. Season with salt and pepper and mix well.

3 Stuff the chicken breasts: lift up the skin along one side of each breast, spread the cheese mixture over the chicken and then gently press the skin back on top. Put the chicken breasts into an ovenproof dish and brush with the melted butter.

4 Roast the chicken in a preheated oven at 190°C (170°C fan, Gas 5) for 25–30 minutes until the chicken is cooked through. Cut each breast into diagonal slices, and serve hot.

Tarragon chicken with lime

🕐 SERVES 4   428 CALS PER SERVING

60 g (2 oz) butter, softened

grated zest of 1 lime and juice of 2 limes

4 skinless, boneless chicken breasts

1 tbsp chopped fresh tarragon

salt and black pepper

150 ml (¼ pint) full-fat crème fraîche

lime segments and fresh tarragon to garnish

1 Put the butter into a bowl, and beat in the lime zest. Prepare the chicken breasts (see box, below).

2 Put the chicken breasts into a roasting tin. Sprinkle with the lime juice, tarragon, and salt and pepper, and roast in a preheated oven at 200°C (180°C fan, Gas 6) for 20 minutes or until the chicken is cooked through.

3 Transfer the chicken breasts to warmed serving plates and keep warm.

4 Put the tin on the hob, add 1 tbsp water to the cooking juices, stirring to dissolve the sediment, and bring to a boil, stirring. Cook, stirring, for 1–2 minutes. Stir in the crème fraîche and heat gently until warmed through.

5 Serve the chicken with the sauce, and garnish each serving with the lime segments and fresh tarragon.

Preparing the chicken

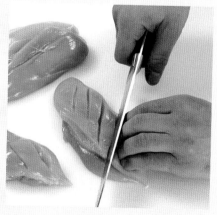

Make 3–4 deep diagonal cuts in each chicken breast with a sharp knife. Spread the top of each breast with one-quarter of the lime butter.

Bacon-wrapped chicken breasts

SERVES 6   **528 CALS PER SERVING**

6 skinless, boneless chicken breasts

4 tbsp coarse-grain mustard

black pepper

18 streaky bacon rashers, rinds removed

snipped fresh chives to garnish

1 Spread both sides of the chicken breasts with the mustard, and season with pepper.

2 Take 3 bacon rashers, stretch them with the back of a knife, and arrange them side by side and slightly overlapping. Wrap a chicken breast with the bacon (see box, below). Repeat with the remaining bacon and chicken.

3 Place the chicken breasts with the bacon seam-side down in a roasting tin, and roast in a preheated oven at 190°C (170°C fan, Gas 5) for 25–30 minutes until the bacon is crisp and brown and the chicken cooked through. Serve at once, garnished with snipped chives.

♥ Healthy note

Use lean back bacon and trim off all the fat along the top edge of each rasher. Allow 12 rashers rather than 18 – it does not matter if some of the chicken peeps through.

Wrapping a chicken breast in bacon

Place a chicken breast at one end of the overlapped bacon rashers, and then wrap the rashers diagonally (working from side to side) around the chicken to make a neat parcel.

Chicken cordon bleu

SERVES 4   **602 CALS PER SERVING**

4 skinless, boneless chicken breasts

4 thin slices of Gruyère cheese

4 thin slices of cooked ham

salt and black pepper

1 egg, beaten

125 g (4 oz) fresh white breadcrumbs

30 g (1 oz) butter

3 tbsp sunflower oil

1 With a sharp knife, cut each chicken breast horizontally, leaving it attached at one side.

2 Open out each chicken breast, place between 2 sheets of greaseproof paper, and pound to a 3 mm (⅛ in) thickness with a rolling pin. Fill and fold the chicken breasts (see box, below).

3 Dip each folded chicken breast into the beaten egg, then dip each breast into the breadcrumbs, making sure each one is evenly coated. Cover and chill for 15 minutes.

4 Melt the butter with the sunflower oil in a large frying pan. When the butter is foaming, add the chicken breasts, and cook for 10 minutes on each side or until the breadcrumb coating is crisp and golden and the chicken is cooked through. Remove the chicken breasts with a slotted spoon and drain thoroughly on paper towels. Cut into 1 cm (½ in) slices, and serve at once.

Folding the chicken

Place 1 slice of cheese and 1 slice of ham on half of each chicken breast, season with salt and pepper, and fold the breast over to cover the filling.

Chicken pinwheels

This is an elegant dinner party dish that is simple and economical to make, yet it looks stunning. An accompaniment of fresh tagliatelle goes well with the tomato and herb sauce.

SERVES 4   **423 CALS PER SERVING**

4 skinless, boneless chicken breasts

melted butter for greasing

basil sprigs to garnish

FILLING

125 g (4 oz) full-fat soft cheese with garlic and herbs

2 tbsp sun-dried tomatoes in oil, drained and chopped

4 tbsp shredded fresh basil

salt and black pepper

TOMATO & HERB SAUCE

1 tbsp olive oil

1 small onion, chopped

1 x 400 g can chopped tomatoes

1 tbsp chopped fresh herbs, such as parsley, chives, and thyme

1 Make the filling: combine the cheese, sun-dried tomatoes, and basil. Season with salt and pepper, and mix well to combine.

2 Put the chicken breasts between sheets of cling film, and pound with a rolling pin until 5 mm (¼ in) thick. Spread one-quarter of the filling over each breast, and tightly roll up each one.

3 Brush 4 squares of foil with melted butter and wrap each chicken roll in a square, twisting the ends to seal them tightly. Put the rolls into a shallow pan of gently simmering water, cover, and poach for 15 minutes.

4 Meanwhile, make the tomato and herb sauce: heat the oil in a pan, add the onion, and cook, stirring often, for a few minutes until soft. Stir in the tomatoes with half of their juice, bring to a boil, and simmer for 3 minutes.

5 Purée the tomato mixture in a food processor until smooth. Work the purée through a sieve, and add more tomato juice if the sauce is too thick. Stir in the chopped fresh herbs, and season with salt and pepper.

6 Unwrap the chicken, and slice on the diagonal. Serve with the tomato and herb sauce, and garnish with basil.

Chicken with sage and orange

SERVES 6   **435 CALS PER SERVING**

boneless chicken breasts, with the skin on

tbsp plain flour

ange segments and fresh sage leaves to garnish

MARINADE

0 ml (½ pint) orange juice

tbsp light soy sauce

garlic cloves, crushed

tbsp chopped fresh sage

cm (½ in) piece of fresh root ginger, peeled
d grated

lt and black pepper

1 Make the marinade: combine the orange juice, soy sauce, garlic, sage, ginger, and salt and pepper. Toss the chicken in the marinade, cover, and leave to marinate in the refrigerator for 20–30 minutes.

2 Reserve the marinade, and arrange the chicken breasts, skin-side up, in a large roasting tin.

3 Roast the chicken in a preheated oven at 190°C (170°C fan, Gas 5) for 10 minutes. Pour the reserved marinade over the chicken, and continue roasting for 10 minutes or until the chicken is cooked through.

4 Remove the chicken with a slotted spoon, and arrange on a warmed platter. Cover and keep warm.

5 Pour all but 2 tbsp of the marinade into a jug, and reserve. Add the flour to the marinade remaining in the roasting tin, and mix to a smooth paste.

6 Put the roasting tin on the hob, and cook, stirring, for 1 minute. Gradually stir in the reserved marinade. Bring to a boil, simmer for 2 minutes, and taste for seasoning. Strain, pour a little around the chicken breasts, and garnish with the orange segments and fresh sage. Serve the remaining sauce separately.

Yogurt and mint barbecued chicken

🍴 SERVES 4   279 CALS PER SERVING

8 chicken thighs on the bone, with the skin left on

couscous salad (made with chopped fresh mint, spring onions, red pepper, cherry tomatoes, and pine nuts tossed in vinaigrette dressing) to serve

MARINADE

4 tbsp olive oil

juice of ½ lemon

3 garlic cloves, crushed

30 g (1 oz) fresh mint, chopped

150 g (5 oz) plain yogurt

¼ tsp each ground cumin and turmeric

salt and black pepper

1 Combine the marinade ingredients in a shallow non-metallic dish. Add the chicken and turn to coat, then cover and leave to marinate in the refrigerator for up to 24 hours.

2 Barbecue the chicken, turning and basting or brushing with the marinade, for 15–20 minutes or until the juices run clear.

3 Serve the chicken thighs hot or cold, on a bed of couscous salad, or with couscous salad served separately in a bowl.

Orange and rosemary barbecued chicken

🍴 SERVES 4   330 CALS PER SERVING

4 chicken breasts, with the skin left on

a few rosemary sprigs

MARINADE

75 ml (2½ fl oz) olive oil

75 ml (2½ fl oz) white wine vinegar

juice of 1 orange

2 tbsp clear honey

4 garlic cloves, crushed

salt and black pepper

ORANGE SALSA

2 oranges, peeled, segmented, and diced

1 red pepper, halved, seeded, and diced

¼ tsp crushed dried red chillies (chilli flakes)

1 tbsp clear honey

1 Combine the marinade ingredients in a shallow non-metallic dish. Add the chicken and turn to coat, then cover and leave to marinate in the refrigerator for up to 24 hours.

2 Lay the rosemary sprigs on the barbecue rack, put the chicken on top, and barbecue for 15–20 minutes until the juices run clear. Turn the chicken over several times during cooking, and baste or brush with the marinade.

3 Mix together the ingredients for the salsa. Serve the chicken breasts sliced diagonally, with the salsa alongside.

Fruity coriander barbecued chicken

🍴 SERVES 4   312 CALS PER SERVING

8 chicken drumsticks, with the skin left on

MARINADE

75 ml (2½ fl oz) olive oil

juice of 1 lime

2 tbsp mango chutney

2.5 cm (1 in) piece of fresh root ginger, peeled and grated

30 g (1 oz) fresh coriander, chopped

salt and black pepper

MANGO SALSA

1 ripe large mango, diced (page 420)

1 cm (½ in) piece of fresh root ginger, peeled and grated

3 spring onions, finely chopped

1 tbsp mango chutney

1 tbsp lime juice

1 Combine the marinade ingredients in a shallow non-metallic dish. Slash the drumsticks, add to the marinade, and turn to coat. Cover and leave to marinate in the refrigerator for up to 24 hours.

2 Barbecue the drumsticks, turning and basting or brushing with the marinade, for 15–20 minutes or until the juices run clear.

3 Mix together the ingredients for the salsa. Serve the drumsticks hot, with the mango salsa alongside.

Successful marinating

A marinade will give poultry or meat extra flavour before it is cooked over a barbecue, and it may help tenderize it at the same time.

A marinade is a mixture of liquids and seasonings. There is always an acid such as lemon juice, wine, or vinegar, which helps make poultry or meat more tender.

An oil, such as olive, sesame, or sunflower, keeps the meat or poultry moist and carries the flavours of the seasonings into the food.

Seasonings usually include salt and pepper, but all kinds of spices and herbs can be used as well. Marinades often include garlic, onions, and fresh root ginger, which also add flavour.

Allow enough time for large pieces of poultry or meat to pick up the flavour of the marinade. Smaller pieces will pick up the flavour more quickly.

Turn the food in the marinade occasionally to ensure an even coating, and baste or brush with the marinade when barbecuing.

Opposite, clockwise from top: Orange and rosemary barbecued chicken, Fruity coriander barbecued chicken, Yogurt and mint barbecued chicken

Chicken thighs with chestnut stuffing

You do not need to roast a whole bird to enjoy the classic combination of chicken with a savoury stuffing. In this recipe, chicken thighs are wrapped around a nutty filling of chestnuts and bacon, and served with cranberry sauce.

 **SERVES 4   598 CALS PER SERVING**

8 boneless chicken thighs, with the skin left on

150 ml (¼ pint) chicken stock

1 tbsp cranberry or redcurrant jelly

STUFFING

15 g (½ oz) butter

2 streaky bacon rashers, rinds removed, diced

1 small onion, finely chopped

125 g (4 oz) frozen chestnuts, thawed and finely chopped

30 g (1 oz) fresh brown breadcrumbs

1 tbsp chopped parsley

salt and black pepper

1 egg yolk

1 Make the stuffing: melt the butter in a frying pan, add the bacon and onion, and cook over a medium heat for 3–5 minutes until the bacon is crisp and the onion soft but not coloured.

2 Add the chestnuts, and cook, stirring occasionally, for 5 minutes. Remove from the heat, add the breadcrumbs, and parsley, and season with salt and pepper, then bind with the egg yolk.

3 Place the chicken thighs, skin-side down, on a chopping board, and divide the stuffing among them. Roll up each thigh to enclose the stuffing.

4 Arrange the chicken thighs in a single layer in a roasting tin, and cook in a preheated oven at 190°C (170°C fan, Gas 5) for 20–25 minutes until the chicken is lightly browned and cooked through. Lift the chicken thighs out of the roasting tin, and keep hot.

5 Spoon off any excess fat, put the tin on the hob, and pour in the stock. Bring to a boil, and boil for 3–5 minutes until syrupy, stirring to dissolve any sediment and cooking juices.

6 Stir in the cranberry or redcurrant jelly, and cook for 1 minute to melt the jelly. Taste for seasoning. Strain the sauce, and serve at once, with the chicken thighs.

Herb-marinated chicken breasts

SERVES 4   641 CALS PER SERVING

4 boneless chicken breasts, with the skin left on

30 g (1 oz) butter

2 tbsp sunflower oil

150 ml (¼ pint) chicken stock

1 bunch of watercress, tough stalks removed, to serve

chopped parsley to garnish

MARINADE

2 tbsp olive oil

1 tbsp lemon juice

3 garlic cloves, crushed

3 tbsp chopped parsley

2 tbsp chopped mixed fresh herbs, eg parsley, chives, tarragon, or thyme

salt and black pepper

1 Make the marinade: combine the oil, lemon juice, garlic, parsley, and herbs, and season with salt and pepper. Turn the chicken in the marinade, cover, and marinate in the refrigerator for at least 30 minutes.

2 Remove the chicken from the marinade, and dry on paper towels.

3 Melt the butter with the oil in a large frying pan. When the butter is foaming, add the chicken breasts, skin-side down, and cook for 10 minutes. Turn the chicken, and cook for a further 5 minutes or until golden and cooked through.

4 Using a slotted spoon, remove the chicken breasts, and keep hot.

5 Pour the chicken stock into the pan, and boil until reduced to about 8 tbsp.

6 Arrange the chicken breasts on beds of watercress, and strain over the hot sauce. Serve hot, garnished with chopped parsley.

Spicy chicken breasts

Substitute 1 tsp paprika and ¼ tsp crushed dried red chillies (chilli flakes) for the herbs in the marinade.

Devilled chicken drumsticks

MAKES 12   138 CALS EACH

12 chicken drumsticks

2 tbsp sesame seeds

tortilla chips to serve

SPICY COATING

2 tbsp olive oil

2 tbsp white wine vinegar

2 tbsp tomato ketchup

1 tbsp Dijon mustard

1 small onion, quartered

2 tbsp dark muscovado sugar

1 large garlic clove, coarsely crushed

¼ tsp chilli powder

salt and black pepper

1 Make the spicy coating: put the oil, vinegar, ketchup, mustard, onion, sugar, garlic, and chilli powder in a food processor. Season with salt and pepper, and purée until fairly smooth.

2 Make 3 deep cuts in each chicken drumstick, arrange in a single layer in a shallow ovenproof dish, and spoon the coating over them. Sprinkle with half of the sesame seeds.

3 Roast in a preheated oven at 190°C (170°C fan, Gas 5) for 30 minutes or until the drumsticks are cooked through. Turn and baste halfway through cooking, and sprinkle with the remaining sesame seeds. Serve hot or cold, with tortilla chips.

Chilli-roasted drumsticks with bacon

Use a different spicy coating: combine 3 tbsp lemon juice, 4 crushed garlic cloves, 1½ tbsp paprika, 1 tbsp mild chilli powder, 1 tsp ground cumin, and ¼ tsp oregano. Coat the drumstick with the mixture, then wrap each one in a streaky bacon rasher.

♡ Healthy note

Chicken is a very lean meat, but the skin is high in fat. If you want to reduce the fat content of these drumsticks, strip the skin off before marinating. The marinade will compensate for the lack of skin, and will keep the chicken moist during cooking.

ove: Coronation chicken.

oronation chicken

SERVES 6   580 CALS PER SERVING

sp sunflower oil

g (4 oz) spring onions, chopped

p mild curry paste

ml (¼ pint) red wine

ed zest and juice of 1 lemon

sp tomato purée

sp apricot jam

ml (½ pint) mayonnaise

g (5 oz) plain yogurt

and pepper

g (1 lb) cooked chicken, cut into
-sized pieces

ercress sprigs to garnish

leat the oil in a small saucepan, add
he spring onions, and cook for about
inutes until beginning to soften but not
our. Stir in the curry paste, and cook,
ng, for 1 minute.

Add the red wine, lemon zest and juice,
and tomato purée. Simmer, uncovered,
ng, for 5 minutes or until reduced to
sp. Strain into a bowl, cover, and leave
ool.

Work the apricot jam through the sieve,
hen stir it into the curry paste and wine
ure. Add the mayonnaise and yogurt,

season with salt and pepper, then stir well
to blend evenly. The mixture should have
a coating consistency, and be the colour
of pale straw.

4 Add the chicken pieces to the
mayonnaise mixture, and stir to coat
evenly. Garnish with watercress sprigs
before serving.

Marinated chicken with peppers

SERVES 6   376 CALS PER SERVING

1.7 kg (3½ lb) chicken

2 tbsp olive oil

1 large red pepper, halved, seeded, and cut
into thin strips

1 large yellow pepper, halved, seeded, and cut
into thin strips

125 g (4 oz) pitted black olives

MARINADE

4 tbsp olive oil

2 tbsp clear honey

juice of ½ lemon

1 tbsp chopped mixed fresh herbs, such as parsley,
thyme, and basil

salt and black pepper

1 Put the chicken into a roasting tin, rub the
breast with oil, and roast in a preheated
oven at 190°C (170°C fan, Gas 5) for
20 minutes per 500 g (1 lb). Twenty minutes
before the end of the roasting time, remove
from the oven, and spoon off the fat. Add
the peppers and return to the oven for
20 minutes.

2 Remove the chicken and peppers from
the tin with a slotted spoon, and leave
to stand until cool.

3 Meanwhile, make the marinade: in
a large bowl, combine the olive oil,
honey, lemon juice, and herbs, and
season with salt and pepper.

4 Strip the chicken flesh from the carcass,
and cut it into small bite-sized strips. Toss
the strips in the marinade, cover, and leave
to cool completely.

5 Spoon the chicken on to a platter,
arrange the peppers and olives around
the edge, and serve at room temperature.

🔍 Cook's know-how

If time is short, use a ready-cooked chicken
and toss with roasted peppers from a jar.
If the peppers are packed in oil they will be
very moist, so you will only need half the
amount of marinade.

Ballotine of chicken

A ballotine is a bird or cut of meat that has been boned, stuffed, and rolled. It is slowly cooked in the oven, allowed to cool, then chilled for several hours or overnight until firm. With its colourful, pistachio-studded filling, this ballotine makes an excellent centrepiece for a buffet party, and is easy to slice and serve.

 **SERVES 10   494 CALS PER SERVING**

2 kg (4 lb) chicken, boned (page 148)

4 thin slices of cooked ham

125 g (4 oz) pistachio nuts, shelled

60 g (2 oz) butter, softened

600 ml (1 pint) chicken stock

STUFFING

500 g (1 lb) belly pork

375 g (12 oz) chicken livers, trimmed

250 g (8 oz) streaky bacon rashers, rinds removed, coarsely chopped

2 shallots, quartered

2 garlic cloves

4 tbsp brandy

2 tsp chopped fresh thyme

1 tsp chopped fresh sage

½ tsp ground ginger

½ tsp ground cinnamon

salt and black pepper

1 Make the stuffing: chop the pork into 5 mm (¼ in) pieces, and place in a bowl.

2 Purée the chicken livers, bacon, shallots, garlic, and brandy in a food processor until smooth. Add to the pork in the bowl with the thyme, sage, ginger, and cinnamon, and season generously with salt and pepper. Stir well to combine.

3 Place the boned chicken, skin-side down, between 2 pieces of cling film and pound to an even thickness with a rolling pin.

4 Remove the cling film from the chicken, and assemble the ballotine (see box, opposite). Tie several pieces of string around the chicken to keep it in shape.

5 Spread the softened butter over the chicken skin, and season generously with salt and pepper. Place the chicken roll on a wire rack in a roasting tin.

6 Bring the stock to a boil, and pour over the chicken in the roasting tin. Cook in a preheated oven at 160°C (140°C fan, Gas 3), basting occasionally and adding more stock if necessary, for 2 hours or until the juices run clear when the chicken is pierced.

7 Transfer the ballotine to a plate, and leave to cool. Cover and chill overnig Cut into thin slices to serve.

Cook's know-how

Classic French ballotine recipes wrap the chicken roll in muslin before cooking, but this is not necessary.

Assembling the ballotine

Spread half of the stuffing over the chicken, to within 2.5 cm (1 in) of the edges. Arrange the ham slices on top. Scatter the pistachio nuts on top of the ham.

Spoon on and spread the remaining stuffing over the pistachio nuts.

Fold the chicken over the stuffing to form a sausage shape, and sew the edges together with thin string or fasten them with small metal skewers.

Greek chicken salad

🥘 SERVES 6   264 CALS PER SERVING

500 g (1 lb) cooked chicken, cut into bite-sized pieces

pitta bread to serve

1 spring onion, cut into strips, to garnish

SAUCE

150 g (5 oz) Greek yogurt

150 ml (¼ pint) crème fraîche

8 spring onions, thinly sliced

2 tbsp chopped fresh mint

1 tbsp chopped flat-leaf parsley

2 tbsp lemon juice

a pinch of sugar

salt and black pepper

1 Make the sauce: in a large bowl, combine the yogurt, crème fraîche, spring onions, mint, parsley, lemon juice, and sugar, and season with salt and pepper.

2 Toss the chicken pieces in the sauce.

3 Sprinkle the bread with a little water and cook under a hot grill for 1 minute on each side. Garnish the chicken with the spring onion strips, and serve with the pitta bread.

Warm chicken salad with mango and avocado

This unusual salad combines refreshing slices of mango and avocado with spicy chicken breast and a warm, rum-flavoured dressing. The combination of flavours makes a truly tropical dish.

🥘 SERVES 4   411 CALS PER SERVING

3 skinless, boneless chicken breasts, cut into 2.5 cm (1 in) strips

1 round lettuce, leaves separated

1 bunch of watercress, trimmed

1 avocado, peeled, stoned (page 327), and sliced lengthways

1 mango, peeled, stoned (page 420), and sliced lengthways

4 tbsp dark rum

paprika to garnish

MARINADE

2 tbsp olive oil

2 tbsp lemon juice

2 tsp balsamic vinegar

2 garlic cloves, crushed

1 tbsp paprika

1 mild fresh red chilli, halved, seeded, and finely chopped

½ tsp ground cumin

salt

1 Make the marinade: combine the oil, lemon juice, vinegar, garlic, paprika, chilli, and cumin, and season with salt. Toss in the chicken strips, cover, and leave to marinate for a few minutes.

2 Arrange beds of lettuce and watercress on 4 serving plates. Arrange the avocado and mango slices on top.

3 Heat a large frying pan, and add the chicken strips with the marinade. Cook over a high heat, stirring, for 5–6 minutes until golden on all sides and cooked through.

4 Using a slotted spoon, remove the chicken strips from the pan, and arrange on top of the avocado and mango.

5 Return the frying pan to the heat, and pour in the rum. Let it bubble, stirring constantly to dissolve any sediment in the frying pan and incorporate the cooking juices, for about 1 minute. Pour the hot rum mixture over the salads, sprinkle with a little paprika, and serve at once.

Christmas roast turkey

If you have a large number to cater for at Christmas, be sure to order a fresh turkey well in advance from your butcher. You can collect it on Christmas Eve or store it for up to 2 days in the refrigerator. If you buy a frozen turkey, make sure that it is thoroughly thawed before cooking – see page 146 for thawing times.

 SERVES 12   675 CALS PER SERVING

pared zest of 1 lemon

a few parsley stalks

a few thyme sprigs

2 celery stalks, roughly sliced

5 kg (10 lb) oven-ready turkey, with giblets

75 g (3 oz) butter, softened

salt and black pepper

250 g (8 oz) streaky bacon rashers (optional)

CHESTNUT STUFFING

30 g (1 oz) butter

1 onion, finely chopped

90 g (3 oz) streaky bacon, finely chopped

375 g (12 oz) frozen chestnuts, thawed, or 175 g (6 oz) dried chestnuts, soaked, finely chopped

175 g (6 oz) pork sausagemeat

3 tbsp chopped parsley

1 tbsp chopped fresh thyme

salt and black pepper

1 small egg, beaten

GRAVY

30 g (1 oz) plain flour

600 ml (1 pint) giblet stock (page 147) or chicken stock

about 2 tbsp port, Madeira or sherry

redcurrant jelly to taste (optional)

TO SERVE

bread sauce

cranberry sauce

bacon rolls

chipolatas

1 Prepare the stuffing: melt the butter in a frying pan, add the onion and bacon, and cook until the onion is soft and both the onion and bacon are golden. Transfer to a large bowl, mix in the remaining stuffing ingredients, and leave until cold.

2 Place the lemon zest, parsley stalks, thyme, and celery into the cavity of the turkey. Fill the neck end with stuffing. Put the leftover stuffing into an ovenproof dish and set aside.

3 Shape the stuffed end ot the turkey into a neat round and secure the loose skin with fine skewers. Tie the legs with string to give a neat shape.

4 Weigh the turkey and calculate the cooking time, allowing 20 minutes per 500 g (1 lb). Arrange 2 large sheets of foil across a large roasting tin. Place the turkey on top and spread the butter over the bird, concentrating on the breast in particular.

5 Season with a little salt and plenty of pepper. If you are using the bacon rashers, overlap them across the turkey, again concentrating on the breast.

6 Fold the sheets of foil loosely over the turkey, leaving a large air gap between the turkey and the foil. Cook the turkey in a preheated oven at 220°C (200°C fan, Gas 7) for 30 minutes.

7 Reduce the oven temperature to 160°C (140°C fan, Gas 3) and cook for the remainder of the calculated cooking time.

8 Thirty minutes before the end of the cooking time, fold back the foil and remove the bacon (if used), to allow the breast to brown, then baste with the cooking juices. To check if the turkey is thoroughly cooked, pierce the thickest part of the thigh with a fine skewer: the juices should run clear, not pink or red.

9 Lift the turkey on to a warmed serving platter, cover with fresh foil, and leave to stand in a warm place for 30 minutes before carving.

10 Meanwhile, put the dish of stuffing in the oven and cook for 25–30 minutes. Now make the gravy: spoon all but 2 tbsp of fat from the roasting tin, leaving behind the cooking juices. Place the tin over a low heat on the hob, add the flour, and cook, stirring, for 1 minute. Add the stock and port, Madeira or sherry to taste, then cook, stirring, until thickened. Season to taste, and add some redcurrant jelly if you think the gravy is too sharp.

11 Carve the turkey and serve with the extra stuffing, gravy, bread sauce, cranberry sauce, bacon rolls, and chipolatas.

Classic accompaniments

Bread sauce
Insert 8 whole cloves into 1 onion. Put it into a pan with 900 ml (1½ pints) milk, 1 bay leaf, and 6 whole black peppercorns. Bring to a boil, remove from the heat, cover, and leave to infuse for 1 hour. Strain the milk and return to the pan. Gradually add about 175 g (6 oz) fresh white breadcrumbs, then bring to a boil, stirring. Simmer for 2–3 minutes. Season with salt and black pepper, and stir in 60 g (2 oz) butter. If liked, stir in 4 tbsp double cream before serving. Serve hot.

Cranberry sauce
Put 500 g (1 lb) fresh cranberries into a saucepan with 125 ml (4 fl oz) water. Bring to a boil and simmer for about 5 minutes, until the cranberries have begun to break down. Stir in 125 g (4 oz) caster sugar and simmer until the sugar has dissolved. Stir in 2 tbsp port before serving. Serve hot or cold.

Bacon rolls
With the back of a knife, stretch 6 streaky bacon rashers until twice their original size. Cut in half and roll up loosely. Thread on to skewers and cook under a hot grill, turning, for 6 minutes or until browned.

Chipolatas
Twist 6 chipolata sausages in the centre and cut in half, to make 12 small sausages. Cook under a hot grill for 10–15 minutes until cooked through and browned all over.

Roast turkey with garlic and tarragon

🕐 SERVES 4   296 CALS PER SERVING

1.25 kg (2½ lb) turkey breast joint

1 tsp plain flour

300 ml (½ pint) chicken stock

salt and black pepper

watercress sprigs to garnish

MARINADE

3 tbsp sunflower oil

grated zest and juice of 1 lemon

1 small onion, sliced

1 garlic clove, crushed

1 large tarragon sprig

1 large lemon thyme sprig

1 Make the marinade: combine the oil, lemon zest and juice, onion, garlic, tarragon, and thyme. Spoon the marinade over the turkey, cover, and leave to marinate in the refrigerator, turning occasionally, for 8 hours.

2 Put the turkey into a roasting tin. Strain the marinade, and pour around the turkey. Cover with foil, and cook in a preheated oven at 190°C (170°C fan, Gas 5) for 20 minutes per 500 g (1 lb). Remove the foil after 20 minutes of cooking to brown the turkey.

3 Test whether the turkey is done by inserting a fine skewer into the thickest part: the juices will run clear when it is cooked. Remove the turkey from the roasting tin, and keep warm while you make the gravy.

4 Put the tin on the hob, add the flour to the juices in the tin, and cook, stirring, for 1 minute until lightly browned. Add the stock, and bring to a boil, stirring constantly until thickened slightly. Simmer for 2–3 minutes, season with salt and pepper, and strain into a warmed gravy boat.

5 Garnish the turkey with watercress, and serve the gravy separately.

Turkey schnitzel

🕐 SERVES 4   394 CALS PER SERVING

3 tbsp plain flour

salt and black pepper

1 large egg, beaten

60 g (2 oz) fresh breadcrumbs

4 x 175 g (6 oz) turkey breast escalopes

2 tbsp sunflower oil

15 g (½ oz) butter

lemon slices and chopped parsley to garnish

1 Sprinkle the flour on to a plate, and season generously with salt and pepper. Pour the beaten egg on to another plate, and sprinkle the breadcrumbs on to a third plate.

2 Coat each escalope with the seasoned flour, shaking off any excess. Dip each floured escalope into the beaten egg, then dip into the breadcrumbs.

3 With a sharp knife, score the escalope in a criss-cross pattern. Cover and chill in the refrigerator for 30 minutes.

4 Heat the oil with the butter in a large frying pan. When the butter is foaming, add the escalopes, and cook over a high heat until golden on both sides.

5 Lower the heat and cook for 10 minutes or until the escalopes are tender. Test the escalopes by piercing with a fine skewer: the juices should run clear.

6 Lift the escalopes out of the pan, and drain on paper towels. Garnish with lemon slices and chopped parsley, and serve at once.

🔍 Cook's know-how

If you can't find turkey breast escalopes, buy breast fillets. Put them between 2 sheets of cling film, and pound with the bottom of a saucepan until they are about 5 mm (¼ in) thick.

Turkey with soured cream and chives

🍴 **SERVES 4**   **542 CALS PER SERVING**

0 g (1 oz) butter

tbsp sunflower oil

00 g (1¼ lb) turkey breast fillets, cut diagonally
to 1 cm (½ in) strips

streaky bacon rashers, rinds removed, diced

large onion, sliced

50 g (8 oz) button mushrooms, halved

0 g (1 oz) plain flour

50 ml (¼ pint) turkey or chicken stock

alt and black pepper

50 g (5 oz) full-fat soured cream

tbsp snipped fresh chives

Melt the butter with the oil in a large
frying pan until foaming. Add the turkey,
nd cook over a high heat, stirring, for
minutes. Remove the turkey from the
an with a slotted spoon, and keep warm.

Lower the heat and add the bacon,
onion, and mushrooms. Cook gently,
rring occasionally, for 3–5 minutes until
e onion is soft but not coloured. Sprinkle
the flour and cook, stirring, for about
minute.

Pour in the stock, and bring to a boil,
stirring until thickened. Add the turkey,
d season with salt and pepper. Cover
d simmer for about 5 minutes or until
e turkey is tender.

Stir in the soured cream, and heat
gently without boiling. Serve at once,
inkled with the chives.

Turkey and lemon stir-fry

🍴 **SERVES 4**   **342 CALS PER SERVING**

600 g (1¼ lb) turkey breast fillets, cut diagonally
into 2.5 cm (1 in) strips

375 g (12 oz) courgettes

1 large green pepper

1 tbsp olive oil

250 g (8 oz) baby sweetcorn

salt

chopped parsley and lemon twists to garnish

MARINADE

125 ml (4 fl oz) dry white wine

grated zest and juice of 1 large lemon

2 tbsp olive oil

black pepper

1 Make the marinade: combine the wine,
lemon zest and juice, oil, and season with
pepper. Toss the turkey strips in the marinade,
cover, and marinate in the refrigerator for at
least 30 minutes.

2 Slice the courgettes thickly on the
diagonal. Halve the green pepper and
remove the seeds, then cut the pepper
halves into long thin strips.

3 Heat the oil in a wok, add the courgettes,
sweetcorn, and green pepper, and stir-fry
over a high heat for 2 minutes. Remove with
a slotted spoon, and keep warm.

4 Remove the turkey strips from the
marinade, reserving the marinade.
Add the turkey to the wok, and stir-fry over
a high heat for 5 minutes or until golden.

5 Pour the reserved marinade over the
turkey and cook for 3 minutes or until
tender. Return the vegetables to the wok,
and heat through. Taste for seasoning.
Serve at once, garnished with parsley
and lemon twists.

Stir-fried turkey meatballs

🍴 SERVES 4   232 CALS PER SERVING

3 tsp sunflower oil

1 onion, thinly sliced

1 green pepper, halved, seeded, and cut into bite-sized pieces

1 courgette, sliced

4–6 mushrooms, thinly sliced

125 g (4 oz) bean sprouts

MEATBALLS

375 g (12 oz) minced turkey

45 g (1½ oz) parsley stuffing mix or breadcrumbs

1 onion, finely chopped

4 garlic cloves, crushed

3 tbsp soy sauce

1 cm (½ in) piece of fresh root ginger, peeled and grated

salt and black pepper

1 Make the meatballs: in a bowl, combine the turkey, stuffing or breadcrumbs, onion, garlic, 1 tbsp of the soy sauce, and the ginger. Season with salt and pepper, then shape into meatballs (see box, below).

2 Heat 1 tsp of the oil in a wok, add the onion, green pepper, and courgette, and stir-fry for 2–3 minutes.

3 Remove the vegetables with a slotted spoon. Heat another 1 tsp of the oil, add the mushrooms, and stir-fry for 2–3 minutes. Remove with a slotted spoon.

4 Heat the remaining oil in the wok, add the meatballs, and cook gently, turning, for 6–7 minutes or until cooked through. Return the vegetables to the wok, add the bean sprouts and the remaining soy sauce, and heat through for 1 minute. Serve hot.

Shaping meatballs

Break off pieces of the turkey mixture and, with dampened hands to prevent the mixture sticking, roll into 5 cm (2 in) meatballs.

Turkey casserole with peppers and cider

🍴 SERVES 6   234 CALS PER SERVING

30 g (1 oz) butter

1 tbsp sunflower oil

750 g (1½ lb) turkey pieces

1 onion, sliced

1 garlic clove, crushed

1 red pepper, halved, seeded, and thinly sliced

1 yellow pepper, halved, seeded, and thinly sliced

300 ml (½ pint) dry cider

salt and black pepper

chopped parsley to garnish

1 Melt the butter with the oil in a flameproof casserole. When the butter is foaming, add the turkey pieces, and cook over a high heat for 5 minutes or until golden on all sides. Lift out with a slotted spoon, and drain on paper towels.

2 Lower the heat, add the onion, garlic, and red and yellow pepper slices to the casserole, and cook for 5 minutes or until the vegetables are just beginning to soften.

3 Return the turkey to the casserole, pour in the cider, and bring to a boil. Season with salt and pepper, cover, and cook in a preheated oven at 160°C (140°C fan, Gas 3) for 1 hour or until the turkey is tender.

4 Using a slotted spoon, transfer the turkey and vegetables to a warmed platter. Put the casserole on the hob and boil, stirring, until the cooking juices are thickened slightly. Taste for seasoning.

5 Spoon the sauce over the turkey and vegetables, garnish with chopped parsley, and serve at once.

Turkey and apple casserole

Substitute 2 cored, halved, and sliced eating apples for the red and yellow peppers, and add them 20 minutes before the end of the cooking time.

Turkey mole

🍴 SERVES 6   334 CALS PER SERVING

2 tbsp sunflower oil

750 g (1½ lb) turkey pieces

300 ml (½ pint) turkey or chicken stock

salt and black pepper

MOLE SAUCE

1 x 400 g can chopped tomatoes

1 small onion, coarsely chopped

90 g (3 oz) blanched almonds

30 g (1 oz) raisins (optional)

20 g (¾ oz) plain chocolate, coarsely chopped

1 garlic clove

1 tbsp sesame seeds

1 tbsp hot chilli powder

1 tsp ground cinnamon

½ tsp ground cloves

½ tsp ground coriander

½ tsp ground cumin

¼ tsp ground aniseed (optional)

1 Make the mole sauce: put the tomatoes, onion, almonds, raisins (if using), chocolate, garlic, sesame seeds, chilli powder, cinnamon, cloves, coriander, cumin, aniseed (if using), and 4 tbsp water into a food processor and process briefly.

2 Heat the sunflower oil in a large saucepan, add the turkey pieces, and cook over a high heat for about 5 minutes until golden on all sides.

3 Add the mole sauce mixture, and cook, stirring, for 2 minutes. Pour in the stock, and bring to a boil. Cover and simmer very gently for 40 minutes or until the turkey is tender. Season with salt and pepper before serving.

🔍 Cook's know-how

If you would rather not use the almonds, you can use 15 g (½ oz) plain flour to thicken the sauce instead.

Turkey salad with mango and grapes

SERVES 4   734 CALS PER SERVING

.25 kg (2½ lb) turkey breast joint

onion, quartered

carrot, sliced

few parsley sprigs

ared zest of 1 lemon

black peppercorns

bay leaf

00 ml (7 fl oz) lemon mayonnaise

bunch of watercress, tough stalks removed

ripe mango, peeled, stoned, and cut into
ubes (page 420)

25 g (4 oz) seedless green grapes

0 g (3 oz) walnut pieces

1 Put the turkey joint into a large saucepan, and cover with cold water. Add the onion, carrot, parsley, lemon zest, peppercorns, and bay leaf, and bring to a boil. Cover and simmer very gently for 1 hour or until the turkey is tender. Remove from the heat, and leave the turkey to cool completely in the poaching liquid.

2 Lift the turkey out of the poaching liquid, and remove the flesh from the carcass. Discard the skin and bones, then cut the meat into bite-sized pieces.

3 Put the turkey pieces into a large bowl, and add the lemon mayonnaise. Stir well to coat the turkey pieces thoroughly and evenly.

4 Arrange the watercress on individual serving plates, and pile the turkey mixture on top. Arrange the mango cubes and grapes around the edge, sprinkle with the walnut pieces, and serve at room temperature.

Waldorf turkey salad

Substitute 2 cored and cubed red eating apples, and 2 sliced celery stalks for the mango and grapes, and then add to the turkey and lemon mayonnaise mixture.

Healthy note

To reduce the fat content of this salad, use equal quantities of low-fat plain yogurt and reduced-calorie mayonnaise instead of the lemon mayonnaise, and omit the walnuts.

Christmas roast goose

Goose is a traditional Christmas bird in Britain and northern Europe, and it is a favourite festive alternative to turkey when a small group of people is to be served. It is simple to cook and tastes delicious with a fruit stuffing and spicy accompaniments.

 SERVES 6–8   1228–921 CALS PER SERVING

5–6 kg (10–12 lb) goose, with giblets reserved for stock

1 onion, quartered

1 cooking apple, quartered

a few sage sprigs

salt and black pepper

30 g (1 oz) plain flour

450 ml (¾ pint) goose giblet stock (page 147)

150 ml (¼ pint) dry white wine

spiced stuffed apples (see box, right) to serve

watercress sprigs to garnish

PORK AND APPLE STUFFING

300 g (10 oz) pork sausagemeat

60 g (2 oz) fresh breadcrumbs

2 tsp dried sage

30 g (1 oz) butter

1 onion, finely chopped

1 large cooking apple, peeled, cored, and finely chopped

1 Make the pork and apple stuffing: in a bowl, combine the sausagemeat, breadcrumbs, and sage.

2 Melt the butter in a pan, add the onion, and cook gently, stirring occasionally, for 3–5 minutes until soft but not coloured.

3 Add the cooking apple, and cook for 5 minutes. Stir the onion and apple into the sausagemeat mixture, season with salt and pepper, and leave to cool.

4 Remove any fat from the cavity of the goose. Put the onion and apple quarters into the cavity together with the sage. Spoon the stuffing into the neck end of the goose, pat it into a rounded shape, and secure the skin flap with a small skewer. Weigh the goose.

5 Prick the skin of the goose all over with a fork, and rub with salt and pepper. Place the goose, breast-side down, on a wire rack in a large roasting tin, and cook in a preheated oven at 220°C (200°C fan, Gas 7) for 30 minutes.

6 Turn the goose breast-side up, and cook for 20 minutes. Reduce the oven temperature to 180°C (160°C fan, Gas 4) and cook for 20 minutes per 500 g (1 lb).

7 Test the goose by inserting a fine skewer into the thickest part of a thigh: the juices should run clear when the meat is thoroughly cooked.

8 Lift the goose on to a warmed serving platter, and then leave to rest, covered with foil, for about 20 minutes.

9 Make the gravy while the goose is resting: pour off all but 2 tbsp of the fat from the roasting tin. Put the tin on the hob, add the flour, and cook, stirring, for 1 minute. Add the stock and wine, and bring to a boil, stirring constantly. Simmer for 2–3 minutes, then taste for seasoning. Strain into a warmed gravy boat.

10 To serve, arrange the spiced stuffed apples around the goose, and garnish with watercress. Hand the gravy separately.

Spiced stuffed apples

Core 8 eating apples, keeping them whole. For the stuffing, combine 2 tbsp Calvados in a small bowl with 1 tsp ground cinnamon, ½ tsp ground allspice, and 8 finely chopped ready-to-eat prunes.

Place the apples in a buttered ovenproof dish, and spoon the stuffing into the centres. Melt 60 g (2 oz) butter, pour over the apples, and cover with foil. Bake in a preheated oven at 180°C (160°C fan, Gas 4) for 1 hour or until tender.

🔍 Cook's know-how

Goose is even richer and fattier than duck. Putting it on a wire rack in the roasting tin ensures it does not sit in the fat during cooking and this gives it a good, crisp skin.

Lacquered duck

🍴 SERVES 4   269 CALS PER SERVING

4 skinless duck breasts, 150–175 g (5–6 oz) each, cut diagonally into 1 cm (½ in) strips

2 tbsp sunflower oil

8 spring onions, trimmed and cut into 2.5 cm (1 in) lengths

salt and black pepper

1 tbsp sesame seeds, toasted

MARINADE

2 large garlic cloves, crushed

1 tbsp soy sauce

1 tbsp olive oil

2 tbsp clear honey

1 Put the duck in a bowl with the marinade ingredients and mix well. Cover and marinate in the refrigerator for about 2 hours, or overnight if time allows.

2 Heat the sunflower oil in a wok or large frying pan. Lift the duck from the marinade (reserving it), and stir-fry over a high heat for about 3–4 minutes or until browned all over. Add the spring onions, and stir-fry for a further 2–3 minutes or until the duck is cooked.

3 Pour the marinade and 5 tbsp water into the pan, bring quickly to a boil, and simmer for a few moments until the sauce has a syrupy consistency – take care not to overcook or the marinade may burn. Season with salt and pepper, scatter over the sesame seeds, and serve immediately.

Spring onions have crisp stems and are milder than most onions. Their crunchy texture makes them a favourite in stir-fries.

Chinese chicken with mango

🍴 SERVES 6   251 CALS PER SERVING

3 skinless, boneless chicken breasts (about 125 g/4 oz each), cut into thin strips

about 2 tbsp sunflower oil

1 large red pepper, halved, seeded, and cut into strips

250 g (8 oz) button chestnut mushrooms, halved

2 tsp cornflour blended with 5 tbsp cold chicken stock or water

salt and black pepper

250 g (8 oz) bean sprouts

about 200 g (7 oz) pak choi, coarsely sliced

60 g (2 oz) roasted cashew nuts, salted or unsalted

1 large ripe mango, peeled and sliced lengthways (see page 420)

chopped fresh coriander to serve (optional)

MARINADE

1 tbsp soy sauce

3 tbsp rice wine vinegar or white wine vinegar

3 tbsp clear honey

1 Put the chicken in a bowl with the marinade ingredients and mix well. Cover and marinate in the refrigerator for about 2 hours, more if time allows.

2 Heat 1 tbsp oil over a high heat in a wok or large frying pan. Lift half the chicken from the marinade (reserving it), and stir-fry for 1–2 minutes until golden all over and nearly cooked. Remove the chicken and set aside, then repeat with the remainder.

3 Heat the remaining oil in the pan, add the red pepper and mushrooms, and stir-fry for 1–2 minutes.

4 Return the chicken to the wok. Stir the cornflour mixture and pour it into the wok, then add the reserved marinade. Season with salt and pepper and bring to a boil. Add the bean sprouts and pak choi, and stir-fry until the pak choi has just wilted, about 2 minutes. Stir in the cashew nuts and mango slices, and serve at once, sprinkled with chopped coriander if you like.

Turkey to go

🍴 SERVES 6   439 CALS PER SERVING

about 750 g (1½ lb) turkey breast fillets, cut into thin strips

1 tsp ground coriander

1 tsp ground cumin

salt and black pepper

12 soft tortilla wraps

about 2 tbsp sunflower oil

1 large red pepper, halved, seeded, and thinly sliced

TO SERVE

soured cream

tomato salsa or mango chutney

shredded Romaine lettuce

1 Put the turkey strips in a bowl with the coriander and cumin. Season with salt and pepper, then mix well to coat the turkey in the spices. Cover and marinate in the refrigerator for about 30 minutes, more if time allows.

2 When you are ready to cook the turkey, warm the tortillas (see page 218). Heat the oil in a wok or large frying pan and fry the turkey in batches with the red pepper strips until golden brown and cooked through, about 4 minutes. You may need to add more oil with each batch.

3 Transfer the warm tortillas to a basket and spoon the turkey and peppers into a serving dish. Let each person spread their tortillas with soured cream and salsa or chutney, top this with some shredded lettuce and turkey, then roll into a fat cigar shape. The filled tortillas are easy to eat with your hands if they are sliced in half on the diagonal.

> 🔍 **Cook's know-how**
>
> Soft tortillas are flat Mexican breads that can be made from wheat or corn (both are suitable for this recipe). They are widely available at supermarkets, and some are flavoured with tomato, garlic, or herbs.

Opposite, clockwise from top left: Lacquered duck, Chinese chicken with mango, Turkey to go

Shaping and cooking Chinese pancakes

Pour the sesame oil into a bowl. Take 2 balls of dough, dip half of 1 ball into the oil, then press the oiled half on to the second ball.

Flatten the dough balls with the palms of your hands and roll out to a pancake about 15 cm (6 in) in diameter. Heat a frying pan. Put the double pancake into the pan and cook for 1 minute. Flip over and cook the other side for 1 minute.

Remove from the pan, and peel the 2 pancakes apart. Repeat with the remaining dough, to make 18 pancakes in all. Cover the pancakes with a damp tea towel to stop them drying out.

Peking duck

This Chinese dish is great fun to make, but you can buy the pancakes if you are short of time – they are sold at most large supermarkets. Let everyone help themselves to some crisp-skinned duck, spring onions, cucumber, and hoisin sauce, so they can assemble their own pancakes.

 SERVES 6   **848 CALS PER SERVING**

2.5 kg (5 lb) duck, with any giblets removed

3 tbsp dry sherry

3 tbsp clear honey

3 tbsp soy sauce

CHINESE PANCAKES

275 g (9 oz) plain flour

200 ml (7 fl oz) boiling water

2 tbsp sesame oil

TO SERVE

6 spring onions, cut into matchstick-thin strips

½ cucumber, peeled and cut into matchstick-thin strips

90 ml (3 fl oz) hoisin sauce, sprinkled with sesame seeds

spring onions to garnish

1 Remove any fat from the cavity of the duck. Put the duck into a bowl, pour boiling water over it, then remove and dry inside and out.

2 Mix together the sherry, honey, and soy sauce, and brush over the duck. Leave to stand, uncovered and at room temperature, for 4 hours or until the skin is dry.

3 Put the duck, breast-side down, on a wire rack in a roasting tin, and roast in a preheated oven at 200°C (180°C fan, Gas 6) for 25 minutes or until browned. Turn over and roast for a further 1–1¼ hours or until tender.

4 Meanwhile, make the pancake dough: sift the flour into a large bowl, add the boiling water, and mix to form a soft dough. Knead until smooth. Cover and leave to stand for about 30 minutes.

5 Knead the dough for 5 minutes. Shape into a roll about 2.5 cm (1 in) in diameter. Cut into 18 pieces, then roll into balls. Shape and cook the pancakes (see box, right).

6 When the duck is cooked, leave it to stand for about 15 minutes. Meanwhile, stack the pancakes on a plate in a steamer, cover, and steam for 10 minutes. Cut the duck into small pieces. Serve with the pancakes, spring onions, cucumber, and hoisin sauce, and garnish with spring onions.

Roast duck with cranberries

any people like the flesh of roast duck
reast a little pink, but the legs need to be
ell cooked, or they may be tough. To
ccommodate the difference, serve the
reast meat first, and return the duck to
e oven for 15 minutes to finish cooking
e legs.

SERVES 4   580 CALS PER SERVING

kg (5 lb) duck, with any giblets reserved
 stock

anberry sauce to serve (page 176)

tercress sprigs to garnish

ANBERRY STUFFING

g (1 oz) butter

mall onion, finely chopped

5 g (6 oz) fresh brown breadcrumbs

5 g (4 oz) cranberries

sp chopped parsley

sp ground mixed spice

t and black pepper

gg, beaten

GRAVY

1 tsp plain flour

300 ml (½ pint) duck giblet stock (page 147)

1 Make the cranberry stuffing: melt the
butter in a pan, add the onion, and cook
gently for 3–5 minutes until softened.

2 Stir in the breadcrumbs, cranberries,
parsley, and mixed spice, and season
with salt and pepper. Bind with the egg,
and leave to cool.

3 Remove any fat from the cavity of the
duck. Spoon the stuffing into the neck
end of the duck, secure the skin flap over
the stuffing with a small skewer, and pat into
a rounded shape. Put any leftover stuffing
into an ovenproof dish and set aside.

4 Prick the skin of the duck all over with a
fork, and rub salt and pepper into the
skin. Place the duck, breast-side down, on
a wire rack in a deep roasting tin, and roast
in a preheated oven at 200°C (180°C fan,
Gas 6) for 25 minutes or until golden brown.

5 Pour off some of the fat from the tin to
reduce splashing. Turn the duck breast-
side up, and roast for another 20 minutes or
until brown.

6 Reduce the oven temperature to 180°C
(160°C fan, Gas 4), and roast the duck,
without basting, for 1–1¼ hours. Cook any
leftover stuffing with the duck for the last
40 minutes.

7 Test the duck by inserting a fine skewer
into the thickest part of a thigh: the juices
will run clear when it is cooked. Keep warm,
uncovered, while you make the gravy.

8 Pour off all but 1 tbsp of the fat from the
roasting tin. Set the tin on the hob, add
the flour, and cook, stirring, for 2 minutes.
Pour in the stock, and bring to a boil, stirring
until lightly thickened. Taste for seasoning,
and strain into a warmed gravy boat.

9 Put the stuffing into a serving dish, carve
the duck (page 150), and garnish with
watercress. Serve with the gravy and
cranberry sauce.

Sauces for duck

Orange sauce
Put 2 finely chopped shallots, 300 ml
(½ pint) chicken stock, and the juice of
2 oranges into a pan, and bring to a boil.
Simmer until reduced by half, then season
with salt and pepper. Push through a sieve,
add the pared zest of 1 large orange, cut into
fine strips, and reheat gently. Serve hot.

Honey sauce
Cook 2 finely chopped shallots in 30 g (1 oz)
butter until soft. Add 1 tbsp plain flour, and
cook, stirring, for 1 minute. Blend in 300 ml
(½ pint) chicken stock and 75 ml (2½ fl oz)
dry white wine. Boil, stirring, until thick. Add
3 tbsp clear honey, 1 tbsp white wine vinegar,
and a pinch each of salt and pepper, and cook
for 1 minute. Push through a sieve, and add
3 tbsp finely chopped parsley. Serve hot.

Blackcurrant sauce
Put 250 g (8 oz) blackcurrants and 300 ml
(½ pint) water into a saucepan, and bring
slowly to a boil. Simmer for 10 minutes until
tender. Add 250 g (8 oz) caster sugar and
1 tbsp port, and cook gently until the sugar
has dissolved. Serve hot or cold.

Duck breasts with raspberry sauce

🍴 SERVES 4   975 CALS PER SERVING

4 x 250–300 g (8–10 oz) duck breasts, with the skin left on

salt and black pepper

RASPBERRY SAUCE

150 ml (¼ pint) port

75 ml (2½ fl oz) water

45 g (1½ oz) caster sugar

250 g (8 oz) raspberries

1 tsp cornflour

juice of 2 oranges

salt and black pepper

1 Make the raspberry sauce: pour the port and measured water into a small saucepan. Add the sugar, and bring to a boil, stirring until the sugar has dissolved. Add the raspberries, bring back to a boil, then cover and simmer very gently for 5 minutes.

2 With a wooden spoon, push the raspberry mixture through a sieve to extract the seeds. Return the raspberry purée to the saucepan, and bring back to a boil.

3 Mix the cornflour with the orange juice. Add a little of the raspberry purée to the cornflour mixture, and blend together. Return to the saucepan, and bring back to a boil, stirring constantly until thickened. Season with salt and pepper, and set aside.

4 Score and season each duck breast (see box, opposite, right).

5 Place the duck breasts under a hot grill, 10 cm (4 in) from the heat, and cook for 8 minutes on each side or until the skin is crisp and the duck is tender but still slightly pink inside.

6 Slice the duck breasts, skin-side up, and arrange in a fan shape on warmed plates. Spoon raspberry sauce around each of the servings, and serve at once.

Hot and spicy stir-fried duck

🍴 SERVES 4   453 CALS PER SERVING

4 x 250–300 g (8–10 oz) skinless duck breasts, cut diagonally into 1 cm (½ in) strips

2 tbsp sunflower oil

8 spring onions, cut into 2.5 cm (1 in) lengths

125 g (4 oz) carrots, cut into matchstick-thin strips

250 g (8 oz) mangetout

1 x 200 g can water chestnuts, drained, rinsed, and sliced

MARINADE

2 tsp dark soy sauce

2 tsp red wine vinegar

2.5 cm (1 in) piece of fresh root ginger, peeled and grated

2 fresh red chillies, halved, seeded, and coarsely chopped

grated zest and juice of 1 orange

1 tsp sesame oil

1 tsp cornflour

1 tsp caster sugar

salt and black pepper

1 Make the marinade: in a large bowl, combine the soy sauce, vinegar, ginger, chillies, orange zest and juice, sesame oil, cornflour, and sugar, then season with salt and pepper.

2 Toss the duck strips in the marinade, cover, and leave to stand for 10 minutes.

3 Lift the duck strips out of the marinade, reserve the marinade, and drain the duck on paper towels.

4 Heat the oil in a wok or large frying pan, add the duck, and stir-fry over a high heat for 5 minutes or until browned all over. Add the spring onions and carrots, and stir-fry for 2–3 minutes. Add the mangetout, and stir-fry for 1 minute.

5 Pour the marinade into the wok, and stir-fry for about 2 minutes or until the duck is just tender. Stir in the water chestnuts, heat through, and taste for seasoning. Serve hot.

Oriental duck with ginger

🍴 SERVES 4   445 CALS PER SERVING

4 x 250–300 g (8–10 oz) skinless duck breasts

1 tbsp sunflower oil

8 baby sweetcorn

bean sprouts and 1 tbsp toasted sesame seeds to garnish

MARINADE

200 ml (7 fl oz) orange juice

3 tbsp dark soy sauce

1 tbsp sesame oil

1 tbsp Chinese rice wine or dry sherry

1 tbsp clear honey

5 cm (2 in) piece of fresh root ginger, peeled and grated

1 garlic clove, crushed

salt and black pepper

1 Make the marinade: in a large bowl, combine the orange juice, soy sauce, sesame oil, rice wine or sherry, honey, fres root ginger, and garlic, then season with s and pepper.

2 With a sharp knife, make several diagonal slashes in each duck breast. Pour the marinade over the duck breasts, turn them over, then cover and marinate in the refrigerator for about 30 minutes.

3 Lift the duck breasts out of the marinade, reserving the marinade. Heat the oil in a large frying pan, add the duck breasts, and cook over a high heat turning frequently, for 10–12 minutes until tender. Add the marinade and simmer fo 2–3 minutes until slightly reduced.

4 Meanwhile, blanch the baby sweetco in boiling salted water for 1 minute. Drain, then make lengthways cuts in eac one, leaving them attached at the stem.

5 To serve, slice each duck breast, and arrange on 4 individual plates. Spoon the hot sauce over the duck, add the sweetcorn, then garnish with bean sprou and the toasted sesame seeds. Serve ho

Duck breasts with red wine sauce

🍴 **SERVES 4   906 CALS PER SERVING**

x 250–300 g (8–10 oz) duck breasts, with
e skin left on

25 ml (4 fl oz) beef stock

25 ml (4 fl oz) red wine

tsp tomato purée

tsp lemon juice

5 g (½ oz) butter

alt and black pepper

tbsp chopped fresh rosemary to garnish

MARINADE

garlic cloves, sliced

tbsp balsamic vinegar

tbsp chopped fresh rosemary

1 Make the marinade: in a bowl, combine the
garlic, vinegar, and rosemary. Score the duck
breasts (see box, right), and put them, skin-side
down, in a shallow dish. Spoon the marinade
over the top. Chill for 30 minutes.

2 Put the duck breasts, skin-side down, with
the marinade, in a frying pan and cook
for 5–7 minutes. Turn, and cook for a further
5 minutes. Remove from the pan, and
keep warm.

3 Spoon any excess fat from the frying pan.
Add the stock and wine, and boil over
a high heat until reduced to a dark glaze,
then add the tomato purée and lemon juice.

4 Remove from heat, and whisk in the butter,
letting it thicken the sauce as it melts. Taste
for seasoning.

5 Slice the duck, and arrange on warmed
plates. Spoon the sauce around the duck,
sprinkle with the chopped rosemary, and
serve hot.

Scoring and seasoning the duck

With a sharp knife, score the skin
of each duck breast with criss-cross
lines. Season both sides with salt
and pepper.

Mushroom-stuffed quail

Whole quail make an impressive dinner party dish. They can be quite fiddly to eat, so boning and stuffing them makes it much easier for your guests. If you are short of time to bone the birds yourself, you can buy them ready boned at supermarkets, or ask the butcher to do it.

SERVES 6   651 CALS PER SERVING

12 quail, boned (page 148)

30 g (1 oz) butter, plus extra for greasing

1 tbsp lime marmalade

MUSHROOM STUFFING

60 g (2 oz) butter

3 shallots, finely chopped

375 g (12 oz) button mushrooms, coarsely chopped

60 g (2 oz) fresh white breadcrumbs

salt and black pepper

1 egg, beaten

LIME SAUCE

150 ml (¼ pint) chicken stock

juice of 1 lime

200 ml (7 fl oz) full-fat crème fraîche

4 tbsp chopped parsley

1 Make the mushroom stuffing: melt the butter in a saucepan, add the shallots, and cook gently, stirring occasionally, for 3–5 minutes until soft but not coloured.

2 Add the mushrooms and cook for 2 minutes, then remove from the heat. Stir in the breadcrumbs, season with salt and pepper, then stir in the egg and leave to cool. Stuff the quail (see box, right).

3 Put the quail into a buttered roasting tin. Melt the butter gently in a saucepan, add the lime marmalade, and heat gently, stirring, until combined. Brush over the quail, and cook in a preheated oven at 200°C (180°C fan, Gas 6) for 15–20 minutes until golden brown and tender. Remove from the tin and keep warm.

4 Make the lime sauce: put the roasting tin on the hob. Add the stock, and bring to a boil, then stir for 5 minutes or until reduced a little.

5 Stir in the lime juice and crème fraîche, and heat gently, stirring constantly, until the sauce has a smooth, creamy consistency.

6 Add half of the parsley and season with salt and pepper. Serve the quail with the lime sauce, and garnish with the remaining parsley.

Stuffing the quail

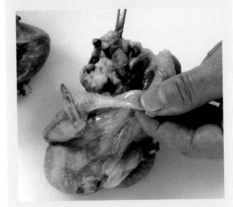

Spoon some of the stuffing into the cavity of each quail; secure the skin with a wooden cocktail stick.

Traditional roast pheasant

Pheasants are often sold in pairs (called a brace) – a cock and a hen. Make sure you get young pheasants for this recipe; old ones are not suitable for roasting and can be very tough unless they are cooked slowly in a casserole.

SERVES 4   660 CALS PER SERVING

2 pheasants, any giblets reserved

90 g (3 oz) butter, softened

salt and black pepper

4 streaky bacon rashers

1 tsp plain flour

300 ml (½ pint) pheasant giblet stock or chicken stock (page 146)

1 tsp redcurrant jelly

watercress sprigs to garnish

TO SERVE

fried breadcrumbs (see box, right)

game chips (see box, right)

bread sauce (page 176)

1 Spread the pheasants with the butter, and season. Lay two bacon rashers crosswise over each breast.

2 Put the pheasants into a roasting tin, and cook in a preheated oven at 200°C (180°C fan, Gas 6), basting once, for 1 hour or until tender.

3 Test the pheasants by inserting a fine skewer in the thickest part of a thigh: the juices should run clear when they are cooked.

4 Lift the pheasants on to a warmed serving platter, cover with foil, and keep warm. Pour off all but 1 tbsp of the fat from the roasting tin, reserving any juices. Put the tin on the hob, add the flour, and cook, stirring, for 1 minute.

5 Add the stock and redcurrant jelly, and bring to a boil, stirring until lightly thickened. Simmer for 2–3 minutes, then taste for seasoning. Strain into a warmed gravy boat.

6 To serve, garnish the pheasants with the watercress sprigs, and serve with fried breadcrumbs, game chips, bread sauce and the gravy.

Pheasant stew

SERVES 6–8   633–475 CALS PER SERVING

[t]bsp sunflower oil

[p]heasants, cut into serving pieces (page 147)

[...]5 g (12 oz) shallots, chopped

[...]5 g (4 oz) piece of smoked streaky bacon, [cu]t into strips

[g]arlic cloves, crushed

[t]bsp plain flour

[...]0 ml (1 pint) game stock or chicken stock [(pa]ge 146)

[...]0 ml (½ pint) red wine

[h]ead of celery, separated into stalks, sliced

[...]0 g (8 oz) button mushrooms

[t]bsp tomato purée

[sal]t and black pepper

[cho]pped parsley to garnish

Heat the oil in a large flameproof
[...] casserole. Add the pheasant pieces and
[co]ok over a high heat until browned. Lift
[ou]t and drain.

[...] Add the shallots and bacon and cook for
[...] 5 minutes. Add the garlic and flour and
[co]ok, stirring, for 1 minute. Add the stock and
[win]e and bring to a boil. Add the celery,
[mu]shrooms, tomato purée, and season.
[Sim]mer for 5 minutes.

[...] Add the pheasant, bring back to a boil,
[...] cover, and cook in a preheated oven
[at 1]60°C (140°C fan, Gas 3) for 2 hours.
[Gar]nish with parsley.

Normandy pheasant

[App]les and cream are traditional
[ingr]edients in the cuisine of Normandy.
[Her]e, apples and a rich sauce perfectly
[com]plement the pheasant, which is
[coo]ked slowly and gently in wine and
[stoc]k to keep it moist and tender.

SERVES 6–8   751–563 CALS PER SERVING

[30 g] (1 oz) butter

[1 tbs]p sunflower oil

[2 ph]easants, cut into serving pieces (page 147)

[2 co]oking apples, quartered, cored, and sliced

[2 ce]lery stalks, sliced

[1 oni]on, sliced

[1 tbs]p plain flour

[300 m]l (½ pint) chicken or game stock (page 146)

[150 m]l (¼ pint) dry white wine

---

salt and black pepper

150 ml (¼ pint) double cream

apple rings to serve (see box, below)

chopped parsley to garnish

1 Melt the butter with the oil in a flameproof
casserole. When the butter is foaming, add
the pheasant pieces, and cook for about
5 minutes until browned. Lift out and drain.

2 Lower the heat, add the apples, celery,
and onion, and cook for 5–6 minutes
until soft.

3 Add the flour and cook, stirring, for
1 minute. Pour in the stock and wine,
season with salt and pepper, and bring
to a boil, stirring until lightly thickened.

4 Return the pheasant to the casserole
and spoon the sauce over the top.
Bring back to a boil, cover with greaseproof
paper and the casserole lid, and cook in a
preheated oven at 180°C (160°C fan, Gas 4)
for 1–1½ hours until tender. Remove the
pheasant from the casserole with a slotted
spoon and keep warm.

5 Strain the sauce into a saucepan. Whisk
in the cream, taste for seasoning, then
reheat gently. Arrange the pheasant on
serving plates with the apple rings. Spoon
the sauce over the pheasant and serve at
once, garnished with parsley.

Apple rings

Core 2 cooking apples, leaving them whole,
and slice crosswise into 5 mm (¼ in) rings.
Melt 30 g (1 oz) butter in a frying pan, add
the apple rings, and sprinkle with a little caster
sugar. Cook over a high heat for 3 minutes,
turning once, until caramelized and golden.

♥ Healthy note

Instead of cream, use low-fat crème fraîche
and only 150 ml (¼ pint) stock. Crème fraîche
is runnier than double cream, so less liquid
is needed.

Extras for game

These traditional accompaniments can
be served with roast pheasant and many
other game dishes, including grouse
and partridge.

Fried breadcrumbs

Melt 30 g (1 oz) butter with 1 tbsp sunflower
oil. When the butter is foaming, add 90 g
(3 oz) fresh white breadcrumbs and cook,
stirring, for 3-5 minutes until golden.

Game chips

Using a mandoline or the finest blade
on a food processor, slice 500 g (1 lb) old
potatoes finely, then dry them. Heat some
sunflower oil in a deep-fat fryer, add the
potato slices, and deep-fry for 3 minutes
or until crisp and golden. Drain, then
sprinkle with salt.

Stuffing balls

Combine 125 g (4 oz) fresh white
breadcrumbs, 60 g (2 oz) grated cold butter,
1 beaten egg, 2 tbsp chopped parsley, and
the finely grated zest of 1 lemon. Season
with salt and pepper, stir to mix well, then
roll into 12 small balls. Melt 30 g (1 oz)
butter with 1 tbsp olive oil in a frying pan.
When the butter is foaming, add the stuffing
balls, and cook for 5 minutes or until golden
all over. Drain thoroughly.

Game pie with fennel and carrots

🍴 SERVES 6   672 CALS PER SERVING

2 tbsp sunflower oil

750 g (1½ lb) boneless game meat, cut into strips or dice

2 large carrots, sliced

1 fennel bulb, sliced

1 large onion, chopped

2 tsp plain flour

300 ml (½ pint) game stock or chicken stock (page 146)

150 ml (¼ pint) red wine

1 tbsp redcurrant jelly

salt and black pepper

plain flour for dusting

250 g (8 oz) ready-made puff pastry

beaten egg for glazing

chopped parsley to garnish

2 litre (3½ pint) pie dish

1 Heat the oil in a large flameproof casserole. Add the game in batches and cook over a high heat until browned all over. Lift out and drain on paper towels.

2 Lower the heat, add the carrots, fennel, and onion, and cook, stirring occasionally, for 5 minutes or until softened. Add the flour and cook, stirring, for about 1 minute.

3 Gradually pour in the stock and bring to a boil, stirring until thickened slightly. Add the game, wine, and redcurrant jelly, and season with salt and pepper. Cover tightly and simmer very gently for 1 hour. Leave to cool.

4 Lightly flour a work surface. Roll out the puff pastry until 2.5 cm (1 in) larger than the pie dish. Invert the dish on to the dough and cut around the edge. Cut a long strip of pastry from the trimmings and press on to the rim of the pie dish. Reserve the remaining trimmings. Spoon in the game and vegetable mixture. Brush the pastry strip with water, top with the pastry lid, and crimp the edge with a fork.

5 Make a hole in the top of the pie to let the steam escape. Roll out the reserved pastry and cut decorative shapes with a pastry cutter. Brush the bottoms of the shapes with beaten egg, and arrange on the pie. Glaze with beaten egg.

6 Bake the pie in a preheated oven at 200°C (180°C fan, Gas 6) for 25–30 minutes until the pastry is well risen and golden. Garnish with parsley.

Ruby hare casserole

🍴 SERVES 4   1068 CALS PER SERVING

1 hare, cut into serving pieces

30 g (1 oz) butter

2 tbsp olive oil

125 g (4 oz) piece of streaky bacon, cut into strips

16 small shallots

250 g (8 oz) chestnut mushrooms, halved

30 g (1 oz) plain flour

900 ml (1½ pints) game stock or chicken stock (page 146)

2 large thyme sprigs

2 large parsley sprigs

salt and black pepper

stuffing balls (page 191)

fresh thyme to garnish

MARINADE

300 ml (½ pint) ruby port

4 tbsp olive oil

1 large onion, sliced

2 bay leaves

1 Make the marinade: in a large bowl, combine the port, oil, onion, and bay leaves. Add the hare pieces, turn in the marinade, cover, and leave to marinate in the refrigerator for 8 hours.

2 Remove the hare from the marinade, reserving the marinade. Melt the butter with the oil in a large flameproof casserole. When the butter is foaming, add the hare pieces and cook over a high heat until browned all over. Lift out and drain on paper towels.

3 Lower the heat, add the bacon and shallots, and cook for 5 minutes or until lightly browned. Add the mushrooms and cook for 2–3 minutes. Remove and drain on paper towels. Add the flour and cook, stirring for 1 minute. Gradually add the stock and bring to a boil, stirring until thickened.

4 Return the hare, bacon, shallots, and mushrooms to the casserole with the strained marinade. Add the thyme and parsley, season with salt and pepper, and bring to a boil. Cover and cook in a preheated oven at 160°C (140°C fan, Gas 3) for 2 hours.

5 Taste for seasoning. Place the stuffing balls on top, garnish with fresh thyme and serve hot.

Guinea fowl Madeira

🍽 SERVES 6   613 CALS PER SERVING

bsp sunflower oil

× 1.25 kg (2½ lb) guinea fowl, cut into serving eces (page 147)

hallots, halved

bsp plain flour

0 ml (1 pint) chicken stock

0 ml (¼ pint) dry white wine

bsp Madeira

lt and black pepper

5 g (12 oz) seedless green grapes

0 ml (¼ pint) double cream

opped parsley to garnish

1 Heat the oil in a flameproof casserole, and cook the guinea fowl pieces in batches for a few minutes until browned all over. Lift out and drain. Lower the heat, add the shallots, and cook, stirring, for 5 minutes or until softened. Lift out and drain.

2 Add the flour, and cook, stirring, for 1 minute. Pour in the stock, and bring to a boil, stirring. Add the wine and Madeira, and season with salt and pepper. Add the guinea fowl and shallots, and bring to a boil. Cook in a preheated oven at 160°C (140°C fan, Gas 3) for 1 hour or until just tender.

3 Transfer the casserole to the hob, add the grapes, and cook for 15 minutes. Add the cream, and heat gently. Garnish with parsley and serve hot.

Rather special game pie

This raised game pie follows a classic recipe that takes about 6 hours to make, over 3 days, but it is well worth the effort. Boned mixed game meats – usually pheasant, hare, and venison – are available in large supermarkets and food halls. There is chicken in the pie too, which goes very well with game, but you could use turkey.

SERVES 20   507 CALS PER SERVING

2 kg (4 lb) chicken, boned and skinned (page 148)

1 kg (2 lb) boneless mixed game meats, cut into 1 cm (½ in) pieces

375 g (12 oz) belly pork, coarsely chopped

500 g (1 lb) piece of streaky bacon, cut into small pieces

butter for greasing

hot-water crust pastry (see box, right)

about 2 tsp salt

black pepper

1 egg, beaten

450 ml (¾ pint) jellied stock (page 147)

MARINADE

150 ml (¼ pint) port

1 small onion, finely chopped

3 garlic cloves, crushed

leaves of 4 thyme sprigs, chopped

1 tsp grated nutmeg

29 cm (11½ in) springform or loose-bottomed cake tin

1 Make the marinade: in a bowl, combine the port, onion, garlic, thyme, and grated nutmeg.

2 Cut the chicken breast into long strips, about 1 cm (½ in) wide, and set aside. Cut the rest of the chicken into 1 cm (½ in) chunks. Add the chunks to the marinade with the game meats, belly pork, and bacon. Cover and leave to marinate in the refrigerator for 8 hours.

3 Lightly butter the tin. Take two-thirds of the hot-water crust pastry, pat it out over the bottom of the tin, and push it up the side, until it stands 1 cm (½ in) above the rim.

4 Season the meat mixture with plenty of salt and pepper, and spoon half into the pastry shell. Smooth the surface evenly.

5 Arrange the reserved chicken breast strips on top of the meat, radiating from the middle. Season with salt and pepper.

6 Top with the remaining meat mixture. Brush the top edge of the pastry with beaten egg. Roll out the remaining pastry, and cover the pie, reserving the trimmings. Pinch around the edge to seal, then crimp.

7 Decorate the pie with the pastry trimmings, attaching them with beaten egg. Make 3 steam holes in the pastry lid, and glaze the pie with beaten egg.

8 Bake in a preheated oven at 220°C (200°C fan, Gas 7) for 1 hour. If the pastry browns too quickly, cover with foil. Reduce the heat to 160°C (140°C fan, Gas 3) and cook for 2–2¼ hours.

9 Test the pie by piercing the centre with a skewer: the juices will run clear and the meat will feel tender when it is done. Leave the pie to cool in the tin for 8 hours.

10 Put the jellied stock into a saucepan and heat until melted. Using a funnel, slowly pour the stock through the holes in the pie. Cover and chill for 6 hours or until the stock has set. Unmould the pie and cut into wedges to serve.

Hot-water crust pastry

Sift 750 g (1½ lb) plain flour and 1 tsp salt into a large bowl. Put 400 ml (14 fl oz) water and 300 g (10 oz) white vegetable fat into a saucepan and heat until the water is boiling and the fat has melted.

Pour on to the flour and mix quickly with a wooden spoon until the mixture holds together.

Turn the dough on to a floured surface, invert the bowl over the top to keep the dough moist, and leave to cool until lukewarm.

Rabbit with mustard and marjoram

🕐 **SERVES 4**   **548 CALS PER SERVING**

bsp Dijon mustard

sp chopped fresh marjoram

abbit portions

g (1 oz) butter

bsp olive oil

arge onion, chopped

arlic cloves, crushed

g (3 oz) piece of smoked streaky bacon,
 into pieces

p plain flour

ml (¾ pint) chicken stock

 and black pepper

ml (¼ pint) single cream

sp chopped parsley to garnish

Mix the mustard and marjoram, and
spread over the rabbit pieces. Place
a shallow dish, cover, and leave to
rinate in the refrigerator for 8 hours.

Melt the butter with the oil in a large
flameproof casserole. When the butter
aming, add the rabbit, and cook for
out 5 minutes until browned all over.
out and drain on paper towels.

Add the onion, garlic, and bacon to
the casserole and cook for 3–5 minutes.
d the flour and cook, stirring, for
inute. Gradually blend in the stock
 bring to a boil, stirring until thickened.

Return the rabbit to the casserole, season
with salt and pepper, and bring back to
bil. Cover and cook in a preheated oven
60°C (140°C fan, Gas 3) for 1½ hours or
 the rabbit is tender.

ransfer the rabbit to a warmed platter
nd keep hot. Boil the sauce for
nutes until reduced. Stir in the cream,
e for seasoning, and spoon over the
bit. Garnish with parsley.

Healthy note

decrease the amount of saturated fat,
iit the bacon and use low-fat crème fraîche
stead of cream. Crème fraîche is runnier
an cream, so reduce the amount of chicken
ck to 300 ml (½ pint) to compensate.

Braised rabbit with mushrooms and cider

🕐 **SERVES 4**   **506 CALS PER SERVING**

30 g (1 oz) butter

1 tbsp sunflower oil

4 rabbit portions

8 small shallots

375 g (12 oz) mushrooms, quartered

300 ml (½ pint) dry cider

a few parsley sprigs

3–4 tarragon sprigs

salt and black pepper

300 ml (½ pint) single cream

2 tbsp chopped parsley to garnish

1 Melt the butter with the oil in a flameproof
casserole. When the butter is foaming,
add the rabbit, and cook for about
5 minutes until browned all over. Lift out
the rabbit with a slotted spoon and drain
on paper towels.

2 Add the shallots to the casserole and
cook over a high heat, stirring, for
about 3 minutes until golden. Add the
mushrooms, and cook, stirring occasionally,
for 3–4 minutes until softened.

3 Return the rabbit to the casserole,
and add the cider, parsley sprigs, and
tarragon. Season with salt and pepper,
and bring to a boil. Cover and cook in a
preheated oven at 160°C (140°C fan, Gas
3) for 1½ hours or until the rabbit is tender.

4 Transfer the rabbit to a warmed platter
and keep warm. Remove and discard
the parsley and tarragon. Bring the sauce
in the casserole to a boil on the hob, then
boil until slightly reduced. Stir in the cream,
taste for seasoning, and reheat gently.

5 Pour the sauce over the rabbit, and
serve at once, garnished with parsley.

Braised rabbit with prunes

Substitute 125 g (4 oz) ready-to-eat pitted
prunes for the mushrooms. Add to the casserole
30 minutes before the end of the cooking time.

Venison casserole

SERVES 6   466 CALS PER SERVING

1 kg (2 lb) stewing venison, cut into 2.5 cm (1 in) cubes

2 tbsp olive oil

6 celery stalks, thickly sliced on the diagonal

150 g (5 oz) chestnut mushrooms, quartered

30 g (1 oz) plain flour

salt and black pepper

125 g (4 oz) small carrots

parsley for garnish

MARINADE

450 ml (¾ pint) red wine

3 tbsp sunflower oil

1 onion, sliced

1 tsp ground allspice

a few parsley sprigs

1 bay leaf

1 Make the marinade: in a large bowl, combine the red wine, oil, onion, allspice, parsley sprigs, and bay leaf. Toss the venison cubes in the marinade to coat them thoroughly, cover, and leave to marinate in the refrigerator, turning occasionally, for 2 days.

2 Lift the venison and onion out of the marinade and pat dry. Strain and reserve the marinade.

3 Heat the oil in a large flameproof casserole, add the venison and onion, and cook for 3–5 minutes until well browned. Lift out and drain on paper towels.

4 Lower the heat, add the celery and mushrooms, and cook for 2–3 minutes until softened. Remove with a slotted spoon. Add the flour and cook, stirring, for 1 minute. Gradually blend in the marinade and bring to a boil, stirring until thickened.

5 Return the venison, onion, celery, and mushrooms to the casserole, and season with salt and pepper. Bring to a boil, cover, and cook in a preheated oven at 160°C (140°C fan, Gas 3) for 1½ hours.

6 Add the carrots, and return to the oven for 30 minutes or until the venison is tender. Serve hot, garnished with parsley.

Pot roast venison

SERVES 6   454 CALS PER SERVING

1.25–1.5 kg (2½–3 lb) boned venison shoulder, rolled and tied

30 g (1 oz) butter

2 tbsp sunflower oil

1 large onion, chopped

2 large carrots, sliced

2 celery stalks, sliced

300 ml (½ pint) beef stock

salt and black pepper

1 tbsp redcurrant jelly

MARINADE

300 ml (½ pint) red wine

2 tbsp olive oil

pared zest of 1 orange

pared zest of 1 lemon

2 tsp crushed juniper berries

6 black peppercorns

1 garlic clove, crushed

1 large thyme sprig

1 large parsley sprig

1 Make the marinade: in a large bowl, combine the wine, oil, orange and lemon zests, juniper berries, black peppercorns, garlic, thyme, and parsley. Turn the venison the marinade, cover, and marinate in the refrigerator, turning occasionally, for 2–3 day

2 Lift the venison out of the marinade, straining and reserving the marinade, and pat dry. Melt the butter with the oil in a large flameproof casserole. When the butt is foaming, add the venison and cook over high heat for 5 minutes or until well browned over. Remove the venison from the casserole

3 Lower the heat and add the onion, carrots, and celery to the casserole. Cover and cook very gently for 10 minutes Place the venison on top of the vegetable add the stock and the strained marinade, then season with salt and pepper and brin to a boil. Cover with a piece of greasepro paper and the casserole lid, and cook in a preheated oven at 160°C (140°C fan, Gas 3) for 2½–3 hours until tender.

4 Lift out the venison and keep warm. Strain the liquid in the casserole, spoor off the fat, then return the liquid to the casserole. Add the redcurrant jelly, and bo for a few minutes until syrupy. Slice the venison, and arrange on a warmed platte Pour over the sauce, and serve hot.

Meat Dishes

Under 45 minutes

BARBECUE

Steaks with smoked oyster relish
Steaks rubbed with garlic, and sprinkled with smoked oyster relish flavoured with parsley.

SERVES 4   278 CALS PER SERVING

Takes 15–20 minutes   Page 212

DINNER PARTY

Chateaubriand with béarnaise sauce
Grilled steak basted with butter, served with a béarnaise sauce flavoured with tarragon.

SERVE 2   761 CALS PER SERVING

Takes 25 minutes   Page 213

Beef Stroganoff
Classic Russian dish: strips of rump steak cooked with shallots and button mushrooms and mixed with soured cream.

SERVES 6   329 CALS PER SERVING

Takes 20 minutes   Page 2

MEXICAN CLASSIC

Beef tacos
Minced beef and tomatoes richly seasoned with garlic, chilli, and coriander. Served in taco shells with lettuce and soured cream.

SERVES 4   407 CALS PER SERVING

Takes 25 minutes   Page 231

Saltimbocca
Veal escalopes topped with sage leaves and Parma ham, and cooked with garlic. Served with a wine and cream sauce.

SERVES 4   342 CALS PER SERVING

Takes 25 minutes   Page 234

HIGH PROTEI

Pork steaks with mixed peppercorns
Lean meat encrusted with peppercorns, served with a white wine, beef stock, and cream sauce.

SERVES 4   567 CALS PER SERVING

Takes 30 minutes, **plus standing**   Page

Veal schnitzels
Veal escalopes coated in beaten egg and fresh white breadcrumbs, chilled, then cooked until lightly golden brown. Served with anchovy fillets, capers, lemon wedges, and parsley.

SERVES 4   373 CALS PER SERVING

Takes 20 minutes, **plus chilling**   Page 233

JAPANESE CLASSIC

Teriyaki beef
Strips of tender rump steak marinated in soy sauce, Japanese rice wine, and sugar. Stir-fried with onion and red pepper.

SERVES 4   329 CALS PER SERVING

Takes 15 minutes, **plus marinating**   Page 215

ORIENTAL CLASS

Pork with chilli and coconut
Strips of pork in a dry marinade of ginger, chilli, and curry powder. Cooked with coco spring onions, and red pepper.

SERVES 6   332 CALS PER SERVING

Takes 40 minutes, **plus marinating**   Page

FAMILY CHOICE

ver and bacon with onion sauce
rips of liver simmered with onion, bacon,
ef stock, tomato ketchup, and
rcestershire sauce.
RVES 4   441 CALS PER SERVING
kes 15 minutes   Page 236

eak Diane
mbéed rump steaks served with a light
uce combining onion, beef stock, lemon
ce, Worcestershire sauce, and parsley.
VES 4   373 CALS PER SERVING
kes 25 minutes   Page 215

urnedos Roquefort
unchy and nutritious: grilled tournedos steaks
ped with a mixture of melted Roquefort
ese, butter, and chopped walnuts.
VES 4   430 CALS PER SERVING
kes 20 minutes   Page 215

lf's liver with sage
es of calf's liver, coated with seasoned
ur, and cooked quickly. Served with pan
es flavoured with sage and lemon juice.
VES 4   364 CALS PER SERVING
kes 10 minutes   Page 234

rned beef hash
ick and nourishing: chunks of corned beef
ked with onion, pieces of potato, and stock,
d grilled until crispy and brown.
VES 4   444 CALS PER SERVING
es 30 minutes   Page 225

nb with mint glaze
f and lamb chops glazed with white wine,
egar, mint sprigs, honey, and Dijon
stard, then barbecued or grilled.
ES 4   304 CALS PER SERVING
es 15 minutes, **plus standing**   Page 244

amed sweetbreads
's sweetbreads simmered with onion,
sley, and bay leaf.
ES 6   230 CALS PER SERVING
es 40 minutes, **plus soaking**   Page 234

Over 60 minutes

TRADITIONAL

English roast beef
Traditional succulent family roast: rolled beef
sirloin basted and cooked until tender. Served
with vegetables, Yorkshire puddings, a rich
red wine gravy, and creamy horseradish sauce.
SERVES 8   394 CALS PER SERVING
Takes 3¼ hours   Page 208

Thai red beef curry
Cubes of chuck steak cooked with cardamom,
bay leaves, cloves, ginger, garlic, paprika,
tomatoes, yogurt, and red pepper.
SERVES 6   327 CALS PER SERVING
Takes 2½ hours   Page 223

Boeuf bourguignon
Rich casserole: cubes of chuck steak cooked
with shallots, bacon, red Burgundy, beef stock,
mushrooms, and herbs.
SERVES 6   490 CALS PER SERVING
Takes 2¾ hours   Page 220

TRADITIONAL

Beef pot roast with winter vegetables
Topside of beef in a casserole with onions,
swede, celery, carrot, wine, and herbs.
SERVES 6   360 CALS PER SERVING
Takes 3½ hours   Page 209

Hungarian goulash
Cubes of chuck steak cooked with stock, onion,
tomatoes, red pepper, potatoes, paprika, and
soured cream.
SERVES 6   474 CALS PER SERVING
Takes 2½ hours   Page 221

Spinach-stuffed lamb
Succulent and nutritious: boned leg of lamb
stuffed with spinach and garlic, and roasted
with wine and anchovies.
SERVES 6–8   459–344 CALS PER SERVING
Takes 2½ hours, **plus cooling**   Page 242

Over 60 minutes

Beef olives with vegetable julienne
Slices of topside wrapped around stir-fried vegetables, and cooked with beef stock.

SERVES 6   257 CALS PER SERVING

Takes 2¼ hours   Page 225

FAMILY CHOICE

Cottage pies with cheesy potato topping
Minced beef cooked with vegetables and stock. Topped with mashed potato and cheese.

SERVES 6   567 CALS PER SERVING

Takes 1½ hours   Page 228

Danish meatballs
Minced pork seasoned with onion, thyme, a paprika and shaped into ovals. Cooked in a tomato sauce, and topped with Greek yogurt

SERVES 4–6   586–391 CALS PER SERVING

Takes 1½ hours   Page 2

Roast leg of pork
Tender and nourishing: pork roasted with carrot and onion until crackling is crisp. Served with gravy and apple sauce.

SERVES 6–8   338–254 CALS PER SERVING

Takes 2¼ hours   Page 255

TRADITIONAL

Roast leg of lamb with red wine gravy
Lamb flavoured with herbs, roasted and served with red wine gravy and mint sauce

SERVES 4–6   517–344 CALS PER SERVING

Takes 2 hours   Page

Rack of lamb with a walnut and herb crust
Rack of lamb coated with a walnut and par crust, and roasted.

SERVES 4–6   626–417 CALS PER SERVING

Takes 1¾ hours, **plus chilling**   Page

AFRICAN CLASSIC

...obotie
...nced beef baked with garlic, apricots,
...nonds, chutney, lemon, and milk-soaked
...ead. Topped with eggs and almonds.
...VES 6–8   656–492 CALS PER SERVING
...kes 1 hour 5 minutes   Page 230

Shoulder of lamb with lemon and olives
Lamb rolled with an olive, lemon, and herb
stuffing, and roasted in wine and stock.
SERVES 6–8   460–345 CALS PER SERVING
Takes 2¾ hours   Page 243

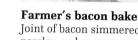

FAMILY CHOICE

Farmer's bacon bake
Joint of bacon simmered with vegetables,
parsley, and peppercorns, cut into pieces,
and baked with a cheese sauce.
SERVES 6–8   510–383 CALS PER SERVING
Takes 2¼ hours   Page 260

...lt beef with mustard sauce
...ed salt beef cooked with carrots, celery,
...atoes, turnips, and leeks. Served with a
...stard sauce flavoured with wine vinegar.
...VES 6–8   575–431 CALS PER SERVING
...es 2¼ hours, **plus soaking**   Page 210

Traditional steak and kidney pie
Rich and satisfying: cubes of beef and kidney
cooked with stock, Worcestershire sauce, and
mushroom. Topped with shortcrust pastry.
SERVES 6   577 CALS PER SERVING
Takes 3¼ hours, **plus cooling**   Page 224

Marinated loin of pork with pineapple
Pork marinated in pineapple juice, maple
syrup, soy sauce, and herbs, then roasted.
SERVES 8   320 CALS PER SERVING
Takes 2½ hours, **plus marinating**   Page 253

...w-roast shoulder of lamb
...ulder of lamb, stuffed with rosemary and
...ic, roasted in beef stock, and served with
...b fat, stock, and port gravy.
...ES 4   656 CALS PER SERVING
...es 4½ hours, **plus standing**   Page 249

TRADITIONAL

Shepherd's pie
Minced lamb baked with mushrooms, carrot,
onion, garlic, stock, and mushroom ketchup.
Topped with mashed potato.
SERVES 6   383 CALS PER SERVING
Takes 1½ hours   Page 251

DINNER PARTY

Mustard-glazed ham
Smoked gammon cooked with cider, glazed
with sugar and mustard, roasted, and served
with a lemon mustard sauce.
SERVES 16–20   477–382 CALS PER SERVING
Takes 4 hours, **plus soaking**   Page 261

Meat know-how

For centuries, meat has been the protein food around which the majority of meals have been planned. Today that tradition has been turned on its head, with healthy eating advice to make meat and other protein foods just one part of a healthy diet, not the major part. Nevertheless, meat is enjoyed by most families several times a week, and it still forms the traditional centrepiece for many celebration meal By making sure the cooking method suits the cut of meat you are preparing – quick cooking for lean meats, long, slow cooking for tougher cuts – you will always have perfectly moist and tender results.

Buying and storing

If possible, buy your meat from a good local butcher, or the butcher in a supermarket, because he's most likely to have just the cut you want (or will be prepared to cut it for you), and he will also advise you how to cook it. Wherever you shop, choose meat that looks fresh and moist (not wet), with a good colour and no greyish tinge. Check that pieces are neatly trimmed, without excess fat and splinters of bone. If the meat is packaged, check the use-by date. Appetites vary, but as a general guide, allow 125-175 g (4-6 oz) of lean boneless meat per person, and about 250 g (8 oz) each if the meat has a reasonable amount of bone.

Store all meat in the refrigerator, with raw kept separate from cooked and on a lower shelf (also below any food that will not be cooked before eating). Mince and offal are more perishable than other kinds of meat, so cook them within 1 day of purchase.

Chops, steaks, and joints can be kept for about 3 days: remove the wrapping and replace with fresh. Eat cooked meat within 2-3 days.

Freezing

Meat to be frozen must be very fresh. Wrap it tightly and thoroughly so that all the air is excluded. Pad any sharp bones so that they don't pierce the wrapping. If packing chops, cutlets, steaks, or hamburgers, separate them with cling film or freezer wrap. The larger the piece of meat the longer it will keep. Mince and sausages can be stored in a freezer for 3 months; offal, chops, and cutlets for 4 months; joints and steaks for 6 months. Thaw frozen meat, in its wrapping and on a plate to catch any juices, at the bottom of the refrigerator.

Microwaving

Because microwave cooking is so fast, meat does not have time to brown and become crisp. This can be overcome by using a special browning dish, which sears meat in the way a frying pan does.

The microwave is very useful for thawing frozen meat. This must be done evenly at the manufacturer's recommended setting to prevent some parts of the meat beginning to cook before others are totally thawed. wrapping should be removed from the meat before thawing to ensure that the meat does not start to cook.

Preparing meat for cooking

Trim off excess fat before cooking and remove any visible gristle, sinew, and tou connective tissue. If grilling or frying stea chops, or bacon rashers, slash or snip a fat at intervals to prevent the meat from curling up during cooking.

Marinate very lean joints to be roaste or lean cuts to be grilled or barbecued t keep them moist during cooking.

Meat stock
Ask your butcher to saw 2 kg (4 lb) bones into 6 cm (2½ in) pieces. Beef and veal bones are best.

1 Roast the bones in a preheated oven at 230°C (210°C fan, Gas 8) for 30 minutes. If you have time, add 2–3 roughly chopped onions, carrots, and celery stalks and roast for another 30 minutes.

2 Transfer the bones and vegetables to a large stockpot. Add 4 litres (7 pints) water, a bouquet garni made of 1–2 bay leaves, a few parsley stalks, and 1–2 sprigs of thyme, and a few black peppercorns.

3 Bring to a boil. Skim off scum, then cover and simmer for 4–6 hours. Ladle into a sie to strain. Skim off fat, or let cool and lift off solidified fat.

Basic cooking techniques

Tougher pieces of meat should be cooked slowly by stewing or braising to make them beautifully tender. Those cuts that are naturally tender can be cooked quickly by frying or grilling or by roasting.

Braising

Brown the meat on all sides in a flameproof casserole, to add flavour and a rich colour. Remove the meat from the casserole.

Add chopped vegetables and cook until they are beginning to brown. Return the meat and add liquid and any flavourings. Bring to a boil, then cover and cook gently on the hob or in the oven, as instructed in the recipe.

Stewing

Cut the meat into even cubes. Put into a flameproof casserole with any vegetables and liquid to cover plus any flavourings. Bring to a boil, then cover and simmer on the hob, or cook in the oven. Alternatively, heat some oil in the casserole and brown the cubes of meat, then brown the vegetables. Add the liquid and any flavourings. Bring to a boil, cover, and simmer as above.

Roasting

1 Take the joint from the refrigerator and allow it to come to room temperature.

2 Preheat the oven. Rub the meat with fat or oil and seasonings, or make incisions all over and insert herbs or slivers of garlic. Insert a meat thermometer, if using.

3 Put the joint and any vegetables in a roasting tin. Roast, basting with the fat and juices in the tin, until cooked to your taste (page 207). If not using a meat thermometer (or an instant-read thermometer), test whether the meat is cooked by inserting a skewer into the centre. If the juices that run out are bloody, the meat is rare; if pink, medium; if clear, well-done.

4 Transfer the joint to a carving board and leave to rest for 10–15 minutes while making gravy. Carve the joint (page 206) and serve.

Grilling and barbecuing

Preheat the grill to hot, or light the barbecue (it will take 20–30 minutes to reach cooking temperature unless it is gas, which will heat up immediately).

Put the meat on the grill rack and put under the hot grill, or arrange on the grid over charcoal. Brush with oil or a marinade, and cook the meat until it is browned on both sides, turning and re-brushing as necessary.

For sausages or thicker pieces of meat that need to be well cooked, reduce the heat or move the meat further away from the heat, to complete cooking.

Stir-frying

1 Cut the meat into uniform pieces for even cooking. Heat a wok or heavy frying pan, then add a little oil.

2 When the oil is hot, start adding the meat, a little at a time – adding too much at once will lower the temperature of the oil. Using a slotted spoon or a spatula, stir and toss the meat constantly until it is evenly browned.

3 If some of the pieces of meat are cooked before others, they can be pushed up the side of the wok or to the side of the pan where they will keep warm but not overcook.

Frying and sautéing

1 Dry the meat with paper towels (if too moist it will not brown quickly and evenly). Heat oil or a mixture of oil and butter in a heavy frying pan until it is very hot, then add the meat, taking care not to crowd the pan.

2 Cook until well browned on both sides. Reduce the heat and continue cooking until the meat is done to your taste. When turning meat, use tongs rather than a fork, as a fork pierces the meat and allows the juices to run out.

Boning and butterflying a leg of lamb

A boned leg of lamb is much easier to carve than meat still on the bone. Tunnel boning leaves a pocket that can be filled with a savoury stuffing. If the leg is cut open to lie flat, this is known as butterflying.

1 To tunnel bone, trim the skin and most or all of the fat from the lamb. Cut around the pelvic bone, at the wide end of the leg, to separate it from the meat. Sever the tendons that connect it to the leg bone. Remove the pelvic bone.

2 At the narrow end of the leg, cut around the shank bone and then scrape the meat away from the whole length of the bone using short strokes.

3 Cut away the meat to expose the joint that joins the shank bone to the leg bone. Sever the tendons and then remove the shank bone.

4 Cut around each end of the leg bone. Ease the leg bone out, cutting and scraping away the meat as you twist and pull the bone out. Trim off the tendons.

5 If you want to butterfly the boned leg, carefully insert a large chef's knife into the cavity left by the leg bone and cut to one side to slit open the meat.

6 Open out the boned leg into a "butterfly" shape. Cut through any thick portions of meat so that the whole leg can be opened out flat and is roughly even in thickness. Trim off excess fat and any remaining tendons.

Boning a shoulder of lamb

A special boning knife, with a narrow, pointed blade, is useful for preparing shoulders of lamb, pork, and veal. If you don't have such a knife, a small, sharp chef's knife can be used instead.

1 Remove the skin and fat. Set the shoulder meat-side up. Cut through the meat to the blade bone, and then cut away the meat on either side, keeping the knife as close to the bone as possible, until the bone is revealed.

2 Cut through the ball and socket joint that li between the blade bone and the central shoulder bone. This will separate the 2 bones.

3 Cut beneath the ball and socket joint to f the end. Hold it firmly in one hand and pu the blade bone away from the meat.

4 Cut around the central shoulder bone, severing the tendons, and cutting and scraping away the meat. Pull out the bone. If necessary, enlarge the pocket left by the bone so that it will accommodate a stuffing

Preparing a best end of neck or rack of lamb

Best end of neck, or rack of lamb, is a tender joint for roasting or grilling. A single rack, which is one side of the upper ribcage, comprises 6-9 cutlets and serves 2-3 people. Two racks can be used to make impressive joints such as a guard of honour or crown roast.

Rack of lamb

If the butcher hasn't done so, remove the backbone (chine) from the meaty end. Pull off the skin. Score through the fat and meat 5 cm (2 in) from the ends of the rib bones.

2 Turn the rack over and set it at the edge of the chopping board, so the ends of the rib bones are suspended. Score the meat along the rack, about 5 cm (2 in) from the ends of the rib bones, cutting through the meat to the bones.

3 Cut out the meat from between the bones, cutting from the crosswise cuts to the ends. Turn the rack over and scrape the ends of the bones clean.

4 Trim away most of the fat from the meat.

Guard of honour

Crown roast

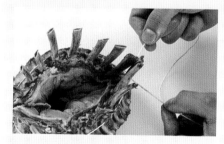

Two racks of lamb are tied together in the shape of a crown.

Prepare 2 racks as above. Slit the membrane between the rib bones at the meaty end so that the racks can be bent.

Stand the racks, meat-side in, on a work surface and curve to form a crown shape. Bend the bones so that the crown will stand upright.

Tie string around the middle of the 2 racks, to hold them in place.

Fill the centre of the roast with a stuffing, then roast (or add a filling just before serving). Carve the roast by cutting down between the rib bones.

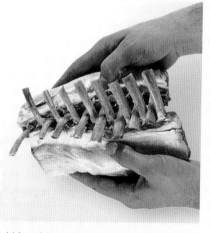

Hold 1 rack in each hand, meat-side out, and push them together, interlocking the rib bones. Cover the exposed bones with foil, if desired, to prevent them from charring during cooking, then cook as directed in the recipe.

Stuffing, rolling, and tying a joint

Joints that have been boned and opened out can be rolled around a savoury stuffing, which adds moisture and flavour to the meat during cooking.

1 Open out the meat and spread with an even layer of stuffing, leaving a small border clear around the edge.

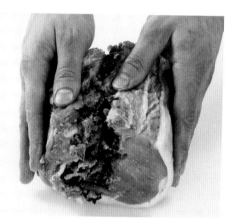

2 Roll up or fold the joint around the stuffing, to make a compact bolster shape. Turn it so that the joint is underneath.

3 Tie string around the meat at regular intervals, to hold in shape during cooking. Remove the string before carving.

Carving a joint on the bone

Once a joint of meat has finished cooking, transfer it to a carving board, cover with foil, and let it "rest" in a warm place for 10–15 minutes. During this time, the temperature of the joint will even out, and the flesh will reabsorb most of the juices. To carve, use a very sharp, long carving knife and a 2-pronged carving fork.

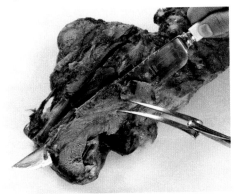

Shoulder of lamb

1 Insert the fork into the shank end. Cut a narrow, wedge-shaped piece from the centre, in the meatiest part between the angle formed by the blade bone and the shoulder bone.

2 Carve neat slices from either side of this wedge-shaped cut until the blade and central shoulder bones are reached. Turn the shoulder over and cut horizontal slices lengthways.

Whole ham

1 Cut a few horizontal slices from one side of the ham, to make a flat surface. Turn the ham over on to this surface. Insert the carving fork into the meat at the shank end. Make 3 or 4 cuts through to the bone at the shank end.

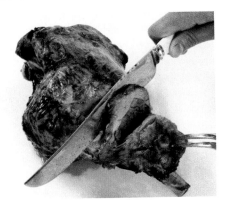

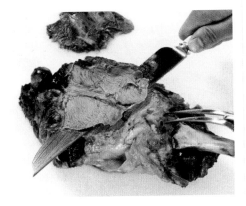

Leg of lamb

1 Set the joint with the meaty side up, and insert the carving fork firmly into the meat at the knuckle end. Cut a narrow, wedge-shaped piece from the centre of the meaty portion, cutting all the way to the bone.

2 Carve neat slices from either side of this wedge-shaped cut, gradually changing the angle of the knife to make the slices larger. Turn the leg over. Trim off the fat, then carve off horizontal slices.

2 Insert the knife into the last cut and slide it along the bone, to detach the slices. Make a few more cuts in the ham and continue to remove the slices in the same way. Turn over and carve off horizontal slices.

Rib of beef

1 Set the roast upright on a carving board, insert the carving fork into the meaty side, to steady the joint, and cut close to the large rib bones at the base of the meat, to remove them.

2 Hold the now boneless roast upright on the board. With the knife at a slight angle, carve the meat into slices that are about 2 cm (¾ in) thick.

Using a meat thermometer

The most accurate way to test if a large piece of meat is cooked is to use a meat thermometer, which registers the internal temperature. Before cooking, insert the spike of the thermometer into the middle or thickest part of the joint. Make sure that the thermometer does not touch a bone as bones become hotter than meat and will therefore give a false reading. Start checking the temperature reading towards the end of the suggested cooking time. Alternatively use an instant-read thermometer, which is inserted near the end of the calculated cooking time. A joint will continue to cook by retained heat for 5–10 minutes after it is removed from the oven.

Making gravy

A delicious gravy can be made from the richly flavoured sediment and juices from roasting meat. Boost flavour with a splash of red or fortified wine, redcurrant jelly, Worcestershire sauce, or lemon juice, to taste.

Pour all but about 2 tbsp fat from the roasting tin, leaving the juices and sediments. Set the tin on the hob and heat until sizzling. Stir in 2 tbsp plain flour. Whisk briskly to mix the flour with the juices, and scrape the bottom and sides of the tin to dislodge any sediment and make a well-browned paste.

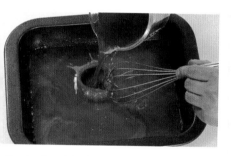

Gradually add 1 litre (1¾ pints) stock or vegetable cooking water, whisking constantly to combine with the flour paste. Whisk until smooth. Simmer, stirring frequently, until the gravy reaches the desired consistency. Season and flavour to taste, then strain if wished. Serve piping hot, in a warmed gravy boat.

Preparing offal

Although not as popular as it used to be, offal, which includes liver, kidneys, sweetbreads, and tongue, is both nutritious and delicious. Flavour and texture vary according to the animal from which the offal comes - offal from veal has the most delicate flavour and texture; offal from pork has the strongest and toughest.

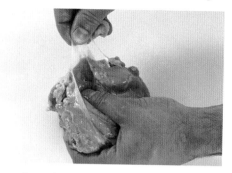

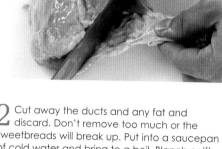

Sweetbreads

1 Soak the sweetbreads in cold water with 1 tbsp lemon juice for 2–3 hours to clean them. Drain, and rinse well. Cut away any discoloured parts. Use your fingers to carefully peel off the thin membrane surrounding the sweetbreads.

2 Cut away the ducts and any fat and discard. Don't remove too much or the sweetbreads will break up. Put into a saucepan of cold water and bring to a boil. Blanch calf's sweetbreads for 5 minutes, and lamb's sweetbreads for 3 minutes.

Lamb's kidneys

1 (If using beef or veal kidneys, first separate them.) Carefully cut through any fine membrane around each kidney and use your fingers to peel it off (cut the ducts from beef or veal kidneys).

2 Set each kidney round-side up and slice lengthways in half (or leave attached at the base, according to recipe directions). With a sharp pair of scissors, snip out the small fatty, white core and the tubes.

Roasting meat

As all ovens are different, these times are intended as a general guide only. When calculating timings, add an extra 500 g (1 lb) on the weight of your joint if it weighs less than 1.5 kg (3 lb). Be sure to preheat the oven before putting the meat in to cook.

Meat		Oven temperature	Time	Internal temperature
Beef	Rare	180°C (160°C fan, Gas 4)	15 mins per 500 g (1 lb)	60°C (140°F)
	Medium	180°C (160°C fan, Gas 4)	20 mins per 500 g (1 lb)	70°C (160°F)
	Well-done	180°C (160°C fan, Gas 4)	25 mins per 500 g (1 lb)	80°C (175°F)
Veal	Well-done	180°C (160°C fan, Gas 4)	25 mins per 500 g (1 lb)	80°C (175°F)
Lamb	Medium rare	180°C (160°C fan, Gas 4)	20 mins per 500 g (1 lb)	75°C (170°F)
	Well-done	180°C (160°C fan, Gas 4)	25 mins per 500 g (1 lb)	80°C (175°F)
Pork	Medium	180°C (160°C fan, Gas 4)	25 mins per 500 g (1 lb)	80°C (175°F)
	Well-done	180°C (160°C fan, Gas 4)	30 mins per 500 g (1 lb)	85°C (180°F)

English roast beef

🍴 **SERVES 8**   **394 CALS PER SERVING**

3.25 kg (6½ lb) prime rib of beef on the bone

vegetable oil for brushing

salt and black pepper

1 onion, quartered

TO SERVE

Yorkshire puddings (see box, opposite)

gravy of your choice (page 232)

horseradish sauce (see box, right)

1 Insert a meat thermometer, if using, into the middle of the meat. Put the beef into a roasting tin, brush all over the meat with oil, and season with salt and pepper. Add the onion quarters to the tin and roast with the beef in a preheated oven at 200°C (180°C fan, Gas 6) for 20 minutes.

2 Meanwhile, make the Yorkshire pudding batter and set aside.

3 After the beef has been roasting for 20 minutes, baste it with the juices from the tin, and lower the oven temperature to 180°C (160°C fan, Gas 4).

4 Roast, basting frequently, for a further 1½ hours for rare beef, 1¾ hours for medium, and 2 hours for well-done, or until the meat thermometer registers 60°C (140°F), 70°C (160°F), or 80°C (175°F).

5 Transfer the beef to a carving board, cover with foil, and leave to stand in a warm place. Increase the oven temperature to 220°C (200°C fan, Gas 7) and bake the Yorkshire puddings.

6 While the puddings are in the oven and the meat is resting, make the gravy in the roasting tin according to the instructions on page 232.

7 Serve the beef with the Yorkshire puddings, gravy, and horseradish sauce.

Horseradish sauce

Mix 2–3 tbsp grated fresh horseradish with 1 tbsp white wine vinegar in a bowl. In another bowl, whisk 150 ml (¼ pint) whipping cream until thick. Fold the cream into the horseradish mixture, and add salt, black pepper and caster sugar to taste. Cover and leave to chill until ready to serve.

Yorkshire puddings

Sift 125 g (4 oz) plain flour and a pinch of salt into a bowl. Make a well, and add 3 beaten eggs and a little milk taken from 200 ml (7 fl oz).

Whisk the milk and egg together in the well with a little of the flour from the sides, then whisk in the remaining milk, gradually drawing in all of the flour to make a smooth batter.

Put some white vegetable fat into each cup of a 12-hole bun tin and heat in a preheated oven at 220°C (200°C fan, Gas 7) until very hot. Remove the tin from the oven. Whisk the batter and pour into the cups in the tin. Bake the Yorkshire puddings in the oven for 15 minutes or until well risen, golden, and crisp. Serve immediately.

French-style braised beef

🍴 SERVES 4–6   604–402 CALS PER SERVING

1 kg (2 lb) piece of lean braising steak (eg chuck steak)

2 tbsp olive oil

125 g (4 oz) piece of lean bacon, cut into strips

1 onion, sliced

250 g (8 oz) carrots, thickly sliced

250 g (8 oz) mushrooms, quartered

500 g (1 lb) tomatoes, chopped

125 g (4 oz) pitted black olives

600 ml (1 pint) beef stock

salt and black pepper

chopped parsley to garnish

MARINADE

500 ml (16 fl oz) red wine

3 tbsp red wine vinegar

2 large garlic cloves

1 strip of orange zest

1 bouquet garni

1 Make the marinade: combine the wine, vinegar, garlic, orange zest, and bouquet garni. Add the beef, cover, and leave to marinate in the refrigerator overnight.

2 Remove the beef from the marinade and pat dry with paper towels. Strain the marinade and reserve. Heat the oil in a large flameproof casserole, add the beef and bacon, and brown all over. Lift out and drain on paper towels.

3 Add the onion, carrots, and mushrooms and cook, stirring, for 5 minutes or until lightly browned.

4 Add the beef, bacon, tomatoes, olives, and reserved marinade. Pour in sufficient stock to cover the meat and season with salt and pepper.

5 Bring to a boil, cover tightly, and cook in a preheated oven at 180°C (160°C fan, Gas 4) for 1½–2 hours or until the meat is very tender.

6 Slice the meat and arrange on a warmed platter with the vegetables. Skim the sauce and pour over the meat. Garnish with parsley before serving.

Beef pot roast with winter vegetables

🍴 SERVES 6   360 CALS PER SERVING

2 tbsp sunflower oil

1.15 kg (2½ lb) beef topside or silverside

4 onions, quartered

1 large swede, cut into thick chunks

2 celery stalks, thickly sliced

2 large carrots, thickly sliced

150 ml (¼ pint) dry white wine

150 ml (¼ pint) hot water

1 bouquet garni

salt and black pepper

chopped parsley to garnish

1 Heat the sunflower oil in a large flameproof casserole. Add the beef and cook over a high heat, turning occasionally, for about 10 minutes until browned all over.

2 Lift the beef out of the casserole and put in the onions, swede, celery, and carrots. Stir well to coat the vegetables in the oil, then cook, stirring occasionally, for about 5 minutes.

3 Push the vegetables to the side of the casserole, and place the meat in the middle, with the vegetables around it.

4 Add the wine, measured water, and bouquet garni, and season with salt and pepper. Bring to a boil, then cover tightly, and cook in a preheated oven at 150°C (130°C fan, Gas 2) for 2½–3 hours until the meat is tender.

5 Transfer the meat and vegetables to a warmed platter, cover, and keep warm.

6 Spoon the fat from the surface of the cooking liquid, then boil over a high heat until the liquid is reduced by half. Taste for seasoning, and strain into a warmed gravy boat. Carve the meat into thin slices, garnish with parsley, and serve with the gravy and vegetables.

Salt beef with mustard sauce

🍴 SERVES 6–8   575–431 CALS PER SERVING

1 kg (2 lb) salted silverside

500 g (1 lb) baby carrots

8 potatoes, halved

8 celery stalks, cut into chunks

250 g (8 oz) turnips, cut into chunks

chopped parsley to garnish

MUSTARD SAUCE

30 g (1 oz) butter

30 g (1 oz) plain flour

150 ml (¼ pint) milk

4 tsp white wine vinegar

2 tsp mustard powder

2 heaped tsp caster sugar

salt and black pepper

1 Put the salt beef into a large bowl. Cover with cold water and leave to soak overnight to remove any excess salt.

2 Rinse the beef under cold running water, place in a large saucepan, and cover with cold water. Cover the pan with its lid, bring to a boil, and simmer very gently, topping up the water in the pan when necessary, for about 1 hour.

3 Add the carrots, potatoes, celery, and turnips and cook for 40 minutes or until the beef and vegetables are tender.

4 Transfer the meat to a warmed platter. Lift out the vegetables with a slotted spoon, reserving the liquid, and arrange around the meat. Cover and keep warm.

5 Make the sauce: melt the butter in a saucepan, add the flour, and cook, stirring, for 1 minute. Remove from the heat and gradually blend in the milk

and 150 ml (¼ pint) of the cooking liquid from the beef. Bring to a boil, stirring constantly, until the sauce thickens. Simm for 2 minutes.

6 In a jug, combine the vinegar, mustar powder, and sugar, and stir into the sauce. Cook for 1 minute, then season w salt and pepper. (Be careful not to add t much salt because the liquid from the be is salty.)

7 Slice the beef and arrange on warme serving plates with the vegetables. Po the mustard sauce over the beef, and sprinkle with parsley.

Beef with roast vegetable salad

 SERVES 4–6   522–348 CALS PER SERVING

kg (2 lb) beef fillet cut from the centre, trimmed

bsp tapenade (black olive paste)

bsp black peppercorns, coarsely crushed

bsp olive oil

opped parsley to garnish

)AST VEGETABLE SALAD

bsp olive oil

aubergine, cut into 5 mm (¼ in) slices

:ourgettes, cut into 5 mm (¼ in) slices

ennel bulb, cut lengthways into
nm (¼ in) pieces

ed pepper, halved, seeded, and cut into
nm (¼ in) strips

ellow pepper, halved, seeded, and cut into
nm (¼ in) strips

t and black pepper

sp balsamic vinegar

Tie the beef to retain its shape, if
necessary. Spread the black olive paste all
er the beef, then press on the peppercorns.

Pour the oil into a roasting tin and heat
in a preheated oven at 220°C (200°C
1, Gas 7).

Insert a meat thermometer, if using, into
the middle of the beef.

Put the beef into the hot oil, and roast
for 25 minutes for rare beef, 35 minutes
medium, or 40 minutes for well-done,
until the meat thermometer registers
C (140°F), 70°C (160°F), or 75°C (170°F).

Meanwhile, put the olive oil for the roast
vegetable salad into a large bowl. Add
aubergine, courgettes, fennel, and red
yellow peppers, and toss in the oil.

When the beef is cooked to your liking,
remove it from the roasting tin and leave
il cold. Meanwhile, put the vegetables
the hot tin and sprinkle with salt and
pper. Cook in the oven, turning the
etables once, for 30 minutes or until
der. Leave to cool, then sprinkle with
balsamic vinegar and toss to coat.

When the beef is cold, slice very thinly
nd serve with the roast vegetable
d. Garnish with parsley.

Beef Wellington

Inside a puff pastry case is a succulent
piece of prime beef and a rich stuffing
of liver pâté and mushrooms. The pastry
locks in all the juices and ensures none of
the wonderful flavours are lost. Serve with
a mushroom and red wine gravy.

 SERVES 8   580 CALS PER SERVING

1.5 kg (3 lb) beef fillet, trimmed and tied

salt and black pepper

2 tbsp sunflower oil

45 g (1½ oz) butter

1 small onion, finely chopped

250 g (8 oz) flat mushrooms, finely chopped

175 g (6 oz) smooth liver pâté

400 g (13 oz) ready-made puff pastry

1 egg, beaten

thin mushroom gravy to serve (page 232)

1 Season the beef with black pepper.
Heat the oil in a large frying pan, add
the beef, and cook over a high heat until
browned all over.

2 Put the beef fillet in a roasting tin and
cook in a preheated oven at 220°C
(200°C fan, Gas 7) for 25 minutes for rare
beef, 35 minutes for medium, or 40 minutes
for well-done. Leave to cool completely.

3 Meanwhile, melt the butter in the frying
pan, add the onion and mushrooms, and
cook, stirring, for 3 minutes or until softened.
Increase the heat to high, and cook until the
excess moisture has evaporated. Turn into a
bowl and leave to cool completely.

4 Add the liver pâté to the mushroom
and onion mixture, season with salt
and pepper, and stir well to combine.

5 Wrap the beef in the pastry (see box,
right).

6 Bake at 220°C (200°C fan, Gas 7) for
45 minutes or until the pastry is crisp and
golden. Cover with foil after 30 minutes to
prevent the pastry becoming too brown.
Leave to stand for about 10 minutes, then
slice and serve with the gravy.

Individual beef Wellingtons

Cut the raw beef into 8 slices. Brown the slices
in a frying pan, cool, then wrap each one in
pastry with a little of the pâté mixture. Bake
for 25–30 minutes.

Wrapping the beef in pastry

Roll out 300 g (10 oz) of the pastry to a 30 x 40
cm (12 x 16 in) rectangle. Spread half of the
pâté mixture down the middle, leaving a 10 cm
(4 in) border on each side.

Remove the string from the beef and place
the beef on the pâté mixture. Cover with
remaining pâté mixture.

Brush the pastry border with beaten egg. Fold
the short sides of the pastry over the beef.

Fold over the long ends and turn the parcel
over. Brush with beaten egg. Roll out the
remaining pastry, and cut into strips, 5 mm
(¼ in) wide. Arrange in a lattice pattern on
top of the pastry, then glaze the strips with
beaten egg.

Steaks with smoked oyster relish

🍴 SERVES 4   278 CALS PER SERVING

4 x 175 g (6 oz) rump steaks

salt and black pepper

2 garlic cloves, crushed

1 tbsp olive oil

smoked oyster relish (see box, right) and lemon wedges to serve

1 Season the steaks with salt and pepper, rub with the garlic, and brush with the oil.

2 Heat a frying pan over a high heat, add the steaks, and cook for 3–4 minutes on each side for rare steaks, 4–5 minutes for medium steaks, or 7–8 minutes for well-done steaks. Transfer the steaks to warmed serving plates.

3 Generously spoon the smoked oyster relish over the steaks, and serve at once, accompanied by lemon wedges.

Classic carpetbag steaks

Melt 15 g (½ oz) butter and cook 2 chopped shallots until softened. Remove from the heat and add 6 chopped fresh oysters, 125 g (4 oz) fresh breadcrumbs, 1 tbsp chopped parsley, and salt and pepper. Cut a pocket in each steak and fill with the stuffing.

Smoked oyster relish

Drain 1 x 100 g can smoked oysters. Finely chop 1 small onion and 1 handful of parsley sprigs.

Chop the drained smoked oysters with a large, sharp chef's knife.

Put the oysters, onion, and parsley into a small bowl and mix well. Chill until needed.

Savoury butters

These simple butters are quickly made, and ideal for adding an elegant touch to plain grilled meats such as steaks, chops, and noisettes.

Coriander butter
Soften 125 g (4 oz) butter and blend in 2 tbsp chopped fresh coriander, 1 tbsp lemon juice, 1 tsp ground coriander, and season with salt and black pepper. Chill. Garnish with a coriander sprig and a sprinkling of ground coriander.

Anchovy butter
Soften 125 g (4 oz) butter and blend in 2 tbsp finely chopped anchovies, 1 tbsp lemon juice, 1 tsp ground coriander, and season with black pepper. Chill. Garnish with anchovy fillets.

Parsley butter
Soften 125 g (4 oz) butter and blend in 2 tbsp chopped parsley, 1 tbsp lemon juice, and season with salt and black pepper. Chill. Garnish with a lemon twist and a parsley sprig.

Mustard butter
Soften 125 g (4 oz) butter and blend in 2 tbsp Dijon mustard, 2 tbsp chopped fresh tarragon, and season with salt and black pepper. Chill. Garnish with a tarragon sprig.

Pepper steaks

SERVES 4   489 CALS PER SERVING

x 150–175 g (5–6 oz) fillet steaks, about
5 cm (1 in) thick, trimmed

lt and black pepper

tbsp black peppercorns

g (1 oz) butter

tbsp sunflower oil

tbsp brandy

0 ml (¼ pint) double cream

opped parsley to garnish

Season the steaks on both sides with
salt. Crush the peppercorns and spread
em on a plate. Coat the steaks with the
eppercorns (see box, below).

Melt the butter with the oil in a frying
pan. When the butter is foaming, add
e steaks, and cook over a high heat for
minutes on each side.

Lower the heat and continue cooking
until the steaks are to your liking: rare
eaks need 1–2 minutes on each side,
edium steaks 3 minutes on each side,
d well-done steaks 4–5 minutes on each
e. Lift out of the pan and keep warm.

Pour the brandy into the frying pan,
and boil rapidly to drive off the alcohol.
en the brandy has almost disappeared,
in the cream, and add salt and pepper
aste. Gently reheat the sauce, pour it
er the steaks, and garnish with parsley.
ve hot.

oating steaks

ess each steak firmly on to the peppercorns,
til both sides are well coated.

Chateaubriand with béarnaise sauce

SERVES 2   761 CALS PER SERVING

400 g (13 oz) Chateaubriand steak (a thick piece
of fillet from the middle of the tenderloin)

30 g (1 oz) butter, melted

black pepper

béarnaise sauce (see box, right)

1 Cut the steak crosswise in half. Brush one
side of each half with melted butter and
season with pepper.

2 Put the steaks, buttered-side up, under
a hot grill, 7 cm (3 in) from the heat,
and cook for 2 minutes or until browned.
Turn the steaks over, brush with melted
butter, and season with pepper. Grill for
about 2 minutes until browned.

3 Lower the heat and cook, turning
once and brushing with the butter, for
4–5 minutes. Cover and leave to stand for
5 minutes. Slice the steaks, and serve with
the béarnaise sauce.

Béarnaise sauce

Put 4 tbsp tarragon vinegar, 1 finely chopped
shallot, and 1 tbsp chopped tarragon into a
pan and boil for a few minutes until reduced
by one-third. Leave to cool. Pour 2 egg yolks
into a bowl over a saucepan of simmering
water, add the vinegar mixture, and whisk
over a gentle heat until thick and fluffy.

Melt 90 g (3 oz) butter and gradually add
to the sauce, whisking constantly until thick.
Season with salt and white pepper.

Teriyaki beef

 SERVES 4   329 CALS PER SERVING

0 g (1 lb) rump steak, trimmed and cut into
n strips

bsp sunflower oil

arge onion, thinly sliced

ed pepper, halved, seeded, and cut into strips

pring onions, sliced, to garnish

MARINADE

5 ml (4 fl oz) dark soy sauce

ml (3 fl oz) Japanese rice wine or dry sherry

bsp caster sugar

Make the marinade: in a bowl, combine
the soy sauce, rice wine or sherry, and
gar. Toss the steak strips in the marinade,
ver, and leave in the refrigerator overnight.

Remove the steak strips from the
marinade, reserving the marinade.
at 1 tbsp of the oil in a wok, add the
on and red pepper, and stir-fry for about
ninutes. Remove from the wok with
lotted spoon and set aside. Heat the
naining oil, and stir-fry the steak strips
5 minutes or until just cooked through.

Return the onion and red pepper to the
wok with the marinade and cook for
ninutes or until heated through. Garnish
n the spring onions before serving.

Steak Diane

 SERVES 4   373 CALS PER SERVING

50–175 g (5–6 oz) rump steaks, trimmed

(1 oz) butter

sp sunflower oil

sp brandy

all onion, finely chopped

ml (½ pint) beef stock

p Worcestershire sauce

p lemon juice

p chopped parsley

and black pepper

ace the steaks between 2 sheets of
reaseproof paper and pound with a
g pin until 5 mm (¼ in) thick.

Melt the butter with the sunflower oil in
large frying pan. When the butter is

site: Teriyaki beef.

---

foaming, add the pounded steaks and
cook over a high heat for about 3 minutes
on each side until browned. Lift the steaks
out of the frying pan and cover with foil to
keep warm.

3 Pour the brandy into the pan, and add
the onion. Cook over a high heat, stirring
occasionally, for a few minutes until the
onion has softened and absorbed most of
the brandy. Stir in the stock, Worcestershire
sauce, lemon juice, and parsley, season
with salt and pepper, and cook for about
2 minutes.

4 Return the steaks to the pan and spoon
over the sauce. Reheat quickly and
briefly, and serve hot.

Beef and bean burritos

 SERVES 4   471 CALS PER SERVING

375 g (12 oz) rump steak, trimmed of fat and cut into thin strips

salt and black pepper

2 tbsp olive oil

1 garlic clove, crushed

½–1 fresh red chilli, halved, seeded, and chopped

½ tsp cumin seeds

1 x 400 g can tomatoes, drained, juice reserved

1 x 400 g can pinto or black beans, drained

8 flour tortillas

4 tbsp soured cream or crème fraîche

chopped fresh coriander to garnish

1 Season the steak strips with salt and
pepper. Heat the olive oil in a large
frying pan, add the steak, crushed garlic,
chopped chilli, and cumin seeds, and cook,
stirring, for 5 minutes or until lightly browned.

2 Add the tomatoes to the pan and cook
for about 3 minutes. Pour in the reserved
tomato juice and boil for 8–10 minutes until
the liquid is reduced.

3 Add the beans and cook until heated
through. Taste for seasoning, cover, and
keep hot. Warm the tortillas (page 218).

4 Divide the steak and tomato mixture
among the tortillas and roll them up.
Serve topped with soured cream and
garnished with coriander.

Tournedos Roquefort

 SERVES 4   430 CALS PER SERVING

125 g (4 oz) Roquefort cheese, crumbled

60 g (2 oz) walnut pieces, roughly chopped

30 g (1 oz) butter, softened

salt and black pepper

4 x 125 g (4 oz) tournedos (small fillet steaks),
2.5 cm (1 in) thick

chopped parsley to garnish

1 In a small bowl, combine the Roquefort,
walnuts, butter, and pepper to taste.

2 Season the tournedos steaks on both
sides with salt and pepper, and place
them under a hot grill, 7–10 cm (3–4 ins)
from the heat. Grill for 3–4 minutes on each
side for rare steaks, 4–5 minutes for medium
steaks, or 7–8 minutes for well-done steaks.

3 Two minutes before the steaks are
ready, sprinkle with the Roquefort
mixture, and return to the hot grill until
the cheese has melted. Serve hot,
garnished with chopped parsley.

 Healthy note

Roquefort cheese and walnuts are a classic
French topping for steak, but they are both
high in fat and calories. If you prefer to
keep these down, try this tasty mushroom
topping instead. Finely chop 250 g (8 oz)
chestnut mushrooms in a food processor,
then finely chop 1 shallot with a sharp
knife, and crush 1 garlic clove. Cook the
shallot and garlic with a few tablespoons
of water, stock, or wine in a non-stick
frying pan for 2-3 minutes until softened.
Add the mushrooms, stir well, and cook for
15 minutes until softened and quite dry.
Stir in 2 tbsp chopped parsley and 1 tsp
finely grated lemon zest, and season with
salt and pepper. Spoon the mixture on top
of the steaks, and serve at once.

Chargrilled steaks with red vegetables

SERVES 6   258 CALS PER SERVING

6 x 150 g (5 oz) fillet steaks

2 roasted red peppers in olive oil (from a jar), cut into strips, with oil reserved

salt and black pepper

2 red onions, cut into chunky wedges

2 garlic cloves, coarsely chopped

2 tbsp lime juice

fresh coriander to garnish

1 Heat a ridged cast iron chargrill pan over a medium heat until very hot. Brush the fillet steaks with a little of the reserved oil from the peppers, and season with salt and pepper. When the pan is hot, chargrill the steaks for about 3–4 minutes on each side for rare meat, 4–5 minutes on each side for medium, and 7–8 minutes on each side for well-done. Remove the steaks from the pan and leave to rest.

2 Turn down the heat under the pan to low, add the red onion wedges, and cook for about 5–8 minutes, turning them occasionally, until they are charred and softened. Add the red pepper strips, the garlic and lime juice, and stir-fry for 1–2 minutes until hot and sizzling. Season with salt and pepper.

3 Serve the steaks whole or sliced thickly on the diagonal, with a garnish of fresh coriander and the red peppers and onions spooned alongside.

Guacamole

Roughly mash the flesh of 1 large ripe avocado in a bowl with a fork. Add ½ finely chopped onion, 1 tbsp chopped fresh coriander, and the juice of 1 lime, Mix well, and season to taste. Chill for no more than 30 minutes before serving, or the avocado will discolour.

Red onions have a sweet, mild taste, that is enhanced by grilling and roasting. When roasted or grilled, they can stand alone as side dishes.

Vegetarian enchiladas

SERVES 6   242 CALS PER SERVING

4 large tortilla wraps, about 23 cm (9 ins) in diameter

1 x 175 g can red kidney beans, drained

60 g (2 oz) feta cheese, grated

60 g (2 oz) Cheddar cheese, grated

1 tbsp olive oil

MEXICAN TOMATO SAUCE

1 tbsp olive oil

½ small onion, finely chopped

1 green chilli, halved, seeded, and finely chopped

1 garlic clove, crushed

1 x 400 g can chopped tomatoes

grated zest of ½ lime

2 tbsp chopped fresh coriander

salt and black pepper

1 Make the tomato sauce. Heat the oil in a pan, add the onion, chilli and garlic, and fry over a high heat for a few minutes. Add the tomatoes and simmer without a lid over a low heat, stirring from time to time, for about 10 minutes until the mixture is fairly thick (the consistency of chutney). If it is still a little runny, reduce it by boiling over a high heat, stirring continuously. Add the lime zest and coriander, and season with salt and pepper.

2 Take one tortilla and spread half of the tomato sauce over it to within 2.5 cm (1 in) of the edge. Top with half of the red kidney beans, and sprinkle over half of both the cheeses. Put another tortilla on top and press down a little with your hand so the two tortillas are sandwiched together. Make a separate tortilla sandwich (enchilada) with the remaining ingredients.

3 Heat the oil in a frying pan with a wide base, so the tortillas can fit in flat. Fry each enchilada for 3–4 minutes on each side or until the tortillas are golden brown and crisp, the filling is hot, and the cheese melted. Slice each enchilada into 6 wedges to serve.

Mexican bean salad

SERVES 6   245 CALS PER SERVING

350 g (12 oz) mixed dried beans, eg red kidney, haricot, black eye, and aduki, soaked in cold water overnight, or 2 x 400 g cans beans

3 celery stalks, finely chopped

1 red onion, finely chopped

2 garlic cloves, crushed

DRESSING

4 tbsp olive oil

2 tbsp lime juice

2 tbsp chopped fresh coriander

1 tsp Dijon mustard

1 tsp clear honey

salt and black pepper

1 Drain the soaked dried beans into a colander and rinse well under cold running water. Tip them into a large saucepan, cover with cold water, and bring to a boil. Half cover the pan and simmer for 1 hour or until all the beans are tender.

2 Drain the beans, rinse under hot water, and tip into a large bowl. If using canned beans, drain and rinse them before putting them in the bowl.

3 Whisk together all the dressing ingredients with plenty of salt and pepper, pour over the beans, and add the celery, red onion, and garlic. Toss well, cover the bowl, and leave to marinate until cold, or overnight.

Refried beans

Heat 1–2 tbsp sunflower oil in a frying pan. Add ½ finely chopped onion, and cook for 8 minutes, until lightly browned. Add 1 crushed garlic clove, and cook for 2 minutes. Drain and rinse 1 x 400 g can red kidney beans, and add to the pan. Cook over a gentle heat until warmed through, mashing the beans with a potato masher or fork and adding 1–2 tbsp water if necessary, to prevent sticking.

Opposite, clockwise from top r
Vegetarian enchiladas with guaca
Refried beans, Chargrilled steaks
red vegetables, Mexican bean s

Winter beef casserole

 SERVES 4–6   680–454 CALS PER SERVING

2 tbsp sunflower oil

1 kg (2 lb) braising steak, trimmed and cut into 2.5 cm (1 in) cubes

3 streaky bacon rashers, rinds removed, cut into strips

1 large onion, chopped

45 g (1½ oz) plain flour

500 g (1 lb) passata (sieved tomatoes)

450 ml (¾ pint) beef stock

150 ml (¼ pint) red wine

6 celery stalks, sliced

250 g (8 oz) carrots, cut into thin strips

1 garlic clove, crushed

1 tsp chopped fresh marjoram or oregano

salt and black pepper

chopped parsley to garnish

1 Heat the oil in a large flameproof casserole, add the beef and bacon, and cook over a moderately high heat for 2–3 minutes until browned. Remove with a slotted spoon, and drain on paper towels.

2 Add the onion and cook, stirring occasionally, for a few minutes until soft but not coloured.

3 Add the flour and cook, stirring, for 1 minute. Add the passata, stock, and wine and bring to a boil, stirring until smooth and thickened. Return the meat to the pan, add the celery, carrots, garlic, and marjoram or oregano, and season with salt and pepper.

4 Bring to a boil, cover and cook in a preheated oven at 160°C (140°C fan, Gas 3) for 2 hours or until the beef is tender. Taste for seasoning and garnish with chopped parsley before serving.

Fajitas

This Mexican speciality features slices of steak marinated in spices and fruit juice. Serve with tortillas, avocado, soured cream, and *pico de gallo* relish.

 SERVES 4   543 CALS PER SERVING

500 g (1 lb) piece of rump steak

8 tortilla wraps

chopped coriander to garnish

1 avocado, stoned, peeled (page 327), and diced

soured cream

MARINADE

juice of 1 orange and 1 lime

3 garlic cloves, crushed

2 tbsp chopped fresh coriander

a few drops of Tabasco sauce

salt and black pepper

PICO DE GALLO RELISH

6 tomatoes, diced

10 radishes, coarsely chopped

5 spring onions, thinly sliced

1–2 green chillies, halved, seeded, and chopped

4 tbsp chopped fresh coriander

juice of ½ lime

1 Make the marinade: in a large bowl, combine the orange and lime juice, garlic, coriander, and Tabasco, and season with salt and pepper. Turn the steak in the marinade, cover, and leave to marinate in the refrigerator overnight.

2 Make the pico de gallo relish: in a bowl, combine the tomatoes, radishes, spring onions, chillies, coriander, lime juice, and salt to taste. Cover and chill until ready to serve.

3 Remove the steak from the marinade and pat dry. Put the steak under a hot grill, 7–10 cm (3–4 in) from the heat, and grill for 3 minutes on each side for rare steak, 4 minutes for medium steak, or 5–6 minutes for well-done steak. Cover with foil and leave to stand for 5 minutes.

4 Meanwhile, warm the tortillas (see box, right).

5 Slice the steak, arrange on serving plates, and sprinkle with coriander. Serve with the tortillas, pico de gallo relish, diced avocado, and soured cream.

Warming tortillas

Sprinkle each tortilla with a little water, and stack the tortillas in a pile.

Wrap the tortillas in foil and warm in a preheated oven at 140°C (120°C fan, Gas 1) for 10 minutes.

eef Stroganoff

ERVES 6   329 CALS PER SERVING

1 oz) butter

sunflower oil

(1½ lb) rump steak, trimmed and cut into
(see box, right)

lots, quartered

(10 oz) button mushrooms, halved

d black pepper

(½ pint) soured cream

ed parsley to garnish

lt the butter with the oil in a large
ng pan. When the butter is foaming,
he steak strips, in batches if necessary,
ook over a high heat for 5 minutes or
rowned all over. Remove from the
vith a slotted spoon.

2 Add the shallots and mushrooms and
cook for about 5 minutes until soft
and browned.

3 Return the steak strips to the pan, and
season with salt and pepper. Stir in the
soured cream and heat gently. Garnish
with parsley, and serve at once.

Healthy note

Stroganoff is a classic dish of steak pan-fried
in butter and oil with mushrooms and soured
cream, but there are ways of cutting down
on the fat without compromising the flavours
in the dish. Use a non-stick pan and omit
the butter, then use just 150 ml (¼ pint)
low-fat crème fraîche instead of the soured
cream. Crème fraîche becomes very runny
when heated, which is why you do not need
as much.

Cutting the beef

Slice the beef at an angle into thin strips,
5 mm (¼ in) wide and 5 cm (2 in) long, using
a sharp chef's knife.

Boeuf bourguignon

SERVES 6 **490 CALS PER SERVING**

2 tbsp sunflower oil

1 kg (2 lb) braising steak, trimmed and cut into 5 cm (2 in) cubes

250 g (8 oz) thickly sliced smoked bacon, rinds removed, cut into strips

12 shallots

30 g (1 oz) plain flour

300 ml (½ pint) red Burgundy or any good red wine

150 ml (¼ pint) beef stock

1 bouquet garni

1 garlic clove, crushed

salt and black pepper

250 g (8 oz) button mushrooms

1 Heat the oil in a large flameproof casserole. Add the beef in batches, and cook over a high heat, turning occasionally, until browned on all sides. Remove with a slotted spoon and set aside to drain on paper towels.

2 Add the bacon and shallots and cook gently, stirring occasionally, for 3 minutes or until the bacon is crisp and the shallots are softened. Lift out and drain on paper towels.

3 Add the flour and cook, stirring, for 1 minute. Gradually blend in the wine and stock and bring to a boil, stirring until thickened.

4 Return the beef and bacon to the casserole, add the bouquet garni and garlic, and season with salt and pepper. Cover and cook in a preheated oven at 160°C (140°C fan, Gas 3) for 1½ hours.

5 Return the shallots to the casserole, add the whole button mushrooms, and cook for 1 hour or until the beef is very tender.

6 Remove the bouquet garni and discard. Taste the sauce for seasoning before serving.

Carbonnade of bee

SERVES 6 **465 CALS PER SERVING**

2 tbsp sunflower oil

1 kg (2 lb) braising steak, trimmed and cut into 5 cm (2 in) cubes

2 large onions, sliced

1 garlic clove, crushed

2 tsp light muscovado sugar

1 tbsp plain flour

450 ml (¾ pint) beer or lager

150 ml (¼ pint) beef stock

1 tbsp red wine vinegar

1 bouquet garni

salt and black pepper

½ baguette, cut into 1.25 cm (½ in) slices

Dijon mustard for spreading

thyme sprigs to garnish

1 Heat the oil in a large flameproof casserole, add the beef in batches, and cook over a high heat for a few minutes until browned. Lift out with a slotted spoon.

2 Lower the heat and add the onions, garlic, and sugar. Cook, stirring, for 4 minutes or until browned. Add the flour and cook, stirring, for 1 minute. Add the beer or lager, and stock, and bring to a boil, stirring until thickened.

3 Return the meat to the casserole, add the vinegar and bouquet garni, and season with salt and pepper. Bring back to a boil, cover, and cook in a preheated oven at 150°C (130°C fan, Gas 2) for 2½ hours or until the meat is really tender. Remove from the oven, lift out the bouquet garni, and discard. Taste for seasoning.

4 Increase the oven temperature to 1 (170°C fan, Gas 5). Toast the baguette slices, and spread with mustard on one Put them, mustard-side up, in the casserole and baste with sauce.

5 Return the casserole to the oven, uncovered, for 10 minutes or until the croûtes are just crisp. Garnish with thyme sprigs before serving.

Chianti beef casserole

SERVES 4–6   512–342 CALS PER SERVING

) g (2 oz) sun-dried tomatoes in oil, roughly hopped, with oil reserved

kg (2 lb) braising steak, trimmed and cut into cm (2 in) cubes

large onions, roughly chopped

large garlic cloves, crushed

5 g (1½ oz) plain flour

50 ml (¼ pint) Chianti or any good red wine

)0 ml (½ pint) beef stock

few fresh thyme sprigs

lt and black pepper

x 400 g can artichoke hearts, drained and halved

2 pitted black olives

heaped tbsp mango chutney

Heat 2 tbsp of the reserved oil from the sun-dried tomatoes in a large frying pan, nd brown the beef on all sides (you may eed to do this in batches). Remove with slotted spoon and keep warm.

) Heat another 2 tbsp sun-dried tomato oil in a large flameproof casserole, add the nions and garlic, and cook for 2–3 minutes.

3 Add the flour and cook, stirring, for 1 minute. Blend in the wine and stock, ring to a boil, and add the tomatoes and yme (reserving a sprig for garnish). Season ith salt and pepper.

Return the beef to the casserole, cover, and reduce the heat. Simmer for ½–2 hours or until the meat is tender.

5 Add the artichokes, olives, and mango chutney, and simmer for 10 minutes. aste for seasoning and garnish with thyme efore serving.

ack olives taste milder than green olives and e picked when fully ripe. Pitting exposes the ive to the brine, which makes the flesh softer.

Hungarian goulash

SERVES 6   474 CALS PER SERVING

2 tbsp sunflower oil

1 kg (2 lb) braising steak, trimmed and cut into 5 cm (2 in) cubes

2 large onions, sliced

1 garlic clove, crushed

1 tbsp plain flour

1 tbsp paprika

600 ml (1 pint) beef stock

1 x 400 g can tomatoes

2 tbsp tomato purée

salt and black pepper

2 large red peppers, halved, seeded, and cut into 2.5 cm (1 in) pieces

4 potatoes, peeled and quartered

150 ml (¼ pint) soured cream

paprika to garnish

1 Heat the sunflower oil in a large flameproof casserole, add the beef in batches, and cook over a high heat until browned.

2 Lift out the beef with a slotted spoon. Lower the heat slightly, add the

onions and garlic, and cook gently, stirring occasionally, for a few minutes until soft but not coloured.

3 Add the flour and paprika and cook, stirring, for 1 minute. Pour in the stock and bring to a boil, stirring.

4 Return the meat to the casserole, add the tomatoes and tomato purée, and season with salt and pepper. Bring back to a boil, cover, and cook in a preheated oven at 160°C (140°C fan, Gas 3) for 1 hour.

5 Add the red peppers and potatoes and continue cooking for 1 hour or until the potatoes and meat are tender.

6 Taste for seasoning, and stir in the soured cream. Sprinkle with a little paprika before serving.

♡ Healthy note

Soured cream is the classic finish for goulash, but to reduce the fat content of this dish you can omit it. To compensate for its richness, add 250 g (8 oz) chestnut mushrooms, sliced, in step 5, and stir in a good handful of chopped flat-leaf parsley in step 6.

Country beef casserole

 SERVES 8   405 CALS PER SERVING

3 tbsp sunflower oil

1 kg (2 lb) braising steak, trimmed and cut into 5 cm (2 in) cubes

500 g (1 lb) carrots, thickly sliced

250 g (8 oz) turnips, cut into large chunks

250 g (8 oz) parsnips, thickly sliced

2 onions, sliced

1 large leek, sliced

1 tbsp plain flour

600 ml (1 pint) beef stock

1 x 400 g can chopped tomatoes

2 tbsp chopped fresh herbs, such as parsley and thyme

1 large bay leaf

salt and black pepper

herb dumplings (see box, below)

1 Heat the oil in a large flameproof casserole, add the beef in batches, and cook over a high heat until browned. Lift out the beef with a slotted spoon.

2 Add the carrots, turnips, parsnips, onions, and leek, and cook over a high heat, stirring occasionally, for 5 minutes or until the vegetables are softened.

3 Add the flour and cook, stirring, for 1 minute. Add the stock and tomatoes, and 1 tbsp of the herbs, and season with salt and pepper. Bring to a boil, then return the meat to the casserole. Cover and cook in a preheated oven at 160°C (140°C fan, Gas 3) for 2 hours.

4 Place the dumplings on top of the meat. Increase the oven temperature to 190°C (170°C fan, Gas 5) and cook for 20–25 minutes until the dumplings are firm. Serve hot, sprinkled with the remaining chopped herbs.

Herb dumplings

Sift 125 g (4 oz) self-raising flour into a bowl, and add 60 g (2 oz) shredded vegetable suet, 1 tbsp chopped fresh thyme or parsley, and salt and pepper. Add 4–5 tbsp water to make a soft dough. Shape into 12–16 balls with your hands.

Chilli con carne

 SERVES 6   362 CALS PER SERVING

250 g (8 oz) dried red kidney beans

2 tbsp sunflower oil

750 g (1½ lb) braising steak, trimmed and cut into large cubes

2 onions, chopped

2 fresh red chillies, halved, seeded, and finely chopped

1 garlic clove, crushed

1 tbsp plain flour

900 ml (1½ pints) beef stock

2 tbsp tomato purée

1 square of plain chocolate, grated

salt and black pepper

1 large red pepper, halved, seeded, and cut into chunks

chopped coriander to garnish

1 Put the red kidney beans into a large bowl, cover generously with cold water, and leave to soak overnight.

2 Drain the beans, rinse under cold running water, and drain again. Put the beans into a large saucepan. Cover with cold water, bring to a boil, and boil rapidly for 10 minutes. Lower the heat and simmer, partially covered, for 50 minutes or until the beans are just tender. Drain.

3 Heat the oil in a large flameproof casserole. Add the beef and cook in batches over a high heat for 5–7 minutes until browned. Lift out with a slotted spoon.

4 Lower the heat, add the onions, chillies, and garlic, and cook, stirring occasionally, for a few minutes until softened.

5 Add the flour and cook, stirring, for 1 minute. Add the stock, tomato purée, and chocolate, and season with salt and pepper. Return the beef to the casserole, add the beans, and bring to a boil. Cover and cook in a preheated oven at 150°C (130°C fan, Gas 2) for 1½ hours.

6 Add the red pepper and cook for 30 minutes. Taste for seasoning, and garnish with coriander.

Quick chilli con carne

Substitute 1 x 400 g can red kidney beans for the dried beans, and minced beef for the braising steak. Simmer gently on the hob for 45 minutes.

Latimer beef with horseradish

 SERVES 6   298 CALS PER SERVING

2 tbsp sunflower oil

1 kg (2 lb) braising steak, trimmed and cut into strips

12 shallots or button onions

30 g (1 oz) plain flour

2 tsp mild curry powder

2 tsp light muscovado sugar

1 tsp ground ginger

600 ml (1 pint) beef stock

2 tbsp Worcestershire sauce

salt and black pepper

3 tbsp chopped parsley

2 tbsp creamed horseradish

extra chopped parsley to garnish

1 Heat the sunflower oil in a large flameproof casserole, and cook the beef strips over a high heat until browned all over. Lift out with a slotted spoon and drain on paper towels.

2 Lower the heat, add the shallots or button onions, and cook gently, stirring occasionally, for a few minutes until softened. Lift out with a slotted spoon and drain on paper towels.

3 Add the flour, curry powder, sugar, and ginger to the casserole and cook, stirring, for 1 minute. Pour in the stock and bring to a boil, stirring until smooth and thickened. Add the Worcestershire sauce, season with salt and pepper, and return to a boil.

4 Return the beef and shallots to the casserole and stir in the parsley. Bring back to a boil, cover, and cook in a preheated oven at 160°C (140°C fan, Gas 3) for 2–2½ hours until the meat is tender.

5 Stir in the horseradish cream, taste for seasoning, and garnish with parsley.

♡ Healthy note

Creamed horseradish is a mixture of grated horseradish with vinegar, seasonings, and cream. For a less rich finish, use just 1 tbsp bottled grated horseradish.

hai red beef curry

SERVES 6   **327 CALS PER SERVING**

sp sunflower oil

ardamom pods, split

cm (1 in) piece of cinnamon stick

oves

ack peppercorns

g (2 lb) braising steak, trimmed and cut into
cm (1 in) cubes

rge onion, chopped

m (2 in) piece of fresh root ginger, peeled
grated

arlic cloves, crushed

paprika

ground cumin

ground coriander

salt

cayenne pepper or ½ tsp chilli powder

ml (1 pint) water

90 g (3 oz) full-fat plain yogurt

1 x 400 g can chopped tomatoes

1 large red pepper, halved, seeded, and
cut into chunks

1 Heat the oil in a large flameproof
casserole, add the cardamom pods,
cinnamon stick, cloves, and peppercorns,
and cook over a moderate heat, stirring,
for 1 minute. Lift out with a slotted spoon
and set aside on a plate.

2 Add the beef in batches, and cook over
a high heat until browned all over. Lift
out the beef with a slotted spoon and drain
on paper towels.

3 Add the onion to the pan and cook
over a high heat, stirring, for about
3 minutes until beginning to brown. Add
the ginger, garlic, paprika, cumin, coriander,
salt, cayenne or chilli, and 4 tbsp of the
measured water. Cook, stirring, for about
1 minute.

4 Return the beef and spices to the
casserole, then gradually add
the yogurt, stirring. Stir in the remaining
water. Add the tomatoes and red pepper,
and bring to a boil. Cover and cook in
a preheated oven at 160°C (140°C fan,
Gas 3) for 2 hours or until the beef is tender.
Taste for seasoning before serving.

🔎 Cook's know-how

If you are short of time, use 3–4 tbsp
ready-made Thai red curry paste instead of
the whole and ground spices in this recipe.
If you prefer, you can use coconut milk
instead of the yogurt.

escape through the pie funnel. Seal the pastry edges and crimp with a fork, then decorate the top of the pie with pastry trimmings, attaching them with beaten egg.

8 Brush the pastry all over with beaten egg, and bake in a preheated oven at 200°C (180°C fan, Gas 6) for 25–30 minutes until the pastry is crisp and golden. Serve hot.

Steak and kidney pudding

Mix 300 g (10 oz) self-raising flour, 150 g (5 oz) shredded suet, salt and pepper, and 200 ml (7 fl oz) water. Use ¾ pastry to line a 1.7 litre (3 pint) bowl. Add the uncooked filling, top with pastry, and steam for 5 hours.

Meatballs in cider

🍴 SERVES 4   416 CALS PER SERVING

250 g (8 oz) minced beef

125 g (4 oz) minced pork

salt and black pepper

plain flour for dusting

2 tbsp sunflower oil

2 large onions, sliced

1 garlic clove, crushed

300 ml (½ pint) dry cider

3 tbsp tomato purée

4 celery stalks, thickly sliced

1 large red pepper, halved, seeded, and cut into strips

125 g (4 oz) mushrooms, sliced

2 tsp caster sugar

1 Mix together the beef and pork, and season with salt and pepper. On a floured work surface, shape the mixture into 16 even-sized balls.

2 Heat the oil in a flameproof casserole, add the meatballs, and cook over a high heat until browned. Remove and drain on paper towels. Lower the heat, add the onions and garlic, and cook, stirring occasionally, for a few minutes until softened.

3 Return the meatballs to the casserole and add the cider, tomato purée, celery, red pepper, mushrooms, and sugar. Season with salt and pepper, and bring to a boil. Cover and simmer for 20 minutes or until meatballs are cooked through. Serve hot.

Traditional steak and kidney pie

This pie is a classic, but for those who do not like kidneys you can omit them and use double the amount of mushrooms. For convenience, the meat can be cooked a day in advance, then all you have to do on the day of serving is make the pastry and bake the pie in the oven.

🍴 SERVES 6   577 CALS PER SERVING

2 tbsp sunflower oil

1 large onion, chopped

750 g (1½ lb) stewing steak, cut into 2.5 cm (1 in) cubes

250 g (8 oz) beef or lamb's kidney, trimmed (page 207), and cut into 2.5 cm (1 in) cubes

30 g (1 oz) plain flour

300 ml (½ pint) beef stock

2 tbsp Worcestershire sauce

salt and black pepper

250 g (8 oz) button mushrooms

beaten egg for glazing

SHORTCRUST PASTRY

250 g (8 oz) plain flour

125 g (4 oz) butter

about 3 tbsp cold water

1 Heat the oil in a large saucepan, add the onion, and cook, stirring from time to time, for a few minutes until soft but not coloured.

2 Add the beef and kidney and cook until browned. Add the flour and cook, stirring, for 1 minute. Add the stock and Worcestershire sauce, season with salt and pepper, and bring to a boil, stirring. Partially cover, and simmer gently for 2 hours.

3 Add the mushrooms and cook for 30 minutes or until the meat is tender. Taste for seasoning, then leave to cool completely.

4 Make the pastry: sift the flour into a bowl. Add the butter and rub in lightly with your fingertips until the mixture looks like fine breadcrumbs. Add the water and mix with a flat-bladed knife until the dough comes together to form a ball.

5 Roll out the pastry on a floured work surface until 2.5 cm (1 in) larger than the pie dish. Invert the dish over the pastry and cut around the dish. Brush the rim of the dish with water and press on a strip of pastry cut from the trimmings.

6 Put a pie funnel into the middle of the dish, then spoon in the meat mixture.

7 Lightly brush the pastry strip with water and top with the pastry lid, making a hole in the middle so the steam can

Corned beef hash

SERVES 4   **444 CALS PER SERVING**

g (2 oz) butter

arge onion, chopped

0 g (1½ lb) potatoes, cut into small chunks

0 ml (½ pint) beef stock

t and black pepper

325 g can corned beef, cut into chunks

opped parsley to garnish

Melt the butter in a large frying pan, add the onion, and cook gently, stirring casionally, for a few minutes until softened.

Add the potatoes and stir to coat in the butter. Pour in the stock, and season h salt and pepper. Simmer for 10–15 nutes until the potatoes are tender and e stock absorbed.

Stir in the corned beef and heat to warm through. Put the pan under a hot grill, m (3 in) from the heat, to brown the top. rnish with parsley.

Beef olives with vegetable julienne

SERVES 6   **257 CALS PER SERVING**

8 thin slices of beef topside, total weight about 750 g (1½ lb)

2 tbsp sunflower oil

375 g (12 oz) piece of celeriac, peeled and cut into matchstick-thin strips

250 g (8 oz) carrots, cut into matchstick-thin strips

2 small leeks, cut into matchstick-thin strips

salt and black pepper

30 g (1 oz) plain flour

1 onion, sliced

1 garlic clove, sliced

450 ml (¾ pint) beef stock

1 Pound each slice of topside between 2 sheets of cling film with a rolling pin until 3 mm (⅛ in) thick.

2 Heat 1 tbsp of the oil in a large frying pan, add the celeriac, carrots, and leeks, and stir-fry over a high heat for 1 minute.

Season with salt and pepper, then lift out and drain. Leave to cool.

3 Divide the vegetables among the beef slices. Roll up and secure with wooden cocktail sticks.

4 Lightly coat the beef olives in half of the flour, shaking off any excess. Heat the remaining oil in a flameproof casserole, add the beef olives, and cook over a high heat for 5–7 minutes until browned. Lift out with a slotted spoon.

5 Add the onion and garlic and cook gently until softened. Add the remaining flour and cook, stirring, for 1 minute. Gradually blend in the stock, season with salt and pepper, and bring to a boil, stirring until thick.

6 Return the beef olives to the casserole, bring to a boil, cover, and cook in a preheated oven at 180°C (160°C fan, Gas 4) for 1½ hours. Lift out the beef and set aside. Sieve the sauce, then reheat. Thinly slice the beef, removing the cocktail sticks. Serve hot, with the sauce.

Below: Beef olives with vegetable julienne.

Thai beef burgers

SERVES 6   **160 CALS PER SERVING**

500 g (1 lb) best-quality minced beef

1 tbsp red Thai curry paste

2 tbsp chopped fresh coriander

2.5 cm (1 in) piece of fresh root ginger, peeled and finely grated

salt and black pepper

1 tbsp olive oil

1 Put the beef in a bowl with the curry paste, fresh coriander, grated ginger and salt and pepper. Mix together thoroughly.

2 Shape the mixture into six even-sized burgers. Put on a large plate, cover and refrigerate for about 30 minutes (they will keep for up to 24 hours).

3 Heat the oil in a large non-stick frying pan or lightly coat a preheated ridged griddle pan with a little oil. Cook the burgers over a medium heat for about 3–4 minutes on each side until they are brown. They are best served just pink in the middle, but they can be cooked another minute or two on each side if you prefer them more done than this.

Lamb burgers

SERVES 8   **270 CALS PER SERVING**

1–2 tbsp olive oil

1 small onion, finely chopped

1 garlic clove, crushed

500 g (1 lb) best-quality minced lamb

1 tsp ground cumin

2 tbsp chopped fresh mint

salt and black pepper

TO SERVE

4 warm pitta breads, halved

about 8 tbsp tzatziki (ready-made or see page 239)

1 Heat 1 tbsp oil in a frying pan and cook the onion and garlic until completely softened – this can take up to 10 minutes. Allow to cool completely.

2 Mix the cooled onion and garlic with the remaining ingredients, then shape into 8 small burgers. Put on a large plate, cover and refrigerate for about 30 minutes (they will keep for up to 24 hours).

3 Heat a large non-stick frying pan or lightly coat a preheated ridged griddle pan with a little oil. Cook the burgers over a medium heat until browned and cooked through, about 3–4 minutes on each side. Serve in warm pitta pockets, with tzatziki.

Veggie burgers

SERVES 6   **216 CALS PER SERVING**

1 small red onion, finely chopped

3 tbsp chopped parsley

1 x 400 g can cannellini beans, drained

1 x 300 g can red kidney beans, drained

60 g (2 oz) no-need-to-soak dried apricots, snipped into pieces

175 g (6 oz) carrots, grated

60 g (2 oz) Cheddar cheese, grated

salt and black pepper

30 g (1 oz) pine nuts, toasted

about 2–3 tbsp olive oil

1 Purée the onion and parsley in a food processor until fairly smooth. Add the remaining ingredients, except the pine nuts and oil, and blitz until smooth. (If you haven't got a processor, mash the beans and mix with the other ingredients except the pine nuts and oil.) Season really well.

2 Add the toasted pine nuts and pulse the machine to mix them in. Shape the mixture into 12 small burgers. Put on a large plate, cover, and refrigerate for about 1 hour (they will keep for up to 24 hours).

3 Place the burgers on a grill tray lined with foil, under a hot grill 7 cm (3 in) from the heat. Brush the burgers frequently with oil, for 4 minutes each side until until they are hot right through.

Toppings for burgers

Chilli aïoli
In a small bowl, combine 2 egg yolks, 1 tbsp lemon juice, 1 tsp Dijon mustard, and salt and pepper to taste, and whisk until thick. Gradually add 250 ml (8 fl oz) olive oil, whisking constantly until the mixture is very thick. Stir in 1 crushed garlic clove, ½ tsp chilli powder, and ¼ tsp ground cumin. Taste for seasoning. Cover and refrigerate until ready to serve. Use on the day of making.

Barbecue sauce
Heat 1 tbsp sunflower oil in a saucepan and cook 1 finely chopped onion and 1 crushed garlic clove until soft but not coloured. Add 1 x 400 g can chopped tomatoes, 2 tbsp water, 2 tbsp lemon juice, 1 tbsp brown sugar, 1 tbsp Worcestershire sauce, 2 tsp Dijon mustard, ½ tsp each paprika and chilli powder, and salt and pepper. Bring to a boil, and simmer for 20 minutes. Serve warm or cold.

Fresh root ginger is pungent and hot. Used in small quantities, it adds a refreshing flavour and spiciness to a dish.

Opposite from top left: Thai burgers, Lamb burgers, Veggie burgers.

Meat loaf

SERVES 6   **478 CALS PER SERVING**

750 g (1½ lb) minced beef

1 x 400 g can chopped tomatoes

90 g (3 oz) herby stuffing mix

1 onion, chopped

1 carrot, coarsely shredded

3 garlic cloves, crushed

2 tbsp chopped parsley

1 egg, beaten

1 tbsp Worcestershire sauce

salt and black pepper

4–5 streaky bacon rashers, rinds removed

1 kg (2 lb) loaf tin

1 Combine the minced beef, tomatoes, stuffing mix, onion, carrot, garlic, parsley, beaten egg, and Worcestershire sauce, and season with salt and pepper.

2 Arrange bacon rashers crosswise in the loaf tin, letting them hang over the sides. Put the beef mixture into the tin and fold over the bacon. Turn the loaf out into a roasting tin and bake in a preheated oven at 190°C (170°C fan, Gas 5), basting once or twice, for 1 hour.

3 Increase the heat to 230°C (210°C fan, Gas 8) and bake for 15 minutes or until the meat loaf is firm. Spoon off any fat, slice the loaf, and serve hot (or leave whole and serve cold).

Parsley has a fresh, herbaceous flavour with a light, peppery note. It retains its distinct, spicy aroma when used in a cooked dish.

Cottage pies with cheesy potato topping

The minced beef mixture can be made a day ahead of serving, and kept in the refrigerator overnight. If you prefer you can omit the cheese in the potato topping, and use olive oil instead of butter.

SERVES 6   **576 CALS PER SERVING**

2 tbsp sunflower oil

1 large onion, finely chopped

1 celery stalk, finely chopped

1 large carrot, finely chopped

750 g (1½ lb) minced beef

2 tsp plain flour

300 ml (½ pint) beef stock

1 tbsp tomato purée

2 tbsp Worcestershire sauce

salt and black pepper

TOPPING

750 g (1½ lb) potatoes, cut into chunks

30 g (1 oz) butter

2–3 tbsp hot milk

125 g (4 oz) mature Cheddar cheese, grated

1 Heat the oil in a large saucepan, add the onion, celery, and carrot, and cook for 3 minutes. Add the minced beef, and cook for 5 minutes or until browned.

2 Add the flour and cook, stirring, for 1 minute. Add the stock, tomato purée, and Worcestershire sauce, season with salt and pepper, and bring to a boil. Cover and simmer, stirring occasionally, for 45 minutes. Remove from the heat and spoon into 6 individual ovenproof dishes, or 1 large dish. Leave to cool.

3 Prepare the potato topping: cook the potatoes in boiling salted water for 20 minutes or until tender. Drain. Add the butter and hot milk to the potatoes and mash until soft, then stir in the cheese and season with salt and pepper.

4 Cover the minced beef mixture with the mashed potato (see box, right). Cook in a preheated oven at 200°C (180°C fan, Gas 6), allowing 20–25 minutes for small pies, 35–40 minutes for a large one, until the potato topping is golden brown and the meat mixture is bubbling. Serve hot.

Covering the pies

Spoon the mashed potato on to the beef mixture, and spread over the top to cover completely.

Score the surface of the mashed potato, using a fork, to make a decorative topping.

Opposite: Cottage pies cheesy potato topp

Above: Bobotie.

Bobotie

🍴 SERVES 6–8   656–492 CALS PER SERVING

1 slice of white bread, crusts removed

300 ml (½ pint) milk

30 g (1 oz) butter

1 large onion, chopped

2 garlic cloves, crushed

1 kg (2 lb) minced beef

1 tbsp medium–hot curry powder

90 g (3 oz) ready-to-eat dried apricots, coarsely chopped

90 g (3 oz) blanched almonds, coarsely chopped

2 tbsp fruit chutney

1 tbsp lemon juice

salt and black pepper

2 eggs

30 g (1 oz) flaked almonds

1 Put the bread into a shallow dish. Sprinkle over 2 tbsp of the milk and leave to soak for 5 minutes.

2 Meanwhile, melt the butter in a large frying pan, add the onion and garlic, and cook gently, stirring occasionally, for a few minutes until soft.

3 Increase the heat, add the beef, and cook, stirring, for 5 minutes or until browned. Spoon off any excess fat.

4 Add the curry powder and cook, stirring, for 2 minutes. Add the chopped apricots and almonds, the chutney, lemon juice, and salt and pepper to taste.

5 Mash the bread and milk in the dish, then stir into the minced beef. Turn into an ovenproof dish and bake in a preheated oven at 180°C (160°C fan, Gas 4) for 35 minutes.

6 Break the eggs into a bowl, and whisk in the remaining milk, and salt and pepper to taste. Pour over the minced beef mixture, sprinkle with the flaked almonds, and bake for 25–30 minutes until the topping is set.

Beef Florentine

Filo provides a quick and easy way to cover a pie, and it gives a lovely crisp topping. If you prefer not to use butter you can use olive oil instead and, to make a lighter dish, you can use reduced-fat Cheddar cheese and low-fat soft cheese, and omit the Gruyère or Emmental.

🍴 SERVES 8   576 CALS PER SERVING

11 sheets of filo pastry

60 g (2 oz) butter, melted

BEEF LAYER

30 g (1 oz) butter

1 kg (2 lb) lean minced beef

1 tbsp plain flour

1 x 400 g can chopped tomatoes

2 tbsp tomato purée

2 garlic cloves, crushed

1 tsp caster sugar

salt and black pepper

SPINACH AND CHEESE LAYER

625 g (1¼ lb) spinach leaves, tough stalks removed, roughly chopped

90 g (3 oz) mature Cheddar cheese, grated

90 g (3 oz) Gruyère or Emmental cheese, grated

125 g (4 oz) full-fat soft cheese

2 eggs, lightly beaten

1 Prepare the beef layer: melt the butter i a large saucepan, add the minced bee and cook, stirring, for 10–15 minutes or unti the meat is browned all over.

2 Add the flour and cook, stirring, for 1 minute. Add the tomatoes, tomato purée, garlic, and sugar, season with salt and pepper, and bring to a boil. Cover an simmer, stirring occasionally, for 35 minutes Taste for seasoning.

3 Meanwhile, prepare the spinach and cheese layer: wash the spinach and p it into a large saucepan. Cook over a gentle heat until the spinach wilts. Drain thoroughly, squeezing to remove excess water. Mix the spinach with the Cheddar, Gruyère or Emmental, soft cheese, and eggs, and season with salt and pepper.

4 Spoon the beef mixture into a shallow ovenproof dish, then spoon the spinac mixture over the top.

5 Prepare the filo topping (see box, below).

6 Bake in a preheated oven at 200°C (180°C fan, Gas 6) for 20–25 minutes u the filo pastry is crisp and golden. Serve h

Preparing the filo topping

Brush 3 of the filo pastry sheets with a little of the melted butter and layer them on top of the spinach mixture, trimming to fit the dish if necessary.

Arrange the remaining 8 filo pastry sheets over the dish, lightly brushing with a little butter and scrunching each one up, in order to completely cover the lower layer of filo pastry.

Beef tacos

🕐 SERVES 4   407 CALS PER SERVING

- tbsp sunflower oil
- 75 g (12 oz) minced beef
- onion, chopped
- garlic cloves, crushed
- tsp chilli powder
- tsp paprika
- tsp ground cumin (optional)
- x 225 g can chopped tomatoes
- lt and black pepper
- fresh green chilli, halved, seeded, and inly sliced
- bsp chopped fresh coriander
- aco shells
- ettuce leaves, finely shredded
- bsp soured cream
- opped coriander to garnish

1 Heat the oil in a large frying pan, add the minced beef, onion, and garlic, and cook, stirring, for 5 minutes or until the beef is browned and the onion and garlic are softened.

2 Add the chilli powder, paprika, and cumin (if using), and cook, stirring, for 2 minutes.

3 Stir in the tomatoes, cover, and cook over a medium heat for 5 minutes. Add salt and pepper to taste, remove from the heat, and stir in the chilli and coriander.

4 Warm the taco shells in a preheated oven at 180°C (160°C fan, Gas 4) for 2–3 minutes, or according to packet instructions. Fill the taco shells (see box, right), and serve hot.

Filling taco shells

Holding each shell in one hand, put a layer of shredded lettuce into the bottom. Add a generous spoonful of the meat mixture and top with soured cream and a sprinkling of chopped coriander.

Lemon roast veal with spinach stuffing

Loin of veal is a lean cut, so it has a tendency to be dry. Marinating for 2 days before roasting makes it more succulent. Loin of pork can be marinated and cooked in the same way.

 SERVES 6–8   444–333 CALS PER SERVING

1.25 kg (2½ lb) boned veal roasting joint, such as loin

150 ml (¼ pint) dry white wine

150 ml (¼ pint) chicken stock

MARINADE

3 tbsp olive oil

grated zest and juice of 1 lemon

4 thyme sprigs

black pepper

STUFFING

30 g (1 oz) butter

1 shallot, finely chopped

2 streaky bacon rashers, rinds removed, finely chopped

175 g (6 oz) spinach leaves, coarsely shredded

grated zest of 1 lemon

60 g (2 oz) fresh brown breadcrumbs

salt and black pepper

1 small egg, lightly beaten

1 Combine the marinade ingredients. Turn the veal in the marinade, cover, and leave to marinate in the refrigerator for 2 days.

2 Make the stuffing: melt the butter, add the shallot and bacon, and cook for 5 minutes or until the shallot is softened. Stir in the spinach and cook for 1 minute. Remove from the heat, add the lemon zest and breadcrumbs, and season with salt and pepper. Mix well, then bind with the egg. Leave to cool completely.

3 Remove the veal from the marinade, reserving the marinade. Spread the stuffing over the veal and roll up (see box, right).

4 Weigh the veal, insert a meat thermometer, if using, into the middle of the meat, and place in a roasting tin. Pour the marinade around the meat. Roast in a preheated oven at 180°C (160°C fan, Gas 4) for 25 minutes per 500 g (1 lb), until the juices run clear or until the thermometer registers 80°C (175°F). Transfer to a platter,

cover loosely with foil, and leave to stand in a warm place for 10 minutes.

5 Meanwhile, spoon the fat from the tin, and remove the thyme sprigs. Put the tin on the hob, add the wine and stock, and bring to a boil, stirring to dissolve the sediment from the bottom of the tin. Boil for 5 minutes or until thickened and reduced by about half.

6 Taste the gravy for seasoning, and pour into a warmed gravy boat. Carve the veal, and serve hot.

Rolling up the veal

Bring the 2 sides of the veal together, enclosing the stuffing. Tie fine string around the veal at regular intervals.

Gravies for meat

Mushroom gravy
Melt 30 g (1 oz) butter in a saucepan. Add 1 finely chopped shallot and cook for 2 minutes until softened. Add 250 g (8 oz) sliced mushrooms and cook gently for 5 minutes. Pour in 300 ml (½ pint) beef stock, and simmer for about 5 minutes. Add 1 tbsp chopped parsley, 1 tsp chopped fresh thyme, and salt and black pepper to taste.

Onion gravy
Heat 1 tbsp sunflower oil and 30 g (1 oz) butter in a saucepan. Add 1 sliced onion and cook for 5–7 minutes until golden. Add 1 tbsp plain flour and cook, stirring, for 1 minute. Add 300 ml (½ pint) chicken stock. Simmer for about 5 minutes. Add salt and pepper to taste.

Red wine gravy
Melt 30 g (1 oz) butter in a saucepan. Add 1 sliced small onion and cook for 5 minutes or until beginning to brown. Add 1 tbsp plain flour and cook, stirring, for 1 minute. Add 100 ml (3½ fl oz) red wine and 300 ml (½ pint) beef stock. Simmer for about 5 minutes. Pour in any juices from the meat, and add salt and pepper to taste.

Pressed tongue

 SERVES 10   392 CALS PER SERVING

2–2.5 kg (4–5 lb) salted ox tongue, trimmed

1 onion, quartered

1 bay leaf

1 tbsp gelatine powder

3 tbsp cold water

15 cm (6 in) round cake tin or stainless steel saucepan

1 Put the ox tongue, onion, and bay leaf in a large saucepan, cover with cold water, and bring to a boil. Simmer very gently for 3 hours until tender. Test the water after 2 hour if it is very salty, replace it with fresh water.

2 Lift the tongue out of the saucepan, reserving the cooking liquid, and leave to cool slightly. Remove and discard the skin, then cut the tongue in half lengthway

3 Sprinkle the gelatine over the measure water in a small bowl. Leave to stand f 3 minutes or until the gelatine is spongy. Pu the bowl into a saucepan of gently simmeri water and leave for 3 minutes or until the gelatine has dissolved.

4 Add 150 ml (¼ pint) of the cooking liquid to the gelatine and mix well.

5 Squash one half of the tongue, cut-side down, into the cake tin or saucepan, and put in the other half, cut-side up. Pou in the gelatine mixture, cover with a small plate, and weigh down with weights or heavy cans. Chill in the refrigerator overnig

6 Dip the base of the tin or saucepan in a bowl of hot water, just long enough melt the jelly slightly so that it comes awa from the bottom. Serve the tongue chillec and very thinly sliced.

Oxtail stew

🍴 SERVES 6   337 CALS PER SERVING

tbsp sunflower oil

25 kg (2½ lb) oxtail, cut into 5 cm (2 in) slices
d trimmed

g (1 oz) plain flour

0 ml (1½ pints) beef stock

arge onions, sliced

bsp tomato purée

bsp chopped parsley

bsp chopped fresh thyme

ay leaf

t and black pepper

elery stalks, thickly sliced

pped parsley to garnish

Heat the oil in a large flameproof
casserole, add the oxtail, and cook over
high heat for 10 minutes or until browned
over. Remove the oxtail and drain on
per towels.

Add the flour and cook, stirring
occasionally, for about 1 minute. Blend
he beef stock and bring to a boil, stirring
il the sauce has thickened.

Return the oxtail to the casserole, and
add the onions, tomato purée, parsley,
me, and bay leaf. Season with salt and
per, and bring to a boil. Cover and
mer gently for 2 hours.

Add the celery and cook for a further
1½–2 hours or until the meat can be
oved from the bones easily. Skim off
fat, then taste the sauce for seasoning.
nkle with parsley before serving.

Cook's know-how

tail stew needs long, slow cooking to develop
rich brown gravy and to make the meat so
t that it falls off the bone. If possible, make
e stew the day before serving; the excess fat
n then be easily lifted from the surface of
e cooled stew before reheating. If you have
y leftover stew, thin it down with stock or
ter to make a tasty and nutritious soup.

Veal schnitzels

🍴 SERVES 4   373 CALS PER SERVING

4 x 60–90 g (2–3 oz) veal escalopes

salt and black pepper

1 egg, beaten

125 g (4 oz) fresh white breadcrumbs

60 g (2 oz) butter

1 tbsp sunflower oil

TO SERVE

8 anchovy fillets, drained and halved lengthways

2 tbsp coarsely chopped capers

lemon wedges

parsley

1 Put each veal escalope between 2 sheets
of cling film and pound to a 3 mm (⅛ in)
thickness with a rolling pin. Season with salt
and pepper.

2 Spread the beaten egg over a plate,
and sprinkle the breadcrumbs over

another plate. Dip each escalope into the
beaten egg, then into the breadcrumbs,
to coat evenly. Chill in the refrigerator for
about 30 minutes.

3 Melt the butter with the oil in a large
frying pan until foaming, add 2 of the
escalopes, and cook for 2 minutes on each
side until golden. Drain on paper towels and
keep warm while cooking the remaining
escalopes. Serve the veal escalopes hot,
with anchovy fillets, capers, lemon wedges,
and parsley.

💙 Healthy note

Traditional Austrian Wienerschnitzel is cooked
in butter to give it a really good golden colour,
but if you use a non-stick frying pan you can
omit the butter and use 2 tbsp sunflower oil.

Calf's liver with sage

🍴 SERVES 4   364 CALS PER SERVING

2 tbsp plain flour

salt and black pepper

500 g (1 lb) calf's liver, sliced

60 g (2 oz) butter

1 tbsp sunflower oil

juice of 1 lemon

3 tbsp roughly chopped fresh sage

sage leaves and lemon slices to garnish

1 Sprinkle the flour on to a plate and season with salt and pepper. Coat the liver slices in the seasoned flour, shaking off any excess.

2 Melt half of the butter with the oil in a large frying pan. When the butter is foaming, add half of the liver slices and cook over a high heat for about 1 minute on each side until browned all over. Lift out with a slotted spoon and keep warm. Repeat with the remaining liver slices.

3 Melt the remaining butter in the pan, and add the lemon juice and sage, stirring to dissolve any sediment from the bottom of the pan. Pour the pan juices over the liver, garnish with sage leaves and lemon slices, and serve at once.

Calf's liver with apple

Halve and slice 1 eating apple and add to the pan with the lemon juice and sage. Cook, stirring, for 3 minutes, and serve with the liver.

🔍 **Cook's know-how**

Overcooking liver will toughen it, so make sure that the butter and oil are really hot, then the liver will cook quickly.

Creamed sweetbreads

🍴 SERVES 6   230 CALS PER SERVING

500 g (1 lb) calf's sweetbreads

2 tbsp lemon juice

1 small onion, chopped

a few parsley sprigs

1 bay leaf

salt and black pepper

45 g (1½ oz) butter

45 g (1½ oz) plain flour

300 ml (½ pint) milk

chopped parsley to garnish

1 Put the sweetbreads into a bowl, cover with cold water, add 1 tbsp of the lemon juice. Leave to soak for 2–3 hours.

2 Drain, rinse, and trim the sweetbreads (page 207).

3 Put the sweetbreads into a large saucepan with the onion, parsley, bay leaf, and a sprinkling of salt and pepper. Cover with cold water and bring slowly to a boil. Simmer gently for 5 minutes or until just tender, skimming off any scum as it rises to the surface.

4 Drain the sweetbreads, and reserve 300 ml (½ pint) of the cooking liquid. Cut the sweetbreads into bite-sized pieces.

5 Melt the butter in a saucepan, add the flour, and cook, stirring, for 1 minute. Remove the pan from the heat, and gradually blend in the milk and reserved cooking liquid. Bring to a boil, stirring constantly, and boil for 2–3 minutes until the mixture thickens. Add the remaining lemon juice and season with salt and pepper.

6 Add the sweetbreads to the sauce and simmer gently for about 5 minutes to warm through. Transfer to warmed plates and garnish with chopped parsley before serving.

Saltimbocca

🍴 SERVES 4   342 CALS PER SERVING

4 x 60–90 g (2–3 oz) veal escalopes

8–12 fresh sage leaves

4 thin slices of Parma ham, trimmed of fat

2 tbsp plain flour

salt and black pepper

30 g (1 oz) butter

1 garlic clove, crushed

125 ml (4 fl oz) dry white wine

4 tbsp double cream

1 Put each veal escalope between 2 sheets of cling film and pound until 3 mm (⅛ in) thick with a rolling pin.

2 Lay 2 or 3 sage leaves on each escalope, and press a slice of Parma ham firmly on top. Sprinkle the flour on to a plate and season with salt and pepper. Lightly coat both sides of the escalopes with the flour, shaking off any excess.

3 Melt half of the butter in a large frying pan until foaming. Add half of the escalopes and cook for 2 minutes on each side, sprinkling them with half of the garlic as they cook. Lift out and keep warm while you cook the remaining escalopes in the same way, with the remaining butter and garlic.

4 Pour the white wine into the empty pan and boil for a few minutes until it is reduced to about 2 tbsp.

5 Stir in the cream and heat gently, then taste for seasoning. Pour the sauce over the escalopes on warmed plates, and serve at once.

💗 **Healthy note**

Omit the ham, wine, and cream. Before serving, squeeze the juice of 1 lemon over the veal, and sprinkle with 2 tbsp shredded fresh basil and salt and pepper to taste.

Opposite: Saltimbocca

Veal stew with olives and peppers

SERVES 8   355 CALS PER SERVING

2 tbsp plain flour

salt and black pepper

1.5 kg (3 lb) stewing veal, cut into 3.5 cm (1½ in) cubes

2–3 tbsp olive oil

2 garlic cloves, crushed

1 red, 1 green, and 1 yellow pepper, halved, seeded, and cut into strips

250 ml (8 fl oz) dry white wine

2 x 400 g cans chopped tomatoes

4 tbsp tomato purée

1 tsp chopped rosemary

250 g (8 oz) pitted black olives

1 tbsp chopped fresh rosemary to garnish

1 tbsp chopped parsley to garnish

1 Put the flour into a plastic bag and season with salt and pepper. Toss the veal in the seasoned flour to coat lightly.

2 Heat the oil in a large flameproof casserole. Add the veal and sprinkle with half of the garlic, then cook for 5–7 minutes until browned all over. Lift out the veal and set aside.

3 Add the peppers and cook, stirring, for 3 minutes, until almost soft. Remove from the casserole and set aside.

4 Return the veal to the casserole, and add the wine, tomatoes, tomato purée, remaining garlic, and rosemary. Cover and simmer for 1 hour.

5 Return the peppers to the casserole and cook for a further 30 minutes or until the meat is very tender.

6 Stir the olives into the casserole and heat through. Serve hot, lightly sprinkled with rosemary and parsley.

Veal Marsala

SERVES 4   239 CALS PER SERVING

4 x 60–90 g (2–3 oz) veal escalopes

1 tbsp plain flour

salt and black pepper

45 g (1½ oz) butter

1 large onion, finely chopped

125 ml (4 fl oz) Marsala

125 ml (4 fl oz) chicken stock

chopped parsley to garnish

1 Put each veal escalope between 2 sheets of cling film and pound until 3 mm (⅛ in) thick with a rolling pin.

2 Season the flour with salt and pepper and use lightly to coat the escalopes.

3 Melt 30 g (1 oz) of the butter in a frying pan, and cook the escalopes, in batches if necessary, for 2 minutes on each side or until golden. Remove from the pan and keep hot.

4 Melt the remaining butter, add the onion, and cook gently for about 5 minutes until soft and lightly browned. Pour in the Marsala and boil, stirring, until reduced to 2 tbsp. Add the stock and boil until reduced to 90 ml (3 fl oz).

5 Return the escalopes to the pan, spoon over the sauce, and warm the escalopes through. Sprinkle with chopped parsley.

Below: Liver and bacon with onion sauce.

Liver and bacon with onion sauce

SERVES 4   441 CALS PER SERVING

2 tbsp sunflower oil

1 large onion, thinly sliced

125 g (4 oz) streaky bacon rashers, rinds removed, cut into strips

500 g (1 lb) calf's liver, trimmed and cut into 1 cm (½ in) strips

2 tbsp plain flour

600 ml (1 pint) beef stock

3 tbsp tomato ketchup

a dash of Worcestershire sauce

salt and black pepper

chopped fresh tarragon to garnish

1 Heat the oil in a large frying pan, add the onion and bacon, and cook gently, stirring occasionally, for a few minutes until the onion is soft and the bacon crisp. Add the liver and cook, stirring, for 2 minutes. Remove with a slotted spoon and keep warm.

2 Add the flour to the pan and cook, stirring, for 1 minute. Pour in the stock and bring to a boil, stirring until thickened.

3 Add the ketchup and Worcestershire sauce, and season with salt and pepper. Return the onion, bacon, and liver to the pan, cover, and simmer for 5 minutes. Sprinkle with tarragon before serving.

Liver Stroganoff

Use 150 ml (¼ pint) chicken stock instead of the beef stock and omit the ketchup and Worcestershire sauce. Stir in 150 ml (¼ pint) soured cream.

Osso buco

Originally from Milan, the name of this Italian classic means "bone with a hole", it is made from thick slices of veal shin that have the central bone in – they are called shanks by some butchers. For authenticity, serve with gremolata and creamy Risotto Milanese (page 316).

SERVES 6   354 CALS PER SERVING

30 g (1 oz) plain flour

Salt and black pepper

6 veal shanks (bone-in), cut about 3.5–5 cm (1½–2 in) thick

30 g (1 oz) butter

1 tbsp olive oil

2 onions, finely chopped

175 g (6 oz) carrots, finely chopped

2 celery stalks, finely chopped

2 garlic cloves, crushed

300 ml (½ pint) dry white wine

300 ml (½ pint) chicken stock

400 g can chopped tomatoes

1 tbsp chopped fresh oregano

1 bay leaf

Gremolata (see box, right) to serve

1 Put the flour into a large plastic bag and season with salt and pepper. Put the veal shanks into the bag and shake until all the meat is evenly coated with flour.

2 Melt the butter with the oil in a large flameproof casserole. When the butter is foaming, add the veal and cook in batches, for 10 minutes or until golden all over. Lift out and drain on paper towels. Lower the heat, add the onions, carrots, celery, and garlic, and cook for 5 minutes.

3 Pour in the wine and boil until reduced by half. Add the stock, tomatoes, oregano, and bay leaf, and bring to a boil. Return the veal to the casserole, bring back to a boil, cover, and cook in a preheated oven at 160°C (140°C fan, Gas 3) for 1½–2 hours until very tender.

4 If the sauce in the casserole is too thin, lift out the veal and keep hot, then boil the sauce until reduced to a thicker consistency. Taste for seasoning. Sprinkle the gremolata over the veal just before serving.

Gremolata

Put 2 tbsp chopped parsley, the finely grated zest of 1 lemon, and 1 finely chopped garlic clove into a small bowl and stir to mix thoroughly.

🔍 Cook's know-how

In Italy the veal is sold with the marrow in the middle of the bone because it is a traditional custom to scoop it out of the bone after finishing the meat. It tastes really good spread on fresh crusty bread.

Veal with tuna mayonnaise

⏱ SERVES 8   636 CALS PER SERVING

1.5 kg (3 lb) boned and rolled veal roasting joint, such as loin

2 large rosemary sprigs

2 garlic cloves, cut into slivers

salt and black pepper

250 ml (8 fl oz) dry white wine

TUNA MAYONNAISE

1 x 200 g can tuna in oil, drained

2 tbsp lemon juice

1 garlic clove, crushed

2 tbsp capers

1 tsp chopped fresh thyme

a dash of Tabasco sauce

125 ml (4 fl oz) olive oil

250 ml (8 fl oz) mayonnaise

TO GARNISH

black olives

1 red pepper, halved, seeded, and cut into strips

fresh basil

1 Make incisions in the veal and push 1 or 2 rosemary leaves and a sliver of garlic into each incision. Season, and rub with any remaining rosemary and garlic.

2 Place the veal in a large roasting tin and pour the wine around it. Cover with foil and roast in a preheated oven at 160°C (140°C fan, Gas 3) for 2–2½ hours or until tender.

3 Remove the veal from the oven, and leave to cool completely in the cooking liquid. Remove any fat that solidifies on the surface. Slice the veal thinly and arrange the slices on a serving platter.

4 Make the tuna mayonnaise: purée the tuna, reserving a little for the garnish, with the lemon juice, garlic, capers, thyme, and Tabasco sauce in a food processor until smooth. Gradually blend in the oil, then add the mayonnaise, and season with salt and pepper. Pour over the veal. At this stage you can garnish and serve, or cover and refrigerate overnight to serve the next day.

5 To serve, garnish with the reserved tuna, the black olives, red pepper, and basil. Serve at room temperature (if refrigerated overnight, take it out for about 1 hour before serving).

Veal chops with mushrooms and cream

⏱ SERVES 4   604 CALS PER SERVING

15 g (½ oz) dried porcini mushrooms

250 ml (8 fl oz) warm water

2 tbsp plain flour

salt and black pepper

4 x 250 g (8 oz) veal loin chops

45 g (1½ oz) butter

8 shallots, chopped

3 garlic cloves, crushed

250 g (8 oz) button mushrooms, thinly sliced

250 ml (8 fl oz) dry white wine

300 ml (½ pint) single cream

1 tbsp chopped fresh tarragon, plus extra to garnish

1 Put the dried mushrooms into a bowl, pour over the warm water, and leave to soak for 30 minutes or until soft.

2 Sprinkle the flour on to a plate, and season with salt and pepper. Lightly coat the chops with the flour.

3 Melt half of the butter in a frying pan, add the veal chops, and cook for about 4 minutes on each side.

4 Remove the chops and keep warm. Melt the remaining butter in the pan, add the shallots and garlic, and cook gently, stirring occasionally, for a few minutes until softened.

5 Drain the dried mushrooms, reserving the soaking liquid. Add the dried and button mushrooms to the pan and cook for 3 minutes or until tender. Remove the shallots and mushrooms from the pan and keep warm.

6 Pour in the wine and boil until reduced to about 3 tbsp. Add the mushroom liquid and boil until reduced to about 125 ml (4 fl oz).

7 Stir in the cream and heat gently. Add the tarragon, and season with salt and pepper. Return the chops, shallots, and mushrooms to the pan and heat through gently. Transfer to serving plates, sprinkle with the extra chopped tarragon, and serve hot.

Greek roast lamb

⏱ SERVES 6   328 CALS PER SERVING

2 kg (4 lb) leg of lamb

4 garlic cloves, cut into slivers

2 large rosemary sprigs, chopped

1 tbsp olive oil

salt and black pepper

chopped fresh rosemary to garnish

1 With a sharp knife, make small incisions in the lamb and insert a sliver of garlic into each incision.

2 Rub the lamb with the rosemary, olive oil, and salt and pepper, then put it in a roasting tin.

3 Roast in a preheated oven at 220°C (200°C fan, Gas 7) for 30 minutes or until the lamb is browned. Lower the oven temperature to 140°C (120°C fan, Gas 1), cover, and cook for a further 3½ hours or until the lamb is very tender.

4 Cover the lamb with foil and leave to rest in a warm place for 10 minutes. Carve the lamb and serve hot, garnished with rosemary. Any cooking juices can be served with the meat, if you like.

Sauces for lamb

Mint sauce
In a small bowl, combine 3 tbsp finely chopped fresh mint with 1–2 tbsp caster sugar, to taste. Add 3 tbsp white wine vinegar or cider vinegar and stir well to mix.

Cumberland sauce
Put 4 tbsp redcurrant jelly into a small saucepan and heat gently until melted. Add 125 ml (4 fl oz) red wine and the grated zest of 1 orange. Bring to simmering point, and simmer, whisking constantly, for 5 minutes. Add the juices of 1 orange and ½ lemon and simmer for a further 5 minutes. Strain, then add salt and pepper. Serve hot.

Tzatziki sauce
Put 150 g (5 oz) Greek yogurt, the grated zest and juice of 1 lemon, 1 crushed garlic clove, 1 tbsp chopped fresh mint, and salt and pepper into a small bowl. Mix well to combine, then taste for seasoning. Cover and chill until required.

oast leg of lamb
ith red wine gravy

...h gravy that incorporates all the
...oursome juices from the meat is traditional
...roast lamb. Red wine boosts the gravy's
...our, and you can add a spoonful of
...currant jelly too, plus a squeeze of lemon
...e and a dash of Worcestershire sauce if
...like.

ERVES 4–6   517–344 CALS PER SERVING

...(4 lb) leg of lamb

...nd black pepper

...p chopped fresh rosemary

...p plain flour

...l (½ pint) lamb or chicken stock

...(3 fl oz) red wine

...sauce (see recipe, opposite) to serve

...ary and thyme to garnish

1 Trim the skin and excess fat from the lamb.
Score the fat (see box, right).

2 Insert a meat thermometer, if using, into the
middle of the meat. Put the lamb, fat-side
up, on a rack in a roasting tin, and rub with salt
and pepper and the rosemary.

3 Roast the lamb in a preheated oven at 200°C
(180°C fan, Gas 6) for 20 minutes. Lower the
oven temperature to 180°C (160°C fan, Gas 4)
and roast for 20 minutes per 500 g (1 lb) for
medium-done meat, 25 minutes per 500 g (1 lb)
for well-done meat, until the meat thermometer
registers 75–80°C (170–175°F), and the fat is crisp
and golden.

4 Remove the lamb, cover with foil, and leave
to stand for 10 minutes.

5 Meanwhile, make the gravy: spoon all but
1 tbsp fat from the tin. Put the tin on the hob,
add the flour, and cook, stirring, for 1 minute.
Pour in the stock and wine, and bring to a boil,
stirring to dissolve any sediment.

6 Simmer the gravy for about 3 minutes,
season with salt and pepper, then strain if
you like. Serve the gravy and mint sauce with
the lamb, garnished with rosemary
and thyme.

Scoring the fat

Score the fat in a criss-cross pattern
using a small, sharp knife, making
sure that only the fat is cut, and that
the meat underneath remains
completely untouched.

Beef and red onion kebabs

🍴 SERVES 4   263 CALS PER SERVING

500 g (1 lb) rump steak, cut into chunks

2 red onions, cut into wedges

salt and black pepper

olive oil for brushing

MARINADE

50 ml (2 fl oz) olive oil

50 ml (2 fl oz) port, sherry, or Marsala

2 tbsp Dijon mustard

1 Combine the marinade ingredients, add the beef, and stir well. Cover and leave to marinate in the refrigerator for at least 2 hours, turning the meat occasionally.

2 Thread the beef and onions on to skewers, season, and brush with olive oil. Barbecue for 2–3 minutes on each side for rare beef, 3–4 minutes for medium, and 4–5 minutes for well-done.

Oriental pork kebabs

🍴 SERVES 4   378 CALS PER SERVING

500 g (1 lb) pork fillet (tenderloin), cut into chunks

1 red pepper, halved, seeded, and cut into chunks

1 green pepper, halved, seeded, and cut into chunks

1 onion, cut into chunks

¼ fresh pineapple, peeled and cut into chunks

MARINADE

90 ml (3 fl oz) sunflower oil

90 ml (3 fl oz) soy sauce

juice of 1 lime

3 garlic cloves, crushed

3 tbsp sugar

¼ tsp ground ginger

1 Combine the marinade ingredients in a bowl. Add the pork, peppers, onion, and pineapple, and stir well. Cover and chill for at least 2 hours.

2 Thread the meat on to skewers, alternating with peppers, onions, and pineapple. Baste with any remaining marinade. Barbecue for 4–5 minutes on each side, basting, until the pork is cooked.

Curried lamb kebabs

🍴 SERVES 4   203 CALS PER SERVING

500 g (1 lb) boneless loin or leg of lamb, trimmed and cut into chunks

lime wedges to serve

MARINADE

3 tbsp plain yogurt

juice of ½ lime

4 garlic cloves, crushed

3 tbsp chopped fresh coriander

1 tbsp chopped fresh mint

2 tsp curry powder

1 Combine the marinade ingredients in a large bowl. Stir in the lamb, cover, and marinate in the refrigerator for at least 2 hours, turning the meat occasionally.

2 Thread the lamb on to skewers. Barbecue for 4 minutes on each side for medium lamb, or 5 minutes for well-done, basting with the marinade a few times. Serve with lime wedges.

Sausage and sesame kebabs

🍴 SERVES 4   225 CALS PER SERVING

16 cocktail sausages

8 button mushrooms

8 cherry tomatoes

2 courgettes, each cut into 4 thick slices on the diagonal

salt and black pepper

olive oil, for brushing

about 2 tbsp mango chutney

about 2 tbsp toasted sesame seeds

1 Thread the sausages lengthways on to skewers, putting 4 sausages on each skewer, then thread the vegetables on to 4 skewers, alternating the mushrooms, tomatoes, and courgettes. Season and brush with olive oil.

2 Barbecue for 4–5 minutes on each side, until cooked through. While the sausages are still hot, brush them with mango chutney and sprinkle with toasted sesame seeds.

Successful barbecues

Cooking over charcoal requires no special skills, but it helps to know a few simple rules before you start.

Meat is best if it is marinated before being cooked over a barbecue. The basis of a marinade should be an oil to keep the food moist, an acid such as lemon or lime juice to help tenderize the meat, and herbs, spices, or other seasonings to add flavour.

Basting or brushing with the marinade while the meat is cooking will help keep it moist.

Light the barbecue well before you want to start cooking – the coals should have stopped glowing and be covered in grey ash or the food may singe and burn on the outside before it is cooked inside. It takes about 30 minutes to get to this stage.

If you are using bamboo skewers for kebabs, soak them in warm water for 30 minutes before use so that they don't burn.

Opposite, top platter: Beef and red ● kebabs (left) with Oriental pork kebabs. **B** ● platter: Sausage and sesame kebab ● and middle); Curried lamb ke ●

Spinach-stuffed lamb

The lamb in this recipe is distinctively flavoured with spinach, wine, and anchovies. Stuffed mushrooms are a perfect accompaniment.

SERVES 6–8   **459–344 CALS PER SERVING**

2 kg (4 lb) leg of lamb, boned but left whole (page 204)

150 ml (¼ pint) dry white wine

4 canned anchovy fillets, chopped

about 150 ml (¼ pint) lamb or chicken stock

salt and black pepper

SPINACH STUFFING

30 g (1 oz) butter

3–4 garlic cloves, crushed

250 g (8 oz) spinach leaves, coarsely shredded

60 g (2 oz) fresh brown breadcrumbs

1 egg, beaten

1 Make the stuffing: melt the butter in a pan. Add the garlic and cook, stirring, for 2–3 minutes until soft. Stir in the spinach, season with salt and pepper, and cook for 1 minute. Add the breadcrumbs, cool, then mix in the egg.

2 Stuff the lamb (see box, right). Secure with fine skewers or thin string.

3 Put the lamb on a rack in a roasting tin and roast in a preheated oven at 200°C (180°C fan, Gas 6) for 15 minutes. Turn, insert a meat thermometer, if using, and cook for 15 minutes.

4 Drain the fat from the tin, then add the wine and anchovies. Cover the lamb loosely with foil, lower the oven temperature to 180°C (160°C fan, Gas 4), and cook for 1½ hours or until the juices run slightly pink. The thermometer should register 75–80°C (170–175°F).

5 Remove the lamb from the tin. Leave to stand, covered with the foil, in a warm place for about 10 minutes.

6 Pour the cooking liquid into a measuring jug and make up to 300 ml (½ pint) with stock.

7 Return the cooking liquid to the tin. Bring to a boil, stirring to dissolve the sediment. Season, and strain into a warmed gravy boat. Serve the lamb, and hand the gravy separately.

Stuffing the lamb

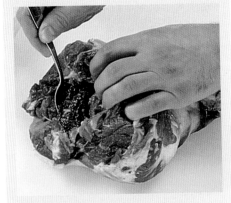

Season the cavity of the lamb with salt and pepper, then spoon in the cold spinach stuffing, packing it in tightly.

Shoulder of lamb with garlic and herbs

SERVES 6   **464 CALS PER SERVING**

2 kg (4 lb) shoulder of lamb, trimmed of excess f⟨

haricot bean cassoulet (page 338) to serve

HERB BUTTER

90 g (3 oz) butter, softened

2 garlic cloves, crushed

1 tbsp chopped fresh thyme

1 tbsp chopped fresh rosemary

1 tbsp chopped fresh mint

2 tbsp chopped parsley

salt and black pepper

GRAVY

1 tbsp plain flour

150 ml (¼ pint) red wine

150 ml (¼ pint) lamb or chicken stock

1 Make the herb butter: mix the butter, garlic, thyme, rosemary, mint, and parsley, and season with salt and peppe⟨

2 Slash the lamb at regular intervals wit⟨ a sharp knife, then push the herb but⟨ into the cuts. Rub any remaining butter ⟨ the lamb. Weigh the lamb.

3 Put the lamb on a rack in a roasting ⟨ and insert a meat thermometer, if usi⟨ into the middle of the meat. Cook in a preheated oven at 200°C (180°C fan, Gas 6) for 30 minutes.

4 Lower the temperature to 180°C (160°C fan, Gas 4) and cook for 20 minutes per 500 g (1 lb). The thermomet⟨ should register 75–80°C (170–175°F).

5 Remove the lamb. Cover loosely wit⟨ and leave to stand in a warm place ⟨ about 10 minutes.

6 Make the gravy: drain all but 1 tbsp the fat from the tin. Set the tin on the hob, add the flour, and cook, stirring, fo⟨ 1 minute. Pour in the wine and stock, br⟨ to a boil, and simmer for 2–3 minutes. T⟨ for seasoning, and strain into a warmec gravy boat. Serve with the lamb and creamed haricot beans.

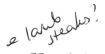
& lamb steaks?

emon-grilled lamb

 SERVES 6–8   425–318 CALS PER SERVING

.5 kg (4–5 lb) leg of lamb, butterflied (page 204)

RINADE

e of 3 lemons

sp clear honey

rge garlic cloves, quartered

sp coarse-grain mustard

Make the marinade: in a non-metallic
dish, mix together the lemon juice,
ney, garlic, and mustard. Turn the lamb
he marinade, cover, and leave to
rinate in the refrigerator, turning the
b occasionally, for 1–2 days.

Remove the lamb from the marinade.
Strain and reserve the marinade. Cook
lamb under a hot grill, 15 cm (6 in) from
heat, basting from time to time with the
rinade, for 20–25 minutes on each side.

est the lamb: insert a skewer into the
thickest part – the juices will run clear
en it is cooked.

Leave the lamb to stand, covered with
foil, in a warm place for 5–10 minutes.
on the fat from the grill pan, strain the
es into a gravy boat, and serve with
lamb.

Cook's know-how

terflied leg of lamb is a good cut for
king on the barbecue as well as under
grill because the meat is thin enough to
k quickly without becoming too charred
he outside. The marinade in this recipe
ks equally well for lamb chops and cutlets,
ch can also be grilled or barbecued.

Shoulder of lamb with lemon and olives

 SERVES 6–8   460–345 CALS PER SERVING

2 kg (4 lb) shoulder of lamb, boned

2 garlic cloves, cut into slivers

150 ml (¼ pint) dry white wine

150 ml (¼ pint) lamb or chicken stock

LEMON AND OLIVE STUFFING

1 tbsp olive oil

1 shallot, finely chopped

125 g (4 oz) fresh breadcrumbs

30 g (1 oz) pitted black olives, roughly chopped

finely grated zest of 1 lemon

1 tbsp chopped fresh thyme

1 tbsp chopped fresh rosemary

1 small egg, beaten

salt and black pepper

1 Make the stuffing: heat the olive oil in
a small pan, add the shallot, and cook
for about 5 minutes. Remove from the heat
and add the breadcrumbs, olives, lemon
zest, herbs, and egg. Season with salt and
pepper, stir, and leave to cool.

2 Make incisions in the meat side of
the lamb, insert the garlic slivers into
them, then sprinkle with salt and pepper
and spread with the stuffing. Roll up and
secure with skewers, then weigh the lamb.

3 Put the lamb into a roasting tin and
insert a meat thermometer, if using,
into the middle of the meat. Pour over the
wine and stock and cook in a preheated
oven at 200°C (180°C fan, Gas 6) for 20–25
minutes. Lower the temperature to 180°C
(160°C fan, Gas 4) and cook for 20 minutes
per 500 g (1 lb) or until the juices run clear.
The meat thermometer should register
75–80°C (170–175°F).

4 Remove the lamb, cover loosely with
foil, and leave to stand for 10 minutes.
Put the tin on the hob and spoon off any
fat. Bring to a boil, and boil for 5 minutes,
stirring to dissolve any sediment from the
tin. Season, strain, and serve.

Lamb chops with minted hollandaise sauce

Instead of the traditional mint sauce, lamb chops are served here with a creamy hollandaise sauce flavoured with fresh mint. The sauce is easy to make, as long as you take care not to get the melted butter too hot.

 SERVES 4   **611 CALS PER SERVING**

4 chump lamb chops

a little olive oil

salt and black pepper

minted hollandaise sauce to serve (see box, below)

1 Brush the chops on both sides with a little oil, and season with salt and pepper.

2 Put the chops under a hot grill, 10 cm (4 in) from the heat, and cook for 3–4 minutes on each side for medium–rare chops, slightly longer for well-done.

3 Arrange the lamb chops on warmed serving plates and serve at once with the warm minted hollandaise sauce.

Minted hollandaise sauce

Whisk together 2 tsp lemon juice, 2 tsp white wine vinegar, and 3 egg yolks at room temperature. Put over a pan of simmering water and whisk until thick. In another pan, gently melt 125 g (4 oz) unsalted butter (do not let it get too hot). Pour into a jug. Pour the melted butter, a little at a time, into the egg-yolk mixture, whisking constantly until the sauce thickens. Remove from the heat, stir in 2 tbsp chopped fresh mint, and season with salt and pepper. Pour into a sauce boat and serve at once.

Lamb with mint glaze

SERVES 4   **304 CALS PER SERVING**

8 best end lamb chops, well trimmed

MINT GLAZE

3 tbsp dry white wine

1 tbsp white wine vinegar

4 mint sprigs, leaves stripped and chopped

1 tbsp clear honey

1 tsp Dijon mustard

salt and black pepper

1 Make the mint glaze: combine the wine, vinegar, mint, honey, and mustard, and season with salt and pepper. Brush the glaze over the chops, and leave to marinate for about 30 minutes.

2 Place the chops over a barbecue or under a hot grill, 7 cm (3 in) from the heat, and cook, brushing often with the glaze, for 4–6 minutes on each side, until done to your liking.

Lamb with orange glaze

Instead of the mint glaze, combine 3 tbsp orange juice with 1 tbsp each white wine vinegar, orange marmalade, and chopped fresh thyme, and 1 tsp Dijon mustard. Season with salt and pepper.

Blanquette of lamb

SERVES 6   **439 CALS PER SERVING**

1 kg (2 lb) boneless shoulder of lamb, trimmed and cut into chunks

1.25 litres (2 pints) water

8 button onions

2 large carrots, thickly sliced

2 bay leaves

juice of ½ lemon

salt and black pepper

250 g (8 oz) button mushrooms

45 g (1½ oz) butter

45 g (1½ oz) plain flour

150 ml (¼ pint) single cream

1 egg yolk

chopped parsley to garnish

1 Put the chunks of lamb into a large saucepan, cover with cold water, and bring to a boil. Drain, then rinse the meat thoroughly to remove the scum.

2 Return the meat to the saucepan and pour in the measured water. Add the button onions, carrots, bay leaves, and lemon juice, and season with salt and pepper. Bring to a boil, cover, and simmer gently for 1 hour.

3 Add the mushrooms and simmer for 3 minutes. Lift out the lamb and vegetables reserving the liquid, and keep hot.

4 Melt the butter in a small pan. Add the flour and cook, stirring occasionally, 1 minute. Gradually blend in the reserved cooking liquid, stirring constantly. Bring to a boil, stirring, then simmer until the sauce thickens.

5 In a bowl, whisk together the cream and egg yolk. Blend in 2 tbsp of the sauce. Take the saucepan off the heat, stir the cream mixture into the sauce, then reheat very gently. Taste for seasoning. the sauce over the lamb and garnish with parsley before serving.

❤ **Healthy note**

Substitute 1 x 400 g can chopped tomatoes and 300 ml (½ pint) dry white wine for the water. Cook the lamb as in the recipe here but do not make the white sauce. This will not be a classic blanquette, but it will cut down on the fat content.

iced lamb
anks

RVES 4   **869 CALS PER SERVING**

sunflower oil

lamb shanks

ts, diced

ns, coarsely chopped

cloves, crushed

½ oz) plain flour

e-spice powder

(16 fl oz) lager

(7 fl oz) beef stock

3 tbsp soy sauce

2 tsp tomato purée

1 tbsp brown sugar

salt and black pepper

1 Heat 1 tbsp of the oil in a large flameproof casserole, and brown the lamb shanks over a high heat until golden on all sides. Remove the lamb from the pan, and set aside.

2 Heat the remaining oil in the pan, add the vegetables and garlic, and fry over a medium heat for about 5 minutes. Sprinkle in the flour and five-spice powder, and fry for 1 minute. Gradually blend in the lager and stock, whisk over a high heat until

boiling and smooth, then add the soy sauce, tomato purée, and sugar, and season with salt and pepper. Return the lamb to the pan, cover, and bring to a boil.

3 Cook in a preheated oven at 160°C (140°C fan, Gas 3) for 2–2½ hours until the lamb is tender and just falling off the bones. Check the seasoning before serving.

Herbed butterfly chops

SERVES 4   320 CALS PER SERVING

4 butterfly lamb chops

1 tbsp olive oil

black pepper

4 rosemary sprigs

4 mint sprigs

4 thyme sprigs

1 Place the lamb chops on a grill rack and brush each one with half of the oil. Sprinkle with black pepper and scatter with the herb sprigs.

2 Place the chops under a hot grill, 10 cm (4 in) from the heat, and cook for 4–6 minutes. Remove from the heat, lift off the herbs, and turn the chops over. Brush the chops with the remaining oil, replace the herbs, and grill for 4–6 minutes until done to your liking. Serve hot.

Irish stew

SERVES 4   539 CALS PER SERVING

1 kg (2 lb) main-crop potatoes, cut into 5 mm (¼ in) slices

2 large onions, sliced

1 kg (2 lb) middle neck lamb chops, trimmed

a few parsley stalks

1 thyme sprig

1 bay leaf

salt and black pepper

300–500 ml (10–16 fl oz) water

chopped parsley to garnish

1 Put half of the potatoes into a flameproof casserole, cover with half of the onions, then add the chops, parsley, thyme, and bay leaf, and season with salt and pepper. Add the remaining onions, then the remaining potatoes, seasoning each layer with salt and pepper.

2 Pour in enough water to half-fill the casserole, and then bring to a boil. Cover tightly and cook in a preheated oven at 160°C (140°C fan, Gas 3) for 2–2½ hours until the lamb and potatoes are just tender.

3 Remove the lid, increase the oven temperature to 220°C (200°C fan, Gas 7), and cook for 20–30 minutes to brown the topping. Sprinkle with parsley before serving.

Lancashire hot pot

SERVES 4   689 CALS PER SERVING

2 tbsp sunflower oil

1 kg (2 lb) middle neck lamb chops, trimmed

3 lamb's kidneys, trimmed (page 207) and halved

1 kg (2 lb) potatoes, cut into 5 mm (¼ in) slices

500 g (1 lb) carrots, sliced

2 large onions, chopped

1 tsp caster sugar

salt and black pepper

1 bay leaf

1 rosemary sprig

a few parsley sprigs

600–750 ml (1–1¼ pints) lamb or chicken stock, or water

chopped parsley to garnish

1 Heat the oil in a flameproof casserole, add the lamb in batches, and brown over a medium heat for 5 minutes. Remove and set aside. Add the kidneys and cook for 3–5 minutes. Remove and set aside.

2 Add the potatoes, carrots, and onions, and cook for 5 minutes. Remove from the casserole.

3 Make layers of lamb chops, kidneys, and vegetables in the casserole, sprinkling with the sugar and a little salt and pepper, and putting the herbs in the middle.

4 Top with a neat layer of potatoes. Pour in enough stock or water to come up to the potato layer. Cover tightly and cook in a preheated oven at 160°C (140°C fan, Gas 3) for 2 hours or until the meat and vegetables are tender.

5 Remove the casserole lid, increase the oven temperature to 220°C (200°C fan, Gas 7), and cook for 20–30 minutes to brown the potato topping. Sprinkle with parsley before serving.

Country hot pot

Omit the kidneys, and substitute 250 g (8 oz) swede for half of the carrots. Layer the meat and vegetables with 60 g (2 oz) pearl barley.

Lamb noisettes wit orange and honey

SERVES 4   457 CALS PER SERVING

8 lamb noisettes

2 lamb's kidneys, trimmed (page 207) and quartered (optional)

chopped fresh thyme and rosemary to garnish

MARINADE

grated zest and juice of 1 orange

4 tbsp clear honey

3 tbsp olive oil

2 garlic cloves, crushed

1 tbsp chopped fresh thyme

1 tbsp chopped fresh rosemary

salt and black pepper

1 Make the marinade: in a shallow, non-metallic dish, combine the orang zest and juice, honey, oil, garlic, thyme, and rosemary, and season with salt and pepper. Add the lamb noisettes to the marinade, turn them, then cover, and le to marinate in the refrigerator overnight.

2 Lift the lamb noisettes out of the marinade, reserving the marinade. Place a piece of kidney, if using, in the middle of each lamb noisette.

3 Put under a hot grill, 10 cm (4 in) from the heat, and cook for 7 minutes on each side until the lamb is tender.

4 Meanwhile, strain the marinade into a small saucepan, bring to a boil, an simmer for a few minutes until it reaches a syrupy consistency. Taste for seasoning spoon over the lamb noisettes, and gar with thyme and rosemary.

Cook's know-how

Noisettes are taken from the loin of the la The eye of meat is cut away, then rolled, ti and cut into thick slices. It is an expensive but gives neat portions of tender, lean mea with no waste.

ack of lamb
ith a walnut
nd herb crust

called best end of neck, a rack
mb usually has 6–8 bones, which
called cutlets. The bones should be
ped clean of all fat – this is called
nch trimmed" by some butchers.

ERVES 4–6   626–417 CALS PER SERVING

ared racks of lamb (page 205)

, beaten

UT AND HERB CRUST

l oz) fresh wholemeal breadcrumbs

oz) parsley, chopped

coarsely chopped walnut pieces

garlic cloves, crushed

grated zest of 1 lemon

walnut oil

d black pepper

ND GRAPE SAUCE

(¼ pint) dry white wine

(¼ pint) lamb or chicken stock

4 oz) seedless green grapes, halved

1 Brush the outsides of the racks of lamb with some of the beaten egg.

2 Prepare the walnut and herb crust: combine the breadcrumbs, parsley, walnuts, garlic, lemon zest, and oil, season with salt and pepper, and bind with the remaining egg. Chill for 30 minutes.

3 Coat the racks with the walnut and herb crust (see box, right), and put them crust-side up into a roasting tin. Cook in a preheated oven at 200°C (180°C fan, Gas 6) for 30 minutes.

4 Remove the lamb, cover with foil, and leave to stand in a warm place for 10 minutes.

5 Meanwhile, make the sauce: spoon all but 1 tbsp of the fat from the roasting tin. Set the tin on the hob, pour in the wine, and bring to a boil, stirring to dissolve any sediment from the bottom of the tin.

6 Add the stock and boil, stirring occasionally, for 2–3 minutes. Taste the sauce for seasoning, strain into a warmed sauce boat, and stir in the grapes. Serve with the lamb.

Coating the lamb

Press half of the walnut and herb crust mixture on to the meaty side of each rack of lamb, using a palette knife.

Indian spiced lamb

🍳 SERVES 6   379 CALS PER SERVING

1.5 kg (3 lb) shoulder or leg of lamb

1 tsp lemon juice

salt and black pepper

cashew nuts and chopped coriander to garnish

SPICED YOGURT MARINADE

4 garlic cloves, coarsely chopped

7 cm (3 in) piece of fresh root ginger, peeled and grated

2 tbsp clear honey

1 tbsp lemon juice

seeds of 5 cardamom pods

1 tsp ground cumin

1 tsp turmeric

¼ tsp cayenne pepper

1 tsp salt

½ tsp ground cinnamon

¼ tsp ground cloves (optional)

150 g (5 oz) Greek yogurt

1 Make the spiced yogurt marinade: purée the garlic, ginger, honey, lemon juice, cardamom, cumin, turmeric, cayenne, salt, cinnamon, cloves (if using), and yogurt in a blender or food processor.

2 Spread the mixture over the lamb (see box, below). Cover and leave to marinate in the refrigerator for at least 2 hours, or overnight.

3 Put the lamb on a rack in a roasting tin and cook in a preheated oven at 160°C (140°C fan, Gas 3) for 3½ hours or until the meat is tender.

4 Remove the lamb and keep hot. Spoon the fat from the tin. Set the tin on the hob and stir in the lemon juice and enough water to make a sauce. Bring to a boil, stirring, and season with salt and pepper.

5 Cut the lamb from the bone, then cut the meat into chunks and mix with the sauce on the hob. Serve hot, garnished with cashew nuts and chopped coriander.

Coating the lamb

Make incisions in the lamb, then spread the marinade over the whole joint, making sure it goes into the incisions.

Aromatic lamb with lentils

🍳 SERVES 8   475 CALS PER SERVING

1.5 kg (3 lb) lamb neck fillet, trimmed and cut into chunks

2 tbsp olive oil

2 onions, chopped

125 g (4 oz) brown or green Puy lentils, rinsed

175 g (6 oz) ready-to-eat dried apricots

salt and black pepper

600 ml (1 pint) lamb or chicken stock

MARINADE

175 ml (6 fl oz) orange juice

2 tbsp olive oil

3 garlic cloves, crushed

1 tsp ground ginger

1 tsp ground coriander

½ tsp ground cinnamon

1 Make the marinade: in a large bowl, combine the orange juice, oil, garlic, ginger, coriander, and cinnamon.

2 Turn the chunks of lamb in the marinade, cover loosely, and then leave to marinate in the refrigerator overnight.

3 Remove the lamb from the marinade, reserving the marinade. Heat the olive oil in a large flameproof casserole, add the lamb in batches, and cook over a high heat for 5 minutes or until browned all over. Lift out the lamb chunks with a slotted spoon.

4 Lower the heat slightly, add the onions, and cook gently, stirring occasionally, for a few minutes until just soft but not coloured. Lift out of the casserole.

5 Make layers of lamb, onions, lentils, and apricots in the casserole, sprinkling each layer with salt and pepper. Pour in the stock and the reserved marinade and bring to a boil. Cover and cook in a preheated oven at 160°C (140°C fan, Gas 3) for 2 hours or until the meat is tender. Taste for seasoning before serving.

Fragrant lamb korma

This aromatic lamb dish is enriched with yogurt instead of cream, which makes it healthier than a traditional korma. The fresh mint and paprika garnish adds to both flavour and presentation. For an authentic accompaniment, serve with spiced red lentils.

🍳 SERVES 6   508 CALS PER SERVING

5 cm (2 in) piece of fresh root ginger, peeled and grated

3 large garlic cloves, peeled

2 large green chillies, halved and seeded

60 g (2 oz) salted cashew nuts (optional)

2 tsp ground cumin

2 tsp ground cardamom

2 tsp turmeric

6 tbsp water

3 tbsp sunflower oil

1 kg (2 lb) lamb neck fillet, trimmed and cut int 4 cm (1½ in) cubes

2 large onions, roughly chopped

300 ml (¼ pint) full-fat Greek yogurt

salt and black pepper

about 1 tbsp lemon juice

fresh mint and paprika to garnish

1 Place the ginger, garlic, chillies, cash nuts (if using), cumin, cardamom, turmeric, and measured water in a food processor or blender, and purée until smo

2 Heat 2 tbsp of the oil in a large flameproof casserole, and brown th lamb on all sides (you may need to do in batches). Remove with a slotted spoo and set aside to drain on kitchen pape

3 Heat the remaining oil in the same p and fry the onions over a high heat 2–3 minutes. Return the lamb to the pa add the puréed spice blend, and stir in yogurt. Season with salt and pepper, c and simmer gently for about 1½–2 hou until the lamb is tender.

4 Just before serving, add the lemon j and check the seasoning. Garnish w sprinkling of mint and paprika, and serv

ow-roast shoulder of lamb

ERVES 4–6   656–437 CALS PER SERVING

g (3 lb) shoulder of lamb, bone in

e garlic cloves, sliced

mary sprigs, snipped into pieces

n, cut into quarters

grated zest and juice of 1 lemon

olive oil

d black pepper

(1 pint) beef stock

plain flour

port

1 With the tip of a small pointed knife, make incisions through the skin of the lamb into the meat. Push the garlic and rosemary into the slits.

2 Scatter the onion quarters over the bottom of a roasting tin, and sit the lamb skin-side up on top. Sprinkle over the lemon zest and juice and the olive oil, and season with salt and pepper. Pour the stock into the tin around the lamb.

3 Roast in a preheated oven at 220°C (200°C fan, Gas 7) for 30–40 minutes until the lamb is brown on top. Lower the oven temperature to 150°C (130°C fan, Gas 2), and roast for a further 3–3½ hours until the lamb is completely tender, basting from time to time.

4 Transfer the lamb to a board, and cover with foil. Leave to stand in a warm place for about 15 minutes.

5 Meanwhile, skim off the fat from the roasting tin, then put 3 tbsp of the fat into a saucepan. Tip the stock and onions into a sieve held over a bowl, and strain the liquid through, pressing on the onions to extract their juices. Measure 600 ml (1 pint) liquid, making it up with a little stock or water if necessary. Heat the fat in the saucepan, sprinkle in the flour, and whisk over a high heat to combine. Gradually blend in the measured stock, whisk until boiling and smooth, then stir in the port and continue boiling until the gravy has reduced by half. Check the seasoning, and serve with the lamb.

Lamb tagine

🍽 SERVES 8   412 CALS PER SERVING

¼ tsp saffron threads

150 ml (¼ pint) hot water

3 tbsp olive oil

1.5 kg (3 lb) boneless shoulder of lamb, well trimmed and cut into 2.5 cm (1 in) cubes

1 fennel bulb or 4 celery stalks, trimmed and sliced crosswise

2 green peppers, halved, seeded, and cut into strips

1 large onion, sliced

30 g (1 oz) plain flour

½ tsp ground ginger

450 ml (¾ pint) lamb or chicken stock

grated zest and juice of 1 orange

125 g (4 oz) ready-to-eat dried apricots

salt and black pepper

mint sprigs to garnish

1 Prepare the saffron (see box, right). Heat the oil in a flameproof casserole, add the lamb in batches, and cook over a high heat for 5 minutes or until browned. Lift out and drain on paper towels.

2 Lower the heat, add the fennel or celery, peppers, and onion, and cook gently, stirring, for 5 minutes.

3 Sprinkle the flour and ginger into the vegetables and cook, stirring occasionally, for 1 minute. Add the saffron liquid to the casserole, return the cubes of lamb, then add the stock and orange zest (retaining a pinch for garnish), and season with salt and pepper. Bring to a boil, cover, and cook in a preheated oven at 160°C (140°C fan, Gas 3) for 1 hour.

4 Add the orange juice and apricots and cook for about 30 minutes until the lamb is very tender. Taste for seasoning and garnish with mint sprigs and orange zest before serving.

Preparing saffron

Put the saffron threads into a small bowl, add the measured hot water, and leave to soak for 10 minutes.

Spiced lamb with coconut

🍽 SERVES 6   496 CALS PER SERVING

1 kg (2 lb) lamb neck fillet, trimmed and cut into 2.5 cm (1 in) cubes

30 g (1 oz) butter

1 tbsp sunflower oil

1 large Spanish onion, sliced

2 large garlic cloves, crushed

1 tbsp plain flour

1 x 400 g can chopped tomatoes

150 ml (¼ pint) lamb or chicken stock

grated zest and juice of 1 lime

2 tbsp mango chutney

60 g (2 oz) creamed coconut, chopped

250 g (8 oz) Greek yogurt

coriander sprigs to garnish

SPICE MIX

2.5 cm (1 in) piece of fresh root ginger, peeled and grated

1 tbsp ground cumin

1 tbsp ground coriander

1 tbsp mild curry powder

salt and black pepper

1 Toss the meat in the ginger, cumin, coriander, and curry powder, and season with salt and pepper.

2 Melt the butter with the oil in a large flameproof casserole. When the butter is foaming, add the lamb in batches, and cook over a high heat for about 5 minutes until browned all over.

3 Lift out with a slotted spoon and set aside. Lower the heat, add the onion and garlic, and cook gently, stirring occasionally, for a few minutes until soft but not coloured.

4 Sprinkle in the flour and cook, stirring, 1 minute. Add the tomatoes, stock, lime zest and juice, and chutney, and season with salt and pepper. Bring to a boil, stir.

5 Return the lamb to the casserole, add the coconut, and bring back to a boil. Cover and cook in a preheated oven at 160°C (140°C fan, Gas 3) for 2 hours or until the lamb is tender.

6 Stir in the yogurt and taste for seasoning. Garnish with coriander sprigs before serving.

Shepherd's pie

🍽 SERVES 6   383 CALS PER SERVING

0 g (1½ lb) minced lamb

5 g (4 oz) mushrooms, sliced

carrots, diced

arge onion, chopped

arlic clove, crushed

g (1 oz) plain flour

0 ml (¼ pint) beef stock

bsp Worcestershire sauce

t and black pepper

g (1½ lb) potatoes

out 4 tbsp hot milk

g (1 oz) butter

Put the minced lamb into a large frying pan and heat gently until the fat runs. rease the heat and cook, turning and shing the meat, until it browns. Using otted spoon, lift the lamb out of the n and spoon off the excess fat.

Add the mushrooms, carrots, onion, and garlic to the pan, and cook gently, ing occasionally, for a few minutes until beginning to soften.

Return the lamb to the frying pan. Sprinkle in the flour and cook, stirring, about 1 minute.

w: Shepherd's pie.

4 Add the stock and the Worcestershire sauce, and season with salt and pepper. Bring to a boil, cover, and simmer gently for 30 minutes.

5 Meanwhile, cook the potatoes in boiling salted water for 15–20 minutes until tender. Drain. Add the milk and butter to the potatoes and mash until soft, then season with salt and pepper.

6 Taste the lamb mixture for seasoning. Turn into an ovenproof dish, then spread the potato on top. With a fork, score the potato in a decorative pattern. Cook in a preheated oven at 200°C (180°C fan, Gas 6) for about 20 minutes until the potato topping is golden and the meat mixture bubbling.

Moussaka

🍽 SERVES 6   965 CALS PER SERVING

750 g (1½ lb) lean minced lamb

2 large onions, finely chopped

2 garlic cloves, crushed

2 tbsp plain flour

2 x 400 g cans chopped tomatoes

4 tbsp tomato purée

salt and black pepper

3 large aubergines, cut into 1 cm (½ lb) slices

olive oil for shallow-frying

TOPPING

60 g (2 oz) butter

60 g (2 oz) plain flour

150 ml (¼ pint) milk

1 x 500 g carton full-fat crème fraîche

125 g (4 oz) Parmesan cheese, grated

2 tsp ready-made English mustard

1 large egg, beaten

wide-based 2.2 litre (4 pint) ovenproof dish

1 Heat a large, deep non-stick frying pan until hot, and fry the lamb until browned, breaking up any lumps with a wooden spoon. Stir in the onions and garlic, and fry for 5 minutes more. Sprinkle in the flour, blend in the tomatoes and tomato purée, and season with salt and pepper. Bring to a boil, then cover and lower the heat. Simmer gently for 45 minutes, stirring occasionally.

2 Meanwhile, bring a saucepan of salted water to a boil. Add the aubergine slices, and bring back to a boil, then blanch for 2 minutes until they are just starting to cook but are still firm. Drain, and dry well with paper towels.

3 Heat 2 tbsp olive oil in a large frying pan, and fry a single layer of aubergine slices until light golden on each side. Do this in batches, using more oil as necessary. As each batch is done, remove from the pan with a fish slice, and set aside.

4 Make the topping: melt the butter in a saucepan, sprinkle in the flour, and cook, stirring, for 1 minute. Remove from the heat, and gradually blend in the milk followed by the crème fraîche. Bring to a boil, stirring constantly until thickened. Simmer for 2–3 minutes, remove from the heat, and stir in half of the Parmesan. Add the mustard, season with salt and pepper, and stir until combined. Leave to cool for 5 minutes, then add the egg and stir well to mix.

5 Spoon the lamb into the ovenproof dish, and level the surface. Arrange the aubergine slices over the lamb, cover with the topping, and sprinkle with the remaining Parmesan. Bake in a preheated oven at 200°C (180°C fan, Gas 6) for 40–45 minutes until golden and bubbling. Leave to stand for a few minutes before serving.

Boned loin of pork with apricot stuffing

Succulent boned loin of pork, with an apricot stuffing flavoured with lemon juice and lemon thyme, is served here with a white wine gravy. The crackling is cooked separately, in the top half of the oven, to ensure that it is deliciously crisp.

SERVES 8   **428 CALS PER SERVING**

1.5 kg (3 lb) boned loin of pork, skin removed and scored at 1 cm (½ in) intervals

sunflower oil for brushing

APRICOT STUFFING

30 g (1 oz) butter

1 small onion, finely chopped

90 g (3 oz) fresh brown breadcrumbs

90 g (3 oz) ready-to-eat dried apricots, coarsely chopped

1 tbsp chopped parsley

1 tbsp lemon juice

2 tsp chopped fresh lemon thyme

1 egg, beaten

salt and black pepper

GRAVY

1 tbsp plain flour

150 ml (¼ pint) chicken stock

150 ml (¼ pint) dry white wine

1 Make the stuffing: melt the butter in a saucepan and cook the onion gently until soft.

2 Remove from the heat and add the breadcrumbs, apricots, parsley, lemon juice, lemon thyme, and egg. Season with salt and pepper, mix well, and leave until cold.

3 Brush the scored side of the pork skin with a little oil, and sprinkle generously with salt and pepper. Place the skin on a rack in a roasting tin.

4 Remove as much fat as possible from the pork, expecially on the top where the skin has been removed. Season the meat well, then stuff and roll (see box, below).

5 Place the pork skin in the top of a preheated oven at 180°C (160°C fan, Gas 4). Put the pork into another roasting tin, brush with oil, and season generously. Insert a meat thermometer, if using, into the middle of the loin, and cook the pork in the oven for 2 hours or until the thermometer registers 80°C (175°F).

6 Transfer the pork to a carving board, cover with foil, and leave to stand for 10 minutes. If the crackling is not really crisp, increase the oven temperature to 200°C (180°C fan, Gas 6) and let it continue to cook while making the gravy.

7 Put the roasting tin on the hob and spoon off all but 1 tbsp of the fat. Sprinkle in the flour, and cook, stirring to dissolve any sediment from the bottom of the tin, for 1 minute. Pour in the stock and wine, and bring to a boil, stirring constantly. Simmer for 3 minutes. Season to taste and strain into a gravy boat. Serve with the pork.

Bacon-wrapped pork in vermouth sauce

SERVES 6   **547 CALS PER SERVING**

2 pork fillets (tenderloins), about 375 g (12 oz) each, trimmed

2 tbsp Dijon mustard

salt and black pepper

375 g (12 oz) streaky bacon rashers, rinds removed

VERMOUTH SAUCE

30 g (1 oz) butter

1 tbsp olive oil

1 shallot, finely chopped

1 tbsp plain flour

200 ml (7 fl oz) chicken stock

90 ml (3 fl oz) dry vermouth

125 g (4 oz) button or chestnut mushrooms, sliced

1 Spread the pork fillets with the mustard and season with salt and pepper. Stretch the bacon rashers with the back of a knife and wrap around the fillets (see box, below).

2 Place the fillets in a roasting tin and cook in a preheated oven at 220°C (200°C fan, Gas 7), turning the fillets halfway through cooking, for 30–35 minutes until the juices from the pork run clear and the bacon is crisp and golden.

3 Meanwhile, make the sauce: melt the butter with the oil in a small pan. When the butter is foaming, add the shallot, and cook gently until softened.

4 Add the flour and cook, stirring, for 1 minute. Gradually blend in the stock and vermouth. Bring to a boil, add the mushrooms, and simmer for 15 minutes.

5 Transfer the pork to a warmed platter. Spoon off the fat from the roasting tin and strain the juices into the sauce. Heat through and taste for seasoning. Serve with the pork.

Stuffing and rolling a loin of pork

Open out the loin of pork and spread the stuffing over the meat.

Roll the pork around the stuffing and tie at intervals with fine string, or use skewers.

Wrapping pork fillets

Overlap half of the bacon rashers on a work surface. Lay 1 pork fillet across the bacon and plait the rashers around the meat. Secure with a fine skewer. Repeat with the second pork fillet.

Boston baked beans

SERVES 6–8   433–325 CALS PER SERVING

5 g (12 oz) dried haricot beans

g (2 oz) dark muscovado sugar

bsp tomato purée

sp black treacle

sp golden syrup

sp mustard powder

sp salt

ck pepper

) g (8 oz) piece of streaky bacon, cut into
cm (1 in) cubes

nions, quartered

ml (1 pint) water

Put the haricot beans into a large bowl,
cover with plenty of cold water, and
ave to soak overnight.

Drain the beans, and rinse under cold
running water. Put the beans into
aucepan, cover with cold water, and
g to a boil. Boil rapidly for 10 minutes,
n partially cover the pan and simmer
30 minutes. Drain and set aside.

Put the sugar, tomato purée, black
treacle, golden syrup, and mustard
a large flameproof casserole. Season
salt and pepper and heat gently,
ng constantly.

Add the bacon and onions to the
casserole with the drained beans
d measured water. Bring to a boil,
er tightly, and cook in a preheated
n at 140°C (120°C fan, Gas 1), stirring
casionally, for 4½–5 hours. Taste for
soning before serving.

Marinated loin of pork with pineapple

SERVES 8   320 CALS PER SERVING

1.5 kg (3 lb) boned loin of pork, skin removed

grilled pineapple rings and parsley sprigs to serve

MARINADE

250 ml (8 fl oz) pineapple juice

2 tbsp maple syrup

2 tbsp soy sauce

2 garlic cloves, crushed

2 tbsp chopped fresh thyme

1 tsp ground coriander

1 Make the marinade: in a large non-
metallic bowl, combine the pineapple
juice, maple syrup, soy sauce, garlic, thyme,
and coriander. Add the pork, cover, and
marinate in the refrigerator, turning
occasionally, for 8 hours.

2 Remove the pork from the marinade,
reserving the marinade. Put the pork
flat, fat-side up, in a small roasting tin.
Insert a meat thermometer, if using, into
the middle of the pork. Cover loosely with
foil and cook in a preheated oven at 220°C
(200°C fan, Gas 7) for 1 hour.

3 Remove the foil and pour the marinade
over the pork. Return to the oven and
cook for 20–30 minutes or until the marinade
has darkened and the juices run clear
when the meat is pierced with a fine
skewer. The meat thermometer should
register 80°C (175°F).

4 Transfer the pork to a carving board,
cover with foil, and leave to stand
for 10 minutes. Strain the cooking juices
and remove the fat (see box, below), then
reheat. Serve the pork sliced, with the juices
poured over, garnished with pineapple
and parsley.

Removing the fat

Skim the layer of fat from the surface of the
juices, using a skimmer or spoon.

Madeira pork with paprika

SERVES 4 **560 CALS PER SERVING**

30 g (1 oz) butter

2 tbsp sunflower oil

750 g (1½ lb) pork fillet (tenderloin), trimmed and cut diagonally into 1 cm (½ in) slices

1 onion, chopped

1 large red pepper, halved, seeded, and cut into strips

1 tbsp paprika

1 tbsp plain flour

300 ml (½ pint) chicken stock

75 ml (2½ fl oz) Madeira

175 g (6 oz) button mushrooms

1 tsp tomato purée

150 ml (¼ pint) single cream

salt and black pepper

1 Melt the butter with the oil in a large frying pan. When the butter is foaming, add the pork slices, in batches if necessary and cook over a high heat for about 3 minutes until just beginning to brown. Lift out with a slotted spoon and drain on paper towels.

2 Add the onion and red pepper and cook, stirring, for 2 minutes. Add the paprika and flour, and cook, stirring, for 1 minute. Remove the pan from the heat and blend in the stock. Return to the heat and add the Madeira, mushrooms, and tomato purée. Simmer for 2–3 minute

3 Return the pork to the pan and seaso with salt and pepper. Cover and simm very gently for 20 minutes or until the por is tender. Stir in the cream, taste for seasoning, and heat through gently. Serve hot.

Slow-roast belly of pork

SERVES 6 **558 CALS PER SERVING**

1.35 kg (3 lb) boned belly of pork, skin scored at 1 cm (½ in) intervals

1 tbsp sunflower oil

salt and black pepper

apple sauce or fruit jelly (eg apple, medlar, gooseberry) to serve

GRAVY

a large knob of butter

3 tbsp plain flour

600 ml (1 pint) beef stock

3 tbsp port

a few drops of Worcestershire sauce

a dash of gravy browning

1 Brush the skin of the pork with the oil. Season with salt and pepper, and rub well into the skin. Sit the pork skin-side up in a small roasting tin, and pour 1.3 litres (2¼ pints) cold water around the meat.

2 Roast the pork in a preheated oven at 150°C (130°C fan, Gas 2) for 4–5 hours until the meat feels very soft and tender.

3 Increase the oven temperature to 220°C (200°C fan, Gas 7), and roast the pork for another 30 minutes or until the skin is crisp and golden.

4 Transfer the pork to a board, and pour any juices from the roasting tin into a jug. Tent the pork loosely with foil (do not cover closely or the crackling will soften), and leave to stand in a warm place for about 15 minutes.

5 Meanwhile, make the gravy: melt the butter in a saucepan, sprinkle in the flour, and stir over a high heat to combine. Gradually blend in the stock, and whisk over a high heat until boiling and smooth. Stir in the port and any pork juices, then lower the heat and add the Worcestershire sauce and gravy browning. Season with a little salt and pepper, and stir well to combine.

6 Carve the pork into 6 slices. Serve hot, with the gravy and apple sauce or fruit jelly.

Cook's know-how

The pork can be cooked the day before. Cool after the long, slow cooking in step 2, and keep covered in the refrigerator overnight. Bring back to room temperature, then roast in a preheated oven at 220°C (200°C fan, Gas 7) for about 30 minutes until the crackling is crisp and the meat is hot.

Healthy note

The cream makes the sauce both look and taste rich, but it can be omitted and the sauce will still be good. Pork fillet (tenderloin) is an excellent cut of meat to us if you are trying to cut down on fat becaus it is very lean and yet tender and succulen

Sauces for pork

Apricot sauce

Melt 30 g (1 oz) butter, and cook 1 thinly sliced small onion until soft. Add 125 g (4 oz) chopped ready-to-eat dried apricots, 150 ml (¼ pint) each chicken stock and dry white wine, and ¼ tsp ground cinnamon. Season with salt and pepper, and simmer for about 20 minutes until pulpy.

Apple sauce

Peel, core, and slice 500 g (1 lb) cooking apples and put into a saucepan with the finely grated zest of 1 lemon and 2-3 tbsp water. Cover tightly and cook gently for about 10 minutes until soft. Stir in 30 g (1 oz) caster sugar. Beat the sauce until smooth, then stir in 15 g (½ oz) butter if you like.

Sweet and sour sauce

Finely slice 1 onion, 1 leek, and 2 celery stalks. Cut 2 carrots into matchstick-thin strips. Heat 2 tbsp sunflower oil in a pan and cook the vegetables for 3 minutes or until softened. Blend 2 tbsp tomato ketchup, 1 tbsp soy sauce, 1 tbsp white wine vinegar, 4 tsp cornflour, and 2 tsp caster sugar, then blend in 300 ml (½ pint) water. Add to the pan and bring to a boil, stirring until thickened.

Roast leg of pork

🍴 SERVES 6–8   338–254 CALS PER SERVING

2 kg (4 lb) leg of pork, skin removed and scored at 1 cm (½ in) intervals

sunflower oil for brushing

salt and black pepper

1 carrot, thickly sliced

1 onion, thickly sliced

1 tbsp plain flour

300 ml (½ pint) chicken stock

apple sauce to serve (see box, left)

1 Brush the scored side of the pork skin with a little oil, and sprinkle generously with salt and black pepper. Place on a rack in a small roasting tin.

2 Remove as much fat as possible from the pork, especially on top where the skin has been removed. Put the pork into another roasting tin, and arrange the carrot and onion around it. Brush the meat with a little oil, season well, and insert a meat thermometer, if using, into the middle of the pork.

3 Put both roasting tins in a preheated oven at 180°C (160°C fan, Gas 4), with the pork skin at the top.

4 Roast for 2½ hours or until the thermometer registers 80°C (175°F). Transfer the pork to a carving board, cover with foil, and leave to stand for 10 minutes. If the crackling is not really crisp, increase the oven temperature to 200°C (180°C fan, Gas 6) and let it continue to cook while making the gravy.

5 Put the roasting tin on the hob. Remove the carrot and onion and spoon off all but 1 tbsp of the fat from the tin.

6 Add the flour and cook, stirring to dissolve any sediment from the bottom of the tin, for 1 minute. Pour in the stock and bring to a boil. Simmer for 3 minutes, then season, and strain into a gravy boat. Serve the pork with the gravy and apple sauce.

🔍 Cook's know-how

The high oven temperature needed for crisp crackling can make meat tough and dry. Removing the skin and cooking it separately, above the pork, avoids this problem.

Above: Pork chops with spinach and mushroom stuffing.

Pork chops with spinach and mushroom stuffing

Tender pork loin chops are topped with a spinach and chestnut mushroom stuffing mixture, and finished off under the grill with Gruyère cheese. A wedge of the stuffing accompanies each chop as a delicious extra.

🍽 **SERVES 6**   **345 CALS PER SERVING**

6 lean pork loin chops, on the bone

olive oil for brushing

about 90 g (3 oz) Gruyère cheese, cut into 6 thin slices

SPINACH AND MUSHROOM STUFFING

1 tbsp olive oil

1 large onion, chopped

150 g (5 oz) chestnut mushrooms, roughly chopped

250 g (8 oz) baby spinach leaves, shredded

90 g (3 oz) fresh breadcrumbs

salt and black pepper

1 Make the stuffing: heat the oil in a large frying pan, add the onion, cover, and cook gently for about 15 minutes or until soft.

2 Uncover the pan, increase the heat, and add the mushrooms. Stir-fry for 2–3 minutes, then add the spinach and stir-fry until it has just wilted. Add the breadcrumbs, season with salt and pepper, and stir well. Leave to cool.

3 Brush the chops on each side with oil, and season well. Put under a hot grill, 10 cm (4 in) from the heat, and grill for 7–8 minutes each side or until cooked through and golden brown.

4 Spoon 1 tablespoon of the stuffing mixture on top of each chop, and top with a slice of cheese. Grill for 3–4 minutes until the cheese has melted.

5 Meanwhile, heat a little oil in a small non-stick frying pan. Put the remaining stuffing into the pan, then press down and level with a wooden spoon so that the stuffing forms a thick pancake.

6 Fry the stuffing for about 5 minutes until the underside is brown and crisp. Transfer the pan to the grill for 2–3 minutes to brown the top. Turn upside down on to a plate, and slice into 6 wedges. Serve a wedge of stuffing with each chop.

Pork chops with oranges

🍽 **SERVES 6**   **361 CALS PER SERVING**

6 boneless pork loin chops

3 tbsp coarse-grain mustard

125 g (4 oz) demerara sugar

3 small oranges

90 ml (3 fl oz) orange juice

salt and black pepper

1 Spread both sides of each pork chop with the mustard, and sprinkle one side with half of the demerara sugar. Arrange the chops, sugared-side down, in a single layer in a shallow ovenproof dish.

2 With a sharp knife, carefully peel the oranges, removing all the pith. Cut the oranges into thin slices.

3 Cover the chops with the orange slices. Pour the orange juice over the top, season with salt and pepper, and sprinkle with the remaining sugar.

4 Cook, uncovered, in a preheated oven at 200°C (180°C fan, Gas 6) for about 35 minutes, basting the chops occasionally until cooked through. Serve hot.

Sweet and sour Chinese spare ribs

🍽 **SERVES 4**   **491 CALS PER SERVING**

1.25 kg (2½ lb) pork spare ribs

salt and black pepper

spring onions to garnish (optional)

SWEET AND SOUR SAUCE

2.5 cm (1 in) piece of fresh root ginger, peeled and grated

2 garlic cloves, crushed

2 tbsp soy sauce

2 tbsp rice wine or dry sherry

2 tbsp hoisin sauce

2 tbsp tomato purée

1 tbsp sesame oil (optional)

1 tbsp caster sugar

1 Lay the ribs in 1 layer in a roasting tin, season with salt and pepper, and cook in a preheated oven at 140°C (120°C fan, Gas 1) for 1½ hours.

2 Make the sauce: combine all the ingredients in a small pan and heat gently.

3 Spoon the sauce over the ribs, turning them to coat. Increase the oven temperature to 180°C (160°C fan, Gas 4) and cook for 25–30 minutes. Serve hot, garnished with spring onions if you like.

Spicy spare ribs

Add 1 tbsp brown sugar, ½ tsp grated nutmeg and ¼ tsp each ground cloves and ground cinnamon to the sauce.

Grilled pork chops with mango sauce

🍴 SERVES 4   347 CALS PER SERVING

pork loin chops, on the bone

sunflower oil for brushing

salt and black pepper

ripe mango

flat-leaf parsley to garnish

MANGO SAUCE

ripe mango

150 ml (¼ pint) chicken stock

tbsp mango chutney

Cut through the fat at regular intervals
on the edge of each pork chop (this
will help prevent the chops from curling up
during cooking).

Brush the chops on each side with oil
and sprinkle with black pepper. Put
under a hot grill, 10 cm (4 in) from the heat,
and grill for 6 minutes on each side or until
cooked through (timing depends on size
of chops).

Meanwhile, make the mango sauce:
peel, stone, and cube the mango
(page 420), then purée in a food processor
until smooth.

Put into a small saucepan with the
stock, mango chutney, and salt and
pepper. Bring to a boil and simmer for
about 3 minutes until heated through.
Taste for seasoning.

Peel the remaining mango and cut
it into 2 pieces lengthways, slightly
off centre to miss the stone. Cut the flesh
from around the stone. Slice the flesh into
thin strips.

Arrange the mango strips on the chops,
garnish with flat-leaf parsley, and serve
with the mango sauce.

Pork with chilli and coconut

🍴 SERVES 6   332 CALS PER SERVING

750 g (1½ lb) pork fillet (tenderloin), trimmed
and cut into 5 mm (¼ in) strips

2 tbsp sunflower oil

8 spring onions, cut into 2.5 cm (1 in) pieces

1 large red pepper, halved, seeded, and cut
into thin strips

1 x 400 g can chopped tomatoes

60 g (2 oz) creamed coconut, coarsely chopped

4 tbsp water

2 tbsp chopped fresh coriander

1 tbsp lemon juice

salt and black pepper

coriander sprigs to garnish

SPICE MIX

2.5 cm (1 in) piece of fresh root ginger, peeled
and grated

2 fresh red chillies, halved, seeded, and
finely chopped

1 garlic clove, crushed

1 tbsp mild curry powder

1 Make the spice mix: in a bowl, combine
the ginger, chillies, garlic, and curry
powder, and season with salt and pepper.
Turn the pork in the mix, cover, and leave to
marinate in the refrigerator for 2 hours.

2 Heat a wok or large frying pan, add the
oil, and heat until hot. Add the strips of
pork in batches, and stir-fry over a high heat
for 5 minutes or until browned all over.

3 Add the spring onions and stir-fry for
1 minute. Add the red pepper and
stir-fry for 1 minute, then add the tomatoes,
coconut, and measured water. Bring to
a boil, cover, and simmer very gently for
15 minutes or until the pork is tender.

4 Add the chopped coriander, lemon
juice, and salt and pepper to taste.
Garnish with coriander sprigs before serving.

Pork steaks with mixed peppercorns

🍴 SERVES 4   567 CALS PER SERVING

4 lean boneless pork steaks

salt

3–4 tbsp mixed or black peppercorns

30 g (1 oz) butter

350 ml (12 fl oz) dry white wine

350 ml (12 fl oz) chicken stock

175 ml (6 fl oz) double cream

1 Season the steaks on each side with salt. Coarsely crush the peppercorns, spread them on a plate, and press the steaks into them to encrust the surface of the meat. Turn the steaks over and repeat on the other side. Cover and set aside for about 30 minutes, if you have the time.

2 Melt the butter in a large frying pan, add the steaks, and cook over a medium heat for 5 minutes on each side or until the meat is just cooked through but still juicy. Lift the steaks out, and keep hot.

3 Pour the wine into the pan and boil until it has reduced by half, stirring to mix in the peppercorns and the sediment from the bottom of the pan.

4 Pour in the stock and cook for 5 minutes. Strain the sauce to remove the peppercorns, then return to the pan and boil for 3 minutes or until the sauce is reduced but not too thick.

5 Add the cream and cook, stirring, over a high heat until the sauce is reduced and thickened. Return the pork steaks to the pan, heat through, and serve at once.

Wiltshire pork casserole

SERVES 8   402 CALS PER SERVING

- tbsp sunflower oil
- 5 kg (3 lb) shoulder of pork, trimmed and cut to 3.5 cm (1½ in) cubes
- g (1½ oz) plain flour
- 0 ml (¾ pint) chicken stock
- bsp white wine vinegar
- bsp clear honey
- bsp soy sauce
- 0 g (8 oz) large mushrooms, quartered
- g (8 oz) ready-to-eat pitted prunes
- and black pepper
- opped parsley to garnish

Heat the oil in a large flameproof casserole. Add the pork in batches d cook over a medium to high heat 5 minutes or until golden brown all over.

Return all of the meat to the casserole, sprinkle in the flour, and cook, stirring, 1 minute.

Stir in the chicken stock, white wine vinegar, honey, and soy sauce, season salt and pepper, and bring to a boil. ver and cook in a preheated oven at °C (140°C fan, Gas 3) for 2 hours.

Stir the mushrooms and prunes into the casserole and cook for 1 hour or until pork is tender. Taste for seasoning and nish with parsley before serving.

idneys turbigo

SERVES 4   455 CALS PER SERVING

- mb's kidneys
- (2 oz) butter
- (8 oz) thin chipolata sausages
- (8 oz) button mushrooms
- utton onions, peeled, with roots left intact
- plain flour
- l (½ pint) lamb or chicken stock
- medium sherry
- tomato purée
- leaf
- nd black pepper
- chopped parsley to garnish
- es (page 44) to serve (optional)

1 Prepare the kidneys (page 207). Melt the butter in a large frying pan, add the kidneys, and cook, stirring, over a high heat for about 3 minutes until browned.

2 Lift the kidneys out and drain on paper towels. Add the sausages and cook for 3 minutes or until browned. Lift out and drain on paper towels.

3 Add the mushrooms and onions to the pan and cook for 3–5 minutes until browned.

4 Sprinkle in the flour and cook, stirring, for 1 minute. Add the stock, sherry, and tomato purée, and bring to a boil, stirring constantly. Add the bay leaf, and season with salt and pepper.

5 Slice the sausages thickly. Return to the pan with the kidneys, cover and simmer for 20–25 minutes until tender.

6 Spoon the kidney mixture on to a warmed platter, garnish with parsley, and serve with croûtes if you like.

Danish meatballs

SERVES 4–6   586–391 CALS PER SERVING

- 500 g (1 lb) minced pork
- 1 small onion, very finely chopped
- 30 g (1 oz) plain flour, plus extra for coating
- 1 tsp chopped fresh thyme
- ¼ tsp paprika
- 1 egg, beaten
- salt and black pepper
- a little milk
- 30 g (1 oz) butter
- 1 tbsp sunflower oil

Below: Danish meatballs.

- Greek yogurt or soured cream to serve
- chopped fresh thyme to garnish

TOMATO SAUCE
- 30 g (1 oz) butter
- 30 g (1 oz) plain flour
- 450 ml (¾ pint) chicken stock
- 1 x 400 g can chopped tomatoes
- 1 tbsp tomato purée
- 1 garlic clove, crushed
- 1 bay leaf

1 Mix the pork, onion, flour, thyme, paprika, and egg. Season, and add enough milk to give a soft, not sticky, texture.

2 Shape the mixture into 20 ovals, using 2 dessertspoons or your hands. Roll lightly in flour, then chill in the refrigerator.

3 Make the tomato sauce: melt the butter in a pan, sprinkle in the flour, and cook, stirring, for 1 minute.

4 Blend in the stock, then add the tomatoes, tomato purée, garlic, and bay leaf, and season with salt and pepper. Bring to a boil, stirring until thickened. Cover and simmer for 20–25 minutes.

5 Meanwhile, melt the butter with the oil in a flameproof casserole. Cook the meatballs in batches, for 5 minutes or until browned all over. Lift out and drain on paper towels.

6 Pour the fat out of the casserole. Return the meatballs, add the sauce, and bring to a boil. Cover and cook in a preheated oven at 180°C (160°C fan, Gas 4) for 30 minutes. Spoon over a little yogurt or soured cream and garnish with thyme. Serve hot.

Above: Farmer's bacon bake.

Farmer's bacon bake

🍳 **SERVES 6–8**   **510–383 CALS PER SERVING**

1 x 750 g (1½ lb) bacon joint

a few parsley stalks

6 black peppercorns

1 bay leaf

4 potatoes, cut into large chunks

4 carrots, thickly sliced

4 celery stalks, thickly sliced

chopped parsley to garnish

CHEESE SAUCE

45 g (1½ oz) butter

45 g (1½ oz) plain flour

200 ml (7 fl oz) milk

90 g (3 oz) mature Cheddar cheese, grated

salt and black pepper

1 Put the bacon joint into a large pan, cover with cold water, and bring to a boil. Drain, rinse, and cover with fresh cold water. Add the parsley stalks, peppercorns, and bay leaf, and bring to a boil. Cover and simmer very gently for 45 minutes.

2 Add the potatoes, carrots, and celery and bring back to a boil. Cover and simmer very gently for 20 minutes or until the meat and vegetables are tender. Drain, reserving the cooking liquid, and allow the bacon to cool slightly.

3 Remove the rind and fat from the bacon, cut the meat into bite-sized pieces, and place in a shallow baking dish with the vegetables. Keep hot.

4 Make the cheese sauce: melt the butter in a saucepan, sprinkle in the flour, and cook, stirring, for 1 minute. Remove from the heat and gradually blend in the milk and 250 ml (8 fl oz) of the reserved cooking liquid. Bring to a boil, stirring constantly until the mixture thickens. Simmer for 2–3 minutes. Add three-quarters of the cheese, and season with salt and pepper.

5 Pour the sauce over the meat and vegetables and sprinkle with the remaining cheese. Bake in a preheated oven at 180°C (160°C fan, Gas 4) for 30 minutes or until the cheese topping is bubbling. Garnish with chopped parsley before serving.

Pasticcio

🍳 **SERVES 6**   **679 CALS PER SERVING**

1 tbsp sunflower oil

500 g (1 lb) minced pork or beef

2 onions, chopped

3 garlic cloves, crushed

1 x 400 g can chopped tomatoes

90 g (3 oz) tomato purée

90 ml (3 fl oz) red wine

2 bay leaves

1 tsp sugar

1 tsp oregano

½ tsp ground cinnamon (optional)

250 g (8 oz) short-cut macaroni

salt and black pepper

CHEESE SAUCE

30 g (1 oz) butter

30 g (1 oz) plain flour

300 ml (½ pint) milk

175 g (6 oz) mature Cheddar cheese, grated

1 egg yolk

1 tsp Dijon mustard

1 Heat the sunflower oil in a large frying pan, add the meat, onions, and garlic, and cook over a medium heat for 5 minut[es] or until lightly browned.

2 Add the tomatoes, tomato purée, and wine. Bring to a boil and simmer for 15 minutes.

3 Add the bay leaves, sugar, oregano, a[nd] cinnamon (if using), and season with s[alt] and pepper. Simmer gently for about 10 minutes or until the sauce is thickened.

4 Meanwhile, cook the macaroni in boiling salted water for 8–10 minutes until just tender. Drain and set aside.

5 Make the cheese sauce: melt the but[ter] in a saucepan, sprinkle in the flour, an[d] cook, stirring, for 1 minute. Remove from [the] heat and gradually blend in the milk. Brin[g] to a boil, stirring constantly, until the mixt[ure] thickens. Simmer for 2–3 minutes. Remove from the heat and stir in the cheese, egg yolk, and mustard, and season with salt and pepper.

6 Spoon half of the meat mixture into an ovenproof dish and add half of th[e] macaroni. Cover with the remaining me[at] mixture, then top with the remaining macaroni and the cheese sauce.

7 Bake the pasticcio in a preheated oven at 180°C (160°C fan, Gas 4) fo[r] 40 minutes or until the topping is golden[.]

Mustard-glazed ham

Gammon tastes best when it is cooked on the bone, especially if it is home-baked. Here, gammon slowly steam-roasts in its own juices, spiked with cider, and it is coated with a tangy glaze. Watercress and orange slices are the perfect finishing touch. Once gammon is cooked it is properly called ham.

SERVES 16–20   477–382 CALS PER SERVING

5 kg (8–10 lb) smoked gammon

0 ml (14 fl oz) cider or apple juice

bsp English mustard

g (3 oz) demerara sugar

MON MUSTARD SAUCE

sp olive oil

e of 1 lemon

sp caster sugar

p coarse-grain mustard

and black pepper

ml (¼ pint) crème fraîche

Put the gammon into a large container, cover with cold water, and leave to soak at least 12 hours.

Drain and rinse the gammon. Arrange 2 pieces of foil, long enough to cover gammon, across a large roasting tin.

Pour the cider or apple juice into the foil. Stand a wire rack on the foil and stand the gammon on the rack. Insert a meat thermometer, if using, into the thickest part of the meat.

4 Wrap the foil loosely over the gammon, leaving plenty of space for air to circulate. Place the gammon just below the middle of a preheated oven and cook at 160°C (140°C fan, Gas 3) for 20 minutes per 500 g (1 lb). The meat thermometer should register 75°C (170°F). Remove the ham from the oven and leave to cool for a few minutes.

5 Increase the oven temperature to 230°C (210°C fan, Gas 8). Transfer the ham to a board, drain the cooking juices from the foil, and discard. Glaze the gammon with the mustard and sugar (see box, right).

6 Return the ham to the rack in the roasting tin. Cover any lean parts with foil, return to the oven, and cook, turning the roasting tin if necessary, for 15–20 minutes until the glaze is golden brown all over.

7 Meanwhile, make the lemon mustard sauce: put the olive oil, lemon juice, caster sugar, and mustard into a screw-top jar, season with salt and pepper, and shake vigorously to mix the ingredients together.

8 Put the crème fraîche into a bowl and stir in the lemon and mustard mixture. Taste for seasoning and leave to chill in the refrigerator until needed.

9 Carve the ham into slices and serve either warm or cold, with the lemon mustard sauce.

Glazing ham

Cut away the skin with a sharp knife, leaving behind a thin layer of fat. Discard the skin.

Score the fat all over in a diamond pattern, so that the glaze penetrates the fat.

Spread a generous layer of mustard over the fat, using a palette knife or your hands.

Press the demerara sugar on to the layer of mustard, making sure it is evenly coated all over.

Sausage cassoulet

Cassoulet is a hearty dish from Languedoc in the south-west of France. This is a simple and satisfying version. The types of meat used in more traditional recipes may include duck, goose, or lamb.

SERVES 8   **619 CALS PER SERVING**

375 g (12 oz) dried haricot beans

2 tbsp olive oil

500 g (1 lb) coarse pork sausages, such as Toulouse

250 g (8 oz) piece of smoked bacon, cut into strips

2 large onions, sliced

250 g (8 oz) piece of garlic sausage, cut into 2.5 cm (1 in) chunks

2 x 400 g cans chopped tomatoes

300 ml (½ pint) chicken stock

150 ml (¼ pint) dry white wine

2 tbsp tomato purée

2 garlic cloves, crushed

1 bouquet garni

salt and black pepper

125–175 g (4–6 oz) fresh white breadcrumbs

chopped parsley to garnish

1 Put the haricot beans into a large bowl, cover with plenty of cold water, and leave to soak overnight.

2 Drain the beans, and rinse under cold running water. Put the beans into a saucepan, cover with fresh cold water, and bring to a boil. Boil rapidly for 10 minutes, then simmer for 30 minutes or until just tender. Drain.

3 Heat the olive oil in a large flameproof casserole, add the sausages and bacon, and cook for 5 minutes or until browned all over. Lift out and drain on paper towels. Thickly slice the sausages.

4 Pour off all but 1 tbsp of the fat from the casserole. Add the onions and cook gently, stirring occasionally, for a few minutes until soft but not coloured.

5 Return the bacon and sausages to the casserole, add the beans, the garlic sausage, tomatoes, stock, wine, tomato purée, garlic, and bouquet garni. Season with salt and pepper and bring to a boil.

6 Cover and cook in a preheated oven at 160°C (140°C fan, Gas 3) for 1 hour, then sprinkle the breadcrumbs over the top and continue cooking, uncovered, for 30 minutes or until the topping is golden brown. Garnish with chopped parsley before serving.

Toad in the hole with onion sauce

SERVES 4   **802 CALS PER SERVING**

400 g (13 oz) pork sausagemeat

1 leek, finely chopped

2 tbsp chopped fresh sage

1 tbsp chopped parsley

3 tbsp sunflower oil

3 onions, chopped

2 tbsp plain flour

300 ml (½ pint) milk

250 ml (8 fl oz) chicken stock

chopped parsley to garnish

BATTER

125 g (4 oz) self-raising flour

3 eggs, beaten

300 ml (½ pint) milk

1 tbsp chopped parsley

salt and black pepper

1 Make the batter: sift the flour into a bowl. Make a well in the middle and add the eggs and a little milk. Blend to a smooth paste, then gradually whisk in the remaining milk until the batter has the pouring consistency of cream.

2 Add the chopped parsley, season with salt and pepper, and whisk again.

3 In another bowl, combine the sausagemeat, leek, sage, and parsley, and season with salt and pepper. Shape into 12 balls and set aside.

4 Heat the oil in a saucepan, add the onions, and cook for a few minutes until soft but not coloured. Transfer one-third of the onions to 4 small ovenproof dishes or 1 large dish. Set aside the remainder.

5 Add the sausage balls to the dishes or dish and bake in a preheated oven at 220°C (200°C fan, Gas 7) for about 10 minutes until brown.

6 Add the batter mixture, and return at once to the oven. Bake for 20–25 minutes until the batter is risen and golden.

7 Meanwhile, add the plain flour to the onions in the pan and cook, stirring, for 1 minute. Remove from the heat and gradually blend in the milk and stock. Bring to a boil, stirring constantly, and simmer for 2–3 minutes until the mixture thickens. Serve the toad in the hole hot, sprinkled with parsley, with the sauce handed separately.

Sausage bake

SERVES 6   **712 CALS PER SERVING**

1 tbsp sunflower oil

1 kg (2 lb) coarse-cut pork sausages

500 g (1 lb) leeks, thickly sliced

750 g (1½ lb) potatoes, cut into 5 mm (¼ in) slices

90 g (3 oz) red lentils

salt and black pepper

2 bay leaves

2 cloves

1 garlic clove, crushed

900 ml (1½ pints) chicken stock

chopped parsley to garnish

1 Heat the oil in a large flameproof casserole and brown the sausages. Lift out, then cut into thick slices.

2 Layer the leeks, potatoes, sausages, and lentils in the casserole, adding seasoning and placing the bay leaves, cloves, and garlic among the layers. Top with a layer of potatoes.

3 Pour in the stock and bring to a boil. Cover tightly and cook in a preheated oven at 160°C (140°C fan, Gas 3) for 2½ hours, checking the liquid level occasionally.

4 Remove the lid, increase the oven temperature to 200°C (180°C fan, Gas 6), and cook for 20–25 minutes until the potato is browned. Garnish with parsley and serve hot.

Vegetarian Dishes

Under 45 minutes

Red lentil and coconut curry
Lentils cooked with coconut and seasoned with ginger, chilli, garlic, and turmeric. Topped with mustard-seed butter.

SERVES 6 **481 CALS PER SERVING**
Takes 40 minutes Page 285

Vegetarian burgers
Butter beans with mushrooms, leeks, garlic, and chilli. Shaped into burgers, and served with crunchy dressed lettuce.

SERVES 6 **134 CALS PER SERVING**
Takes 30 minutes Page 284

45-60 minutes

Couscous with roasted peppers
Tasty and simple to make: couscous with ch[...] peas, courgettes, carrots, and spices. Toppe[...] with peppers and almonds.

SERVES 4–6 **418–279 CALS PER SERVING**
Takes 45 minutes Page [...]

Mixed bean bake
Aduki and butter beans simmered with mushrooms, tomatoes, and parsley. Topped with leeks and a cheese sauce.

SERVES 6 **376 CALS PER SERVING**
Takes 60 minutes Page[...]

Roast vegetables niçoise
Black olives, courgettes, tomatoes, red oni[...] and garlic, sprinkled with capers, herbes [...] Provence, and pepper, and baked.

SERVES 4 **237 CALS PER SERVING**
Takes 60 minutes Pag[...]

Tomato and olive tart
Poppyseed pastry base baked with a toppi[...] of onions, tomatoes, tomato purée, basil, garlic, vignotte cheese, and black olives.

SERVES 8 **377 CALS PER SERVING**
Takes 60 minutes, plus chilling Pag[...]

Dairy-free lasagne
Tomato sauce layered with lasagne, lightl[...] browned aubergine slices, and spinach, [...] topped with courgettes, and baked.

SERVES 4–6 **364–243 CALS PER SERVING**
Takes 60 minutes, plus standing Pag[...]

Spinach roulade
Combined spinach, butter, and eggs, briefly baked, sprinkled with Parmesan, and rolled with a crème fraîche and mushroom filling.

SERVES 6–8 **250–187 CALS PER SERVING**
Takes 30 minutes, plus chilling Page 289

Over 60 minutes

...nach gnocchi with tomato sauce
...mplings of spinach, ricotta and Parmesan
...eses, and eggs, served with tomato sauce.
...ES 4   738 CALS PER SERVING
...es 1¼ hours, **plus chilling**   Page 275

DINNER PARTY

Spiced aubergines with filo crust
Diced aubergine, onions, Caerphilly cheese,
lentils, red peppers, spices, and oregano, in
filo pastry.
SERVES 6   569 CALS PER SERVING
Takes 1¼ hours, **plus standing**   Page 282

HIGH PROTEIN

Christmas nut loaf
Brown rice blended with ceps, mushrooms,
carrots, parsley, and rosemary, and baked with
nuts, and Cheddar cheese. Served in slices
accompanied with cranberry sauce.
SERVES 6–8   600–450 CALS PER SERVING
Takes 2½ hours, **plus soaking**   Page 288

Aubergine parmigiana
Rich and tangy: aubergine slices layered with
garlic- and basil-flavoured tomato sauce, and
mozzarella and Parmesan cheeses.
SERVES 6   516 CALS PER SERVING
Takes 1¼ hours, **plus standing**   Page 272

...to, celeriac, and Parmesan gratin
...toes and celeriac baked with cream and
...ta cheese, breadcrumbs, and Parmesan.
...S 6   451 CALS PER SERVING
...s 1¾ hours   Page 272

ECONOMICAL

Country vegetable pies
Carrots and parsnips baked with onion, garlic,
and parsley sauce. Topped with mashed potato
for a nourishing meal.
SERVES 6   428 CALS PER SERVING
Takes 1¼ hours   Page 268

Chestnut loaf
Chestnuts baked with potatoes and celery,
flavoured with garlic, parsley, soy sauce, and
tomato purée. Served with spicy tomato salsa.
SERVES 6   226 CALS PER SERVING
Takes 1¼ hours   Page 288

Stuffed red peppers
Baked peppers with a nourishing stuffing of
button mushrooms, onion, rice, red lentils,
stock, pine nuts, and parsley.
SERVES 4   622 CALS PER SERVING
Takes 1½ hours   Page 273

...er vegetable terrine
...colourful layers of puréed carrot,
...ac, and broccoli, baked and served
...es.
4–6   142–95 CALS PER SERVING
...1¾ hours, **plus chilling**   Page 278

Mushroom lasagne
Lasagne layered with mushroom and tomato
sauce, spinach balls, béchamel sauce, and
grated Cheddar cheese, then baked.
SERVES 6   684 CALS PER SERVING
Takes 1¼ hours   Page 274

Cheese-topped baked aubergines
Aubergines spiked with garlic slivers dipped
in herbs and olive oil. Topped with Gorgonzola
and Cheddar cheeses.
SERVES 4   447 CALS PER SERVING
Takes 1¼ hours   Page 273

Cheese and vegetable pie
A variety of vegetables mixed with parsley and
marjoram, in a Cheddar cheese and mustard
sauce. Topped with cheese pastry.
SERVES 6   406 CALS PER SERVING
Takes 1½ hours, **plus chilling**   Page 268

Vegetarian know-how

There are two basic types of vegetarian diet. A vegan diet is the strictest – vegans do not eat any meat, poultry, fish, eggs, or dairy products – while a vegetarian diet excludes meat, poultry, and fish but may include eggs and dairy products. In addition, there is the "demi-vegetarian" diet, which ca include fish and even poultry. With such a great variety of foods from which to choose, vegetarian diets, based largely on complex carbohydrates, pulses, vegetables, fruits, nuts, and seeds, can be imaginative and nutritious.

Maintaining a balanced diet

Fish, meat, poultry, dairy products, and eggs are high-quality protein foods – they contain all the essential dietary amino acids (the building blocks of protein) that the body needs. Many vegetarians replace fish, meat, and poultry with eggs, cheese, and other dairy products, but this is not the ideal solution as many dairy foods are high in saturated fats and calories.

A healthy alternative in a vegetarian diet is to focus on protein-rich pulses, nuts, and seeds. The protein these foods offer does not contain all 8 of the essential amino acids (with the exception of that from soya beans, which is "complete"), but it is easy to enhance their nutritional value – simply eat them with bread, pasta, and rice or other grains. Examples of vegetarian protein combinations drawn from cuisines around the world are beans or dhal (lentils) and rice, hummus and pitta bread, or a mixed nut, lentil, and vegetable salad.

Another dietary interaction that vegetarians should be aware of is that between iron and vitamin C. The form of iron found in meat is easily absorbed by the body, whereas the iron in vegetables, nuts, grains, pulses, and eggs needs a helping hand. This is provided by vitamin C, which enhances iron uptake. So, when planning meals, include vitamin C-rich foods such as fresh fruit (in particular citrus, berries, and kiwi fruit) and vegetables (peppers, tomatoes, broccoli, mangetout, and cabbages are all good sources).

Vegetable stock

Add any vegetable trimmings you have (celery tops or tomato skins, for example), or va the ingredients to emphasize the flavour of the dish in which you want to use the stock

1 Coarsely chop 2 onions, 1 leek, 3 celery stalks, and 2–3 carrots. Put into a large saucepan or stockpot and add 1 large bouquet garni, plus 1 crushed garlic clove, if wished.

2 Add 1.25 litres (2 pints) water and bring t a boil. Skim off any scum that rises to the surface, then lower the heat and simmer for 30 minutes.

3 Strain the stock through a sieve. If not us immediately, leave to cool, then cover store in the refrigerator for up to 5 days or in freezer for up to 1 month.

Tofu

Tofu is a high-protein food manufactured from soya beans. It is low in fat and calories, so can make a healthy basis for many vegetarian dishes. It is very bland (unless it is smoked), but easily absorbs flavours from marinades and sauces. Silken tofu has a soft, creamy texture: use it in sauces, dips, and puddings. Firm tofu, which has a texture similar to feta cheese, can be stir-fried, grilled, or casseroled. Other vegetarian meat substitutes include TVP (textured vegetable protein), which is also made from soya beans, and Quorn.

A gelatine substitute

Gelatine is a natural protein found in the bones, skin, and connective tissues of animals. Commercial powdered gelatine is derived from pig skin, and is thus unacceptable in a vegetarian diet. The most common substitutes are agar-agar (or kanten) and carrageen (or Irish moss both of which are derived from seaweed They have stronger setting properties th. gelatine, so less is needed. Follow the packet instructions for amounts to use.

ooking pulses

lses are the dried, edible seeds of the legume family – beans, peas, and lentils. Stored
a cool, dark place, they will keep for up to 6 months. They're easy to prepare, but if
u want to save time you can use canned pulses, which are already cooked.

ut the pulses into a large bowl and cover
ith plenty of cold water. Leave to soak for
recommended time (see below). Drain and
in cold water.

2 Put into a saucepan and add cold water –
about twice their volume. Bring to a boil
and fast boil for 10–15 minutes. Cover and
simmer until tender (see below).

Soaking and cooking times of pulses

ooking times depend on the variety of pulse and whether it is recently dried or
has been stored a long time and thus is very dry. The cooking times given below
re therefore only a guide.

Pulse	Soaking	Cooking
Aduki beans	8–12 hours	45 minutes
Black-eyed beans	8–12 hours	1 hour
Butter beans	8–12 hours	1–1½ hours
Chick peas	8–12 hours	2 hours
Flageolet beans	8–12 hours	1–1½ hours
Haricot beans	8–12 hours	1–1½ hours
Red lentils	not required	20–30 minutes
Green lentils	not required	30–45 minutes
Mung beans (whole)	8–12 hours	45 minutes
Red kidney beans	8–12 hours	1¾ hours
Soya beans	10–12 hours	2½–4 hours
Split peas	not required	2 hours

Warning Most pulses contain toxins that we cannot digest, and these can cause symptoms of
vere food poisoning. To destroy the toxins, boil the pulses rapidly for 10–15 minutes at the start
cooking, then reduce the heat to carry on cooking at a simmer. Chick peas, lentils, and split peas
not need this fast boil.

Pulses know-how

Pulses are usually soaked for at least 8 hours,
but you can speed up the process: boil for
3 minutes, then cover and soak for 1–2 hours.

Add salt towards the end of cooking: if it is
added at the beginning, it could toughen the
skins of the pulse.

Pulses double in size and weight when cooked,
so if a recipe calls for 250 g (8 oz) cooked
pulses, you will need 125 g (4 oz) dried weight.

Adding bicarbonate of soda to the cooking water
can adversely affect the nutritional value of
pulses.

Grains

Whole grains are first-class sources of
carbohydrate, fibre, vitamins, and minerals.

Bulgur wheat

Also known as burghul wheat, this is made
from steamed, dried, and crushed wheat
kernels. It cooks very quickly, or can just be
soaked and used in salads. Cracked wheat is
similar, but is not pre-cooked and so takes
longer to cook than bulgur wheat.

Couscous

Made from semolina, the wheat flour also
used for pasta, couscous only needs to be
soaked to allow the grains to swell and
soften. For extra flavour, steam the couscous
over a vegetable stew in a colander set over
a large pot.

Pearl barley

The nutty flavour and chewy texture of this
grain is delicious in vegetable soups and
stews. The starch in the grain acts as
a thickener too.

Polenta

Made from ground maize or corn, and also
known as cornmeal, polenta is added to
simmering water and stirred constantly
until it is very thick. Instant polenta takes
only about 8 minutes to cook. Serve warm,
or leave to cool and set, then slice and grill.

Millet

Available as flakes or whole grains, millet
has a delicate, slightly nutty flavour. Add
a small handful to soups to thicken them.

Oats

Oatflakes, also called rolled oats, are the
basis of porridge and muesli. Fine oatmeal
can be used to make biscuits, bread, and
oatcakes – and to thicken soups; coarser
varieties can be cooked into porridge.

Quinoa

A tiny grain from South America with a
slightly sweet taste, quinoa can be used like
brown rice and other whole grains. Rinse it
well before cooking.

Above: Country vegetable pies.

Country vegetable pies

🍴 SERVES 6   428 CALS PER SERVING

8 carrots, diced

8 parsnips, diced

300 ml (½ pint) vegetable stock

2 tbsp olive oil

1 onion, chopped

1 head of garlic, separated into cloves and peeled

750 g (1½ lb) potatoes, diced

salt and black pepper

4 tbsp hot milk

45 g (1½ oz) butter

paprika to garnish

PARSLEY SAUCE

45 g (1½ oz) butter

45 g (1½ oz) plain flour

150 ml (¼ pint) milk

4 tbsp chopped parsley

1 Blanch the carrots and parsnips in the stock for 1 minute. Drain, reserving the stock. Put the oil into an ovenproof dish, add the vegetables and half of the garlic, and stir well. Roast in a preheated oven at 200°C (180°C fan, Gas 6) for 30 minutes.

2 Meanwhile, cook the potatoes and the remaining garlic in boiling salted water for 15–20 minutes until tender. Drain, return to the pan, and add the hot milk and 30 g (1 oz) of the butter. Mash, and season with salt and pepper.

3 Remove the roasted vegetables with a slotted spoon, divide among 6 small ovenproof dishes, and season well.

4 Make the parsley sauce: melt the butter in a small pan, add the flour, and cook, stirring, for 1 minute. Remove from the heat and blend in the milk and reserved stock. Bring to a boil, stirring, until thick. Simmer for 2–3 minutes, then stir in the parsley and season with salt and pepper.

5 Pour the sauce over the vegetables, top with the potato, and dot with the remaining butter. Bake for 20 minutes. Serve hot, with paprika sprinkled on top.

Cheese and vegetable pie

🍴 SERVES 6   406 CALS PER SERVING

30 g (1 oz) butter

1 onion, chopped

2 carrots, sliced

500 g (1 lb) courgettes, sliced

2 large tomatoes, chopped

125 g (4 oz) mushrooms, sliced

2 tbsp chopped parsley

½ tsp fresh marjoram or oregano

salt and black pepper

CHEESE SAUCE

30 g (1 oz) butter

30 g (1 oz) plain flour

300 ml (½ pint) milk

60 g (2 oz) mature Cheddar cheese, grated

1 tsp English mustard

pinch of cayenne pepper

CHEESE PASTRY

125 g (4 oz) plain flour, plus extra for rolling

60 g (2 oz) butter

60 g (2 oz) mature Cheddar cheese, grated

1 small egg, beaten

1 Make the cheese pastry: sift the flour into a bowl. Add the butter and rub in lightly until the mixture resembles fine breadcrumbs. Stir in the cheese, then bind to a soft but not sticky dough with 1 tbsp of the beaten egg and 1 tbsp cold water. Chill for 30 minutes.

2 Melt the butter in a large pan, add the onion, and cook gently for 3–5 minutes until softened. Add the carrots and cook f about 5 minutes.

3 Add the courgettes, tomatoes, mushrooms, and herbs, and season wit salt and pepper. Cook over a low heat, stirring occasionally, for 10–15 minutes until softened. Remove from the heat.

4 Make the cheese sauce: melt the butt in a saucepan, add the flour, and cool stirring, for 1 minute. Remove from the hea and gradually blend in the milk.

5 Bring to a boil, stirring until the mixture thickens. Simmer for 2–3 minutes, then stir in the cheese, mustard, and cayenne, and season with salt and pepper. Stir the vegetables into the sauce, remove from the heat, and leave to cool.

6 Roll out the pastry on a floured work surface. Invert a pie dish on to the pastry and cut around the edge. Reserve the trimmings.

7 Transfer the vegetable and sauce mixture to the pie dish and top with the pastry. Crimp the edges with a fork and make a hole in the top of the pastry to allow steam to escape.

8 Decorate the pie with the pastry trimmings, attaching them with beaten egg. Brush the pastry all over with the remaining beaten egg. Bake in a preheated oven at 200°C (180°C fan, Gas 6) for 30 minutes or until the pastry is crisp and golden all over.

oast vegetables içoise

SERVES 4   237 CALS PER SERVING

g (1½ lb) courgettes, sliced

rge red onion, thinly sliced

arlic cloves, crushed

sp olive oil, more if needed

g (4 oz) black olives, pitted

fresh mixed herbs

sp capers

k pepper

g (8 oz) cherry tomatoes, halved

sp shredded fresh basil

ut the courgettes, red onion, and garlic
an ovenproof dish, drizzle with 4 tbsp
and toss to mix.

Arrange the black olives on top of the
vegetables, then sprinkle with the herbs
capers, and plenty of pepper.

Roast in a preheated oven at 190°C
170°C fan, Gas 5) for 25 minutes, then
the tomatoes and roast for a further
inutes, checking occasionally to see
e surface is getting too dry. If it is, drizzle
le more olive oil over the vegetables.

prinkle the dish with the shredded fresh
asil. Serve hot or cold.

Mixed bean bake

SERVES 6   376 CALS PER SERVING

2 tbsp olive oil

3 large leeks, trimmed and sliced

1 garlic clove, crushed

250 g (8 oz) mushrooms, sliced

1 x 400 g can aduki or red kidney beans, drained and rinsed

1 x 400 g can butter beans, drained and rinsed

1 x 400 g can chopped tomatoes

3 tbsp tomato purée

4 tbsp chopped parsley

salt and black pepper

CHEESE SAUCE

30 g (1 oz) butter

30 g (1 oz) plain flour

300 ml (½ pint) milk

1 egg, beaten

125 g (4 oz) Cheddar cheese, grated

1 Heat the olive oil in a large saucepan. Add the leeks and cook gently, stirring, for a few minutes until softened but not coloured. Lift out with a slotted spoon and set aside.

2 Add the garlic and mushrooms and cook, stirring occasionally, for about 5 minutes. Add the canned beans, tomatoes, tomato purée, and 3 tbsp of the parsley. Season with salt and pepper. Bring to a boil, cover, and simmer very gently for about 20 minutes.

3 Meanwhile, make the cheese sauce: melt the butter in a small saucepan, add the flour, and cook, stirring, for 1 minute. Remove the pan from the heat and gradually blend in the milk. Bring to a boil, stirring constantly until the mixture thickens. Simmer for 2–3 minutes, then leave to cool slightly. Stir in the egg and cheese, and season with salt and black pepper.

4 Transfer the bean mixture to an ovenproof dish and arrange the leeks on top. Pour the cheese sauce over the leeks, and bake in a preheated oven at 190°C (170°C fan, Gas 5) for 30 minutes or until the top is golden. Serve hot, sprinkled with the remaining parsley.

Below: Mixed bean bake.

Roasted vegetable medley

🍴 **SERVES 4**   **245 CALS PER SERVING**

175 g (6 oz) small new potatoes, scrubbed and halved

8 baby carrots, scrubbed and trimmed

2 red onions, cut into wedges

2 garlic cloves, sliced

salt and black pepper

about 2 tbsp olive oil

a few rosemary sprigs

250 g (8 oz) cherry tomatoes

125 g (4 oz) French beans

1 small cauliflower, broken into florets

1 x 400 g can butter beans, drained

2 tbsp balsamic vinegar

2 tbsp coarse-grain mustard

a handful of chopped fresh herbs (eg parsley, chives, basil, chervil)

1 Put the potatoes, carrots, onions and garlic in a roasting tin. Season and add the olive oil, then turn to coat. Tuck in the rosemary sprigs, and roast in a preheated oven at 190°C (170°C fan, Gas 5) for 40–45 minutes or until the vegetables are tender, stirring in the tomatoes about 15–20 minutes before the end.

2 Meanwhile, cook the French beans and cauliflower in boiling salted water for 4 minutes. Drain and set aside.

3 Mix the roasted vegetables with the French beans, cauliflower, and butter beans, then gently mix in the balsamic vinegar, mustard, and herbs. Serve hot.

Roasted vegetable gratin

Transfer the vegetables to an ovenproof dish. Sprinkle with 90 g (3 oz) grated Cheddar cheese mixed with 60 g (2 oz) fresh breadcrumbs. Return to the oven for about 10–15 minutes until golden.

Mushroom Stroganoff

🍴 **SERVES 4**   **177 CALS PER SERVING**

20 g (¾ oz) dried mushrooms (porcini)

2 tbsp olive oil

1 onion, chopped

1 garlic clove, crushed

500 g (1 lb) chestnut mushrooms

2 red peppers, halved, seeded, and sliced

2 tsp paprika

salt and black pepper

30 g (1 oz) cornflour

300 ml (½ pint) cold vegetable stock

1 x 400 g can artichoke hearts, drained

2 tbsp dry white or red wine

1 tbsp tomato purée

low-fat crème fraîche or plain yogurt to serve

1 Soak the dried mushrooms in 150 ml (¼ pint) warm water for 20 minutes, then drain and reserve the soaking water.

2 Heat the oil in a flameproof casserole, add the onion and garlic, and cook for 3–5 minutes until softened.

3 Add the mushrooms, peppers, and paprika, and season with salt and pepper. Cook, stirring, for 5 minutes. Mix the cornflour and stock, add to the pan with the artichokes, wine, mushroom water, and tomato purée and bring to a boil. Simmer gently for 10–15 minutes. Taste for seasoning. Serve hot, with crème fraîche or yogurt.

Mushroom vol-au-vent

When cooking the mushrooms, increase the heat to reduce and thicken the sauce. Warm through a ready-made large vol-au-vent shell, and fill with the hot Mushroom Stroganoff.

Spicy pumpkin casserole

🍴 **SERVES 4**   **196 CALS PER SERVING**

2 tbsp olive oil

2 onions, cut into wedges

2 potatoes, cut into 2.5 cm (1 in) cubes

2 parsnips, cut into 2.5 cm (1 in) cubes

500 g (1 lb) pumpkin, peeled and cut into 2.5 cm (1 in) cubes

1–2 tbsp curry paste

375 ml (13 fl oz) vegetable stock

salt and black pepper

chopped fresh coriander to garnish

1 Heat the olive oil in a flameproof casserole. Add the onions and cook gently for 3–5 minutes or until softened.

2 Add the vegetable cubes, curry paste and stock. Season and bring to a boil. Cover and simmer, stirring, for 20 minutes.

3 Remove the vegetables with a slotted spoon and transfer to a warmed serving dish. Bring the sauce to a boil and boil until reduced and thickened. Spoon the sauce over the vegetables, garnish with coriander and serve hot.

Spicy pumpkin in a pie

Cool the vegetables and sauce, transfer to a pie dish, and top with ready rolled pastry. Bake at 190°C (170°C fan, Gas 5) for 15 minutes or until the pastry is cooked and the filling is hot.

Opposite, clockwise from top: Spicy pumpkin casserole, Mushroom Stroganoff, Roasted vegetable medley

Aubergine parmigiana

SERVES 6 **516 CALS PER SERVING**

1.5 kg (3 lb) aubergines

2 eggs, lightly beaten

60 g (2 oz) plain flour

3 tbsp olive oil, more if needed

2 onions, chopped

3 x 400 g cans chopped tomatoes, drained

1 x 140 g can tomato purée

2 garlic cloves, crushed

2 tbsp chopped fresh basil

¼ tsp caster sugar

salt and black pepper

350 g (11 oz) mozzarella cheese, sliced

125 g (4 oz) Parmesan cheese, grated

1 Cut the aubergines into 1 cm (½ in) slices. Dip into the beaten eggs, then into the flour, shaking off any excess.

2 Heat 1 tbsp olive oil in a large frying p add the aubergine slices in batches, and cook for 3–4 minutes on each side u golden, adding more oil between batch if necessary. Lift out with a slotted spoon and drain on paper towels.

3 Heat another tablespoon of olive oil ir a saucepan, add the onions, and coc gently until soft. Stir in the tomatoes, tomc purée, garlic, and basil. Bring to a boil, th simmer for 10–15 minutes until thickened. the sugar and season with salt and pepp

4 Spoon some of the tomato mixture i a shallow ovenproof dish and cover a layer of aubergine slices, then with a l each of mozzarella and Parmesan. Continue layering, finishing with tomato mixture, mozzarella, and Parmesan.

5 Bake in a preheated oven at 190°C (170°C fan, Gas 5) for 15–20 minutes until the cheese is lightly browned.

♡ Healthy note

For a lighter version of this dish, omit th egg and flour coating for the aubergines step 1. In step 2, lightly brush the slices with olive oil, and grill or chargrill them until golden brown on each side.

Potato, celeriac, and Parmesan gratin

SERVES 6 **451 CALS PER SERVING**

60 g (2 oz) butter, plus extra for greasing

1 onion, sliced

2 garlic cloves, crushed

1 kg (2 lb) floury potatoes, thinly sliced

375 g (12 oz) celeriac, peeled and thinly sliced

300 ml (½ pint) single cream

150 ml (¼ pint) milk

250 g (8 oz) ricotta cheese

3 tbsp snipped fresh chives

salt and black pepper

2 tbsp fresh breadcrumbs

3 tbsp grated Parmesan cheese, plus extra for serving

1 Melt the butter in a frying pan, add the sliced onion and crushed garlic, and cook gently, stirring occasionally, for 3–5 minutes until softened but not coloured. Lightly butter a large gratin dish.

2 Arrange the potatoes, celeriac, and the onion mixture in layers in the prepared gratin dish, finishing with a neat layer of potatoes.

3 In a large bowl, combine the cream, milk, ricotta cheese, and chives, and season with salt and pepper. Beat well together, then pour over the vegetables.

4 In a small bowl, combine the breadcrumbs and 3 tbsp grated Parmesan cheese, and then sprinkle evenly over the potatoes.

5 Bake in a preheated oven at 180°C (160°C fan, Gas 4) for about 1 hour or until the potatoes and celeriac are tender and the top is golden brown.

6 Serve the gratin hot, sprinkled with extra grated Parmesan cheese.

Cheese-topped baked aubergines

SERVES 4   447 CALS PER SERVING

bsp chopped parsley

bsp chopped fresh basil

bsp olive oil

sp salt

medium aubergines

arlic cloves, cut into thin slivers

g (6 oz) Gorgonzola or Danish blue eese, crumbled

g (6 oz) Cheddar or mozzarella cheese, grated

In a small bowl, combine the parsley, half of the basil, the olive oil, and salt.

Prepare the aubergines (see box, below). Put the aubergines into an ovenproof and bake in a preheated oven at 180°C 0°C fan, Gas 4) for 40–50 minutes until y are very tender and soft to the touch.

Remove the aubergines from the oven, sprinkle with the Gorgonzola and eddar cheeses, and bake for 5 minutes ntil the cheese is melted. Serve at e, sprinkled with the remaining basil.

reparing the aubergines

diagonal slits one-third of the way into ch aubergine. Stuff the garlic slivers and n the chopped herb mixture into each slit.

Italian stuffed courgettes

SERVES 4   437 CALS PER SERVING

4 large courgettes

30 g (1 oz) butter

2 tbsp olive oil, plus extra for greasing

1 small onion, finely chopped

4 ripe tomatoes, finely chopped

4 tbsp chopped fresh basil

salt and black pepper

2 tbsp capers, drained and coarsely chopped

250 g (8 oz) Fontina cheese, grated

1 Cut the courgettes in half lengthways. Scoop out the flesh and chop finely.

2 Melt the butter with 1 tbsp of the olive oil in a saucepan.

3 When the butter is foaming, add the onion and cook gently, stirring occasionally, for 3–5 minutes until softened but not coloured.

4 Add the courgette flesh, tomatoes, and basil, and season with salt and pepper. Cook, stirring, for 5 minutes.

5 Brush the insides of the courgette shells with the remaining oil and arrange in a lightly oiled shallow ovenproof dish. Bake the shells in a preheated oven at 180°C (160°C fan, Gas 4) for 5–10 minutes.

6 Divide half of the tomato mixture among the courgette shells. Cover with the chopped capers and a thin layer of cheese. Spoon over the remaining tomato mixture and top with the remaining cheese. Return to the oven and bake for 10–15 minutes until the cheese topping is bubbling.

Stuffed red peppers

SERVES 4   622 CALS PER SERVING

8 small red peppers

4 tbsp water

STUFFING

4 tbsp olive oil

1 large onion, finely chopped

1 garlic clove, crushed

175 g (6 oz) button mushrooms, chopped

250 g (8 oz) long grain rice

90 g (3 oz) dried red lentils

450 ml (¾ pint) vegetable stock

salt and black pepper

60 g (2 oz) pine nuts, toasted

4 tbsp chopped parsley

fresh coriander to garnish

1 Slice the tops off the red peppers and reserve. Cut out and discard the cores, seeds, and white ribs, and set the peppers aside.

2 Make the stuffing: heat the oil in a pan. Add the onion and garlic and cook gently, stirring occasionally, for 3–5 minutes until soft but not coloured. Add the mushrooms and cook for 10 minutes.

3 Add the rice and lentils and stir to coat in the oil. Pour in the stock, season with salt and pepper, and bring to a boil. Cover and simmer very gently for 15–20 minutes until the rice is tender and the liquid has been absorbed. Stir in the pine nuts and parsley, then taste for seasoning.

4 Divide the stuffing among the peppers, stand them upright in a casserole dish that just contains them, and replace the tops.

5 Pour the measured water into the bottom of the casserole, cover, and bake in a preheated oven at 180°C (160°C fan, Gas 4) for about 40 minutes until the peppers are tender. Serve at once, garnished with coriander.

♡ Healthy note

Using a non-stick pan in step 2 will enable you to halve the amount of oil to 1 or 2 tbsp, and cutting out the pine nuts will reduce the fat content even further.

Mushroom lasagne

SERVES 6   **684 CALS PER SERVING**

2 tbsp olive oil

1 large onion, finely chopped

500 g (1 lb) mushrooms, sliced

2 large garlic cloves, crushed

30 g (1 oz) plain flour

2 x 400 g cans chopped tomatoes

1 tbsp chopped fresh basil

1 tsp caster sugar

salt and black pepper

500 g (1 lb) frozen whole leaf spinach, thawed and drained

white sauce made with 90 g (3 oz) each butter and plain flour, 900 ml (1½ pints) milk, and 1 tsp Dijon mustard

300 g (10 oz) mature Cheddar cheese, grated

150 g (5 oz) pre-cooked lasagne sheets

1 Heat the oil in a saucepan, add the onion, mushrooms and garlic and cook for 10 minutes or until soft. Sprinkle in the flour and cook, stirring, for 1 minute.

2 Add the tomatoes, basil, and sugar, and season with salt and pepper. Cover and simmer for 20 minutes.

3 Season the spinach with salt and pepper. Taking 1 teaspoonful at a time, shape it loosely into 24 balls.

4 Spoon one-third of the mushroom mixture into a large ovenproof dish, and place 8 of the spinach balls on top. Cover with one-third of the white sauce and one-third of the cheese. Arrange half of the lasagne on top. Repeat the layers, finishing with cheese.

5 Bake in a preheated oven at 190°C (170°C fan, Gas 5) for 35 minutes or until the pasta is tender. Serve hot.

Healthy note

This is a luxury lasagne for a special occasion. For everyday, halve the amount of white sauce and cheese.

Dairy-free lasagne

SERVES 4–6   364–243 CALS PER SERVING

3 tbsp olive oil, more if needed

 courgettes, sliced

and black pepper

aubergine, cut into 5 mm (¼ in) slices

onions, chopped

d pepper, halved, seeded, and diced

arlic cloves, crushed

400 g cans chopped tomatoes

140 g can tomato purée

sp caster sugar

sp chopped fresh basil

g (5 oz) pre-cooked lasagne sheets

g (8 oz) frozen chopped spinach, thawed,
ned, and seasoned well

Heat 1 tbsp olive oil in a large non-stick
rying pan, add the courgettes, and cook
3 minutes. Turn into a bowl, and sprinkle
n salt.

Heat another tablespoon of oil in the
oan, and cook the aubergine slices for
out 3–5 minutes on each side until
den. Remove and set aside.

Add the onions, red pepper, and garlic
o the pan, with more oil if needed, and
en gently for 3–5 minutes. Add the
atoes, tomato purée, and sugar and
g to a boil. Simmer for 10 minutes until
kened, stir in the basil, and season with
and pepper.

poon one-third of the tomato
auce into a large ovenproof dish
cover with one-third of the lasagne.
the aubergine, then half of the
aining tomato sauce. Add half of
emaining lasagne, then the spinach.
the remaining lasagne and tomato
e, and finish with an overlapping
of courgettes.

ake in a preheated oven at 190°C
70°C fan, Gas 5) for 35 minutes or until
asta is tender and the top is golden.

Spinach gnocchi with tomato sauce

SERVES 4   738 CALS PER SERVING

1 kg (2 lb) spinach leaves

375 g (12 oz) ricotta cheese

3 eggs

4 tbsp grated Parmesan cheese

pinch of grated nutmeg

salt and black pepper

60–75 g (2–2½ oz) plain flour

TOMATO SAUCE

30 g (1 oz) butter

1 small onion, chopped

1 small carrot, chopped

30 g (1 oz) plain flour

1 x 400 g can chopped tomatoes

300 ml (½ pint) vegetable stock

1 bay leaf

1 tsp caster sugar

TO SERVE

125 g (4 oz) butter

grated Parmesan cheese and Parmesan shavings

1 Wash the spinach and put into a saucepan with only the water remaining on the leaves. Cook over a gentle heat until just wilted. Drain the spinach throughly, squeezing to remove any excess water.

2 Put the spinach, ricotta, eggs, Parmesan, and nutmeg into a food processor, season with salt and pepper and purée until smooth. Turn into a bowl and gradually add flour until the mixture just holds its shape.

3 Using 2 dessertspoons, form the mixture into 20 oval shapes. Cover and chill in the refrigerator for 1 hour.

4 Make the tomato sauce: melt the butter in a pan, add the onion and carrot, and cook for 10 minutes or until softened. Sprinkle in the flour and cook, stirring, for 1 minute. Add the tomatoes, stock, bay leaf, and sugar, season with salt and pepper, and bring to a boil. Cover and simmer for 30 minutes. Purée in a food processor until smooth. Keep hot.

5 Cook the gnocchi in batches in boiling salted water for about 5 minutes or until they float to the surface. Lift out and keep hot. Melt the butter and pour over the gnocchi. Serve the gnocchi hot, with the tomato sauce, grated Parmesan, and Parmesan shavings.

Majorcan tumbet casserole

SERVES 6   188 CALS PER SERVING

625 g (1¼ lb) baby new potatoes

500 g (1 lb) courgettes, thickly sliced

500 g (1 lb) Spanish onions, thickly sliced

500 g (1 lb) tomatoes, halved

3 fat garlic cloves, peeled and left whole

olive oil

salt and black pepper

3 tsp chopped fresh rosemary

400 ml (14 fl oz) passata (sieved tomatoes)

Tabasco sauce

3 fresh thyme sprigs, plus extra to garnish

1.8 litre (3 pint) ovenproof dish, about
20 x 28 x 5 cm (8 x 11 x 2 in)

1 Boil the potatoes in salted water for about 15–20 minutes until not quite done. Drain and leave until cool enough to handle, then peel and cut in half.

2 Toss the courgettes, onions, tomatoes, and garlic cloves in a couple of tablespoons of olive oil and season well. Arrange cut-side down on a large baking sheet or in a shallow roasting tin. Roast in a preheated oven at 220°C (200°C fan, Gas 7) for about 30–40 minutes, turning once, until the vegetables are charred and soft.

3 Pick out the garlic, squash it with the back of a knife, and return it to the other vegetables. Layer the vegetables in an ovenproof dish – first the potatoes with some seasoning and rosemary, about 6 tbsp passata, and a good dash of Tabasco, then the onions, tomatoes, and courgettes with seasoning, rosemary, passata, and Tabasco as before. Push 3 sprigs of thyme in near the top.

4 Bake in a preheated oven at 200°C (180°C fan, Gas 6) for about 15–20 minutes, or at 170°C (150°C fan, Gas 3) for 30–40 minutes, until hot and bubbling. Before serving, replace the cooked thyme with fresh thyme. Good served with Vegetarian Burgers (see page 284).

Kilkerry pie

SERVES 6   494 CALS PER SERVING

90 g (3 oz) butter

500 g (1 lb) leeks, trimmed and thickly sliced

60 g (2 oz) plain flour

300 ml (½ pint) apple juice

300 ml (½ pint) milk

1 tsp coarse-grain mustard

salt and black pepper

4 hard-boiled eggs, roughly chopped

150 g (5 oz) mature Cheddar cheese, grated

500 g (1 lb) potatoes, cut into 5 mm (¼ in) slices (not peeled)

5 sheets of filo pastry, each about
25 x 38 cm (10 x 15 in)

shallow ovenproof dish, about 25 cm
(10 in) square

1 Melt 60 g (2 oz) of the butter in a large frying pan, and cook the leeks for about 8–10 minutes until softened. Stir in the flour and cook for 1 minute, then gradually add the apple juice and milk, stirring constantly until boiling. It may look slightly curdled at this stage, but don't worry, it will come together. Reduce the heat, and simmer gently for 2–3 minutes. Add the mustard and season well.

2 Remove the sauce from the heat and stir in the roughly chopped eggs and the cheese. Now cook the potatoes in boiling salted water for 4–5 minutes until just tender. Drain, and mix into the sauce, then season, and pour into the dish.

3 Melt the remaining butter. Brush one of the filo sheets with butter and put it over the mixture in the dish, scrunching up the edges to fit. Repeat with the remaining filo sheets, scrunching up the last sheet before putting it on top of the pie. You can leave the pie for up to 6 hours at this stage, then bake it when you need it.

4 Bake in a preheated oven at 200°C (180°C fan, Gas 6) for 30–40 minutes until the filo is crisp and golden and the pie is hot right through.

Tuscan cannelloni

SERVES 4   482 CALS PER SERVING

8 sheets of fresh lasagne, or dried lasagne cooke according to packet instructions

500 g (1 lb) passata (sieved tomatoes) or ready-made fresh tomato and basil pasta sauce

2–3 tbsp grated fresh Parmesan cheese

a small handful of chopped fresh basil

FILLING

a little olive oil

2 shallots, finely chopped

1 garlic clove, crushed

2 x 300 g cans cannellini beans, drained

60 g (2 oz) sun-blushed or sun-dried tomatoes, snipped into pieces

150 g (5 oz) Dolcelatte cheese, roughly choppe

2 heaped tbsp chopped fresh basil

salt and black pepper

shallow ovenproof dish, about 28 x 20 cm
(11 x 8 in)

1 Make the filling: heat the oil in a small pan, and cook the shallots and garlic until soft. Allow to cool. Crush the beans with a fork so that most are mashed but a few still retain some shape, then mix them with the shallots and garlic, tomato Dolcelatte, and basil. Season well, taste, and add more seasoning if necessary.

2 Lay the lasagne sheets flat, divide th filling among them, and roll up from short ends to enclose the filling. Put the cannelloni seam-side down into an oiled buttered ovenproof dish – they should fi snugly. Season, then pour over the pass or pasta sauce.

3 Cover and cook in a preheated ove at 190°C (170°C fan, Gas 5) for 45–5 minutes until the pasta is cooked and th filling piping hot. (If pre-cooked pasta w used, bake for 25–30 minutes.) Scatter the Parmesan and basil over the top before serving.

Opposite, clockwise from top
Tuscan cannelloni, Kilker
Majorcan tumbet cas

Polenta with grilled vegetables

🍴 SERVES 6   319 CALS PER SERVING

175 g (6 oz) polenta

150 ml (¼ pint) cold water

600 ml (1 pint) boiling salted water

30 g (1 oz) butter

2 courgettes, halved and thickly sliced lengthways

2 tomatoes, cored and sliced

1 fennel bulb, trimmed and quartered lengthways

1 red onion, thickly sliced

melted butter for brushing

MARINADE

4 tbsp olive oil

2 tbsp red wine vinegar

3 garlic cloves, chopped

2–3 tbsp chopped parsley

salt and black pepper

1 Put the polenta into a saucepan, cover with the measured cold water, and leave to stand for 5 minutes.

2 Add the boiling salted water to the pan, return to a boil, and stir for 10–15 minutes, until smooth and thickened.

3 Sprinkle a baking tray with water. Stir the butter into the polenta, then spread the mixture over the tray in a 1 cm (½ in) layer. Leave to cool.

4 Combine the marinade ingredients in a bowl. Add the courgettes, tomatoes, fennel, and onion. Cover and marinate in the refrigerator for 30 minutes.

5 Lift the vegetables out of the marinade and cook over a hot barbecue for 2–3 minutes on each side. Cut the polenta into strips and cook over a hot barbecue, brushing with melted butter, for 1–2 minutes on each side until golden. Serve hot.

🔍 Cook's know-how

Instead of barbecuing the polenta and vegetables, you can cook them on a ridged cast-iron chargrill pan, or under a preheated grill, for the same length of time.

Winter vegetable terrine

🍴 SERVES 4–6   142–95 CALS PER SERVING

375 g (12 oz) carrots, coarsely chopped

2.5 cm (1 in) piece of fresh root ginger, peeled and grated

salt and black pepper

375 g (12 oz) celeriac, peeled and coarsely chopped

375 g (12 oz) broccoli

sunflower oil for greasing

3 eggs

1 kg (2 lb) loaf tin or terrine

1 Cook the carrots with the ginger in boiling salted water for 10–15 minutes until the carrots are just tender. Cook the celeriac in boiling salted water for 8–10 minutes until tender.

2 Cut the stalks off the broccoli and cook them in boiling salted water for 8–10 minutes until almost tender, then add the broccoli florets and cook for 1 minute longer.

3 Drain all of the vegetables separately and rinse in cold water. Line the base of the oiled loaf tin with greaseproof paper.

4 Put the broccoli in a food processor, add 1 egg, and season with salt and pepper. Purée until smooth, then turn the mixture into the loaf tin and level the surface.

5 Put the celeriac in the food processor, add another egg, and season with salt and pepper, then purée until smooth. Spread over the broccoli mixture and level the surface.

6 Purée the carrots and ginger with the remaining egg and salt and pepper in the food processor until smooth. Spread over the celeriac and level the surface.

7 Tightly cover the tin with oiled foil. Put the tin into a roasting tin and pour in boiling water to come halfway up the sides. Cook in a preheated oven at 180°C (160°C fan, Gas 4) for 1 hour or until firm.

8 Remove from the water, and leave to cool in the loaf tin. Chill thoroughly in the refrigerator. Turn out the terrine, and cut in slices to serve.

ouscous with oasted peppers

SERVES 4–6   418–279 CALS PER SERVING

ge red pepper

ge yellow pepper

g (6 oz) couscous

ml (1 pint) hot vegetable stock

p olive oil

(2 oz) blanched almonds

urgettes, sliced

ge red onion, chopped

ge carrot, thinly sliced

arlic cloves, crushed

00 g can chick peas, drained and rinsed

ground cumin

curry powder

tsp crushed dried red chillies

nd black pepper

ped coriander to garnish

1 Cook the peppers under a hot grill, 10 cm (4 in) from the heat, for 10 minutes or until charred. Seal in a plastic bag and leave to cool.

2 Put the couscous into a bowl and stir in the hot stock. Cover and leave to stand for 10 minutes.

3 Meanwhile, heat the oil in a large frying pan, add the almonds, and cook gently, stirring, for 3 minutes or until lightly browned. Lift out with a slotted spoon and drain on paper towels.

4 Add the courgettes, onion, carrot, and garlic to the pan, and cook, stirring, for about 5 minutes.

5 Stir in the chick peas, cumin, curry powder, and crushed chillies, and cook, stirring occasionally, for a further 5 minutes. Stir in the couscous, and cook for 3–4 minutes until heated through. Season to taste.

6 Remove the skins, cores, and seeds from the grilled peppers, and cut the flesh into thin strips.

7 Divide the couscous among warmed serving plates and arrange the pepper strips on top. Serve at once, sprinkled with the almonds and chopped coriander.

Niramish

SERVES 6   303 CALS PER SERVING

2 tbsp sunflower oil

3 tbsp curry paste

½ tsp chilli powder

2.5 cm (1 in) piece of fresh root ginger, peeled and grated

1 large onion, chopped

2 garlic cloves, crushed

3 tbsp mango chutney

1 small cauliflower, cut into florets

2 potatoes, cut into chunks

2 large carrots, sliced

2 red peppers, halved, seeded, and cut into chunks

1 x 400 g can chopped tomatoes

1 x 400 g can coconut milk

250 g (8 oz) green beans, chopped into short lengths

salt and black pepper

juice of 1 lime

fresh coriander leaves to garnish

1 Heat the oil in a large saucepan, add the curry paste and chilli powder, and cook, stirring constantly, for 1 minute. Add the ginger, onion, garlic, and mango chutney, and cook, stirring, for 3–5 minutes until the onion is softened but not coloured.

2 Add the cauliflower, potatoes, and carrots to the pan, and stir well to coat in the spices. Cook, stirring occasionally, for 5 minutes.

3 Add the red peppers, tomatoes, and coconut milk to the pan and bring to a boil, then add the beans and season with salt and pepper. Stir well.

4 Cover and simmer gently for 25–30 minutes or until all the vegetables are tender. Stir in the lime juice and taste for seasoning. Serve hot, garnished with coriander leaves.

Sag aloo

SERVES 6   143 CALS PER SERVING

500 g (1 lb) new potatoes

salt

2 tbsp sunflower oil

1 tsp mustard seeds

1 tsp cumin seeds

2 onions, sliced

3 garlic cloves, chopped

2.5 cm (1 in) piece of fresh root ginger, peeled and grated

1 small fresh green chilli, halved, seeded, and finely chopped

2 tsp ground coriander

½ tsp turmeric

250 ml (8 fl oz) water

500 g (1 lb) fresh baby leaf spinach

2 tbsp lime or lemon juice

plain yogurt to serve

1 Cook the potatoes in a saucepan of boiling salted water for 10 minutes. Drain and leave to cool. Cut into bite-sized pieces and set aside.

2 Heat the oil in a large, heavy frying pan. Add the mustard and cumin seeds and cook, stirring, for a few seconds until they pop. Add the onions, garlic, ginger, and chilli and cook for about 5 minutes until soft.

3 Add 1 tsp salt, the ground coriander, and the turmeric. Cook, stirring, for 1 minute. Add the potatoes and turn to coat in the spices, then pour in the water and bring to a boil. Cover and cook over a gentle heat for 15 minutes or until the potatoes are tender.

4 Remove the lid and stir in the spinach. Increase the heat and cook, stirring occasionally, for about 10 minutes or until the spinach wilts right down into the sauce. Stir in the lime or lemon juice and taste for seasoning. Serve hot, with yogurt.

Dhal

SERVES 6   275 CALS PER SERVING

225 g (8 oz) green lentils

1 bay leaf

2 tbsp vegetable oil

1 large carrot, chopped

1 large green pepper, halved, seeded, and chopped

1 large onion, chopped

1 garlic clove, crushed

1 cm (½ in) piece of fresh root ginger, peeled and finely grated

½ tsp each ground cinnamon, cumin, and coriander

1 x 400 g can chopped tomatoes

salt and black pepper

1 Rinse and drain the lentils, put them into a large saucepan, and pour in enough cold water to cover. Bring to a boil and add the bay leaf, then cover and simmer for 30 minutes or until the lentils are tender. Drain and remove the bay leaf.

2 Heat the oil in the saucepan, add the vegetables, garlic, and ginger, and fry for 10 minutes, stirring occasionally. Add the lentils, ground spices, and tomatoes and cook gently for 10 minutes or until the carrot is soft.

3 Purée the mixture in 3 batches in a blender or food processor. Do not purée for longer than about 30 seconds for each batch because the dhal should not be too smooth – it should retain some of the texture of the lentils. Reheat in the rinsed-out pan and add salt and pepper to taste.

Accompaniments

- tomato and coriander relish
- cucumber raita
- grated carrot salad
- mango chutney
- poppadoms
- basmati rice
- naan bread

Opposite, clockwise from top right: Yogurt, cucumber raita, Niramish, Sag aloo,

Spiced aubergines with filo crust

 SERVES 6   569 CALS PER SERVING

2 tbsp olive oil

2 large onions, chopped

2 tbsp mild curry paste

2 aubergines, cut into 1 cm (½ in) dice

2 red peppers, halved, seeded, and diced

salt and black pepper

175 g (6 oz) dried red lentils

250 g (8 oz) Caerphilly cheese, diced

300 g (10 oz) filo pastry

60 g (2 oz) melted butter

26 cm (10½ in) springform cake tin

1 Heat the oil in a large saucepan or deep frying pan. Cook the onions over a low heat, stirring occasionally, for 3–5 minutes until softened. Stir in the curry paste, and cook for 2 minutes.

2 Add the aubergines and the red peppers and cook for 10–15 minutes until soft. Season with salt and pepper and leave to cool.

3 Meanwhile, put the lentils into a pan, cover with water, and bring to a boil. Simmer for 15 minutes or until just soft. Drain and cool.

4 Stir the lentils and diced cheese into the aubergine mixture. Taste for seasoning.

5 Using two-thirds of the filo, line the bottom and side of the cake tin,

brushing each sheet with melted butter, and letting them overhang the rim of the tin. Spoon in the aubergine mixture and the filo over the top. Brush the remaining with butter, crumple, and arrange on top.

6 Bake in a preheated oven at 190°C (170°C fan, Gas 5) for 40 minutes or u the pastry is golden. Serve hot.

Cook's know-how

If you are short of time, omit the filo. Sprea the aubergine, pepper, and lentil mixture in baking dish and grate the cheese over the t

Carrot roulade

SERVES 6–8   483–363 CALS PER SERVING

5 g (4 oz) butter, plus extra for greasing

large garlic clove, crushed

red pepper, halved, seeded, and finely chopped

200 g can tomatoes

0 g (1½ lb) carrots, grated

ggs, separated

LING

ucumber, seeded and diced

and black pepper

g (4 oz) goat's cheese

g (4 oz) full-fat soft cheese

pring onions, thinly sliced

rge garlic clove, crushed

tbsp finely chopped parsley

k if needed

23 cm (13 x 9 in) Swiss roll tin

Put the diced cucumber for the filling nto a colander, sprinkle with salt, and ve to stand for 20 minutes.

Butter the tin and line with baking parchment. Butter the parchment.

Melt the butter, add half of the garlic, the red pepper, and tomatoes, and k gently for 5 minutes.

Add the carrots and cook gently for 2 minutes or until soft. Turn the carrot ture into a large bowl and beat in the yolks. Season with salt and pepper. In ther bowl, whisk the egg whites until but not dry, then fold into the carrot ure.

our the carrot mixture into the Swiss roll n and bake in a preheated oven at C (180°C fan, Gas 6) for 10 minutes or golden. Cover and leave to cool.

Make the filling: rinse the cucumber and at dry with paper towels. Turn into a and combine with the goat's cheese, cheese, spring onions, garlic, parsley, black pepper to taste. If the mixture is thick, stir in 1–2 tbsp milk.

urn the roulade out on to a sheet of aking parchment and peel off the lining r. Trim the edges. Spread the filling over oulade, leaving a 2.5 cm (1 in) border ach side. Roll up the roulade from one side, using the baking parchment for ort. Cover and chill for 30 minutes. Cut lices to serve.

Tomato and olive tart

SERVES 8   377 CALS PER SERVING

3 tbsp olive oil

2 large onions, coarsely chopped

3 garlic cloves, crushed

1 x 400 g can chopped tomatoes

1 x 140 g can tomato purée

2 tsp chopped fresh basil

1 tsp caster sugar

125 g (4 oz) vignotte or mozzarella cheese, grated

90 g (3 oz) pitted black olives

shredded fresh basil to garnish

POPPYSEED BASE

250 g (8 oz) plain flour

125 g (4 oz) butter

90 g (3 oz) poppyseeds

1 tbsp light muscovado sugar

salt and black pepper

about 4 tbsp cold water

1 Make the base: put the flour, butter, poppyseeds, and sugar in a food processor, season with salt and pepper, and pulse until the mixture resembles fine breadcrumbs.

2 Add the water and process until the mixture forms a ball. Turn out and knead lightly, then roll out to a 30 cm (12 in) round on a baking sheet and pinch the edge to form a rim. Prick the base all over with a fork and chill for 30 minutes.

3 Heat the oil in a pan, add the onions and garlic, and cook gently for 3–5 minutes until soft. Add the tomatoes, tomato purée, basil, and sugar. Season and bring to a boil. Boil for 5–7 minutes until thick. Leave to cool slightly.

4 Bake the poppyseed base in a preheated oven at 220°C (200°C fan, Gas 7) for 15 minutes. Spread the tomato mixture over the base, sprinkle with the cheese and olives, and bake for 15–20 minutes. Serve hot or cold, sprinkled with basil.

Cook's know-how

If you are short of time, use ready-made shortcrust pastry instead of the poppyseed base. You will need a 500 g (1 lb) packet.

Spinach and ricotta samosas

SERVES 4   307 CALS PER SERVING

4 sheets of filo pastry

60 g (2 oz) melted butter, plus extra for greasing

FILLING

30 g (1 oz) butter

1 small onion, finely chopped

300 g (10 oz) spinach leaves, shredded

125 g (4 oz) ricotta cheese

pinch of grated nutmeg

salt and black pepper

tomato sauce (page 275) to serve

1 Make the filling: melt the butter in a saucepan, add the onion, and cook gently for 3–5 minutes until softened.

2 Add the spinach to the onion and cook for 1–2 minutes. Leave to cool. Add the ricotta and nutmeg, season with salt and pepper, and mix well. Divide into 8 portions.

3 Lightly butter a baking tray. Cut each sheet of filo pastry lengthways into 2 long strips. Brush 1 strip with melted butter, covering the remaining strips with a damp tea towel. Fill and fold the parcels (see box, below).

4 Bake in a preheated oven at 200°C (180°C fan, Gas 6) for 20 minutes or until the pastry is crisp and golden. Serve with the tomato sauce.

Filling and folding the parcels

Spoon 1 portion of filling on to a corner of the filo strip. Fold over opposite corner to form a triangle.

Fold the filled triangle until you reach the end of the strip. Brush with melted butter and put on to the baking tray. Butter, fill, and fold the remaining filo strips.

Falafel with sesame yogurt sauce

SERVES 6   326 CALS PER SERVING

1 x 400 g can chick peas, drained and rinsed

6 spring onions, chopped

30 g (1 oz) fresh white bread

1 egg

grated zest and juice of ½ lemon

1 garlic clove, roughly chopped

2 tbsp roughly chopped fresh coriander

2 tbsp roughly chopped parsley

1 tbsp tahini paste

1 tsp ground coriander

1 tsp ground cumin

½ tsp ground cinnamon

pinch of cayenne pepper

salt and black pepper

sunflower oil for shallow-frying

chopped fresh coriander to garnish

warmed mini pitta breads to serve

SESAME YOGURT SAUCE

4 tbsp plain yogurt

2 tbsp olive oil

1 tbsp lemon juice

1 tbsp tahini paste

1 Put the chick peas into a food processor, add the onions, bread, egg, lemon zest and juice, garlic, coriander, parsley, tahini, ground coriander, cumin, cinnamon, and cayenne pepper, and season with salt and pepper. Purée until smooth.

2 Turn into a bowl, cover, and leave to stand for at least 30 minutes.

3 Meanwhile, make the sesame yogurt sauce: in a bowl, combine the yogurt, oil, lemon juice, tahini, and salt and pepper to taste.

4 With dampened hands, shape the falafel mixture into balls about the size of a walnut, then flatten them into patties.

5 Pour enough oil into a non-stick frying pan just to cover the base, and heat until hot. Shallow-fry the falafel in batches for 2–3 minutes on each side until golden. Lift out and drain on paper towels. Garnish with coriander and serve warm, with mini pitta breads and sesame yogurt sauce.

Vegetarian burgers

SERVES 6   134 CALS PER SERVING

15 g (½ oz) butter

125 g (4 oz) chestnut mushrooms, finely chopped

1 small leek, finely chopped

1 small green chilli, halved, seeded, and finely chopped

1 tsp sugar

1 garlic clove, crushed

2 x 400 g cans butter beans or cannellini beans (or use one of each), drained and rinsed

salt and black pepper

plain flour for coating

4 tbsp olive or sunflower oil

DRESSED LETTUCE

4 tbsp reduced-calorie mayonnaise

2 tbsp Dijon mustard

dash of lemon juice

½ small iceberg lettuce, finely shredded

1 small onion, thinly sliced

1 Melt the butter in a frying pan, add the mushrooms and leek, and cook over a high heat for 2–3 minutes until fairly soft. Add the chilli, sugar, and garlic, and stir fry for 2–3 minutes. Add the beans and cook, stirring, for 1 minute.

2 Remove from the heat, season well, and mash with a potato masher until the beans are broken into a rough mixture with no large lumps. Shape into 6 burgers.

3 Spinkle some flour on to a plate and season with salt and pepper. Coat both sides of each burger in flour.

4 Heat the oil in a frying pan, add the burgers, and cook for about 3–4 minutes on each side until golden brown and heated right through.

5 Make the dressed lettuce: combine the mayonnaise, mustard, and lemon juice. Stir in the lettuce and onion. Serve with the burgers.

Red bean and tomato curry

SERVES 4   218 CALS PER SERVING

bsp sunflower oil

rge onion, sliced

arlic cloves, crushed

fresh green chillies, halved, seeded, and sliced

cm (1 in) piece of fresh root ginger, peeled d grated

sp Madras or other hot curry powder

400 g can chopped tomatoes

400 g cans red kidney beans, drained rinsed

sp lemon juice

h coriander leaves to garnish

Heat the oil in a large frying pan, add he onion, garlic, chillies, and ginger, and k, stirring occasionally, for a few minutes all the aromas are released, and the on is softened but not coloured.

Add the curry powder and season with salt, then cook, stirring, for 2 minutes.

Add the tomatoes with most of their uice and cook for about 3 minutes. Add beans and cook for a further 5 minutes ntil the beans are warmed through and sauce is thickened. Add the lemon juice serve hot, garnished with coriander.

Red lentil and coconut curry

SERVES 6   481 CALS PER SERVING

300 g (10 oz) red lentils

900 ml (1½ pints) water

2.5 cm (1 in) piece of fresh root ginger, peeled and grated

1½ fresh green chillies, halved, seeded, and finely chopped

4 garlic cloves

90 g (3 oz) creamed coconut, grated

½ tsp turmeric

1 tbsp lemon juice

salt

30 g (1 oz) butter

4 tsp black mustard seeds

1 Put the lentils into a pan and add the water. Bring to a boil and simmer for about 20 minutes or until tender.

2 Using a pestle and mortar, crush the fresh root ginger, two-thirds of the chillies, and 2 of the garlic cloves until smooth. Add to the lentils.

3 Add the creamed coconut, turmeric, lemon juice, and a pinch of salt. Cook gently, stirring, until the coconut dissolves, then increase the heat and cook for 5 minutes or until any excess liquid has evaporated. Taste for seasoning.

4 Crush the remaining garlic and set aside. Melt the butter in a frying pan and add the mustard seeds. As soon as they begin to pop, remove the frying pan from the heat and stir in the crushed garlic and the remaining chopped chilli.

chillies add a piquancy and spicy aroma ies, sauces, marinades, and stews. Look for green, firm, and smooth-skinned chillies.

Peking tofu with plum sauce

🍴 SERVES 6   269 CALS PER SERVING

sunflower oil, for frying

250 g (8 oz) tofu, cut into 1.5 cm (just over ½ in) cubes

18 Chinese pancakes (ready-made or see page 186)

6 spring onions, trimmed and cut into matchsticks

¼ cucumber, peeled, seeded, and cut into matchsticks

PLUM SAUCE

250 g (8 oz) dark red plums, halved and stoned

1 small cooking apple, peeled, cored, and sliced

1 fresh red chilli, halved, seeded, and finely chopped

90 g (3 oz) caster sugar

50 ml (2 fl oz) white wine vinegar

1 Make the plum sauce: put the plums, apple, chilli, sugar, vinegar, and 25 ml (1 fl oz) water into a pan. Heat gently to dissolve the sugar, then bring to a boil. Partially cover and simmer gently for about 30–40 minutes until the fruits have cooked down and only a little liquid remains. Remove from the heat and allow to cool.

2 Pour enough oil into a non-stick frying pan to cover the base. Heat until hot, then fry the tofu for 3–4 minutes until golden brown all over, turning carefully. Remove and drain on kitchen paper.

3 To serve, spread a pancake with a little plum sauce, top with a little crispy fried tofu, spring onions, and cucumber and roll up to eat.

Plums have a sweet, tart flavour, and cook well in sauces. Avoid hard, wrinkled, or shrivelled plums, and those with brown patches.

Japanese noodle soup

🍴 SERVES 6   213 CALS PER SERVING

1.5 litres (2⅓ pints) miso soup (3 sachets)

1 tsp five-spice paste or 1 tsp five-spice powder mixed to a paste with a little water

300 g (10 oz) udon noodles (made from wheat flour)

250 g (8 oz) tofu, cut into 1 cm (½ in) cubes

3 spring onions, trimmed and shredded

1 Make the miso soup, bring to a boil and add the five-spice paste. Simmer for 5 minutes, then add the noodles and simmer for 2 minutes, gently separating them with chopsticks or a fork.

2 Add the tofu and heat through for 1 minute. Ladle into soup dishes and scatter over the shredded spring onions before serving.

Firecracker stir-fry

🍴 SERVES 4   129 CALS PER SERVING

250 g (8 oz) pak choi

2–3 tbsp sunflower or sesame oil

250 g (8 oz) sugarsnap peas, trimmed

1 red pepper, halved, seeded, and cut into strips

1 yellow pepper, halved, seeded, and cut into strips

2–3 hot fresh red chillies, halved, seeded, and sliced

300 g (10 oz) shiitake mushrooms, sliced

2–3 tbsp soy sauce

salt and black pepper

boiled or steamed long grain rice, to serve

1 Cut the leafy tops off the pak choi, shred the leaves coarsely, and reserve. Slice the stems in half, or into quarters if they are large.

2 Heat the oil in a wok or large frying pan. Add the peas, peppers and chilli and stir-fry over a high heat for about 3–4 minutes. Add the mushrooms and pak choi stems and continue to stir-fry for another 2–3 minutes.

3 When the vegetables are just about tender, add the shredded pak choi leaves with a dash of soy sauce. Taste and add salt and pepper if needed, plus more soy sauce if you like. Serve immediately, with rice.

Thai curry

🍴 SERVES 4   296 CALS PER SERVING

1 tbsp sunflower or sesame oil

1 fresh green chilli, halved, seeded, and finely chopped

2.5 cm (1 in) piece of fresh root ginger, peeled and grated

1 tbsp Thai green curry paste

1 large cauliflower, cut into bite-sized florets

375 g (12 oz) fine green beans, halved

1 x 400 g can coconut milk

150 ml (¼ pint) vegetable stock

1 fresh lemon grass stalk, bruised by bashing with a rolling pin

salt and black pepper

1 x 200 g can water chestnuts

3 tbsp chopped fresh coriander, to garnish

boiled or steamed Thai jasmine rice, to serve

1 Heat the oil in a wok or large non-stick frying pan and stir-fry the chilli and ginger for 2 minutes. Add the curry paste and stir-fry for a further minute.

2 Add the cauliflower and beans and stir evenly to coat the vegetables in the spices. Pour in the coconut milk and stock, then add the lemon grass and seasoning. Bring to a boil and simmer gently for about 20–30 minutes until the beans and cauliflower are just cooked (take care not to overcook them). Add the water chestnuts for the last 5 minutes. Remove and discard the lemon grass, scatter over the coriander and serve with rice.

Opposite, clockwise from top: Thai with jasmine rice, Firecracker s with long grain rice, Japanese r soup, Peking tofu with plum

Christmas nut loaf

SERVES 6–8   600–450 CALS PER SERVING

75 g (2½ oz) brown rice

salt and black pepper

15 g (½ oz) dried ceps

30 g (1 oz) butter

2 carrots, grated

1 small onion, finely chopped

1 garlic clove, crushed

250 g (8 oz) button mushrooms, chopped

2 tbsp chopped parsley

1 tbsp chopped fresh rosemary

125 g (4 oz) walnuts, toasted and chopped

125 g (4 oz) Brazil nuts, toasted and chopped

60 g (2 oz) pine nuts, toasted

175 g (6 oz) Cheddar cheese, grated

1 egg, beaten

sunflower oil for greasing

rosemary sprigs to garnish

cranberry sauce (page 176) to serve

1 kg (2 lb) loaf tin

1 Cook the rice in boiling salted water for 30–35 minutes until tender.

2 Meanwhile, soak the ceps in a bowl of warm water for about 20–30 minutes.

3 Drain the rice when it is ready. Drain the ceps, pat dry, and chop finely.

4 Melt the butter in a frying pan, add the carrots, onion, and garlic, and cook gently, stirring occasionally, for 5 minutes. Stir in the chopped mushrooms, rice, ceps, parsley, and rosemary, and cook until softened.

5 Purée the mixture in a food processor. Stir in the walnuts, Brazil nuts, pine nuts, cheese, and egg. Season with salt and pepper.

6 Lightly grease the loaf tin, spoon in the mixture, and level the top. Cover with foil and bake in a preheated oven at 190°C (170°C fan, Gas 5) for 1½ hours or until firm. Turn out, cut into slices, and garnish. Serve hot, with cranberry sauce.

Chestnut loaf

SERVES 6   226 CALS PER SERVING

250 g (8 oz) frozen chestnuts, thawed

1 tbsp olive oil, plus extra for greasing

1 onion, coarsely chopped

2 celery stalks, chopped

2 garlic cloves, crushed

250 g (8 oz) potatoes, boiled and mashed

125 g (4 oz) fresh wholemeal breadcrumbs

1 egg, beaten

2 tbsp chopped parsley

1 tbsp soy sauce

1 tbsp tomato purée

salt and black pepper

red pepper strips and watercress sprigs to garnis

spicy tomato salsa (see box, below) to serve

1 kg (2 lb) loaf tin

1 Coarsely chop half of the chestnuts, a finely chop the remainder.

2 Heat the oil in a pan, add the onion, celery, and garlic, and cook, stirring, for 3–5 minutes until soft. Remove from the heat.

3 Stir in the chestnuts, potatoes, breadcrumbs, egg, parsley, soy sauc and tomato purée, and season with salt and pepper.

4 Spoon the mixture into the greased l tin, and level the top. Cover with foil and cook in a preheated oven at 180°C (160°C fan, Gas 4) for 1 hour or until firm Turn out, cut into slices, and garnish. Ser hot or cold, with the spicy tomato salsa.

Spicy tomato salsa

Dice 8 large tomatoes, and put into a bowl. S in 2 chopped spring onions, 1 seeded and fin chopped fresh green chilli, the zest and juice of 2 limes, 3 tbsp chopped fresh coriander, ar 1 tsp caster sugar. Season with salt and pepp and chill.

Glamorgan sausages

SERVES 4   526 CALS PER SERVING

g (5 oz) fresh white breadcrumbs

g (4 oz) Caerphilly or Cheddar cheese, grated

mall leek, finely chopped

g (1 oz) walnuts, finely chopped

sp chopped fresh sage or parsley

p grated lemon zest

p mustard powder

(2 oz) Welsh goat's cheese, coarsely chopped

gs

sp milk

and black pepper

flour for coating

sp sunflower oil

sage or parsley to garnish

n a bowl, combine the breadcrumbs,
cheese, leek, walnuts, sage or parsley,
on zest, and mustard. Blend the goat's
ese into the mixture.

Separate 1 egg, reserving the white and
adding the yolk to the remaining egg.
the egg and yolk into the cheese
ure with the milk, and season with salt
pepper.

Divide the mixture into 8 pieces and roll
nto sausages about 7 cm (3 in) long.
er and chill for about 1 hour to allow
flavours to develop.

prinkle some flour on to a plate and
eason with salt and pepper. Brush the
ages with the reserved egg white, then
nto the seasoned flour until lightly
ed all over. Shake off any excess flour.

eat the oil in a frying pan, add the
ausages, and cook over a medium
, turning occasionally, for 8–10 minutes
golden. Drain on paper towels, and
hot, garnished with sage or parsley.

t's cheese nuggets

ne goat's cheese into 16 cubes. Combine
readcrumbs with the other ingredients as
e. Mould the mixture around the goat's
se cubes, forming small balls. Chill, then
and cook as in steps 4 and 5.

Spinach roulade

SERVES 6–8   250–187 CALS PER SERVING

560 g (1 lb 2 oz) spinach leaves

30 g (1 oz) butter, plus extra for greasing

4 eggs, separated

¼ tsp grated nutmeg

1 tbsp finely grated Parmesan cheese

FILLING

15 g (½ oz) butter

250 g (8 oz) button mushrooms, sliced

juice of ½ lemon

salt and black pepper

200 ml (7 fl oz) crème fraîche

2 tbsp chopped parsley

33 x 23 cm (13 x 9 in) Swiss roll tin

1 Make the filling: melt the butter in a pan,
add the mushrooms and lemon juice,
and season with salt and pepper. Cook
for 3 minutes until just softened, then leave
to cool.

2 Wash the spinach and put into a pan with
only the water remaining on the leaves.
Cook over a gentle heat for 1–2 minutes until
the spinach has just wilted. Drain well, and
squeeze out the excess water.

3 Butter the tin and line with baking
parchment. Butter the parchment.

4 Coarsely chop the spinach, turn into
a large bowl, and beat in the butter,
egg yolks, and nutmeg. Season with salt
and pepper. In another bowl, whisk the
egg whites until firm but not dry, then fold
gently into the spinach mixture.

5 Pour the spinach mixture into the Swiss
roll tin and bake in a preheated oven at
220°C (200°C fan, Gas 7) for 10–12 minutes
until firm.

6 Sprinkle the Parmesan cheese on to
a sheet of baking parchment. Turn the
roulade out on to the cheese, leave to
cool for 5–10 minutes, then peel off the
lining paper. Trim the edges of the roulade.

7 Drain the mushrooms, reserving some
of the cooking liquid. Put them into
a bowl, add the crème fraîche, parsley,
and season to taste. Add a little of the
reserved liquid if too thick. Spread the filling
over the roulade, leaving a 2.5 cm (1 in)
border. Roll up from one long side. Cover
and chill for 30 minutes. Cut into slices
to serve.

Halloumi and vegetable kebabs

SERVES 4   722 CALS PER SERVING

1 small baguette

250 g (8 oz) halloumi cheese

1 large red pepper, halved and seeded

150 ml (¼ pint) olive oil, plus extra for greasing

16 large cherry tomatoes

grated zest and juice of 1 lemon

1 garlic clove, crushed

2 tbsp chopped fresh basil

1 tbsp snipped fresh chives

salt and black pepper

8 metal skewers

1 Cut the bread into 8 thick slices and cut each slice in half. Cut the halloumi into 16 cubes and cut the red pepper into 8 pieces.

2 Oil the skewers and thread alternately with the tomatoes, bread, cheese, and red pepper. Place in a shallow flameproof dish.

3 Mix the oil, lemon zest and juice, garlic, and herbs, and season with salt and pepper. Drizzle over the kebabs.

4 Cook the kebabs under a hot grill, 10 cm (4 in) from the heat, turning once and basting with the marinade, for 3–4 minutes until the cheese is lightly browned.

Tofu and vegetable kebabs

Substitute smoked tofu for the halloumi cheese, and 8 button mushrooms for the red pepper.

Vegetable stir-fry with tofu

SERVES 4   335 CALS PER SERVING

250 g (8 oz) firm tofu, cut into bite-sized pieces

2 tbsp sesame oil

1 tbsp sunflower oil

1 head of chicory, halved lengthways

4 carrots, thinly sliced diagonally

5 cm (2 in) piece of fresh root ginger, peeled and grated

250 g (8 oz) shiitake mushrooms, sliced

8 spring onions, sliced into 2.5 cm (1 in) pieces

250 g (8 oz) bean sprouts

3 tbsp toasted sesame seeds

MARINADE

3 tbsp soy sauce

3 tbsp dry sherry

1 garlic clove, crushed

salt and black pepper

1 Make the marinade: in a bowl, combine the soy sauce, sherry, and garlic, and season with salt and pepper. Turn the tofu in the marinade, cover, and leave to marinate at room temperature for at least 15 minutes.

2 Drain the tofu, reserving the marinade. Heat the sesame and sunflower oils in a wok or large frying pan, add the tofu, and carefully stir-fry over a high heat for 2–3 minutes, being careful not to break up the tofu. Remove from the wok with a slotted spoon and drain on paper towels.

3 Separate the chicory halves into leaves. Add the carrots and ginger to the wok and stir-fry for about 2 minutes. Add the mushrooms and spring onions and stir-fry for a further 2 minutes, then add the bean sprouts and chicory leaves and stir-fry for 1 minute.

4 Return the tofu to the wok, pour the reserved marinade over the top, and boil quickly until almost all of the marinade has evaporated and the tofu has warmed through. Generously sprinkle with the toasted sesame seeds, taste for seasoning, and serve at once.

Mexican chilli with tofu

SERVES 6   257 CALS PER SERVING

3 onions, chopped

3 garlic cloves, roughly chopped

1 fresh green chilli, halved, seeded, and roughly chopped

2 tsp paprika

1 tbsp mild chilli powder

4 tbsp sunflower oil

1 x 400 g can chopped tomatoes, drained and juice reserved

500 ml (16 fl oz) hot vegetable stock

625 g (1¼ lb) firm tofu, cut into bite-sized pieces

1 x 400 g can red kidney beans, drained

salt and black pepper

chopped fresh coriander to garnish

1 Put the onions, garlic, green chilli, and spices into a food processor and proc until fairly chunky.

2 Heat the oil in a large frying pan. Add the onion mixture and cook for a few minutes, stirring occasionally, until soften and fragrant.

3 Add the tomatoes to the pan and c stirring occasionally, until reduced ar thickened. Pour in the stock and cook fo 5–10 minutes more until thickened again

4 Add the tofu, kidney beans, and the reserved tomato juice, and cook, spooning the sauce over the tofu piece for 5–8 minutes until heated through. Do stir the tofu as it may break up. Season, serve hot, sprinkled with coriander.

Cook's know-how

Halloumi is a semi-hard Greek cheese, which is usually made from ewe's milk. It is best eaten hot, straight from the grill, as it becomes rubbery when it cools down.

Cook's know-how

Reducing a sauce involves cooking it over high heat to allow the moisture to evapora and the flavours to become concentrated.

Pasta, Rice, and Noodles

Under 45 minutes

Persian pilaf
Rice cooked with cumin and cardamom seeds, cinnamon, cloves, and bay leaves. Combined with pistachio nuts and raisins.

SERVES 4 426 CALS PER SERVING

Takes 40 minutes   Page 315

Fettuccine primavera
Asparagus, broccoli, courgette, pepper, garlic, tomatoes, petits pois, and cream mixed with fettuccine. Served with basil and Parmesan.

SERVES 6 554 CALS PER SERVING

Takes 35 minutes   Page 303

Pasta spirals with herby meatballs
Minced turkey or chicken, breadcrumbs, Parmesan cheese, parsley, and thyme in a tomato–basil sauce.

SERVES 8 384 CALS PER SERVING

Takes 35 minutes   Page

Cannelloni with ricotta and spinach
Cannelloni tubes filled with spinach and ricotta cheese, and topped with tomato sauce.

SERVES 6 462 CALS PER SERVING

Takes 40 minutes   Page 309

Risi e bisi
Risotto rice cooked with peas, stock, and Parma ham. Flavoured with garlic, onion, Parmesan cheese, and parsley.

SERVES 6 390 CALS PER SERVING

Takes 40 minutes   Page

Penne with spinach and Stilton
Pasta quills with mushrooms, cream, and garlic, mixed with spinach, Stilton cheese, and lemon juice.

SERVES 4 976 CALS PER SERVING

Takes 15 minutes   Pag

Stir-fried Chinese noodles
Egg noodles stir-fried with mangetout, be sprouts, shiitake mushrooms, garlic, and ginger, served sprinkled with spring onio

SERVES 4 476 CALS PER SERVING

Takes 20 minutes, **plus soaking**   Pag

Spaghetti bolognese
Traditional Italian dish: spaghetti served a sauce of minced beef simmered with c garlic, tomato, and redcurrant jelly.

SERVES 6 602 CALS PER SERVING

Takes 15 minutes   Pag

45-60 minutes

TRADITIONAL

dgeree
glo-Indian breakfast dish: long grain rice
.ed with smoked haddock, hard-boiled eggs,
am, and lemon juice. Mixed with parsley.

/ES 4   470 CALS PER SERVING
.es 45 minutes   Page 316

HIGH PROTEIN

Tuna and fennel pasta bake
Fresh and aromatic: fennel and onion baked
with white sauce, pasta shells, tuna, eggs, and
Cheddar cheese.

SERVES 6   512 CALS PER SERVING
Takes 45 minutes
                                            Page 304

VEGETARIAN

li alla napoletana
:oli, shiitake mushrooms, red pepper, courgettes, and
ard-flavoured white sauce baked with pasta twists.

6   475 CALS PER SERVING
. 55 minutes   Page 308

Over 60 minutes

FAMILY CHOICE

Classic lasagne
Pasta layered with minced beef, simmered
with stock, tomatoes, celery, white sauce, and
Cheddar and Parmesan cheeses.

SERVES 8   641 CALS PER SERVING
Takes 1½ hours   Page 310

Smoked haddock lasagne
Lasagne sheets layered with smoked haddock
fillets, button mushrooms, Cheddar cheese,
and creamy white sauce.

SERVES 8   473 CALS PER SERVING
Takes 1¼ hours   Page 309

Three-cheese macaroni
Macaroni baked with a sauce flavoured with
Cheddar and light mozzarella cheeses, topped
with breadcrumbs.

SERVES 8   436 CALS PER SERVING
Takes 1 hour 5 minutes   Page 308

Paella
Chicken and rice are cooked with bacon,
stock, tomatoes, onion, peppers, peas, saffron,
mussels, and prawns.

SERVES 6   718 CALS PER SERVING
Takes 1¼ hours   Page 320

Pasta, rice, and noodles know-how

Both pasta and rice are natural convenience foods: they are so quick to cook and they do not need any elaborate preparation. They are also endlessly versatile, working well with almost every ingredient imaginable to make starters, soups, main dishes, side dishes, salads, snacks, and even a few desserts.

Pasta and rice are very nutritious, being high in starchy carbohydrates, and in their wholegrain forms also offering vitamins, minerals, and fibre. As long as rich ingredients such as butter, cream, and cheese are kept to a minimum, pasta and rice dishes can be very low in fat and calories.

Buying and storing

Pasta is available both fresh and dried as well as vacuum-packed, in a huge variety of shapes, both plain and stuffed. The best commercial dried pasta is made from durum wheat. Egg is sometimes added to dried pasta, while the fresh pasta sold in packets in supermarkets is most often enriched with eggs. Pasta is also coloured and flavoured - with spinach or tomato, for example. Fresh pasta is convenient because it cooks quickly, but its texture is not necessarily as good as some dried pasta. A good Italian brand of dried pasta, made from 100% durum wheat (*semola di grano duro*), is often of superior quality.

Dried pasta, in a tightly closed packet, will keep almost indefinitely in the storecupboard (up to 2 years); fresh pasta must be refrigerated and can only be kept for 2–3 days (check the use-by date). For longer storage, freeze it (see below).

Rice is another good storecupboard stand-by. As long as it is stored in an airtight container in a cool, dry, dark place, it will keep for up to a year. But make sure that the container is tightly closed to prevent moisture or insects from getting in.

Store any leftover cooked pasta or rice in a tightly closed container in the refrigerator. Use pasta within 2 days. Rice should be eaten on the day it is cooked as it is susceptible to toxins that cause food poisoning.

Freezing

Fresh uncooked pasta can be frozen for up to 3 months and then cooked from frozen. Layered or filled pasta dishes such as cannelloni, lasagne, and macaroni cheese freeze very well and can also be stored for up to 3 months. Put them in foil or other freezerproof containers that can go straight from the freezer into the oven.

There is no advantage to freezing cooked rice as it takes a long time to thaw - longer than it would take to cook a fresh batch.

It is not advisable to freeze pasta and rice in soups and other dishes that contain a lot of liquid because the pasta and rice become mushy when thawed. Instead, add when reheating the soup or casserole.

Microwaving

There is no advantage to cooking pasta in a microwave because it takes just as long as conventional cooking. However, many pasta sauces can be microwaved quickly and successfully, dishes containing layered or filled pasta cook really well in the microwave, and it is also an excellent way to reheat cooked pasta (be careful not to overcook it). The microwave is excellent for cooking rice, plain or turned into a pilaf or risotto, and the liquid does not have to be brought to a boil before the rice is added. Risotto turns out as tender and creamy as one made by the classic method that involves constant stirring, and yet it can be left totally unattended in the microwave.

Oriental noodles

Oriental noodles are made from a variety flours. The most popular types are availa in supermarkets and delicatessens; other can be found in Chinese or Japanese shop

Wheat noodles
The most common of Oriental noodles, these are made from wheat flour usually enriched with egg. They are available bot flat and round and in a variety of widths.

Cellophane noodles
Sometimes referred to as transparent noodles or bean thread noodles, these ar very fine and white. They are made from ground mung beans.

Rice noodles
Rice vermicelli are long, thin, white stran made from rice flour. Sold dried or fresh bundles, they are used in soups and are deep-fried.

Rice sticks
Made from the same dough as rice nood rice sticks are broad ribbons. They are usually served in a broth or sauce.

Soba
These thin, brownish Japanese noodles a made from buckwheat flour. They are oft served with a dipping sauce.

Udon
Made from white wheat flour, these are from Japan.

Noodles know-how
Store Oriental noodles in the same way a pasta. Most Oriental noodles need only be soaked or briefly cooked in boiling water before being added to soups and broths, vegetable dishes, and stir-fries.

asta shapes

the many pasta shapes available there
e some that are traditionally served with
rtain sauces – spaghetti with bolognese
uce, for example. But you can mix and
atch as you wish.

ng, thin varieties

pelli d'angelo or angel hair, vermicelli,
aghettini, spaghetti, and bucatini are best
ved with a thin oily sauce that clings
hout making the strands stick together.

ng flat ribbons

sta such as linguine, fettuccine, and
liatelle is usually served with a creamy
ce such as alfredo.

bular pasta

caroni, penne (quills), and rigatoni are
t with rich sauces that will run inside
ir tubes.

teresting shapes

re is a vast range of small pasta shapes,
more are being created every day. The
st common include ditali (thimbles),
lli (spirals), conchiglie (shells), farfalle
ws), gnocchi (fluted shells), lumache
ils), orecchiette (ears), and radiatori
ls). Sauce them like tubular pasta.

up pasta

y small pasta shapes, such as
chigliette, ditalini, farfallette, and orzo,
used in soup.

led pastas

olotti, capelletti, ravioli, and tortellini
some of the shapes stuffed with ground
ts or mixtures such as spinach and
tta, and served with a simple sauce.

et pasta

sheets of lasagne are layered with sauce
baked. Fresh lasagne, and cooked dried
gne, can be rolled around a filling to
e cannelloni.

Coloured and flavoured pasta

Jot only does pasta come in a vast range
f shapes, you can also choose from
variety of colours and flavours. Green is
e most common colour, and is derived
om spinach. Other colours include red,
om tomato purée, pink, coloured with
eetroot, yellow, from saffron, and even
lack pasta, coloured with squid ink.
hese colourings affect the taste very
ttle. Flavoured pasta usually has
gredients such as herbs, garlic, or
ack pepper added to the dough. Serve
ith a complementary sauce.

Cooking times and quantities for pasta

These times can only be a guide because
they depend on the freshness of fresh
pasta and the age of dried pasta, as well
as shape and thickness. Start timing as
soon as the water returns to a boil, and
for fresh pasta, start testing three-quarters
of the way through the suggested cooking
time. If using dried pasta, start testing
as soon as the minimum time given on
the packet is reached. Fresh, store-
bought pasta takes 2–4 minutes, 7–10
minutes if filled. Most dried pastas cook
in 8–12 minutes (less for fine pasta such
as capelli d'angelo and vermicelli).

In Italy, pasta is usually eaten as a first
course. Use 500 g (1 lb) fresh or dried
pasta (uncooked weight) to serve 6
people as a first course and 4 people as
a main dish. If the dish has a rich sauce
or filling it will stretch even further. As
an accompaniment to another dish, this
amount would serve 6–8 people.

Pre-cooked lasagne

The sheets of dried lasagne that are
labelled "pre-cooked" or "no pre-cooking
required" are a great boon to the busy,
time-stretched cook because they can
be taken straight from the packet and
layered with the other ingredients.
However, this lasagne needs to absorb
liquid during cooking, so if you are
using it in a recipe that calls for fresh
pasta or for ordinary dried lasagne,
increase the quantity of sauce and make
it thinner and runnier. Or briefly soak
the sheets in a dish of hot water for
about 5 minutes to moisten and soften
them before layering in the baking dish.

Pasta know-how

To test pasta, lift out a piece and bite it –
it should be tender but still a little firm.
The Italians call this al dente, literally
"to the tooth".

If you are going to use cooked pasta in
a baked dish, undercook it slightly before
mixing it with sauce. This will help
prevent it from being overcooked when
it comes out of the oven.

Cooking pasta

There is one golden rule when cooking
pasta: use plenty of water and salt – at
least 2 litres (3½ pints) water and 2 tsp
salt for every 250 g (8 oz) of pasta.

1 Bring the salted water to a boil. Add the
pasta and stir to separate. If cooking
spaghetti, let the ends soften before stirring.
Return the water to a boil as quickly as possible.
Reduce the heat so that the water is bubbling
briskly and cook, uncovered.

2 When the pasta is al dente (see box, left),
immediately tip it into a large colander, and
shake to drain the pasta thoroughly.

3 Return the pasta to the pan or transfer to a
warmed bowl. Toss with olive oil or butter, add
plenty of ground black pepper and chopped
fresh herbs, if liked, and serve immediately.

Rice varieties

There are many varieties of rice, each with a distinct flavour and aroma. Here are the most common.

Camargue red

Similar to brown rice in texture, flavour, and cooking time.

Basmati

Available in brown or white varieties. Used mainly in Indian dishes. Cook for 10–15 minutes.

Brown

Has a slightly chewy texture with a mild nutty flavour. Cook for 30–35 minutes.

Easy-cook

Part-cooked so the grains stay separate. Cook for 10–12 minutes.

Long grain

Mild in flavour. The most widely used type of white rice. Cook for 12–15 minutes.

Short grain

Italian short grain (eg arborio, carnaroli) is used for risotto; Spanish paella rice is similar but less creamy (the best is said to come from Valencia). Short grain rice is also used for rice pudding. Cook for 20–25 minutes.

Wild

Not a true rice, but an aquatic grass from North America. Cook for 35–40 minutes.

Boiling rice

Long grain rice should be rinsed well before and after boiling, to remove starch that would cause stickiness.

Put the rice into a large bowl of cold water. Swirl it around with your fingertips until the water becomes milky. Drain and repeat until the water stays clear. Drain again. Bring a large pan of salted water to a boil and add the rice.

Bring the water back to a boil. Reduce the heat so that the water is simmering quite vigorously. Cook until the rice is just tender. Drain well and rinse with boiling water to remove any excess starch.

Cooking with rice

The length of the rice grain determines how it should be cooked and used. Short grain rice is almost round in shape and very starchy. It is best cooked by absorption, so that remains moist and sticky, and used for puddings, risottos, paella, stir-fried rice, and croquettes. The grains of long grain rice are separate, dry, and fluffy after cooking so it can be boiled and then used in pilafs, salads, and other savoury dishes.

White rice has been milled to remove the husk, bran, and germ, whereas for brown rice only the tough outer husk has been removed, leaving the nutritious bran layer. Thi gives it its distinctive colour and nutty flavour.

Cooking rice by absorption

Cook the rice very gently in simmering salted water. Use 2 parts water to 1 part rice.

1 Bring the salted water to a boil and add the rice. Return to a boil and stir once. Cover, reduce the heat, and cook gently until the water is absorbed.

2 Remove the pan from the heat and leav to stand, covered, for at least 5 minutes. Fluff up the rice with chopsticks or a fork just before serving.

Cooking risotto rice

An authentic risotto requires constant attention as the hot liquid (usually stock) must stirred into the rice very gradually. This basic technique can be varied in many ways adding shellfish, mushrooms, herbs, ham, and so on.

1 Heat butter or oil in a large saucepan and soften the onion, garlic, or other flavourings as specified in the recipe.

2 Add the rice and stir to coat the grains the fat (this will keep them separate dur cooking). Cook, stirring, for 1–2 minutes or u the rice grains look translucent.

3 Add a ladleful, about 150 ml (¼ pint), of the hot stock. Stir and cook until absorbed. Add another ladleful and cook until absorbed.

4 Continue adding stock, stirring, for 25–3 minutes. When the rice is tender but stil to the bite, you have added enough stock

Pasta alla marinara

SERVES 6   531 CALS PER SERVING

g (1 lb) pasta bows

and black pepper

sp olive oil

rge onion, finely chopped

rge garlic clove, crushed

ml (4 fl oz) dry white wine

g (4 oz) squid, cut into strips or rings

g (2 oz) button mushrooms, sliced

g (4 oz) scallops, halved

g (4 oz) cooked peeled prawns

ml (¼ pint) double cream or full-fat
me fraîche

sp chopped parsley

Cook the pasta bows in a large
saucepan of boiling salted water for
0 minutes until just tender.

Meanwhile, heat the oil in a large pan,
add the onion and garlic, and cook
tly, stirring occasionally, for 3–5 minutes
I softened but not coloured.

Pour in the white wine and boil to reduce
the liquid in the saucepan to about
sp, stirring constantly. Add the squid
cook for 1 minute, then add the
hrooms and scallops, and cook, stirring,
a further 2 minutes. Add the prawns,
m, and half of the parsley, and heat
ugh.

Drain the pasta bows thoroughly, and
add to the seafood mixture, stirring well
ombine. Season with salt and black
per, and serve at once, garnished with
remaining chopped parsley.

Healthy note

food and cream are a classic combination
a pasta sauce, but you may prefer a slightly
rich alternative. In fact, you can omit the
am altogether and use a few tablespoons of
pasta cooking water instead. Italian cooks
n use this technique.

Tagliatelle with prawns

SERVES 4   294 CALS PER SERVING

2 tbsp olive oil

1 large onion, chopped

1 garlic clove, crushed

375 g (12 oz) button mushrooms, halved

500 g (1 lb) tomatoes, chopped into small pieces,
cores removed — tinned?

salt and black pepper

500 g (1 lb) tagliatelle

375 g (12 oz) cooked peeled prawns

125 ml (4 fl oz) full-fat crème fraîche

4 tbsp chopped parsley to garnish

1 Heat the oil in a large pan, add the onion
and garlic, and cook gently, stirring, for
3–5 minutes until softened but not coloured.
Add the mushrooms and cook over a high
heat, stirring, for about 5 minutes.

2 Add the tomatoes, season with salt and
pepper, and simmer gently, uncovered,
for about 20 minutes or until the mixture has
thickened.

3 Meanwhile, cook the tagliatelle in a
large saucepan of boiling salted water
for 8–10 minutes until just tender.

4 Add the prawns and crème fraîche
to the tomato mixture and cook gently
for about 2 minutes until the prawns are
heated through. Taste for seasoning.

5 Drain the tagliatelle thoroughly and pile
on to warmed serving plates. Spoon the
prawn mixture on top, sprinkle with parsley,
and serve at once.

Pasta with smoked salmon and prawns

Substitute 125 g (4 oz) smoked salmon, cut into
bite-sized pieces, for 125 g (4 oz) of the prawns.
Add the smoked salmon after the prawns have
been heated through in step 4.

Spaghetti alle vongole

SERVES 4   626 CALS PER SERVING

about 3 dozen fresh clams in their shells,
cleaned (page 107)

2 tbsp olive oil, plus extra for tossing

1 onion, chopped

1 garlic clove, crushed

¼ tsp chilli powder

1 x 400 g can chopped tomatoes

4 tbsp dry white wine

salt and black pepper

500 g (1 lb) spaghetti

2 tbsp chopped parsley

1 Holding each clam in a tea towel, insert
a thin knife blade between the shells and
twist the knife to open the shells. Reserve
4 clams for garnish. Remove the remaining
clams from their shells, cut them into bite-
sized pieces, and set aside with any juices.

2 Heat the olive oil in a large pan, add the
onion and garlic, and cook gently, stirring
occasionally, for 3–5 minutes until softened
but not coloured. Add the chilli powder and
cook gently, stirring, for 1 minute.

3 Add the tomatoes and wine, season with
salt and pepper, and bring to a boil.
Simmer, uncovered, for about 15 minutes or
until the mixture has thickened.

4 Meanwhile, cook the spaghetti in a large
saucepan of boiling salted water for
8–10 minutes until just tender. Drain, then toss
the spaghetti in a little olive oil to prevent
sticking. Transfer to warmed serving bowls.

5 Add the parsley, and the clams and their
juices to the tomato mixture, and cook for
2 minutes. Do not cook longer or the clams
will toughen.

6 Taste for seasoning, then spoon the
sauce over the spaghetti. Serve at
once, garnished with the reserved clams
in their shells.

Cook's know-how

Live clams should be tightly closed in their
shells. If any are open, give them a sharp tap
on the work surface, then discard any that do
not close.

Pasta shells with scallops

SERVES 4   753 CALS PER SERVING

8 large scallops, each cut into 3 slices

75 ml (2½ fl oz) water

juice of 1 lemon

1 slice of onion

6 black peppercorns

1 small bay leaf

500 g (1 lb) pasta shells

15 g (½ oz) butter

chopped parsley and lemon slices to garnish

SAUCE

45 g (1½ oz) butter

125 g (4 oz) button mushrooms, sliced

30 g (1 oz) plain flour

150 ml (¼ pint) double cream or full-fat crème fraîche

1 tbsp tomato purée

salt and black pepper

1 Put the scallops into a pan with the measured water, half the lemon juice, the onion, peppercorns, and bay leaf.

2 Bring to a gentle simmer, cover, and poach very gently for 2–3 minutes or until the scallops are opaque.

3 Remove the scallops with a slotted spoon, strain the liquid, and reserve.

4 Make the sauce: melt the butter in a saucepan, add the mushrooms, and cook gently, stirring occasionally, for 2 minutes. Sprinkle in the flour and cook, stirring, for 1 minute. Remove from the heat and blend in the strained poaching liquid. Cook, stirring, for 1 minute until thickened.

5 Add the cream and tomato purée and bring to a boil, stirring constantly until the mixture thickens. Simmer for 2 minutes, then add salt and pepper to taste.

6 Cook the pasta shells in a large saucepan of boiling salted water for 8–10 minutes or until tender. Drain, then toss with the butter and the remaining lemon juice. Add the scallops to the sauce, and heat through very gently.

7 Pile the pasta on warmed serving plates, and spoon the sauce on top. Serve at once, garnished with the parsley and lemon slices.

Tagliatelle with vegetable ribbons

SERVES 4   294 CALS PER SERVING

375 g (12 oz) courgettes

250 g (8 oz) carrots, peeled

salt

375 g (12 oz) fresh tagliatelle

scant 1 tbsp olive oil

1 garlic clove, crushed

200 ml (7 fl oz) full-fat crème fraîche

2 tbsp pesto (page 346) or use ready-made

60 g (2 oz) dolcelatte cheese

chopped parsley to garnish

1 Thinly slice the courgettes and carrots into wide, thin ribbons (page 326).

2 Bring a large pan of salted water to a boil, add the tagliatelle, courgettes, and carrots, and cook for 3 minutes. Drain and refresh under cold running water.

3 Heat the oil in a large frying pan, add the garlic, and stir-fry for about 1 minute.

4 Add the crème fraîche and pesto, then crumble in the cheese. Simmer and stir the sauce for 2–3 minutes, then add the tagliatelle and vegetables. Mix gently, turn into a warmed serving dish, and sprinkle with chopped parsley. Serve immediately.

Penne with asparagus

SERVES 6   462 CALS PER SERVING

125 g (4 oz) goat's cheese, cut into small pieces

3 tbsp olive oil

3 garlic cloves, crushed

3 tbsp shredded fresh basil

500 g (1 lb) penne or spaghetti

salt and black pepper

500 g (1 lb) asparagus

1 In a small bowl, combine the goat's cheese, olive oil, garlic, and shredded fresh basil.

2 Cook the pasta in a large saucepan of boiling salted water for 8–10 minutes until just tender.

3 Meanwhile, trim any woody ends from the asparagus and peel the spears if they are not young. Cut the asparagus into bite-sized pieces and cook in boiling salted water for about 3 minutes until just tender.

4 Drain the pasta thoroughly, add the goat's cheese mixture, and toss together. Drain the asparagus and add to the pasta mixture. Toss lightly together, season with salt and black pepper, and serve at once.

Penne with spinach and Stilton

SERVES 4   976 CALS PER SERVING

500 g (1 lb) penne

salt and black pepper

45 g (1½ oz) butter

2 large garlic cloves, crushed

250 g (8 oz) chestnut mushrooms, sliced

300 ml (½ pint) double cream

1 egg, lightly beaten (optional)

90 g (3 oz) spinach leaves, coarsely shredded

90 g (3 oz) blue Stilton cheese, crumbled

juice of ½ lemon

pinch of grated nutmeg

1 Cook the pasta quills in boiling salted water for 8–10 minutes until just tender.

2 Meanwhile, melt the butter in a large pan, add the garlic, and cook, stirring for 1 minute. Add the mushrooms and cook stirring occasionally, for 2 minutes. Stir in cream and boil for 2–3 minutes until the mixture reaches a coating consistency.

3 Drain the pasta, add to the mushroom and cream mixture with the egg (if using), stir well, and heat through. Add the spinach, Stilton cheese, lemon juice, nutmeg, and pepper to taste, and stir well to coat the pasta. Serve at once.

Penne with broccoli and Stilton

Substitute 125 g (4 oz) small broccoli florets for the spinach. Cook in boiling salted water 3–4 minutes or until just tender. Add to the pasta with the cheese, lemon juice, nutmeg and pepper, omitting the egg. Stir well, and serve at once.

Opposite: Penne with spinach and S

Fusilli with double tomatoes

⚫ SERVES 4　　464 CALS PER SERVING

375 g (12 oz) fusilli tricolore

250 g (8 oz) asparagus tips, cut into 5 cm (2 in) lengths

3 tbsp olive oil

2 garlic cloves, crushed

90 g (3 oz) chestnut mushrooms, sliced

500 g (1 lb) ripe cherry tomatoes, halved

60 g (2 oz) sun-blushed or sun-dried tomatoes, each piece snipped into three

salt and black pepper

TO SERVE

30 g (1 oz) pine nuts, toasted

a small handful of fresh basil leaves, shredded

1 Cook the pasta in boiling salted water according to packet instructions until just tender, adding the asparagus 2 minutes before the end of cooking. Drain the pasta and asparagus together and refresh under cold running water. Drain well.

2 Heat the oil in a large frying pan, add the garlic and mushrooms, and fry over a high heat for a couple of minutes. Add both kinds of tomatoes and continue to stir-fry over a high heat until they are just heated through. Season well.

3 Quickly toss the pasta and asparagus through the tomato mixture in the pan until everything is hot, then scatter over the pine nuts and basil. Serve at once.

💙 **Healthy note**

Tomatoes contain beneficial amounts of vitamins C and E. More importantly, they are a rich source of lycopene, a powerful antioxidant that can help to protect the body from harmful free radical damage. Lycopene is most easily absorbed from tomatoes that have been heat processed in some way; a little oil helps absorption, too. Cherry tomatoes are also especially rich in antioxidants. All these ingredients make this recipe a perfect addition to a healthy diet.

Red hot ragù

⚫ SERVES 6　　517 CALS PER SERVING

375 g (12 oz) rigatoni or other tubular pasta

60 g (2 oz) Parmesan cheese, coarsely grated

3 tbsp chopped parsley, or 175 g (6 oz) young spinach leaves, shredded

SAUCE

500 g (1 lb) good-quality pork sausages with herbs

a little olive oil

3 garlic cloves, crushed

2 small red chillies, halved, cored, and finely chopped

2 x 400 g cans chopped tomatoes

1 large onion, finely chopped

1 good tbsp sun-dried tomato purée

1 tbsp chopped fresh basil

½–1 tsp caster or granulated sugar, to taste

salt and black pepper

1 Make the sauce. Cut long slits in each sausage and remove the skins. Heat a little oil in a non-stick frying pan and add the garlic and sausagemeat. Fry over a medium heat for about 4–5 minutes, breaking the meat up with a wooden spatula until it is brown, with a minced pork consistency. Stir in the remaining sauce ingredients. Bring to a boil, cover, and simmer gently for 40–50 minutes or until the sausagemeat is cooked. Check the seasoning.

2 Meanwhile, cook the pasta in boiling salted water according to packet instructions until just tender.

3 Drain the pasta and mix it into the sauce in the pan with half the Parmesan, then check the seasoning again. Scatter the parsley and remaining Parmesan over individual servings.

Note: If using spinach, stir it into the bubbling sauce and cook for a couple of minutes until it wilts before adding the pasta and half the Parmesan.

Rigatoni with mushrooms and rocket

⚫ SERVES 6　　355 CALS PER SERVING

375 g (12 oz) rigatoni or other tubular pasta

150 ml (5 fl oz) dry white wine

1 small onion, finely chopped

500 g (1 lb) mixed wild or cultivated mushrooms, such as shiitake, oyster, ceps, coarsely sliced

salt and black pepper

6 tbsp double cream

4 tbsp good-quality pesto (ready-made or see page 346)

60 g (2 oz) rocket leaves

coarsely grated Parmesan cheese, to serve

1 Cook the pasta in boiling salted water according to packet instructions until just tender.

2 Meanwhile, pour the wine into a large frying pan, add the onion and cook over a low heat until the onion has softened, about 10–15 minutes. Add the mushrooms and stir over a high heat for a few minutes until the mushrooms are cooked and the liquid has reduced (there should be about 2 tablespoons left). Sea with salt and pepper, add the cream, an pesto, and stir to mix.

3 Drain the pasta and add to the mushroom mixture in the pan. Check the seasoning. At the last moment, stir in rocket leaves, and allow to wilt for abou 2 minutes. Serve immediately, scattered with Parmesan.

Note: The warm, peppery, pungent taste of rocket is one people love or hate. If you love it and you're making your own pesto for this dis try substituting rocket for basil in the pesto re on page 346.

Opposite, clockwise from top left: Red hot Rigatoni with mushrooms and r Fusilli with double tom

Spaghetti all'Amatriciana

A speciality of Amatrice, near Rome, this tomato-based sauce is spiked with chilli and garlic, and richly flavoured with diced bacon and roast peppers.

 SERVES 6   431 CALS PER SERVING

1 red pepper

1 green pepper

4 tbsp olive oil

5 unsmoked bacon or pancetta rashers, any rinds removed, diced

½–1 fresh green chilli, halved, seeded, and thinly sliced

3 garlic cloves, crushed

2 ripe tomatoes, finely chopped

2 tbsp chopped flat-leaf parsley

salt and black pepper

500 g (1 lb) spaghetti

shavings of Parmesan cheese to serve

1 Halve the red and green peppers, and remove the cores and seeds. Roast and peel the peppers (page 345). Cut the flesh into thin strips.

2 Heat the oil in a frying pan, add the bacon, and cook over a high heat for 5 minutes or until crisp. Add the roasted pepper strips and the chilli, and cook for 2 minutes. Stir in the garlic and cook for about 1 minute.

3 Add the tomatoes and parsley and cook for 3 minutes or until thickened. Remove from the heat and season with salt and pepper.

4 Cook the spaghetti in a large saucepan of boiling salted water for 8–10 minutes until just tender.

5 Drain the spaghetti thoroughly. Add the sauce and toss with the spaghetti. Serve at once, topped with Parmesan cheese shavings.

Spaghetti all'arrabbiata

Melt 30 g (1 oz) butter with 2 tbsp olive oil in a frying pan, add 3 crushed garlic cloves and ½–1 tsp crushed dried red chillies (chilli flakes), and cook gently. Drain 1 x 400 g can chopped tomatoes, stir the tomatoes into the pan, and bring slowly to a boil. Simmer until reduced and thickened, add ¼ tsp fresh oregano, and season with salt and black pepper. Toss with the spaghetti, and serve at once.

Stir-fried Chinese noodles

 SERVES 4   476 CALS PER SERVING

5 dried shiitake mushrooms

250 ml (8 fl oz) hot vegetable stock

375 g (12 oz) Chinese egg noodles

salt

about 2 tsp soy sauce

1 tbsp sunflower oil

250 g (8 oz) mangetout

3 garlic cloves, crushed

5 mm (¼ in) piece of fresh root ginger, peeled and grated

¼ tsp sugar (optional)

125 g (4 oz) bean sprouts

about ½ tsp crushed dried red chillies (chilli flakes)

TO SERVE

3 spring onions, sliced

2 tsp sesame oil

1 tbsp chopped fresh coriander

1 Put the mushrooms into a bowl, pour over the hot vegetable stock, and leave to soak for about 30 minutes.

2 Drain the mushrooms, reserving the liquid. Squeeze the mushrooms dry, then cut into thin strips.

3 Cook the noodles in a large saucepan of boiling salted water for 3 minutes or according to packet instructions. Drain the noodles, toss with soy sauce to taste, and set aside.

4 Heat the sunflower oil in a wok or large frying pan, add the mushrooms, mangetout, garlic, and ginger, and stir-fry for 2 minutes. Add the sugar, if using, bean sprouts, crushed chillies to taste, and 3 tbsp of the reserved mushroom soaking liquid. Stir-fry for 2 minutes.

5 Add the egg noodles and stir-fry for 2 minutes or until heated through. Serve at once, sprinkled with the spring onions, sesame oil, and coriander.

Tortellini with peas and bacon

 SERVES 6   643 CALS PER SERVING

500 g (1 lb) tortellini

salt and black pepper

1 tbsp sunflower oil

250 g (8 oz) bacon or pancetta rashers, any rinds removed, diced

175 g (6 oz) frozen petits pois

300 ml (½ pint) double cream

grated Parmesan cheese to serve

1 Cook the tortellini in boiling salted water for about 10–12 minutes, or according to packet instructions, until tender.

2 Meanwhile, heat the oil in a frying pan, add the bacon, and cook over a high heat, stirring, for 3 minutes or until crisp.

3 Cook the petits pois in boiling salted water for about 2 minutes until just tender. Drain.

4 Drain the tortellini thoroughly and return to the saucepan. Add the bacon, petits pois, and cream, and season with salt and pepper. Heat gently for 1–2 minutes to warm through. Serve at once, sprinkled with grated Parmesan cheese.

♡ Healthy note

Use just 150 ml (¼ pint) low-fat crème fraîche instead of the double cream. Then do what the Italians do - splash a few ladlefuls of the pasta water into the sauce and stir vigorously to make enough sauce to coat the pasta.

ettuccine rimavera

SERVES 6   554 CALS PER SERVING

g (4 oz) asparagus, trimmed and cut into
 sized pieces

g (4 oz) broccoli florets

urgette, sliced

nd black pepper

p olive oil

d and ½ yellow pepper, halved, seeded,
 diced

lic cloves, crushed

00 g can chopped tomatoes

(3 oz) frozen petits pois

l (4 fl oz) double cream

 (1 lb) fettuccine

 shredded fresh basil

(3 oz) Parmesan cheese, grated, to serve

1 Cook the asparagus, broccoli, and
courgette in boiling salted water for
3 minutes or until just tender. Drain, rinse
under cold running water, and set aside.

2 Heat the oil in a large, deep frying
pan, add the peppers and garlic,
and cook, stirring, for 4 minutes or until
the peppers are softened.

3 Add the tomatoes and the petits pois,
and cook for 5 minutes or until the liquid
in the pan is reduced by half.

4 Add the asparagus, broccoli,
and courgette, stir in the cream, and
boil for 1–2 minutes to reduce the liquid
and concentrate the flavour. Add salt and
pepper to taste, and remove from the heat.

5 Cook the fettuccine in a large saucepan
of boiling salted water for 8–10 minutes
until just tender.

6 Drain the fettuccine thoroughly, add
to the sauce, and toss over a high heat.
Stir in the shredded basil and serve at
once, sprinkled with Parmesan cheese.

🍂 Healthy note

For a lighter, less creamy version of this
classic dish use 1 x 400 g can chopped
tomatoes and omit the cream. Instead of
sprinkling with Parmesan to serve, sprinkle
with more shredded fresh basil.

Spaghetti bolognese

SERVES 4   **904 CALS PER SERVING**

3 tbsp olive oil

500 g (1 lb) minced beef

1 large onion, finely chopped

2 celery stalks, sliced

1 tbsp plain flour

2 garlic cloves, crushed

90 g (3 oz) tomato purée

150 ml (¼ pint) beef stock

150 ml (¼ pint) red wine

1 x 400 g can chopped tomatoes

1 tbsp redcurrant jelly

salt and black pepper

500 g (1 lb) spaghetti

grated Parmesan cheese to serve

1 Heat 2 tbsp of the oil in a saucepan. A the minced beef, onion, and celery, a cook, stirring, for 5 minutes or until the bee is browned. Add the flour, garlic, and tomato purée, and cook, stirring, for abou 1 minute.

2 Pour in the stock and wine. Add the tomatoes and redcurrant jelly, season with salt and pepper, and bring to a boil. Cook, stirring, until the mixture has thicken

3 Lower the heat, partially cover the po and simmer very gently, stirring occasionally, for about 1 hour.

4 Meanwhile, cook the spaghetti in boi salted water for 8–10 minutes until jus tender. Drain thoroughly.

5 Return the spaghetti to the saucepar add the remaining oil, and toss gentl to coat.

6 Divide the spaghetti among warmec serving plates and ladle some of the sauce on top of each serving. Sprinkle v a little Parmesan cheese and hand arou the remainder separately.

Tuna and fennel pasta bake

SERVES 6   **512 CALS PER SERVING**

250 g (8 oz) pasta shells (conchiglie)

salt and black pepper

1 tbsp sunflower oil

1 fennel bulb, trimmed and finely sliced

1 onion, finely sliced

60 g (2 oz) butter

60 g (2 oz) plain flour

600 ml (1 pint) milk

1 x 200 g can tuna in brine, drained and flaked

3 hard-boiled eggs, coarsely chopped

125 g (4 oz) mature Cheddar cheese, grated

2 tbsp chopped parsley to garnish

1 Cook the pasta shells in boiling salted water for 8–10 minutes until just tender. Drain thoroughly and set aside.

2 Heat the sunflower oil in a large frying pan, add the fennel and onion, and cook for 3–5 minutes until softened but not coloured. Set aside.

3 Melt the butter in a large saucepan, sprinkle in the flour, and cook, stirring, for 1 minute. Remove from the heat and gradually blend in the milk. Bring to a boil, stirring until the mixture thickens. Simmer for 2–3 minutes.

4 Stir in the pasta, the fennel and onion, tuna, eggs, and cheese. Season with salt and pepper, then turn the mixture into a shallow ovenproof dish.

5 Bake in a preheated oven at 200°C (180°C fan, Gas 6) for about 30 minutes or until heated through and golden brown on top. Serve hot, sprinkled with chopped parsley.

♡ Healthy note

To reduce fat, boil the fennel and onion with the pasta, make half the quantity of sauce in step 3, and make up the volume with pasta cooking water. You could also omit the eggs and halve the amount of cheese.

Spaghetti alla carbonara

🍴 SERVES 4   906 CALS PER SERVING

0 g (1 lb) spaghetti

lt and black pepper

5 g (6 oz) diced pancetta or streaky bacon, y rinds removed

arlic clove, crushed

ggs

5 g (4 oz) Parmesan cheese, grated

ml (¼ pint) single cream

opped parsley to garnish

Cook the spaghetti in a large saucepan of boiling salted water for 8–10 minutes il just tender.

Meanwhile, put the pancetta or bacon into a frying pan and heat gently for inutes until the fat runs. Increase the at and add the garlic. Cook for 2–3 utes or until the bacon is crisp.

Break the eggs into a bowl. Add the bacon and garlic mixture, using a ted spoon. Add the Parmesan cheese, ison generously with salt and pepper, d whisk until well blended.

Drain the spaghetti and return to the hot pan. Stir in the bacon and egg mixture d toss quickly until the egg just begins to Stir in the cream and heat gently. Serve nce, sprinkled with parsley.

ghetti alfredo

150 ml (¼ pint) double cream with 30 g) butter until the mixture has thickened. Set e. Cook the pasta, drain, then add to the m mixture. Add 90 ml (3 fl oz) more cream, (3 oz) Parmesan cheese, a pinch of grated eg, and season with salt and pepper. Heat ly until thickened, and serve.

Cook's know-how

s best to buy a whole piece of Parmesan ese and grate the quantity you need for a en dish. Ready grated Parmesan in packets ss economical and lacks the flavour of shly grated Parmesan.

Pasta spirals with herby meatballs

🍴 SERVES 8   384 CALS PER SERVING

500 g (1 lb) pasta spirals (fusilli)

shredded fresh basil to garnish

TOMATO–BASIL SAUCE

1 tbsp olive oil

1 onion, coarsely chopped

2 garlic cloves, crushed

2 x 400 g cans chopped tomatoes

1 tsp caster sugar

salt and black pepper

1 tbsp chopped fresh basil

MEATBALLS

500 g (1 lb) minced turkey or chicken

2 tbsp chopped parsley

1 tsp chopped fresh thyme

60 g (2 oz) Parmesan cheese, grated

60 g (2 oz) fresh breadcrumbs

1 egg, beaten

a little olive oil, for frying

1 Make the tomato basil sauce: heat the oil in a deep frying pan, add the onion and garlic, and cook gently, stirring occasionally, for 3–4 minutes.

2 Add the tomatoes and sugar, season with salt and pepper, and stir well. Simmer, uncovered, for about 20 minutes, stirring occasionally, until the onion is soft and the sauce reduced.

3 Make the meatballs: in a large bowl, combine the minced turkey or chicken, parsley, thyme, Parmesan cheese, breadcrumbs, and egg, then season with salt and pepper. With dampened hands, shape the mixture into balls about the size of large walnuts.

4 Heat a little oil in a large frying pan, add the meatballs, and cook for about 8 minutes until browned and cooked through. Lift out with a slotted spoon and drain on paper towels. Add to the tomato sauce and heat gently for about 5 minutes.

5 Meanwhile, cook the pasta in a large pan of boiling salted water for 8–10 minutes until tender. Drain thoroughly, and top with the meatballs and sauce. Serve at once, garnished with shredded basil.

Filling and cooking the ravioli

1 Place 18 spoonfuls of filling at regular intervals on to one half of the pasta. Lightly brush the pasta between the filling with water.

2 Roll the remaining pasta around a rolling pin and unroll over the filling. Press the pasta around the edges and the spoonfuls of filling.

3 With a knife, pastry wheel, or pastry cutter, cut into round or square ravioli. Leave for about 30 minutes, turning once, until dried out.

4 Add a little oil to a large saucepan of boiling salted water, add the ravioli, and cook for 4–5 minutes until just tender. Drain and serve immediately.

Basic pasta dough

300 g (10 oz) "00" flour or strong plain white flour

3 eggs

1 tsp salt

1 tbsp olive oil

1 Sift the flour into a mound on a work surface. Make a well in the middle of the flour and add the eggs, salt, and oil. Using your fingertips, gradually draw the flour into the egg mixture until a sticky ball of dough is formed.

2 Knead the dough on a floured work surface for 10 minutes or until the pasta dough is smooth and no longer sticks to the work surface.

3 Shape the dough into a ball, put into an oiled plastic bag, and leave to rest at room temperature for about 30 minutes.

4 Roll out the dough very thinly on a lightly floured work surface into a 37 cm (15 in) square. Leave the pasta uncovered for about 20 minutes to dry out slightly. Cut the pasta in half, and use it to make one of the ravioli recipes on this page.

Chicken and prosciutto ravioli

SERVES 3   464 CALS PER SERVING

15 g (½ oz) butter

90 g (3 oz) cooked chicken, minced

75 g (2½ oz) prosciutto, finely chopped

1 tbsp fresh white breadcrumbs

1 tbsp chopped fresh flat-leaf parsley

2 tsp each water and tomato purée

salt and black pepper

1 quantity Basic Pasta Dough (see above)

1 egg

TO SERVE

tomato basil sauce (page 305)

basil sprigs

1 Make the filling. Melt the butter in a sauce-pan. Add the chicken and fry for 5 minutes. Stir in the remaining ingredients.

2 Fill, cook and drain the ravioli (see box, left). Toss in the tomato basil sauce, and serve at once, garnished with basil sprigs.

Ricotta and spinach ravioli

SERVES 3   341 CALS PER SERVING

125 g (4 oz) ricotta cheese

60 g (2 oz) Parmesan cheese, grated

1 egg, beaten

¼ tsp grated nutmeg

250 g (8 oz) spinach leaves, cooked, squeezed d and chopped

salt and black pepper

1 quantity Basic Pasta Dough (see left)

30 g (1 oz) butter to serve

1 Make the filling. Beat together the ricot half of the Parmesan, the egg, nutmeg and spinach. Season with salt and peppe

2 Fill, cook and drain the ravioli (see bo left). Serve with butter, the remaining Parmesan, and black pepper.

Crab and prawn ravioli

SERVES 3   322 CALS PER SERVING

90 g (3 oz) cooked white crabmeat, flaked

90 g (3 oz) cooked peeled prawns, chopped

60 g (2 oz) full-fat soft cheese

1 spring onion, very finely chopped

salt and black pepper

1 quantity Basic Pasta Dough (see left)

coriander pesto (page 116) to serve

1 Make the filling. Combine the crabme and prawns with the cheese and spri onion, and season with salt and pepper.

2 Fill, cook and drain the ravioli (see b left). Toss with the coriander pesto a serve at once.

Opposite, clockwise from top left: Chicke prosciutto ravioli with tomato basil sauce, R and spinach ravioli with grated Parmesan and prawn ravioli with coriander

Three-cheese macaroni

SERVES 8   **436 CALS PER SERVING**

375 g (12 oz) short-cut macaroni

salt and black pepper

45 g (1½ oz) butter, plus extra for greasing

45 g (1½ oz) plain flour

900 ml (1½ pints) milk

2 tsp Dijon mustard

175 g (6 oz) smoked Cheddar cheese, grated

60 g (2 oz) light mozzarella cheese, grated

90 g (3 oz) mature Cheddar cheese, grated

60 g (2 oz) fresh white breadcrumbs

1 Cook the macaroni in boiling salted water for 8–10 minutes until just tender. Drain and set aside.

2 Melt the butter in a large saucepan. Add the flour and cook, stirring, for 1 minute. Remove the pan from the heat and gradually blend in the milk. Bring to a boil, stirring constantly until the mixture thickens. Simmer for about 5 minutes, stirring.

3 Stir in the mustard, smoked Cheddar and mozzarella cheeses, 60 g (2 oz) of the mature Cheddar cheese, and the cooked macaroni. Season with salt and pepper.

4 Lightly butter a large shallow ovenproof dish and spoon in the macaroni mixture. Sprinkle with the breadcrumbs and the remaining Cheddar cheese and bake in a preheated oven at 200°C (180°C fan, Gas 6) for about 15–20 minutes until golden and bubbling.

Cheese and leek macaroni

Omit the mozzarella cheese. Melt 30 g (1 oz) butter in a saucepan, add 2–3 trimmed and finely sliced leeks, and cook gently for 3–5 minutes until softened. Add the leeks to the sauce with the two Cheddar cheeses and cooked and drained macaroni.

Fusilli alla napoletana

SERVES 4   **713 CALS PER SERVING**

250 g (8 oz) pasta spirals (fusilli)

salt and black pepper

250 g (8 oz) broccoli

15 g (½ oz) butter

1 tbsp olive oil

1 large onion, chopped

2 large garlic cloves, crushed

150 g (5 oz) shiitake mushrooms, coarsely chopped

1 red pepper, halved, seeded, and sliced

250 g (8 oz) courgettes, sliced

75 g (3 oz) Cheddar cheese, grated

SAUCE

60 g (2 oz) butter

60 g (2 oz) plain flour

600 ml (1 pint) milk

1 tsp Dijon mustard

1 Cook the pasta in a large pan of boiling salted water for 8–10 minutes until just tender. Drain thoroughly.

2 Cook the broccoli stalks in boiling salted water for 3 minutes, then add the florets, and cook for 2 minutes longer. Drain and rinse in cold water.

3 Melt the butter with the oil in a large frying pan. Add the onion and garlic and cook gently, stirring occasionally, for 3–5 minutes, until softened.

4 Add the mushrooms, red pepper, and courgette slices, and cook, stirring occasionally, for 3 minutes. Remove from the heat and stir in the broccoli.

5 Make the sauce: melt the butter in a large saucepan, sprinkle in the flour and cook, stirring, for 1 minute. Remove from the heat and gradually blend in the milk. Bring to a boil, stirring constantly until thickened. Simmer for 2–3 minutes. Add the mustard, and season with salt and pepper.

6 Remove the sauce from the heat, add the vegetables and pasta, and stir well to coat.

7 Divide the mixture among 4 individual gratin dishes, sprinkle with the Cheddar cheese, and bake in a preheated oven at 200°C (180°C fan, Gas 6) for 20–25 minutes until golden. Serve hot.

♡ Healthy note

For a lighter, and quicker, version of this baked pasta dish, make it without the sauce in step 5 and simply toss the hot vegetables with the freshly cooked pasta, moistening with a few spoonfuls of the pasta cooking water or 1–2 tbsp olive oil if you prefer. Serve at once.

Smoked haddock lasagne

🍴 SERVES 8   473 CALS PER SERVING

fresh lasagne sheets

knob of butter

[2]0 g (8 oz) button mushrooms, sliced

[7]0 g (1½ lb) undyed smoked haddock fillets, [ski]nned and cut into large pieces

[5]0 g (2 oz) mature Cheddar cheese, grated

[SA]UCE

[9]0 g (3 oz) butter

[la]rge onion, chopped

[9]0 g (3 oz) plain flour

[600] ml (1 pint) milk

[1 x] 200 g carton crème fraîche

[5]0 g (2 oz) mature Cheddar cheese, grated

[1 t]sp Dijon mustard

[2]0 g (¾ oz) fresh dill, finely chopped

[juic]e of ½ lemon

[salt] and black pepper

[1.75 l]itre (3 pint) ovenproof dish, about
[15 x]25 x 5 cm (6 x 10 x 2 in)

[Im]merse the sheets of lasagne in a dish
[of] hot water, and leave to stand until
[read]y to use. This will soften them before
[cook]ing, and ensure they cook properly
[whe]n layered with the fish and sauce.

[Ma]ke the sauce: melt the butter in
[a] large saucepan, add the onion, and
[cook]over a high heat for 1 minute. Turn the
[hea]t down to low, cover the pan, and
[coo]k for about 10 minutes until the onion
[has]softened. Remove the lid, increase the
[hea]t to medium, and sprinkle in the flour.
[Coo]k, stirring, for 1 minute, then remove
[from] the heat, and gradually blend in the
[milk] followed by the crème fraîche. Bring
[to a]boil, stirring constantly until thickened.
[Simm]er for 2–3 minutes, remove from the
[heat], and stir in the cheese. Add the
[must]ard, dill, and lemon juice, season with
[salt a]nd pepper, and stir until combined.
[Set a]side.

[M]elt the knob of butter in a frying pan,
[a]nd fry the mushrooms over a medium
[heat]for a few minutes until tender. Increase
[the h]eat to high, and continue frying for
[2 m]inutes to drive off any liquid, stirring
[cons]tantly. Tip the mushrooms into the
[sauc]e, and stir well to combine.

4 Scatter one-third of the haddock pieces over the bottom of the ovenproof dish, and pour over one-third of the sauce. Drain the lasagne sheets, and dry with paper towels. Arrange 3 sheets of lasagne over the sauce, without overlapping the edges (you may have to trim the pasta to fit neatly). Repeat the layers, then top with the remaining haddock and sauce, and cover with the cheese.

5 Bake in a preheated oven at 200°C (180°C fan, Gas 6) for 25–30 minutes until bubbling, cooked through, and golden on top. Leave to stand for about 5 minutes before serving.

Cannelloni with ricotta and spinach

🍴 SERVES 6   462 CALS PER SERVING

butter for greasing

18 cannelloni tubes

30 g (1 oz) Parmesan cheese, grated

TOMATO SAUCE

1 tbsp olive oil

2 celery stalks, chopped

1 small onion, chopped

1 carrot, chopped

1 garlic clove, crushed

300 ml (½ pint) chicken or vegetable stock

2 x 400 g cans chopped tomatoes

2 tbsp tomato purée

salt and black pepper

60 g (2 oz) sun-dried tomatoes in oil, drained and chopped

FILLING

2 tbsp olive oil

1 small onion, chopped

1 garlic clove, crushed

500 g (1 lb) spinach leaves, chopped

500 g (1 lb) ricotta cheese

¼ tsp grated nutmeg

1 Make the tomato sauce: heat the oil in a saucepan, add the celery, onion, carrot, and garlic, and cook gently for 3–5 minutes until softened. Stir in the stock, tomatoes, and tomato purée, season with salt and pepper, and bring to a boil. Cover and simmer, stirring occasionally, for 30 minutes.

2 Meanwhile, make the filling: heat the oil in a large pan, add the onion and garlic, and cook for 3–5 minutes until softened. Add the spinach and cook over a high heat for 1–2 minutes. Cool slightly, add the ricotta and nutmeg, and season with salt and pepper.

3 Purée the tomato sauce in a food processor, then stir in the chopped sun-dried tomatoes.

4 Grease an ovenproof dish. Spoon the spinach filling into the cannelloni. Arrange in the dish, cover with the sauce, and sprinkle with Parmesan. Bake in a preheated oven at 200°C (180°C fan, Gas 6) for 30 minutes. Serve hot.

Below: Cannelloni with ricotta and spinach.

Caribbean rice and peas

SERVES 4–6   435–290 CALS PER SERVING

2 tbsp olive oil

8 spring onions, sliced

3 smoked bacon rashers, rinds removed, diced

2 garlic cloves, crushed

250 g (8 oz) long grain rice

1 x 200 g can tomatoes

3 tbsp chopped parsley

2 bay leaves

1 small green chilli, halved, seeded, and thinly sliced

½ tsp turmeric

½ tsp cumin seeds

1 tsp fresh thyme leaves

1 x 400 g can red kidney beans or black-eyed beans, drained and rinsed

375 ml (13 fl oz) chicken stock

1 lime, cut into wedges, to serve

1 Heat the oil in a pan, add the spring onions and bacon, and cook for about 5 minutes or until the bacon is crisp. Add the garlic and cook for 2 minutes.

2 Add the rice and stir to coat the grains in the oil. Add the tomatoes with their juice, 2 tbsp of the parsley, the bay leaves, chilli, turmeric, cumin, and thyme, and cook for 2 minutes.

3 Add the beans and stock and bring to a boil. Cover and cook over a low heat for 15 minutes until the rice is tender and the liquid has been absorbed.

4 Sprinkle with remaining parsley, and serve at once, with lime wedges.

Cook's know-how

Don't be misled by the name of this dish – there are no peas in it, but this is not a mistake. In the Caribbean the dish is traditionally made with small round beans, which are known as pigeon peas, hence the name of the dish. Red kidney beans make a good substitute when pigeon peas are not available.

Savoury rice

SERVES 4   356 CALS PER SERVING

2 tbsp olive oil

1 onion, chopped

1 carrot, diced

200 g (7 oz) long grain rice

250 g (8 oz) tomatoes, finely chopped

500 ml (16 fl oz) hot chicken or vegetable stock

150 g (5 oz) sweetcorn kernels

90 g (3 oz) frozen peas

2 tbsp tomato purée

salt and black pepper

1 garlic clove, crushed

chopped parsley to garnish

1 Heat the oil in a frying pan, add the onion and carrot, and cook gently, stirring, for 3–5 minutes until the onion is softened but not coloured.

2 Add the rice, and stir to coat the grains in the oil. Add the tomatoes and stock.

3 Add the sweetcorn, peas, and tomato purée, and bring to a boil. Simmer, stirring occasionally, for 12–15 minutes or until the rice is tender and the liquid has been absorbed.

4 Add salt and pepper to taste, and stir in the garlic. Serve at once, sprinkled with parsley.

Classic lasagne

SERVES 8   641 CALS PER SERVING

125 g (4 oz) mature Cheddar cheese, grated

30 g (1 oz) Parmesan cheese, grated

175 g (6 oz) pre-cooked lasagne sheets

chopped parsley to garnish

MEAT SAUCE

2 tbsp olive oil

1 kg (2 lb) minced beef

45 g (1½ oz) plain flour

300 ml (½ pint) beef stock

1 x 400 g can chopped tomatoes

6 celery stalks, sliced

2 onions, chopped

2 large garlic cloves, crushed

4 tbsp tomato purée

1 tsp sugar

salt and black pepper

WHITE SAUCE

60 g (2 oz) butter

45 g (1½ oz) plain flour

600 ml (1 pint) milk

1 tsp Dijon mustard

¼ tsp grated nutmeg

1 Make the meat sauce: heat the oil in a saucepan, add the beef, and cook, stirring, until browned.

2 Sprinkle in the flour and stir for 1 minute then add the stock, tomatoes, celery, onions, garlic, tomato purée, and sugar. Season with salt and pepper and bring to a boil. Cover and simmer for 1 hour.

3 Meanwhile, make the white sauce: me the butter in a saucepan, sprinkle in th flour and cook, stirring, for 1 minute. Remo from the heat and gradually blend in the milk. Bring to a boil, stirring until the mixtur thickens. Simmer for 2–3 minutes. Stir in th mustard and nutmeg, and season with so and pepper.

4 Spoon one-third of the meat sauce in a large shallow ovenproof dish, cover with one-third of the white sauce, and one-third of the Cheddar and Parmesan cheeses. Arrange half of the lasagne in a single layer. Repeat the layers, finishing with the Cheddar and Parmesan cheese

5 Bake in a preheated oven at 190°C (170°C fan, Gas 5) for 45–60 minutes until the pasta is tender and the topping a golden brown colour. Serve at once, sprinkled with parsley.

Opposite: Classic las

Singapore noodles

SERVES 6   324 CALS PER SERVING

250 g (8 oz) rice noodles

2 tbsp sunflower oil

375 g (12 oz) pork fillet or tenderloin, cut into thin strips

1 tsp crushed dried red chillies (chilli flakes)

90 g (3 oz) shiitake mushrooms, sliced

200 g (7 oz) pak choi, coarsely chopped, keeping white and green parts separate

2 tbsp mild curry powder

2 tbsp soy sauce

2 tbsp oyster sauce

juice of ½ lime

4 tbsp coconut cream

chopped fresh coriander to garnish

1 Cook the noodles according to packet instructions. Drain, refresh under cold running water, and set aside.

2 Heat 1 tbsp oil in a large wok or non-stick frying pan and stir-fry the pork over a high heat for about 2 minutes until brown and cooked through. Remove from the pan with a slotted spoon and set aside.

3 Heat the remaining oil in the pan. Add the chilli flakes, mushrooms, and the white parts of the pak choi, and stir-fry for 1–2 minutes. Add the curry powder, soy sauce, oyster sauce, lime juice, and coconut cream, and stir-fry for a further few minutes.

4 Add the green parts of the pak choi, then return the pork and add noodles to the pan. Stir-fry for a few minutes until piping hot, then scatter over the coriander.

Pak choi brings a crunchy, mildly sweet flavour to noodle dishes. Choose fresh ones that have bright, green leaves and stalks that snap easily.

Szechuan noodles with water chestnuts

SERVES 6   367 CALS PER SERVING

375 g (12 oz) medium egg noodles

1 tbsp olive oil

250 g (8 oz) minced pork

2.5 cm (1 in) piece of fresh root ginger, peeled and finely grated

2 garlic cloves, crushed

2 spring onions, trimmed and sliced on the diagonal, keeping white and green parts separate

1 red pepper, halved, seeded, and finely sliced

3 tbsp soy sauce, or more, to taste

3 tbsp black bean sauce

2 tsp caster or granulated sugar

90 g (3 oz) bean sprouts

1 x 220 g can water chestnuts, drained and halved

salt and black pepper

1 Cook the noodles according to packet instructions. Drain, refresh under cold running water, and set aside.

2 Heat the oil in a wok or large non-stick frying pan and stir-fry the pork for about 2 minutes until brown. Add the ginger, garlic, white parts of the spring onions, and the red pepper, and stir-fry for a few minutes more.

3 Stir in the 3 tbsp soy sauce, the black bean sauce, sugar, and 5 tbsp water, and boil for few minutes. Add the bean sprouts and water chestnuts, and the noodles to the pan, then toss over a high heat for about 2 minutes until everything is hot. Check the seasoning, and add more soy sauce if you like. Serve immediately, with the green spring onions scattered on top.

Pad Thai with tiger prawns

SERVES 6   245 CALS PER SERVING

250 g (8 oz) thick rice noodles

2 tbsp olive oil

2 skinless, boneless chicken breasts (about 125 g/4 oz each), cut into thin strips

1 small fresh red chilli, halved, seeded, and finely chopped

2.5 cm (1 in) piece of fresh root ginger, peeled and finely grated

2.5 cm (1 in) piece of fresh lemongrass from the lower part of the stalk, very finely chopped

125 g (4 oz) peeled raw tiger prawns

90 g (3 oz) oyster mushrooms, thinly sliced

125 g (4 oz) sugarsnap peas, trimmed and sliced on the diagonal

3 tbsp soy sauce

2 tbsp lime juice

1 tbsp fish sauce

salt and black pepper

TO SERVE

30 g (1 oz) salted or unsalted peanuts, coarsely chopped

a handful of fresh coriander, chopped

1 Cook the noodles according to packet instructions. Drain, refresh under cold running water, and set aside.

2 Heat 1 tbsp of the oil in a wok or large non-stick frying pan, and stir-fry the chicken over a high heat for 2 minutes or until golden brown and cooked through. Remove with a slotted spoon and set aside.

3 Heat the remaining oil in the pan, add the chilli, ginger, lemongrass, prawns, mushrooms, and peas and stir-fry for 1 minute. Add the soy sauce, lime juice, and fish sauce and season with salt and pepper. Return the chicken to the pan, add the noodles. Stir-fry until the prawns pink and everything is piping hot, for 2– minutes. Serve hot, with peanuts and coriander scattered on top.

Opposite, clockwise from top right: Sing noodles, Pad Thai with tiger pr Szechuan noodles with water che

Portuguese rice with tuna

🍴 SERVES 4   603 CALS PER SERVING

3 streaky bacon rashers, rinds removed, cut into strips

3 tbsp olive oil

1 small onion, thinly sliced

250 g (8 oz) long grain brown rice

600 ml (1 pint) hot chicken stock

salt and black pepper

375 g (12 oz) fresh tuna, cut into chunks

1 x 400 g can pimientos, drained and cut into strips

16 black olives

dill sprigs and lemon slices to garnish

1 Put the bacon into a large, heavy saucepan and heat until it begins to sizzle. Add the olive oil, and onion, and c[ook] gently, stirring occasionally, for 3–5 minut[e] until soft but not coloured. Add the rice [and] stir to coat the grains in the oil.

2 Pour the stock into the pan, season with salt and pepper, and bring to a boil. Cover and simmer for 25–30 minu[tes.]

3 Add the tuna, pimientos, and olives, and cook for 5 minutes or until all the liquid has been absorbed and the rice [and] tuna are tender. Season, garnish with dil[l] sprigs and lemon slices, and serve at on[ce.]

Portuguese rice with canned tuna

Substitute 2 x 200 g cans tuna in brine for th[e] fresh tuna. Drain the tuna well, and flake it roughly with a fork.

Risi e bisi

🍴 SERVES 6   390 CALS PER SERVING

60 g (2 oz) butter

1 onion, finely chopped

60 g (2 oz) Parma ham, diced, or 90 g (3 oz) unsmoked lean bacon rashers, rinds removed, diced

2 garlic cloves, crushed

300 g (10 oz) risotto rice

300 g (10 oz) frozen peas

salt and black pepper

1 litre (1¾ pints) hot chicken or vegetable stock

60 g (2 oz) Parmesan cheese, grated, and 2 tbsp chopped parsley to garnish

1 Melt the butter in a large pan. When it is foaming, add the onion, Parma ham, and garlic, and cook gently, stirring occasionally, for 3–5 minutes until the onion is soft but not coloured.

2 Add the rice and stir to coat in the butter. Add the frozen peas and seasoning.

3 Pour in half of the stock and cook, stirring constantly, over a low heat until it is absorbed. Add a little more stock and cook, stirring, until it has been absorbed.

4 Continue adding the stock in this way until the rice is just tender and the mixture is thick and creamy. It should take about 25 minutes.

5 Serve hot, sprinkled with the grated Parmesan cheese and chopped parsley.

ersian pilaf

SERVES 4   **426 CALS PER SERVING**

mall cinnamon stick

p cumin seeds

lack peppercorns

ds of 4 cardamom pods, crushed

loves

sp sunflower oil

nall onion, chopped

p turmeric

g (8 oz) long grain rice

litres (2 pints) hot vegetable or chicken stock

y leaves, torn into pieces

and black pepper

(2 oz) shelled pistachio nuts,
rsely chopped

(1 oz) raisins

coriander to garnish

1 Heat a heavy pan and add the cinnamon stick, cumin seeds, peppercorns, cardamom seeds, and cloves.

2 Dry-fry the spices over a medium heat for 2–3 minutes until they begin to release their aromas.

3 Add the oil to the pan and, when it is hot, add the onion and turmeric. Cook gently, stirring occasionally, for about 10 minutes until the onion is softened.

4 Add the rice and stir to coat the grains in the oil. Slowly pour in the hot stock, add the bay leaves, season with salt and pepper, and bring to a boil. Lower the heat, cover, and cook very gently for about 10 minutes without lifting the lid.

5 Remove the saucepan from the heat and leave to stand, still covered, for about 5 minutes.

6 Add the pistachio nuts and raisins to the pilaf, and fork them in gently to fluff up the rice. Garnish with fresh coriander, and serve at once.

Wild rice gratin

SERVES 6   **446 CALS PER SERVING**

375 g (12 oz) mixed basmati and wild rice

salt and black pepper

250–375 g (8–12 oz) broccoli

15 g (½ oz) butter

2 onions, chopped

3 garlic cloves, crushed

125 ml (4 fl oz) full-fat soured cream or crème fraîche

125 g (4 oz) mozzarella cheese, grated

60 g (2 oz) Parmesan cheese, grated

1 tbsp chopped fresh rosemary

1 Cook the rice in boiling salted water for about 35 minutes, or according to packet instructions. Drain thoroughly and rinse with cold water. Drain again.

2 Meanwhile, cut the stalks off the broccoli and cook them in boiling salted water for 8–10 minutes until almost tender, then add the florets, and cook for 2 minutes longer. Drain and rinse in cold water. Drain again and set aside.

3 Melt the butter in a frying pan, add the onions, and cook gently, stirring occasionally, for 3–5 minutes until softened. Add the garlic, and cook, stirring occasionally, for 3–5 minutes until the onions are lightly browned.

4 Coarsely chop the broccoli, then stir into the rice with the onion and garlic mixture, soured cream, three-quarters of the mozzarella and Parmesan cheeses, and the rosemary. Season with salt and pepper.

5 Turn the mixture into an ovenproof dish and sprinkle with the remaining mozzarella and Parmesan cheeses. Bake in a preheated oven at 180°C (160°C fan, Gas 4) for about 20 minutes until the cheese has melted. Serve hot.

♡ Healthy note

Reduce the fat content by using low-fat crème fraîche instead of soured cream, reduced-fat mozzarella, and just 2 tbsp grated Parmesan.

Risotto Milanese

🍴 SERVES 6   403 CALS PER SERVING

90 g (3 oz) butter

1 onion, chopped

375 g (12 oz) risotto rice

1.25 litres (2 pints) hot vegetable or chicken stock

a few pinches of saffron strands

salt and black pepper

60 g (2 oz) Parmesan cheese, grated

Parmesan shavings to serve

1 Melt 30 g (1 oz) of the butter in a large saucepan, add the chopped onion, and cook gently, stirring occasionally, for 3–5 minutes until softened but not coloured.

2 Add the rice, stirring to coat the grains in the butter, and cook for 1 minute. Add a ladleful of hot stock to the pan, and cook gently, stirring constantly, until all the stock has been absorbed.

3 Sprinkle in the saffron strands and season with salt and pepper. Continue to add the stock, a ladleful at a time, stirring constantly, until the risotto is thick and creamy and the rice tender. This will take 20–25 minutes.

4 Stir in the remaining butter and the Parmesan cheese, and season to taste with salt and pepper. Serve at once, topped with Parmesan shavings.

🔍 Cook's know-how

Risotto Milanese is the traditional accompaniment to Osso Buco (page 237), but you can serve it with any other dish of meat or poultry, or as a first course on its own. In the past, it was traditionally cooked with the marrow from the veal shanks used for the Osso Buco, but nowadays the finished risotto is sometimes topped with a few spoonfuls of the juices from a veal roast to give it a more traditional and authentic flavour. If you want to reduce the fat content in this recipe, omit the butter in step 4.

Chicken liver risotto

🍴 SERVES 4–6   619–413 CALS PER SERVING

75 g (2½ oz) butter

1 tbsp sunflower oil

125 g (4 oz) smoked bacon rashers, rinds removed, diced

1 onion, chopped

1 garlic clove, crushed

175 g (6 oz) risotto rice

60 g (2 oz) wild rice

600 ml (1 pint) hot chicken stock

250 g (8 oz) chicken livers, sliced

125 g (4 oz) wild mushrooms, sliced

60 g (2 oz) sun-dried tomatoes in oil, drained and chopped

salt and black pepper

30 g (1 oz) Parmesan cheese, grated

1 tbsp chopped fresh rosemary

1 Melt 60 g (2 oz) of the butter with the oil in a large frying pan. When the butter is foaming, add the bacon, onion, and garlic, and cook gently, stirring occasionally, for 3–5 minutes until the onion is soft but not coloured.

2 Add the risotto rice and wild rice, stirring to coat the grains in the oil, then pour in the hot chicken stock. Cover and simmer for 25 minutes.

3 Meanwhile, melt the remaining butter in a saucepan. Add the chicken livers, and cook, stirring, for 2–3 minutes until a rich brown colour. Add the mushrooms, and cook, stirring occasionally, for 5–7 minutes.

4 Stir the chicken livers into the rice. Add the sun-dried tomatoes, season with salt and pepper, and cook for 5 minutes or until all the liquid has been absorbed. Serve hot, garnished with Parmesan and rosemary.

Kedgeree

🍴 SERVES 4   470 CALS PER SERVING

175 g (6 oz) long grain rice

¼ tsp turmeric

375 g (12 oz) smoked haddock fillet

2 hard-boiled eggs

60 g (2 oz) butter, plus extra for greasing

juice of ½ lemon

150 ml (¼ pint) single cream

salt

cayenne pepper

2 tbsp finely chopped parsley

1 Simmer the rice and turmeric, covered in boiling salted water for 12–15 minutes until tender. Rinse with boiling water, drain and keep warm.

2 Meanwhile, put the haddock, skin-side down, in a frying pan, cover with cold water, and poach for 8–10 minutes.

3 Cut 1 egg lengthways into quarters and reserve for garnish. Coarsely chop the second egg.

4 Drain the haddock, remove the skin and bones, then flake the fish. Put the fish into a large bowl, add the rice, chopped egg, butter, lemon juice, and cream, and season with salt and cayenne pepper. Stir gently to mix.

5 Butter an ovenproof dish, add the kedgeree, and bake in a preheated oven at 180°C (160°C fan, Gas 4), stirring occasionally, for 10–15 minutes.

6 To serve, stir in the parsley and garnish with the reserved egg quarters.

🔍 Cook's know-how

Some smoked haddock is dyed bright yellow, so look out for smoked haddock that is pale in colour and labelled "undyed" if you want to avoid artificial colourings.

Opposite: Ked

Quick nasi goreng

SERVES 6   296 CALS PER SERVING

375 g (12 oz) long grain rice

2 tbsp vegetable oil

1 onion, chopped

½ tsp paprika

1 tsp ground ginger

125 g (4 oz) button mushrooms, sliced

60 g (2 oz) bean sprouts

1 tsp soy sauce

125 g (4 oz) cooked peeled prawns

2 spring onions, finely sliced

chopped coriander to garnish

1 Cook the rice in boiling salted water, for 12–15 minutes until tender. Drain, rinse with boiling water, drain again, and set aside.

2 Heat 1 tbsp of the oil in a frying pan or wok, add the onion, and cook for 3–5 minutes until soft. Add the paprika and ginger, and cook over a low heat for 1 minute. Add the mushrooms and bean sprouts and cook for 2–3 minutes until softened. Remove from the pan.

3 Heat the remaining oil in the pan, add the rice, and cook over a gentle heat, stirring, for 7–8 minutes to warm through. Stir in the soy sauce. Return the onions and vegetables to the pan and add the prawns. Serve hot, garnished with coriander.

Vegetarian nasi goreng

SERVES 6   379 CALS PER SERVING

375 g (12 oz) long grain rice

salt

2 tbsp tamarind paste (optional)

2 tbsp vegetable oil

1 red pepper, halved, seeded, and thinly sliced

1 large onion, chopped

3 garlic cloves, crushed

1 cm (½ in) piece of fresh root ginger, peeled and grated

2 tsp curry powder

¼ tsp each crushed dried red chillies (chilli flakes) and turmeric

½ small hard white cabbage, thinly sliced

1 x 200 g can chopped tomatoes

3 tbsp soy sauce

TO GARNISH

3 tomatoes, cut into strips

½ cucumber, cut into strips

omelette strips (see below)

1 Cook the rice in boiling salted water for 12–15 minutes until tender. Drain, rinse with boiling water, and drain again. Stir in the tamarind paste (if using) and set aside.

2 Heat 1 tbsp of the oil in a large frying pan or wok, add the red pepper and onion, and cook for 3–5 minutes until softened. Add the garlic, ginger, curry powder, crushed chillies, and turmeric, and cook gently, stirring, for 1 minute.

3 Add the cabbage and cook for 3–5 minutes. Add the tomatoes and cook for 2–3 minutes. Remove from the pan.

4 Heat the remaining oil in the pan, add the rice, and cook gently until lightly browned. Return the vegetables to the pan. Add the soy sauce and heat gently to warm through.

5 Serve hot, garnished with tomato, cucumber, and omelette strips.

Omelette garnish

Whisk 2 eggs with plenty of salt and pepper. Melt 30 g (1 oz) butter in an omelette pan or small frying pan. Add the eggs to the pan and cook until set. Slide the omelette out of the pan and roll it up, then leave to cool before slicing across into fine strips.

Chicken nasi goreng

SERVES 6   622 CALS PER SERVING

375 g (12 oz) long grain rice

salt and black pepper

90 ml (3 fl oz) olive oil

6 streaky bacon rashers, chopped

2 large onions, chopped

3 garlic cloves, crushed

¼ tsp chilli powder

2 tsp mild curry powder

2 cooked chicken breasts, skinned and cubed

90 ml (3 fl oz) soy sauce

6 spring onions, chopped

60 g (2 oz) cooked peeled prawns

60 g (2 oz) almonds, halved, and toasted (page 162)

TO GARNISH

coriander sprigs

6 fried eggs (optional)

prawn crackers

1 Cook the rice in boiling salted water for 12–15 minutes until tender. Drain, rinse with boiling water, drain again, and set aside.

2 Heat 1 tbsp of the oil in a large frying pan or wok, add the bacon, and cook for 3–5 minutes until browned. Add the remaining oil, the onions, and garlic, and cook over a gentle heat for 3–5 minutes until the onions are soft but not coloured.

3 Add the chilli and curry powders and cook, stirring, for 1 minute or until fragrant. Add the chicken and cook for 5–6 minutes until just beginning to brown.

4 Add the soy sauce and half of the rice and stir well. Add the remaining rice, and season with salt and pepper. Cook over a gentle heat, stirring, for 7–8 minutes until the rice is heated through. Stir in the spring onions, prawns, and almonds, and heat through.

5 Serve hot, garnished with coriander sprigs, and fried eggs if you like. Serve prawn crackers in a separate bowl.

Opposite, clockwise from top
Chicken nasi goreng, Vegetarian
nasi goreng, Quick nasi goreng

Egg-fried rice

SERVES 4   441 CALS PER SERVING

250 g (8 oz) long grain rice

salt and black pepper

3 tbsp sunflower oil

60 g (2 oz) bacon rashers, rinds removed, diced

125 g (4 oz) frozen peas

2 eggs, beaten

125 g (4 oz) bean sprouts

6 spring onions, sliced

1 Cook the rice in boiling salted water for 12–15 minutes until tender. Drain.

2 Heat the oil in a wok or large frying pan, add the bacon, and cook over a high heat, stirring, for 2 minutes. Add the rice and peas and cook, stirring, for 5 minutes.

3 Add the eggs and bean sprouts, and stir-fry for 2 minutes until the eggs have just set. Taste for seasoning, sprinkle with the sliced spring onions, and serve at once.

Special egg-fried rice

Add 125 g (4 oz) cooked peeled prawns when you add the rice and peas in step 2, and sprinkle with 60 g (2 oz) toasted cashew nuts just before serving.

Bean sprouts are nutritious and crunchy, making them ideal for stir-fries. They do not keep well, so use soon after purchase.

Risotto al verde

SERVES 4   734 CALS PER SERVING

15 g (½ oz) butter

3 garlic cloves, crushed

250 g (8 oz) risotto rice

1 litre (1¾ pints) hot vegetable stock

175 ml (6 fl oz) single cream

90 g (3 oz) blue cheese, crumbled

4 tbsp ready-made pesto

90 g (3 oz) Parmesan cheese, grated

4 tbsp pine nuts, lightly toasted

4 tbsp shredded fresh basil

1 Melt the butter in a large saucepan. When it is foaming, add the garlic and cook gently for 1 minute.

2 Add the risotto rice, stirring to coat the grains in the butter, and cook for 2 minutes. Add a ladleful of the hot vegetable stock, and cook gently, stirring constantly, until the stock has been absorbed. Continue to add the stock, a ladleful at a time, and cook for 20–25 minutes or until the rice is just tender.

3 Add the cream, and cook gently, stirring, until it has been absorbed. Stir in the blue cheese, then the pesto, Parmesan, and pine nuts. Garnish with shredded fresh basil, and serve.

Chicken and mushroom risotto

Add 125 g (4 oz) sliced mushrooms to the saucepan with the garlic in step 1 and cook for 3–5 minutes until the mushrooms are soft. Substitute chicken stock for the vegetable stock, omit the blue cheese and pesto, then add 250 g (8 oz) cooked diced chicken with the cream in step 3.

Asparagus risotto

Add 1 finely chopped onion to the pan with the garlic in step 1, cook for 3–5 minutes until soft. Omit the blue cheese and pesto, and add 375 g (12 oz) trimmed and chopped asparagus in step 2, about 5 minutes before the end of the cooking time.

Paella

SERVES 6   718 CALS PER SERVING

3 tbsp olive oil

6 chicken thighs

250 g (8 oz) smoked bacon, rind removed, cut into strips

1 large onion, chopped

1 litre (1¾ pints) chicken stock

250 g (8 oz) tomatoes, chopped

2 garlic cloves, crushed

a few pinches of saffron threads, soaked in a little hot water

500 g (1 lb) short grain rice

1 red and 1 green pepper, halved, seeded, and sliced

125 g (4 oz) frozen peas

salt and black pepper

500 g (1 lb) mussels, cleaned (page 107)

125 g (4 oz) cooked peeled prawns

TO FINISH

12 black olives, pitted

6 large cooked prawns, unpeeled

lemon wedges

2 tbsp chopped parsley

1 Heat the oil in a paella pan or a large, deep frying pan or sauté pan. Add the chicken and cook over a medium heat for 10 minutes until browned all over. Add the bacon and onion and cook for 5 minutes.

2 Stir in the stock, tomatoes, garlic, and saffron with its soaking liquid, and bring a boil. Add the rice, red and green pepper and peas, and season with salt and pepper. Cover and bake in a preheated oven at 180°C (160°C fan, Gas 4) for 35–40 minutes until the rice is nearly tender and the stock has been absorbed.

3 Meanwhile, put the mussels into a large pan with about 1 cm (½ in) water. Cover tightly, and cook, shaking the pan occasionally, for 5 minutes or until the shells open. Drain the mussels, and throw away any that have not opened: do not try to force them open.

4 Stir the peeled prawns into the paella, cover, and cook gently on the hob for about 5 minutes. Taste for seasoning. Arrange the mussels around the pan, and the olives, large prawns, and lemon wedges on top. Serve hot, sprinkled with parsley.

Vegetables and Salads

Under 45 minutes

Pasta and mackerel salad
Pasta shells tossed with courgettes, French beans, orange segments, mackerel, walnuts, and a dressing of oils and orange juice.

SERVES 6   643 CALS PER SERVING
Takes 30 minutes, **plus chilling**   Page 356

ITALIAN CLASSIC

Tricolore salad
Thinly sliced beefsteak tomatoes arranged with slices of mozzarella cheese and avocado, and drizzled with olive oil.

SERVES 4   509 CALS PER SERVING
Takes 20 minutes   Page 351

Cauliflower and broccoli cheese
Tasty and nutritious: Cauliflower and brocco florets, boiled and drained, and baked with cheese sauce. Served hot.

SERVES 4   513 CALS PER SERVING
Takes 35–40 minutes   Page 3

Celeriac remoulade
Matchstick-thin strips of celeriac tossed wi yogurt and mayonnaise dressing flavoured with capers and mustard.

SERVES 4–6   100–66 CALS PER SERVING
Takes 15 minutes   Page

Salad niçoise
Lettuce, French beans, and cucumber topped with tomatoes, eggs, tuna, anchovies, olives, and a garlic and mustard dressing.

SERVES 4   530 CALS PER SERVING
Takes 25 minutes   Page 355

Roasted fennel and sweet potato gra
Fennel bulbs, boiled with sweet potatoes, coated with butter and seasoning, and bak with cheese. Served hot.

SERVES 4   312 CALS PER SERVING
Takes 35–40 minutes   Page

Tomato and basil salad

Assortment of tomatoes and chunks of yellow pepper dressed in oil and balsamic vinegar. Sprinkled with basil.

SERVES 4–6   146–97 CALS PER SERVING

Takes 10 minutes, **plus standing**   Page 354

Creamed spinach

Creamy and nutritious: lightly cooked spinach mixed with crème fraîche, Parmesan cheese, chives, and nutmeg, then grilled.

SERVES 4   250 CALS PER SERVING

Takes 20 minutes   Page 335

Sweet and sour beetroot

Juicy and well-flavoured: diced beetroot cooked with onions, garlic, lemon juice, and mint. Served warm or cold.

SERVES 4   242 CALS PER SERVING

Takes 20 minutes   Page 335

Aromatic Brussels sprouts

Tender and tangy: Brussels sprouts simmered, then tossed with mustard-seed butter, and flavoured with lemon juice.

SERVES 6–8   125–94 CALS PER SERVING

Takes 15 minutes   Page 337

Asparagus with Parmesan

Asparagus marinated in olive oil, wine, vinegar, and garlic. Rolled in Parmesan cheese, and baked with marinade.

SERVES 4   215 CALS PER SERVING

Takes 35 minutes, **plus marinating**   Page 342

Crunchy oriental salad

Iceberg lettuce, bean sprouts, spring onions, and green pepper tossed with ginger dressing, and sprinkled with sesame seeds.

SERVES 6   141 CALS PER SERVING

Takes 10 minutes, **plus soaking**   Page 347

Waldorf salad

Fruity salad: celery and apple flavoured with lemon and coated with mayonnaise. Mixed with pieces of walnut.

SERVES 4   469 CALS PER SERVING

Takes 15 minutes, **plus chilling**   Page 347

Greek salad

Tomato wedges with cucumber, green pepper, feta cheese, and olives. Flavoured with olive oil, lemon, and oregano.

SERVES 4–6   503–335 CALS PER SERVING

Takes 10 minutes   Page 350

ergine with fresh pesto

iterranean flavours: slices of aubergine grilled until lightly wned, cooled, then spread with pesto, and sprinkled with basil.

S 4   499 CALS PER SERVING

s 20 minutes, **plus standing**   Page 346

ed carrots and turnips

s of carrot and whole baby turnips glazed chicken stock, butter, and sugar. ured with fresh mint and parsley.

S 4   115 CALS PER SERVING

 20 minutes   Page 337

Summer peas and beans

Shelled peas cooked with French beans, then combined with cooked young broad beans, butter, and mint.

SERVES 6–8   107–80 CALS PER SERVING

Takes 20 minutes   Page 339

Under 45 minutes

Caesar salad
Pieces of cos lettuce tossed with olive oil, lemon juice, and hard-boiled egg quarters. Mixed with croûtons and Parmesan cheese.

SERVES 4   421 CALS PER SERVING

Takes 20 minutes   Page 348

Pepperata salad
Courgette slices tossed with roasted peppers, watercress, and vinaigrette dressing.

SERVES 4–6   310–207 CALS PER SERVING

Takes 20 minutes, **plus cooling**   Page 345

Potato, apple, and celery salad
Hearty salad: pieces of boiled potato tossed with vinaigrette dressing, mixed with apple, celery, onion, and mayonnaise.

SERVES 6   332 CALS PER SERVING

Takes 30 minutes, **plus chilling**   Page 349

Three-bean salad
French beans, chick peas, and red kidney beans combined with olives in a Greek yogurt dressing, flavoured with vinegar and mustard.

SERVES 4   315 CALS PER SERVING

Takes 15 minutes, **plus standing**   Page 354

Couscous salad
Couscous cooked with sultanas and ginger. Mixed with chilli oil, raspberry vinegar, tomatoes, onion, spring onions, and mint.

SERVES 6   280 CALS PER SERVING

Takes 20 minutes, **plus cooling**   Page 354

45–60 minutes

FRENCH CLASS

Pommes Anna
Thinly sliced potatoes, layered in frying pan, dotted with butter, and seasoned with salt and pepper, then cooked until tender.

SERVES 6   205 CALS PER SERVING

Takes 55 minutes   Page 332

Sweet and sour red cabbage
Shredded red cabbage cooked with bacon, apple, sugar, red wine, vinegar, sultanas, caraway seeds, cinnamon, and nutmeg.

SERVES 8   225 CALS PER SERVING

Takes 55 minutes   Page 336

Swiss rösti
Grated potatoes seasoned with pepper, and shaped into a cake. Lightly cooked in butter until golden.

SERVES 8   230 CALS PER SERVING

Takes 45 minutes, **plus chilling**   Page

Garlic creamed potatoes
Hearty and satisfying: boiled potato, mashed then mixed with roasted garlic, warm milk, and butter. Sprinkled with chives.

SERVES 6   227 CALS PER SERVING

Takes 45 minutes   Page

Over 60 minutes

FRENCH CLASSIC

DINNER PARTY

aricot bean cassoulet
arty dish: haricot beans skimmed with
rot, onion, and herbs. Thickened with
réed beans and garnished with chopped
rsley.
VES 6   167 CALS PER SERVING
es 1½ hours, **plus soaking**   Page 338

Gratin dauphinois
Rich and creamy: thinly sliced potato layered
with cream, garlic, and grated Gruyère cheese,
then baked until golden.
SERVES 8   279 CALS PER SERVING
Takes 1¾ hours   Page 331

Hasselback potatoes
Simple to make: whole potatoes sliced almost
through at intervals. Brushed with butter,
sprinkled with Parmesan, and baked.
SERVES 8   183 CALS PER SERVING
Takes 1 hour 5 minutes   Page 333

Potatoes lyonnaise
Mouthwateringly delicious: thickly sliced
potatoes layered with onion. Baked until the
potatoes are tender.
SERVES 6   246 CALS PER SERVING
Takes 1¾ hours   Page 330

Roast potatoes
Classic accompaniment to roast meat or
poultry: briefly simmered pieces of potato
roasted in a little fat until crisp and golden.
SERVES 6   192 CALS PER SERVING
Takes 1¼ hours   Page 330

Spinach and cheese baked potatoes
Hearty and healthy: baked potatoes scooped
out and mixed with spinach, onion, and
ricotta cheese.
SERVES 4–8   291–146 CALS PER SERVING
Takes 1¾ hours   Page 333

Ratatouille
Slices of aubergine, courgette, and red pepper
cooked with tomatoes. Flavoured with onion,
garlic, and basil.
SERVES 4–6   236–157 CALS PER SERVING
Takes 1½ hours, **plus standing**   Page 344

ter of vegetables
xcellent vegetable dish made by arranging celeriac purée and
ed vegetables in rows on a platter, seasoned with salt and pepper.
S 6   190 CALS PER SERVING
s 1¼ hours   Page 341

Vegetables and salads know-how

On every shopping trip there seem to be more new vegetables to try – strangely shaped squashes and roots like kohlrabi, tomatoes and peppers of all colours, exotic mushrooms, Chinese cabbages, and salad greens such as wild rocket, mizuna, and red chard – as well as different varieties of familiar vegetables like potatoes, each suitable for particular cooking methods. Imported produce adds to the bounty of our own seasonal vegetables. And for added convenience, chilled ready-prepared vegetables and salads are widely available. This wonderful variety enables a cook to be innovative, creating nutritious, appetizing dishes with minimum effort.

Buying and storing

When choosing vegetables and salad leaves, look for the freshest available. Their colour should be bright and their texture firm and crisp. Any vegetables that are bruised or show signs of age – those that are discoloured, shrivelled, or flabby – are past their best. In general, small, young vegetables are more tender than large, older ones, although very small baby vegetables can be quite tasteless.

Some vegetables, including onions, garlic, roots such as potatoes, parsnips and swede, and pumpkin, can be stored in a cool, dark, well-ventilated place. More perishable vegetables, such as peas, sweetcorn, celery, salad leaves, spinach, and ripe tomatoes, should be chilled. Keep them in the special salad drawer in the refrigerator, unwrapping them or piercing their bags to prevent moisture build-up.

Many vegetables can be prepared ahead of time and kept in sealed plastic bags in the fridge. The exceptions to this are vegetables such as celeriac and Jerusalem artichokes that discolour when cut and exposed to the air. Salad leaves can also be prepared in advance, but do not dress until ready to serve or they will wilt.

Nutrition

A healthy, well-balanced diet should include plenty of vegetables, because they supply essential vitamins, minerals, fibre, and disease-fighting compounds. And vegetables are low in calories and fat. To get the maximum benefit from the vegetables you eat:

- choose the freshest produce
- keep it in the fridge, or in a cool, dark place, and do not store for too long
- prepare as close to cooking or eating as possible
- leave on the peel or skin as it provides fibre, and nutrients are often concentrated just under the skin

- rinse thoroughly but don't soak before cooking, particularly if the vegetable is peeled or cut
- cut large pieces if boiling or steaming
- use the cooking liquid in a sauce or soup

Freezing

Most vegetables freeze very well, whether plain, in a sauce, or in a prepared dish. The exceptions are potatoes and watery vegetables like cucumber and tomatoes. Vegetables that are to be frozen plain should be very fresh. Before freezing blanch them in boiling water, then cool quickly in iced water; this will set the fresh colour. Vegetables can be kept in the freezer for 6–12 months, and can be cooked directly from frozen.

Microwaving

The microwave is ideal for cooking small quantities of vegetables: little water is used so they retain their nutrients as well as colours and flavours. Cut vegetables into uniform pieces, or pierce skins of those that are left whole. Arrange them so that the tender parts are in the centre of the dish, to prevent overcooking. Add salt when serving. Keep the dish tightly covered during cooking, and turn or stir once or twice if necessary.

Cutting vegetables

Keep pieces to a uniform size and shape to ensure they cook evenly.

Julienne
Cut into 5 mm (¼ in) slices. Stack the slices then cut into sticks, 5 mm (¼ in) thick.

Dice
Cut into 1 cm (½ in) strips, then cut across the strips to form neat dice.

Ribbons
Using a vegetable peeler, carefully shave off thin, wide ribbons.

Preparing vegetables

Knowing the most efficient way to prepare vegetables will save you time and effort in the kitchen. For most tasks, a chopping board and a sharp chef's knife, small knife, vegetable peeler are all you'll need. Here's how the professionals deal with more unusual vegetables.

Dicing fresh chillies

1 Cut the chilli in half lengthways. Remove the stalk and core and scrape out the fleshy white ribs and seeds.

2 Set the chilli cut-side up and cut into thin strips. Hold the strips together and cut across to make dice. (See know-how box right.)

Chopping fresh root ginger

1 With a small knife, peel off the skin. Slice the ginger across the fibrous grain.

2 Set the flat of a knife on top of the slices and crush. Chop the crushed slices.

Preparing peppers

1 Cut around the stalk and the core. Twist and pull them out in one piece.

2 Cut the pepper in half. Scrape out the fleshy white ribs and the seeds.

Chopping garlic

1 Set the flat side of a knife on top of the clove and crush it lightly. Peel off the skin.

2 With a sharp chef's knife, chop the crushed garlic clove finely.

Preparing vegetables know-how

The juices produced by **fresh chillies** can burn the skin, so it's best to wear rubber gloves when cutting them and to avoid touching your eyes or lips.

The more finely you chop **garlic**, the stronger the flavour. Garlic crushed in a press will have the strongest flavour of all.

Avocados discolour quickly, so brush cut surfaces with lemon juice, and use as soon as possible.

Other vegetables that discolour when cut and exposed to the air include globe artichokes, celeriac and Jerusalem artichokes.

Preparing asparagus

Cut off any woody ends from the asparagus and make the spears uniform in length. If you like, peel them: using a vegetable peeler, and working down towards the end of the spear, shave off the tough layer of skin from all sides.

Preparing avocado

Cut the avocado in half lengthways around the stone and twist the 2 halves to separate them. Remove the stone. If the avocado is to be mashed, the flesh can simply be scooped out of the skin with a teaspoon. To serve in slices, lightly score the skin into 2 or 3 strips, then peel off the strips of skin and slice the flesh.

Cooking vegetables

Choose the right cooking method to bring out the best in vegetables and create exciting accompaniments or main dishes. If cooking a variety of vegetables at the same time, remember that some take longer to cook than others, so you may have to add them in stages.

Baking

Potatoes, sweet potatoes, aubergines, and pumpkin are all delicious baked. Prick the skins of whole vegetables or, if cut, moisten cut surfaces with oil or butter. Push a skewer through the centres of large vegetables to conduct heat and speed up cooking time.

Roasting

Cut any root vegetables into large chunks and parboil them. Drain well. Put olive oil or duck fat into a roasting tin and heat in a preheated 180°C (160°C fan, Gas 4) oven. Add the vegetables to the tin and turn to coat with the fat. Roast, turning occasionally, until well browned.

Stir-frying

Cut the vegetables into small, even-sized piec[es]. Heat a little oil in a wok. When it is hot, add the vegetables, starting with those that need the longest cooking time. Keep the heat high, and toss and stir the vegetables constantly. Cook for just a few minutes until the vegetables are tender but still crisp.

Boiling

Drop vegetables (both greens and roots) into a large pan of boiling salted water and bring back to the boil as quickly as possible. Simmer until just tender, then drain. To stop further cooking and set the colour of green vegetables, rinse briefly under cold running water.

Braising

Carrots, celery, and other root vegetables are ideal for braising. Put the vegetables into a heavy pan or flameproof casserole, add a small amount of water or stock, and bring to the boil. Cover tightly and cook over a gentle heat until just tender. Boil to evaporate the liquid or drain.

Sautéing

Vegetables can be sautéed in oil or a mixtur[e of] oil and butter (butter alone burns if it becom[es] too hot). Cook the vegetables over a high h[eat], stirring and turning constantly, until they start [to] brown. Reduce the heat and continue cook[ing,] stirring occasionally, until tender.

Steaming

This method is ideal for delicate vegetables such as cauliflower, broccoli, and asparagus. Bring water to the boil in a steamer base. Put the vegetables in a single layer on the rack, cover, and steam until just tender. If you don't have a steamer, use a large saucepan with a steamer basket, or a wok and a bamboo steamer.

Chargrilling

Many types of quick-cooking vegetables can be cooked on a chargrill, as well as under a grill or on a barbecue. Halve the vegetables or cut into thick slices. Brush with oil and chargrill, turning at least once, until tender. For extra flavour, marinate vegetables first (page 342).

Deep-frying

Most vegetables (except roots like potatoes) need a protective coating such as batter be[fore] being deep-fried. Heat oil in a deep-fat fryer [to] the required temperature. Add the vegetabl[es in] batches and fry until golden, bringing the oil back to the required temperature between [each] batch. Drain on paper towels.

Mayonnaise

This always useful sauce is the base for many others – add crushed garlic and you have aïoli – and for salad dressings. It can be made by hand, with a balloon whisk, or more quickly in a food processor or blender. For a lighter result use 1 whole egg rather than egg yolks, and sunflower oil alone.

Traditional mayonnaise

Put a bowl on a tea towel to steady it. Add 2 egg yolks, 1 tsp Dijon mustard, and salt and pepper to taste, and beat together with a balloon whisk until the egg yolks have thickened slightly.

2 Whisk in 150 ml (¼ pint) olive or sunflower oil, or a mixture of the two, just a drop at a time at first, whisking until the mixture is thick. Stir in 2 tsp white wine vinegar or lemon juice. Check the seasoning, adding sugar to taste if liked. Serve at once, or chill. This makes 200 ml (7 fl oz).

Food-processor mayonnaise

Put 2 whole eggs, 2 tsp Dijon mustard, and salt and pepper to taste in the bowl of a food processor or blender. Process briefly to combine.

2 With blades turning, slowly add 300 ml (½ pint) olive or sunflower oil, or a mixture of the two. Finish as for traditional mayonnaise above.

Salad dressings

Most salad dressings can be made in a matter of seconds – for vinaigrette the ingredients only need to be shaken together in a screw-topped jar, and the basic mixture can be endlessly varied. Other dressings are simply made by whisking flavourings into a creamy mixture based on mayonnaise.

Vinaigrette dressing

Put 6 tbsp olive oil, 2 tbsp white wine vinegar, 1 tbsp lemon juice, 1 tbsp Dijon mustard, ¼ tsp caster sugar, and salt and pepper to taste into a screw-topped jar. Shake until combined. This makes 150 ml (¼ pint).

Nutty vinaigrette

Use red wine vinegar instead of the white wine vinegar and lemon juice in the recipe above, and replace 2 tbsp of the olive oil with walnut or hazelnut oil.

Easy coleslaw dressing

Whisk 5 tbsp cider vinegar and 1 tbsp caster sugar into 150 ml (¼ pint) mayonnaise. Season with salt and pepper to taste. If liked stir in a pinch of caraway seeds.

Blue cheese dressing

Put 150 ml (¼ pint) each of mayonnaise and soured cream into a bowl with 90 g (3 oz) mashed blue cheese, 1 tsp white wine vinegar, 1 crushed garlic clove, and black pepper to taste. Whisk until smooth.

Green mayonnaise dressing

Put 50 g (2 oz) each watercress sprigs and flat-leaf parsley in a blender or food processor with 4 chopped spring onions and 1 garlic clove. Process until finely chopped. Whisk into a mixture of 150 ml (¼ pint) each mayonnaise and soured cream or Greek-style yogurt.

Herb vinaigrette

Add 2 tbsp chopped fresh herbs (eg dill, tarragon, chervil, or flat-leaf parsley) to the vinaigrette just before serving.

Salad dressings know-how

If mayonnaise curdles, add 1 tbsp hot water and beat well, or start again with fresh egg yolks and oil and slowly add the curdled mixture once the eggs and oil thicken.

For best results have the eggs for mayonnaise at room temperature.

Keep mayonnaise, tightly covered, in the refrigerator for no more than 1–2 days (remember that it contains raw eggs).

Vinaigrette dressing can be kept in its screw-topped jar in the fridge for up to 1 week. Shake well before serving.

Potatoes lyonnaise

SERVES 6   246 CALS PER SERVING

90 g (3 oz) butter, plus extra for greasing

1 large onion, sliced

1 kg (2 lb) floury potatoes, thickly sliced

salt and black pepper

chopped parsley to garnish

1 Lightly butter a gratin dish. Melt the butter in a frying pan, add the onion, and cook gently, stirring occasionally, for 3–5 minutes until the onions are softened but not coloured.

2 Layer the potatoes and onion in the gratin dish, seasoning each layer with salt and pepper, and finishing with a neat layer of potatoes.

3 Pour any butter left in the frying pan over the potatoes. Bake in a preheated oven at 190°C (170°C fan, Gas 5) for 1–1½ hours until the potatoes are tender. Garnish with parsley, and serve hot.

Roast potatoes

SERVES 6   192 CALS PER SERVING

1 kg (2 lb) floury potatoes, cut into even-sized pieces

3 tbsp goose or duck fat, or sunflower oil

salt

1 Put the potatoes into a large saucepan, cover with cold water, and bring to a boil. Simmer for 1 minute, then drain thoroughly.

2 Return the potatoes to the saucepan and shake over a gentle heat to roughen the surfaces and dry the potatoes thoroughly.

3 Put the fat into a roasting tin, heat until very hot, then add the potatoes, turning to coat them in the fat. Roast the potatoes in a preheated oven at 220°C (200°C fan, Gas 7), turning and basting occasionally, for 45–60 minutes until tender, crisp, and golden. Sprinkle with salt, and serve at once.

Cook's know-how

Roughening the outside of blanched potatoes before roasting helps make them really crisp. If you like, you can also score them roughly with a fork.

Swiss rösti

SERVES 8   230 CALS PER SERVING

1.5 kg (3 lb) large baking potatoes, scrubbed

black pepper

60 g (2 oz) butter

2 tbsp sunflower oil

fresh thyme to garnish

1 Cook the potatoes in boiling salted water for about 10 minutes until just tender. Drain the potatoes thoroughly, leave to cool, then peel. Cover and chill for about 4 hours.

2 Coarsely grate the potatoes into a large bowl, season with pepper, and stir carefully to mix.

3 Melt 30 g (1 oz) of the butter with 1 tbsp of the oil in a frying pan, add the grated potato, and flatten into a cake with a fish slice. Cook over a low heat for about 15 minutes until the base is crisp and golden brown. Turn on to a large buttered plate.

4 Melt the remaining butter and oil in the frying pan, slide in the potato cake, and cook for 5–10 minutes to brown the second side. Turn out on to a warmed platter, garnish, and serve cut into wedges.

Celeriac rösti

Substitute 750 g (1½ lb) celeriac for half of the potato. Before boiling in step 1, peel the celeriac, and toss in lemon juice to prevent discoloration.

Onion rösti

Heat 1 tbsp sunflower oil in a frying pan, add 1 large chopped onion, and cook for 3–5 minutes until softened but not coloured. Fork the onion into the grated potato in step 2, before seasoning with pepper.

Chipped potatoes

SERVES 6   281 CALS PER SERVING

750 g (1½ lb) floury potatoes

sunflower oil for deep-frying

salt

deep-fat fryer

1 Cut the potatoes into 5 x 1 cm (2 x ½ in) sticks, put into a bowl of cold water, and leave to soak for 5–10 minutes.

2 Heat the oil in a deep-fat fryer to 160°C (325°F). Dry the chips thoroughly, then lower them into the deep-fat fryer, in batches if necessary, and deep-fry for 5–6 minutes until soft and very pale golden.

3 Lift the basket out of the fryer. Increase the temperature of the oil to 190°C (375°F). Carefully return the basket of chips to the fryer and deep-fry for 3–4 minutes until crisp and golden brown. Lift out the basket and drain the chips on paper towel. Sprinkle with salt, and serve hot.

French fries

Cut the potatoes into 5 cm x 5 mm (2 x ¼ in) sticks and leave to soak as directed. Heat the oil as directed and deep-fry the sticks for 4–5 minutes. Lift out of the fryer, increase the heat as directed, return and deep-fry the sticks for 1–2 minutes. Sprinkle with salt, and serve at once.

Cook's know-how

Good chips should be crisp and golden on the outside and soft and tender in the middle. The secret is to cook the potatoes first in medium hot oil until tender, then lift them out, increase the temperature of the oil, and cook the chips quickly to brown and crisp the outsides. Drain well on paper towels before serving.

ratin dauphinois

SERVES 8   279 CALS PER SERVING

r for greasing

nl (¼ pint) single cream

nl (¼ pint) double cream

ge garlic clove, crushed

(2 lb) main-crop potatoes

nd black pepper

(4 oz) Gruyère cheese, grated

ghtly butter a shallow gratin dish. Put
e single and double creams into
wl, add the garlic, and stir to mix.

hinly slice the potatoes, preferably
ith the slicing disc of a food processor.

repare the gratin dauphinois (see
ox, right).

ake in a preheated oven at 160°C
40°C fan, Gas 3) for 1½ hours or until
otatoes are tender and the topping
den brown. Serve at once.

Preparing the gratin dauphinois

Arrange a layer of potatoes, slightly overlapping,
in the bottom of the gratin dish. Season with salt
and pepper.

Pour a little of the cream mixture over the
potatoes, then sprinkle with grated cheese.
Continue layering the potatoes, cream, and
cheese, and adding salt and pepper, then finish
with a layer of cheese.

Garlic creamed potatoes

SERVES 4 **227 CALS PER SERVING**

750 g (1½ lb) floury potatoes, cut into large chun[k]

4 garlic cloves, unpeeled

salt and black pepper

about 150 ml (¼ pint) milk

60 g (2 oz) butter

2 tbsp snipped fresh chives

1 Cook the potatoes and whole garlic cloves in boiling salted water for 20–30 minutes until tender. Drain thoroughly, an[d] peel the skins off the garlic cloves.

2 Return the potatoes to the saucepan and toss over a gentle heat for a few seconds to dry thoroughly, shaking the saucepan so that the potatoes do not b[u]

3 Mash the potatoes and garlic togethe[r] or work through a sieve for a finer pur[e] then push them to one side of the pan.

4 Pour the milk into the saucepan and heat until almost boiling. Beat the mil[k] into the potatoes and garlic with the but[ter] and salt and pepper to taste. Sprinkle wi[th] chives, and serve hot.

Herb and cheese creamed potatoes

Omit the garlic, and add 2 tbsp chopped parsley and 60 g (2 oz) finely grated Chedd[ar] cheese when you beat in the milk.

Creamed potatoes with swede

Omit the garlic and fresh chives. Substitute 250 g (8 oz) swede, cut into small chunks, for 250 g (8 oz) of the potatoes, and add a pinch of grated nutmeg just before servin[g]

Pommes Anna

SERVES 6 **205 CALS PER SERVING**

750 g (1½ lb) floury potatoes

90 g (3 oz) butter, plus extra for greasing

salt and black pepper

1 Slice the potatoes very thinly, preferably with the slicing disc of a food processor.

2 Generously butter the base and sides of an ovenproof frying pan. Layer the potatoes in the frying pan, seasoning each layer with salt and pepper, and dotting with the butter.

3 Cover the pan tightly with buttered foil and the lid, and cook over a medium heat for about 15 minutes or until the base of the potato cake is light golden brown.

4 Transfer the pan to a preheated oven and cook at 190°C (170°C fan, Gas 5) for 30 minutes or until the potato cake is tender.

5 Invert a warmed serving platter over the pan, and turn out the potato cake so that the crisp layer is on the top. Serve at once, cut into wedges.

Individual pommes Anna

Layer the sliced potatoes in well-buttered individual patty tins, seasoning the layers and dotting with butter as in step 2. Omit the cooking on the hob in step 3, and bake, uncovered, in the hottest part of a preheated oven at 220°C (200°C fan, Gas 7) for 30–35 minutes or until the potatoes are tender and golden brown.

> **Cook's know-how**
>
> Arrange the potatoes in the frying pan as soon as they have been sliced. Don't leave them to soak in water or the starch in them will leach out and they will not hold together to make the cake.

pinach and cheese aked potatoes

SERVES 4–8   291–146 CALS PER SERVING

aking potatoes, scrubbed

g (8 oz) spinach leaves

osp olive oil

mall onion, finely chopped

g (4 oz) ricotta cheese

sp grated nutmeg

and black pepper

Prick the potatoes all over with a fork.
Bake in a preheated oven at 220°C
0°C fan, Gas 7) for 1–1¼ hours until tender.

Meanwhile, wash the spinach and put
it into a saucepan with only the water
haining on the leaves. Cook over a gentle
t for 1–2 minutes until the spinach has just
ed. Drain thoroughly, squeezing to remove
ess water. Chop the spinach finely.

Heat the olive oil in a small saucepan,
add the onion, and cook gently, stirring
casionally, for 3–5 minutes until softened
not coloured.

Cut the potatoes in half lengthways,
scoop out the flesh and turn it into a
vl. Add the spinach, onion, any oil left in
pan, the ricotta cheese, and nutmeg.
son with salt and pepper, and mix
oughly. Fill the potato skins with the
ure, return to the oven at the same
perature as before, and cook for
ninutes or until piping hot. Serve hot.

ing onion and hummus ed potatoes

e the potatoes, cut in half lengthways, and
p out the flesh. Mix with 4 finely chopped
g onions, 150 g (5 oz) hummus, and season
salt and pepper. Fill the potato skins and
e as in step 4.

Hasselback potatoes

SERVES 8   183 CALS PER SERVING

8 large floury potatoes

60 g (2 oz) butter, melted, plus extra for greasing

salt and black pepper

4 tbsp grated Parmesan cheese

parsley to garnish

1 Peel the potatoes, then slice them (see box, right).

2 Put the potatoes into a buttered roasting tin and brush with the melted butter, separating the slices slightly so a little of the butter goes between them. Season with salt and pepper.

3 Bake in a preheated oven at 220°C (200°C fan, Gas 7) for 45 minutes, then sprinkle with the Parmesan cheese and return to the oven for 10–15 minutes or until the potatoes are tender.

4 Transfer to a warmed serving platter, garnish with parsley, and serve at once.

Slicing the potatoes

Cut a thin slice off one side of each potato, and place the potato cut-side down on a board. Make vertical cuts, three-quarters of the way through, at 5 mm (¼ in) intervals.

Cook's know-how

To make it easier to slice the potatoes, push a skewer lengthways through the lower part of each potato, and slice as far down as the skewer. Remove the skewer before cooking.

Cauliflower and broccoli cheese

SERVES 4   513 CALS PER SERVING

1 head of cauliflower, weighing about 500 g (1 lb)

1 head of broccoli, weighing about 500 g (1 lb)

salt and black pepper

butter for greasing

60 g (2 oz) mature Cheddar cheese, grated

CHEESE SAUCE

60 g (2 oz) butter

60 g (2 oz) plain flour

600 ml (1 pint) milk

60 g (2 oz) Parmesan cheese, grated

60 g (2 oz) mature Cheddar cheese, grated

1 tsp Dijon mustard

1 Trim off and discard any thick, woody cauliflower and broccoli stalks. Break the heads into large florets, then cut off the thin, tender stalks and reserve.

2 Bring a saucepan of salted water to a boil. Add the cauliflower florets with half of the reserved stalks, and bring back to a boil. Boil for 2 minutes, then add the broccoli florets and boil for a further 3 minutes, or until the vegetables are just cooked but still have bite (they should not be soft). Drain and rinse under cold running water. Drain again, then spread out in a buttered, shallow ovenproof dish with the florets facing upwards.

3 Make the cheese sauce: melt the butter in a saucepan, sprinkle in the flour, and cook, stirring, for 1 minute. Remove from the heat, and gradually blend in the milk. Bring to a boil, stirring constantly until thickened. Simmer for 2–3 minutes, remove from the heat, and stir in the Parmesan and Cheddar cheeses. Add the mustard, season with salt and pepper, and stir until combined.

4 Pour the sauce over the vegetables, and sprinkle with the Cheddar cheese. Bake in a preheated oven at 200°C (180°C fan, Gas 6) for 20 minutes or until golden and bubbling. Serve hot.

Opposite: Cauliflower and broccoli cheese.

Spiced yams

SERVES 4   381 CALS PER SERVING

45 g (1½ oz) butter

2 garlic cloves, crushed

2 yams, total weight 1 kg (2 lb), trimmed but unpeeled, cubed

1 tsp mild chilli powder

¼ tsp paprika

¼ tsp ground cinnamon

1 x 200 g can chopped tomatoes

salt

plain yogurt and chopped parsley to serve

1 Melt the butter in a large pan. When it is foaming, add the garlic, and cook gently, stirring occasionally, for 1–2 minutes until soft but not coloured.

2 Add the yams to the pan and toss over a medium to high heat for 1–2 minutes.

3 Stir in the chilli powder, paprika, and cinnamon, then add the tomatoes, and cook the mixture over a medium heat for 1–2 minutes.

4 Season with salt, cover, and simmer for 15–20 minutes until the yams are tender. Turn the yams occasionally with a palette knife, but do not stir or they will break up. Serve hot, topped with yogurt and parsley.

Ginger parsnips

SERVES 8   249 CALS PER SERVING

1 kg (2 lb) parsnips, cut into matchstick-thin strips

salt and black pepper

60 g (2 oz) butter

2.5 cm (1 in) piece of fresh root ginger, peeled and grated

300 ml (½ pint) full-fat crème fraîche

1 Blanch the parsnips in a large saucepan of boiling salted water for 2 minutes. Drain the parsnips.

2 Melt the butter in the saucepan. Add the ginger and cook gently, stirring, for 2–3 minutes. Add the parsnips, tossing to coat in the butter. Season with salt and pepper, then turn the mixture into a large, shallow ovenproof dish.

3 Pour the crème fraîche over the parsnip mixture and bake in a preheated oven at 190°C (170°C fan, Gas 5) for 10–15 minutes until tender. Serve hot.

Creamed spinach

SERVES 4   250 CALS PER SERVING

750 g (1½ lb) fresh spinach leaves

45 g (1½ oz) butter

125 ml (4 fl oz) full-fat crème fraîche

¼ tsp grated nutmeg

salt and black pepper

1–2 tbsp grated Parmesan cheese

1 Cut any coarse outer leaves and stalks off the spinach and discard, then wash the spinach thoroughly in plenty of cold water.

2 Melt the butter in a saucepan, add the spinach, and stir until it has absorbed the butter.

3 Add half of the crème fraîche, season with the nutmeg and salt and pepper, and heat through.

4 Transfer to a shallow flameproof dish, pour the remaining crème fraîche on top, and sprinkle with grated Parmesan. Put under a hot grill for a few minutes until lightly browned. Serve hot.

Sweet and sour beetroot

SERVES 4   242 CALS PER SERVING

3 tbsp olive oil

2 onions, chopped

2 garlic cloves, crushed

30 g (1 oz) caster sugar

4 cooked beetroot, diced

juice of 1 lemon

2 tsp chopped fresh mint

salt and black pepper

fresh mint to garnish

1 Heat the olive oil in a large saucepan, add the onions and garlic, and cook gently, stirring occasionally, for 3–5 minutes until the onions are softened but not coloured.

2 Stir in the sugar, beetroot, half of the lemon juice, and the mint. Cook gently, stirring, for 10 minutes. Taste for seasoning, adding salt and pepper, and more lemon juice if needed.

3 Serve warm or cold, garnished with fresh mint.

Sweet and sour red cabbage

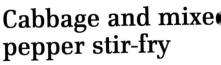 **SERVES 8**   **225 CALS PER SERVING**

1 tbsp sunflower oil

4 streaky bacon rashers, rinds removed, diced

125 g (4 oz) light soft brown sugar

2 onions, chopped

1 red cabbage, weighing about 1 kg (2 lb), shredded

1 tart apple, cored and diced

250 ml (8 fl oz) red wine

4 tbsp red wine vinegar

60 g (2 oz) sultanas

2 tsp caraway seeds

¼ tsp ground cinnamon

pinch of grated nutmeg (optional)

salt and black pepper

1 Heat the sunflower oil in a large saucepan, add the diced bacon, and cook for about 5 minutes until crisp and browned.

2 Stir in 90 g (3 oz) of the sugar and cook gently, stirring constantly, for 1–2 minutes, taking care that it does not burn.

3 Add the onions, cabbage, and apple, and cook, stirring occasionally, for about 5 minutes.

4 Pour in the wine and half of the wine vinegar, then add the sultanas, caraway seeds, cinnamon, and nutmeg (if using). Season with salt and pepper. Cover and cook over a low heat for 30 minutes or until the cabbage is tender but still firm. If there is too much liquid, uncover, and boil rapidly until the liquid evaporates completely.

5 Stir in the remaining sugar and wine vinegar, heat through, and taste for seasoning. Serve hot.

Vegetarian red cabbage with chestnuts

Omit the bacon. Add 125 g (4 oz) coarsely chopped peeled chestnuts in step 3, with the onions, cabbage, and diced apple.

Cabbage and mixed pepper stir-fry

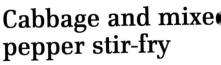 **SERVES 6–8**   **128–96 CALS PER SERVING**

2–3 tbsp olive oil

1 large onion, finely sliced

6 celery stalks, sliced diagonally

2 red peppers, halved, seeded, and cut into thin strips

1 yellow pepper, halved, seeded, and cut into thin strips

175 g (6 oz) mushrooms, quartered

salt and black pepper

1 small white cabbage, finely shredded

1 Heat 1 tbsp olive oil in a wok or large frying pan, add the sliced onion, and stir-fry over a high heat for about 2 minut until beginning to brown.

2 Add the sliced celery and stir-fry for about 1 minute, then lower the heat and stir-fry for 2 minutes.

3 Add another tablespoon of olive oil to the wok. When it is hot, add the pepp and mushrooms, season with salt and pepper, and stir-fry for 3 minutes.

4 Add the cabbage, with the remainin oil if needed, and stir-fry for 2 minutes or until tender–crisp. Taste for seasoning.

Savoy cabbage stir-fry

Heat 1 tbsp sunflower oil in a wok and stir-fr 1 finely sliced large onion, and 2 crushed g cloves for a few minutes. Add a further 1 tb sunflower oil, then 1 shredded small Savoy cabbage, and stir-fry for 2 minutes. Sprinkle with 2 tbsp soy sauce and 1 tsp sesame oil.

🔍 Cook's know-how

This is a good vegetable dish to serve when entertaining. Prepare and stir-fry the vegetables up to the end of step 3. The fina cooking of the cabbage can be done just before serving.

e: Glazed carrots and turnips.

azed carrots
d turnips

🍴 ERVES 4   115 CALS PER SERVING

(12 oz) carrots, cut into 5 cm (2 in) strips

(12 oz) baby turnips

l (½ pint) chicken stock

1 oz) butter

caster sugar

d black pepper

mixed chopped fresh mint and parsley

t the vegetables into a pan with
e stock, butter, and sugar. Season
salt and pepper, and bring to a boil.
r and cook for about 10 minutes until
egetables are almost tender.

emove the lid and boil rapidly until
e liquid in the pan has evaporated
ormed a glaze on the vegetables.
the herbs, and serve hot.

Garlic spring greens

🍴 SERVES 6   103 CALS PER SERVING

1 kg (2 lb) spring greens, tough stalks removed

salt

2 tbsp olive oil

3 garlic cloves, coarsely chopped

1 Roll up the spring greens, a few leaves
at a time, and cut across into thin strips.
Blanch in boiling salted water for 2 minutes.

2 Drain and rinse in iced water to cool.
Drain thoroughly, squeezing to remove
excess water.

3 Heat the olive oil in a large saucepan,
add the garlic, and cook gently for
1 minute or until lightly browned. Add the
spring greens, toss to coat thoroughly in
the garlic and oil, and cook for 2–3 minutes
until the spring greens are heated through.

4 Season with salt to taste. Serve hot
or cold.

Aromatic Brussels sprouts

🍴 SERVES 6–8   125–94 CALS PER SERVING

1 kg (2 lb) Brussels sprouts

salt and black pepper

45 g (1½ oz) butter

2 tsp mustard seeds

1 tbsp lemon juice

1 Cut a cross in the base of each sprout,
and simmer the sprouts in boiling salted
water for 5–10 minutes until just tender. Drain.

2 Melt the butter in a large saucepan,
add the mustard seeds, cover,
and cook over a low heat for 1–2 minutes
until the mustard seeds have stopped
popping and the butter is lightly browned.
Do not let the butter burn.

3 Add the sprouts to the pan, tossing to
heat them through and coat them in
the mustard-seed butter. Add the lemon
juice, season with salt and pepper, and
serve at once.

Above: Haricot bean cassoulet.

Haricot bean cassoulet

SERVES 6   167 CALS PER SERVING

250 g (8 oz) dried haricot beans

30 g (1 oz) butter

1 small carrot, finely chopped

1 small onion, finely chopped

1 bouquet garni or bunch of fresh mixed herbs

salt and black pepper

2 tbsp chopped parsley

1 Put the beans into a large bowl, cover with cold water, then leave to soak for at least 8 hours.

2 Drain the beans. Rinse under cold water and drain again. Put the beans into a saucepan and cover with cold water. Bring to a boil and boil rapidly for 10 minutes. Drain.

3 Melt the butter in a heavy saucepan, add the carrot and onion, and cook, stirring, for 3–4 minutes until beginning to soften.

4 Add the beans and bouquet garni or fresh herbs, and pour in enough cold water to cover the beans generously. Bring to a boil, cover, and simmer gently for 1 hour or until the beans are soft but not breaking up.

5 Drain the bean mixture, reserving the cooking liquid. Discard the bouquet garni or herbs. Purée one-third of the bean mixture in a food processor.

6 Stir the purée back into the unpuréed bean mixture in the pan, adding a little of the reserved cooking liquid to make a sauce-like consistency. Season with salt and pepper. Reheat gently and serve hot, sprinkled with chopped parsley,

French-style peas

SERVES 4–6   237–158 CALS PER SERVING

1 small round lettuce, shredded

6 spring onions, chopped

60 g (2 oz) butter

1 tbsp chopped parsley

1 tsp caster sugar

500 g (1 lb) shelled fresh peas (they must be young)

4 tbsp water

salt and black pepper

1 Line the bottom of a saucepan with lettuce. Add the spring onions, butte parsley, and sugar, and top with the pe Add the water, season with salt and pe and bring to a boil.

2 Simmer gently, uncovered, for 15–2(minutes until the liquid has evapora and the peas are tender. Taste for seasoning and serve hot.

elery and leek ir-fry

SERVES 6   235 CALS PER SERVING

(1 oz) butter

sp olive oil

g (1 lb) young leeks, trimmed and thinly sliced

elery stalks, thinly sliced on the diagonal

and black pepper

p snipped fresh chives

g (4 oz) salted cashew nuts to garnish

Melt the butter with the olive oil in a wok r large frying pan.

When the butter is foaming, add the eeks, and cook over a high heat, ng occasionally, for 5 minutes.

Add the celery, and cook for 3–5 minutes. Add salt and pepper, then stir e snipped fresh chives. Garnish with the d cashew nuts, and serve at once.

Healthy note

elery is a good source of potassium, and known to help prevent and reduce high ood pressure.

Glazed shallots

SERVES 6   150 CALS PER SERVING

750 g (1½ lb) small shallots or pickling onions

90 g (3 oz) butter

1 tbsp caster sugar

1 tbsp chopped fresh thyme

salt and black pepper

chopped parsley to garnish

1 Place the shallots in a single layer in a large frying pan and cover with cold water.

2 Add the butter, sugar, and thyme, and season with salt and pepper. Cover and bring to a boil. Uncover, and simmer gently for 10–15 minutes until the shallots are golden and the liquid almost evaporated. Shake the pan vigorously at intervals, to prevent the shallots sticking.

3 Garnish the shallots with parsley, and serve hot.

Summer peas and beans

SERVES 6–8   107–80 CALS PER SERVING

250 g (8 oz) shelled fresh broad beans (they must be young)

salt and black pepper

250 g (8 oz) shelled peas (they must be young)

250 g (8 oz) French beans, halved

30 g (1 oz) butter

2 tbsp chopped fresh mint

fresh mint to garnish

1 Cook the broad beans in a saucepan of boiling salted water for a few minutes until just tender. Add the peas and French beans and cook for another 5–10 minutes or until tender (the timing depends on their freshness).

2 Drain all the vegetables, and return to the pan. Add the butter and mint and stir until the butter melts. Taste for seasoning, and serve hot, garnished with fresh mint.

Below: Summer peas and beans.

Roasted fennel and sweet potato gratin

SERVES 4–6   312–208 CALS PER SERVING

2 large fennel bulbs

500 g (1 lb) sweet potatoes

salt and black pepper

60 g (2 oz) butter

90 g (3 oz) Parmesan cheese, grated

1 Cut each fennel bulb lengthways in half, then cut each half lengthways into 3 pieces, keeping the root ends intact. Peel the sweet potatoes, and cut the flesh into 3.5 cm (1½ in) cubes.

2 Bring a saucepan of salted water to a boil. Add the fennel, bring back to a boil, and boil for 7 minutes. Add the sweet potatoes, and boil for a further 3 minutes. Drain the vegetables, rinse under cold running water, and dry well.

3 Melt the butter in the saucepan, and return the vegetables to the pan. Toss to coat in the butter, and season with salt and pepper.

4 Tip the mixture into a shallow ovenproof dish, level the surface, and sprinkle with the cheese. Roast in a preheated oven at 220°C (200°C fan, Gas 7) for 20–25 minutes until golden brown. Serve hot.

Below: Roasted fennel and sweet potato gratin.

Golden roasted pumpkin

SERVES 6–8   93–70 CALS PER SERVING

1 kg (2 lb) piece of pumpkin, skinned, seeded, and cut into large chunks

2–3 tbsp olive oil

1 tsp balsamic or red wine vinegar

3 garlic cloves, crushed

1 tsp chopped fresh thyme

1 tsp paprika

salt and black pepper

fresh thyme to garnish

1 Put the pumpkin chunks on a baking tray. Mix the oil, vinegar, garlic, thyme, and paprika, season with salt and pepper, and pour over the pumpkin.

2 Roast in a preheated oven at 190°C (170°c fan, Gas 5) for 15–20 minutes until the pumpkin is tender and lightly browned on top. Garnish with thyme, and serve at once. If preferred, leave to cool and serve with a vinaigrette dressing (page 329).

Italian fennel

SERVES 8   108 CALS PER SERVING

4 fennel bulbs, trimmed and quartered lengthwe

salt and black pepper

butter for greasing

250 g (8 oz) mozzarella cheese, grated

chopped parsley to garnish

1 Cook the fennel in boiling salted water for 3–5 minutes until just tender. Drain thoroughly.

2 Butter a shallow ovenproof dish. Add the fennel and season with salt and pepper. Sprinkle the grated mozzarella cheese on top.

3 Bake in a preheated oven at 200°C (180°C fan, Gas 6) for 15–20 minutes until the cheese topping is golden and bubbling. Sprinkle with chopped parsley and serve hot.

atter of vegetables

ERVES 6   190 CALS PER SERVING

(1½ lb) celeriac, peeled and cut into
(1½ in) pieces

nd black pepper

full-fat crème fraîche

(1 lb) baby new potatoes, scraped

(1 lb) small Chantenay carrots, trimmed

e pointed cabbage, core removed
aves finely shredded

1 oz) butter

c clove, crushed

t the celeriac pieces into a large
ucepan. Cover with cold water, add
e salt, and bring to a boil. Cover, and
er for 15–20 minutes or until tender. Lift
e celeriac with a slotted spoon, and
e in a food processor or blender until
th. Stir in the crème fraîche, and
on with salt and pepper.

2 Bring the water in the pan back to a
boil. Add the potatoes, cover, and
simmer for 10–12 minutes or until tender.
Remove from the pan with a slotted spoon,
rinse under cold running water, and set
aside to drain.

3 Add the carrots to the boiling water in
the pan, and boil for 8 minutes or until
tender. Remove from the pan with the
slotted spoon, rinse under cold running
water, and set aside to drain.

4 Add the cabbage to the boiling water
in the pan, and simmer for 3 minutes or
until tender. Drain in a colander, rinse under
cold running water, and squeeze to remove
as much water as possible.

5 Melt the butter in the pan. Brush a large
ovenproof platter with some of the
butter, then add the garlic to the butter in
the pan and heat for a minute. Toss in the
potatoes, and season with salt and pepper.

6 Put the celeriac purée, potatoes, carrots,
and cabbage in rows on the platter, and
season with salt and pepper. Cover with foil,
and refrigerate until needed.

7 To serve, reheat the vegetables on the
foil-covered platter in a preheated oven
at 220°C (200°C fan, Gas 7) for about 25
minutes until hot and steaming. Serve
immediately, or the cabbage will lose
its colour.

Cook's know-how

This is an excellent vegetable dish for
entertaining, and it goes especially well
with a Sunday roast. It can be prepared up
to the end of step 6 as long as 24 hours
ahead, then all you have to do before the
meal is reheat it in the oven.

Asparagus with Parmesan

SERVES 4   **215 CALS PER SERVING**

625 g (1¼ lb) asparagus

90 g (3 oz) Parmesan cheese, grated

lemon wedges and flat-leaf parsley sprigs to garnish

MARINADE

2 tbsp olive oil

2 tsp white wine vinegar

3 garlic cloves, crushed

salt and black pepper

1 Trim the woody ends from the asparagus. Make the marinade: in a shallow dish, combine the oil, vinegar, garlic, a pinch of salt, and plenty of pepper.

2 Roll the asparagus in the marinade, cover, and leave to marinate for 15 minutes.

3 Sprinkle the Parmesan on to a plate. Roll the asparagus in the Parmesan, then arrange in a single layer in a large ovenproof dish.

4 Pour any remaining marinade over the asparagus, and roast in a preheated oven at 200°C (180°C fan, Gas 6) for 10–15 minutes until lightly browned and sizzling hot. Garnish with the lemon wedges and parsley sprigs, and serve hot.

Cook's know-how

To save time, you can omit the marinating and cook the asparagus on a ridged cast-iron chargrill pan. The charred stripes from the pan will boost the flavour of the asparagus and make it look attractive too.

Chargrilled vegetable platter

SERVES 4   **194 CALS PER SERVING**

4 baby aubergines

salt and black pepper

4 baby courgettes

1 red pepper

1 yellow pepper

1 large red onion

500 g (1 lb) asparagus

4 large mushrooms

175 g (6 oz) pattypan squash

olive oil for brushing

8–10 wooden cocktail sticks

1 Prepare the vegetables. Trim the aubergines, cut in half lengthways, and score a criss-cross pattern on the cut surfaces.

2 Cut the courgettes in half lengthways. Cut the red and yellow peppers in half lengthways and cut out the fleshy ribs and seeds. Peel the red onion and cut lengthways into 4–6 wedges. Trim the woody ends from the asparagus and cut the spears to an even length.

3 Gently wipe the mushrooms with damp paper towels and remove the stalks. Trim the squash if necessary.

4 Place the asparagus spears side by side in groups of 3 or 4 (depending on thickness). Gently push a cocktail stick through the asparagus, about 1 cm (½ in) from the tips, until they are all skewered. Insert a second cocktail stick at the bases of the spears. Repeat for the remaining groups of asparagus spears.

5 Brush all of the vegetables generously with olive oil and season with salt and pepper to taste.

6 Place a batch at a time over a hot barbecue or on a preheated ridged griddle pan, and cook for 10–15 minutes, turning occasionally, until the vegetables are lightly charred. Keep each batch warm while you cook the remaining vegetables.

Adding extra flavour

If you are cooking the vegetables over a barbecue, lay some woody herbs such as thyme or rosemary over the rack before you put the vegetables on. Another way of injecting flavour into the vegetables is to soak them in a well-flavoured marinade for about an hour before cooking – you can leave them overnight if this suits you better.

Herb and garlic marinade
Put 250 ml (8 fl oz) olive oil, 2 finely chopped garlic cloves, 1 tbsp chopped fresh rosemary, oregano, or thyme, and salt and pepper to taste into a bowl and whisk to mix thoroughly.

Honey and mustard marinade
Put 250 ml (8 fl oz) sunflower oil, 2 tbsp soy sauce, 1 tbsp clear honey, 2 tsp Dijon mustard, and salt and pepper to taste into a small bowl and whisk to mix.

Flavoured oils

Flavoured oils are easy to make and add an individual touch. One of these flavoured oils can be used to baste the vegetables during chargrilling instead of the olive oil in Chargrilled Vegetable Platter.

Thai perfumed oil
Lightly bruise 2–3 sprigs coriander and 3 x 5 cm (2 in) pieces fresh lemon grass. Put the coriander, lemon grass, and 2 dried chillies into a clean jar or bottle. Pour in 500 ml (16 fl oz) groundnut oil or corn oil and seal the bottle. Leave in a cool, dark place for 2 weeks, remove the coriander and lemon grass, and use to baste as directed.

Paprika oil
Spoon 2 tbsp paprika into a clean jar or bottle. Pour in 500 ml (16 fl oz) extra-virgin olive oil and seal the bottle. Leave in a cool, dark place, shaking the bottle from time to time, for 1 week. Line a funnel with a double layer of muslin and then strain the oil into another bottle. Use the oil to baste as directed.

Mixed herb oil
Lightly bruise 1 rosemary sprig and 1 thyme sprig. Put the herbs, 1 bay leaf, and 6 black peppercorns into a clean jar or bottle. Pour in 500 ml (16 fl oz) extra-virgin olive oil and seal the bottle. Leave in a cool, dark place for about 2 weeks. Use to baste as directed.

Opposite: Chargrilled vegetable platter

Herbed roasted tomatoes

SERVES 4   106 CALS PER SERVING

500 g (1 lb) cherry tomatoes

fresh herb sprig to garnish

HERB BUTTER

45 g (1½ oz) butter, softened

2 tbsp chopped fresh herbs (eg coriander, basil, flat-leaf parsley)

1 garlic clove, crushed

½ tsp lemon juice

salt and black pepper

1 Arrange the tomatoes in a single layer in an ovenproof dish. Roast in a preheated oven at 230°C (210°C fan, Gas 8) for 15–20 minutes until the tomatoes are tender but still retain their shape.

2 Meanwhile, make the herb butter: put the butter into a small bowl and beat in the herbs, garlic, and lemon juice. Season with salt and pepper. Garnish and serve hot, dotted with the herb butter.

Okra with chilli

SERVES 4–6   152–101 CALS PER SERVING

3 tbsp sunflower oil

1 small onion, sliced

1 garlic clove, crushed

500 g (1 lb) okra, trimmed

1 large fresh red chilli, halved, seeded, and diced

salt and black pepper

1 Heat the oil in a wok or large frying pan, add the onion, and stir-fry over a high heat for 3 minutes or until golden. Add the garlic and stir-fry for 1 minute.

2 Add the okra and chilli and stir-fry over a high heat for 5–10 minutes until the okra is tender, but still retains some crispness. Add salt and pepper to taste. Serve hot.

Cook's know-how

Because of its shape, okra is sometimes known as ladies' fingers. Trim the ends carefully so that the sticky juices and seeds are not exposed and released.

Ratatouille

SERVES 4–6   236–157 CALS PER SERVING

4 tbsp olive oil

1 large onion, sliced

1 large garlic clove, crushed

1 large aubergine, cut into 1 cm (½ in) slices

4 courgettes, sliced

6 juicy ripe tomatoes, sliced

1 large red pepper, halved, seeded, and sliced

1 tsp caster sugar

salt and black pepper

1 tbsp chopped fresh basil to garnish

1 Heat the olive oil in a large frying pan, add the onion and garlic, and cook gently, stirring occasionally, for 3–5 minutes until softened.

2 Add the aubergine slices, cover, and simmer gently for 20 minutes.

3 Add the courgettes, tomatoes, red pepper, and sugar. Season with salt and pepper. Cover and cook gently, stirring occasionally, for 30 minutes or until the vegetables are soft.

4 Taste for seasoning and serve hot or cold, sprinkled with the chopped fresh basil.

Mixed vegetable stir-fry

SERVES 4   155 CALS PER SERVING

1 tbsp olive oil

250 g (8 oz) courgettes, sliced thinly on the diagonal

1 yellow pepper, halved, seeded, and thinly sliced

250 g (8 oz) mixed mushrooms, sliced

salt and black pepper

1 tbsp lemon juice

60 g (2 oz) flaked almonds, toasted

1 Heat the olive oil in a wok or large frying pan, add the courgettes, and stir-fry for 3–4 minutes until the courgettes are just beginning to colour.

2 Add the yellow pepper and mushrooms and stir-fry for 2 minutes. Add salt and pepper, stir in the lemon juice, and leave the mixture to bubble for about 1 minute. Sprinkle with the toasted flaked almonds, and serve hot.

Yankee succotash

SERVES 6   491 CALS PER SERVING

2 tbsp sunflower oil

1 large onion, chopped

8 thick streaky bacon rashers, rinds removed, di

500 g (1 lb) sweetcorn kernels

250 ml (8 fl oz) single cream

1 x 400 g can beans, such as borlotti or broad beans, drained

salt

Tabasco sauce

3–4 tbsp snipped fresh chives

fresh chives to garnish

1 Heat the sunflower oil in a large frying pan, add the onion and bacon, and cook gently, stirring occasionally, for 7 minutes or until lightly browned.

2 Stir in the sweetcorn and cream and simmer for 2 minutes. Purée 3–4 tbsp the sweetcorn mixture in a food process until quite smooth, then stir back into the frying pan.

3 Add the beans and return to a boil. Simmer, stirring occasionally, for 5–10 minutes until the mixture is thickened.

4 Add salt and Tabasco sauce to taste and stir in the snipped chives. Serve at once, garnished with chives.

Healthy note

Succotash is a Native American dish traditionally made rich with bacon and cream, but you can omit these two ingredients from this recipe and use vegetable stock instead of the cream.

epperata salad

ERVES 4–6   310–207 CALS PER SERVING

urgettes, sliced lengthways

olive oil

peppers

ow peppers

(5 oz) watercress

grette dressing (page 329)

1 Brush the courgette slices on both sides with the olive oil, and cook under a hot grill, about 10 cm (4 in) from the heat, for 1–2 minutes on each side until golden. Leave to cool.

2 Halve the peppers lengthways and remove the cores and seeds. Roast and peel the peppers (see box, right). Cut the flesh into chunks. Cut the courgette slices crosswise.

3 Put the watercress into a large serving bowl. Mix in the peppers and courgettes, pour over the dressing, and toss to coat. Serve at once.

♡ Healthy note

Red peppers are an excellent source of vitamin C and carotenes, which are linked to reduced risk of heart disease and strokes, and many forms of cancer.

Roasting and peeling peppers

Cook the pepper halves, cut-side down, under a hot grill, 10 cm (4 in) from the heat, until the skin is black and blistered. Seal in a plastic bag and leave to cool. Peel off the skin, using your fingers.

Aubergine with fresh pesto

🍴 SERVES 4   499 CALS PER SERVING

1 large aubergine

75 ml (2½ fl oz) olive oil, plus extra for greasing

2–3 tsp balsamic or wine vinegar

fresh pesto (see box, right)

shredded fresh basil to garnish

1 Cut the aubergine crosswise into thin slices and arrange in a single layer on a lightly oiled baking tray. Brush the slices with one-quarter of the oil, place under a hot grill, 7 cm (3 in) from the heat, and grill for 5 minutes or until lightly browned. Turn, brush with one-third of the remaining oil, and grill 5 minutes more.

2 Sprinkle the remaining oil and the vinegar over the aubergine slices. Leave to cool. Spread pesto over one side of each slice, garnish with fresh basil, and serve at room temperature.

Fresh pesto

Purée 60 g (2 oz) grated Parmesan cheese, 1 garlic clove, 60 g (2 oz) pine nuts, 60 g (2 oz) fresh basil leaves, and salt and pepper to taste in a food processor until almost smooth.

Add 4 tbsp olive oil gradually, with the blades turning, scraping the side of the bowl occasionally with a rubber spatula to ensure that all of the mixture is incorporated.

Spinach and bacon salad

🍴 SERVES 6   436 CALS PER SERVING

g (1 lb) baby spinach leaves, all
lks removed

arge slices of thick-cut white bread,
usts removed

osp sunflower oil

arlic clove, crushed

streaky bacon rashers, rinds removed,
into strips

tbsp vinaigrette or blue cheese dressing
ge 329)

and black pepper

Tear the spinach leaves into large pieces
and put them into a salad bowl.

Make the croûtons: cut the bread into
small cubes. Heat the sunflower oil in
ying pan, add the garlic, and cook for
inute. Add the bread cubes and cook,
ing, for 1–2 minutes until golden and
o. Lift out the croûtons and drain on
per towels.

Add the bacon to the pan and fry for
5 minutes or until crisp. Lift out and drain
paper towels.

Sprinkle the bacon over the spinach.
Spoon the dressing over the salad,
son with salt and pepper, and toss
tly. Scatter the croûtons over the
d, and serve at once.

Mixed leaf salad

🍴 SERVES 4–6   117–78 CALS PER SERVING

p lettuce, such as iceberg or romaine

ch of watercress, tough stalks removed

(2 oz) lamb's lettuce

(2 oz) rocket

t 4 tbsp vinaigrette dressing (page 329)

snipped fresh chives

ar the lettuce leaves into bite-sized
eces and put them into a large salad
l. Add the watercress, lamb's lettuce,
rocket, and mix together.

our the dressing over the salad and
ss gently. Sprinkle with the chives,
serve at once.

Red salad bowl

🍴 SERVES 4–6   387–258 CALS PER SERVING

1 small head of radicchio

1 small oak leaf lettuce

1 small lollo rosso lettuce

1 small red onion, thinly sliced

125 g (4 oz) seedless red grapes

DRESSING

150 ml (¼ pint) olive oil

3 tbsp balsamic vinegar

1 garlic clove, crushed (optional)

½ tsp caster sugar, or to taste

salt and black pepper

1 Tear the radicchio leaves and the oak
leaf and lollo rosso lettuce leaves into
bite-sized pieces. Put them into a large
salad bowl and mix together, then add
the onion and grapes.

2 Make the dressing: combine the oil,
vinegar, and garlic, if using, with sugar,
salt, and pepper to taste.

3 Pour just enough dressing over the salad
to cling to the leaves, toss gently, and
serve at once.

Waldorf salad

🍴 SERVES 4   469 CALS PER SERVING

500 g (1 lb) crisp red-skinned apples, cored
and diced

juice of ½ lemon

4 celery stalks, thickly sliced

150 ml (¼ pint) mayonnaise (page 329)

salt and black pepper

90 g (3 oz) walnut pieces, coarsely chopped

chopped parsley to garnish

1 Put the diced apples into a bowl, pour
the lemon juice over the top, and stir to
coat thoroughly to prevent discoloration.
Transfer to a salad bowl and add
the celery.

2 Spoon the mayonnaise over the salad,
season with salt and pepper, and toss
gently to mix. Cover and chill until required.
Stir in the walnut pieces and garnish with
chopped parsley just before serving.

Crunchy oriental salad

🍴 SERVES 6   141 CALS PER SERVING

1 iceberg or romaine lettuce

175 g (6 oz) bean sprouts

6 spring onions, thinly sliced on the diagonal

1 green pepper, halved, seeded, and thinly sliced

2 tbsp toasted sesame seeds

DRESSING

3 tbsp sunflower or olive oil

1 tsp sesame oil

1 tbsp white wine vinegar

1 garlic clove, crushed

1 cm (½ in) piece of fresh root ginger, peeled
and grated

½ tsp caster sugar, or to taste

salt and black pepper

1 Tear the lettuce leaves into bite-sized
pieces. Put the lettuce, bean sprouts,
spring onions, and pepper into a salad
bowl and mix together.

2 Make the dressing: combine the oils,
vinegar, garlic, and ginger, and season
to taste with sugar, salt, and pepper.

3 Toss the salad with the dressing, sprinkle
with the sesame seeds, and serve.

Romaine lettuce has a crisp texture, making
it an ideal choice for crunchy salads.

Caesar salad

 SERVES 4   421 CALS PER SERVING

1 cos or romaine lettuce

4 tbsp olive oil

2 tbsp lemon juice

salt and black pepper

2 hard-boiled eggs, peeled

30 g (1 oz) Parmesan cheese, coarsely grated

CROÛTONS

3 large slices of thick-cut white bread,
crusts removed

4 tbsp olive oil

1 garlic clove, crushed

1 Make the croûtons: cut the bread into small cubes. Heat the olive oil in a frying pan, add the garlic, and cook for 1 minute. Add the bread cubes and cook, stirring, for 1–2 minutes until crisp. Lift out and drain on paper towels.

2 Tear the lettuce leaves into bite-sized pieces and put them into a salad bowl. Whisk the olive oil and lemon juice, season with salt and pepper, and toss with the leaves.

3 Cut the hard-boiled eggs into quarters, and add to the salad. Add the croûtons and Parmesan cheese and toss gently. Serve at once.

Caesar salad with anchovies

Coarsely chop 6 canned anchovy fillets and add to the salad with the hard-boiled eggs in step 3.

Cook's know-how

If you prefer a lighter salad, you can toast the bread to make the croûtons rather than frying it in oil. For a sophisticated change, use 4 hard-boiled quails' eggs, halved, instead of hens' eggs.

Crunchy coleslaw

SERVES 8   245 CALS PER SERVING

white cabbage, weighing about 750 g (1½ lb)

ml (¼ pint) vinaigrette dressing (page 329)

mall onion, finely chopped

sp Dijon mustard

t and black pepper

elery stalks, thinly sliced

arrots, grated

g (2 oz) sultanas

-90 ml (2½–3 fl oz) mayonnaise (page 329)

Cut the cabbage into quarters lengthways and cut out the core. Shred e cabbage finely, using either a sharp fe or the slicing blade of a food processor.

Put the cabbage into a large bowl, add the vinaigrette, onion, and Dijon ustard, and season with salt and pepper. s to mix thoroughly. Cover the bowl tly, and leave to chill for about 8 hours.

Add the celery, carrots, and sultanas, and toss to mix thoroughly. Stir in the yonnaise. Cover and chill until ready erve. Toss the coleslaw well and taste seasoning before serving.

arrot julienne alad

SERVES 4–6   79–53 CALS PER SERVING

arrots

and black pepper

SSING

sp olive oil

white wine vinegar

rlic clove, crushed

chopped parsley

n and fresh chives to garnish

Cut the carrots into matchstick strips. anch in a saucepan of salted boiling er for 2–3 minutes. Drain, refresh under running water, and drain again.

Make the dressing: combine the oil, white wine vinegar, garlic, and parsley, season with salt and pepper.

ut the carrots into a salad bowl, pour ver the dressing, and toss to coat ly. Leave to cool. Garnish with lemon chives before serving.

Potato, apple, and celery salad

SERVES 6   332 CALS PER SERVING

750 g (1½ lb) new potatoes, scrubbed

salt and black pepper

75 ml (2½ fl oz) vinaigrette dressing (page 329)

6 celery stalks, sliced

1 small red onion, very finely sliced

2 red-skinned apples, such as Red Delicious or Spartan, cored and diced

125 ml (4 fl oz) mayonnaise (page 329)

2 tbsp snipped fresh chives to garnish

1 Put the potatoes into a large saucepan of boiling salted water and simmer gently for 10–15 minutes until just tender. Drain, leave to cool, then cut the potatoes in half.

2 Put the potatoes into a large salad bowl, add the vinaigrette dressing, and toss gently while the potatoes are still warm. Leave to cool.

3 Add the celery, onion, and apples to the cold potatoes. Mix gently until all the ingredients are thoroughly coated with dressing, then season with salt and pepper. Cover and chill for at least 1 hour.

4 Gently stir in the mayonnaise, taste for seasoning, then sprinkle with the chives, and serve at once.

Celeriac remoulade

SERVES 4–6   100–66 CALS PER SERVING

500 g (1 lb) celeriac

juice of 1 lemon

sliced gherkin and chopped parsley to garnish

DRESSING

150 ml (¼ pint) plain yogurt

2 tbsp mayonnaise (page 329)

1 tsp finely chopped capers

½ tsp Dijon mustard

salt and black pepper

1 Make the dressing: combine the yogurt, mayonnaise, capers, and Dijon mustard, and season with salt and pepper.

2 Peel the celeriac, cut into matchstick-thin strips, and place in a bowl of cold water. Add the lemon juice and toss to prevent discoloration.

3 Drain the celeriac and transfer to a salad bowl. Pour over the dressing and toss gently to mix. Garnish with the gherkins and chopped parsley, and serve at once.

Below: Celeriac remoulade.

Potato salad

SERVES 8   357 CALS PER SERVING

1 kg (2 lb) new potatoes, scrubbed

salt and black pepper

1 small mild onion, very finely chopped

4 tbsp vinaigrette dressing (page 329)

250 ml (8 fl oz) mayonnaise (page 329), or less if preferred

2 tbsp snipped fresh chives, plus extra to garnish

1 Put the potatoes into a large saucepan of boiling salted water and simmer for 15–20 minutes until tender. Drain the potatoes thoroughly. Cut them into even-sized pieces.

2 Put the potatoes into a large salad bowl and add the chopped onion.

3 While the potatoes are still quite warm, spoon the vinaigrette dressing over them and then toss gently to mix all the ingredients thoroughly.

4 Add the mayonnaise and the chives, and mix together gently. Add salt and pepper to taste, cover, and chill for about 30 minutes (the salad is best served not too cold). Garnish with extra chives before serving.

Greek salad

SERVES 4–6   503–335 CALS PER SERVING

4 beefsteak or slicing tomatoes

1 cucumber, sliced

250 g (8 oz) feta cheese, diced

24 black olives, pitted

125 ml (4 fl oz) extra virgin olive oil

4 tbsp lemon juice

salt and black pepper

2 tbsp chopped fresh oregano or flat-leaf parsley

1 Halve the tomatoes lengthways, cut out the cores, and cut each half into 4 wedges.

2 Put the tomatoes into a large salad bowl, and add the cucumber, feta cheese, and olives.

3 Spoon over the olive oil and lemon juice, and add salt and black pepper to taste (do not use too much salt as feta is a salty cheese), then toss gently to mix.

4 Sprinkle the salad with the oregano or parsley before serving.

Avocado salad

SERVES 6   240 CALS PER SERVING

60 g (2 oz) pine nuts

250 g (8 oz) mixed salad leaves

2 oranges

2 avocados

DRESSING

finely grated zest of 1 orange

3 tbsp orange juice

1 tbsp walnut oil

1–2 tsp caster sugar

salt and black pepper

1 Spread the pine nuts on a baking tray, and toast under a hot grill for 2 minutes.

2 Put the salad leaves into a large salad bowl. Peel the oranges, removing the rind and pith, and separate into segments (page 421).

3 Halve, stone, and peel the avocados (page 327). Slice lengthways and mix with the orange segments and pine nuts.

4 Whisk together the dressing ingredients, and pour over the salad. Toss gently and serve.

Cucumber salad

SERVES 4–6   75–50 CALS PER SERVING

1 cucumber, peeled and cut in half lengthways

1 tbsp chopped fresh dill

DRESSING

2 tbsp hot water

2 tbsp white wine vinegar

1 tbsp sunflower oil

2 tbsp caster sugar

salt and black pepper

1 Scoop out the cucumber seeds. Cut the flesh crosswise into thin slices, and arrange in a serving dish.

2 Make the dressing: whisk together the water, wine vinegar, oil, sugar, and salt and pepper to taste.

3 Pour the dressing over the cucumber and sprinkle with the dill before serving.

Serving suggestion

This Danish-style salad goes well with both grilled or baked fresh fish and smoked fish.

Mushroom salad

SERVES 6   102 CALS PER SERVING

3 tbsp sunflower oil

½ tsp ground coriander

750 g (1½ lb) button mushrooms

salt and black pepper

4 celery stalks, thinly sliced

shredded fresh basil to garnish

DRESSING

150 ml (¼ pint) plain yogurt

1 tbsp lemon juice

1 tbsp white wine vinegar

1 tsp Dijon mustard

1 garlic clove, crushed

1 Heat the oil in a frying pan, add the ground coriander, and cook gently, stirring, for 1 minute. Add the mushrooms, season lightly, and cook over a high heat stirring, for 5 minutes. Lift out with a slotted spoon. Leave to cool.

2 Make the dressing: combine the yogu lemon juice, vinegar, Dijon mustard, garlic, and salt and pepper to taste. Pour the dressing over the mushrooms, and tos to mix. Cover and chill for 8 hours. Stir in t celery and garnish with basil before servir

Tomato and onion salad

SERVES 6   166 CALS PER SERVING

750 g (1½ lb) ripe but firm tomatoes, thinly slice

1 mild onion, cut into thin rings

1 tbsp snipped fresh chives

DRESSING

90 ml (3 fl oz) extra virgin olive oil

2 tbsp red wine vinegar

¼ tsp caster sugar

salt and black pepper

1 Overlap the tomato slices in circles of diminishing size in a large shallow dish Arrange the onion rings on top.

2 Make the dressing: combine the olive oil, red wine vinegar, and caster suga and add salt and pepper to taste.

3 Spoon the dressing over the tomatoe and onions, cover, and leave to chill for about 2 hours. Sprinkle with the snipp chives before serving.

ricolore salad

SERVES 4   **509 CALS PER SERVING**

efsteak or slicing tomatoes

and black pepper

g (8 oz) mozzarella cheese

ocados

p lemon juice

bsp extra virgin olive oil

sprigs to garnish

1 Slice the tomatoes thinly, put into a bowl, and sprinkle with salt and pepper. Thinly slice the mozzarella.

2 Cut the avocados in half lengthways. Twist to loosen the halves and pull them apart. Remove the stones (page 327), score and peel off the skin, then cut the halves crosswise.

3 Cut the avocado quarters into slices lengthways, then sprinkle with lemon juice to prevent discoloration.

4 Arrange the tomato, mozzarella, and avocado slices attractively on a platter. Drizzle with the extra virgin olive oil and garnish with basil sprigs before serving.

Basil, an aromatic and peppery herb, lends a warm flavour to salads. Since its leaves bruise easily, they are added as garnish just before serving.

Italian pesto salad

 SERVES 4–6   252–168 CALS PER SERVING

375 g (12 oz) broccoli, cut into bite-sized florets

375 g (12 oz) cauliflower, cut into bite-sized florets

about 12 black olives, pitted

PESTO

30 g (1 oz) fresh basil

1 garlic clove

1 tbsp pine nuts

30 g (1 oz) Parmesan cheese, grated

salt and black pepper

5 tbsp extra virgin olive oil

1 Make the pesto: put the basil, garlic, pine nuts, Parmesan and seasoning into a small food processor and process until the basil is finely chopped. With the machine running, add the oil in a fine stream until the paste is creamy. Check the seasoning.

2 Blanch the broccoli and cauliflower florets in boiling salted water for about 2 minutes (they should retain plenty of bite, so take care not to overcook them). Drain and refresh under cold running water. Drain again, then toss with the pesto. Scatter with the olives and chill before serving.

 Healthy note

Broccoli and cauliflower are both cruciferous vegetables (the name crucifer comes from the cross shape of their 4-petalled flowers), known to be excellent nutrition boosters. They are rich in the antioxidants vitamin C, vitamin E, and carotenes, which can help guard against heart disease and strokes, and they have a strong link to a lower risk of cancer. Crucifers are also rich in folate and iron, minerals that help prevent and correct anaemia, and in potassium, a mineral that helps avoid and regulate high blood pressure.

Puy lentil salad

 SERVES 6   181 CALS PER SERVING

250 g (8 oz) Puy lentils, rinsed

3 tbsp olive oil

2 tbsp balsamic vinegar

salt and black pepper

1 bunch of spring onions, trimmed and finely sliced

3 tbsp chopped fresh flat-leaf parsley

1 Pour the lentils into a medium saucepan, cover with plenty of cold water, and bring to a boil. Reduce the heat, cover, and simmer for 15 minutes or until the lentils are tender.

2 Drain the lentils well, tip into a serving bowl, and add the olive oil and vinegar, and plenty of seasoning (warm lentils absorb the flavours of dressing better than cold lentils). Leave to cool, then mix in the spring onions and chopped parsley just before serving.

Tabbouleh

 SERVES 4   193 CALS PER SERVING

125 g (4 oz) bulgur wheat

3 tbsp extra virgin olive oil

juice of 2 lemons

salt and black pepper

¼ bunch spring onions, finely sliced

½ cucumber, peeled, seeded, and finely diced

6 tbsp chopped fresh mint

6 tbsp chopped fresh flat-leaf parsley

1 Soak the bulgur wheat in boiling water for 30 minutes. Drain well, tip into a serving bowl, and add the olive oil, lemon juice, and plenty of seasoning. Do this immediately while the wheat is still warm so that it absorbs the maximum flavour.

2 Add the spring onions, cucumber, and freshly chopped herbs to the bowl. Stir well and check the seasoning. Chill before serving.

Herb salad with orange and mustard dressing

 SERVES 4–6   207–138 CALS PER SERVING

125 g (4 oz) fine asparagus

salt and black pepper

½ romaine lettuce

60 g (2 oz) lamb's lettuce

60 g (2 oz) rocket

1 small bunch of flat-leaf parsley, stalks removed

60 g (2 oz) pine nuts, toasted

60 g (2 oz) sun-blushed or sun-dried tomatoes, snipped into small pieces

DRESSING

1 orange

2 tbsp olive oil

1 tsp maple syrup

1 tsp wholegrain mustard

1 Trim the asparagus and cut into 2.5 cm (1 in) lengths. Cook in boiling salted water for about 3 minutes until just tender. Drain and refresh under cold running water.

2 Break the romaine lettuce into manageable pieces and mix with the lamb's lettuce, rocket, and parsley leaves in a salad bowl. Add the asparagus, pine nuts, and tomatoes, and toss gently.

3 Remove the zest of the orange with a zester and add the strips to the salad. Squeeze the juice from half of the orange to give about 3 tbsp, then mix with the remaining dressing ingredients and seasoning to taste. Toss the salad with the dressing just before serving.

Opposite, clockwise from top: Herb salad with orange and mustard dressing, Puy lentil salad, Tabbouleh, Italian pesto salad

Couscous salad

SERVES 6   280 CALS PER SERVING

½ tsp crushed dried red chillies

90 ml (3 fl oz) olive oil

250 g (8 oz) couscous

500 ml (16 fl oz) boiling water

3–4 tbsp sultanas

5 cm (2 in) piece of fresh root ginger, peeled and grated

salt and black pepper

3–4 tbsp white wine vinegar

5 ripe tomatoes, diced

1 onion, chopped

3 spring onions, thinly sliced

2 tbsp chopped fresh mint

mint sprigs to garnish

1 Combine the chillies and olive oil, and set aside.

2 Put the couscous into a bowl, stir in the measured water, sultanas, ginger, and a good pinch of salt. Cover and leave to stand for 10 minutes.

3 Stir in the chilli oil, vinegar, tomatoes, onion, spring onions, and mint. Season with salt and pepper to taste, and garnish with mint sprigs before serving.

Bulgur wheat salad

SERVES 4   280 CALS PER SERVING

175 g (6 oz) bulgur wheat

4–5 tbsp vinaigrette dressing (page 329)

juice of 1 lemon

3 tomatoes, diced

4 spring onions, chopped

3 tbsp chopped parsley

3 tbsp chopped fresh mint

salt and black pepper

parsley sprigs to garnish

1 Put the bulgur wheat into a large bowl, cover with cold water, and leave to stand for 30 minutes.

2 Drain the bulgur wheat, pressing out as much of the liquid as possible. Transfer to a salad bowl, and mix in the vinaigrette dressing, lemon juice, tomatoes, spring onions, parsley, and mint. Season with salt and pepper, toss well, and garnish with parsley. Serve at room temperature.

Tomato and basil salad

SERVES 4–6   146–97 CALS PER SERVING

2 beefsteak or slicing tomatoes

4 ripe salad tomatoes

125 g (4 oz) cherry tomatoes

1 yellow pepper, cored, deseeded, and cut into chunks

2 tbsp shredded fresh basil

DRESSING

3 tbsp extra virgin olive oil

2 tsp balsamic vinegar

¼ tsp caster sugar

salt and black pepper

1 Make the dressing: combine the olive oil, vinegar, sugar, and salt and pepper to taste.

2 Cut the beefsteak tomatoes in half lengthways, cut out the core, and cut each half into 4 wedges. Thickly slice the salad tomatoes. Halve the cherry tomatoes.

3 Put all the tomatoes and the yellow pepper into a salad bowl, and sprinkle with the dressing. Cover and leave to stand for 1 hour to let the flavours mingle. Sprinkle with the basil just before serving.

Wild rice salad

SERVES 6   369 CALS PER SERVING

250 g (8 oz) mixed long grain and wild rice

salt and black pepper

175 g (6 oz) French beans, cut in half crosswise

2 tbsp chopped parsley

60 g (2 oz) button mushrooms, thinly sliced

60 g (2 oz) walnut pieces

DRESSING

4 tbsp sunflower oil

2 tbsp walnut oil

2 tbsp white wine vinegar

1 tsp Dijon mustard

1 Cook the rice in boiling salted water for 15 minutes, or according to packet instructions, until just tender. Drain, rinse in boiling water, and drain again. Transfer to a large bowl.

2 Cook the beans in boiling salted water for 4–5 minutes until just tender. Drain, rinse in cold water, and drain again.

3 Make the dressing: combine the oils, vinegar, mustard, and salt and pepper to taste. Pour over the rice while still warm, stir, and leave to cool.

4 Add the beans, parsley, mushrooms, and walnuts to the rice. Stir before serving.

Three-bean salad

SERVES 4   315 CALS PER SERVING

250 g (8 oz) French beans, cut in half crosswise

salt and black pepper

1 x 400 g can chick peas, drained and rinsed

1 x 400 g can red kidney beans, drained and rinsed

10 pitted black olives, halved

chopped parsley to garnish

DRESSING

4 tbsp Greek yogurt

3 tbsp olive oil

3 tbsp red wine vinegar

2 tsp Dijon mustard

¼ tsp caster sugar, or to taste

1 Cook the French beans in boiling salted water for 4–5 minutes until just tender. Drain, rinse under cold running water, and drain again.

2 Make the dressing: combine the Greek yogurt, oil, red wine vinegar, and mustard, and season with sugar, salt, and pepper to taste.

3 Put the chick peas, red kidney beans, and French beans into a large bowl. Pour the dressing over the beans and stir gently to mix. Cover and leave to stand 1 hour. Add the olives, sprinkle with the chopped parsley, and serve at once.

Three-bean salad with bacon

Substitute 250 g (8 oz) cooked, shelled and skinned broad beans for the chick peas, and omit the olives. Cut 60 g (2 oz) streaky bacon rashers into strips, and dry-fry until crisp and golden. Sprinkle over the salad just before serving.

Salade niçoise

SERVES 4   530 CALS PER SERVING

50 g (8 oz) French beans, cut in half crosswise

salt and black pepper

hard-boiled eggs

cos or romaine lettuce

cucumber, sliced

tomatoes, quartered

x 200 g can tuna, drained

small mild onion, very thinly sliced

x 50 g can anchovy fillets, drained

2 pitted black olives

chopped parsley to garnish

DRESSING

150 ml (¼ pint) olive oil

3 tbsp white wine vinegar

1 garlic clove, crushed

½ tsp Dijon mustard

1 Cook the French beans in boiling salted water for 4–5 minutes until just tender. Drain, rinse under cold running water, and drain again.

2 Peel the shells from the eggs, and cut the eggs into wedges lengthways.

3 Make the dressing: combine the oil, vinegar, garlic, and mustard, and season with salt and pepper.

4 Tear the lettuce leaves into pieces and place on a large serving plate. Arrange the cucumber and beans on top of the lettuce.

5 Arrange the tomatoes and eggs on the serving plate. Coarsely flake the tuna with a fork and place in the middle. Arrange the onion, anchovy fillets, and olives over the tuna. Pour over the dressing, garnish with parsley, and serve at once.

Above: Pasta and mackerel salad.

Pasta and mackerel salad

🍴 SERVES 6   643 CALS PER SERVING

500 g (1 lb) pasta shells

salt and black pepper

2 courgettes, sliced

125 g (4 oz) French beans, cut in half crosswise

2 oranges

375 g (12 oz) peppered smoked mackerel fillets

30 g (1 oz) walnut pieces

DRESSING

juice of 1 orange

2 tbsp sunflower oil

1 tbsp walnut oil

2 tbsp chopped parsley

1 Cook the pasta shells in a large saucepan of boiling salted water for 8–10 minutes until just tender. Drain, rinse under cold running water, and drain again.

2 Cook the courgettes and French beans in another pan of boiling salted water for 4–5 minutes until tender. Drain, rinse, and drain again.

3 Peel and segment the oranges (page 421) and set aside. Remove the skin and any bones from the mackerel, then flake the flesh into large pieces.

4 Make the dressing: combine the orange juice, sunflower and walnut oils, and parsley, and season with salt and pepper.

5 Put the pasta, courgettes, French beans, orange segments, flaked mackerel, and walnut pieces into a large salad bowl. Add the dressing and toss gently so that the fish does not break up. Leave to chill in the refrigerator for at least 30 minutes before serving.

Rice salad

🍴 SERVES 6   345 CALS PER SERVING

250 g (8 oz) long grain rice

salt and black pepper

125 g (4 oz) frozen peas

125 g (4 oz) frozen sweetcorn kernels

1 red pepper, halved, seeded, and diced

2 tbsp chopped fresh coriander

DRESSING

90 ml (3 fl oz) olive oil

3 tbsp white wine vinegar

1 tsp Dijon mustard

1 garlic clove, crushed

1 Cook the rice in boiling salted water for 12–15 minutes until just tender, adding the peas and sweetcorn for the last 3 minutes. Drain, rinse in boiling water, and drain again. Transfer to a bowl.

2 Make the dressing: combine the olive oil, wine vinegar, mustard, and garlic, and season with salt and pepper. Pour over the rice while still warm, stir gently, and leave to cool.

3 Add the red pepper, and coriander to the rice, and stir to combine. Serve at once.

Pasta salad with peppers

🍴 SERVES 6   370 CALS PER SERVING

500 g (1 lb) pasta bows

salt and black pepper

1 red pepper, halved, seeded, and diced

1 green pepper, halved, seeded, and diced

3 spring onions, sliced diagonally

4 tbsp mayonnaise (page 329)

spring onion tops, sliced, to garnish

1 Cook the pasta bows in a large saucepan of boiling salted water for 8–10 minutes until just tender.

2 Drain, rinse under cold running water, and drain again. Leave to cool.

3 Put the pasta, peppers, and spring onions into a salad bowl, and season with salt and pepper. Add the mayonnaise, stir well to coat all the ingredients evenly, then chill for 30 minutes. Garnish with spring onions before serving.

Pasta salad with mangetout and sesame seeds

Substitute 125 g (4 oz) blanched mangetout for the red and green peppers. Omit the mayonnaise. Mix together 2 tbsp white wine vinegar, 1 tbsp sunflower oil, and 1 tsp sesame oil, and pour over the salad. Taste for seasoning. Substitute 2 tbsp toasted sesame seeds for the spring onion garnish, and serve at once.

💚 **Healthy note**

If you prefer not to use mayonnaise for the dressing, use 2 tbsp olive oil whisked with the juice of 1 lemon, 1 tsp Dijon mustard, and a good handful of roughly chopped herbs. Fresh basil, dill, parsley, chervil, and chives can all be used, on their own or mixed together.

Yeast Cookery

Under 45 minutes

Dinner rolls
A simple dough shaped into rolls and baked until golden. Served warm or cool and spread with butter.

MAKES 18   95 CALS EACH
Takes 40 minutes, **plus rising**   Page 364

TRADITIONAL

Hot cross buns
Slightly sweet spiced buns studded with currants and mixed peel, decorated with pastry crosses, and baked until golden.

MAKES 12   279 CALS EACH
Takes 35 minutes, **plus rising**   Page 3

Spicy deep-pan pizza
Thick, crisp-crusted pizza covered with tomatoes, pepperoni sausage, mozzarella, Parmesan cheeses. Spiked with green chilli

MAKES 1 LARGE PIZZA   3596 CALS
Takes 35 minutes, **plus rising**   Page

Brioches
Classic and rich: an egg- and butter-enriche dough baked until golden brown in characteristic fluted moulds.

MAKES 12   149 CALS EACH
Takes 35 minutes, **plus rising**   Page

Jam doughnuts
Old-fashioned favourite: doughnuts filled w raspberry jam, deep-fried, and sprinkled w cinnamon and sugar.

MAKES 16   269 CALS EACH
Takes 40 minutes, **plus rising**   Page

Focaccia
Italian classic: flat pizza-like bread flavoured with olive oil and fresh rosemary. Sprinkled with coarse sea salt.

MAKES 1 LARGE LOAF   2989 CALS
Takes 35 minutes, **plus rising**   Page 368

FAMILY CHOICE

Bath buns
Sweetened rich dough with sultanas and mixed peel. Shaped into buns, topped with crushed sugar, and baked until golden.

MAKES 18   196 CALS EACH
Takes 40 minutes, **plus rising**   Page 378

TRADITIONAL

mhouse loaf

ole to make: white flour loaf dusted with
and baked until well risen and golden.
s a large and tender crumb.

S 1 LARGE LOAF   2790 CALS
s 50 minutes, **plus rising**   Page 363

Chelsea buns

A plain dough rolled with a filling of sultanas,
currants, orange zest, and mixed spices.
Sliced, baked, and glazed with honey.

MAKES 12   298 CALS EACH
Takes 60 minutes, **plus rising**   Page 379

Over 60 minutes

Pissaladière with Mediterranean vegetables

A delicious pizza with roasted aubergine
cubes, red peppers, and cheese topping,
drizzled with vinegar and olive oil and
sprinkled with basil. Served hot.

SERVES 6   434 CALS PER SERVING
Takes 1¼ hours   Page 371

Sourdough rye bread

Sourdough starter gives a slightly tangy
flavour to this hearty loaf. Studded with
caraway seeds.

MAKES 2 LARGE LOAVES   3329 CALS PER LOAF
Takes 1 hour 5 minutes, **plus rising**   Page 368

Lardy cake

Traditional English cake made tender and
crisp with lard and studded with mixed fruit.
Baked until dark golden brown.

MAKES 1 LARGE LOAF   8186 CALS
Takes 1 hour 5 minutes, **plus rising**   Page 375

HIGH FIBRE

-grain loaf

ritious wholemeal and white flour loaf
ed with wheat flakes, linseed and
wer seeds, then lightly brushed with
sprinkled with wheat flakes, and baked.

2 SMALL LOAVES   1495 CALS PER LOAF
60 minutes, **plus rising**   Page 367

Croissants

Classic French breakfast roll: made rich and
flaky with butter. Shaped into crescents,
glazed, and baked until golden.

MAKES 12   352 CALS EACH
Takes 55 minutes, **plus chilling**   Page 374

Yeast cookery know-how

The pleasure of baking bread is legendary. From making and kneading the dough to slicing a fresh baked loaf, the experience is a thoroughly satisfying one that cooks the world over have shared for centuries. Indeed, yeast cookery is perhaps the most popular of all kitchen crafts.

From this rich history comes a wide variety of recipes, both sweet and savoury, many of which are easily made; others are more time-consuming to prepare. Crumpets and hot cross buns, Danish pastries and croissants, wholemeal bread and crispy, thin-crusted pizzas are all equally delicious.

Yeast cookery ingredients

There is a large range of flours from which to choose, each with its own unique texture and flavour. The different types of yeast, on the other hand, vary simply in their method of preparation.

Flour

The best flours to use for yeast doughs are those labelled "strong". These are milled from hard wheat with a high gluten content and produce a good open-textured bread. Ordinary plain flour, which contains a higher proportion of soft wheat, can be used for yeast doughs, but the result will be a more close-textured and crumbly loaf.

The flour most commonly used for breadmaking is white wheat flour. Other wheat flours include wholemeal flour, also called whole wheat, which is milled from the entire wheat kernel, including the bran and germ; brown or wheatmeal flour, which contains more of the bran and wheat germ than white flour; granary flour, which is brown flour with malted wheat flakes and cracked and whole wheat grains added.

Other grains and cereals, such as barley, buckwheat, maize (corn), millet, oats, and rye, are milled into flour for bread-making. Soya beans are also ground into a flour-like powder. Most of these flours are low in gluten, or contain no gluten at all, so they are normally combined with wheat flour to prevent the bread from being too dense.

Fresh yeast

This form of yeast, which looks like creamy-grey putty, is perishable and so needs to be refrigerated (keep it in an airtight container for up to 4–5 days). You will find it at a bakery where they bake on the premises or at a healthfood shop. Fresh yeast should be almost odourless, with only a slightly yeasty smell, and it should break apart cleanly. It needs to be blended with warm liquid and "fed" with sugar, then left to become frothy before mixing with flour. To substitute fresh yeast for dried yeast, use double the weight, ie 15 g (½ oz) fresh yeast for 7 g (¼ oz) dried.

Dried yeast

Fast-action dried yeast (also known as easy-blend) is added directly to flour with other dry ingredients. Ordinary dried yeast needs to be blended with warm liquid and a little sugar before mixing with flour. After 5 minutes or so, the yeast should dissolve and the mixture should be foamy. If this is not the result, discard the yeast and start again. Dried yeast will keep for up to 6 months in a cool place.

Lukewarm water (40–43°C/105–110°F) should be used to blend and dissolve both fresh and ordinary dried yeast. If the water is too hot it will kill the yeast.

Bread machines

Although keen bakers maintain that bread made in a machine can never be as good to eat as a loaf made by hand, bread machines are increasingly popular, perhaps because they mean you can enjoy a freshly baked loaf at any time. Pop in the ingredients and the machine will mix, knead, raise, knock up, and bake for you. Just be sure to follow the manufacturer's recipes and instructions.

Freezing

It is a good idea to halve or quarter loaves before freezing so you can take out what you need. Pack in moisture-proof wrapping and seal well. Most loaves can be frozen for up to 4 months; if enriched with milk or fruit, storage time is 3 months. Thaw, still wrapped, at room temperature. Bread with a crust, such as baguette, does not freeze well as the crust lifts off.

Successful home baking

The quantity of liquid given in a recipe can only be a guide because the absorbency of flour can vary. The quantity of liquid that flour can absorb depends on temperature and humidity, how much hard wheat the flour contains (proportions vary from one brand to another) and whether it is wholemeal or white.

Dough can be kneaded in a food processor or an electric mixer fitted with a dough hook, as well as by hand.

Dough rises quickest in a warm environment. A slow rise, such as in the fridge overnight, gives bread more flavour.

To test if dough has risen sufficiently, push in a finger; when withdrawn, an indentation should remain in the dough.

Making a yeast dough

Making bread is not difficult, nor does it take up a lot of time – the most lengthy parts of the procedure, the rising and baking, are done by the bread itself. Here are the basic techniques, using fast-action dried yeast.

1 Sift the flour into a large bowl, and then mix in the yeast and any other dry ingredients. Make a well in the middle and pour in almost all the measured liquid (the precise amount is difficult to gauge).

2 Using your fingers, mix the liquid ingredients together, then gradually incorporate the flour. Mix thoroughly until a soft, quite sticky dough is formed, adding the remaining liquid if it is needed.

3 Turn the dough on to a lightly floured work surface and knead: fold it over towards you, then push it down and away with the heel of your hand. Turn the dough, fold it, and push it away again. Continue kneading for 5–10 minutes until the dough is elastic and smooth. Doughs made with strong wheat flour take longer to knead than those made with soft flour.

4 Shape the dough into a ball. Put the dough into a lightly oiled bowl and turn to coat it all over with oil. Cover with oiled cling film or a damp tea towel and leave to rise in a warm, draught-free place such as an airing cupboard (or in a cool place for a longer time).

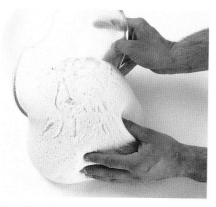

5 When the dough has doubled in size, turn it on to a lightly floured work surface and knock out the air by punching the dough firmly. Knead the dough vigorously for 2–3 minutes until smooth and elastic.

6 Shape the dough as directed. Cover loosely with cling film or a dry tea towel and leave in a warm, draught-free place to rise until doubled in size again. Bake according to the recipe.

Testing loaves

At the end of cooking, bread should be well risen, firm, and golden brown. To test if it is thoroughly cooked, tip out of the tin or lift off the baking tray and tap the base. The bread should have a hollow, drum-like sound. If it does not sound hollow, return it to the oven to bake for a further 5 minutes, then remove it and test again.

Glazes and toppings

Breads and rolls can be glazed before or after baking to add flavour and, depending on the glaze, to make the crust soft or shiny and crisp. Apply the glaze thinly, using a pastry brush. Here are a few suggestions for different glazes:

- water (before baking) for a crisp crust
- milk or cream (before baking) for a soft crust
- egg or egg yolk beaten with a pinch of salt (before baking) or butter (after baking) for a shiny crust
- sugar and water (after baking) for a shiny crust

Toppings such as wheat or barley flakes, woody herbs such as rosemary, sunflower or sesame seeds, poppyseeds, grated cheese, chopped nuts, and coarse sea salt can be sprinkled over glazed breads and rolls before baking. Sweetened breads are often sprinkled with sugar or a spice-and-sugar mixture after cooking.

Shaping loaves

Because of the elastic quality of dough, it can very easily be formed into a variety of different shapes. Here are some of the more traditional ones.

Cottage loaf
Cut off one-third of the dough. Roll each piece into a ball and put the small ball on top of the large ball. Push a forefinger through the middle all the way to the base.

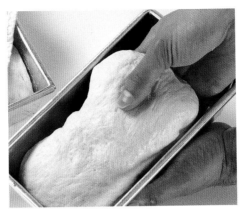

Tin loaf
Shape the dough into a cylinder a little longer than the tin, then tuck the ends under so the shape will just fit the tin. Place the dough in the tin, with the joins underneath.

Round loaf
Roll the dough into a ball, then pull up the sides of the ball to the middle, to make a tight, round ball. Turn the ball over and put on a baking tray.

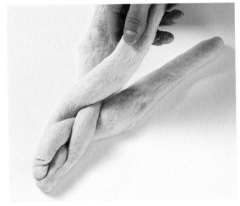

Plaited loaf
Divide the dough into 3 and roll each piece into a strand. Place them side by side and pinch together at one end. Plait the strands, pinching them together at the other end to secure.

Crown loaf
Divide the dough into 9 even-sized pieces and shape each into a ball. Place 8 balls around the side of a deep cake tin, then place one ball in the middle to form a crown. The balls will rise to fill the tin.

Butter shapes

When you are entertaining, butter looks much better if it is shaped rather than just being left in a block. These shapes can be prepared in advance, tray frozen, and packed in freezer bags, then thawed when needed. If you like, flavour the butter with herbs, garlic, or mustard to serve with savoury breads, and spices, honey, or sugar for sweet breads.

Discs Use butter at room temperature. Beat it with a wooden spoon until it is soft, then beat in any flavourings. Spoon on to a sheet of greaseproof paper and spread into a rough sausage, then roll in the paper until it forms a neat sausage shape. Wrap the butter tightly in the greaseproof paper and twist the ends to secure. Chill in the refrigerator until firm. Unwrap and slice the butter across into thin discs. Use immediately or keep chilled, or freeze until required.

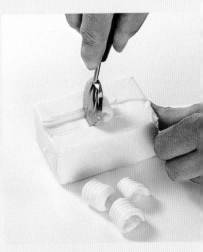

Curls Use a well-chilled block of butter. Warm a butter curler in hot water, then dry it. Pull the curler lengthways along the surface of the block, to shave off curls. Use the butter curls immediately, or keep them in iced water in the refrigerator until required.

Devon flat baps

MAKES 16   135 CALS EACH

g (1 lb) strong white flour, plus extra for dusting

g (1½ oz) butter

sp salt

7 g sachet fast-action dried yeast

out 150 ml (¼ pint) very hot water

out 150 ml (¼ pint) milk

sp clear honey

flower oil for greasing

Put the flour into a large bowl. Add the butter and rub in with the fingertips until e mixture resembles fine breadcrumbs. Stir the salt and yeast, and make a well in e middle. Mix the water, milk, and honey gether, and add to the flour until a soft, ite sticky, dough is formed.

Knead the dough on a lightly floured surface until smooth and elastic. Shape o a round and place in a lightly oiled ge bowl. Cover with oiled cling film and ave to rise in a warm place for 1–1½ hours until doubled in size.

Turn out the dough on to a lightly floured surface and knock back with your fists. ead for 2–3 minutes until the dough is ooth and elastic.

Lightly oil 2 baking trays. Divide the dough into 16 even-sized pieces. Knead and l into rounds and place well apart on the aking trays. With the heel of your hand, tten each round so that it measures 7 cm in) across.

Cover loosely with oiled cling film and leave to rise in a warm place for about minutes or until the dough has doubled size.

Lightly flour the baps and bake in a preheated oven at 200°C (180°C fan, as 6) for 15–20 minutes until golden. Leave cool on a wire rack.

Cook's know-how

If you are short of time, just mix and shape these baps, omitting the first rise in step 2 and giving them just one rise in step 5. The texture of the bread will not be quite as light, but it will still be good.

Farmhouse loaf

MAKES 1 LARGE LOAF   2790 CALS

750 g (1½ lb) strong white flour, plus extra for dusting

30 g (1 oz) butter or margarine

2 tsp salt

1 x 7 g sachet fast-action dried yeast

about 450 ml (¾ pint) lukewarm water

sunflower oil for greasing

1 kg (2 lb) loaf tin

1 Put the flour into a bowl, rub in the butter with the fingertips until the mixture resembles breadcrumbs, then stir in the salt and yeast, and make a well in the middle. Add enough water to mix to a soft dough that is quite sticky.

2 Knead the dough on a lightly floured surface until smooth and elastic. Shape into a round and place in a lightly oiled large bowl.

3 Cover the bowl with oiled cling film and leave to rise in a warm place for 1–1½ hours or until the dough has doubled in size.

4 Turn out the dough on to a lightly floured surface and knock back with your fists. Knead vigorously for 2–3 minutes until the dough is smooth and elastic.

5 Lightly oil the loaf tin. Shape the dough to fit the tin, tucking the ends under to give a smooth top, and place in the tin. Cover loosely with oiled cling film and leave to rise in a warm place for 30 minutes or until the dough reaches the top of the tin.

6 Lightly dust the top of the loaf with flour and bake in a preheated oven at 230°C (210°C fan, Gas 8) for 30–35 minutes until golden. Turn the loaf out and tap the base: it should sound hollow if it is cooked. Leave the loaf to cool on a wire rack.

Dinner rolls

⏱ MAKES 18   95 CALS EACH

500 g (1 lb) strong white flour

1 tsp salt

1 x 7 g sachet fast-action dried yeast

about 350 ml (12 fl oz) lukewarm water

sunflower oil for greasing

1 Put the flour into a large bowl, then stir in the salt and yeast. Make a well in the middle and pour in enough water to make a soft, quite sticky, dough.

2 Knead the dough on a lightly floured surface until smooth and elastic. Shape into a round and place in a lightly oiled large bowl. Cover with oiled cling film and leave to rise in a warm place for 1–1½ hours or until doubled in size.

3 Lightly oil 2 or 3 baking trays. Divide the dough into 18 pieces. Shape into balls, folding the sides to the middles to form round balls. Arrange on the trays, leaving room for expansion. Cover loosely with oiled cling film and leave to rise in a warm place for 20 minutes or until doubled in size.

4 Bake in a preheated oven at 190°C (170°C fan, Gas 5) for 20 minutes or until golden. Leave to cool on a wire rack.

Wholemeal country loaf

⏱ MAKES 1 LARGE LOAF   2975 CALS

750 g (1½ lb) strong wholemeal flour, plus extra for dusting

30 g (1 oz) butter or margarine

1 tbsp caster sugar

2 tsp salt

1 x 7 g sachet fast-action dried yeast

about 450 ml (¾ pint) lukewarm water

sunflower oil for greasing

milk for glazing

cracked wheat for sprinkling

20 cm (8 in) round cake tin

1 Put the flour into a large bowl. Rub in the butter with the fingertips, then stir in the sugar, salt, and yeast. Make a well in the middle and add enough water to mix to a soft, quite sticky, dough.

2 Knead the dough on a lightly floured surface until smooth and elastic, then shape into a round.

3 Place the dough in a lightly oiled large bowl, cover with oiled cling film, and leave to rise in a warm place for 1–1½ hours or until the dough has doubled in size.

4 Turn out the dough on to a lightly floured surface and knock back with your fists. Knead for 2–3 minutes until smooth.

5 Shape the dough into a round and put it into the lightly oiled cake tin. Flatten with your hand, then mark into 8 wedges with a knife. Cover loosely with oiled cling film and leave to rise in a warm place for 1–1½ hours or until doubled in size.

6 Brush the loaf with milk and sprinkle with cracked wheat. Bake in a preheated oven at 230°C (210°C fan, Gas 8) for 20–25 minutes. Tap the base to see if the loaf is cooked: it should sound hollow. Leave to cool on a wire rack.

Milk rolls

⏱ MAKES 18   188 CALS EACH

750 g (1½ lb) strong white flour, plus extra for dusting

60 g (2 oz) butter or white vegetable fat

2 tsp salt

1 x 7 g sachet fast-action dried yeast

about 450 ml (¾ pint) lukewarm milk

sunflower oil for greasing

1 egg, beaten

poppyseeds and sesame seeds for sprinkling

1 Put the flour into a large bowl, rub in the butter, then stir in the salt and yeast. Make a well in the middle and add enough milk to mix to a soft, quite sticky, dough.

2 Knead the dough on a lightly floured surface until smooth and elastic. Shape into a round and place in a lightly oiled large bowl. Cover with oiled cling film and leave to rise in a warm place for 1–1½ hours or until doubled in size.

3 Turn out the dough on to a lightly floured surface and knock back with your fists. Knead for 2–3 minutes until smooth and elastic.

4 Divide the dough into 18 even-sized pieces and shape into balls, folding the sides to the middles to form tight round balls, or shape as required (see box, right).

5 Lightly oil 2 or 3 baking trays. Arrange the rolls on the baking trays, leaving enough room between them for the dough to expand, cover loosely with oiled cling film, and leave to rise in a warm place for 15–20 minutes or until doubled in size.

6 Brush the rolls with the beaten egg to glaze and sprinkle with poppyseeds and sesame seeds. Bake in a preheated oven at 230°C (210°C fan, Gas 8) for about 15 minutes until golden. Leave to cool on a wire rack.

Shaping milk rolls

Form each piece of dough into a long rope and tie into a single knot.

Roll each piece of dough into a thin strand. Fold in half and twist together, sealing the ends well to form a twist. Shape each piece of dough into a ball or an oval. Snip tops with scissors.

Opposite: Dinner roll

Walnut bread

⊘ MAKES 2 SMALL LOAVES   1657 CALS PER LOAF

650 g (1 lb 5 oz) strong white flour, plus extra for dusting

2 tsp salt

30 g (1 oz) butter or margarine

125 g (4 oz) walnut pieces, coarsely chopped

2 tbsp chopped parsley

1 x 7 g sachet fast-action dried yeast

about 400 ml (14 fl oz) lukewarm water

sunflower oil for greasing

1 Put the flour and salt into a large bowl. Rub in the butter, then stir in the walnuts, parsley, and yeast. Make a well in the middle and add enough water to mix to a soft, quite sticky, dough.

2 Knead the dough on a lightly floured surface until smooth and elastic. Shape into a round and place in a lightly oiled large bowl. Cover loosely with oiled cling film and leave in a warm place for 1–1½ hours or until doubled in size.

3 Lightly oil 2 baking trays. Knock back the dough with your fists, then knead for 2–3 minutes until smooth and elastic.

4 Divide the dough in half, shape each half into a round, and then place on a baking tray.

5 Cover the rounds loosely with oiled cling film, and leave to rise in a warm place for 20–30 minutes.

6 Dust each loaf with flour, slash the tops in a criss-cross pattern, and bake in a preheated oven at 220°C (200°C fan, Gas 7) for about 10 minutes; reduce the oven temperature to 190°C (170°C fan, Gas 5), and bake for 20 minutes or until the bread is golden brown.

7 Tap the bases to see if the loaves are cooked: they should sound hollow. Best eaten while still warm.

Cheese and herb bread

⊘ MAKES 1 MEDIUM LOAF   2707 CALS

500 g (1 lb) strong white flour, plus extra for dusting

90 g (3 oz) mature Cheddar cheese, grated

30 g (1 oz) Parmesan cheese, grated

2 tsp mustard powder

2 tbsp chopped parsley

1½ tsp salt

1 x 7 g sachet fast-action dried yeast

about 350 ml (12 fl oz) lukewarm milk

sunflower oil for greasing

beaten egg for glazing

2 tbsp grated Cheddar cheese for sprinkling

1 Put the flour into a large bowl and stir in the cheeses, mustard powder, parsley, salt, and yeast, mixing thoroughly. Make a well in the middle and add enough milk to mix to a soft, quite sticky, dough.

2 Knead the dough on a lightly floured surface until smooth and elastic.

3 Shape the dough into a round and place in a lightly oiled bowl. Cover with oiled cling film, and leave to rise in a warm place for 1–1½ hours or until doubled in size.

4 Turn the dough on to a floured surface and knock back. Knead for 2–3 minutes until smooth and elastic.

5 Lightly flour a baking tray. Shape the dough into a 15 cm (6 in) round and place on the baking tray. Cover loosely with oiled cling film and leave to rise in a warm place for 20–30 minutes.

6 Brush with the egg to glaze, cut a shallow cross in the top, and sprinkle with the grated Cheddar cheese. Bake in a preheated oven at 230°C (210°C fan, Gas 8) for 10 minutes; reduce the oven temperature to 200°C (180°C fan, Gas 6), and bake for 20 minutes, covering the loaf loosely with foil halfway through baking if it is browning too much. Leave to cool on a wire rack.

Potato bread

⊘ MAKES 2 SMALL LOAVES   1002 CALS PER LO[...]

500 g (1 lb) strong white flour, plus extra for dusti[...]

1 tsp salt

15 g (½ oz) butter

1 x 7 g sachet fast-action dried yeast

250 g (8 oz) cold mashed potato

about 250 ml (8 fl oz) lukewarm water

sunflower oil for greasing

2 x 500 g (1 lb) loaf tins

1 Put the flour and salt into a large bowl[...] rub in the butter, then stir in the yeast. Add the potato, rubbing it loosely into the[...] flour. Make a well in the middle of the ingredients and add enough water to mi[...] to a soft, quite sticky, dough.

2 Knead the dough on a floured surfac[...] until smooth and elastic, then shape [...] a round. Place in a lightly oiled large bo[...] cover with oiled cling film, and leave to rise in a warm place for 1 hour or until doubled in size.

3 Turn out the dough on to a lightly flou[...] surface and knock back with your fis[...] Knead until smooth and elastic.

4 Lightly oil the loaf tins. Divide the dou[...] in half, and shape to fit the tins, tuck[...] the ends underneath. Place in the tins. Cover loosely with oiled cling film and le[...] in a warm place to rise for 30 minutes or[...] until the dough reaches the tops of the t[...]

5 Bake in a preheated oven at 230°C (210°C fan, Gas 8) for 10 minutes; reduce the oven temperature to 200°C (180°C fan, Gas 6), and bake for 20–25 minutes until golden. Tap the bases of th[...] loaves to see if they are cooked: they should sound hollow. Serve warm or col[...]

🔍 Cook's know-how

Always add the measured liquid gradually when making dough. Recipes cannot specif[...] exact amounts because flours vary in how much liquid they will absorb.

ulti-grain loaf

MAKES 2 SMALL LOAVES   **1495 CALS PER LOAF**

- g (5 oz) wheat flakes
- (1½ oz) linseed
- ml (½ pint) boiling water
- g (1 lb) strong white flour, plus extra for dusting
- g (4 oz) strong wholemeal flour
- (2 oz) sunflower seeds
- (¾ oz) salt
- g sachet fast-action dried yeast
- t 350 ml (12 fl oz) lukewarm water
- ower oil for greasing
- or glazing
- t flakes to decorate

- 0 g (1 lb) loaf tins

1 Put the wheat flakes and linseed into a large bowl, pour the boiling water over, and stir. Cover and set aside for 30 minutes or until the water has been absorbed.

2 Stir the flours, sunflower seeds, salt, and yeast into the wheat-flake mixture. Make a well in the middle and add enough water to mix to a soft, quite sticky, dough.

3 Knead the dough on a lightly floured surface until smooth and elastic. Shape into a round and place in a lightly oiled large bowl. Cover with oiled cling film and leave to rise in a warm place for 1–1½ hours or until doubled in size.

4 Turn out the dough on to a floured surface and knock back with your fists. Knead for 2–3 minutes until smooth and elastic once again.

5 Oil the tins. Divide the dough in half, and shape into oblongs, tucking the ends under to give smooth tops. Place in the tins. Alternatively, shape into 2 rounds and place on oiled baking trays. Cover loosely with oiled cling film and leave to rise in a warm place for 20–30 minutes.

6 Brush the loaves with milk to glaze and sprinkle with wheat flakes. Bake in a preheated oven at 230°C (210°C fan, Gas 8) for 10 minutes; reduce the oven temperature to 200°C (180°C fan, Gas 6), and bake for 20–25 minutes. Tap the bases to see if the loaves are cooked: they should sound hollow. Leave to cool on a wire rack.

Olive and sun-dried tomato breads

MAKES 2 SMALL LOAVES   **1139 CALS PER LOAF**

400 g (13 oz) strong white flour

60 g (2 oz) buckwheat flour

1 tsp salt

1 x 7 g sachet fast-action dried yeast

black pepper

about 300 ml (½ pint) lukewarm water

1 tbsp olive oil, plus extra for greasing

125 g (4 oz) pitted black olives, coarsely chopped

125 g (4 oz) sun-dried tomatoes in oil, drained and chopped

1 tbsp chopped parsley

1 tbsp chopped fresh basil

1 tbsp coarse sea salt

1 Put the flours into a large bowl. Stir in the salt and yeast and season with black pepper. Make a well in the middle. Pour in the water and oil and mix to a soft but not sticky dough.

2 Knead until smooth and elastic, shape into a round, and place in a lightly oiled large bowl. Cover with oiled cling film, and leave to rise in a warm place for 1–1½ hours or until doubled in size.

3 Lightly oil a baking tray. Knock back the dough, then knead for 2–3 minutes. Divide the dough into 2 pieces. Roll out each piece until about 23 x 25 cm (9 x 10 in). Spread one of the pieces with the olives and the other with the sun-dried tomatoes, parsley, and basil.

4 Roll up each piece of dough from one long end and place, seam-side down, on the tray. Make 4–5 diagonal slashes on the top of each loaf, cover loosely with oiled cling film, and leave to rise in a warm place for 20–30 minutes.

5 Brush the top of each loaf with water and lightly sprinkle with sea salt. Bake in a preheated oven at 230°C (210°C fan, Gas 8) for 15 minutes; reduce the oven temperature to 190°C (170°C fan, Gas 5), and bake for a further 15 minutes or until golden.

6 Tap the bases to see if the loaves are cooked: they should sound hollow. Leave to cool on a wire rack.

Sourdough rye bread

A satisfying and tasty country bread from Eastern Europe, this rye bread is not difficult to make but, because the starter has to be left to ferment for a couple of days, it does require a little forward planning.

MAKES 2 LARGE LOAVES   **3329 CALS PER LOAF**

1.5 kg (3 lb) strong white flour, plus extra for sprinkling

1 x 7 g sachet fast-action dried yeast

250 ml (8 fl oz) lukewarm water

3 tbsp caraway seeds (optional)

1 tbsp salt

sunflower oil for greasing

polenta for sprinkling

SOURDOUGH STARTER

250 g (8 oz) strong white flour

1 tsp fast-action dried yeast

250 ml (8 fl oz) lukewarm water

SPONGE

200 g (7 oz) rye flour

250 ml (8 fl oz) lukewarm water

1 Make the sourdough starter: put the flour into a large bowl and stir in the yeast. Make a well in the middle, pour in the lukewarm water, and mix together.

2 Cover tightly and leave at room temperature for 2 days. Alternatively, leave the starter in the refrigerator for up to 1 week.

3 Make the sponge: put the rye flour into a large bowl, add the sourdough starter and the lukewarm water, and stir to mix. Cover tightly and leave at room temperature for 8 hours or chill in the refrigerator for up to 2 days.

4 Put the flour into a bowl, add the sponge mixture, yeast, lukewarm water, caraway seeds, if using, and salt, and mix to a soft and slightly sticky dough.

5 Turn the dough into a large ungreased bowl, sprinkle the top with flour, cover loosely with oiled cling film, and leave to rise in a warm place for 2 hours or until doubled in size.

6 Lightly sprinkle 2 baking trays with polenta. Turn out the dough on to a lightly floured surface and knock back

with your fists. Knead for 3–4 minutes until smooth and elastic. Halve the dough and form into 2 rounds. Score the tops with a sharp knife.

7 Place on the baking trays, cover loosely with oiled cling film, and leave to rise in a warm place for 45 minutes or until doubled in size.

8 Place the loaves in a preheated oven 220°C (200°C fan, Gas 7). Fill a roasting tin with boiling water and place at the bottom of the oven. Bake the loaves for about 35 minutes until they are lightly browned. Tap the bases to see if the loaves are cooked: they should sound hollow. Leave to cool on wire racks.

Focaccia

MAKES 1 LARGE LOAF   **2989 CALS**

750 g (1½ lb) strong white flour, plus extra for dusting

1 x 7 g sachet fast-action dried yeast

3–4 tbsp chopped fresh rosemary

3 tbsp olive oil, plus extra for greasing

about 450 ml (¾ pint) lukewarm water

2 tsp coarse sea salt

1 Put the flour into a bowl, and add the yeast and rosemary. Make a well in the middle, add the oil and enough water to make a soft but not sticky dough. Knead the dough until smooth and elastic, then shape into a round.

2 Place the dough in a lightly oiled large bowl, cover loosely with oiled cling film, and leave to rise in a warm place for about 1 hour or until the dough has doubled in

3 Turn out the dough on to a lightly floured surface and knock back with your fists. Knead for 2–3 minutes until smooth. Roll out the dough to a round 5 cm (2 in) thick. Cover loosely with oiled cling film and leave in a warm place for 1 hour or until doubled in size.

4 Brush with olive oil and sprinkle with salt. Bake in a preheated oven at 190°C (170°C fan, Gas 5) for 20 minutes until golden. Best eaten warm.

Opposite: Foca

Spicy deep-pan pizza

MAKES 1 LARGE PIZZA   **3596 CALS**

125 g (4 oz) tomato purée

1 x 400 g can chopped tomatoes, drained

60 g (2 oz) pepperoni sausage, sliced

300 g (10 oz) mozzarella cheese, grated

60 g (2 oz) Parmesan cheese, grated

2 tbsp sliced pickled green chillies (from a can or jar)

DOUGH

500 g (1 lb) strong white flour

1 x 7 g sachet fast-action dried yeast

½ tsp salt

2 tbsp olive oil, plus extra for greasing

about 300 ml (½ pint) lukewarm water

deep dish 35 cm (14 in) round pizza pan

1 Make the dough: mix the flour, yeast, salt, and 2 tbsp oil in a large bowl. Add enough water to mix to a soft, quite sticky, dough. Knead on a lightly floured surface for 5–10 minutes until smooth and elastic.

2 Put into an oiled large bowl, turn to coat with the oil, cover with oiled cling film and leave to rise in a warm place for 1 hour or until doubled in size.

3 Lightly oil the pizza pan. Knock back the dough on a floured surface, roll out, and shape into a 35 cm (14 in) round. Put into the pan and shape the edge to form a rim.

4 Spread the tomato pureé over the base. Top with the tomatoes and pepperoni. Sprinkle over the mozzarella, Parmesan, and green chillies.

5 Bake in a preheated oven at 240°C (220°C fan, Gas 9) for 10–15 minutes until the crust is golden and the cheese topping melted. Serve hot.

Calzone

MAKES 4   **899 CALS EACH**

3 tbsp olive oil

2 large onions, sliced

1 tsp balsamic vinegar

3 Romano peppers, halved, seeded, and chopped

250 g (8 oz) chestnut mushrooms, thickly sliced

salt and black pepper

1 x 400 g can chopped tomatoes, drained

4 tbsp tomato purée

30 g (1 oz) pitted black olives, halved

175 g (6 oz) mature Cheddar cheese, grated

DOUGH

500 g (1 lb) strong white flour

1 x 7 g sachet fast-action dried yeast

3 tbsp olive oil, plus extra for greasing

300 ml (½ pint) lukewarm water

beaten egg to seal and glaze

1 Make the dough: put the flour, yeast, olive oil, and water into an electric mixer, and mix with the dough hook for about 5 minutes until a dough forms. If making the dough by hand, put the dry ingredients into a large bowl, add the oil and water, and mix with the hands until combined.

2 Knead the dough on a lightly floured surface for 5–10 minutes until smooth, shape into a ball, and place in a lightly oiled large bowl. Cover with oiled cling film, and leave to rise in a warm place for 1–1½ hours or until doubled in size.

3 Knock back the dough on a lightly floured surface, and knead until smooth. Cut into 4 equal pieces, and roll out each piece to a 23 cm (9 in) round.

4 Make the filling: heat 2 tbsp of the olive oil in a frying pan, add the onions, and fry over a high heat for 1 minute. Turn the heat down to low, cover, and cook for 15 minutes or until the onions are soft. Remove the lid, increase the heat to high, and fry for a few minutes, stirring frequently, to evaporate any liquid. Transfer the onions to a bowl with a

slotted spoon, add the vinegar, and stir to mix. Heat the remaining 1 tbsp olive oil in frying pan, add the peppers, and fry for 4 minutes. Add the mushrooms, and fry fo 2–3 minutes until just cooked, then drain c any liquid. Mix the peppers and mushroor with the onions, season with salt and pepper, and leave to cool.

5 Mix the drained tomatoes and tomato purée together in a bowl. Spread one quarter of this mixture over one half of ec piece of dough. Top with one-quarter of vegetable mixture, and one-quarter of th olives and cheese. Season well. Brush the edges of the dough with beaten egg, ar fold each round in half to enclose the filli Press and crimp the edges together to se (see box, below).

6 Lay the calzone on an oiled baking tr and brush with beaten egg. Bake in c preheated oven at 240°C (220°C fan, Ga for about 15 minutes until light golden bro and crisp. Serve hot or warm.

Filling the calzone

Put one-quarter of the filling on to half of eac dough round.

Brush the edges of the dough with beaten eg and fold over to enclose the filling. Seal the edges and crimp as shown, then brush the to with egg.

issaladière with Mediterranean vegetables

SERVES 6   **434 CALS PER SERVING**

ubergines, cut into 2 cm (¾ in) cubes

and black pepper

sp olive oil

d peppers, halved, seeded, and cut into n (¾ in) cubes

ge onions, roughly chopped

h of sugar

g (4 oz) Emmental or Gruyère cheese, grated

balsamic vinegar

olive oil

es from 1 small bunch of basil

GH

g (6 oz) self-raising flour

baking powder

salt

(2 oz) butter, cubed

60 g (2 oz) Parmesan cheese, grated

1 large egg

about 100 ml (3½ fl oz) milk

1 Make the topping: spread the aubergine cubes out in a large roasting tin, season with salt and pepper, and drizzle with 1 tbsp of the olive oil. Spread the peppers out in another large roasting tin, season with salt and pepper, and drizzle with another 1 tbsp of the olive oil.

2 Roast the aubergines and peppers in a preheated oven at 200°C (180°C fan, Gas 6) for about 25 minutes until the vegetables are tender and the aubergine is golden.

3 Meanwhile, heat the remaining olive oil in a frying pan, and fry the onions over a high heat for 1 minute. Lower the heat, cover the pan, and cook for about 10 minutes until the onions are soft. Add the sugar, increase the heat, and fry for a few minutes more.

4 Tip the onions into a bowl, add aubergines and peppers, and stir gently to combine. Leave the oven on.

5 Make the dough: mix the flour, baking powder, and salt in a large bowl. Add the butter, and rub in with the fingertips until the mixture resembles fine breadcrumbs. Stir in the Parmesan. Beat the egg in a measuring jug with a fork, then pour in enough milk to make up to 150 ml (¼ pint). Gradually add the egg and milk to the flour, mixing with the hands to form a soft dough – not all of the liquid may be necessary.

6 Turn the dough on to a floured large baking tray. Knead lightly, roll out to a 28 cm (11 in) round, and flute the edge. Bake for 15 minutes or until the edge of the dough just begins to colour.

7 Spoon the vegetables over the dough, and sprinkle with the cheese. Bake for a further 15 minutes or until the cheese is light golden and the base is cooked. Transfer to a serving plate, drizzle with the vinegar and olive oil, and top with the basil leaves. Cut into 6 wedges, and serve hot or warm.

Four seasons pizza

🍴 MAKES 1 LARGE PIZZA (SERVES 4)
457 CALS PER SLICE

1 x 400 g can chopped tomatoes, drained

1 pizza base (see box, below)

salt and black pepper

60 g (2 oz) thinly sliced salami

½ tsp oregano

60 g (2 oz) small button mushrooms, sliced

30 g (1 oz) mozzarella cheese, chopped

30 g (1 oz) anchovy fillets, drained

12 pitted black olives

2–3 pieces of bottled red peppers (in oil), thinly sliced

2 tbsp olive oil

grated Parmesan and fresh basil leaves to finish

1 Spread the tomatoes over the pizza base and season to taste.

2 Put salami and oregano on one quarter of the pizza, the mushrooms and mozzarella on a second quarter, the anchovies and olives on a third, the peppers on the fourth. Lightly sprinkle with olive oil. Bake, following the instructions in step 3 (see box, below). Sprinkle with Parmesan and basil after baking.

Mini pizzas

🍴 MAKES 12   458 CALS EACH

1 x 400 g can chopped tomatoes, drained

1 quantity pizza dough (see box, below), shaped into 12 x 7 cm (3 in) rounds

salt and black pepper

2 tbsp olive oil

GOAT'S CHEESE TOPPING

8 sun-dried tomatoes in oil, diced

6 pitted black olives, diced

2 garlic cloves, crushed

60 g (2 oz) goat's cheese, diced

PARMA HAM TOPPING

2 thin slices of Parma ham, diced

6 artichoke hearts in oil, drained and sliced

Spread the tomatoes over the rounds and season. Top half with the sun-dried tomatoes, olives, garlic, and goat's cheese, and half with the Parma ham and artichokes. Sprinkle with the oil. Bake, following the instructions in step 3 (see box, below).

Napoletana pizza

🍴 MAKES 1 LARGE PIZZA (SERVES 4)
404 CALS PER SLICE

1 x 400 g can chopped tomatoes, drained

1 pizza base (see box, below)

1 x 60 g can anchovy fillets, drained

125 g (4 oz) mozzarella cheese, chopped

2 tbsp olive oil

Spread the tomatoes over the pizza base. Halve the anchovies and arrange on top w the remaining ingredients. Bake, following the instructions in step 3 (see box, below).

Tuna and caper pizza

🍴 MAKES 1 LARGE PIZZA (SERVES 4)
466 CALS PER SLICE

1 x 400 g can chopped tomatoes, drained

1 pizza base (see box, below)

1 x 200 g can tuna, drained

2 tbsp capers

125 g (4 oz) mozzarella cheese, chopped

1 tsp oregano

2 tbsp olive oil

Spread the tomatoes over the pizza base Top with the remaining ingredients. Bake, following the instructions in step 3 (see box, below).

Making the thin-crust pizza base

1 Sift 250 g (8 oz) strong white flour on to a work surface and add a heaped ½ tsp fast-action dried yeast and ½ tsp salt. Make a well in the middle and add about 150 ml (5 fl oz) lukewarm water and 1 tbsp olive oil. Draw in the flour with your fingertips or a pastry scraper and work to form a smooth dough.

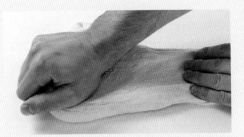

2 Lightly oil a large bowl. Knead the dough for 10 minutes until smooth. Shape into a round and put in the bowl. Cover loosely with oiled cling film and leave in a warm place to rise for about 1 hour or until doubled in size. Turn out of the bowl and knead for 2–3 minutes on a lightly floured surface until smooth.

3 Roll and stretch the dough until it is about 35 cm (14 in) round and about 1 cm (½ in) thick. Make a rim around the edge. Put on a baking tray, add topping, and bake in a preheated oven at 220°C (200°C fan, Gas 7) for 20–30 minutes. Bake mini pizzas for only 12–15 minutes.

Opposite, clockwise from top
Mini pizzas, Four seasons p
Tuna and caper pizza, Napoletana p

Croissants

Croissant is the French word for crescent, the traditional shape for this classic breakfast roll. The dough for croissants is made with butter and milk, so they are rich enough to be served just as they are, but they are even more delicious served warm with butter and jam, or marmalade.

MAKES 12   **352 CALS EACH**

500 g (1 lb) strong white flour

½ tsp salt

300 g (10 oz) butter, at room temperature

1 x 7 g sachet fast-action dried yeast

30 g (1 oz) caster sugar

about 150 ml (¼ pint) milk

about 150 ml (¼ pint) very hot water

sunflower oil for greasing

beaten egg for glazing

1 Put the flour and salt into a large bowl, add 60 g (2 oz) of the butter, and rub in with your fingertips until the mixture resembles fine breadcrumbs. Stir in the yeast and sugar.

2 Make a well in the middle of the dry ingredients. Mix the milk and water together, pour into the well, and mix with a wooden spoon until smooth.

3 Cover the bowl with oiled cling film and chill the dough for 2 hours.

4 Meanwhile, on a sheet of baking parchment, spread out the remaining butter into a 12 x 20 cm (5 x 8 in) rectangle. Cover with another sheet of baking parchment and chill.

5 Roll out the dough on a floured surface into an 18 x 35 cm (7 x 14 in) rectangle, and place the chilled butter on top so that it covers the top two-thirds of the rectangle.

6 Fold the bottom third of the dough over the middle third, and fold the top third, with the butter, over the top to form a neat parcel. Seal the edges with the edge of your hand. Wrap and chill for 30 minutes.

7 Roll out the dough parcel into an 18 x 35 cm (7 x 14 in) rectangle, fold into 3 as before, and seal the edges. Wrap and chill for a few hours until firm enough to roll and shape.

8 Shape the croissants (see box, oppos Place on 2 baking trays and leave fo about 30 minutes until almost doubled in

9 Lightly brush the croissants with the beaten egg and bake in a preheate oven at 220°C (200°C fan, Gas 7) for 12- minutes until crisp and golden brown. Le to cool slightly before serving.

Chocolate croissants

Make the dough. Before rolling the triangle into sausage shapes, sprinkle them with 90 (3 oz) plain chocolate chips.

Shaping the croissants

Roll out the dough into a 35 x 53 cm (14 x 21 in) rectangle, and cut into 2 triangles.

Roll each triangle into a sausage shape, starting from the long side and ending with the point of the triangle.

Bend the ends of each croissant to give the traditional shape.

Lardy cake

🍴 MAKES 1 LARGE LOAF   8186 CALS

500 g (1 lb) strong white flour, plus extra for dusting

1 tsp salt

1 x 7 g sachet fast-action dried yeast

15 g (½ oz) white vegetable fat

about 300 ml (½ pint) lukewarm water

sunflower oil for greasing

FILLING

90 g (3 oz) lard or white vegetable fat

60 g (2 oz) butter, plus extra for greasing

90 g (3 oz) currants

90 g (3 oz) sultanas

60 g (2 oz) chopped mixed candied peel

90 g (3 oz) light muscovado sugar

GLAZE

1 tbsp caster sugar

1 tbsp boiling water

23 x 30 cm (9 x 12 in) roasting tin

1 Mix the flour, salt, and yeast in a bowl. Rub in the fat. Make a well in the middle and pour in enough water to mix to a soft dough.

2 Knead on a lightly floured surface until smooth and elastic, place in a lightly oiled large bowl, and cover with oiled cling film. Leave to rise in a warm place, 1–1½ hours.

3 Turn out the dough on to a lightly floured surface and roll out to a rectangle about 5 mm (¼ in) thick. Dot with one-third each of the vegetable fat and butter. Sprinkle over one-third each of the dried fruit, mixed peel, and sugar.

4 Fold into three, folding the bottom third up and the top third down on top of it. Seal the edges to trap the air, then give the dough a quarter turn. Repeat the rolling and folding twice more, with the remaining fat, fruit, peel, and sugar.

5 Lightly butter the roasting tin. Roll out the dough to fit the tin, and lift it into the tin. Cover with oiled cling film and leave to rise in a warm place for about 30 minutes or until doubled in size.

6 Score the top of the dough in a criss-cross pattern, and bake in a preheated oven at 200°C (180°C fan, Gas 6) for about 30 minutes or until golden brown. Leave to cool in the tin for about 10 minutes.

7 Meanwhile, make the glaze: dissolve the caster sugar in the measured water. Brush the glaze on top of the warm cake and leave to cool.

Brioches

🍴 MAKES 12   149 CALS EACH

275 g (9 oz) strong white flour, plus extra for dusting

30 g (1 oz) caster sugar

60 g (2 oz) butter

1 x 7 g sachet fast-action dried yeast

2 eggs, beaten

about 3 tbsp lukewarm milk

sunflower oil for greasing

beaten egg for glazing

12 individual brioche moulds

1 Sift the flour and sugar into a large bowl. Rub in the butter until the mixture resembles fine breadcrumbs, then stir in the yeast. Make a well in the middle, then pour in the eggs and enough milk to mix to a soft dough.

2 Knead the dough on a lightly floured surface until smooth and elastic. Shape into a round and place in a lightly oiled large bowl. Cover with oiled cling film and leave to rise in a warm place for 1–1½ hours or until doubled in size.

3 Turn out the dough on to a lightly floured surface and knock back with your fists. Knead the dough for 2–3 minutes until smooth.

4 Lightly oil the brioche moulds. Shape the brioches (see box, below).

5 Cover loosely with oiled cling film and leave to rise in a warm place for 20 minutes or until doubled in size.

6 Brush the brioches with a little beaten egg and bake in a preheated oven at 200°C (180°C fan, Gas 6) for 10–12 minutes until golden brown. Tap the bases to see if the brioches are cooked through: they should sound hollow. Leave to cool on a wire rack.

Shaping brioches

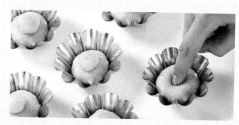

Divide the dough into 12 pieces, then cut one-quarter from each. Shape each piece into a ball. Place the large balls in the moulds, and press a hole in the middle of each. Place the small balls over the holes and press down to seal.

Danish pastries

These melt-in-the-mouth, flaky pastries are quick and easy to make and are particularly good for breakfast. Vary the fillings, bake them ahead, and freeze. Warm the pastries, loosely covered with foil, in a low oven, and serve for a special breakfast or brunch.

 MAKES 16   **480 CALS EACH**

500 g (1 lb) strong white flour, plus extra for dusting

½ tsp salt

375 g (12 oz) butter, plus extra for greasing

1 x 7 g sachet fast-action dried yeast

60 g (2 oz) caster sugar

150 ml (¼ pint) tepid milk

2 eggs, beaten

beaten egg to glaze

FILLING AND TOPPING

250 g (8 oz) white almond paste

4 apricot halves, canned or fresh

about 2 tsp water

125 g (4 oz) icing sugar

60 g (2 oz) flaked almonds

60 g (2 oz) glacé cherries

1 Put the flour and salt into a bowl and rub in 60 g (2 oz) of the butter. Stir in the yeast and sugar. Make a well in the middle, add the lukewarm milk and eggs, and mix to a soft dough.

2 Turn out the dough on to a floured surface and knead for 10 minutes or until smooth. Shape into a round and place in an oiled bowl. Cover with oiled cling film and leave in a warm place to rise for 1 hour or until doubled in size.

3 Turn out the dough on to a lightly floured work surface and knead for 2–3 minutes until smooth. Roll out into a 20 x 35 cm

(8 x 14 in) rectangle. Dot the top two-third of the dough with half of the remaining butter. Fold the bottom third up and the to third down to form a parcel. Seal the edge then give the dough a quarter turn so the folded side is to the left.

4 Roll out the dough into a 20 x 35 cm (8 x 14 in) rectangle as before. Dot wit the remaining butter, fold, and chill for 15 minutes. Roll, fold, and chill twice more.

5 Divide the dough into 4 pieces. Shape and fill the pastries (see box, below). Arrange on buttered baking trays and lec to rise in a warm place for 20 minutes. Bru with beaten egg and bake in a preheate oven at 220°C (200°C fan, Gas 7) for 15 minutes or until golden brown. Transfer to a wire rack.

6 Mix the water and icing sugar and spoon a little over each pastry while s warm. Decorate kites with flaked almonc and pinwheels with glacé cherries. Leave to cool.

Shaping Danish pastries

Crescents

1 Roll out the dough into a 23 cm (9 in) round. Cut into quarters. Place a small roll of almond paste at the wide end of each piece.

Kites

1 Roll out the dough into a 20 cm (8 in) square. Cut into 4 squares. Make cuts around 2 corners of each square, 1 cm (½ in) in from the edge.

Pinwheels and Envelopes

For pinwheels: roll out dough and cut into 4 squares as for kites. Put almond paste in midc of each. Cut from the corners almost to the middle. Fold in alternate points.

2 Starting from the wide end, roll up each dough quarter loosely around the almond paste, then curve the ends to form a crescent.

2 Place a round of almond paste in the middle of each square. Lift each cut corner and cross it over the almond paste to the opposite corner.

For envelopes: roll out the dough, cut into 4, c fill as for pinwheels. Fold 2 opposite corners int the middle. Top with a half apricot, cut-side do

Opposite, clockwise from top: Pinw
Envelopes, Crescents,

Bath buns

MAKES 18   196 CALS EACH

500 g (1 lb) strong white flour

60 g (2 oz) caster sugar

1 tsp salt

1 x 7 g sachet fast-action dried yeast

about 150 ml (¼ pint) lukewarm milk

60 g (2 oz) butter, melted and cooled slightly

1 egg and 2 egg yolks, beaten

150 g (5 oz) sultanas

90 g (3 oz) chopped mixed peel

sunflower oil for greasing

TOPPING

1 egg, beaten

30 g (1 oz) nibbed sugar or coarsely crushed sugar cubes

1 Put the flour and sugar into a large bowl and stir in the salt and yeast. Make a well in the middle and add the milk, butter, egg and egg yolks, sultanas, and mixed peel. Mix to a soft dough.

2 Knead the dough on a lightly floured surface until smooth and elastic.

3 Shape the dough into a round and place in an oiled bowl. Cover with oiled cling film and leave to rise in a warm place for 1–1½ hours or until the dough has doubled in size.

4 Turn the dough on to a lightly floured surface and knock back. Knead the dough for 2–3 minutes until smooth and elastic.

5 Lightly oil 2 or 3 baking trays. Divide the dough into 18 pieces, shape into rolls, and place on the baking trays. Cover loosely with oiled cling film and leave to rise in a warm place for about 30 minutes or until doubled in size.

6 Brush the tops of the buns with the beaten egg and sprinkle with the sugar. Bake in a preheated oven at 190°C (170°C fan, Gas 5) for 15 minutes or until golden brown.

7 Tap the bases of the buns to see if they are cooked through: they should sound hollow. Leave to cool on a wire rack.

Crumpets

MAKES 20   73 CALS EACH

375 g (12 oz) strong white flour

½ tsp salt

1 x 7 g sachet fast-action dried yeast

about 250 ml (8 fl oz) milk

about 300 ml (½ pint) very hot water

sunflower oil for greasing

4 crumpet rings or 4 x 7 cm (3 in) pastry cutters

1 Put the flour into a large bowl, stir in the salt and yeast, and make a well in the middle. Mix the milk and water together, pour in, and beat to form a smooth, thick batter.

2 Cover and leave in a warm place to rise for 1 hour or until the surface is bubbling.

3 Beat the batter mixture for 2 minutes, then pour into a jug. Lightly oil the crumpet rings or pastry cutters and oil a griddle or frying pan. Place the rings or cutters on the griddle and then leave for 1–2 minutes to heat through.

4 Pour 2 cm (¾ in) of batter into each ring and cook for 5–7 minutes until the surface is dry and full of holes, and the crumpets are shrinking away from the sides of the rings.

5 Lift off the rings, turn the crumpets over, and cook for 1 minute until pale golden. Transfer the crumpets to a wire rack and leave to cool.

6 Repeat with the remaining batter, lightly greasing the griddle and rings between each batch. Serve warm.

Jam doughnuts

MAKES 16   269 CALS EACH

500 g (1 lb) strong white flour, plus extra for dusti◼

30 g (1 oz) butter or margarine

90 g (3 oz) caster sugar

1 x 7 g sachet fast-action dried yeast

about 90 ml (3 fl oz) milk

about 90 ml (3 fl oz) very hot water

2 eggs, beaten

sunflower oil for greasing and deep-frying

150 g (5 oz) raspberry jam

125 g (4 oz) caster sugar

2 tsp ground cinnamon

1 Put the flour into a large bowl and rub the butter with the fingertips until the mixture resembles fine breadcrumbs. Stir i◼ the sugar and yeast, and make a well in t◼ middle. Mix the milk and hot water togeth◼ Pour the eggs into the well and mix with th◼ flour, adding enough milk and water to ma◼ a smooth dough.

2 Knead the dough on a lightly floured surface until smooth and elastic. Shap◼ into a round and place in a lightly oiled large bowl.

3 Cover with oiled cling film and leave in a warm place for 1–1½ hours until doubled in size. Turn out on to a lightly floured surface, and knock back with you◼ fists. Knead for 2–3 minutes until smooth.

4 Divide the dough into 16 pieces. Shape◼ each one into a ball, then flatten slight◼ Fill the doughnuts (see box, below). Place t◼ doughnuts on oiled baking trays, cover wit◼ oiled cling film, and leave to rise in a warm place for 30 minutes.

5 Heat the oil in a deep-fat fryer to 160°C◼ (325°F), and cook the doughnuts in batches for 5 minutes until golden. Drain, to◼ in sugar and cinnamon, and serve warm.

Filling the doughnuts

Place 1 tsp raspberry jam in the middle of each doughnut. Gather the edges over the jam and pinch firmly to seal.

Griddled English muffins

⬤ MAKES ABOUT 12   158 CALS EACH

g (1 lb) strong wholemeal flour, plus extra dusting

p salt

7 g sachet fast-action dried yeast

out 250 ml (8 fl oz) milk

out 125 ml (4 fl oz) very hot water

flower oil for greasing

m (3 in) pastry cutter

Put the flour into a large bowl, stir in the salt and yeast, and make a well in the dle. Mix the milk and water together, r in all at once, and mix to a soft dough.

Knead on a lightly floured surface until smooth and elastic, then shape into und. Place the dough in a lightly oiled e bowl, cover with oiled cling film, and ve to rise in a warm place for 45–60 utes until doubled in size.

Knock back the dough, then turn out on to a lightly floured surface and knead 2–3 minutes until smooth and elastic.

Roll out the dough until 1 cm (½ in) thick. Using the cutter, cut into 12 ds, re-rolling and kneading the dough necessary.

ightly dust 2 baking trays with flour, rrange the rounds on the trays, and er loosely with oiled cling film. Leave to n a warm place for about 30 minutes or doubled in size.

ightly oil a griddle or frying pan, and cook the muffins over a medium heat, 4 at a time, for about 7 minutes on h side until golden and cooked through. ot allow the griddle to get too hot or outside of the muffins will burn before nside is cooked.

Chelsea buns

⬤ MAKES 12   298 CALS EACH

500 g (1 lb) strong white flour

1 tsp salt

60 g (2 oz) butter

1 x 7 g sachet fast-action dried yeast

30 g (1 oz) caster sugar

about 200 ml (7 fl oz) lukewarm milk

1 large egg, beaten

sunflower oil for greasing

4 tbsp clear honey

FILLING

60 g (2 oz) butter

30 g (1 oz) light muscovado sugar

60 g (2 oz) sultanas

60 g (2 oz) currants

grated zest of 1 orange

1 tsp ground mixed spice

1 Put the flour into a large bowl and stir in the salt. Rub in the butter and yeast. Stir in the sugar. Make a well in the middle, pour in the milk and egg, and mix to a soft dough.

2 Knead the dough on a lightly floured surface until smooth and elastic, then shape into a round and place in a lightly oiled large bowl. Cover with oiled cling film and leave in a warm place for 1–1½ hours or until doubled in size.

3 Make the filling: cream the butter with the muscovado sugar. In another bowl, combine the sultanas, currants, orange zest, and mixed spice.

4 Lightly oil an 18 x 28 cm (7 x 11 in) roasting tin. Turn out the dough on to a lightly floured surface, and knock back with your fists. Knead for 2–3 minutes until smooth.

5 Roll out into a 30 cm (12 in) square and dot with the butter mixture. Fold in half and roll out into a 30 cm (12 in) square. Sprinkle with the fruit mixture, then roll up.

6 Cut the roll into 12 pieces and arrange cut-side up in the roasting tin. Cover with oiled cling film. Leave in a warm place to rise for about 30 minutes or until the pieces are touching.

7 Bake in a preheated oven at 220°C (200°C fan, Gas 7) for 20–25 minutes, covering the buns loosely with foil after about 15 minutes to prevent them from browning too much. Transfer to a wire rack.

8 Warm the honey in a small pan and brush over the buns to glaze. Pull the buns apart, and serve warm.

Cinnamon rolls

MAKES 16   **450 CALS EACH**

1 kg (2 lb) plain flour

60 g (2 oz) caster sugar

1 x 7 g sachet fast-action dried yeast

1 tsp salt

about 350 ml (12 fl oz) lukewarm milk

2 eggs, lightly beaten

30 g (1 oz) butter, melted

250 g (8 oz) raisins

1 tbsp ground cinnamon

sunflower oil for greasing

milk for glazing

GLAZE

200 g (7 oz) icing sugar

4 tbsp water

1 tsp vanilla extract

1 Sift the flour and 30 g (1 oz) of the sugar into a bowl, then stir in the yeast and salt. Make a well in the middle, pour in the milk, eggs, and butter, and stir to make a sticky dough.

2 Knead the dough on a lightly floured surface until smooth and elastic.

3 Knead in the raisins and half of the cinnamon, then divide the dough into 16 even-sized pieces. Shape each piece into a 20–25 cm (8–10 in) strand, then flatten.

4 Combine the remaining sugar and cinnamon, sprinkle the mixture over the strips of dough, then roll up tightly into spirals.

5 Lightly oil 2 baking trays. Arrange the rolls on the trays, cover loosely with oiled cling film, and leave to rise in a warm place for about 1 hour or until doubled in size.

6 Brush the rolls with milk to glaze, then bake them in a preheated oven at 190°C (170°C fan, Gas 5) for 30–40 minutes until lightly browned. Transfer the rolls to a rack.

7 Meanwhile, make the glaze: in a small bowl, combine the icing sugar, measured water, and vanilla extract. As soon as the cinnamon rolls come out of the oven, brush them with the glaze. Serve the rolls warm or cold.

Hot cross buns

MAKES 12   **279 CALS EACH**

500 g (1 lb) strong white flour

60 g (2 oz) caster sugar

1 x 7 g sachet fast-action dried yeast

1 tsp salt

1 tsp ground mixed spice

1 tsp ground cinnamon

½ tsp grated nutmeg

about 150 ml (¼ pint) milk

about 75 ml (2½ fl oz) very hot water

60 g (2 oz) butter, melted and cooled slightly

1 egg, beaten

90 g (3 oz) currants

60 g (2 oz) chopped mixed peel

sunflower oil for greasing

60 g (2 oz) shortcrust pastry

GLAZE

2 tbsp caster sugar

2 tbsp water

1 Sift the flour into a large bowl, stir in the sugar, yeast, salt, mixed spice, cinnamon, and nutmeg, and make a well in the middle. Mix the milk and water together and add to bowl with the butter, egg, currants, and mixed peel. Mix to a soft dough.

2 Knead the dough on a lightly floured surface until smooth and elastic, then shape into a round.

3 Put into an oiled large bowl, cover with oiled cling film, and leave to rise in a warm place for 1–1½ hours or until doubled in size.

4 Knock back the dough with your fists, then turn on to a lightly floured surface and knead for 2–3 minutes until smooth and elastic. Divide the dough into 12 pieces and shape into round rolls.

5 Roll out the shortcrust pastry to 5 mm (¼ in) thickness, cut it into 24 narrow strips, and press 2 strips in the form of a cross on each bun. Secure with a little water.

6 Lightly oil 2 baking trays, arrange the buns on the trays, and cover with oiled cling film. Leave to rise in a warm place for 30 minutes or until doubled in size.

7 Bake the buns in a preheated oven at 220°C (200°C fan, Gas 7) for 15 minutes or until golden brown. Transfer the buns to a wire rack, brush with the glaze, and serve warm or cold.

Pies, Tarts, and Hot Desserts

Under 45 minutes

Jamaican bananas

Banana halves coated in a rich caramel and cinnamon sauce, spiked with rum. Served warm with vanilla ice cream.

SERVES 4   269 CALS PER SERVING

Takes 15 minutes   Page 391

Cherries Jubilee

Morello cherries simmered in sugar and flavoured with almond extract and brandy. Served with vanilla ice cream.

SERVES 4   162 CALS PER SERVING

Takes 20 minutes   Page 391

Fruit fritters

Bite-sized pieces of apple and banana coated in batter, and deep-fried until golden. Sprinkled with sugar and ground cinnamon.

SERVES 6   361 CALS PER SERVING

Takes 25 minutes   Page 393

45-60 minutes

FRENCH CLASSIC

Crêpes Suzette

Delicious crêpes coated with a sweet orange sauce including brandy or orange liqueur, folded in quarters, and served hot.

SERVES 4   604 CALS PER SERVING

Takes 55 minutes   Page 392

Treacle tart

Rich and sweet: pastry shell filled with gold syrup, breadcrumbs, and lemon zest and juice. Served warm.

SERVES 8   386 CALS PER SERVING

Takes 60 minutes, **plus chilling**   Page

French apricot and almond tart

A French classic: apricots in lemon juice, on a bed of crème pâtissière in a pastry shell. Glazed with brandy and flaked almonds.

SERVES 10   398 CALS PER SERVING

Takes 45 minutes, **plus chilling**   Page 411

Double crust apple pie

Family favourite: light and golden puff pas encases tender apple slices in this tradition apple pie.

SERVES 6   432 CALS PER SERVING

Takes 60 minutes, **plus cooling**   Page

TRADITION

Bread and butter pudding

Slices of white bread thickly spread with butter, layered with dried fruit, lemon zes and sugar, and baked in a custard.

SERVES 6   516 CALS PER SERVING

Takes 60 minutes, **plus standing**   Pag

DINNER PARTY

Plum crumble
Sweet and crunchy: juicy plums sprinkled with sugar and ground cinnamon, and baked beneath a golden brown topping.
SERVES 6   436 CALS PER SERVING
Takes 50 minutes   Page 391

Baked apples
Cooked apples filled with sugar and butter, then baked until soft and served hot with their juices spooned over.
SERVES 6   235 CALS PER SERVING
Takes 55 minutes   Page 389

Magic chocolate pudding
Irresistible light chocolate sponge flavoured with cocoa and vanilla extract, and baked in a chocolate sauce.
SERVES 4   361 CALS PER SERVING
Takes 45 minutes   Page 396

Baked apple dumplings
Cooking apples filled with sugar and ground cinnamon, enclosed in a decorative pastry case, and baked until golden.
SERVES 4   781 CALS PER SERVING
Takes 60 minutes, **plus chilling**   Page 402

Key lime pie
Creamy, tangy lime-flavoured filling is set in a baked shortcrust pastry shell, then chilled and served decorated with lime slices.
SERVES 8   489 CALS PER SERVING
Takes 60 minutes, **plus chilling**   Page 412

Baklava
Traditional Greek pastry: layers of buttered filo pastry and walnuts soaked in honey and lemon juice, and cut into squares.
MAKES 20 SQUARES   249 CALS EACH
Takes 60 minutes, **plus chilling**   Page 416

cemeat and almond tart
stry shell filled with mincemeat and topped with a light,
ny almond mixture, then baked until golden.
 10   685 CALS PER SERVING
 60 minutes, **plus chilling**   Page 401

and almond tart
cious tart filled with ripe plums and
marzipan, lightly dusted with icing
and served warm.
6   549 CALS PER SERVING
60 minutes   Page 413

Apple Brown Betty
Layers of spiced apple slices and buttered breadcrumbs sprinkled with caster sugar, then baked until golden brown.
SERVES 6   284 CALS PER SERVING
Takes 55 minutes   Page 390

Over 60 minutes

Hot chocolate soufflés
Light and airy: individual soufflés made from dark chocolate, baked until well risen and fluffy, then dusted with icing sugar.
SERVES 4   494 CALS PER SERVING
Takes 1¼ hours   Page 398

Apple Charlotte
Slices of buttered bread covered with an apple and apricot jam mixture, and topped with a layer of bread triangles.
SERVES 6   428 CALS PER SERVING
Takes 1 hour 5 minutes   Page

Pineapple upside-down pudding
Pineapple rings and chopped apricots bene a light and springy sponge topping, turned and served upside-down.
SERVES 8   375 CALS PER SERVING
Takes 1 hour 5 minutes   Page

Summer berry soufflés with berry compote
Deliciously sweet: soft, spongy, mixed sum berry soufflés, served with a warm berry compote of berries cooked in sugar.
SERVES 6   180 CALS PER SERVING
Takes 1 hour 5 minutes   Page

Rice pudding
Rich and creamy: pudding rice, milk, caste sugar, and lemon zest mixed together, topp with grated nutmeg and butter, and baked.
SERVES 4   210 CALS PER SERVING
Takes 2¾ hours, **plus standing**   Page

Steamed jam pudding
Traditional pudding: a temptingly light sp mixture is steamed over jam. A firm fami favourite.
SERVES 4–6   573–382 CALS PER SERVING
Takes 1¾ hours   Page

Strawberry and rhubarb pie
Sweet strawberries and rhubarb are light spiced, and baked in a pastry shell with a lattice topping.
SERVES 6–8   371–278 CALS PER SERVING
Takes 1¼ hours, **plus chilling**   Pag

Eve's pudding
Warming and filling: sweetened sliced cooking apples, and lemon zest and juice, are topped with a golden sponge.
SERVES 6   414 CALS PER SERVING
Takes 1 hour 5 minutes   Page 389

FAMILY CHOICE

Sticky toffee pudding
Rich pudding flavoured with coffee extract, dates, and walnuts, and served with a deliciously sticky toffee sauce.
SERVES 8   690 CALS PER SERVING
Takes 1 hour 5 minutes   Page 397

Magic lemon pudding
Fresh and tangy: a light lemony mixture separates during cooking into a sponge top and a delicious lemon sauce underne
SERVES 4   295 CALS PER SERVING
Takes 1 hour 5 minutes   Pag

TRADITIONAL

FAMILY CHOICE

mon meringue pie
iciously sweet: golden brown pastry with
gy lemon filling, topped with light and
fy meringue.

VES 8–10   537–430 CALS PER SERVING

es 1¼ hours, **plus chilling**   Page 410

Christmas pudding
Dried fruits are combined with nuts, lemon
zest, and juice. Grated carrot ensures that the
pudding stays deliciosuly moist. Once steamed,
the pudding is liberally laced with rum.

SERVES 8–10   522–418 CALS PER SERVING

Takes 6¼ hours   Page 400

Treacle pudding
Wonderfully sweet and sticky: a simple,
traditional steamed pudding, deliciously
sweetened with golden syrup.

SERVES 4–6   619–413 CALS PER SERVING

Takes 3¼ hours   Page 403

Apple strudel
Sheets of filo pastry enclosing apples, lemon
zest and juice, sugar, spices, and sultanas, and
sprinkled with almonds.

SERVES 8   278 CALS PER SERVING

Takes 1¼ hours   Page 408

Bakewell tart
Traditional sweet dessert: pastry shell spread
with jam, topped with an almond-flavoured
sponge and a pastry lattice.

SERVES 6   560 CALS PER SERVING

Takes 1¼ hours, **plus chilling**   Page 409

Pecan pie
The buttery rich pecan nut kernels are toasted,
then mixed with a lightly spiced syrup, and
flavoured with brandy and vanilla extract.

SERVES 8   458 CALS PER SERVING

Takes 1¼ hours, **plus chilling**   Page 410

Tarte au citron
Light and tangy: pastry shell with a cream and
lemon filling, baked until set, and lightly
dusted with icing sugar.

SERVES 10–12   572–476 CALS PER SERVING

Takes 1¼ hours, **plus chilling**   Page 412

Mississippi mud pie
Popular American dessert: pastry shell with
a sweetened chocolate and coffee filling,
decorated with whipped cream.

SERVES 12   553 CALS PER SERVING

Takes 1¼ hours, **plus chilling**   Page 416

ch apple tart
chunks, jam, sugar, and lemon zest, puréed, and spooned
pastry shell, and topped with apple slices and jam glaze.

10   **474 CALS PER SERVING**

2 hours, **plus chilling**   Page 409

Pies, tarts, and hot desserts know-how

Puddings may no longer be a feature of every family meal, but few people can say that they don't enjoy something sweet from time to time, be it a traditional steamed pudding or comforting bread and butter pudding – one of the nation's favourites – or a glamorous golden pastry filled with fresh fruit or a rich custard. Hot pastry desserts can take very little time to make these days as bought pastry, especially the ready-rolled varieties, is so good. But if you have the time, and you enjoy it, then it's very satisfying to make your own, and you can try all the different types of pastry.

Types of pastry

All pastries are based on a mixture of flour, fat, and a liquid to bind them. Plain white flour is usually used, although wholemeal or a mixture of the two gives a "nuttier" pastry. The liquid used for binding may be water, milk, or egg; the fat may be butter, margarine, lard, white vegetable fat, or a combination.

Shortcrust pastry

A blend of 2 parts flour, 1 part fat, and usually water, shortcrust pastry (right) is used for sweet and savoury pies and tarts.

Pâte sucrée

Bound with egg yolks, pâte sucrée (opposite) is richer than shortcrust pastry and is used for sweet tarts and tartlets. The classic method for mixing the dough is on a flat marble work surface.

Puff pastry

This light, flaky pastry is made by rolling and folding the dough many times to make paper-thin layers of dough and butter. Ready-made fresh or frozen pastry is very convenient, but not all brands are made with butter. Puff pastry is often used as a top crust for sweet and savoury pies, to wrap beef Wellington, and for mille-feuille.

Flaky pastry

This is a short-cut version of puff pastry. The rolling and folding process is repeated only a few times. It is used for pies and tarts.

Quick puff pastry

Like puff and flaky pastry, this is rolled and folded, but the butter is added all at once, in large cubes. Quick puff pastry can be used in the same ways as flaky pastry and for dishes normally made with puff pastry.

Filo and strudel pastry

These are similar types of pastry made from a pliable dough that is stretched and rolled until extremely thin. It is then rolled around a filling or layered with melted butter. Filo and strudel pastries are difficult to make at home, but ready-made varieties are available fresh and frozen. Common uses include strudel and baklava.

Freezing

Most puddings freeze well, particularly baked sponge and steamed suet puddings (before or after cooking), bread and butter pudding (before cooking), crumbles (before or after cooking), and pancakes. Custard-based and milk puddings are not as successful because they tend to separate.

Pastry dough is an excellent freezer standby; thaw before rolling out. Unbaked pastry shells are ideal for last-minute desserts as they can be baked from frozen. It's not a good idea to freeze baked pastries.

Microwaving

The microwave can be a helpful tool when preparing pies, tarts, and hot desserts. For baking pastry-based pies and tarts, however, there really is no substitute for the conventional oven.

The microwave is perfect for cooking fruit fillings for pies and tarts. The fruit remains plump and colourful. It can also be used to melt or soften butter and to heat liquids in which fruit is left to soak. Under careful watch, the microwave can be used to melt chocolate and to make caramel.

Shortcrust pastry

You can also make shortcrust in a food processor: pulse the flour with the fat until like breadcrumbs, then add the water and pulse again briefly (do this briefly or the pastry will be tough). Tip o to a floured surface and knead lightly to mix to a smooth dough. These quantitie make sufficient pastry to line a 23–25 c (9–10 in) flan dish, flan tin, or pie dish.

1 Sift 175 g (6 oz) plain flour into a bowl. Cu 90 g (3 oz) well-chilled butter, margarine, other fat into small pieces and add to the b Stir to coat the fat with flour.

2 Using your fingertips, quickly and lightly the fat into the flour, lifting the mixture to incorporate air, until it resembles fine breadcrumbs. Sprinkle over about 2 tbsp co water and stir gently with a table knife to m the mixture seems too dry to bind together, a little more water.

3 Gather the mixture together and knea briefly until smooth (handle the dough little as possible or the pastry will be tough). dough feels at all sticky, add a little more fl Shape into a ball, wrap, and chill for 30 mi

âte sucrée

is French sweet pastry is traditionally
ade on a marble surface. These
antities make sufficient pastry to line
5 cm (10 in) flan dish, tin, or pie dish.

ift 200 g (7 oz) plain flour on to a work
urface. Make a well in the middle and add
g (3 oz) softened butter, 60 g (2 oz) caster
ar, and 3 egg yolks (for a less rich pastry, use
1 egg yolk). With your fingertips blend
ether the butter, sugar, and egg yolks.

sing your fingertips, gradually work the
fted flour into the blended butter mixture
the mixture resembles coarse crumbs. If the
re seems too sticky, work in a little more flour.

th your fingers or a pastry scraper, gather
e dough into a ball, then knead briefly
is smooth and pliable. Shape the dough
ball again, wrap, and chill for 30 minutes
l it feels just firm.

Quick puff pastry

Ideal for both sweet and savoury pies.
These quantities make sufficient pastry
for a 25 cm (10 in) double-crust pie.

1 Sift 250 g (8 oz) plain flour into a bowl. Add
90 g (3 oz) each of cubed butter and white
vegetable fat, and stir to coat in flour. Add
150 ml (¼ pint) cold water and, with a table
knife, bind to a lumpy dough.

2 Roll out the dough into a rectangle 3 times
as long as it is wide. Fold the bottom third up
and the top third down. Press the edges with
the side of your hand, to seal. Wrap and chill for
15 minutes, then place so the folded edges are
to the sides.

3 Roll out the dough into a rectangle and fold
as before. Turn the dough so the folded
edges are to the sides again. Repeat the rolling,
folding, and turning twice more. Wrap and chill
for 30 minutes.

Making a pastry shell

Careful handling of pastry dough should
ensure it does not shrink or distort
when baking.

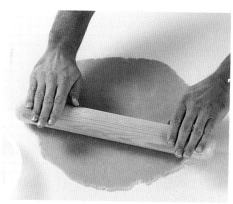

1 Put the pastry dough on a floured work
surface and flour the rolling pin. Roll out into
a round, starting in the middle each time and
lifting and turning the pastry round a quarter
turn after each roll.

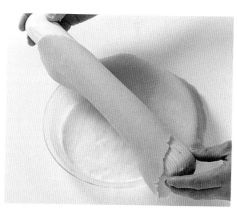

2 If lining a pie dish, roll out the pastry dough
to a round 5 cm (2 in) larger than the top of
the dish; a pastry lid should also be 5 cm (2 in)
larger. Roll the pastry up loosely around the
rolling pin, and unroll over the dish.

3 Gently ease the pastry into the dish, pressing
it firmly and neatly into the bottom edge. Be
very careful not to stretch the pastry. Carefully
trim off the excess pastry with a table knife. If
there are any holes, patch them with bits of
pastry dough.

Baking blind

A pastry shell may be partly baked before adding a filling, to help it stay crisp, or it may be fully baked if the filling itself does not need to be cooked. The shell is filled with baking beans to weigh down the pastry.

1 Prick the pastry shell all over with a fork. Line with a piece of foil or greaseproof paper, allowing it to come high above the rim so that it can be lifted out easily after baking.

2 Fill the shell with ceramic baking beans, dried pulses, or uncooked rice, and bake in a preheated oven at 190°C (170°C fan, Gas 5) for 10 minutes.

3 Remove the beans and foil. Return the shell to the oven and bake for 5 minutes (part-baked) or 15 minutes (fully baked). If the pastry rises during baking, gently press it down with your hand.

Decorative edges

A simple way to give a decorative finish to a pie is to crimp the edge. Place the tips of the thumb and forefinger of one hand against the outside rim of the dish. With the forefinger of your other hand, gently push the pastry edge outwards between the thumb and finger, and pinch the pastry to make a rounded V shape. Repeat this action all around the pastry lid. Alternatively, push and pinch in the opposite direction, working from the outside of the edge inwards.

Decorating pies and tarts

Keep pastry trimmings to make small decorative shapes. Cut them freehand or use cutters. They can be fixed to the edge of a pastry shell or arranged on a lid. If the pastry has a glaze, attach the shapes with water, then apply the glaze all over the pie, brushing it on gently so the shapes are not disturbed.

A pastry lid can be brushed with a glaze before baking. A little milk or beaten egg will give a shiny finish, as will egg white alone - this is a good way to use up whites when the pastry is made with egg yolks. Sprinkle a pastry lid with sugar for a crisp, sweet glaze.

Steamed puddings

Light sponges and rich suet mixtures ca both be gently cooked by steaming. Be sure to make the seal tight so moisture cannot get inside. It is important to keep the water in the saucepan topped up, so boil some water ready to add to the pan when needed.

1 Turn the mixture into a greased, heatproo bowl. Layer a piece of greaseproof pape with a piece of foil and make a pleat across middle, to allow for the pudding's expansion during cooking. Butter the paper.

2 Place the foil and paper, buttered-side d over the top of the bowl. Secure by tying string tightly under the rim. Form a handle w another piece of string. Trim away excess p and foil.

3 Put a trivet or upturned saucer or plate the bottom of a saucepan and half fill water. Bring to a simmer. Lower the bowl in the saucepan; add more boiling water to halfway up the side of the bowl. Cover tigh and steam for the required time. Make sur the water stays at simmering point and top when necessary.

Apple Charlotte

SERVES 6   428 CALS PER SERVING

g (2 lb) cooking apples, quartered, cored,
eled, and sliced

5 g (4 oz) caster sugar

osp water

osp apricot jam

5 g (4 oz) butter, softened, plus extra for greasing

slices of bread, crusts removed

cm (6 in) square cake tin

Put the apples, sugar, and measured water
in a saucepan and cook over a medium
at for about 10–15 minutes until the apples
soft but still holding their shape. Stir in
apricot jam.

Spread the butter on one side of each
slice of bread. Lightly butter the cake tin
assemble the pudding (see box, below).

Bake in a preheated oven at 200°C
(180°C fan, Gas 6) for about 40 minutes
l crisp and golden. Serve hot.

ssembling the Charlotte

8 of the bread slices to line the tin, cutting
m into strips or squares as necessary, and
cing them buttered-side down. Spoon in
apple mixture. Cut the remaining slices of
ad into quarters diagonally. Arrange the
arters, buttered-side up, on top of the
le mixture.

Above: Eve's pudding.

Eve's pudding

SERVES 6   414 CALS PER SERVING

butter for greasing

500 g (1 lb) cooking apples, quartered, cored,
peeled, and sliced

90 g (3 oz) demerara sugar

grated zest and juice of 1 lemon

SPONGE TOPPING

125 g (4 oz) baking margarine, straight from
the refrigerator

125 g (4 oz) caster sugar

2 eggs, beaten

125 g (4 oz) self-raising flour

1 tsp baking powder

1.25 litre (2 pint) ovenproof dish

1 Lightly butter the ovenproof dish and
arrange the apples in the bottom.
Sprinkle over the demerara sugar and the
lemon zest and juice.

2 Make the sponge topping: put the
margarine, sugar, eggs, flour, and baking
powder in a large bowl, and beat until
smooth and well blended. Spoon on top of
the apple slices, and level the surface.

3 Bake in a preheated oven at 180°C
(160°C fan, Gas 4) for about 45 minutes
until the sponge topping is well risen, golden,
and springy to the touch. Serve hot.

Spiced Eve's pudding

Add 1 tsp ground cinnamon to the sponge
topping, and 60 g (2 oz) raisins, 1 tsp ground
cinnamon, and 1 tsp ground mixed spice to
the apple mixture.

Baked apples

SERVES 6   235 CALS PER SERVING

6 cooking apples

90 g (3 oz) light muscovado sugar

90 g (3 oz) butter, diced

3 tbsp water

1 Wipe the apples, and remove the cores
using an apple corer. Make a shallow cut
through the skin around the equator of
each apple.

2 Put the apples into an ovenproof dish
and fill their middles with the sugar and
butter. Pour the water around the apples.

3 Bake in a preheated oven at 190°C
(170°C fan, Gas 5) for 40–45 minutes until
the apples are soft. Serve hot, spooning all
the juices from the dish over the apples.

Citrus baked apples

Add the finely grated zest of 1 orange or
1 lemon to the muscovado sugar.

Baked apples with mincemeat

Use 125 g (4 oz) mincemeat instead of the
sugar and butter.

Apple Brown Betty

Easy to prepare from mainly storecupboard ingredients, this pudding is real comfort food, and it can be made with fruits other than apples if you prefer. Serve it with vanilla or yogurt ice cream, crème fraîche, or whipped cream.

 SERVES 6   284 CALS PER SERVING

30–45 g (1–1½ oz) butter

175 g (6 oz) stale breadcrumbs

1 kg (2 lb) cooking apples, quartered, cored, peeled, and thinly sliced

125 g (4 oz) caster sugar, plus extra for sprinkling

1 tbsp lemon juice

1–2 tsp ground cinnamon

deep 1.5–2 litre (2½–3½ pint) ovenproof dish

1 Melt the butter in a frying pan. Add the breadcrumbs and stir over a medium heat for 5 minutes or until the crumbs are crisp and golden. Remove from the heat.

2 Toss the apples with the caster sugar, lemon juice, and ground cinnamon.

3 Press one-quarter of the crisp breadcrumbs over the bottom of the dish. Cover with half of the apple mixture and sprinkle with a further one-quarter of the breadcrumbs.

4 Arrange the remaining apple mixture on top of the breadcrumbs, spoon over any juices, and cover with the remaining breadcrumbs. Sprinkle the top of the pudding lightly with caster sugar.

5 Cover the dish with foil. Bake in a preheated oven at 200°C (180°C fan, Gas 6) for about 20 minutes.

6 Remove the foil and continue baking for a further 20 minutes or until the apples are tender and the top is golden brown. Serve warm.

Apple and cranberry Brown Betty

Add 175 g (6 oz) fresh or thawed frozen cranberries to the apple mixture. Add a little more sugar if necessary.

Peach Melba Brown Betty

Substitute 3 peeled, stoned, and sliced peaches, and 250 g (8 oz) raspberries for the apples. Omit the lemon juice and cinnamon.

Cook's know-how

White or brown bread can be used for the breadcrumbs. Wholemeal gives a nutty flavour, and granary gives an interesting texture. For best results, the bread should be about 2 days old.

Cherries Jubilee

🍴 SERVES 4   162 CALS PER SERVING

425 g jar or can Morello cherries in syrup

tbsp caster sugar

ml (2½ fl oz) brandy

ew drops of almond extract

illa ice cream to serve

Drain the cherries, reserving 125 ml
(4 fl oz) of the syrup. Put the cherries into
aucepan with the measured syrup and
e sugar.

Heat gently, stirring, until the sugar has
dissolved, then bring to a boil. Simmer
about 5 minutes until the liquid has
ckened and reduced by about half.

Pour the brandy over the cherries,
and add the almond extract. Boil to
aporate the alcohol, then spoon the hot
erries and syrup over scoops of vanilla ice
am, and serve at once.

sh cherries Jubilee

lace the Morello cherries with 500 g (1 lb)
n cherries. Pit the cherries and poach them
50 ml (8 fl oz) red wine and 100 g (3½ oz)
er sugar until tender. Substitute the
ching liquid for the syrup.

maican bananas

🍴 SERVES 4   269 CALS PER SERVING

5 g (1–1½ oz) unsalted butter

bsp dark muscovado sugar

ground cinnamon

l (2 fl oz) dark rum

but ripe bananas, cut in half lengthwise

a ice cream to serve

ut the butter and sugar into a large
eavy frying pan, and heat gently
the butter has melted and sugar
lved. Stir to blend together, then
gently, stirring, for about 5 minutes.

tir the cinnamon and rum into the
aramel mixture, then add the banana
es. Cook for 3 minutes on each side
warmed through.

ansfer the bananas and hot sauce
serving plates. Serve at once, with
ps of vanilla ice cream.

Plum crumble

🍴 SERVES 6   436 CALS PER SERVING

1 kg (2 lb) plums, halved and stoned

60 g (2 oz) light muscovado sugar

1 tsp ground cinnamon

CRUMBLE TOPPING

250 g (8 oz) plain wholemeal flour

125 g (4 oz) butter

90 g (3 oz) light muscovado sugar

1 Put the plums into a shallow ovenproof
dish and sprinkle with the sugar and
cinnamon.

2 Make the topping: put the flour into
a bowl, and rub in the butter with the
fingertips until the mixture resembles fine
breadcrumbs. Stir in the sugar.

3 Sprinkle the topping evenly over the
plums, without pressing it down, and
bake in a preheated oven at 180°C
(160°C fan, Gas 4) for 30–40 minutes until
golden. Serve the crumble hot.

Crunchy apricot crumble

Substitute fresh apricots for the plums, and
omit the cinnamon. Substitute porridge oats
or muesli for half of the flour in the crumble
topping, or use up to 125 g (4 oz) chopped
toasted hazelnuts. You can also use half white
and half wholemeal flour.

Rhubarb and ginger crumble

Substitute 1 kg (2 lb) rhubarb, cut into 2.5 cm
(1 in) pieces, for the plums. Put into a saucepan
with the sugar, 2 tbsp water, and 1 tsp ground
ginger instead of the cinnamon, and cook
gently until the rhubarb is soft.

Crêpes Suzette

⏱ **SERVES 4**   **604 CALS PER SERVING**

juice of 2 oranges

125 g (4 oz) unsalted butter

60 g (2 oz) caster sugar

3–4 tbsp orange liqueur or brandy

CRÊPES

125 g (4 oz) plain flour

1 egg

1 tbsp oil, plus extra for frying

300 ml (½ pint) milk

18–20 cm (7–8 in) frying pan

1 Make the crêpes: sift the flour into a bowl. Make a well in the middle. Mix together the egg, 1 tbsp oil, and the milk, and pour into well. Gradually beat in the flour, to make a fairly thin batter.

2 Heat a little oil in the frying pan, then wipe away the excess oil. Add 2–3 tbsp batter to the pan, tilting it to coat the bottom evenly. Cook for 45–60 seconds, then turn over, and cook the other side for about 30 seconds. Slide the crêpe out on to a warmed plate.

3 Repeat to make 7 more crêpes. Stack the crêpes on top of each other as soon as they are cooked (they will not stick together).

4 Make the orange sauce and add and fold the crêpes (see box, below). Heat to warm through.

Making the sauce and folding the crêpes

Put the orange juice, butter, sugar, and liqueur or brandy into a large frying pan, and boil for 5 minutes until reduced. Place 1 crêpe in the pan, coat with sauce, fold in half, then in half again. Move to one side of the pan. Add another crêpe. Coat with the sauce, and fold as before. Repeat with the remaining crêpes.

French pancakes

⏱ **SERVES 4**   **378 CALS PER SERVING**

60 g (2 oz) butter, softened, plus extra for greasing

60 g (2 oz) caster sugar

2 eggs, beaten

60 g (2 oz) self-raising flour

300 ml (½ pint) milk

apricot jam and caster sugar to serve

8-hole bun tin with 7 cm (3 in) cups

1 Combine the butter and sugar in a bowl and cream together until soft. Beat in the eggs, a little at a time, then fold in the flour.

2 In a small saucepan, heat the milk to just below boiling point. Stir into the creamed mixture.

3 Lightly butter the bun tin cups, and divide the batter equally among them. Bake in a preheated oven at 190°C (170° fan, Gas 5) for about 20 minutes until the pancakes are well risen and golden brown.

4 Slide the pancakes out of the cups, and serve with apricot jam and caster sugar. To eat, place a little jam in the middle of each pancake, fold in half, and sprinkle with sugar.

Below: Crêpes Suzette.

Fruit fritters

SERVES 6   **361 CALS PER SERVING**

pples

ananas

:e of ½ lemon

flower oil for deep-frying

g (2 oz) caster sugar

p ground cinnamon

TER

g (4 oz) plain flour

sp icing sugar

gg, separated

ml (¼ pint) mixed milk and water

Quarter, core, and peel the apples. Cut the apples and bananas into bite-sized ces. Toss the pieces in the lemon juice prevent discoloration.

Make the batter: sift the flour and sugar into a bowl, and make a well. d the egg yolk and a little of the milk ture and whisk together. Whisk in half he remaining milk mixture, drawing in flour to form a smooth batter. Add the aining milk.

Whisk the egg white in a separate clean bowl until stiff but not dry. Fold into the ter until evenly mixed.

Heat the oil in a deep-fat fryer to 190°C (375°F). Pat the fruit dry. Dip each piece uit into the batter, lower into the hot oil, cook in batches for 3–4 minutes until den and crisp. Drain on paper towels keep warm while cooking the remainder.

Combine the caster sugar and cinnamon, sprinkle generously over the fritters, and e at once.

Magic lemon pudding

SERVES 4   **295 CALS PER SERVING**

60 g (2 oz) butter, softened, plus extra for greasing

grated zest and juice of 1 large lemon

90 g (3 oz) caster sugar

2 eggs, separated

30 g (1 oz) plain flour

175 ml (6 fl oz) milk

lemon or lime slices to decorate

600 ml (1 pint) ovenproof dish

1 Put the butter, lemon zest, and sugar into a bowl and beat together until pale and fluffy.

2 Add the egg yolks, flour, and lemon juice, and stir to combine. Gradually stir in the milk until evenly mixed.

3 Whisk the egg whites until stiff but not dry. Gradually fold into the lemon mixture.

4 Lightly butter the ovenproof dish. Pour the lemon mixture into the dish, and put the dish into a roasting tin. Add enough hot water to the roasting tin to come almost to the rim of the dish. Bake in a preheated oven at 160°C (140°C fan, Gas 3) for 40 minutes or until the sponge feels springy. Serve hot, decorated with lemon or lime slices. Leftovers are good cold.

Cook's know-how

This "magic" pudding separates during cooking to form a sponge topping with a tangy lemon sauce beneath.

Dark chocolate fondue

SERVES 6   208 CALS PER SERVING

200 g (7 oz) good-quality dark chocolate

30 g (1 oz) caster sugar

125 ml (4 fl oz) water

finely grated zest of 2 oranges (optional)

dippers of your choice (see box, right)

1 Break the dark chocolate into small pieces and put them into a heatproof bowl. Sit the bowl on top of a small saucepan of gently simmering water, making sure that the bottom of the bowl does not touch the water, or the chocolate may get too hot and "seize" into a ball. Heat the chocolate very gently, stirring only once or twice, until the chocolate has just melted, then remove the saucepan from the heat, keeping the bowl over the hot water.

2 Put the sugar into another saucepan, pour in the measured water, and bring to a boil. Simmer for 5 minutes, then slowly stir this sugar syrup into the melted chocolate and whisk until smooth. Stir in the orange zest, if using.

3 Pour the chocolate fondue into a fondue pot and place over a low flame to keep warm. Serve with dippers of your choice.

White chocolate fondue

SERVES 6   278 CALS PER SERVING

175 g (6 oz) good-quality white chocolate

150 ml (¼ pint) double cream

dippers of your choice (see box, right)

1 Roughly chop the chocolate and put the pieces into a heatproof bowl. Sit the bowl on top of a small saucepan of gently simmering water, making sure the bottom of the bowl does not touch the water or the chocolate may get too hot and "seize" into a ball. Heat very gently, stirring only once or twice, until the chocolate has just melted, then remove the bowl from the pan and set aside.

2 Pour the cream into a heavy-based saucepan and bring almost to boiling point (you should see bubbles beginning to break around the edge of the cream). Slowly pour the hot cream on to the melted chocolate, stirring gently.

3 Pour the chocolate fondue into a fondue pot and place over a low flame to keep warm. Serve with dippers of your choice.

Chocolate fudge fondue

SERVES 6   416 CALS PER SERVING

1 x 125 g (4 oz) bar caramel and fudge chocolate

90 g (3 oz) good-quality dark chocolate

125 g (4 oz) butter

60 g (2 oz) golden syrup

4 tbsp double cream

dippers of your choice (see box, top right)

1 Roughly chop the caramel and fudge bar and the dark chocolate, and put the pieces into a small saucepan. Cut the butter into small cubes and drop them into the pan, then pour in the golden syrup.

2 Cook the mixture over a very low heat, stirring only once or twice, for 10–12 minutes. Remove from the heat and whisk together until smooth, then whisk in the cream.

3 Pour the chocolate fondue into a fondue pot and place over a low flame to keep warm. Serve with dippers of your choice.

Dippers

Increase the fun of your fondue by offering as wide a choice as possible of ingredients for dipping and dunking. You can be as creative as you like, but bear in mind that the ingredients need to be speared on small forks so they should not be too hard or crisp. Conversely, if the texture of the dippers is soft and crumbly, they will drop into the pot and spoil the fondue. Here is a selection of tried-and-tested dippers.

- Strawberries with hulls intact, either whole fruits or halved if large
- Cherries, still on their stalks if possible
- Banana slices (slightly under-ripe)
- Fig wedges
- Apricots and peaches, stoned and cut into quarters
- Kiwi fruits, cut lengthways into eighths
- Pears, cut into chunky wedges and tossed in lemon juice
- Grapes, the large seedless variety
- Dried fruits, such as apricots, peaches, or mango
- Panettone cake, cut into cubes
- Brioche, cut into squares
- Long biscuits, such as Viennese fingers, langues de chats, or cigarettes russes

Opposite, clockwise from top: Dip
Dark chocolate fondue, White choc
fondue, Chocolate fudge for

Queen of puddings

⬤ SERVES 6   386 CALS PER SERVING

4 egg yolks

600 ml (1 pint) milk

30 g (1 oz) butter, plus extra for greasing

60 g (2 oz) caster sugar

grated zest of 1 orange

90 g (3 oz) fresh white breadcrumbs

3 tbsp strawberry or raspberry jam

MERINGUE TOPPING

4 egg whites

175 g (6 oz) caster sugar

shallow 1.25 litre (2 pint) ovenproof dish

1 In a large bowl, lightly beat the egg yolks. Set aside. Heat the milk in a small saucepan until bubbles appear around the edge. Add the butter, sugar, and orange zest, and heat gently until the butter has melted and the sugar dissolved.

2 Lightly butter the ovenproof dish and set aside. Gradually add the hot milk mixture to the egg yolks, whisking all the time.

3 Stir in the breadcrumbs, then pour into the ovenproof dish. Leave to stand for 15 minutes.

4 Bake the pudding in a preheated oven at 180°C (160°C fan, Gas 4) for about 30 minutes until just set. Remove from the oven and set aside.

5 Warm the jam in a small saucepan until melted. Spread the warmed jam evenly over the surface of the pudding.

6 Make the meringue topping: whisk the egg whites until stiff but not dry. With an electric mixer, whisk in the caster sugar, 1 tsp at a time, keeping the mixer at full speed.

7 Spoon the meringue on top of the pudding, spreading it to the edge and pulling it up to form peaks.

8 Return the pudding to the oven and bake for a further 10–15 minutes until the top of the meringue is crisp and golden brown. Serve at once.

Pineapple upside-down pudding

⬤ SERVES 8   375 CALS PER SERVING

60 g (2 oz) butter, softened, plus extra for greasing

60 g (2 oz) light muscovado sugar

1 x 225 g can pineapple rings in natural juice, drained, and juice reserved

4 ready-to-eat dried apricots, coarsely chopped

SPONGE

125 g (4 oz) butter, softened

125 g (4 oz) caster sugar

2 eggs, beaten

175 g (6 oz) self-raising flour

1 tsp baking powder

18 cm (7 in) round cake tin

1 Lightly butter the tin and line the bottom with baking parchment. Cream together the butter and sugar and spread evenly over the baking parchment.

2 Arrange the pineapple rings on top of the butter and sugar mixture, and sprinkle the chopped dried apricots among the pineapple rings.

3 Make the sponge: put the butter, caster sugar, eggs, flour, and baking powder into a bowl with 2 tbsp of the reserved pineapple juice. Beat for 2 minutes or until smooth and well blended. Spoon the mixture on top of the pineapple rings and level the surface.

4 Bake in a preheated oven at 180°C (160°C fan, Gas 4) for about 45 minutes until the sponge is well risen and springy to the touch. Invert the sponge on to a warmed serving plate, and serve at once.

Apricot upside-down pudding

Substitute 1 x 400 g can apricot halves for the pineapple, and 2 tbsp chopped stem ginger for the dried apricots.

Magic chocolate pudding

⬤ SERVES 4   361 CALS PER SERVING

60 g (2 oz) caster sugar

60 g (2 oz) fine semolina

30 g (1 oz) cocoa powder

1 tsp baking powder

30 g (1 oz) butter, melted, plus extra for greasing

2 eggs, beaten

2–3 drops of vanilla extract

icing sugar for dusting

SAUCE

90 g (3 oz) light muscovado sugar

2 tbsp cocoa powder

300 ml (½ pint) hot water

1 litre (1¾ pint) ovenproof dish

1 Mix together the sugar and semolina in a large bowl. Sift the cocoa powder and baking powder into the bowl, and mix thoroughly.

2 In a separate bowl, whisk together the melted butter, eggs, and vanilla extract with an electric whisk. Add this mixture to the dry ingredients and stir with a wooden spoon until well blended.

3 Lightly butter the ovenproof dish. Pour the mixture into the dish.

4 Make the sauce: mix together the muscovado sugar and cocoa powder, and gradually stir in the measured hot water. Pour the liquid over the pudding.

5 Bake the pudding in a preheated oven at 180°C (160°C fan, Gas 4) for 30 minutes or until the liquid has sunk to the bottom and the sponge is well risen and springy to the touch. Sprinkle with icing sugar, and serve at once.

Nutty chocolate pudding

Add 60 g (2 oz) chopped pecan nuts or walnuts to the dry ingredients in step 1.

Sticky toffee pudding

SERVES 8   690 CALS PER SERVING

0 g (3 oz) butter, softened, plus extra for greasing

50 g (5 oz) light muscovado sugar

eggs, beaten

tbsp coffee extract

75 g (6 oz) self-raising flour

tsp baking powder

75 g (6 oz) stoned dates, roughly chopped

0 g (3 oz) walnuts, roughly chopped

75 ml (6 fl oz) hot water

TOFFEE SAUCE

125 g (4 oz) butter

175 g (6 oz) light muscovado sugar

6 tbsp double cream

60 g (2 oz) walnuts, roughly chopped

deep 18 cm (7 in) square cake tin

1 Butter the cake tin and line the bottom with baking parchment.

2 Put the butter, sugar, eggs, coffee extract, flour, and baking powder into a large bowl. Beat well until smooth and thoroughly blended.

3 Stir in the dates and walnuts, and then the measured hot water. Pour the mixture into the tin.

4 Bake in a preheated oven at 180°C (160°C fan, Gas 4) for 45–50 minutes until the pudding is well risen, browned on top, and springy to the touch.

5 About 10 minutes before the pudding is ready, make the toffee sauce: put the butter and sugar into a small saucepan, and heat gently, stirring, until the butter has melted and the sugar dissolved. Stir in the cream and walnuts and heat gently to warm through.

6 Cut the pudding into 8 even-sized squares, and transfer to serving plates. Spoon over the toffee sauce, and serve at once.

Cook's know-how

Serve the toffee sauce with other hot or cold desserts, such as steamed puddings or ice cream.

Hot chocolate soufflés

🕐 SERVES 4   494 CALS PER SERVING

125 g (4 oz) plain chocolate

2 tbsp water

300 ml (½ pint) milk

45 g (1½ oz) butter, plus extra for greasing

45 g (1½ oz) plain flour

2–3 drops of vanilla extract

60 g (2 oz) caster sugar

4 egg yolks

5 egg whites

sifted icing sugar for dusting

4 x 300 ml (½ pint) soufflé dishes

1 Break the chocolate into pieces, and put into a small saucepan with the meaured water and a few tablespoons of the milk. Heat gently, stirring, until the chocolate has melted. Add the remaining milk, stirring to blend.

2 Melt the butter in a pan, add the flour, and cook, stirring, for 1 minute. Remove from the heat, and gradually add the chocolate and milk mixture. Bring to a boil, stirring, until the sauce has thickened. Stir in the vanilla extract and caster sugar, and leave to cool.

3 Beat the egg yolks into the cooled chocolate mixture. Lightly butter the individual soufflé dishes and set aside.

4 Whisk the egg whites until stiff but not dry. Stir 1 large spoonful of the egg whites into the chocolate mixture, then carefully fold in the remainder. Divide the mixture among the 4 soufflé dishes.

5 Place on a hot baking tray and bake a preheated oven at 190°C (170°C fa Gas 5) for 40–45 minutes until the soufflés are well risen and firm. Dust with sifted icir sugar. Serve the soufflés at once.

> 🔍 **Cook's know-how**
>
> If you prefer, you can make 1 large soufflé instead of individual soufflés. Simply use 1 x 1.25 litre (2 pint) soufflé dish and bake in the oven for 45-50 minutes. Another alternative is to make 8 small soufflés, ideal for a dinner party after a rich main course. If you use 8 x 150 ml (¼ pint) dishes they wi take about 20-30 minutes to bake in the ove

ummer berry
ouflés with
erry compote

SERVES 6   180 CALS PER SERVING

g (13 oz) frozen mixed summer berries

eaped tbsp cornflour

sp cassis (blackcurrant liqueur)

ter for greasing

rge egg whites

g (6 oz) caster sugar

150 ml (¼ pint) soufflé dishes

Measure half of the berries into a
saucepan, and heat gently for a few
utes until the fruit is soft.

Put the cornflour and cassis into a small
bowl, and mix until smooth. Add a little
he hot berry juices to the cornflour mix,
and pour back into the saucepan. Heat,
ng, until thickened, then press through
eve into a bowl, leaving just the pips
hind in the sieve. Set the berry purée
de to cool.

Put a baking tray in the oven, and
preheat the oven to 190°C (170°C fan,
5). Butter the soufflé dishes.

Put the egg whites into a large bowl,
and beat with an electric whisk on high
ed until stiff but not dry. Add 100 g
oz) of the sugar a teaspoon at a time,
keep beating until stiff and shiny. Stir
le of the whites into the berry purée,
carefully fold in the remainder until
nly combined.

poon the mixture into the prepared
dishes, level the tops, then run your
er inside the rim of each dish – this will
ure the soufflés rise evenly. Place the
es on the hot baking tray, and bake for
minutes until the soufflés are well risen
light golden on top.

Meanwhile, make the compote: heat
he remaining berries and sugar in a pan
a low heat, stirring until the sugar has
olved and the fruit has defrosted. Check
harpness, and add a little more sugar
fruit does not taste sweet enough.

erve the soufflés as soon as they come
ut of the oven, with the warm compote.

Rice pudding

SERVES 4   210 CALS PER SERVING

15 g (½ oz) butter, plus extra for buttering the dish

60 g (2 oz) short grain (pudding) rice

600 ml (1 pint) milk

30 g (1 oz) caster sugar

1 strip of lemon zest

¼ tsp grated nutmeg

900 ml (1½ pint) ovenproof dish

1 Lightly butter the ovenproof dish. Rinse
the rice under cold running water and
drain well.

2 Put the rice into the dish and stir in the
milk. Leave for about 30 minutes to
allow the rice to soften.

3 Add the caster sugar and lemon zest to
the rice mixture, and stir to mix. Sprinkle
the surface of the milk with freshly grated
nutmeg and dot with small knobs of butter.

4 Bake in a preheated oven at 150°C
(130°C fan, Gas 2) for 2–2½ hours until
the skin of the pudding is brown. Serve at
once.

Chilled rice with pears

Let the pudding cool, then lift off the skin. Chill
the pudding and serve in glass dishes, topped
with slices of poached fresh or canned pears,
topped with melted strawberry jam.

Bread and butter
pudding

SERVES 6   516 CALS PER SERVING

12 thin slices of white bread, crusts removed

about 125 g (4 oz) butter, softened, plus extra
for greasing

175 g (6 oz) mixed dried fruit

grated zest of 2 lemons

125 g (4 oz) demerara sugar

600 ml (1 pint) milk

2 eggs

1.7 litre (3 pint) ovenproof dish

1 Spread one side of each slice of bread
with a thick layer of butter. Cut each
slice of bread in half diagonally. Lightly
butter the ovenproof dish and arrange
12 of the triangles, buttered-side down,
in the bottom of the dish.

2 Sprinkle over half of the dried fruit, lemon
zest, and sugar. Top with the remaining
bread, buttered-side up. Sprinkle over the
remaining fruit, lemon zest, and sugar.

3 Beat together the milk and eggs, and
strain over the bread. Leave for 1 hour
so that the bread can absorb some of
the liquid.

4 Bake in a preheated oven at 180°C
(160°C fan, Gas 4) for about 40 minutes
until the bread slices on the top of the
pudding are a golden brown colour and
crisp, and the custard mixture has set
completely. Serve at once.

Below: Bread and butter pudding.

Christmas pudding

This is a rich, dark pudding, laden with dried fruit, spices, and alcohol – the traditional way to finish the festive meal. A delicious cold alternative is the Iced Christmas Pudding on page 448.

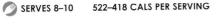 **SERVES 8–10**   **522–418 CALS PER SERVING**

90 g (3 oz) self-raising flour

125 g (4 oz) shredded vegetable suet or grated chilled butter

30 g (1 oz) blanched almonds, shredded

125 g (4 oz) carrot, grated

250 g (8 oz) raisins

125 g (4 oz) currants

125 g (4 oz) sultanas

125 g (4 oz) fresh breadcrumbs

¼ tsp grated nutmeg

60 g (2 oz) mixed candied peel, chopped

90 g (3 oz) light muscovado sugar

grated zest and juice of 1 lemon

2 eggs, beaten

butter for greasing

75 ml (2½ fl oz) dark rum or brandy

brandy butter (see box, below right) to serve

1.25 litre (2 pint) pudding bowl

1 In a large bowl, combine the flour, suet or butter, almonds, carrot, raisins, currants, sultanas, breadcrumbs, nutmeg, candied peel, sugar, and lemon zest. Add the lemon juice and eggs, and stir until well combined.

2 Lightly butter the pudding bowl. Spoon in the pudding mixture and level the surface.

3 Cover with buttered greaseproof paper, then foil, both pleated in the middle. Secure the paper and foil in place by tying string under the rim of the bowl (page 388).

4 Put the bowl into a steamer or saucepan of simmering water, making sure the water comes halfway up the side of the bowl. Cover and steam, topping up with boiling water as needed, for about 6 hours.

5 Remove the bowl from the steamer or pan and leave to cool. Remove the paper and foil covering. Make a few holes in the pudding with a fine skewer, and pour in the rum or brandy.

6 Cover the pudding with fresh greaseproof paper and foil. Store in a cool place for up to 3 months.

7 To reheat for serving, steam the pudding for 2–3 hours. Serve at once, with brandy butter.

Brandy butter

Make your own brandy butter by creaming together 250 g (8 oz) each of unsalted butter and caster sugar or icing sugar, and 90 ml (3 fl oz) brandy. The brandy butter can be frozen for up to 3 months.

Mincemeat and almond tart

s is a rich dessert, ideal for a Christmas
ner party or lunch. For an everyday
dding you could use a little less
ncemeat and add some stewed
ple, which will give a lighter texture
d flavour.

SERVES 10   685 CALS PER SERVING

g (6 oz) butter, softened

g (6 oz) caster sugar

gs

g (6 oz) ground almonds

o almond extract

ut 8 tbsp good-quality mincemeat

TRY

g (8 oz) plain flour

g (4 oz) chilled butter, cut into cubes

(2 oz) caster sugar

g, beaten

TOPPING

175 g (6 oz) icing sugar, sifted

juice of ½ lemon

1–2 tbsp water

60 g (2 oz) flaked almonds

deep 28 cm (11 in) loose-bottomed fluted flan tin

1 Make the pastry: put the flour into a large bowl. Add the butter and rub in with the fingertips until the mixture resembles fine breadcrumbs. Stir in the sugar, then mix in the egg to bind to a soft, pliable dough. Wrap the dough in cling film and chill for about 30 minutes.

2 Roll out the dough on a lightly floured surface and use to line the tin. Prick the bottom with a fork. Cover and chill while preparing the filling.

3 Put the butter and sugar into a large bowl and cream together until pale and fluffy. Add the eggs one at a time, beating well after each addition, then mix in the ground almonds and almond extract.

4 Spread the mincemeat evenly over the bottom of the pastry shell. Pour the almond mixture over the mincemeat.

5 Bake in a preheated oven at 190°C (170°C fan, Gas 5) for about 40 minutes until the filling is golden and firm to the touch. Cover loosely with foil if it is browning too much.

6 Meanwhile, make the topping: stir together the icing sugar, lemon juice, and enough water to make a thin glacé icing. Spread evenly over the tart, then sprinkle with the almonds.

7 Return to the oven for 5 minutes or until the icing is shiny and the almonds lightly coloured. Serve warm or cold.

Strawberry and rhubarb pie

🍴 SERVES 6–8   371–278 CALS PER SERVING

150 g (5 oz) caster sugar, plus extra for sprinkling

45 g (1½ oz) cornflour

750 g (1½ lb) rhubarb, cut into 1 cm (½ in) slices

1 cinnamon stick, halved

375 g (12 oz) strawberries, hulled and halved

SHORTCRUST PASTRY

175 g (6 oz) plain flour

90 g (3 oz) chilled butter, cut into cubes

about 2 tbsp cold water

23 cm (9 in) flan dish or tin

1 Make the pastry: put the flour into a large bowl, add the butter, and rub in with the fingertips until the mixture resembles fine breadcrumbs. Add enough water to bind to a soft, but not sticky dough. Wrap the pastry in cling film and leave to chill in the refrigerator for about 30 minutes.

2 Meanwhile, combine the sugar with the cornflour and toss with the rhubarb, cinnamon, and strawberries. Leave to soak for 15–20 minutes.

3 On a lightly floured surface, divide the dough in half and roll out one half into a thin round to line the bottom and sides of the flan dish.

4 Put the soaked fruit into the pastry shell, removing the cinnamon.

5 Roll out the second half of pastry to the same size as the first round. Cut a 1 cm (½ in) strip from around the edge of the pastry.

6 Cut the remaining pastry into 1 cm (½ in) strips and arrange in a lattice on top of the pie. Brush the ends with water and attach the long strip around the rim of the pie. Sprinkle with 1–2 tbsp sugar.

7 Bake in a preheated oven at 220°C (200°C fan, Gas 7) for 10 minutes; reduce the oven temperature to 180°C (160°C fan, Gas 4), and bake for a further 30–40 minutes until the fruit is just cooked, and the pastry golden. Serve warm or cold.

Steamed jam pudding

🍴 SERVES 4–6   573–382 CALS PER SERVING

125 g (4 oz) soft butter or margarine, plus extra for greasing

3 tbsp jam

125 g (4 oz) caster sugar

2 eggs, beaten

175 g (6 oz) self-raising flour

1 tsp baking powder

about 1 tbsp milk

1.25 litre (2 pint) pudding bowl

1 Lightly grease the pudding bowl, and spoon the jam into the bottom.

2 Put the butter or margarine, sugar, eggs, flour, and baking powder into a large bowl, and beat until smooth and thoroughly blended. Add enough milk to give a dropping consistency.

3 Spoon the mixture into the pudding bowl, and smooth the surface. Cover with greased greaseproof paper and foil, both pleated in the middle. Secure with string (page 388).

4 Put the bowl into a steamer or saucepan of simmering water, making sure the water comes halfway up the side of the bowl. Cover and steam, topping up with boiling water as needed, for about 1½ hours. Turn the pudding out on to a warmed plate, and serve hot.

Baked apple dumplings

🍴 SERVES 4   781 CALS PER SERVING

4 cooking apples, peeled and cored

60 g (2 oz) demerara sugar

½ tsp ground cinnamon

milk for glazing

SHORTCRUST PASTRY

375 g (12 oz) plain flour

90 g (3 oz) chilled butter, cut into cubes, plus extra for greasing

90 g (3 oz) chilled white vegetable fat, cut into cubes

3–4 tbsp cold water

1 Make the pastry: put the flour into a large bowl. Add the butter and white vegetable fat, and rub in with the fingertips until the mixture resembles fine breadcrumbs. Mix in enough water to make a soft, pliable dough. Wrap the dough in cling film and chill for about 30 minutes.

2 Divide the dough into 4 pieces. Roll out each piece on a lightly floured surface and cut into an 18 cm (7 in) round. Reserve the trimmings. Put an apple in the centre each round and make 4 dumplings (see box, below).

3 Cut leaf shapes from the pastry trimmings and use to decorate the tops of the dumplings, attaching them with a little water. Make a hole in the top of each dumpling and lightly brush all over with milk.

4 Bake in a preheated oven at 200°C (180°C fan, Gas 6) for 35–40 minutes until the pastry is golden and the apples tender. Serve hot.

Making the apple dumplings

Fill the apples with the demerara sugar and cinnamon. Draw up a pastry round to enclose each apple, sealing the joins with a little water. Place, with the joins underneath, on a baking tray.

reacle pudding

SERVES 4–6   619–413 CALS PER SERVING

r for greasing

l (3 fl oz) golden syrup

g (4 oz) self-raising flour

g (4 oz) shredded vegetable suet or
ed chilled butter

g (4 oz) fresh white breadcrumbs

(2 oz) caster sugar

t 125 ml (4 fl oz) milk

ml (1½ pint) pudding bowl

1 Lightly butter the bowl and spoon the golden syrup into the bottom.

2 Put the flour, suet or butter, breadcrumbs, and sugar into a bowl and stir to combine. Stir in enough milk to give a dropping consistency. Spoon into the bowl on top of the syrup.

3 Cover the bowl with buttered baking parchment and foil, both pleated in the middle. Secure by tying string under the rim of the bowl (page 388).

4 Put the bowl into a steamer or saucepan of simmering water, making sure the water comes halfway up the side of the bowl if using a saucepan. Cover and steam, topping up with boiling water as needed, for about 3 hours. Turn out the pudding, and serve.

Double crust apple pie

For a successful double crust pie, the pastry underneath should be properly cooked and not soggy. Putting the dish on a hot baking tray at the start of baking is the key.

 **SERVES 6   432 CALS PER SERVING**

500 g (1 lb) cooking apples, preferably Bramley's, quartered, cored, peeled, and sliced

250 g (8 oz) Cox's apples, quartered, cored, peeled, and sliced

about 30 g (1 oz) caster sugar, plus extra for sprinkling

2 tbsp water

rough puff pastry (page 387)

milk for glazing

24 cm (9½ in) pie dish

1 Put the apples into a large pan and add the sugar and water. Cover and cook gently, stirring, for about 10 minutes until the apples are soft and fluffy. Taste for sweetness and add more sugar if necessary. Turn into a bowl and leave the apples to cool.

2 Divide the pastry into 2 portions, 1 portion slightly larger than the other. Roll out the larger portion on a lightly floured surface and use to line the pie dish.

3 Spoon the apple filling on to the pastry shell, spreading it almost to the edge and then doming it in the middle.

4 Roll out the remaining pastry. Brush the edge of the pastry shell with a little water, then lay the pastry lid over the apple filling. Trim the edge, then crimp to seal. Make a small hole in the pastry lid to allow the steam to escape.

5 Use the pastry trimmings to make leaves to decorate the pie, attaching them with milk. Brush the pastry lid with milk and sprinkle with sugar.

6 Put a baking tray in the oven and preheat the oven to 220°C (200°C fan, Gas 7). Put the pie dish on the hot baking tray (this helps ensure a crisp pastry base) and bake for 25–30 minutes until the pastry is golden.

St Clement's apple pie

When cooking the apples, add the grated zest and juice of 1 large lemon, and 3 tbsp fine-cut orange marmalade to the apples.

Tarte Tatin

 **SERVES 6   511 CALS PER SERVING**

90 g (3 oz) butter

90 g (3 oz) demerara sugar

1 kg (2 lb) Cox's apples or similar firm eating apples

grated zest and juice of 1 lemon

PASTRY

175 g (6 oz) plain flour

125 g (4 oz) chilled butter, cut into cubes

30 g (1 oz) icing sugar

1 egg yolk

about 1 tbsp cold water

shallow 23 cm (9 in) round cake tin

1 Make the pastry: put the flour into a large bowl and add the butter. Rub in until the mixture resembles fine breadcrumbs. Stir in the icing sugar, then mix in the egg yolk and enough water to make a soft, but not sticky, dough. Wrap and chill for 30 minutes.

2 Put the butter and sugar into a pan and heat very gently until the sugar dissolves. Increase the heat and cook gently for 4–5 minutes until the mixture turns dark golden brown and is thick, but pourable. Pour evenly over the bottom of the tin.

3 Peel, core, and slice the apples. Toss them with the lemon zest and juice. Arrange in the cake tin (see box, top right).

4 Roll out the pastry on a lightly floured surface into a round slightly larger than the tin. Lay the pastry over the apples, tucking the excess down the side of the tin.

5 Bake in a preheated oven at 200°C (180°C fan, Gas 6) for 25–30 minutes until the pastry is crisp and golden. Invert a serving plate on top of the tin, turn the tin and plate over, and lift the tin to reveal the caramelized apples. Serve warm or cold.

Arranging the apples in the cake tin

Arrange a single layer of the best apple slices in a circular pattern on top of the caramel mixture. Cover evenly with the remaining apple slices.

Sauces for puddings

Sweet white sauce Blend together 3 eggs, 30 g (1 oz) caster sugar, and 1 tsp cornflour. Heat 600 ml (1 pint) milk to just below boiling and stir into the egg mixture. Return to the pan and heat gently, stirring, until thickened. Strain into a cold bowl to prevent further cooking, and serve warm or cold.

Pouring custard Blend 1 tbsp cornflour with 1 tbsp caster sugar, and a little milk taken from 300 ml (½ pint). Bring the remaining milk to a boil and stir into the cornflour mixture. Return to the saucepan and heat gently, stirring, until thickened. If preferred, add flavourings such as grated orange zest, brandy, rum, or vanilla extract to the sauce. Serve warm.

Sabayon sauce Put 4 egg yolks, 60 g (2 oz) caster sugar, and 150 ml (¼ pint) dry white wine into a bowl over a saucepan of gently simmering water. Whisk for 5–8 minutes or until the mixture is frothy and thick. Remove from the heat and whisk in the grated zest of 1 orange. Serve at once or, to serve cool, continue whisking the mixture until cool.

Opposite: Double crust apple

Classic apple crumble

SERVES 6   404 CALS PER SERVING

900 g (2 lb) cooking apples, eg Bramley's

175 g (6 oz) granulated sugar

finely grated zest of 1 lemon

6 tbsp water

TOPPING

175 g (6 oz) plain flour

90 g (3 oz) butter

60 g (2 oz) demerara sugar

1 Quarter, peel, and core the apples, then slice them fairly thinly. Toss the slices in the sugar, lemon zest, and water. Put in a shallow 20 cm (8 in) ovenproof dish.

2 Make the topping: put the flour in a bowl and rub in the butter until the mixture resembles fine breadcrumbs, then stir in the sugar.

3 Sprinkle the topping evenly over the apple mixture in the dish and bake in a preheated oven at 180°C (160°C fan, Gas 4) for 40–45 minutes until golden brown and bubbling. Serve at once.

Cook's know-how

For a crunchier topping on the Classic Apple Crumble, use 125 g (4 oz) wholemeal flour and 60 g (2 oz) porridge oats or muesli instead of the plain flour. To sweeten cooking apples, especially windfall apples that are not at their best, use apricot jam instead of some - or all - of the sugar. Apricot jam gives a gentle sweetness, and it improves the texture of the apples, especially if you are using them for a purée or a pie.

Apple tarte au citron

SERVES 10   463 CALS PER SERVING

4 eggs

250 g (8 oz) caster sugar

finely grated zest and juice of 2 lemons

125 g (4 oz) butter, melted

2 large cooking apples, eg Bramley's, quartered, cored, and peeled – about 350 g (12 oz) prepared weight

2 red eating apples, quartered, cored, and thinly sliced (leave the red skin on)

about 30 g (1 oz) demerara sugar

PASTRY

250 g (8 oz) plain flour

30 g (1 oz) icing sugar

125 g (4 oz) butter, cubed

1 egg, beaten

1 Make the pastry: sift the flour and icing sugar into a bowl and rub in the cubes of butter until the mixture resembles breadcrumbs. Stir in the egg and bring together to form a dough. (If making the pastry in a food processor, process the flour, butter, and icing sugar until like breadcrumbs, pour in the beaten egg, and pulse until the dough forms a ball.) Form the pastry into a smooth ball, put inside a plastic bag, and chill in the refrigerator for at least 30 minutes.

2 Roll out the chilled dough on a lightly floured surface and use to line a deep 25 cm (10 in) loose-bottomed flan tin. Chill again for 30 minutes.

3 Prepare the filling: beat the eggs, caster sugar, and lemon zest and juice in a bowl. Stir in the warm melted butter, then coarsely grate the cooking apples directly into mixture and mix well.

4 Spread the runny lemon mixture in the chilled pastry case. Level the surface with the back of a spoon and arrange the red-skinned apples around the outside edge.

5 Bake on a hot baking sheet in a preheated oven at 200°C (180°C fan, Gas 6) for about 40–50 minutes or until the centre feels firm to the touch and the apples are tinged brown. Serve at once.

Blackberry and apple cobbler

SERVES 4   538 CALS PER SERVING

2 cooking apples, eg Bramley's

500 g (1 lb) blackberries

60 g (2 oz) caster sugar

finely grated zest and juice of 1 lemon

COBBLER TOPPING

250 g (8 oz) self-raising flour

60 g (2 oz) butter, cubed

90 g (3 oz) caster sugar

90 ml (3 fl oz) milk, plus extra for glazing

5 cm (2 in) round fluted biscuit cutter

1 Quarter, peel, and core the apples, the cut the apples into large slices, about 1 cm (½ in) thick.

2 Put the apples into a saucepan with t blackberries, sugar, and lemon zest ar juice. Cover and simmer gently for 10–15 minutes until the apple pieces are tender but not broken up.

3 Meanwhile, make the cobbler topping put the flour into a bowl, add the cub of butter, and rub in with the fingertips ur the mixture resembles fine breadcrumbs. in the sugar, add the milk, and mix to forr a soft dough.

4 Roll out the dough on a lightly floured surface until 1 cm (½ in) thick. Cut ou as many shapes as you can with the bisc cutter, then re-roll the trimmings and cut more. If you do not have a biscuit cutter, stamp out rounds with the rim of a glass coffee mug.

5 Transfer the fruit to an ovenproof dish arrange the pastry shapes on top and brush with milk to glaze.

6 Bake in a preheated oven at 220°C (200°C fan, Gas 7) for 15–20 minutes until the cobbler topping is golden. Serve at once.

Opposite, clockwise from top r
Classic apple crumble, Apple tar
citron, Blackberry and apple col

Above: Treacle tart.

Treacle tart

🥄 **SERVES 8**   **386 CALS PER SERVING**

375 g (12 oz) golden syrup

about 200 g (7 oz) fresh white or brown breadcrumbs

grated zest and juice of 1 large lemon

PASTRY

175 g (6 oz) plain flour

90 g (3 oz) chilled butter, cut into cubes

about 2 tbsp cold water

25 cm (10 in) loose-bottomed fluted flan tin

1 Make the pastry: put the flour into a large bowl, add the butter, and rub in with the fingertips until the mixture resembles fine breadcrumbs. Mix in enough water to make a soft pliable dough.

2 Wrap the dough in cling film and leave to chill in the refrigerator for about 30 minutes.

3 Roll out the dough on a lightly floured surface and use to line the flan tin.

4 Gently heat the golden syrup in a saucepan until melted, and stir in the breadcrumbs and lemon zest and juice. Pour into the pastry shell.

5 Bake in a preheated oven at 200°C (180°C fan, Gas 6) for 10 minutes; reduce the oven temperature to 180°C (160°C fan, Gas 4), and bake for a further 30 minutes or until the pastry is golden and the filling firm.

6 Leave to cool in the tin for a few minutes. Serve warm, cut into slices.

Apple strudel

🥄 **SERVES 8**   **278 CALS PER SERVING**

four 25 x 45 cm (10 x 18 in) sheets of filo pastry

60 g (2 oz) butter, melted

30 g (1 oz) fresh white breadcrumbs

15 g (½ oz) flaked almonds

icing sugar for dusting

FILLING

750 g (1½ lb) cooking apples, quartered, cored, peeled, and sliced

grated zest and juice of 1 lemon

3 tbsp light muscovado sugar

½ tsp ground mixed spice

½ tsp ground cinnamon

125 g (4 oz) sultanas

60 g (2 oz) blanched almonds, roughly chopped

1 Make the filling: mix together the apples, lemon zest and juice, sugar, mixed spice, cinnamon, sultanas, and almonds.

2 Lightly brush 1 sheet of filo pastry with melted butter. Cover with the remaining sheets, brushing each with butter. Add the filling and finish the strudel (see box, right).

3 Brush the strudel with the remaining melted butter and sprinkle with the almonds. Bake in a preheated oven at 190°C (170°C fan, Gas 5) for 40–45 minutes until the pastry is crisp and golden. Dust with icing sugar. Serve warm or cold.

Finishing the strudel

Sprinkle the breadcrumbs over the pastry. Spoon the apple mixture along the middle of the pastry.

Fold the pastry to enclose the filling turn over on to a baking tray, and bend into a horseshoe shape.

akewell tart

SERVES 6   560 CALS PER SERVING

g (4 oz) butter

g (4 oz) caster sugar

gg, lightly beaten

g (4 oz) ground rice or semolina

sp almond extract

sp raspberry jam

g sugar for dusting

TRY

g (6 oz) plain flour

g (1½ oz) chilled butter, cut into cubes

g (1½ oz) chilled white vegetable fat,
into cubes

ut 2 tbsp cold water

for glazing

cm (7½ in) loose-bottomed fluted flan tin

Make the pastry: put the flour into
a large bowl. Rub in the butter and
getable fat until the mixture resembles
breadcrumbs. Mix in enough water to
ke a soft, pliable dough. Wrap in cling
and chill for 30 minutes.

Roll out the pastry on a lightly floured
work surface and use to line the flan
Reserve the trimmings.

Melt the butter in a saucepan, stir in
the caster sugar, and cook for about
inute. Remove from the heat, leave
cool a little, then gradually stir in the
g, ground rice or semolina, and
ond extract.

Spread the jam evenly over the bottom
of the pastry shell, and pour the almond
ture on top.

Roll out the reserved pastry trimmings,
and cut into thin strips, long enough
across the tart. Arrange the strips on
of the almond filling to form a lattice,
ching them to the edge of the pastry
with a little milk.

Bake in a preheated oven at 200°C
180°C fan, Gas 6) for 45–50 minutes
the filling is well risen and golden
springs back when lightly pressed with
ger. If the pastry is browning too much,
er the tart loosely with foil.

emove the tart from the oven. Sprinkle
with icing sugar and serve the tart warm
old.

French apple tart

SERVES 10   474 CALS PER SERVING

90 g (3 oz) butter

1.5 kg (3 lb) cooking apples, quartered, cored,
and cut into chunks

3 tbsp water

6 tbsp apricot jam

125 g (4 oz) caster sugar

grated zest of 1 large lemon

APPLE TOPPING AND GLAZE

375 g (12 oz) eating apples, quartered, cored,
peeled, and sliced

juice of 1 lemon

1 tbsp caster sugar

6 tbsp apricot jam

PASTRY

250 g (8 oz) plain flour

125 g (4 oz) chilled butter, cubed

125 g (4 oz) caster sugar

4 egg yolks

28 cm (11 in) loose-bottomed fluted flan tin

baking beans

1 Make the pastry: put the flour into a bowl
and rub in the butter until the mixture
resembles fine breadcrumbs. Stir in the
sugar, then the egg yolks and a little cold
water, if needed, to make a soft dough.
Wrap and chill for 30 minutes.

2 Melt the butter in a large saucepan,
and add the cooking apples and
water. Cover and cook very gently for
20–25 minutes until the apples are soft.

3 Rub the apples through a nylon sieve
into a clean pan. Add the jam, sugar,
and lemon zest. Cook over a high heat for
15–20 minutes, stirring constantly, until all
the liquid has evaporated and the apple
purée is thick. Leave to cool.

4 Roll out the pastry on a lightly floured
surface and use to line the flan tin. Bake
blind (page 388) in a preheated oven at
190°C (170°C fan, Gas 5) for 10–15 minutes.
Remove the beans and foil and bake for
another 5 minutes. Cool.

5 Spoon the apple purée into the
shell. Arrange the apple slices on top,
brush with lemon juice, and sprinkle with
caster sugar. Return to the oven and bake
for 30–35 minutes until the apples are
tender and their edges lightly browned.

6 Heat the jam, work through a sieve,
then brush over the apples. Serve the
tart warm or cold.

Pecan pie

🍴 SERVES 8   458 CALS PER SERVING

150 g (5 oz) pecan nut halves

30 g (1 oz) unsalted butter

60 g (2 oz) light muscovado sugar

30 g (1 oz) caster sugar

125 ml (4 fl oz) golden syrup

3 tbsp brandy

1 tsp vanilla extract

2 tbsp single cream

¼ tsp ground cinnamon

pinch of grated nutmeg

1 large egg, lightly beaten

2 egg yolks

PASTRY

175 g (6 oz) plain flour

90 g (3 oz) chilled butter, cubed

about 2 tbsp cold water

1 egg white, lightly beaten

23 cm (9 in) loose-bottomed fluted flan tin

baking beans

1 Make the pastry: put the flour into a bowl, add the butter, and rub in with the fingertips until the mixture resembles fine breadcrumbs. Add enough water to make a soft dough. Leave to chill for about 30 minutes.

2 Roll out the pastry on a lightly floured work surface and line the flan tin. Bake blind (page 388) in a preheated oven at 180°C (160°C fan, Gas 4) for 10 minutes.

3 Remove the beans and foil, lightly brush the pastry shell with egg white, and return to the oven for 1–2 minutes. Remove from the oven and set aside.

4 Spread the pecans out on a baking tray, and roast in the oven, turning occasionally, for 10–15 minutes. Reserve a few pecan halves and coarsely chop the remainder. Leave the oven on.

5 Put the butter into a heavy saucepan and cook over a gentle heat until it turns golden brown. Add the sugars and golden syrup, and heat gently until the sugars dissolve. Add the brandy, bring to a boil, and cook for 5 minutes.

6 Remove from the heat and stir in the vanilla extract, cream, cinnamon, and nutmeg.

7 Whisk together the egg and egg yolks. Whisk a little hot syrup into the eggs. Add half of the syrup, little by little, then add the remainder. Leave to cool.

8 Arrange the chopped pecans and pecan halves in the pastry shell. Pour the syrup and egg mixture over them. Bake in the oven for about 40 minutes until golden brown and set. Leave to cool before serving.

Lemon meringue pie

🍴 SERVES 8–10   537–430 CALS PER SERVING

grated zest and juice of 4 large lemons

90 g (3 oz) cornflour

600 ml (1 pint) water

4 egg yolks

175 g (6 oz) caster sugar

MERINGUE

5 egg whites

250 g (8 oz) caster sugar

PASTRY

250 g (8 oz) plain flour

30 g (1 oz) icing sugar

125 g (4 oz) chilled butter, cut into cubes

1 egg yolk

2 tbsp cold water

25 cm (10 in) loose-bottomed fluted flan tin

baking beans

1 Make the pastry: sift the flour and icing sugar into a large bowl. Add the butter and rub in with the fingertips until the mixture resembles fine breadcrumbs.

2 Mix in the egg yolk and enough cold water to make a soft, pliable dough. Wrap the dough in cling film and chill in the refrigerator for about 30 minutes.

3 Roll out the dough on a lightly floured surface and use to line the flan tin. Bake blind (page 388) in a preheated oven at 200°C (180°C fan, Gas 6) for 10 minutes.

4 Remove the baking beans and foil and bake the pastry shell for 5 minute or until the base has dried out. Remove from the oven and reduce the temperatu to 150°C (130°C fan, Gas 2).

5 Mix the lemon zest and juice with the cornflour. Bring the water to a boil, the stir into the lemon mixture. Return to the pan and bring back to a boil, stirring, unt the mixture thickens. Remove from heat.

6 Leave to cool slightly, then stir in the egg yolks and sugar. Return to a low heat and cook, stirring, until just simmering Pour into the pastry shell.

7 Whisk the egg whites until stiff but not dry. Whisk in the sugar 1 tsp at a time. Pile on top of the filling and spread over evenly. Bake for 45 minutes or until crisp and brown. Serve the pie warm or cold.

Below: Lemon meringue pie.

Crème pâtissière

Put 3 eggs, 90 g (3 oz) vanilla sugar, and 60 g (2 oz) plain flour into a large bowl, add a little milk taken from 400 ml (14 fl oz), and mix until smooth. Pour the remaining milk into a heavy saucepan and bring almost to a boil. Pour on to the egg mixture, whisking well.

Rinse out the saucepan to remove any milk residue. Return the egg mixture to the pan, and cook over a gentle heat, stirring continuously, until thickened.

rench apricot and mond tart

ften the star of French pâtissèrie, this
den fruit tart is easy enough to make
ome.

SERVES 10   398 CALS PER SERVING

e pâtissière (see box, right)

ING

(2 lb) fresh apricots, halved and stoned

of 1 lemon

ml (4 fl oz) water

(2½ oz) caster sugar

arrowroot

p brandy

(1 oz) toasted flaked almonds

RY

g (8 oz) plain flour

(4 oz) chilled butter, cubed

(2 oz) caster sugar

, beaten

n (11 in) loose-bottomed fluted flan tin

g beans

ake the pastry: sift the flour into a large
wl. Add the butter and rub in until the
re resembles fine breadcrumbs.

tir in the sugar, then mix in the egg to make
soft, pliable dough. Wrap in cling film and
for 30 minutes.

3 Roll out the pastry on a lightly floured surface and use to line the flan tin. Bake blind (page 388) in a preheated oven at 200°C (180°C fan, Gas 6) for 10 minutes until the pastry shell is beginning to brown at the edge. Remove the beans and foil and bake for another 5–10 minutes. Leave to cool.

4 Put the apricots, cut-side down, in a shallow pan with the lemon juice, measured water, and sugar. Cover tightly and bring to a boil. Lower the heat and simmer gently for 3 minutes or until just soft.

5 Remove the apricots with a slotted spoon, reserving the juices. Drain on paper towels, and leave to cool.

6 Remove the pastry shell from the flan tin and put on a serving plate. Spread the crème pâtissière over the pastry shell, and smooth the surface.

7 Arrange the apricots, cut-side down, on the crème pâtissière. Combine the arrowroot and brandy in a small bowl and stir in the reserved apricot juices.

8 Return the mixture to the pan and bring to a boil, stirring until thick. Add the toasted flaked almonds.

9 Spoon the glaze over the apricots, making sure they are evenly coated. (Add a little water to the glaze if it is too thick.) Leave to stand until the glaze has cooled and set. Serve the tart cold.

Pour into a bowl and cover with cling film, gently pressing it over the surface of the custard to prevent a skin from forming. Leave to cool.

Tarte au citron

SERVES 10–12   572–476 CALS PER SERVING

9 eggs

300 ml (½ pint) double cream

grated zest and juice of 5 large lemons

375 g (12 oz) caster sugar

icing sugar for dusting

lemon twists to decorate

PASTRY

250 g (8 oz) plain flour

125 g (4 oz) chilled butter, cut into cubes

60 g (2 oz) caster sugar

1 egg

28 cm (11 in) loose-bottomed fluted flan tin

baking beans

1 Make the pastry: put the flour into a large bowl. Add the butter and rub in with the fingertips until the mixture resembles fine breadcrumbs.

2 Stir in the caster sugar, then bind together with the egg to make a soft, pliable dough. Wrap in cling film and chill for 30 minutes.

3 Roll out the dough on a lightly floured surface and use to line the flan tin. Bake blind (page 388) in a preheated oven at 200°C (180°C fan, Gas 6) for 10 minutes.

4 Remove the baking beans and foil and bake the pastry shell for 5 minutes or until the base has dried out. Remove from the oven and reduce the oven temperature to 180°C (160°C fan, Gas 4).

5 Beat the eggs in a bowl and add the cream, lemon zest and juice, and caster sugar. Stir until smooth, and pour into the pastry shell.

6 Bake for 35–40 minutes until the lemon filling has set. Cover the tart loosely with foil if the pastry begins to brown too much.

7 Leave the tart to cool a little, then dust with icing sugar. Decorate with lemon twists, and serve warm or at room temperature.

Key lime pie

SERVES 8   489 CALS PER SERVING

300 ml (½ pint) double cream

1 x 400 g can sweetened condensed milk

grated zest and juice of 1 lime

lime slices to decorate

PASTRY

175 g (6 oz) plain flour

90 g (3 oz) chilled butter, cut into cubes

about 2 tbsp cold water

23 cm (9 in) loose-bottomed fluted flan tin

baking beans

1 Make the pastry: put the flour into a large bowl, add the butter, and rub in until the mixture resembles fine breadcrumbs. Add enough cold water to make a soft pliable dough.

2 Wrap the dough in cling film or foil and chill in the refrigerator for 30 minutes.

3 Roll out the dough on a lightly floured surface and use to line the flan tin.

4 Bake the pastry shell blind (page 388) in a preheated oven at 200°C (180°C fan, Gas 6) for about 10 minutes. Remove the baking beans and foil and return the shell to the oven for 5 minutes. Cool slightly.

5 Whip the cream to soft peaks in a large bowl and mix together with the condensed milk. Slowly stir in the lime zest and juice until the mixture thickens.

6 Pour the mixture into the shell and smooth the top, or create a pattern with a palette knife. Chill in the refrigerator for at least 2 hours or until the filling is set firm.

7 Serve the pie chilled, decorated with lime slices.

Banoffi pie

SERVES 8   816 CALS PER SERVING

90 g (3 oz) butter, plus extra for greasing

90 g (3 oz) light soft brown sugar

1 x 397 g can caramel condensed milk

BISCUIT CRUST

90 g (3 oz) butter

175 g (6 oz) digestive biscuits, finely crushed

TOPPING

2 bananas

200 ml (7 fl oz) double or whipping cream, lightly whipped

cocoa powder or chocolate curls

20 cm (8 in) springform or loose-bottomed cake tin

1 Lightly grease the cake tin, and line the bottom with baking parchment.

2 Make the biscuit crust (see box, below) and place in the refrigerator to set.

3 Meanwhile, make the filling: put the butter and sugar into a saucepan, and stir over a low heat until melted and combined. Add the condensed milk, and stir until smooth. Bring to a boil over a high heat, stirring. Boil for 1 minute only then pour immediately over the biscuit c in the tin. Chill for at least 30 minutes, unt set. (The pie can be made up to this stag the day before serving.)

4 Peel the bananas, cut into chunky sli and arrange over the set toffee base Spread the whipped cream over the bananas to cover them completely so th do not discolour. Chill the pie for at least 2 hours until firm enough to cut (it will ke in the refrigerator for up to 6 hours). Befo serving, sift cocoa powder over the crea or decorate with chocolate curls.

Making the biscuit crust

Melt the butter in a saucepan, add the crushed biscuits, and stir well to combine. Press on to the bottom and side of the flan tin. Chill.

um and mond tart

SERVES 6   **549 CALS PER SERVING**

(6 oz) golden marzipan, grated

(1 lb) ripe plums, halved and stoned

sugar for sifting

RY

(8 oz) plain flour

(4 oz) icing sugar, sifted

(4 oz) butter, cubed

ll egg, beaten

milk for glazing

(9 in) fluted flan tin

1 Put a baking tray in the oven, and preheat the oven to 200°C (180°C fan, Gas 6).

2 Make the pastry: put the flour, sugar, and butter into a food processor, and pulse until the mixture resembles fine breadcrumbs. Add the egg, and pulse again until the dough holds together in a ball. (To make by hand, put the flour into a bowl, and rub in the butter with the fingertips, then stir in the sugar and egg.) Knead the dough on a lightly floured surface until smooth, then wrap in cling film and chill for 10 minutes.

3 Remove a little less than half of the pastry for the top of the tart, and return it to the refrigerator. Roll out the remaining pastry on a lightly floured surface, and use

to line the bottom and side of the flan tin, making a rim around the top edge. If the pastry cracks, press it together again, and patch it with rolled-out pastry trimmings if necessary.

4 Prick all over the bottom of the pastry with a fork, and scatter with the grated marzipan. Arrange the plums cut-side down on top. Brush the pastry rim with water. Roll out the reserved pastry to a round that is slightly larger than the diameter of the tin, and place over the plums. Press the pastry edges together to seal, and trim off any excess. Brush with a little milk to glaze.

5 Place the tin on the hot baking tray, and bake for 30–35 minutes until pale golden. Sift icing sugar over the tart, and serve warm.

Raspberry tartlets

🕐 MAKES 16   209 CALS EACH

250 g (8 oz) mascarpone

2 tbsp caster sugar

350 g (12 oz) raspberries

3 tbsp redcurrant jelly

1–2 tsp lemon juice to taste

PASTRY

250 g (8 oz) plain flour

125 g (4 oz) chilled butter, cut into cubes

2 tbsp caster sugar

3–4 tbsp cold water

7 cm (3 in) pastry cutter

16 x 6 cm (2½ in) round tartlet tins

1 Make the pastry: put the flour into a bowl, add the butter, and rub in with the fingertips until the mixture resembles fine breadcrumbs. Stir in the sugar, then add enough cold water to bind to a soft pliable dough. Wrap and chill for at least 30 minutes.

2 On a lightly floured surface, roll out the pastry thinly. Using the pastry cutter, cut out 16 rounds.

3 Gently press the rounds into the tartlet tins. Prick all over with a fork and bake in a preheated oven at 190°C (170°C fan, Gas 5) for 12–15 minutes until golden. Leave in the tins for 10 minutes, then remove and transfer to a wire rack. Leave to cool completely.

4 Beat together the mascarpone and sugar and spoon into the pastry shells. Top with the raspberries, pressing them gently into the filling.

5 Melt the jelly with lemon juice to taste in a small pan, then spoon over the fruits. Leave to set before serving.

Tropical tartlets

🕐 MAKES 10   286 CALS EACH

about 600 ml (1 pint) ready-made thick custard

1 x 200 g can mandarin oranges in natural juice, well drained

1 x 200 g can apricot halves in natural juice, well drained and cut into pieces

about 3 tbsp apricot jam

about 60 g (2 oz) toasted flaked almonds

ALMOND PASTRY

60 g (2 oz) ground almonds

125 g (4 oz) plain flour

2 tbsp caster sugar

90 g (3 oz) chilled butter, cut into cubes

about 3 tbsp cold water

10 x 7 cm (3 in) round tartlet tins or boat-shaped tins (barquette moulds)

1 Make the pastry: combine the almonds, flour, and sugar in a bowl. Add the butter and rub in with the fingertips until the mixture resembles fine breadcrumbs. Add enough cold water to make a soft pliable dough. Wrap and chill for 1 hour.

2 Put the pastry on a floured surface and flatten slightly. Place a large sheet of baking parchment on top and roll out the pastry, beneath the parchment, until about 3 mm (⅛ in) thick. Line the tartlet tins with pastry and chill for 2 hours.

3 Prick the pastry all over and bake in a preheated oven at 190°C (170°C fan, Gas 5) for 10 minutes. Leave the shells to cool in the tins for 10 minutes. Remove and transfer to a wire rack. Leave to cool.

4 Spoon custard into each shell, then top with the mandarin oranges and apricots. Melt the jam in a small pan, sieve, then spoon over the fruit. Sprinkle with the almonds and leave to set before serving.

Blueberry puffs

🕐 MAKES 8   375 CALS EACH

500 g (1 lb) ready-made puff pastry

beaten egg

100 g (4 oz) blueberries

150 ml (5 fl oz) double or whipping cream

1 tbsp caster sugar

1 ripe nectarine or peach, stoned and sliced

icing sugar for dusting

1 Roll out the pastry until 5 mm (¼ in) thick on a lightly floured surface. Cut into strips 7 cm (3 in) wide, then cut the strips diagonally into 8 diamond shapes.

2 With a sharp knife, score each pastry diamond 1 cm (½ in) from the edge, taking care not to cut all the way through. Place on a dampened baking tray and glaze with beaten egg.

3 Bake in a preheated oven at 230°C (210°C fan, Gas 8) for 10–15 minutes until golden. Transfer to a wire rack. Remove the pastry centres, reserving them for lids if desired. Leave to cool.

4 Divide half of the blueberries among the pastry shells. Whip the cream and sugar and divide among the shells. Top with nectarine or peach slices, and the remaining blueberries. Dust the pastry lids with icing sugar, replace, and serve.

Opposite, clockwise from top: Raspberry tar
Blueberry puffs, Tropical tar

Mississippi mud pie

SERVES 12　　**553 CALS PER SERVING**

200 g (7 oz) plain chocolate

125 g (4 oz) butter

1 tbsp coffee extract

3 eggs

150 ml (¼ pint) single cream

175 g (6 oz) dark muscovado sugar

150 ml (¼ pint) whipping cream to decorate

PASTRY

250 g (8 oz) plain flour

125 g (4 oz) chilled butter, cut into cubes

about 2–3 tbsp cold water

25 cm (10 in) loose-bottomed fluted flan tin

baking beans

1 Make the pastry: put the flour into a large bowl. Add the butter and rub in until the mixture resembles fine breadcrumbs. Add enough cold water to make a soft pliable dough.

2 Wrap the dough and chill for 30 minutes.

3 Roll out the dough on a lightly floured surface and use to line the flan tin.

4 Bake the pastry shell blind (page 388) in a preheated oven at 200°C (180°C fan, Gas 6) for about 10 minutes until the pastry edge begins to brown.

5 Remove the baking beans and foil, and bake for a further 5 minutes or until the base has dried out. Remove the pastry shell from the oven, and reduce the oven temperature to 190°C (170°C fan, Gas 5).

6 Break the chocolate into pieces, and place in a heavy pan with the butter and coffee extract. Heat gently, stirring occasionally, until the chocolate and butter have melted. Remove from the heat. Leave the mixture to cool slightly.

7 Beat the eggs, then add to the saucepan with the cream and sugar. Stir thoroughly to mix.

8 Pour the filling into the pastry shell. Bake for 30–35 minutes until the filling has set. Leave to cool.

9 Pipe whipped cream rosettes around the edge of the pie before serving.

Mille-feuille

SERVES 6　　**486 CALS PER SERVING**

250 g (8 oz) puff pastry, thawed if frozen

3 tbsp raspberry jam

150 ml (¼ pint) double or whipping cream, whipped

CRÈME PÂTISSIÈRE

2 eggs, beaten

60 g (2 oz) vanilla sugar

30 g (1 oz) plain flour

300 ml (½ pint) milk

ICING

125 g (4 oz) icing sugar

about 1 tbsp water

1 Make the crème pâtissière (page 411), using the quantities listed above.

2 Roll out the pastry on a floured surface to make a thin, 28 x 33 cm (11 x 13 in) rectangle. Lay it over a dampened baking tray.

3 Prick the pastry with a fork. Bake in a preheated oven at 220°C (200°C fan, Gas 7) for 10–15 minutes until the pastry is crisp and a deep brown colour.

4 Remove from the oven and leave to cool. Reduce the oven temperature to 180°C (160°C fan, Gas 4).

5 Trim the edges of the pastry to a rectangle, then cut into 3 equal rectangles, 10 cm (4 in) wide. Crush the pastry trimmings and set aside.

6 Mix the icing sugar and enough water to make a smooth glacé icing. Spread over 1 of the rectangles, and place on a baking tray.

7 Bake for 2 minutes or until the icing has just set and has a slight sheen. Leave to cool.

8 Place a second pastry rectangle on a serving plate. Spread evenly with the jam and then the whipped cream. Set the third rectangle on top and cover with the crème pâtissière.

9 Top with the iced pastry rectangle. Decorate the long edges of the rectangle with thin rows of crushed pastry trimmings.

10 Chill the mille-feuille in the refrigerator until ready to serve.

Baklava

MAKES 20 SQUARES　　**249 CALS EACH**

250 g (8 oz) walnut pieces, finely chopped

60 g (2 oz) light muscovado sugar

1 tsp ground cinnamon

175 g (6 oz) butter, melted, plus extra for greasing

24 sheets of filo pastry, weighing about 500 g (1 l

90 ml (3 fl oz) clear honey

2 tbsp lemon juice

shallow 18 x 23 cm (7 x 9 in) rectangular cake ti

1 Mix together the walnuts, sugar, and cinnamon.

2 Lightly butter the cake tin and lay 1 sheet of filo pastry in the bottom of the tin, allowing the pastry to come up th sides. (If necessary, cut the sheets in half t fit in the tin.) Brush the pastry with a little melted butter.

3 Repeat with 5 more filo sheets, layerin and brushing each one with the butte Sprinkle with one-third of the nut mixture.

4 Repeat this process twice, using 6 mo sheets of filo pastry each time, brushir each sheet with butter and sprinkling the nut mixture over each sixth sheet. Finish v 6 buttered sheets of filo pastry, and lightl brush the top with melted butter.

5 Trim the edges of the filo, then, using a sharp knife, cut about halfway throu the pastry layers to make 20 squares.

6 Bake in a preheated oven at 220°C (200°C fan, Gas 7) for 15 minutes, then reduce the oven temperature to 180°C (160°C fan, Gas 4) and bake for 10–15 minutes until the pastry is crisp and golden brown. Remove the baklava fror the oven.

7 Heat the honey and lemon juice in a heavy saucepan until the honey hc melted. Spoon over the hot baklava. Lec to cool in the tin for 1–2 hours. Cut into th marked squares, and serve the baklava room temperature.

Chilled Desserts

Under 45 minutes

DINNER PARTY

Baked Alaska
Impressive dessert: sponge case filled with layers of raspberries, strawberries, or other summer fruits, topped with ice cream and meringue, and browned.
SERVES 8   **256 CALS PER SERVING**
Takes 30 minutes   Page 448

LOW FAT

ITALIAN CLASSI◀

Cassata
Layers of ice cream, rum-soaked fruits, and sorbet are frozen to make this traditional Italian dessert.
SERVES 8   **364 CALS PER SERVING**
Takes 30 minutes, **plus freezing**   Page ◀

Orange pannacotta with boozy oranges
Sponged gelatine in warm cream, orange zest, and orange liqueur, chilled in moulds. Served with a spoonful of boozy oranges alongside.
SERVES 4   **782 CALS PER SERVING**
Takes 20 minutes, **plus chilling**   Page 428

Caramelized oranges
Quick and easy: oranges caramelized and served in their own juices, and decorated with strips of orange zest.
SERVES 4   **388 CALS PER SERVING**
Takes 30 minutes, **plus chilling**   Page 427

Quick vanilla ice cream
Plain and simple: fresh eggs and double cream flavoured with vanilla sugar, whiske▶ until light and creamy, and frozen.
SERVES 4–6   **799–533 CALS PER SERVING**
Takes 20 minutes, **plus freezing**   Page ▶

Peach Melba
Deliciously ripe peaches and raspberries, topped with a large scoop of vanilla ice cre▶ and a sweet raspberry sauce.
SERVES 4   **273 CALS PER SERVING**
Takes 15 minutes   Page ▶

Zabaglione
Light dessert: egg yolks, sugar, and Marsal▶ whisked until creamy, and served with boudoir biscuits.
SERVES 6   **114 CALS PER SERVING**
Takes 20 minutes   Page▶

Iced Christmas pudding
Easy and delicious: dried fruit, apricots, cherries, and brandy combined with custa▶ and whipped cream, and frozen.
SERVES 8   **437 CALS PER SERVING**
Takes 20 minutes, **plus freezing**   Page▶

LOW FAT

Old English trifle
Family favourite: sponges layered with peaches or pears, crisp biscuits, custards, and whipped cream. Decorated with toasted almonds.
SERVES 8   **401 CALS PER SERVING**
Takes 35 minutes, **plus chilling**   Page 423

Summer pudding
Ripe and juicy strawberries, redcurrants, blackcurrants, cherries, and raspberries wrapped in juice-soaked bread.
SERVES 6   **240 CALS PER SERVING**
Takes 35 minutes, **plus chilling**   Page 426

45-60 minutes

erry cheesecake
.ck cherries flavoured with Kirsch top a
ghtly sweet and creamy cheese filling with a
sp biscuit base.
VES 8   530 CALS PER SERVING
.es 60 minutes, **plus chilling**   Page 435

Marbled raspberry cheesecake
Crunchy base of walnuts and oats is topped
with a creamy raspberry and cheese filling.
Decorated with whipped cream.
SERVES 10   439 CALS PER SERVING
Takes 45 minutes, **plus chilling**   Page 436

ocolate and brandy mousse
ooth and delicious: an egg and whipped
am mousse flavoured with chocolate and
ndy. Topped with cream and chocolate.
ES 6   585 CALS PER SERVING
es 45 minutes, **plus chilling**   Page 442

FRENCH CLASSIC

Crème caramel
Easy and delicious: velvety vanilla-flavoured
custard coated with a tempting golden brown
caramel sauce.
SERVES 6   255 CALS PER SERVING
Takes 60 minutes, **plus chilling**   Page 443

DINNER PARTY

wberry meringue roulade
ght meringue layer scattered with flaked
onds, spread with whipped cream and
wberries, and rolled into a roulade.
ES 8   349 CALS PER SERVING
s 55 minutes, **plus chilling**   Page 434

The ultimate chocolate roulade
Rich and creamy: a heavenly chocolate-
flavoured sponge filled with rich cream, lightly
dusted with icing sugar before serving.
SERVES 8   469 CALS PER SERVING
Takes 45 minutes, **plus cooling**   Page 441

Over 60 minutes

Pavlova with pineapple and ginger
Crisp meringue case filled with whipped
double cream and ginger, and topped with
pineapple rings and strips of stem ginger.
SERVES 6–8   504–378 CALS PER SERVING
Takes 2½ hours, **plus cooling**   Page 431

Mango and passion fruit meringue
Two light and crunchy meringue rounds are
sandwiched together with cream, mango
slices, strawberries, and passion fruit.
SERVES 6   503 CALS PER SERVING
Takes 1½ hours, **plus cooling**   Page 429

Hazelnut meringue gâteau
Toasted hazelnuts add a rich flavour to
meringue rounds, which are sandwiched with
cream and served with raspberry sauce.
SERVES 8   429 CALS PER SERVING
Takes 1¼ hours   Page 430

Tropical fruit cheesecake
Crunchy coconut biscuit base topped with a
creamy mango mixture, and decorated with
tropical fruits.
SERVES 10   396 CALS PER SERVING
Takes 1¼ hours   Page 435

Chilled desserts know-how

Chilled desserts can be made well in advance so are great for dinner parties. Fruit salads and fools, trifles, creamy mousses and light chilled soufflés, meringue baskets, gâteaux, rich cheesecakes, layered terrines, ice creams, and sorbets – all can be kept in the refrigerator or freezer, to be served when you're ready.

Freezing

Many completed desserts, as well as ingredients and accompaniments for desserts, can be stored in the freezer. Freeze chocolate, caramel, or fruit sauces; thaw at room temperature, or reheat from frozen if serving warm. Tray freeze piped rosettes of cream, then pack in a freezer bag; pack chocolate decorations in rigid containers. Both can be used frozen – they will thaw in minutes. Freeze citrus zest, and thaw, unwrapped, at room temperature. Tray freeze baked meringue shells, gâteau layers, and cheesecake; unwrap and thaw in the refrigerator. Crème caramel can be frozen uncooked in the mould and baked from frozen, allowing extra time.

Egg safety

Some of the chilled desserts in this book, such as mousses and soufflés, contain uncooked eggs. Because of the risk of salmonella poisoning, it is usually recommended that those in vulnerable groups should not eat raw or undercooked eggs (see also page 30).

Dissolving gelatine

Gelatine is a flavourless setting agent used in chilled desserts such as fruit jellies. It is most commonly available as a powder, in sachets. Leaf gelatine can also be used (4 sheets in place of 1 sachet): soften in cold water for 5 minutes, then drain and melt in the hot dessert mixture, whisking well.

1 Put the given quantity of cold water or other liquid into a small heatproof bowl and sprinkle the given quantity of gelatine over the surface. Leave to soak for about 10 minutes until the gelatine has absorbed the liquid and become spongy.

2 Put the bowl of gelatine into a pan of hot water and heat until the gelatine has dissolved and is clear. Use a metal spoon to check that there are no granules left. Use the gelatine at the same temperature as the mixture it is setting.

Preparing mangoes

Mangoes have a large, flat central stone and the flesh clings to it tightly. There are 2 methods of preparation, depending on how the flesh is to be used.

Slicing

For flesh to be used sliced or puréed, cut the flesh from each side of the stone with a sharp knife. Also cut the flesh from the edges of the stone. Then peel and slice or purée.

Dicing

1 Cut the unpeeled flesh away from each side of the stone. With a sharp knife, score the flesh in a criss-cross pattern, cutting just to the skin but not through it.

2 Press in the middle of the skin to open out the cubes of flesh, then cut them away from the skin with a sharp knife.

Preparing a pineapple

When peeling pineapple, cut away the sk in strips, taking out all the "eyes". If ther are any left after peeling, cut them out with the tip of a knife.

Wedges or cubes

1 Cut off the green crown, then cut a slice from the base. Set the pineapple upright or a chopping board and slice away strips of skin cutting from top to bottom.

2 To remove the core, cut the pineapple ir quarters lengthways. Cut the central core from each quarter. Cut the quarters into wedg or cubes as required.

Rings

Do not cut the pineapple lengthways, but c crosswise into 1 cm (½ in) slices. Stamp out t central core from each slice using a biscuit c pastry cutter.

reparing citrus fruits

hen taking the zest from citrus fruits (even if they are unwaxed), first scrub the fruit with
ot soapy water, rinse well, and dry.

ating
ld the grater on a plate. Rub the fruit over the
edium grid of the grater, removing just the zest
d leaving behind the bitter white pith. Use a
stry brush to remove all the zest from the grater.

Peeling
Use a small sharp knife. Cut off a slice of peel
across the top and the base, cutting through
to the flesh. Set the fruit upright on a chopping
board and cut away the peel from top to
bottom, following the curve of the fruit
and cutting away the white pith as well.

ring
a vegetable peeler or small knife to pare
strips of zest, trying not to take any of the
te pith with the zest. Cut the pieces of
lengthways into very fine strips or "julienne".

Segmenting
Hold the peeled fruit over a bowl to catch
the juice. With a sharp knife, cut down one
side of a segment, cutting it from the dividing
membrane. Cut away from the membrane on
the other side, and remove the segment.
Continue all around the fruit.

sting
speedy removal of zest in tiny strips, use
trus zester or a flat ultra-sharp grater.

Citrus tips

To get the maximum juice from citrus
fruits, first roll the fruit gently on a work
surface, pressing lightly. Or heat in the
microwave, on HIGH (100% power) for
30 seconds, just until the fruit feels warm.

If a recipe includes citrus zest, add it
immediately after grating or zesting,
preferably to any sugar in the recipe.
Then the zest won't discolour or dry out,
and all the flavoursome oils from the zest
will be absorbed by the sugar.

Whisking egg whites

A balloon whisk is the classic tool for
whisking egg whites, but an electric
mixer saves time and effort. Ensure
all your equipment is clean, dry, and
grease-free, and that the egg whites
are at room temperature.

Whisk the whites as forcefully as possible (on
maximum speed if using an electric mixer) right
from the start. When they look like a cloud, add
any sugar little by little. The mixture will get stiffer
and stiffer as you add sugar and whisk.

Folding egg whites

To retain as much air as possible, egg
whites should be folded gently and quickly
into a mixture.

Mix a spoonful of the whites into the heavy
mixture to lighten it. Using a rubber spatula or
metal spoon, fold in the remaining whites using
a "figure of eight" motion, cutting straight through
the mixture, then turning it over until well blended.

Preparing a soufflé dish

To give a chilled soufflé the appearance
of having risen above the rim of the dish,
it is set with a raised collar.

Cut out a piece of foil or greaseproof paper
5 cm (2 in) longer than the circumference of
the dish and wide enough to stand 5 cm (2 in)
above it when folded. Fold in half. Wrap around
the dish and secure with tape or string. Remove
before serving.

Decorating with chocolate

Chocolate decorations can transform a dessert, and you don't have to reserve them for desserts made only from chocolate – fruit fools and mousses can also benefit from a contrasting finishing touch.

Grating chocolate
Use chilled chocolate and hold it firmly in a piece of greaseproof paper. Hold the grater on a sheet of greaseproof paper and rub the chocolate over the large grid of the grater.

Chocolate curls
Have the chocolate at room temperature, and use a vegetable peeler to shave off long curls on to a sheet of greaseproof paper. Lift the paper to tip the curls on to the dessert.

Chocolate caraque
1 Spread a smooth, thin layer of melted chocolate, about 1.5 mm (1/16 in) thick, on to a cool work surface (preferably marble), and leave to cool until nearly set.

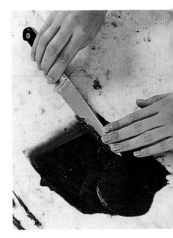

2 Using a long, sharp knife held at an angle, push across the chocolate with a slight sawing action, to shave it into "caraque" curls. Use a cocktail stick to pick up the caraque.

Melting chocolate

Care is needed when melting chocolate, especially white chocolate. Don't allow it to overheat or come into contact with any steam as this could cause it to scorch or harden.

Chop the chocolate and put it into a heatproof bowl set over a pan of hot, not boiling, water. The base of the bowl should not be touching the water. Heat gently, without stirring, until the chocolate becomes soft. Remove from the heat, but leave the bowl over the water. Stir until the chocolate is very smooth and creamy.

Decorating with cream

Piped whipped cream adds a professional touch to desserts and cakes, and with a little practice and some confidence this is not difficult to do. A star-shaped nozzle is the most useful.

1 Drop the nozzle into the piping bag, then tuck the lower half of the piping bag into the nozzle, to prevent the cream from leaking out when filling the bag.

2 Hold the bag in one hand, folding the top of the bag over your hand. Spoon in the whipped cream.

3 When the bag is full, twist the top until there is no c left. Pipe the cream as desir gently squeezing the twisted end to force out the cream a steady stream.

Rosette
Hold the bag upright, just above the surface of the cake. Squeeze gently, moving the bag in a small circle. Stop squeezing and lift the nozzle away.

Swirl
Hold the bag upright, just above the surface of the cake. Squeeze the bag and pipe the cream in a steady stream, guiding the nozzle in an "S" shape.

Rope
Hold the bag at a 45° angle. Pipe a short length of cream to 1 side. Pipe another leng of cream to the opposite sid overlapping the first one.

Winter fruit salad

🍴 SERVES 6   173 CALS PER SERVING

g (2 oz) caster sugar

ml (3 fl oz) water

red zest of ½ lemon

pink grapefruit

oranges

g (8 oz) seedless green grapes, halved

ripe pears, peeled, cored, and sliced

bananas, sliced

Put the sugar and measured water into
a saucepan and heat gently until the
gar has dissolved. Add the lemon zest
d bring the syrup to a boil. Boil for
minute, then strain into a serving bowl.
ave to cool.

Using a sharp serrated knife, cut the
peel and pith from each grapefruit and
ange. Remove the segments by cutting
tween each membrane. Add the
gments to the bowl.

Add the grapes, pears, and bananas to
the serving bowl and gently mix to coat
of the fruit in the sugar syrup.

Cover and chill the fruit salad for up to
1 hour before serving.

mmer berry salad

t 750 g (1½ lb) strawberries in half, then mix
m with 250 g (8 oz) raspberries and 250 g
oz) blueberries. Sift 3 tbsp icing sugar over
fruit, and pour the juice of 2 oranges on
. Stir gently, cover, and chill for 1 hour.

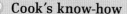

Cook's know-how

you are short of time you can just sprinkle
e fruit with caster sugar to taste rather than
aking a sugar syrup. To prevent the pears
nd bananas from discolouring when sliced
nd exposed to the air, toss the pieces in
mon juice.

Above: Old English trifle.

Old English trifle

🍴 SERVES 8   401 CALS PER SERVING

1 x 400 g can peach or pear halves

6 trifle sponges

4 tbsp red fruit jam

60 g (2 oz) ratafia biscuits or macaroons

75 ml (2½ fl oz) sherry

3 egg yolks

30 g (1 oz) caster sugar

1 tsp cornflour

300 ml (½ pint) milk

300 ml (½ pint) double or whipping cream

30 g (1 oz) flaked almonds, toasted, to decorate

1 Drain and slice the fruit, reserving the juice.

2 Cut the trifle sponges in half horizontally
and sandwich the halves together with
the jam.

3 Line the bottom of a glass serving bowl
with the trifle sponges, and arrange the
fruit and biscuits on top. Drizzle over the
sherry and reserved fruit juice, and leave to
soak while you make the custard.

4 In a bowl, mix together the egg yolks,
sugar, and cornflour. Warm the milk in
a heavy saucepan, then pour it into the egg
yolk mixture, stirring constantly. Return the
mixture to the pan and cook over a low heat,
stirring constantly, until the custard thickens.
Leave the custard to cool slightly.

5 Pour the custard over the sponges, fruit,
and biscuits in the glass bowl. Cover the
surface of the custard with a sheet of cling

film, to prevent a skin from forming, and chill
until set, preferably overnight (to let the
flavours mingle).

6 Whip the cream until thick and spread
over the custard. Scatter the almonds
over the top to decorate. Serve chilled.

Apricot and ginger trifle

Use 1 x 400 g can apricot halves. Sandwich
the sponges with apricot jam and sprinkle with
1 piece of stem ginger in syrup, chopped,
instead of the almonds.

Gooseberry fool

🍴 SERVES 6   396 CALS PER SERVING

500 g (1 lb) gooseberries, topped and tailed

1 tbsp water

60 g (2 oz) butter

2 elderflower heads (optional)

sugar to taste

300 ml (½ pint) double cream, whipped until thick

strips of blanched lime zest to decorate

1 Put the gooseberries into a pan with the
measured water, butter, and elderflowers,
if using. Cover and cook gently for 5–10
minutes until the gooseberries are soft.

2 Beat with a wooden spoon until smooth,
and add sugar to taste. Leave to cool.

3 Fold mixture into the cream. Turn into
serving glasses and chill for 30 minutes.
Decorate with lime zest.

Rhubarb and orange fool

Substitute 500 g (1 lb) chopped rhubarb for the
gooseberries and omit the elderflowers. Cook
the rhubarb until soft with sugar to taste and
the finely grated zest and juice of 1 large orange.

Port and claret jelly

 SERVES 8   201 CALS PER SERVING

8 sheets of leaf gelatine (about 25 g/scant 1 oz)

250 g (8 oz) caster or granulated sugar

450 ml (¾ pint) water

2 tbsp redcurrant jelly

1 cinnamon stick

450 ml (¾ pint) claret

300 ml (½ pint) ruby port

TO SERVE

small seasonal red fruits, eg raspberries, cherries, redcurrants, wild strawberries

cream (optional)

1.5 litre (2⅓ pint) jelly mould or 8 wine glasses

1 Put the sheets of gelatine in a medium bowl and cover with cold water. Leave to soak for about 5 minutes until softened.

2 Meanwhile, put the sugar into a large saucepan, pour in the measured water, and add the redcurrant jelly. Heat gently until the sugar and jelly have dissolved, then add the cinnamon stick, claret, and port. Bring to a boil, bubble for 1 minute, then remove the pan from the heat.

3 Pour the wine through a sieve lined with a double layer of muslin (or a J-cloth) into a bowl. Lift the gelatine out of the water, squeeze it, then add to the wine and stir until the gelatine has dissolved. Cool a little, pour into a mould or glasses, and leave until completely cold. Cover, and chill until set, at least 4 hours. Serve with seasonal fruits, and cream if you like.

Cook's know-how

If you want to use powdered gelatine instead of gelatine leaves, for the Port and Claret Jelly you will need to sprinkle 2 tbsp gelatine powder over 6 tbsp cold water in a small bowl, and for the Cranberry and Vodka Sparkle you will need to sprinkle 1½ tsp gelatine powder 1½ tbsp cold water. Leave to sponge for 10 minutes before stirring into the hot liquid.

Raspberry passion

 SERVES 6   196 CALS PER SERVING

3 ripe passion fruit

500 g (1 lb) plain yogurt

200 ml (7 fl oz) half-fat créme fraîche

375 g (12 oz) raspberries

90 g (3 oz) light muscovado sugar

6 x 300 ml (½ pint) stemmed glasses

1 Using a teaspoon, scoop the seeds and flesh from the passion fruit into a bowl, and mix with the yogurt and crème fraîche.

2 Put an equal quantity of raspberries in each glass, then fill with the crème fraîche mixture. Cover and refrigerate for up to 8 hours.

3 An hour or so before serving, sprinkle with sugar and return to the refrigerator until ready to serve.

Cranberry and vodka sparkle

 SERVES 4   99 CALS PER SERVING

2 sheets of leaf gelatine

175 ml (6 fl oz) cranberry juice

125 ml (4 fl oz) vodka

squeeze of lime juice

dainty red fruits (eg raspberries, cherries, redcurrants, wild strawberries) to serve

4 x 100 ml (3½ fl oz) glasses

1 Put the sheets of gelatine into a medium bowl and cover with cold water. Leave to soak for about 5 minutes until softened.

2 Heat the cranberry juice in a pan. Lift the gelatine out of the water, squeeze it, then add to the cranberry juice and stir until the gelatine has dissolved. Cool slightly, then add the vodka and lime juice. Cool completely, then pour into glasses, cover and chill until set, about 6 hours. Serve topped with dainty red fruits.

Jubilee trifle

 SERVES 6   417 CALS PER SERVING

8 trifle sponges

about 7 tbsp black cherry jam

1 x 420 g can pear quarters in natural juice, drained and juice reserved

1 x 420 g can red cherries, drained and juice reserved

4 tbsp kirsch or other cherry liqueur

500 ml (18 fl oz) custard (ready-made or see page 405 and use double the amount of cornflou

150 ml (¼ pint) whipping cream

6 individual glass dishes, or a 1.5 litre (2⅓ pint) shallow glass dish, about 20 cm (8 in) in diamete

1 Split the trifle sponges in half, spread generously with about 4 tbsp jam, and sandwich together again. Place four in the bottom of 6 individual glass dishes, cutting them to fit.

2 Chop each pear quarter into small pieces, and put some of the pieces around the edges of the dishes, and some in between the sponges. Dot with the cherries.

3 Mix 5 tbsp of the pear juice with the kirsch, and pour half of it over the sponges. Arrange the last four sponges in the dishes, again cutting them to fit, then pour over the remaining juice and kirsch. Leave for a few minutes, then gently squc flat with the back of a spoon. Pour over t custard, level gently, and chill for 1 hour.

4 Lightly whip the cream – it should still b soft and floppy – and spread over the custard. Cover and chill for at least 4 hou (or up to 24 hours).

5 To serve, warm 3 tbsp cherry jam in a small pan with 2 tbsp of the reserved cherry juice until the jam has dissolved. Leave to cool, then sieve to remove any lumps, and drizzle over the trifles.

Opposite, clockwise from top left: Port claret jelly, Raspberry passion, Cranb and vodka sparkle, Jubilee tr

Summer pudding

This classic English summer-time treat is very easy to make, and not at all high in calories. For a perfect, evenly coloured result, reserve half of the cooking juices and pour them over any pale patches of bread after unmoulding the pudding.

🍴 **SERVES 6**   **240 CALS PER SERVING**

8 slices of stale medium-sliced white bread, crusts removed

875 g (1¾ lb) mixed summer fruits such as strawberries, redcurrants, blackcurrants, cherries, and raspberries

150 g (5 oz) caster sugar

75 ml (2½ fl oz) water

2 tbsp framboise or crème de cassis liqueur

crème fraîche or Greek yogurt to serve

1.25 litre (2 pint) pudding bowl

1 Set 2 slices of bread aside for the top of the pudding, then use the remaining slices to line the bowl (see box, right).

2 Hull and halve the strawberries if large, strip the currants from their stalks, and pit the cherries.

3 Place the redcurrants, blackcurrants, and cherries in a saucepan with the sugar and measured water. Heat gently until the juices begin to run. Stir until the sugar has dissolved, and cook until all of the fruit is just tender.

4 Remove from the heat and add the strawberries, raspberries, and liqueur.

5 Spoon the fruit and half of the juice into the lined bowl, reserving the remaining juice. Cover the top of the fruit with the reserved bread slices.

6 Stand the bowl in a shallow dish to catch any juices that may overflow, then put a saucer on top of the bread lid. Place a kitchen weight (or a can of food) on top of the saucer. Leave to chill for 8 hours.

7 Remove the weight and saucer and invert the pudding on to a serving plate. Spoon the reserved juices over the top, paying particular attention to any pale areas, and serve with either crème fraîche or Greek yogurt.

Lining the pudding bowl

Put a slice of bread in the bottom of the bowl, cutting it to fit if necessary, then use the remainder to line the sides. The slices should fit snugly together.

emon syllabub

SERVES 4   470 CALS PER SERVING

ml (¼ pint) dessert wine or sweet white wine

rge lemons

g (3 oz) caster sugar

ml (½ pint) double cream

gg whites

Put the wine into a bowl with the grated
zest and juice of 1 of the lemons, and
sugar. Stir to mix, then leave to stand
about 15 minutes, stirring occasionally,
il the sugar has dissolved.

Meanwhile, remove the zest from the
remaining lemon in long, very thin strips.
nch the strips in a small saucepan of
ling water for 1 minute. Drain, rinse under
d running water, and pat dry.

In a medium bowl, whip the cream
until it just holds its shape. Add the wine
ture very slowly, whisking well between
ch addition to ensure that the mixture
ains thick.

In a separate bowl, whisk the egg
whites until stiff but not dry. Carefully
into the cream and wine mixture.
on into 4 tall syllabub glasses. Decorate
top of each syllabub with a strip of
on zest, and serve at once.

ango and lime
ousse

SERVES 6   354 CALS PER SERVING

ge ripe mangoes

ed zest and juice of 2 limes

(½ oz) powdered gelatine

gs, plus 1 egg yolk

(1½ oz) caster sugar

ml (¼ pint) double or whipping cream,
ped until thick

ORATION

ml (¼ pint) double or whipping cream,
ped until thick

e, thinly sliced

ce the mango flesh away from the
ones (page 421). Peel the flesh, then
e in a blender or food processor. Add
me zest to the purée.

2 Put the lime juice into a small bowl,
sprinkle the gelatine over the top, and
leave for 10 minutes until it becomes spongy.

3 Stand the bowl in a pan of hot water
and heat until the gelatine has dissolved.

4 Combine the eggs, egg yolk, and sugar
in a large bowl and whisk vigorously for
about 10 minutes until the mixture is pale
and very thick. Gradually add the mango
purée, whisking between each addition to
keep the mixture thick.

5 Fold the whipped cream into the mango
mixture. Add the dissolved gelatine in a
steady stream, stirring gently to mix. Pour
the mixture into a glass serving bowl and
chill until set.

6 To decorate, pipe rosettes of whipped
cream (page 422) on top of the mousse.
Cut the lime slices in half, place 2 slices
between each rosette of cream, and
serve chilled.

Caramelized
oranges

SERVES 4   388 CALS PER SERVING

250 g (8 oz) granulated sugar

150 ml (¼ pint) cold water

150 ml (¼ pint) lukewarm water

3 tbsp orange liqueur

8 thin-skinned oranges

1 Put the sugar and measured cold water
into a heavy pan and heat gently until
the sugar dissolves.

2 When all the sugar has dissolved, bring
to a boil and boil steadily until a rich
brown colour. (If the caramel is too light in
colour it will be very sweet, but be careful
not to let it burn.)

3 Protect your hand by covering it with
a cloth, and remove the pan from the
heat. Pour the measured lukewarm water
into the caramel.

4 Return the pan to the heat and stir to
melt the caramel. Pour the caramel into
a heatproof serving dish. Leave to cool for
30 minutes. Stir in the orange liqueur.

5 Pare the zest from 1 of the oranges,
using a vegetable peeler. Cut the
zest into very thin strips (page 421). Cook
for 1 minute in boiling water, drain, rinse
thoroughly under cold running water,
and set aside.

6 Using a sharp knife, remove the peel
and pith from each orange, catching
any juice to add to the caramel in the dish.
Cut each orange into slices crosswise, then
reassemble the oranges, holding the slices
together with cocktail sticks.

7 Place the oranges in the dish of caramel
and spoon the caramel over them.
Scatter the strips of orange zest over the
top. Chill for about 30 minutes. Remove
the cocktail sticks before transferring the
oranges to individual bowls to serve.

Below: Caramelized oranges.

Orange pannacotta with boozy oranges

SERVES 4   782 CALS PER SERVING

sunflower oil for greasing

3 tbsp cold water

2 tsp powdered gelatine

600 ml (1 pint) whipping cream

60 g (2 oz) caster sugar

5 oranges

4 tbsp orange liqueur

4 x 150 ml (¼ pint) metal pudding or dariole moulds

1 Brush the moulds with oil, and stand them on a tray. Measure the water into a small bowl, sprinkle the gelatine over the top, and leave to become spongy.

2 Meanwhile, pour the cream into a saucepan, and add the sugar. Finely grate the zest from the oranges, and add

to the pan with 2 tbsp of the liqueur. Heat the cream until bubbles appear around the edge, stirring until the sugar has dissolved and the cream is smooth. Remove from the heat, and leave to cool slightly.

3 Add the sponged gelatine to the warm cream, and whisk until completely dissolved and smooth. Pour the cream into the prepared moulds. Chill for about 6 hours, ideally overnight, until set.

4 Using a serrated knife, peel and segment the oranges, working over a bowl to catch the juice. Tip the segments into the bowl, and squeeze the thick, white membranes over the bowl to extract the remaining juice. Stir in the remaining liqueur. Chill until serving time.

5 To serve, dip each mould briefly into very hot water, then loosen the pannacotta away from the top of the mould with your fingertips, and carefully turn the pannacotta out on to a plate. Serve chilled, with a spoonful of boozy oranges alongside.

Below: Orange pannacotta with boozy oranges.

Scotch mist

SERVES 6   446 CALS PER SERVING

450 ml (¾ pint) double or whipping cream

4 tbsp whisky

90 g (3 oz) meringues, coarsely crushed

30 g (1 oz) flaked almonds, toasted

1 Whip the cream with the whisky until it just holds its shape. Fold in the crushed meringues.

2 Spoon the mixture into 6 glass serving bowls, cover, and chill for about 20 minutes or until firm.

3 Scatter the toasted flaked almonds ov the desserts just before serving.

Eton mess

Substitute 4 tbsp brandy for the whisky, and add 500 g (1 lb) chopped strawberries to the cream mixture. Decorate with strawberry hal and mint leaves instead of the almonds.

Mango and passion fruit meringue

SERVES 6 **503 CALS PER SERVING**

g whites

g (8 oz) caster sugar

NG

e mango

ssion fruit

ml (½ pint) whipping cream, whipped thick

g (4 oz) strawberries, sliced

ORATION

ml (¼ pint) double or whipping cream, ped until stiff

w strawberries

1 Mark 2 x 20 cm (8 in) circles on 2 sheets of non-stick baking parchment, turn the paper over, and use to line 2 baking trays.

2 Whisk the egg whites with a hand-held electric mixer until stiff but not dry. Add the sugar, 1 tsp at a time, and continue to whisk until all the sugar has been incorporated and the mixture is stiff and glossy.

3 Pipe the meringue, in concentric circles, inside the marked circles on the paper-lined baking trays.

4 Bake the meringue rounds in a preheated oven at 140°C (120°C fan, Gas 1) for 1–1¼ hours until crisp and dry. Leave to cool, then carefully peel off the paper.

5 Dice the mango very finely (page 421). Halve the passion fruit and scoop out the pulp.

6 Spread the whipped cream over 1 of the meringue rounds. Arrange the mango, passion fruit pulp, and strawberries on top, and cover with the remaining meringue round.

7 Decorate with piped rosettes of whipped cream (page 422), strawberry slices, and a whole strawberry.

Peach meringue

Substitute 2 peeled and sliced peaches for the mango, and 125 g (4 oz) raspberries for the strawberries. Decorate the top of the peach meringue with a few whole raspberries.

Chilled lemon soufflé

SERVES 4   883 CALS PER SERVING

3 tbsp cold water

15 g (½ oz) powdered gelatine

3 large eggs, separated

250 g (8 oz) caster sugar

grated zest and juice of 3 lemons

300 ml (½ pint) double or whipping cream, whipped until thick

DECORATION

30 g (1 oz) nibbed almonds, lightly toasted

150 ml (¼ pint) double or whipping cream, whipped until stiff

1 litre (1¾ pint) soufflé dish

1 Prepare the soufflé dish: tie a band of double thickness greaseproof paper or foil around the outside so that it stands about 5 cm (2 in) above the top of the dish (page 421).

2 Put the water into a small bowl and sprinkle the gelatine over the top. Leave for about 10 minutes until it becomes spongy. Stand in a pan of hot water and heat until dissolved.

3 Put the egg yolks and sugar into a heatproof bowl and put over a pan of gently simmering water. Do not let the bottom of the bowl touch the water. Using an electric hand-held mixer, whisk together. Add the lemon zest and juice and whisk at full speed until the mixture is pale and thick.

4 Fold the whipped cream into the lemon mixture, then fold in the dissolved gelatine.

5 In a separate large bowl, whisk the egg whites until stiff but not dry. Fold into the lemon mixture, and carefully pour into the prepared soufflé dish. Level the surface, then chill for about 4 hours until set.

6 Carefully remove the paper collar. Decorate the outside edge of the soufflé with the lightly toasted almonds and sprinkle some in the middle. Pipe the cream (page 422) around the edge of the soufflé, and serve chilled.

Hazelnut meringue gâteau

Crisp meringues made with toasted hazelnuts are sandwiched with a whipped cream filling. The attractive decoration is easy to create: piped rosettes of cream are topped with hazelnuts and raspberries, and the gâteau is accompanied by a raspberry sauce.

SERVES 8   429 CALS PER SERVING

125 g (4 oz) shelled hazelnuts

4 egg whites

275 g (9 oz) caster sugar

½ tsp white wine vinegar

300 ml (½ pint) whipping cream, whipped until thick

icing sugar for dusting

RASPBERRY SAUCE

250 g (8 oz) raspberries

about 4 tbsp icing sugar, sifted

1 Mark 2 x 20 cm (8 in) circles on 2 sheets of non-stick baking parchment. Turn the paper over and use to line 2 baking trays.

2 Spread the hazelnuts on another baking tray and toast in a preheated oven at 190°C (170°C fan, Gas 5) for about 10 minutes. Remove from the oven, then turn the temperature down to 160°C (140°C fan, Gas 3).

3 Tip the hazelnuts on to a clean tea towel and rub together inside the towel to remove the skins. Reserve 8 whole nuts for decoration and grind the remaining nuts in a food processor.

4 Whisk the egg whites until stiff but not dry (if using an electric mixer turn it to high speed). Add the caster sugar, 1 tsp at a time, and continue to whisk, still at high speed, until all of the caster sugar has been incorporated and the mixture is stiff and glossy.

5 Whisk in the white wine vinegar, then fold in the ground hazelnuts.

6 Divide the hazelnut meringue mixture equally between the baking trays, spreading it out evenly within the marked circles.

7 Bake in the oven for about 30 minutes until the top of each meringue round is crisp and a pale beige colour. The insides of the meringues should still be soft like marshmallow.

8 Lift the meringue rounds off the baking trays and peel the lining paper from the bases. Leave to cool on a wire rack.

9 Make the raspberry sauce: reserve 8 whole raspberries for decoration, and put the remainder in a food processor. Blend until smooth, then push through a sieve to remove the seeds. Gradually whisk in icing sugar to taste.

10 Use two-thirds of the whipped cream to sandwich the meringue rounds together. Sift icing sugar on top and decorate with rosettes (page 422) of the remaining whipped cream. Top the rosettes with the reserved whole hazelnuts and raspberries. Serve with the raspberry sauce.

Sauces for desserts

Hot chocolate sauce Heat 175 g (6 oz) plain chocolate, broken into pieces, 2 tsp instant coffee granules, 125 ml (4 fl oz) hot water, and 90 g (3 oz) caster sugar in a pan until the chocolate has melted. Serve hot.

Chocolate marshmallow sauce Heat 60 g (2 oz) chopped plain chocolate, 100 g (3½ oz) marshmallows, 75 ml (2½ fl oz) double cream, and 75 ml (2½ fl oz) honey in a pan until the chocolate and marshmallows have melted. Serve hot.

Butterscotch sauce Heat 60 g (2 oz) butter, 150 g (5 oz) light muscovado sugar, and 150 g (5 oz) golden syrup in a pan until melted. Remove from the heat and add 150 ml (¼ pint) double cream and a few drops of vanilla extract, stirring until smooth. Serve hot.

Peach sauce Put 1 x 400 g can peaches and their juice into a food processor or blender with ¼ tsp almond extract. Work to a smooth purée. Serve chilled.

Pavlova with pineapple and ginger

Pavlova meringue is crisp on the outside, soft and slightly chewy like marshmallows inside. This pineapple and ginger topping is good in winter, but if you want to make a summer pavlova, use sweetened fresh mixed berries instead – and omit the ginger.

SERVES 6–8   **504–378 CALS PER SERVING**

egg whites

0 g (8 oz) caster sugar

½ tsp cornflour

½ tsp white wine vinegar

TOPPING

75 ml (13 fl oz) double or whipping cream

0 g (2 oz) stem ginger in syrup, cut into matchstick-thin strips

x 400 g can pineapple rings, drained

1 Preheat the oven to 160°C (140°C fan, Gas 3). Mark a 23 cm (9 in) circle on a sheet of non-stick baking parchment, turn the paper over, and line a baking tray.

2 Whisk the egg whites until stiff, then add the sugar, 1 tsp at a time, whisking the mixture constantly.

3 Blend the cornflour and vinegar and whisk into the egg white mixture.

4 Spread the mixture inside the circle on the baking parchment, building the sides up so that they are higher than the middle. Place in the oven, then immediately reduce the heat to 150°C (130°C fan, Gas 2).

5 Bake the meringue for 1 hour or until firm to the touch. Turn off the oven and leave the meringue inside for another hour.

6 Peel the lining paper from the meringue, and transfer the meringue to a serving plate. Leave to cool.

7 Before serving, whip the cream until stiff, and stir in half of the stem ginger strips. Spoon the mixture into the middle of the meringue. Top with the pineapple rings and the remaining stem ginger strips.

🔎 Cook's know-how

Keep the oven door closed when you leave the meringue to dry out, but if you have a fan-assisted oven, you should leave the door slightly open. The meringue base can be made a day in advance and kept in an airtight container in a cool place until needed. Add the cream and fruit topping just before serving.

Fresh fruit baskets

MAKES 8   303 CALS EACH

1 quantity Basic Meringue (see recipe, below right)

250 ml (8 fl oz) double cream

berries and mint sprigs (optional) to decorate

RASPBERRY SAUCE

250 g (8 oz) fresh or frozen raspberries

2 tbsp icing sugar

a squeeze of lemon juice, to taste

1 Make the raspberry sauce: purée the raspberries in a blender or food processor, then push the purée through a sieve with a spoon into a bowl (discard the seeds in the sieve). Stir in the sugar and lemon juice to taste. Chill in the refrigerator until ready to use.

2 Pipe 8 meringue baskets (see box, below). Bake in a preheated oven at 120°C (100°C fan, Gas ½) for 1–1½ hours until firm. Leave to cool.

3 Whip the cream until it forms stiff peaks. Fill the baskets with the cream, top with berries, and decorate with mint sprigs if you like. Serve with the chilled raspberry sauce.

Mocha meringue mille-feuilles

MAKES 6   537 CALS EACH

1 quantity Basic Meringue (see recipe, below right)

125 g (4 oz) slivered almonds

icing sugar for dusting

COFFEE CHANTILLY CREAM

250 ml (8 fl oz) double cream

1 tsp instant coffee, dissolved in 1 tbsp water

2–3 tbsp caster sugar

1 Spoon 18 mounds of meringue on to non-stick baking parchment, then spread them flat with a palette knife until they are very thin and about 7.5 cm (3 in) in diameter. Sprinkle over the almonds. Bake in a preheated oven at 120°C (100°C fan, Gas ½) for 1–1½ hours until firm. Cool.

2 Make the coffee Chantilly cream: whip the cream until it forms soft peaks. Add the coffee and sugar to the cream and whip until stiff peaks form.

3 Sandwich the meringue discs together in threes, with the coffee Chantilly cream in between. Dust with a little icing sugar before serving.

Chocolate meringue shells

MAKES 12   231 CALS EACH

1 quantity Basic Meringue (see recipe, below)

60 g (2 oz) plain chocolate, chopped

CHOCOLATE GANACHE

125 g (4 oz) plain chocolate, chopped

125 ml (4 fl oz) double cream

1 Pipe 24 shells (see box, below left). Bak in a preheated oven at 120°C (100°C fan, Gas ½) for 1–1½ hours until firm. Leav to cool. Put the chocolate into a heatpro bowl over a pan of hot water and heat u melted. Drizzle over the meringues and leave to set.

2 Make the ganache: put the choppe chocolate and the cream into a hea based saucepan and heat gently, stirring occasionally, until the chocolate has melt

3 Remove the pan from the heat and whisk the ganache for about 5 minut until the mixture is fluffy and cooled. Sandwich the meringues together with th chocolate ganache.

Basic meringue

MAKES 24   43 CALS EACH

4 egg whites

250 g (8 oz) caster sugar

1 Whisk the egg whites in a scrupulously clean large bowl, with an electric har mixer on maximum speed, until the white are stiff and look like clouds.

2 Keeping the mixer on maximum spee add the caster sugar a teaspoon at time and continue whisking until the mix is stiff and shiny.

3 Pipe, spoon, or spread the meringue as preferred and bake as in the recip above. All ovens vary, so baking times cannot be exact. You will know the meringues are cooked when they can be lifted easily from the parchment.

Piping meringue shapes

Baskets Mark 8 x 10 cm (4 in) circles on non-stick baking parchment; turn over. Spoon the meringue into a piping bag fitted with a medium star nozzle, and pipe inside the circles, building up the sides to form baskets.

Shells Spoon the meringue into a piping bag fitted with a medium star nozzle. Pipe 24 even-sized shells, about 5 cm (2 in) in diameter at the base, on to non-stick baking parchment.

Opposite, clockwise from to
Mocha meringue mille-feuilles, Cho
meringue shells, Fresh fruit ba

Floating islands

🥄 **SERVES 4**   **412 CALS PER SERVING**

butter for greasing
3 eggs, separated
30 g (1 oz) vanilla sugar
1 tsp cornflour
600 ml (1 pint) milk
175 g (6 oz) caster sugar
30 g (1 oz) flaked almonds, toasted

1 Butter 4 individual serving dishes. Line a baking tray with a sheet of baking parchment.

2 In a large bowl, mix together the egg yolks, vanilla sugar, and cornflour. In a heavy saucepan, bring the milk to a bo Add the boiling milk to the egg-yolk mixtu stirring constantly, then pour the mixture back into the pan.

3 Return to the heat and cook gently, stirring constantly, until the froth disappears and the custard is thickened. Pour the custard into the buttered dishes, and leave to cool.

4 Whisk the egg whites until stiff but not dry. Add the caster sugar, 1 tsp at a time, and continue to whisk until all the sugar has been incorporated and the mixture is stiff and glossy.

5 Shape the meringue into 8 ovals by scooping it up between 2 tablespoon Place the ovals on the baking tray.

6 Cook in a preheated oven at 160°C (140°C fan, Gas 3) for 20 minutes until the meringues are set and no longer stick Leave to cool, then arrange on top of the custard. Sprinkle with almonds before servi

Strawberry meringue roulade

🥄 **SERVES 8**   **349 CALS PER SERVING**

sunflower oil for greasing
4 egg whites
250 g (8 oz) caster sugar
45 g (1½ oz) flaked almonds
icing sugar for dusting
FILLING
300 ml (½ pint) double or whipping cream, whipped until thick
250 g (8 oz) strawberries, quartered

23 x 33 cm (9 x 13 in) Swiss roll tin

1 Lightly oil the Swiss roll tin and line with a sheet of baking parchment.

2 Whisk the egg whites until stiff but not dry. Add the sugar, 1 tsp at a time, and continue to whisk, until all the sugar has been incorporated and the mixture is stiff and glossy.

3 Spoon the meringue into the lined tin and tilt to level the surface. Sprinkle over the flaked almonds.

4 Bake near the top of a preheated oven at 200°C (180°C fan, Gas 6) for about 8 minutes until the top is golden brown.

5 Reduce the oven temperature to 160°C (140°C fan, Gas 3), and continue baking for 10 minutes or until the meringue is firm to the touch.

6 Remove the meringue from the oven and turn out on to a sheet of baking parchment. Peel the lining paper from the base and leave the meringue to cool for 10 minutes.

7 Spread the whipped cream evenly over the meringue, and scatter the strawberries over the cream.

8 Roll up the meringue from a long side, using the lining paper to help lift it. Wrap the roulade in baking parchment and leave to chill in the refrigerator for about 30 minutes. Lightly dust with sifted icing sugar before serving.

🔍 **Cook's know-how**

This classic dessert is called îles flottantes in French, although you may also see it described as oeufs à la neige, or "snow eggs" They are one and the same thing. You can b vanilla sugar, or make it yourself.

ropical fruit heesecake

SERVES 10   396 CALS PER SERVING

pe mangoes

ml (¼ pint) mango and apple fruit juice

g (½ oz) powdered gelatine

g (8 oz) full-fat soft cheese, at room temperature

g (4 oz) caster sugar

ggs, separated

ml (¼ pint) whipping cream, whipped until thick

CUIT BASE

g (4 oz) coconut or digestive biscuits, crushed

g (2 oz) butter, melted

g (1 oz) demerara sugar

CORATION

iwi fruit, peeled and sliced

250 g can pineapple pieces in natural
e, drained

cm (9 in) loose-bottomed or springform
e tin

Make the biscuit base: mix together the
biscuits, melted butter, and sugar, and
ess over the bottom of the tin.

Slice the mango flesh away from the
stones (page 421). Peel, then purée in
od processor.

Pour the fruit juice into a heatproof bowl,
and sprinkle the gelatine over the top.
ave for about 10 minutes until it becomes
ngy. Stand the bowl in a small pan of
water, and heat gently until the gelatine
dissolved.

In a large bowl, beat the soft cheese until
smooth and creamy. Beat in half of the
ter sugar, the egg yolks, and the mango
ée. Gradually beat in the gelatine mixture.

In a separate bowl, whisk the egg whites
until stiff but not dry. Whisk in the remaining
ar, 1 tsp at a time, and continue to whisk
high speed until the sugar is incorporated
the mixture is stiff and glossy.

Fold the whipped cream into the cheese
and mango mixture, then fold in the egg
tes. Pour on to the biscuit base and chill
set.

Use a knife to loosen the side of the
cheesecake, then remove from the tin.
e on to a serving plate. Decorate the
with slices of kiwi fruit and pieces of
eapple before serving.

Cherry cheesecake

SERVES 8   530 CALS PER SERVING

375 g (12 oz) full-fat soft cheese

125 g (4 oz) caster sugar

2 eggs, beaten

a few drops of vanilla extract

1 tbsp lemon juice

BISCUIT SHELL

175 g (6 oz) digestive biscuits, crushed

90 g (3 oz) butter, melted

2 tbsp demerara sugar

TOPPING

1 tsp arrowroot

1 x 400 g can pitted black cherries

1 tbsp kirsch

23 cm (9 in) springform cake tin

1 Make the biscuit shell: mix together the crushed biscuits, melted butter, and sugar, and press evenly over the bottom and up the side of the cake tin.

2 Put the soft cheese into a bowl and beat until smooth. Add the caster sugar and beat until well blended. Add the eggs, vanilla extract, and lemon juice. Mix until smooth and creamy.

3 Pour the filling into the biscuit shell. Bake in a preheated oven at 180°C (160°C fan, Gas 4) for 25–30 minutes until just set. Leave to cool completely, then transfer to the refrigerator and leave to chill.

4 Make the topping: dissolve the arrowroot in a little of the cherry juice. Put the cherries and their juice into a small pan and add the arrowroot mixture with the kirsch. Bring to a boil, stirring, until thick. Leave to cool completely.

5 Spoon the cherries on top of the cheese filling. Chill. Use a knife to loosen the side of the cheesecake from the tin, then remove the cheesecake. Serve chilled.

Austrian cheesecake

🍴 SERVES 8   331 CALS PER SERVING

90 g (3 oz) butter, at room temperature, plus extra for greasing

150 g (5 oz) caster sugar

300 g (10 oz) curd cheese

2 eggs, separated

60 g (2 oz) ground almonds

2 tbsp semolina

grated zest and juice of 1 large lemon

60 g (2 oz) sultanas

icing sugar for dusting

20 cm (8 in) loose-bottomed or springform cake tin

1 Lightly butter the tin and line the bottom with a round of baking parchment.

2 Beat the butter with the sugar and curd cheese until light and creamy. Beat in the egg yolks, then stir in the almonds, semolina, and lemon zest and juice. Leave to stand for 10 minutes, then fold in the sultanas.

3 In a separate bowl, whisk the egg whites until stiff but not dry. Carefully fold into the cheese mixture.

4 Turn into the prepared tin and level the surface. Bake in a preheated oven at 190°C (170°C fan, Gas 5) for 30–35 minutes until browned and firm to the touch. Turn off the oven and leave the cheesecake inside to cool for about 1 hour. Chill before serving.

5 Use a knife to loosen the side of the cheesecake from the tin, then remove the cheesecake. Slide on to a serving plate, and dust with sifted icing sugar.

Marbled raspberry cheesecake

The crunchy base of this cheesecake, made with crushed oat biscuits and walnuts, provides a delicious contrast to the creamy filling, marbled with streaks of fresh raspberry purée. It is a delicate cheesecake, so for best results be sure to chill it well before slicing and serving.

🍴 SERVES 10   439 CALS PER SERVING

3 tbsp cold water

15 g (½ oz) powdered gelatine

500 g (1 lb) raspberries

4 tbsp framboise (raspberry liqueur)

250 g (8 oz) full-fat soft cheese, at room temperature

150 ml (¼ pint) soured cream

2 eggs, separated

125 g (4 oz) caster sugar

BISCUIT BASE

125 g (4 oz) sweet oat or digestive biscuits, coarsely crushed

60 g (2 oz) butter, melted

30 g (1 oz) demerara sugar

45 g (1½ oz) walnuts, chopped

DECORATION

150 ml (¼ pint) whipping cream, whipped until stiff

a few raspberries

mint sprigs

23 cm (9 in) loose-bottomed or springform cake tin

1 Make the biscuit base: mix together the biscuits, butter, demerara sugar, and walnuts and press evenly over the bottom of the tin.

2 Put the measured water into a heatproof bowl, sprinkle the gelatine over the top, and leave for about 10 minutes until spongy.

3 Meanwhile, purée the raspberries in a food processor, then push them through a sieve to remove the seeds. Stir in the liqueur. Set aside.

4 Put the soft cheese into a large bowl, and beat until soft and smooth. Add the soured cream and egg yolks, and beat until well blended.

5 Stand the bowl of gelatine in a saucepan of hot water and heat gently until it dissolves. Stir into the cheese mixture.

6 Make the filling (see box, right).

7 Use a knife to loosen the side of the cheesecake from the tin, then remove the cheesecake. Slide on to a serving plate. Pipe whipped cream (page 422) around the edge and decorate with raspberries and mint sprigs.

Making the filling

Whisk the egg whites until stiff but not dry. Add the caster sugar, 1 tsp at a time, and keep whisking until all the sugar is incorporated and the meringue mixture is stiff and glossy.

Turn the cheese mixture into the meringue and fold together, blending well. Leave the mixture to thicken slightly.

Fold in the raspberry purée, swirling it in just enough to give an attractive marbled effect.

Pour the mixture carefully on to the biscuit base and chill until set.

Opposite: Marbled raspberry cheesec●

Tropical island fruit salad

SERVES 6   155 CALS PER SERVING

1 small ripe pineapple

1 ripe charentais or cantaloupe melon

1 ripe mango

250 g (8 oz) seedless black grapes

150 ml (¼ pint) pineapple and coconut juice or pineapple juice

125 g (4 oz) physalis (cape gooseberries)

2 ripe guavas, preferably pink-fleshed

2 Asian (nashi) pears

1 Cut the top and bottom off the pineapple. Remove the skin with a sharp knife, then cut out the brown eyes. Cut the pineapple lengthways into 4 and remove and discard the hard inner core. Cut the flesh into chunks and put into a large glass serving bowl.

2 Cut the melon into quarters, remove and discard the seeds with a spoon. Cut each melon quarter in half, remove the skin with a sharp knife, and cut the flesh into chunks. Add to the pineapple.

3 Peel the mango, cut either side of the large flat stone, and neatly cut the mango flesh into pieces. Add to the bowl with the grapes. Pour over the fruit juice, cover, and chill in the refrigerator for about 4 hours, or overnight.

4 Peel back the paper lanterns on the physalis. Remove the fruits from about half of the physalis, wipe gently with kitchen paper, and add to the bowl.

5 Peel the guavas, halve the fruits, and remove the seeds. Cut the flesh into neat pieces and add to the bowl. Peel and quarter the pears, remove the cores, and slice the flesh neatly into the bowl.

6 Stir the fruits gently together, making sure the pear is submerged in juice or it will discolour. Cover and chill in the refrigerator for about 1 hour. Serve chilled, decorated with the remaining physalis.

Spiced fruit salad

SERVES 4   460 CALS PER SERVING

500 g (1 lb) mixed no-need-to-soak dried fruits, eg pears, peaches, mango, prunes, pineapple, figs, apple

about 900 ml (1½ pints) apple juice

2–3 star anise, to taste

1 vanilla pod

75 g (2½ oz) dried cranberries

75 g (2½ oz) dried cherries

1 Put the mixed fruits into a saucepan with 900 ml (1½ pints) apple juice, the star anise, and vanilla pod. Bring to a boil and simmer gently for about 15 minutes.

2 Add the dried cranberries and cherries to the pan and continue cooking for about 15 minutes, adding more apple juice (or water) if necessary. Serve hot or cold.

Orange passion salad

SERVES 6   89 CALS PER SERVING

8 thin-skinned oranges

juice of 1 small lime

2 ripe papayas (pawpaws)

3 ripe passion fruit

1 Remove the thin orange skin from 2 of the oranges with a zester and set the strips of zest aside. Peel all the oranges and remove all the skin and pith. Slice into rounds and remove any pips.

2 Put the orange slices into a fairly shallow glass bowl with any juice from the oranges and the lime juice.

3 Halve the papayas lengthways and scoop out the seeds. Peel the halves, cut crosswise into fairly thick slices, and add to the bowl. Cut the passion fruit in half crosswise and scoop the juice and pips over the fruit in the bowl. Top the salad with the orange zest, cover, and chill in the refrigerator for at least 2 hours. Stir before serving – there is no need for sugar.

Fruits of the forest salad

SERVES 6   94 CALS PER SERVING

250 g (8 oz) fresh cranberries

60 g (2 oz) caster sugar

250 g (8 oz) strawberries, hulled and halved if large

125 g (4 oz) blueberries

250 g (8 oz) raspberries

250 g (8 oz) blackberries

250 g (8 oz) loganberries, or increase the amount of the other berries if loganberries are unavailable

2–3 tbsp balsamic vinegar

1 tsp green peppercorns in brine or oil, rinsed and lightly crushed

1 Put the cranberries into a stainless steel pan with 5 tbsp water. Cook gently for about 5–10 minutes or until the cranberries pop and are just soft. Remove from the heat, stir in the sugar, and leave until the sugar has dissolved and the mixture has cooled slightly (do not add the sugar at the beginning or it will make the cranberry skins tough).

2 Put the remaining fruit into a serving bowl, add the cooled cranberries and juice, and mix gently together.

3 Add the balsamic vinegar and green peppercorns and mix gently. Cover and chill in the refrigerator for at least 4 hours (or overnight) to allow to juices to develop and the flavours to mellow.

Opposite, clockwise from top right: Spiced fruit salad, Orange passion salad, Tropical island fruit salad, Fruits of the forest salad

Chocolate chip cheesecake

This delicious dessert, with its crunchy muesli base and rich chocolate filling, is ideal for parties. It can be prepared up to a month in advance and frozen in foil. Thaw, wrapped, in the refrigerator for 8 hours, then decorate.

SERVES 8   628 CALS PER SERVING

125 g (4 oz) plain dark chocolate, broken into pieces

3 tbsp cold water

15 g (½ oz) powdered gelatine

250 g (8 oz) full-fat soft cheese

2 eggs, separated

60 g (2 oz) caster sugar

150 ml (¼ pint) soured cream

30 g (1 oz) plain dark chocolate chips, coarsely chopped

BASE

125 g (4 oz) muesli

90 g (3 oz) butter, melted

30 g (1 oz) demerara sugar

DECORATION

300 ml (½ pint) whipping cream, whipped until stiff

chocolate curls or caraque (page 422)

20 cm (8 in) loose-bottomed or springform cake tin

1 Make the base: mix together the muesli, melted butter, and sugar, and press evenly over the bottom of the tin. Chill.

2 Meanwhile, put the chocolate into a small heatproof bowl over a pan of hot water. Heat gently to melt the chocolate, stirring occasionally. Leave to cool.

3 Put the measured water into a heatproof bowl and sprinkle the gelatine over the top. Leave for 10 minutes until spongy. Stand the bowl in a pan of hot water and heat gently until the gelatine has dissolved.

4 Beat the cheese until smooth. Add the egg yolks and sugar and beat until blended. Stir in the soured cream, melted chocolate, chocolate chips, and gelatine. Mix well.

5 In a separate bowl, whisk the egg whites until stiff but not dry. Fold carefully into the chocolate mixture until evenly mixed. Pour on to the muesli base and chill until set.

6 Use a knife to loosen the side of the cheesecake from the tin, then remove the cheesecake. Slide on to a serving plate. Pipe rosettes of whipped cream (page 422) on top and decorate with chocolate curls or caraque.

Cook's know-how

Chocolate chips are convenient, but if you don't have any to hand, simply chop up a bar of plain dark chocolate.

Tiramisu

SERVES 8   508 CALS PER SERVING

eaped tsp instant coffee granules

ml (4 fl oz) boiling water

sp brandy

ggs

g (2½ oz) caster sugar

g (8 oz) full-fat mascarpone cheese

ml (½ pint) double cream, whipped until thick

acket trifle sponges

g (2 oz) plain dark chocolate, coarsely grated

g (1 oz) white chocolate, coarsely grated,
ecorate

Dissolve the coffee in the measured
boiling water and mix with the brandy.

Combine the eggs and caster sugar in
a large bowl and whisk together until
k and light, and the mixture leaves a
on the surface.

Put the mascarpone into a bowl and stir
in a little of the egg mixture. Fold in the
, then fold in the cream.

Cut the trifle sponges horizontally in half.
Layer the tiramisu (see box, below)
half the sponges, half the coffee and
ndy mixture, half the mascarpone
ture, and half the plain chocolate.

Repeat the layers with the remaining
ngredients, decorating the top with
grated white chocolate and the
aining grated plain chocolate. Cover
chill for at least 4 hours before serving.

ayering the tiramisu

e the bottom of a large glass serving bowl
h half of the sponge pieces. Drizzle half of the
ffee and brandy mixture over the sponges.

The ultimate chocolate roulade

SERVES 8   469 CALS PER SERVING

butter for greasing

175 g (6 oz) plain dark chocolate, broken
into pieces

6 large eggs, separated

175 g (6 oz) caster sugar

2 tbsp cocoa powder, sifted

300 ml (½ pint) double or whipping cream

icing sugar for sifting

23 x 33 cm (9 x 13 in) Swiss roll tin

1 Lightly grease the tin, then line with baking
parchment, pushing it into the corners.

2 Put the chocolate into a heatproof bowl.
Put the bowl over a pan of hot water, and
heat gently until the chocolate has melted,
stirring occasionally. Remove the bowl from
the pan, and allow the chocolate to cool
slightly until warm.

3 Put the egg whites into a large bowl, and
beat with an electric whisk on high speed
until stiff but not dry. Put the sugar and egg
yolks into another large bowl, and beat with
the same whisk (no need to wash) on high
speed until light, thick, and creamy. Add the
chocolate to the egg yolk mixture, and stir
until blended.

4 Stir 2 large spoonfuls of the egg whites
into the chocolate mixture, then carefully
fold in the remaining egg whites followed by
the cocoa powder. Turn into the prepared
tin, and gently level the surface.

5 Bake in a preheated oven at 180°C
(160°C fan, Gas 4) for 20–25 minutes
until risen. Remove from the oven, and leave
the cake to cool in the tin (it will dip and
crack a little).

6 When the cake is cold, whip the cream
in a bowl until it just holds its shape. Sift
icing sugar over a large sheet of baking
parchment. Turn the cake out on to the
paper with one of the short edges facing
you, and peel off the lining paper. Spread the
whipped cream over the cake, then make
a shallow cut through the cream and cake
along the short edge nearest to you, about
2 cm (¾ in) in from the edge. Roll up the
roulade away from you, tightly to start with,
and using the paper to help. Don't worry if
it cracks – this is quite normal, and how it
should be. Sift icing sugar over the roulade
before serving.

Cook's know-how

If you like, add some fresh or frozen
raspberries to the filling, and scatter lots of
fresh raspberries around the roulade on a
serving platter - it will look stunning. The filled
roulade can be made a day ahead and kept in
the refrigerator. It can also be frozen, wrapped
in foil or cling film, for up to 2 months.
Defrost overnight in the refrigerator, and
bring to room temperature before serving.

Chocolate and brandy mousse

SERVES 6   **585 CALS PER SERVING**

250 g (8 oz) plain dark chocolate, broken into pieces

3 tbsp brandy

3 tbsp cold water

15 g (½ oz) powdered gelatine

4 eggs, plus 2 egg yolks

90 g (3 oz) caster sugar

150 ml (¼ pint) whipping cream, whipped until thick

DECORATION

150 ml (¼ pint) double or whipping cream, whipped until stiff

chocolate curls or caraque (page 422) to decorate

1 Put the chocolate into a heatproof bowl with the brandy over a pan of hot water. Heat gently until melted. Leave to cool.

2 Put the cold water into a heatproof bowl and sprinkle the gelatine over the top. Leave for about 10 minutes until spongy. Stand the bowl in a pan of hot water and heat gently until dissolved.

3 Combine the eggs, egg yolks, and sugar in a large heatproof bowl, and put over a saucepan of simmering water. Whisk with a hand-held electric mixer until the egg mixture is very thick and mousse-like. Whisk in the dissolved gelatine.

4 Fold the whipped cream into the cool chocolate, then fold into the egg mixture. Carefully pour into a glass serving bowl, cover, and leave in the refrigerator until set.

5 Decorate with piped rosettes of cream and chocolate curls or caraque (page 422). Serve the mousse chilled.

Cook's know-how

Buy a good-quality plain dark chocolate. For the best flavour, look for a brand with at least 70% cocoa solids.

ots au chocolat

SERVES 6   324 CALS PER SERVING

g (6 oz) plain dark chocolate, broken
 pieces

sp strong black coffee

g (½ oz) butter

w drops of vanilla extract

gs, separated

ml (¼ pint) double cream, whipped until stiff,
ecorate

Put the chocolate pieces into a saucepan
with the strong black coffee. Heat gently,
ng, until the chocolate melts.

Leave the chocolate mixture to cool
slightly, then add the butter, vanilla
ract, and egg yolks and stir until well
nded.

Whisk the egg whites until stiff but not
dry. Fold gently but thoroughly into the
ocolate mixture.

Pour the mixture into 6 small custard pots,
ramekins, or other serving dishes, and
ve to chill for about 8 hours.

Decorate each pot of chocolate with a
iped rosette of whipped cream (page
 before serving.

abaglione

SERVES 6   114 CALS PER SERVING

g yolks

(2½ oz) caster sugar

ml (4 fl oz) Marsala

iardi (Italian sponge fingers) or boudoir
its to serve

Whisk the egg yolks and sugar in
 heatproof bowl until light and foamy.
 the Marsala, and whisk to blend.

Put the bowl over a pan of simmering
water, making sure it does not touch
water. Heat gently, whisking the mixture
 it becomes thick and creamy and
ds in soft peaks.

emove from the heat and whisk until
ool. Pour into glass dishes and serve
nce, with savoiardi.

Above: Crème caramel.

Helen's pudding

 SERVES 6   510 CALS PER SERVING

125 g (4 oz) fresh brown breadcrumbs

90 g (3 oz) demerara sugar

75 g (2½ oz) drinking chocolate powder

2 tbsp instant coffee

300 ml (½ pint) double cream

150 ml (¼ pint) single cream

60 g (2 oz) plain dark chocolate, grated

1 In a bowl, mix together the breadcrumbs,
sugar, drinking chocolate, and coffee
granules. In another bowl, whip the creams
together until they form soft peaks.

2 Spoon half of the cream into 6 glass
serving dishes. Cover with the
breadcrumb mixture and then with the
remaining cream. Chill for at least 6 hours,
or overnight for best results.

3 Sprinkle generously with the grated
chocolate just before serving.

Cook's know-how

To make grating chocolate easy, chill it well in
the refrigerator before you grate it, and use the
largest holes on the grater.

Crème caramel

 SERVES 6   255 CALS PER SERVING

175 g (6 oz) granulated sugar

150 ml (¼ pint) water

4 eggs

30 g (1 oz) vanilla sugar

600 ml (1 pint) full-fat milk

6 small ramekins

1 Combine the sugar and water in a
saucepan and heat gently until all the
sugar has dissolved. Bring to a boil, and
cook without stirring, until golden. Pour into
the ramekins.

2 Whisk the eggs and vanilla sugar in
a bowl. Heat the milk until just warm,
then pour into the egg mixture, stirring well.
Strain into the ramekins.

3 Put the ramekins in a roasting tin and
add enough hot water to come halfway
up the sides of the ramekins. Bake in a
preheated oven at 160°C (140°C fan,
Gas 3) for about 40 minutes until just set
and firm to the touch but not solid. Cool,
then chill for 8 hours.

4 Turn out on to individual plates to serve.

Above: Quick vanilla ice cream.

Quick vanilla ice cream

🍴 SERVES 4–6　　799–533 CALS PER SERVING

6 eggs, separated

175 g (6 oz) vanilla sugar or 175 g (6 oz) caster sugar and 1 tsp vanilla extract

450 ml (¾ pint) double cream, whipped until thick

1 Whisk the egg whites (at high speed if using an electric mixer) until stiff but not dry. Add the sugar, 1 tsp at a time, and continue whisking until the sugar has been incorporated and the egg-white mixture is very stiff and glossy.

2 Put the egg yolks into a separate bowl and whisk at high speed with an electric mixer until blended thoroughly.

3 Gently fold the whipped cream and egg yolks into the egg-white mixture. Turn into a large shallow freezerproof container, cover, and leave the mixture to freeze for 8 hours.

4 Transfer the ice cream to the refrigerator for about 10 minutes before serving so that it softens slightly.

Cappuccino ice cream

Substitute caster sugar for the vanilla sugar, and add 3 tbsp each coffee extract and brandy when folding the mixtures in step 3.

Lemon ice cream

Substitute caster sugar for the vanilla sugar, and add the finely grated zest and juice of 3 large lemons when folding the mixtures in step 3.

Crème brûlée

🍴 SERVES 6　　302 CALS PER SERVING

butter for greasing

4 egg yolks

30 g (1 oz) vanilla sugar

600 ml (1 pint) single cream

60 g (2 oz) demerara sugar

6 small ramekins or shallow crème brûlée dishes

1 Lightly butter the ramekins or crème brûlée dishes.

2 In a large bowl, beat the egg yolks with the vanilla sugar. Heat the cream to just below boiling point, then slowly pour into the egg-yolk mixture, stirring all the time.

3 Carefully pour the custard into the ramekins or dishes. Set in a roasting tin and add enough hot water to come halfway up the sides of the ramekins or dishes.

4 Bake in a preheated oven at 160°C (140°C fan, Gas 3) for about 25 minutes, or until just set and firm to the touch. Leave to cool.

5 Sprinkle the demerara sugar evenly over the top of the set custard. Place under a very hot grill until the sugar melts and caramelizes to a rich golden brown colour.

6 Chill the crème brûlées for no more than 2 hours before serving.

Chocolate and meringue bombe

🍴 SERVES 8　　413 CALS PER SERVING

600 ml (1 pint) vanilla ice cream

600 ml (1 pint) chocolate ice cream

150 ml (¼ pint) whipping cream

1 tbsp brandy

125 g (4 oz) meringues, coarsely crushed

1.5 litre (2½ pint) bombe mould or pudding bo

1 Chill the bombe mould in the refrigera Layer the mould with the chocolate a vanilla ice creams (see box, below).

2 Whip the cream with the brandy until just holds its shape. Gently fold in the crushed meringues. Use the cream mixtu to fill the cavity in the mould. Cover and freeze overnight.

3 Dip the mould into cold water and in the chocolate and meringue bombe to a large serving plate. Slice and serve.

Filling the mould

Allow the vanilla ice cream to soften at room temperature for about 20 minutes. Spread it over the base and up the side of the mould. Chill in the freezer until solid.

Soften the chocolate ice cream, then sprea it evenly over the vanilla ice cream to make a hollow inner layer. Return to the freezer until solid.

above: Cassata.

Peach Melba

🌀 SERVES 4   273 CALS PER SERVING

4 ripe peaches, peeled, stoned, and sliced

8 scoops of vanilla ice cream

mint sprigs to decorate

MELBA SAUCE

375 g (12 oz) raspberries

about 4 tbsp icing sugar

1 Make the Melba sauce (see box, below).

2 Arrange the peach slices in 4 glass serving dishes. Top each with 2 scoops of ice cream and some sauce. Decorate with mint sprigs and the remaining raspberries.

Making Melba sauce

Purée 250 g (8 oz) of the raspberries. Push through a sieve to remove the seeds.

Sift the icing sugar over the purée and stir in.

Cassata

🌀 SERVES 8   364 CALS PER SERVING

g (1 oz) candied angelica, rinsed, dried, d chopped

g (1 oz) glacé cherries, rinsed, dried, d chopped

g (1 oz) chopped mixed candied peel

bsp dark rum

0 ml (1 pint) raspberry sorbet

0 ml (¼ pint) double cream, whipped until thick

0 ml (1 pint) vanilla ice cream

0 ml (1½ pint) terrine

Chill the terrine. Put the angelica, glacé cherries, and candied peel in a bowl.

2 Add the rum and stir well, then leave to soak while preparing the ice-cream ayers.

3 Allow the sorbet to soften, then spread it evenly over the bottom of the chilled errine. Chill in the freezer until solid.

4 Fold the fruit and rum mixture into the whipped cream. Spoon into the terrine nd level the surface. Return to the freezer ntil firm.

5 Allow the vanilla ice cream to soften, then spread it evenly over the fruit layer. over and freeze for 8 hours.

6 To turn out, dip the terrine into warm water and invert the cassata on to a rge serving plate. Slice, and serve at once.

Frozen lemon flummery

🌀 SERVES 4   391 CALS PER SERVING

150 ml (¼ pint) double cream

finely grated zest and juice of 1 large lemon

175 g (6 oz) caster sugar

300 ml (½ pint) milk

thinly pared zest of 1 lemon, cut into strips, to decorate

1 Whip the cream until it forms soft peaks. Add the lemon zest and juice, caster sugar, and milk, and mix until evenly blended.

2 Pour into a shallow freezerproof container, cover, and freeze for at least 6 hours or until firm.

3 Cut the mixture into chunks, then transfer to a food processor and work until smooth and creamy. Pour into 4 individual freezerproof dishes and freeze for about 8 hours.

4 Blanch the strips of lemon zest in a pan of boiling water for 1 minute only. Drain, rinse, and pat dry.

5 Decorate the flummery with the strips of lemon zest and serve.

Frozen orange flummery

Substitute the finely grated zest and juice of 1 orange for the lemon, and reduce the caster sugar to 125 g (4 oz). Decorate with blanched strips of orange zest.

Lime sorbet

SERVES 6   169 CALS PER SERVING

250 g (8 oz) granulated sugar

600 ml (1 pint) water

finely grated zest and juice of 6 limes

2 egg whites

strips of lime zest to decorate

1 Put the sugar and measured water into a saucepan and heat gently until the sugar dissolves. Bring to a boil and boil for 2 minutes. Remove from the heat, add the lime zest, and leave to cool completely. Stir in the lime juice.

2 Strain the lime syrup into a shallow freezerproof container and freeze for about 2 hours until just mushy. Turn the mixture into a bowl and whisk gently to break down any large crystals.

3 Whisk the egg whites until stiff but not dry, then fold into the lime mixture. Return to the freezer, and freeze until firm. Transfer the sorbet to the refrigerator to soften for about 30 minutes before serving, and top with strips of lime zest.

Apricot sorbet

SERVES 6   104 CALS PER SERVING

90 g (3 oz) granulated sugar

300 ml (½ pint) water

juice of 1 lemon

750 g (1½ lb) apricots, halved and stoned

2 egg whites

1 Put the sugar, measured water, and lemon juice into a saucepan and heat gently until the sugar has dissolved. Bring to a boil, add the apricots, and simmer for 15 minutes or until very tender. Cool.

2 Peel and slice a few apricots for decoration, and set aside. Press the remainder through a sieve. Mix with the syrup in a freezerproof container, then follow steps 2 and 3 of Lime Sorbet (above). Decorate with the sliced apricots before serving.

Pear and ginger sorbet

SERVES 6   128 CALS PER SERVING

90 g (3 oz) granulated sugar

300 ml (½ pint) water

1 tbsp lemon juice

750 g (1½ lb) pears, peeled and cored

1 piece of stem ginger in syrup, finely chopped

2 egg whites

strips of stem ginger to decorate

1 Put the sugar, measured water, and lemon juice into a saucepan and heat gently until the sugar dissolves. Bring to a boil, add the pears, and poach gently, basting with the sugar syrup from time to time, for 20–25 minutes until the pears are tender. Cool, then purée in a food processor.

2 Add the chopped stem ginger to the pear purée. Pour the pear mixture into a freezerproof container, then follow steps 2 and 3 of Lime Sorbet (left). Decorate with stem ginger before serving.

Raspberry sorbet

SERVES 6   152 CALS PER SERVING

500 g (1 lb) raspberries

175 g (6 oz) granulated sugar

600 ml (1 pint) water

juice of 1 orange

3 egg whites

raspberries and mint sprigs to decorate

1 Purée the raspberries in a food processor, then push through a sieve to remove the seeds. Put the sugar and measured water into a saucepan and heat gently until the sugar dissolves. Bring to a boil, then boil for 5 minutes. Pour into a bowl and cool.

2 Stir in the raspberry purée and orange juice. Pour into a freezerproof container, then follow steps 2 and 3 of Lime Sorbet (top left). Decorate with raspberries and mint sprigs before serving.

Granitas

Italian granitas are similar to sorbets but even easier to make: they are simply flavoured ice crystals.

Coffee
Put 60 g (2 oz) caster sugar and 4 tbsp instant coffee granules into a pan with 750 ml (1¼ pints) water and bring to a boil. Simmer for about 5 minutes. Leave to cool, then pour into a freezerproof container. Freeze, stirring occasionally, for 5 hours.

Lemon
Put 200 g (7 oz) caster sugar into a saucepan, add 500 ml (16 fl oz) water, and bring to a boil. Simmer for 5 minutes. Leave to cool. Add 2 tsp finely grated lemon zest and the juice of 4 lemons to the sugar syrup. Pour into a freezerproof container and freeze, stirring occasionally, for 5 hours.

Watermelon
Remove and discard the rind and seeds from 1 kg (2 lb) watermelon. Purée the flesh in a food processor. Pour into a freezerproof container and mix in 30 g (1 oz) icing sugar and 1½ tsp lemon juice. Freeze, stirring occasionally, for 5 hours.

Opposite, clockwise from top
Lime sorbet, Raspberry sorbet, Pea
ginger sorbet, Apricot s

Baked Alaska

SERVES 8   256 CALS PER SERVING

250 g (8 oz) raspberries, sliced strawberries, or other summer fruits

450 ml (¾ pint) vanilla ice cream

2 egg whites

125 g (4 oz) caster sugar

whole berries to decorate

1 x 20 cm (8 in) sponge flan case

1 Put the sponge flan case into a shallow ovenproof serving dish. Arrange the fruits in the case.

2 Put the ice cream on top of the fruits and put in the freezer to keep the ice cream frozen while making the meringue.

3 Whisk the egg whites (an electric mixer can be used) until stiff but not dry.

4 Add the caster sugar, 1 tsp at a time, and continue to whisk until the sugar has been incorporated and the meringue mixture is stiff and glossy.

5 Pipe or spoon the meringue over the ice cream, covering it completely.

6 Bake immediately in a preheated oven at 230°C (210°C fan, Gas 8) for 3–4 minutes until the meringue is tinged with brown. Serve at once, decorated with raspberries and strawberries.

Cook's know-how

A block of firm ice cream is needed for this recipe – do not use soft-scoop ice cream. Make sure the ice cream is completely covered by the egg white, which stops the ice cream melting.

Rich vanilla ice cream

Home-made ice cream tastes better than commercially made ice cream, and it keeps for up to a month in the freezer. If you have an electric ice-cream maker, you will get a smoother result.

SERVES 4–6   577–385 CALS PER SERVING

4 egg yolks

125 g (4 oz) caster sugar

300 ml (½ pint) milk

300 ml (½ pint) double cream

1½ tsp vanilla extract

strawberries to decorate

1 Put the egg yolks and sugar into a bowl and whisk until light in colour.

2 Heat the milk in a heavy pan to just below boiling point. Add a little of the hot milk to the egg-yolk mixture and stir to blend, then pour in the remaining milk.

3 Pour back into the pan and heat gently, stirring, until the froth disappears and the mixture coats the back of a spoon. Do not boil.

4 Leave the custard to cool, then stir in the cream and vanilla extract.

5 Pour into a container and freeze for 3 hours. Tip into a bowl and mash to break down the ice crystals. Return to container. Freeze for 2 hours. Mash and freeze for another 2 hours. Remove from the freezer 30 minutes before serving, and decorate.

Chocolate ice cream

In step 2, heat the milk with 125 g (4 oz) chopped dark chocolate. Let it melt before adding to the egg-yolk mixture.

Chocolate chip ice cream

In step 2, heat the milk with 125 g (4 oz) chopped white chocolate. Let it melt before adding to the egg-yolk mixture. Stir 60 g (2 oz) dark chocolate chips into the custard with the cream in step 4.

Banana and honey ice cream

Mash 500 g (1 lb) bananas with 3 tbsp lemon juice and 2 tbsp honey. Add to the custard with the cream in step 4.

Iced Christmas pudding

SERVES 8   437 CALS PER SERVING

175 g (6 oz) mixed dried fruit

60 g (2 oz) ready-to-eat dried apricots, chopped

60 g (2 oz) glacé cherries, halved

3 tbsp brandy

3 eggs

125 g (4 oz) caster sugar

450 ml (¾ pint) milk

450 ml (¾ pint) double cream

150 ml (¼ pint) single cream

1.75 litre (3 pint) pudding bowl

1 Combine the dried fruit, apricots, glacé cherries, and brandy. Cover and leave to soak for 8 hours.

2 In a large bowl, whisk together the egg and sugar. Heat the milk in a heavy saucepan to just below boiling point. Pour into the egg mixture, stirring.

3 Pour back into the pan. Cook gently, stirring with a wooden spoon, until the froth disappears and the mixture thicken. Do not boil. Remove from the heat and leave to cool.

4 Whip 300 ml (½ pint) double cream and the single cream together until they are just beginning to hold their shape. Fold into the custard with the fruit and brandy mixture.

5 Turn into a shallow freezerproof container and freeze for 2 hours or until beginning to set but still slightly soft.

6 Remove the pudding from the freezer and mix well to distribute the fruit even. Spoon into the pudding bowl, cover, and return to the freezer. Freeze for 3 hours or until firm.

7 Remove from the freezer about 20 minutes before serving to soften. Turn out on to a serving plate, and spoon the remaining cream, lightly whipped, on top. Slice and serve at once.

Cakes and Teabreads

Under 45 minutes

Blueberry and vanilla muffins
American classic: delicious, and not too
sweet vanilla muffins filled with blueberries.
Served warm for breakfast or with tea.

MAKES 12   249 CALS EACH
Takes 40 minutes   Page 459

Fork biscuits
Plain and simple: a butter-enriched dough,
imprinted with a fork pattern and baked
until crisp and golden.

MAKES 32   104 CALS EACH
Takes 30 minutes, **plus cooling**   Page 477

Mincemeat buns
Rich and fruity: a miniature and quick version
of mince pies. Baked in individual cake cases.

MAKES 32   137 CALS EACH
Takes 40 minutes, **plus cooling**   Page 465

45-60 minutes

Shortbread
Highland classic: a dough made rich with
butter, baked until golden, and sprinkled
with sugar.

MAKES 8 WEDGES   233 CALS EACH
Takes 55 minutes, **plus cooling**   Page 470

Iced lime traybake
Light and delicious: a lime-flavoured cake
batter baked in a rectangular tin, topped
with tangy lime icing, and cut into squares.

MAKES 12 SQUARES   340 CALS EACH
Takes 50 minutes, **plus cooling**   Page 464

Pink almond macaroons
Delicate pink macaroons, flavoured with
almonds, and filled with raspberry jam
and butter cream.

MAKES 40   113 CALS EACH
Takes 55 minutes, **plus cooling**   Page 475

Wimbledon cake
Two layers of golden sponge filled with fresh
whipped cream, sweet and juicy strawberries
and tropical passion fruit.

CUTS INTO 8 SLICES   260 CALS EACH
Takes 60 minutes, **plus cooling**   Page 4

FAMILY CHOIC

Devon scones
An English teatime favourite: a simple dou
makes featherweight scones. Serve spread
with butter and jam.

MAKES 12   133 CALS EACH
Takes 45 minutes, **plus cooling**   Page

FAMILY CHOI

Flapjacks
Rich, chewy, and very easy to make: an
oat-studded batter is spread into a roasting
tin, baked, and cut into fingers.

MAKES 24   102 CALS EACH
Takes 45 minutes, **plus cooling**   Page

Over 60 minutes

TRADITIONAL

Simnel cake
Moist and tender fruit cake, brushed with
apricot jam, topped with almond paste, and
decorated with balls of almond paste.
CUTS INTO 12 SLICES   494 CALS EACH
Takes 2³⁄4 hours, **plus cooling**   Page 467

...sh soda bread
...aditional bread made light and tasty
...n buttermilk. Scored and baked until
...den brown.
INTO 8 WEDGES   227 CALS EACH
...es 45 minutes, **plus cooling**   Page 474

...mon cup cakes with lemon icing
...et and light: cup cakes with a creamy,
...ony icing. Decorated with silver balls
...itter.
...ES 12   332 CALS EACH
...es 45 minutes   Page 463

...il's food cake
...rs of moist, rich chocolate sponge spread
... a sweet, fluffy white American icing.
...ect for family gatherings.
...IN 12 SLICES   513 CALS EACH
...s 60 minutes, **plus cooling**   Page 456

...enburg cake
...sic cake made from chocolate and vanilla
...rs wrapped with almond paste.
...INTO 8 SLICES   425 CALS PER SERVING
...s 60 minutes, **plus cooling**   Page 467

...ss roll
...d favourite: a light golden sponge spread
...rously with a layer of raspberry jam,
...d up, and decorated with sugar.
...INTO 8 SLICES   195 CALS EACH
...s 45 minutes, **plus cooling**   Page 458

Date and walnut loaf
Sweet dates and crunchy walnuts are baked in
a lightly sweetened batter. Delicious sliced and
spread with butter.
CUTS INTO 12 SLICES   269 CALS EACH
Takes 1³⁄4 hours, **plus cooling**   Page 472

Gingerbread
Moist and tasty: a batter made dark and
delicious with treacle and spices. Best
when baked ahead.
MAKES 15 SQUARES   349 CALS EACH
Takes 1¹⁄4 hours, **plus cooling**   Page 471

Cakes and teabreads know-how

Cake-making is often seen as the test of a cook's skills, but there are lots of cakes and teabreads, as well as scones, biscuits, cookies, and American-style muffins that are really quite simple to make and just as delicious as more elaborate creations. If you are a beginner, just remember to follow recipes carefully, and make sure your weighing and measuring is accurate. Use the right equipme and tins, and take the time to prepare cakes properly, and you'll achieve perfect results every time You'll find that once you've gained confidence, you'll be able to experiment with more difficult recipe:

Storing

Most cakes are best eaten freshly made, particularly sponge cakes that don't contain fat, but if you do want to keep a cake, be sure to store it in an airtight container. Put the cake on the upturned lid of the cake tin, then put the tin over the top. This makes it easy to remove the cake from the tin. Fruit cakes and cakes made by the melting method, such as gingerbread, will improve with keeping (store in an airtight tin). Wrap fruit cake in greaseproof paper and then overwrap in foil. Don't put foil directly in contact with a fruit cake as the acid in the fruit may react with the foil. Any cake that has a filling or icing of whipped cream, butter-icing, or soft cheese should be kept in the refrigerator. Scones, American-style muffins, and most teabreads are best eaten freshly made.

Most biscuits can be stored in an airtight tin for a few days; if they soften, crisp them up in a warm oven. Allow cakes and biscuits to cool completely on a wire rack before putting them into a tin. Do not store cakes and biscuits together as the moisture from the cake will soften the biscuits.

Freezing

If baked goods are not eaten immediately freezing is a good way to keep them fresh. Cakes, teabreads, biscuits, American-style muffins, and scones all freeze well.

Wrap plain cakes, fruit cakes and teabreads in foil or freezer wrap. If a cake has been iced or decorated, tray freeze it, then place in a rigid container or freezer bag. Fruit cakes can be stored for up to 12 months; un-iced cakes for 4–6 months; iced cakes for 2–3 months. Unwrap decorated cakes before thawing, but leave other cakes in their wrapping.

Biscuits, muffins, and scones can be stored for 6 months. Interleave biscuits with foil or freezer wrap to keep them separate. Thaw biscuits and muffins at room temperature. Scones can be successfully reheated or toasted from frozen.

Microwaving

Microwave-baked cakes and biscuits can be disappointingly pale in colour and gluey in texture. Instead, in baking the microwave comes into its own when used as an accessory to the conventional oven. Here are good things to use it for:
- melting chocolate: break chocolate into small pieces, put into a bowl, and cook on LOW for 3–5 minutes until melted and shiny; stir halfway
- melting crystallized honey or syrup: heat on HIGH for 1–2 minutes. If kept in the jar, take off the lid
- softening hardened, set sugar: cook on HIGH for 30–40 seconds
- skinning and toasting hazelnuts: place them on paper towels and cook on HIGH for 30 seconds, then remove skins. Cook until golden

Baking ingredients

In baking it is important to use the ingredients specified in a recipe. Choose the best quality available.

Butter and other fats

In simple cakes, biscuits, and teabreads, where flavour is important, always use butter. In other cakes, margarine is acceptable. For all-in-one mixtures soft margarine is best as it is made up of 80% fat and blends easily. Low-fat spreads are not suitable for baking because of their high water content, so check before you buy. If oil is called for, use a mild, light one such as sunflower oil or sweeter corn oil.

Flour

Both plain and self-raising flours are used in baking, either white or wholemeal. Self-raising flour includes a raising agent (usually a mixture of bicarbonate of soda and cream of tartar), so if you want to substitute plain flour, add 2 tsp baking powder to each 250 g (8 oz) flour.

Raising agents

Baking powder and bicarbonate of soda are used to raise cakes, teabreads, and biscuits. When a mixture contains bakir powder, or self-raising flour, be sure to bake without delay, while the chemicals are still active.

Sugar

For most mixtures, it is essential to use a sugar that dissolves easily, such as cas sugar or soft, fine muscovado sugar. Granulated sugar can be used in rubbec in mixtures. Coarse demerara sugar is fine for melted mixtures and is ideal fo sprinkling on the top of cakes, as is icir sugar. Other sweeteners used in baking include golden syrup, honey, molasses, and malt extract, as well as concentrate fruit purée or juice.

Eggs

Eggs at room temperature are more ea: aerated than cold eggs taken straight fr the refrigerator. Cold eggs can also caus some cake mixtures to curdle.

Baking biscuits

When arranging biscuits on prepared baking sheets, leave enough space between them to allow for spreading, i necessary. As biscuits cook quickly, the can easily be baked in batches if you do have enough baking sheets.

At the end of the baking time, many biscuits will still feel a little soft in the middle: they will continue to bake on t hot sheet after being removed from the oven. If the recipe directs, leave them t firm up for 1–2 minutes before transferring to a wire rack. Avoid lettin biscuits cool completely on the sheet o: they may stick.

Whisked cakes

...ght, fatless sponges are raised by air ...isked into eggs. Use a hand-held electric ...xer or a large, table-top mixer. If using ...and-held mixer, set it at high speed.

...Whisk the eggs, or egg yolks, with the sugar ...until the mixture is light, pale, and thick ...ough to leave a trail on the surface when the ...aters are lifted out.

...Gently fold in the flour and any other ...ingredients. If the eggs have been separated, ...whisked egg whites should be folded into ...mixture last of all.

...l-in-one cakes

...sure to use a soft margarine for this ...ck, simple technique.

...ll the ingredients into a large bowl and ...together with a hand-held electric mixer ...combined. You can also mix in a food ...essor or by hand.

Creamed cakes

The creaming method is used for both cakes and biscuits. A wooden spoon, rubber spatula, or electric mixer are all suitable. Be sure to soften the butter or margarine first.

1 Cream the fat and sugar together until the mixture is pale in colour and fluffy in texture. Keep scraping the side of the bowl with a spoon or spatula to incorporate all of the mixture.

2 Lightly beat the eggs. Gradually add the eggs to the creamed mixture, beating well between each addition. If the mixture curdles, which will result in a dense-textured cake, beat in a spoonful of the flour.

3 Sift over the flour and any other dry ingredients. Using a wooden spoon, gently fold in the flour until well combined. Any liquid ingredients should also be added at this stage.

Preparing cake tins

Lightly greasing the tin ensures a cake will turn out easily. Some recipes also call for the tin to be floured or lined with greaseproof paper or baking parchment.

Greasing and flouring

Use melted or softened butter or margarine, or oil, according to the recipe. Brush over the bottom and side of the tin using a pastry brush or paper towels. If flouring, add a spoonful of flour and tilt the tin to coat it with a thin layer. Tip out any excess flour.

Lining

1 Set the cake tin on a sheet of greaseproof paper or parchment and mark around the base with a pencil or the tip of a knife.

2 Cut out the shape, cutting just inside the line, then press smoothly over the bottom of the tin. Lightly grease if directed in the recipe.

Baking, testing, and cooling cakes

Before baking cakes, teabreads, and biscuits, be sure to preheat the oven to the correct temperature. If you need to, adjust the position of the shelves before you turn on the oven.

1 As soon as the mixture is prepared, turn it into the tin and level the surface. Tap the tin on the work surface to break any large air bubbles. Transfer immediately to the oven.

2 When cooked, a cake will shrink slightly from the side of the tin. To test, lightly press the middle with a fingertip; the cake should spring back. Rich cakes should feel firm to the touch.

3 Set the cake tin on a wire rack and leave to cool for about 10 minutes. Run a knife around the side of the cake to free it from the tin.

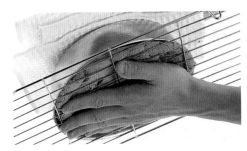

4 Hold a wire rack over the top of the tin, then invert the rack and tin so that the cake falls on to the rack. Carefully lift the tin away from the cake.

5 Peel off the lining paper. With a light-textured cake, turn it over again so the base is on the rack; this will prevent the rack marking the top.

6 To cut the cake in half, steady it by setting one hand gently on top. Cut the cake horizontally, using a gentle sawing action.

Filling and icing cakes

There are many simple ways to fill or decorate cakes. Whipped cream, jam, or chocolate spread make quick and easy fillings. Butter-icing can be made in a variety of flavours, to complement the flavour of the cake.

Chocolate butter-icing

In a bowl, soften 150 g (5 oz) butter. Add 30 g (1 oz) cocoa powder and 250 g (8 oz) sifted ic sugar, and beat together until smooth. Add a li milk if necessary to give a spreading consisten For a citrus icing, omit the cocoa powder an add finely grated orange or lemon zest.

Spreading icing

Only ice a cake when it has cooled comple Use a large palette knife and spread the icir with long, smooth strokes over the top and si of the cake. Dip the palette knife in warm w if the icing sticks to it.

Baking know-how

Be sure to use the correct size tin, as stated in the recipe. To check the dimensions of a cake tin, measure inside the top rim. To work out the depth, measure from the bottom to the top rim on the inside of the tin. To check the capacity of a tin, measure how much water is needed to fill it to the brim.

Bake for the minimum time given in the recipe before opening the oven door. If the door is opened too soon it may cause some cakes to deflate.

If a cake looks as though it is browning too quickly, cover the top loosely with foil. If baking several cake layers, stagger them on the oven shelves so one is not directly beneath another.

When measuring ingredients with a spoon, don't hold the spoon directly over the bowl or you may accidentally add too much.

Testing fruit cakes

For fruit cakes and fruited teabreads, insert a metal skewer or long wooden cocktail stic into the middle: the skewer or stick should come out clean, without any moist crumbs sticking to it.

ourgette loaf

CUTS INTO 12 SLICES   331 CALS EACH

0 g (8 oz) courgettes

ggs

5 ml (4 fl oz) sunflower oil, plus extra for greasing

0 g (8 oz) caster sugar

sp vanilla extract (optional)

5 g (12 oz) self-raising flour

sp ground cinnamon

tsp salt

g (2 oz) walnut pieces, coarsely chopped

g (2 lb) loaf tin

Coarsely grate the courgettes, put them into a sieve, and leave for about 30 nutes to drain.

Beat the eggs until light and foamy. Add the sunflower oil, sugar, vanilla extract (if ng), and courgettes and mix lightly until mbined.

Sift the flour, cinnamon, and salt into a large bowl. Make a well in the middle, ur in the courgette mixture, and stir to mix roughly. Stir in the chopped walnuts.

Pour the mixture into the greased loaf tin and bake in a preheated oven at 180°C 0°C fan, Gas 4) for about 50 minutes until . Turn out and cool.

Cook's know-how

or best results, the courgettes should be oroughly drained. Press into the sieve with ur hand or the back of a spoon to extract e excess juices.

Chocolate and beetroot cake

CUTS INTO 8 SLICES   641 CALS EACH

150 g (5 oz) soft butter, plus extra for greasing

250 g (8 oz) light muscovado sugar

3 large eggs

60 g (2 oz) cocoa powder

200 g (7 oz) self-raising flour

2 tsp baking powder

4 tbsp milk

250 g (8 oz) cooked beetroot, peeled and coarsely grated

CHOCOLATE FUDGE ICING

60 g (2 oz) butter

30 g (1 oz) cocoa powder, sifted

3 tbsp milk

250 g (8 oz) icing sugar, sifted

23 cm (9 in) springform or loose-bottomed cake tin

1 Lightly grease the tin, and line the bottom with baking parchment.

2 Combine all the cake ingredients, except the beetroot, in a large bowl. Beat with an electric whisk until smooth, then fold in the beetroot. Spoon the mixture into the prepared tin.

3 Bake in a preheated oven at 180°C (160°C fan, Gas 4) for 45–55 minutes until the cake is well risen and shrinking away from the side of the tin. Set aside to cool a little, then remove the side of the tin (leaving the cake on the base), and leave to cool completely.

4 Make the icing: melt the butter in a saucepan, add the cocoa powder, and stir over a high heat for 1 minute. Add the milk and icing sugar, and stir to combine. Remove from the heat, and set aside to cool and thicken.

5 Remove the cake from the base of the tin, and peel off the lining paper. Using a serrated knife, slice the cake in half to make 2 equal layers. Spread one-third of the icing on the bottom half, and place the other half on top. Spread the remaining icing over the top and side of the cake to give a thin layer. Serve at once, or keep in the refrigerator for up to 3 days.

Carrot cake

CUTS INTO 10 SQUARES   412 CALS EACH

150 ml (¼ pint) sunflower oil, plus extra for greasing

250 g (8 oz) wholemeal self-raising flour

2 tsp baking powder

150 g (5 oz) light muscovado sugar

60 g (2 oz) walnuts, coarsely chopped

125 g (4 oz) carrots, grated

2 ripe bananas, mashed

2 eggs

1 tbsp milk

TOPPING

250 g (8 oz) low-fat soft cheese, at room temperature

2 tsp clear honey

1 tsp lemon juice

chopped walnuts to decorate

18 cm (7 in) square cake tin

1 Lightly grease the cake tin and line the bottom with baking parchment.

2 Combine all the cake ingredients in a large bowl. Mix well until thoroughly blended. Turn into the prepared cake tin and level the surface.

3 Bake in a preheated oven at 180°C (160°C fan, Gas 4) for about 50 minutes until the cake is well risen, firm to the touch, and beginning to shrink away from the sides of the tin.

4 Leave the cake to cool in the tin for a few minutes. Turn out on to a wire rack, peel off the lining paper, and leave to cool completely.

5 Make the topping: mix together the cheese, honey, and lemon juice. Spread on top of the cake and sprinkle the walnuts over the top. Store the cake in the refrigerator until ready to serve.

Healthy note

A full-fat cream cheese frosting is the traditional topping for carrot cake, but here a low-fat soft cheese is suggested, and it tastes equally good. If you prefer not to have frosting at all, spread clear honey on top of the cake while it is hot from the oven, and sprinkle with chopped walnuts.

1½ tsp baking powder

1 tsp vanilla extract

150 ml (¼ pint) soured cream

AMERICAN FROSTING

400 g (13 oz) caster sugar

2 egg whites

4 tbsp hot water

pinch of cream of tartar

3 x 20 cm (8 in) sandwich cake tins

1 Grease the tins with butter and line the bottoms with baking parchment.

2 Put the chocolate into a pan with the water. Heat gently, stirring, until the chocolate melts. Cool.

3 Combine the butter and sugar in a bo and beat until light and fluffy. Gradua add the eggs, beating well.

4 Stir in the melted chocolate. Sift toget the flour, bicarbonate of soda, and baking powder. Fold into the chocolate mixture until evenly blended, then fold in the vanilla extract and soured cream.

5 Divide the mixture evenly among the prepared tins. Bake in a preheated oven at 190°C (170°C fan, Gas 5) for about 25 minutes until well risen, springy to the touch, and just shrinking away from the sides of the tins.

6 Turn out the cakes on to a wire rack, p off the lining paper, and leave to coo

7 Make the American frosting: combine all the ingredients in a heatproof bowl Set the bowl over a pan of hot water and whisk with an electric mixer for 12 minute or until the mixture is white, thick, and stands in peaks.

8 Use half of the American frosting to sandwich the layers together, then spread the remainder over the top and side of the cake, swirling it decoratively and pulling it into peaks with the flat of a small palette knife.

Above: Heavenly chocolate cake.

Heavenly chocolate cake

🍴 CUTS INTO 8 SLICES   615 CALS EACH

125 g (4 oz) butter, plus extra for greasing

200 g (7 oz) plain dark chocolate, broken into pieces

2 tbsp water

3 eggs, separated

125 g (4 oz) caster sugar

90 g (3 oz) self-raising flour

60 g (2 oz) ground almonds

FUDGE ICING

60 g (2 oz) butter

30 g (1 oz) cocoa powder

3 tbsp milk

250 g (8 oz) icing sugar, sifted

white chocolate curls (page 422) to decorate

deep 20 cm (8 in) cake tin

1 Lightly butter the tin and line the bottom with baking parchment.

2 Put the chocolate into a heatproof bowl with the butter and water. Put the bowl over a pan of hot water and heat gently, stirring, until the mixture has melted. Cool.

3 Combine the egg yolks and caster sugar in a large bowl and whisk together with an electric whisk until fluffy and very light in colour. Stir in the cooled chocolate mixture. Carefully fold in the flour and ground almonds.

4 In a separate bowl, whisk the egg whites until stiff but not dry. Fold into the sponge mixture, gently but thoroughly. Pour the mixture into the prepared tin. Bake in a preheated oven at 180°C (160°C fan, Gas 4) for 50 minutes or until well risen and firm to the touch.

5 Leave the cake to cool in the tin for a few minutes, turn out on to a wire rack, and peel off the lining paper. Cool completely. Make the fudge icing: melt the butter in a pan, add the cocoa powder, and cook, stirring, for 1 minute. Stir in the milk and icing sugar. Beat well until smooth. Leave to cool until thickened.

6 Split the cake in half horizontally and sandwich the layers together with half of the fudge icing. With a palette knife, spread the remaining icing over the top and sides of the cake. Decorate with white chocolate curls.

Devil's food cake

🍴 CUTS INTO 12 SLICES   513 CALS EACH

175 g (6 oz) soft butter or margarine, plus extra for greasing

90 g (3 oz) plain dark chocolate, broken into pieces

175 ml (6 fl oz) hot water

300 g (10 oz) light muscovado sugar

3 eggs, beaten

300 g (10 oz) plain flour

1½ tsp bicarbonate of soda

Victoria sandwich cake

CUTS INTO 8 SLICES   386 CALS EACH

175 g (6 oz) soft butter or margarine, plus extra for greasing

175 g (6 oz) caster sugar

3 eggs

175 g (6 oz) self-raising flour

1 tsp baking powder

FILLING

3 tbsp raspberry or strawberry jam

caster sugar for sprinkling

2 x 18 cm (7 in) sandwich tins

1 Lightly grease the tins and line the bottoms with baking parchment.

2 Combine all the cake ingredients in a large bowl. Beat well for about 2 minutes until smooth.

3 Divide the mixture between the prepared tins and level the surfaces. Bake in a preheated oven at 180°C (160°C fan, Gas 4) for about 25 minutes or until the cakes are well risen, golden, and springy to the touch.

4 Turn out on to a wire rack, peel off the lining paper, and leave to cool.

5 Sandwich the 2 cakes together with jam and sprinkle the top of the cake with caster sugar.

Lemon sandwich cake

Add the finely grated zest of 1 lemon to the cake ingredients before beating. Sandwich the cakes together with lemon curd and 150 ml (¼ pint) whipping cream, whipped until thick. Dust with sifted icing sugar.

Wimbledon cake

CUTS INTO 8 SLICES   260 CALS EACH

butter for greasing

3 eggs

90 g (3 oz) caster sugar

90 g (3 oz) self-raising flour

FILLING AND TOPPING

300 ml (½ pint) whipping cream, whipped until thick

125 g (4 oz) strawberries, sliced

1 passion fruit, halved

strawberries, halved, to decorate

2 x 18 cm (7 in) sandwich cake tins

1 Lightly butter the cake tins, line the bottoms with baking parchment, then butter the parchment.

2 Put the eggs and sugar into a large bowl. Whisk with an electric mixer at high speed until the mixture is pale and thick enough to leave a trail when the whisk is lifted out.

3 Sift in half of the flour and fold in gently. Repeat with the remaining flour.

4 Divide the mixture between the tins. Tilt to spread the mixture evenly.

5 Bake in a preheated oven at 190°C (170°C fan, Gas 5) for 20–25 minutes until well risen, golden, and beginning to shrink away from the sides of the tins. Turn out on to a wire rack, peel off the lining paper, and leave to cool.

6 Spread half of the whipped cream over 1 of the sponges. Top with the sliced strawberries and passion fruit pulp. Put the other sponge on top and press down gently.

7 Spread the remaining cream on top of the cake, smoothing it neatly with a palette knife. Decorate with strawberry halves.

Marbled coffee ring cake

CUTS INTO 12 SLICES   **471 CALS EACH**

250 g (8 oz) soft butter, plus extra for greasing

250 g (8 oz) caster sugar

4 eggs

250 g (8 oz) self-raising flour

2 tsp baking powder

2 tsp instant coffee

1 tbsp hot water

30 g (1 oz) white chocolate

ICING

60 g (2 oz) butter, softened

3 tbsp milk

2 tbsp instant coffee

250 g (8 oz) icing sugar, sifted

1.75 litre (2¾ pint) ring mould

1 Lightly grease the ring mould with butter.

2 Combine the butter, sugar, eggs, flour, and baking powder in a large bowl. Beat until smooth.

3 Put half of the mixture into another bowl. Dissolve the instant coffee in the measured hot water and stir into one half of the cake mixture.

4 Drop tablespoonfuls of the plain mixture into the ring mould, then tablespoonfuls of the coffee mixture on top of the plain mixture. Marble by swirling together with a skewer.

5 Bake in a preheated oven at 180°C (160°C fan, Gas 4) for 40 minutes or until well risen and firm to the touch. Leave to cool for a few minutes, then turn out on to a wire rack set over a tray, and cool completely.

6 Make the icing: combine the butter, milk, and coffee in a pan and heat, stirring, until smooth. Remove from the heat and beat in the icing sugar until smooth and glossy.

7 Leave to cool, then pour over the cake, spreading it over the sides to cover completely. Leave to set.

8 Melt the white chocolate in a heatproof bowl over a pan of hot water. Cool slightly, then spoon into a plastic bag. Snip off a corner of the bag and drizzle the chocolate over the cake. Leave to set.

White chocolate gateau

CUTS INTO 14 SLICES   **391 CALS EACH**

90 g (3 oz) butter, melted and cooled slightly, plus extra for greasing

6 large eggs

175 g (6 oz) caster sugar

125 g (4 oz) self-raising flour

30 g (1 oz) cocoa powder

2 tbsp cornflour

FILLING AND TOPPING

300 ml (½ pint) double or whipping cream, whipped until thick

white chocolate curls (optional – page 422)

deep 23 cm (9 in) round cake tin

1 Lightly butter the cake tin and line the bottom of the tin with baking parchment.

2 Put the eggs and sugar into a large bowl and whisk together with an electric mixer on high speed until the mixture is pale and thick enough to leave a trail on itself when the whisk is lifted out.

3 Sift together the flour, cocoa powder, and cornflour, and fold half into the egg mixture. Pour half of the cooled butter around the edge; fold in gently.

4 Repeat with the remaining flour mixture and butter, folding gently.

5 Turn the mixture into the prepared cake tin and tilt the tin to level the surface. Bake in a preheated oven at 180°C (160°C fan, Gas 4) for 35–40 minutes until the sponge is well risen and firm to the touch. Turn out on to a wire rack, peel off the lining, and cool.

6 Cut the cake in half horizontally and sandwich the layers together with half of the whipped cream. Cover the cake with a thin layer of cream, then pipe the remainder around the top and bottom edges.

7 Press the chocolate curls over the top and side of the cake, if using.

Swiss roll

CUTS INTO 8 SLICES   **195 CALS EACH**

butter for greasing

4 large eggs

125 g (4 oz) caster sugar, plus extra for sprinkling

125 g (4 oz) self-raising flour

icing sugar for sprinkling

FILLING

about 4 tbsp raspberry jam

23 x 33 cm (9 x 13 in) Swiss roll tin

1 Lightly butter the Swiss roll tin, line with baking parchment, then lightly butter the parchment.

2 Put the eggs and sugar into a large bowl. Whisk together with an electric mixer at high speed until the mixture is pa and thick enough to leave a trail when th whisk is lifted out.

3 Sift the flour into the egg mixture and fold in gently but thoroughly.

4 Turn the mixture into the prepared tin and tilt to spread the mixture evenly, particularly into the corners.

5 Bake in a preheated oven at 220°C (200°C fan, Gas 7) for 10 minutes or ur the sponge is golden and starting to shrir away from the side of the tin.

6 Invert the sponge on to a large piece of baking parchment which has been liberally sprinkled with caster sugar. Peel the lining paper and trim the edges of the sponge with a sharp knife.

7 Roll up the sponge and the baking parchment together, from one of the short ends. Leave to stand for 2–3 minute

8 Unroll the sponge, and remove the baking parchment. Spread the spong with warmed jam and roll up again. Wra tightly in baking parchment and leave to cool. Unwrap, dust with icing sugar, and serve in slices.

lueberry and
anilla muffins

MAKES 12   249 CALS EACH

g (8 oz) plain flour

baking powder

g (5 oz) caster sugar

ml (6 fl oz) milk

rge eggs

ml (¼ pint) sunflower oil

(3 oz) blueberries

p 12-hole muffin tin and 12 paper cases

1 Line the muffin tin with the paper cases.

2 Put all the ingredients, except the blueberries, into a bowl. Beat with an electric whisk until evenly combined and smooth (it is quite a thin mixture). Stir in the blueberries.

3 Divide the mixture among the paper cases. Bake in a preheated oven at 180°C (160°C fan, Gas 4) for 25–30 minutes until well risen and light golden. Serve warm.

🔎 Cook's know-how

These traditional American muffins have a dense texture and are not too sweet. They are perfect for breakfast, and to serve with morning coffee or afternoon tea – or whenever you like.

Best-ever brownies

🍴 MAKES 24   336 CALS EACH

375 g (12 oz) plain chocolate, broken into pieces

250 g (8 oz) baking margarine

2 tsp instant coffee

2 tbsp hot water

2 eggs

250 g (8 oz) caster sugar

1 tsp vanilla extract

90 g (3 oz) self-raising flour

175 g (6 oz) walnut pieces

250 g (8 oz) plain chocolate chips

1 Grease a 30 x 23 cm (12 x 9 in) roasting tin, line the base with greaseproof paper, and grease the paper.

2 Put the chocolate and margarine in a bowl and sit the bowl on top of a small saucepan of gently simmering water. Melt the chocolate slowly, then remove the bowl from the pan and let the chocolate cool.

3 Put the coffee in another bowl, pour in the hot water, and stir to dissolve. Add the eggs, sugar, and vanilla extract. Gradually beat in the chocolate mixture. Fold in the flour and walnuts, then the chocolate chips.

4 Pour the mixture into the prepared tin and bake in a preheated oven at 190°C (170°C fan, Gas 5) for about 40–45 minutes or until firm to the touch. Don't overcook – the crust should be dull and crisp, but the middle should still be gooey. Leave to cool in the tin, then cut into 24 pieces.

🔍 Cook's know-how

For brownies to be good they must not be overcooked. The secret is to take them out of the oven just before you think they are done - the middle should be soft and squidgy, not set firm. Do not worry if there is a dip in the middle and a crack on top, this is how it should be, and you will find the mixture firms up on cooling.

Chocolate cup cakes

🍴 MAKES 24   198 CALS EACH

40 g (1½ oz) cocoa powder

about 4 tbsp boiling water

3 eggs

175 g (6 oz) baking margarine

175 g (6 oz) caster sugar

115 g (4½ oz) self-raising flour

1 rounded tsp baking powder

ICING

60 g (2 oz) butter

30 g (1 oz) cocoa powder

about 3 tbsp milk

250 g (8 oz) icing sugar

2 x 12-hole muffin tins and 24 paper cases

1 Line two 12-hole muffin tins with paper cases. Sift the cocoa powder into a bowl, pour in the boiling water, and mix into a thick paste. Add the remaining cake ingredients and mix with an electric hand whisk (or beat well with a wooden spoon).

2 Divide the mixture equally among the 24 paper cases. Bake in a preheated oven at 200°C (180°C fan, Gas 6) for about 10 minutes until well risen and springy to the touch. Cool in the cases on a wire rack.

3 Make the icing. Melt the butter, then pour it into a bowl. Sift in the cocoa powder and stir to mix. Stir in the milk and then sift in the icing sugar a little at a time to make a glossy, spreadable icing. Spread the icing over the cakes and leave to set before serving.

Double-chocolate muffins

🍴 MAKES 12   262 CALS EACH

2 eggs, lightly beaten

125 g (4 oz) full-fat plain yogurt

125 ml (4 fl oz) strong brewed coffee

125 ml (4 fl oz) milk

250 g (8 oz) self-raising flour, sifted

250 g (8 oz) caster sugar

75 g (2½ oz) cocoa powder

pinch of salt

100 g (3½ oz) plain chocolate chips

melted butter for greasing

12-hole muffin tin

1 Combine the eggs, yogurt, coffee, and milk in a large bowl.

2 Sift together the flour, sugar, cocoa powder, and salt, and stir into the milk mixture. Mix well. Stir in the chocolate chips.

3 Butter each cup of the muffin tin, then spoon in the muffin mixture, filling the cups almost to the tops.

4 Bake the muffins in a preheated oven at 200°C (180°C fan, Gas 6) for about 10 minutes; reduce the oven temperature to 180°C (160°C fan, Gas 4), and continue to bake for about 15 minutes until the muffins are golden and firm. Serve warm.

Opposite, clockwise from top
Double-chocolate muffins, Best-ever brownies, Chocolate cup cakes

Lemon cup cakes with lemon icing

MAKES 12   332 CALS EACH

25 g (4 oz) soft butter

25 g (4 oz) self-raising flour

25 g (4 oz) caster sugar

tbsp milk

large eggs

finely grated zest of 1 small lemon

LEMON ICING

25 g (4 oz) soft unsalted butter

50 g (8 oz) icing sugar, sifted

juice of 1 small lemon

edible silver balls or glitter to decorate

deep 12-hole muffin tin and 12 paper cases

Line the muffin tin with the paper cases. Put all the cake ingredients into a bowl, and beat with an electric whisk until evenly combined and smooth.

2 Divide the mixture among the paper cases. Bake in a preheated oven at 180°C (160°C fan, Gas 4) for 20–25 minutes until well risen and light golden brown. Transfer the cakes in their cases to a wire rack, and leave to cool.

3 Make the icing: put the butter and half of the icing sugar into a bowl, and beat with an electric whisk until evenly combined and smooth. Add the lemon juice and the remaining icing sugar, and beat again until light and fluffy. Spread the icing over the cold cup cakes, and decorate with silver balls or glitter.

Chocolate and orange mousse cake

This cake is made of chocolate sponge layers sandwiched together with a deliciously fluffy chocolate and orange mousse. When making the mousse, do not overwhisk the egg whites; when they just flop over at the tip they are ready to fold into the chocolate mixture.

CUTS INTO 12 SLICES   417 CALS EACH

butter for greasing

eggs

25 g (4 oz) caster sugar

g (3 oz) self-raising flour

g (1 oz) cocoa powder

Opposite: Lemon cup cakes with lemon icing.

MOUSSE

175 g (6 oz) plain dark chocolate, broken into pieces

grated zest and juice of 1 orange

1 tsp powdered gelatine

2 eggs, separated

300 ml (½ pint) double cream, whipped until thick

DECORATION

300 ml (½ pint) double or whipping cream, whipped until thick

strips of orange zest, blanched

deep 23 cm (9 in) springform cake tin

1 Lightly butter the tin and line the bottom with baking parchment. Make the sponge (see box, right).

2 Bake the sponge in a preheated oven at 180°C (160°C fan, Gas 4) for 40–45 minutes until the sponge is well risen and beginning to shrink away from the sides of the tin. Turn out on to a wire rack, peel off the lining paper, and leave to cool.

3 Cut the cake in half horizontally. Put one half back into the clean tin.

4 Make the mousse: put the chocolate into a heatproof bowl set over a pan of hot water. Heat gently, stirring occasionally, until the chocolate has melted. Leave to cool slightly.

5 Strain the orange juice into a small heatproof bowl and sprinkle over the gelatine. Leave for 3 minutes or until spongy, then stand the bowl in a saucepan of gently simmering water for 3 minutes or until the gelatine has dissolved.

6 Stir the egg yolks and orange zest into the cooled chocolate. Slowly stir in the dissolved gelatine, then fold in the whipped cream. In a separate bowl, whisk the egg whites until stiff but not dry, then gently fold into the chocolate mixture until well blended.

7 Pour the mousse on top of the cake layer in the tin. Put the remaining cake layer on top. Cover and chill in the refrigerator until the mousse filling is set.

8 Remove the side of the tin and slide the cake on to a serving plate. Decorate with cream and orange zest.

Making the sponge

Combine the eggs and sugar in a large bowl and whisk with an electric mixer at high speed until the mixture is pale and thick enough to leave a trail on itself when the whisk is lifted out.

Sift the flour and cocoa powder over the surface.

Fold in the flour and cocoa until blended.

Turn the mixture into the prepared tin and tilt to level the surface.

Iced lime traybake

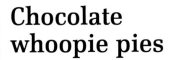 MAKES 12 SQUARES   340 CALS EACH

175 g (6 oz) soft butter or margarine, plus extra for greasing

175 g (6 oz) caster sugar

250 g (8 oz) self-raising flour

1½ tsp baking powder

3 eggs

3 tbsp milk

finely grated zest of 2 limes

ICING

250 g (8 oz) icing sugar

juice of 2 limes

23 x 30 cm (9 x 12 in) cake tin

1 Lightly grease the tin and line the bottom with baking parchment.

2 Combine all the cake ingredients in a large bowl and beat well for about 2 minutes or until smooth and thoroughly blended.

3 Turn into the prepared tin and level the surface. Bake in a preheated oven at 180°C (160°C fan, Gas 4) for 35–40 minutes until the cake is well risen, springy to the touch, and beginning to shrink away from the sides of the cake tin.

4 Leave to cool slightly in the tin, then turn out on to a wire rack, peel off the lining paper, and cool.

5 Make the icing: sift the icing sugar into a bowl. Mix in enough of the lime juice to give a runny consistency. Pour over the cooled cake, spreading carefully with a palette knife, and leave to set. When cold, cut into squares and serve.

Chocolate and mint traybake

Mix 4 tbsp cocoa powder with 4 tbsp hot water and leave to cool. Add to the basic cake ingredients with 4 tbsp chopped fresh mint. For the icing, break 250 g (8 oz) plain dark chocolate into pieces and put into a heatproof bowl with 90 g (3 oz) butter and 4 tbsp hot water. Put the bowl over a saucepan of hot water and heat gently until the chocolate has melted. Beat together until smooth and shiny, then spread over the top of the cooled cake.

Chocolate whoopie pies

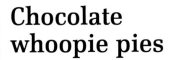 MAKES 15   455 CALS EACH

375 g (12 oz) plain flour

60 g (2 oz) cocoa powder

½ tsp bicarbonate of soda

150 g (5 oz) soft butter

200 g (7 oz) light muscovado sugar

1 large egg

300 ml (½ pint) soured cream

FILLING

125 g (4 oz) soft butter

250 g (8 oz) icing sugar, sifted

1 tsp vanilla extract

TOPPING

125g (5 oz) icing sugar

2 tbsp cocoa powder

2½ tbsp cold water

coloured sprinkles to decorate

1 Line 2 baking trays with baking parchment. Sift the flour, cocoa powder and bicarbonate of soda into a bowl.

2 Put the butter, sugar, egg, and soured cream into another bowl, and beat with an electric whisk until evenly combined and smooth. Add half of the flour mixture, and beat until smooth again, then add the remaining flour mixture and beat until the mixture is very thick and smooth.

3 Divide the mixture in half, and put 15 rounded spoonfuls on each baking tray leaving room between them for the cakes to spread during baking.

4 Bake in a preheated oven at 180°C (160°C fan, Gas 4) for 15–20 minutes until risen and firm to the touch – they will be cracked a little in the middle. Leave to cool slightly, then transfer to a wire rack and leave to cool completely.

5 Make the filling: put the butter into a bowl with half of the icing sugar, and beat with an electric whisk until smooth and creamy. Add the remaining sugar and beat again, then stir in the vanilla extract.

6 Make the topping: sift the icing sugar and cocoa powder into a bowl. Add the water, and mix to a smooth, spreadable icing. Sandwich the pies together with the filling, spread the icing on top, and scatter with coloured sprinkles.

Rich fruit cake

CUTS INTO 10 SLICES   570 CALS EACH

50 g (8 oz) soft butter or margarine, plus extra
for greasing

50 g (8 oz) light muscovado sugar

eggs

50 g (8 oz) self-raising flour

50 g (8 oz) raisins

50 g (8 oz) sultanas

25 g (4 oz) glacé cherries, halved and rinsed

tsp ground mixed spice

tbsp brandy

deep 20 cm (8 in) round cake tin

Lightly grease the tin and line the bottom with greaseproof paper.

Combine all the ingredients in a large bowl and mix well until combined. Turn the mixture into the prepared cake tin and level the surface.

Bake in a preheated oven at 140°C (120°C fan, Gas 1) for 2–2¼ hours. Cover the top of the cake with foil after about 1 hour to prevent the top becoming too brown.

When cooked, the cake should be firm to the touch and a fine skewer inserted in the middle of the cake should come out clean. Leave the cake to cool in the tin before turning out. Store in an airtight container.

Mincemeat buns

MAKES 32   137 CALS EACH

375 g (12 oz) mincemeat

250 g (8 oz) currants

2 eggs

150 g (5 oz) caster sugar

150 g (5 oz) soft butter or margarine

250 g (8 oz) self-raising flour

32 paper cake cases

1 Combine all the ingredients in a large bowl and beat well for about 2 minutes.

2 Divide the cake mixture evenly among the paper cases, putting them into bun tins if preferred.

3 Bake in a preheated oven at 160°C (140°C fan, Gas 3) for 25–30 minutes until golden and springy to the touch. Transfer the cases to a wire rack and leave to cool.

Cook's know-how

Mincemeat is traditionally made with beef suet. If you want a vegetarian version, use vegetable suet or grated chilled butter. Home-made mincemeat is best, but you can improve on commercial ones by adding finely chopped nuts, angelica, dried apricots, peaches, or pears.

Simnel cake

is is now a traditional Easter cake, but iginally it was given by girls to their others on Mothering Sunday. The almond ste balls represent the 11 disciples of hrist, excluding Judas Iscariot.

CUTS INTO 12 SLICES   494 CALS EACH

5 g (6 oz) soft butter or margarine, plus extra greasing

5 g (6 oz) light muscovado sugar

ggs

5 g (6 oz) self-raising flour

5 g (6 oz) sultanas

g (3 oz) currants

g (3 oz) glacé cherries, quartered, rinsed, d dried

g (1 oz) candied peel, roughly chopped

ted zest of 1 large lemon

sp ground mixed spice

LING AND DECORATION

0 g (1 lb) almond paste

osp apricot jam

gg white

ep 18 cm (7 in) round loose-bottomed cake tin

Roll out one-third of the almond paste. Using the base of the cake tin as a ide, cut out an 18 cm (7 in) round.

Grease the cake tin and line the bottom and side with greaseproof paper.

Combine all the cake ingredients in a bowl. Beat well until thoroughly blended. oon half of the cake mixture into the epared tin and smooth the surface. with the round of almond paste.

Spoon the remaining cake mixture on top and level the surface.

Bake in a preheated oven at 150°C (130°C fan, Gas 2) for 2¼ hours or until lden brown and firm to the touch.

Cover the top of the cake with greaseproof paper if it is browning quickly. Leave to cool for 10 minutes, en remove from the tin, and leave to ol completely.

Warm the jam and use to brush the top of the cake.

8 To decorate the cake, roll out half of the remaining almond paste and use the tin to cut out an 18 cm (7 in) round. Put on top of the jam and crimp the edges. Roll the remaining almond paste into 11 even-sized balls. Place around the edge of the cake, attaching them with egg white.

9 Brush the tops of the balls and the almond paste with egg white. Place under a hot grill for 1–2 minutes, until the balls are golden.

Battenburg cake

CUTS INTO 8 SLICES   425 CALS EACH

125 g (4 oz) soft butter or margarine, plus extra for greasing

125 g (4 oz) caster sugar

2 large eggs

60 g (2 oz) ground rice

125 g (4 oz) self-raising flour

½ tsp baking powder

a few drops of vanilla extract

1½ tsp cocoa powder

3 tbsp apricot jam

250 g (8 oz) almond paste

shallow 18 cm (7 in) square cake tin

1 Lightly grease the cake tin with butter. Line the bottom of the tin with baking parchment.

2 Beat the butter, sugar, eggs, ground rice, flour, baking powder, and vanilla extract in a large bowl for 2 minutes or until the mixture is smooth and evenly combined.

3 Spoon half of the mixture into one half of the prepared tin. Dissolve the cocoa in a little hot water to make a thick paste and add to the remaining cake mixture in the bowl. Mix well, then spoon into the other half of the tin.

4 Bake the mixture in a preheated oven at 160°C (140°C fan, Gas 3) for 35 minutes or until the cake is well risen and springy to the touch. Turn out on to a wire rack, peel off the lining paper, and cool.

5 Trim the edges of the cake. Cut it into 4 equal strips down the length of the 2 colours.

6 Warm the apricot jam in a small saucepan. Stack the cake strips, alternating the colours to give a chequerboard effect and sticking them together with the apricot jam.

7 Roll out the almond paste into an oblong that is the same length as the cake and wide enough to wrap around it. Put the cake on top, then brush with jam. Wrap the paste around the cake (see box, below).

8 Score the top with a crisscross pattern and crimp the edges with your fingertips to make a decorative effect.

Wrapping the cake

Wrap the almond paste around the cake, pressing it on gently and making the join in 1 corner. Turn to hide the join.

posite: Simnel cake.

Rich fruit Christmas cake

🍴 CUTS INTO ABOUT 30 SLICES   316 CALS EACH

425 g (14 oz) currants	

250 g (8 oz) sultanas

250 g (8 oz) raisins

300 g (10 oz) glacé cherries, quartered, rinsed, and dried

150 g (5 oz) ready-to-eat dried apricots, snipped into small pieces

75 g (2½ oz) mixed candied peel, roughly chopped

4 tbsp brandy, plus extra for soaking

300 g (10 oz) plain flour

1 tsp ground mixed spice

½ tsp grated nutmeg

300 g (10 oz) soft butter, plus extra for greasing

300 g (10 oz) dark muscovado sugar

5 eggs

60 g (2 oz) whole unblanched almonds, roughly chopped

1 tbsp black treacle

finely grated zest of 1 large lemon

finely grated zest of 1 large orange

deep 23 cm (9 in) round or 20 cm (8 in) square cake tin

1 Combine the fruit and candied peel in a large bowl. Add the brandy, and stir to mix well. Cover and leave overnight.

2 Put the remaining ingredients into a large bowl and beat well with an electric mixer until thoroughly blended. Stir in the soaked fruits and any liquid.

3 Grease the cake tin with butter, line the bottom and sides with a double layer of greaseproof paper, and grease the paper. Spoon the mixture into the prepared tin. Level the surface and cover the top of the cake with greaseproof paper.

4 Bake in a preheated oven at 140°C (120°C fan, Gas 1) for 4¾–5 hours until firm to the touch and a skewer inserted into the middle of the cake comes out clean. Leave the cake to cool in the tin.

5 When the cake has cooled, pierce it in several places with a fine skewer and pour over a little brandy. Remove the cake from the tin, but leave the lining paper on. Wrap the cake in more greaseproof paper, then overwrap with foil. Store the cake in a cool place for up to 3 months, to mature, unwrapping and spooning over more brandy (1–2 tbsp) occasionally.

6 Decorate the cake with glacé fruit, almond paste, or ready-to-use icing (see box, right). Tie a ribbon around the cake, if wished.

Marzipan (almond paste)

🍴 MAKES ENOUGH FOR A 23 CM (9 IN) ROUND OR 20 CM (8 IN) SQUARE CAKE

250 g (8 oz) ground almonds

250 g (8 oz) caster sugar

250 g (8 oz) icing sugar, sifted, plus extra for dusting

6 drops of almond extract

about 4 egg yolks, or about 2 whole eggs

1 Mix the ground almonds in a bowl with the two different types of sugar until evenly combined. Lightly beat together the extract and egg yolks or whole eggs. Add almost all of this mixture to the dry ingredients and mix together until a stiff paste forms; it is best to do this with your hands. Add the remaining egg if needed so that the mixtures comes together well.

2 Dust a flat surface lightly with icing sugar, turn out the mixture on to it, and knead with your hands to make a stiff paste. Take care not to over-knead or the paste will be oily. Wrap in cling film and store in the refrigerator until required.

Royal icing

🍴 MAKES ENOUGH FOR A 23 CM (9 IN) ROUND OR 20 CM (8 IN) SQUARE CAKE

2 egg whites

500 g (1 lb) icing sugar, sifted

4 tsp lemon juice

1 Whisk the egg whites in a large bowl lightly with a fork until bubbles begin to form on the surface. Add about half the icing sugar and all of the lemon juice and beat well with a wooden spoon for about 10 minutes until brilliant white.

2 Gradually stir in the remaining icing sugar until the consistency is just right for spreading or piping. If not using immediately, keep the bowl covered with a damp cloth to prevent the icing drying out.

Cake decorations

Whichever cake you choose, you need to melt and sieve about 90 g (3 oz) apricot jam before you apply any of the decorations or icing. The jam prevents the cake from drying out and suppresses any crumbs.

Candied fruit cake
This looks most dramatic if it is made in a square tin. Brush the jam over the top of the cake and then arrange nuts and whole or sliced candied fruits and peel in a decorative pattern while the jam is still warm and sticky. Glaze with more jam and leave until set firmly in place before tying a ribbon around the sides of the cake.

Snow white cake
Brush the jam over the top and sides of the cake. Roll out the marzipan and use it to cover the cake completely, then smooth it in place with your hands and trim off any excess. Let the marzipan dry out for a few days before covering with royal icing. Use a palette knife to rough up the icing into peaks, immediately after you have spread it all over the cake. If you are using bought decorations for the top of the cake (here, silver dragées and fresh cranberries), you need to gently press them in before the icing sets hard.

Opposite, clockwise from t
Candied fruit cake, Snow white ca

Shortbread

MAKES 8 WEDGES   **233 CALS EACH**

125 g (4 oz) plain flour

60 g (2 oz) semolina or cornflour

125 g (4 oz) butter, plus extra for greasing

60 g (2 oz) caster sugar, plus extra for sprinkling

1 Mix the flour with the semolina or cornflour in a bowl. Add the butter and rub in with the fingertips. Stir in the sugar. Knead the mixture lightly until it forms a smooth dough.

2 Lightly butter a baking tray. Roll out the dough on a lightly floured work surface into an 18 cm (7 in) round. Lift on to the baking tray. Crimp the edges to decorate, prick all over with a fork, and mark into 8 wedges with a sharp knife. Chill until firm.

3 Bake in a preheated oven at 160°C (140°C fan, Gas 3) for 35 minutes or until a pale golden brown colour. Mark the wedges again and sprinkle the shortbread with sugar.

4 Allow the shortbread to cool on the baking tray for about 5 minutes, then lift off carefully with a palette knife and transfer to a wire rack to cool completely. Cut into wedges to serve.

Below: Shortbread.

Fruity banana bread

CUTS INTO 12 SLICES   **334 CALS EACH**

125 g (4 oz) butter or margarine, plus extra for greasing

250 g (8 oz) self-raising flour

175 g (6 oz) caster sugar

125 g (4 oz) sultanas

60 g (2 oz) walnuts, roughly chopped

125 g (4 oz) glacé cherries, quartered, rinsed, and dried

2 large eggs, beaten

500 g (1 lb) bananas, weight with peel, peeled and mashed

1 kg (2 lb) loaf tin

1 Grease the loaf tin and line the bottom with greaseproof paper.

2 Put the flour into a bowl, add the butter, and rub in with the fingertips until the mixture resembles fine breadcrumbs. Mix in the caster sugar, sultanas, chopped walnuts, and glacé cherries.

3 Add the eggs and mashed bananas and beat the mixture until well blended. Spoon into the prepared tin.

4 Bake in a preheated oven at 160°C (140°C fan, Gas 3) for about 1¼ hours until well risen and firm to the touch. A fine skewer inserted into the middle of the loaf should come out clean.

5 Leave the loaf to cool slightly in the tin, then turn out on to a wire rack, and pe off the lining paper. Leave the loaf to cool completely before slicing and serving.

Dundee cake

CUTS INTO 12 SLICES   **384 CALS EACH**

150 g (5 oz) butter, at room temperature, plus extra for greasing

150 g (5 oz) light muscovado sugar

3 eggs

250 g (8 oz) plain flour

1 tsp baking powder

175 g (6 oz) sultanas

90 g (3 oz) currants

90 g (3 oz) raisins

60 g (2 oz) glacé cherries, quartered, rinsed, and dried

60 g (2 oz) chopped mixed candied peel

2 tbsp ground almonds

grated zest of 1 large lemon

60 g (2 oz) whole almonds, blanched and halved to decorate

deep 20 cm (8 in) round loose-bottomed cake t

1 Lightly butter the cake tin and line the bottom with greaseproof paper.

2 Combine the butter, sugar, eggs, flour, and baking powder in a bowl and bee for 2 minutes or until well blended. Stir in th fruit, mixed peel, ground almonds, and lemon zest.

3 Spoon the mixture into the prepared tin. Level the surface and arrange the halved almonds neatly in concentric circl on top.

4 Bake in a preheated oven at 160°C (140°C fan, Gas 3) for 1½ hours or until well risen, golden, and firm to the touch. A fine skewer inserted into the middle of the cake should come out clean. Cover the cake with foil halfway through baking if it is browning too quickly.

5 Leave the cake to cool in the tin for a few minutes, then turn out on to a wire rack and leave to cool completely. Store in an airtight container for about 1 week before eating.

Bara brith

5 g (12 oz) mixed dried fruit

0 g (8 oz) light muscovado sugar

0 ml (½ pint) strong hot tea, strained

tter for greasing

0 g (10 oz) self-raising flour

egg, beaten

g (2 lb) loaf tin

Combine the dried fruit, sugar, and hot tea in a large bowl. Stir the mixture, then ver and leave to steep for at least 8 hours.

Lightly butter the loaf tin and line the bottom with greaseproof paper. Stir e flour and egg into the dried fruit and tea xture, mixing thoroughly. Turn the mixture o the loaf tin and level the surface.

Bake in a preheated oven at 150°C (130°C fan, Gas 2) for 1½–1¾ hours until ell risen and firm to the touch. A fine ewer inserted into the middle should me out clean.

Leave to cool in the tin for about 10 minutes, then turn out on to a wire rack, d peel off the lining paper. Leave to cool mpletely. Serve sliced, and buttered if shed.

Cornbread

flower oil for greasing

5 g (6 oz) polenta or fine yellow cornmeal

5 g (4 oz) plain flour

tbsp brown sugar

p baking powder

p salt

0 ml (½ pint) lukewarm milk

ggs, lightly beaten

g (2 oz) butter, melted and cooled slightly

cm (7 in) square cake tin

Lightly oil the cake tin. Put the polenta, flour, sugar, baking powder, and salt into arge bowl and make a well in the ddle. Pour in the milk, eggs, and butter, d beat the ingredients to form a batter.

Pour the mixture into the cake tin and bake in a preheated oven at 200°C 0°C fan, Gas 6) for 25–30 minutes until den. Leave to cool, then cut into squares.

Gingerbread

250 g (8 oz) butter or margarine, plus extra for greasing

250 g (8 oz) dark muscovado sugar

250 g (8 oz) black treacle

375 g (12 oz) plain flour

5 tsp ground ginger

2 tsp ground cinnamon

2 eggs, beaten

3 pieces of stem ginger in syrup, drained and roughly chopped

300 ml (½ pint) milk

2 tsp bicarbonate of soda

23 x 30 cm (9 x 12 in) cake tin

1 Lightly grease the tin and line the bottom with greaseproof paper.

2 Heat the butter, sugar, and treacle in a pan, stirring, until smooth. Cool slightly.

3 Sift in the flour and ground spices. Stir well, then beat in the eggs and stem ginger.

4 Warm the milk in a small heavy saucepan, and add the bicarbonate of soda. Pour into the gingerbread mixture and stir gently until thoroughly blended.

5 Pour the mixture into the prepared tin. Bake in a preheated oven at 160°C (140°C fan, Gas 3) for about 1 hour until well risen and springy to the touch.

6 Leave to cool in the tin for a few minutes, then turn out on to a wire rack, and peel off the paper. Leave to cool completely, then store in an airtight container for 2–3 days (it improves with keeping). Cut into squares to serve.

Date and walnut loaf

🍴 CUTS INTO 12 SLICES   269 CALS EACH

90 g (3 oz) soft butter or margarine, plus extra for greasing

250 g (8 oz) dates, stoned and roughly chopped

150 ml (¼ pint) boiling water

90 g (3 oz) caster sugar

1 egg

250 g (8 oz) self-raising flour

1 tsp baking powder

90 g (3 oz) walnuts, roughly chopped

1 kg (2 lb) loaf tin

1 Lightly grease the loaf tin with butter and line with greaseproof paper.

2 Put the dates into a bowl, pour over the measured boiling water, and leave for about 15 minutes.

3 Combine the butter, sugar, egg, flour, and baking powder in a large bowl and beat until well blended. Add the walnuts and dates, plus the soaking liquid, and stir to mix.

4 Spoon into the prepared loaf tin and bake in a preheated oven at 180°C (160°C fan, Gas 4) for 1¼–1½ hours until well risen and firm to the touch. A fine skewer inserted into the middle of the loaf should come out clean.

5 Leave to cool in the loaf tin for a few minutes, then turn out on to a wire rac and peel off the lining paper. Leave to co completely. Serve sliced and buttered, if wished.

Cherry and banana loaf

Omit the dates and walnuts, and add 125 g (4 oz) quartered glacé cherries and 2 mashe large ripe bananas in step 3.

Wholemeal drop scones

g (6 oz) wholemeal self-raising flour

p baking powder

g (1½ oz) caster sugar

rge egg

ml (7 fl oz) milk

flower oil for greasing

den syrup or butter and jam to serve

Combine the flour, baking powder, and sugar in a bowl, and stir to mix. Make well in the middle of the dry ingredients d add the egg and half of the milk. Beat ell to make a smooth, thick batter.

Add enough milk to give the batter the consistency of thick cream.

Heat a flat griddle or heavy frying pan and grease with oil. Drop spoonfuls of tter on to the hot griddle or pan, spacing em well apart. When bubbles rise to the face, turn scones over and cook til golden.

As each batch is cooked, wrap the scones in a clean tea towel to keep em soft. Serve warm, with syrup or butter d jam.

ain drop scones

ostitute plain self-raising flour for the wholemeal -raising flour, and use a little less milk.

Welsh cakes

g (8 oz) self-raising flour

p baking powder

g (4 oz) butter

g (3 oz) caster sugar

g (3 oz) currants

sp ground mixed spice

gg, beaten

ut 2 tbsp milk

flower oil for greasing

m (3 in) pastry cutter

Sift the flour and baking powder into a arge bowl. Add the butter and rub in with fingertips until the mixture resembles fine adcrumbs.

Above: Devon scones.

2 Add the sugar, currants, and mixed spice, and stir to mix. Add the egg and enough milk to form a soft, but not sticky, dough.

3 On a lightly floured work surface, roll out the dough to a thickness of 5 mm (¼ in). Cut into rounds with pastry cutter.

4 Heat a flat griddle or a heavy frying pan and grease with a little oil. Cook the Welsh cakes on the hot griddle or pan over a low heat for about 3 minutes on each side until cooked through and golden brown.

5 Leave to cool on a wire rack. Serve on the day of making, if possible.

Devon scones

60 g (2 oz) butter, plus extra for greasing

250 g (8 oz) self-raising flour

2 tsp baking powder

30 g (1 oz) caster sugar

1 egg

about 150 ml (¼ pint) milk, plus extra for glazing

butter and jam to serve

5 cm (2 in) pastry cutter

1 Lightly butter a large baking tray.

2 Sift the flour and baking powder into a bowl. Rub in the butter with the fingertips until the mixture resembles fine breadcrumbs. Stir in the sugar.

3 Break the egg into a measuring jug and make up to 150 ml (¼ pint) with milk. Beat lightly to mix. Add to the bowl and mix to a soft dough.

4 Lightly knead the dough until smooth. Roll out until 1 cm (½ in) thick, cut into rounds with the pastry cutter, and put on the baking tray. Brush with milk.

5 Bake in a preheated oven at 220°C (200°C fan, Gas 7) for about 10 minutes until risen and golden. Cool on a wire rack. Serve on the day of making, if possible, with butter and jam.

Cheese scones

Omit the sugar, and add 125 g (4 oz) grated mature Cheddar cheese and ½ tsp mustard powder to the dry ingredients before mixing in the egg and milk. Roll out the dough into a 15 cm (6 in) round and cut it into wedges. Brush with milk and sprinkle with finely grated cheese. Bake as directed.

Irish soda bread

CUTS INTO 8 WEDGES   227 CALS EACH

500 g (1 lb) plain white flour, plus extra for dusting

1 tsp bicarbonate of soda

1 tsp salt

300 ml (½ pint) buttermilk, or half milk and half plain yogurt

90 ml (3 fl oz) lukewarm water

sunflower oil for greasing

1 Sift the flour, bicarbonate of soda, and salt into a large bowl. Pour in the buttermilk, or milk and yogurt, and the measured water. Mix with a wooden spoon or your hands to form a very soft dough.

2 Lightly oil a baking tray. Turn out the dough on to a lightly floured work surface and shape into a round measuring 18 cm (7 in) in diameter.

Below: Irish soda bread.

3 Place the loaf on the prepared baking tray and cut a deep cross in the top.

4 Bake in a preheated oven at 200°C (180°C fan, Gas 6) for 30 minutes. Turn the bread over and bake for a further 10 minutes or until the loaf sounds hollow when tapped on the base. Cool on a wire rack. Serve on the day of making.

Potato farls

MAKES 12   113 CALS EACH

175 g (6 oz) plain flour

1 tbsp baking powder

60 g (2 oz) butter, plus extra for greasing

45 g (1½ oz) caster sugar

125 g (4 oz) freshly boiled and mashed potato

3 tbsp milk

1 Sift the flour and baking powder into a bowl. Rub in the butter until the mixture resembles fine breadcrumbs. Stir in the sugar and mashed potato. Add enough milk to bind to a soft, but not sticky, dough.

2 Turn out the dough on to a floured surface and knead lightly until blended. Roll out until 1 cm (½ in) thick and cut into rectangles or triangles.

3 Place the farls on a buttered baking tray and bake in a preheated oven at 220°C (200°C fan, Gas 7) for 12–15 minutes until risen and golden. Leave to cool on a wire rack. Serve on the day of making.

Almond tuiles

MAKES 30   45 CALS EACH

2 egg whites

125 g (4 oz) caster sugar

60 g (2 oz) plain flour

½ tsp vanilla extract

60 g (2 oz) butter, melted and cooled

30 g (1 oz) flaked almonds

1 Line a baking tray with baking parchment. Put the egg whites into a bowl and beat in the sugar until frothy. Stir in the flour and vanilla extract, then add the melted butter.

2 Put 6 teaspoonfuls of the mixture on to the baking tray, spacing them well apart to allow for spreading. Flatten each with a fork.

3 Sprinkle with the almonds. Bake in a preheated oven at 180°C (160°C fan, Gas 4) for about 6 minutes until golden brown around the edges but still pale in the middle.

4 Allow the biscuits to cool on the baking tray for a few seconds, then lift off with a fish slice and gently lay them over a greased rolling pin to give the traditional curved shape.

5 Allow the biscuits to set, then lift off on to a wire rack and leave to cool.

6 Cook and shape the remaining mixture in batches, cooking one batch while another is setting on the rolling pin.

ove: Pink almond macaroons.

Pink almond
macaroons

MAKES 40   113 CALS EACH

g (7 oz) icing sugar, sifted

g (7 oz) ground almonds

g (7 oz) caster sugar

bsp cold water

arge eggs, separated

sp almond extract

food colouring

LING

g (3 oz) soft butter

g (5 oz) icing sugar, sifted

pberry jam

ing bag fitted with 1 cm (½ in) plain nozzle

Line 2 baking trays with baking parchment. Combine the icing sugar d almonds in a bowl, and set aside.

Put the caster sugar and water into a stainless steel pan. Heat gently over ow heat, stirring, until the sugar has solved. Bring to a boil, and boil for ew minutes without stirring, until you ve a shiny, clear syrup, the consistency single cream. If you have a sugar ermometer it should read 110°C, no re. Remove from the heat, and leave cool slightly.

Put 2 of the egg whites into a bowl, and beat with an electric whisk on high eed until stiff but not dry. Slowly pour in

the sugar syrup in a thin, steady stream, beating constantly until all the syrup is used and you have a shiny meringue.

4 Add the remaining 2 unbeaten egg whites to the sugar and almonds, and mix to a very thick paste with a wooden spoon. Add the almond extract, and stir in just enough food colouring to make the mixture pink. Add a heaped tablespoonful of the meringue, beat well, then carefully fold in the remaining meringue until the mixture is an even pink colour. Do not overmix or it will be too runny.

5 Fill the piping bag with the mixture. Pipe 40 small rounds, each about 3.5 cm (1½ in) in diameter, on to each baking tray. If you do not have a piping bag, use 2 teaspoons to spoon the mixture on to the trays. Set aside to dry for about an hour until a skin forms on top.

6 Bake in a preheated oven at 150°C (130°C fan, Gas 2) for about 25 minutes until firm and glossy on top. Turn the oven off, and leave the macaroons to cool in the oven for about an hour. Transfer to a wire rack with a damp palette knife, and leave to cool completely.

7 Make the filling: cream the butter and half of the icing sugar in a bowl, beating until pale and fluffy. Beat in the remaining sugar a little at a time until the mixture is smooth. Using a small palette knife, spread a little jam and butter cream over the bottom of 40 macaroons, then sandwich together with the remaining macaroons.

Coconut macaroons

MAKES 26   116 CALS EACH

3 egg whites

175 g (6 oz) icing sugar

175 g (6 oz) ground almonds

a few drops of almond extract

175 g (6 oz) desiccated coconut

about 13 whole almonds, blanched and halved

1 Line 2 baking trays with baking parchment.

2 Whisk the egg whites thoroughly until stiff but not dry. Sift in the icing sugar and fold it in gently. Fold in the ground almonds, almond extract, and desiccated coconut.

3 Put teaspoonfuls of the coconut mixture on to the baking trays. Top each with an almond half.

4 Bake in a preheated oven at 150°C (130°C fan, Gas 2) for about 25 minutes until golden brown and crisp on the outside and soft in the middle.

5 Leave the macaroons to cool on a wire rack. Best served on the day of making.

Flapjacks

MAKES 24   102 CALS EACH

125 g (4 oz) butter, plus extra for greasing

90 g (3 oz) golden syrup

90 g (3 oz) light muscovado sugar

250 g (8 oz) rolled oats

roasting tin or shallow cake tin, about 20 x 30 cm (8 x 12 in)

1 Lightly butter the roasting tin or cake tin.

2 Combine the butter, syrup, and sugar in a saucepan and heat gently until the ingredients have melted and dissolved. Stir in the oats and mix well.

3 Spoon into the prepared tin and smooth the surface with a palette knife. Bake in a preheated oven at 180°C (160°C fan, Gas 4) for about 30 minutes.

4 Leave to cool in the tin for about 5 minutes, then mark into 24 fingers. Leave to cool completely, then cut and remove from the tin.

Below: Flapjacks.

Fridge cookies

MAKES 50   59 CALS EACH

250 g (8 oz) plain flour

1 tsp baking powder

125 g (4 oz) butter, plus extra for greasing

175 g (6 oz) caster sugar

60 g (2 oz) walnuts, finely chopped

1 egg, beaten

1 tsp vanilla extract

1 Sift the flour and baking powder into a bowl. Rub in the butter with the fingertips until the mixture resembles breadcrumbs. Mix in the sugar and walnuts. Add the beaten egg and vanilla extract, and stir to form a smooth dough.

2 Shape the dough into a cylinder about 5 cm (2 in) in diameter. Wrap in foil, roll to give smooth sides, and refrigerate for about 8 hours.

3 Lightly butter several baking trays. Cut the cylinder into thin slices and place the biscuits on the baking trays. Bake in a preheated oven at 190°C (170°C fan, Gas 5) for 10–12 minutes until golden.

Pinwheel biscuits

MAKES 18   98 CALS EACH

VANILLA DOUGH

60 g (2 oz) butter, at room temperature

30 g (1 oz) caster sugar

90 g (3 oz) plain flour

a few drops of vanilla extract

about 1 tbsp water

COFFEE DOUGH

60 g (2 oz) butter, at room temperature

30 g (1 oz) caster sugar

90 g (3 oz) plain flour

1 tbsp coffee extract

milk for brushing

1 Combine the ingredients for the vanilla dough in a bowl and mix well, adding just enough water to bind. Knead lightly, then wrap and chill for at least 2 hours until very firm.

2 Mix the ingredients for the coffee dough, using the coffee extract to bin Wrap and chill for at least 2 hours until very firm.

3 On a lightly floured work surface, roll out each dough to a rectangle about 18 x 25 cm (7 x 10 in).

4 Brush the coffee dough with a little mil then place the vanilla dough on top. Roll up together like a Swiss roll, starting at a narrow end.

5 Wrap the roll tightly in foil and leave to c in the refrigerator for about 30 minutes or until firm.

6 Lightly grease 1–2 baking trays. Cut the dough roll into about 18 thin slices and place them well apart on the baking tray

7 Bake in a preheated oven at 180°C (160°C fan, Gas 4) for about 20 minute until the vanilla dough is a very pale golden colour.

8 Leave the biscuits to cool on the bakir trays for a few minutes, then lift off on a wire rack and leave to cool completely

🔍 Cook's know-how

If the doughs become too soft and difficult to roll out, put each piece of dough between sheets of greaseproof paper before rolling.

Viennese fingers

🔘 MAKES 12   215 CALS EACH

5 g (6 oz) butter, plus extra for greasing

g (2 oz) caster sugar

5 g (6 oz) self-raising flour

g (3 oz) plain dark chocolate, broken
 pieces

Lightly butter 2 baking trays. Combine
 the butter and sugar in a bowl and
eam together until pale and fluffy. Stir
the flour and beat until well combined.

Spoon the mixture into a piping bag
 with a medium star nozzle. Pipe into
cm (3 in) lengths on the baking trays.
ke in a preheated oven at 160°C
40°C fan, Gas 3) for about 20 minutes
til golden. Cool on a wire rack.

Put the chocolate into a heatproof bowl.
 Set the bowl over a pan of hot water and
at gently until the chocolate has melted.
 both ends of each biscuit into the
ocolate. Leave to set on the wire rack.

Ginger snaps

🔘 MAKES 15   81 CALS EACH

g (2 oz) butter, plus extra for greasing

g (3 oz) golden syrup

5 g (4 oz) self-raising flour

p ground ginger

p ground cinnamon

sp bicarbonate of soda

sp caster sugar

Lightly grease 2 baking trays with butter.
 Combine the butter and golden syrup in
mall saucepan and heat gently until
elted. Leave the mixture to cool slightly.

Sift the flour, spices, and bicarbonate
 of soda into a bowl, and stir in the
gar. Add the cooled syrup mixture, and
to mix to a soft but not sticky dough.

Roll the dough into balls about the size
 of walnuts and place well apart on the
king trays. Flatten the dough balls slightly
h the heel of your hand.

Bake in a preheated oven at 190°C
 (170°C fan, Gas 5) for about 15 minutes.
ave the biscuits to cool on the baking
ys for a few minutes, then transfer them to
wire rack and leave to cool completely.

Above: Fork biscuits.

Fork biscuits

🔘 MAKES 32   104 CALS EACH

250 g (8 oz) butter, at room temperature, plus extra
for greasing

125 g (4 oz) caster sugar

300 g (10 oz) self-raising flour

1 Lightly grease 2 baking trays with butter.
Put the butter into a large bowl and beat
with a wooden spoon to soften it. Gradually
beat in the caster sugar, then stir in the flour.
Use your hands to gather the mixture
together into a soft but not sticky dough.

2 Roll the dough into balls about the size
of walnuts and place well apart on the
baking trays. Dip a fork into cold water and
press on top of each ball to flatten it and
imprint the fork pattern.

3 Bake in batches in a preheated
oven at 180°C (160°C fan, Gas 4) for
15–20 minutes until the biscuits are a very
pale golden colour. Transfer the biscuits
from the baking tray to a wire rack and
leave to cool completely.

Brandy snaps

🔘 MAKES 15   107 CALS EACH

90 g (3 oz) butter

90 g (3 oz) demerara sugar

90 g (3 oz) golden syrup

90 g (3 oz) plain flour

¾ tsp ground ginger

¾ tsp lemon juice

1 Line a baking tray with baking parchment.
Combine the butter, sugar, and syrup in a
saucepan and heat gently until the
ingredients have melted and dissolved.
Cool slightly, then sift in the flour and ginger.
Add the lemon juice and stir well.

2 Place 3–4 teaspoonfuls of the mixture
on the baking tray, leaving plenty of
room for the biscuits to spread out.

3 Bake in a preheated oven at 160°C
(140°C fan, Gas 3) for about 8 minutes
until the mixture spreads out to form large,
thin, dark golden rounds. While the biscuits
are baking, oil the handles of 4 wooden
spoons.

4 Remove the biscuits from the oven and
leave for 1–2 minutes to firm slightly.

5 Lift a biscuit from the paper using a fish
slice or palette knife, turn the biscuit over
so that the rough side is on the outside, and
wrap around an oiled wooden spoon
handle. Repeat with the remaining biscuits.
Transfer to a wire rack and cool until firm.
Slip from the spoon handles.

6 Continue baking, shaping, and cooling
the remaining mixture in batches.

Coffee éclairs

🌀 **MAKES 10–12**   **263–219 CALS EACH**

butter for greasing

1 quantity choux pastry (see box, below)

1 egg, beaten

300 ml (½ pint) whipping cream, whipped

COFFEE ICING

1 tsp instant coffee

15 g (½ oz) butter

2 tbsp water

90 g (3 oz) icing sugar

1 Butter a baking tray and sprinkle with water. Spoon the choux into a piping bag fitted with a 1 cm (½ in) plain nozzle, pipe into 7 cm (3 in) lengths and brush with beaten egg. Bake in a preheated oven at 220°C (200°C fan, Gas 7) for 10 minutes, then bake at 190°C (170°C fan, Gas 5) for 20 minutes. Split in half and cool on a rack.

2 Spoon the whipped cream into the bottom halves of the éclairs.

3 Make the icing: put the coffee, butter, and water in a bowl over a pan of water. Heat gently until the butter melts. Remove from the heat and beat in the icing sugar. Dip the top half of each eclair in the icing, then place on top of the cream. Leave the icing to cool before serving.

Religieuses

🌀 **MAKES 10**   **366 CALS EACH**

butter for greasing

1 quantity choux pastry (see box, below)

1 egg, beaten

300 ml (½ pint) whipping cream, whipped

1 quantity warm Wicked Chocolate Icing (Chocolate Profiteroles, right)

1 Butter a baking tray and sprinkle with water. Spoon the choux into a piping bag fitted with a 1 cm (½ in) plain nozzle, pipe 10 small and 10 slightly larger balls, and brush with beaten egg. Bake in a preheated oven at 220°C (200°C fan, Gas 7) for 10 minutes, then bake at 190°C (170°C fan, Gas 5) for 20 minutes. Split one side of each bun and cool on a rack.

2 Reserve about 3 tbsp of the whipped cream. Fill the balls with the remaining whipped cream, spooning it in the sides.

3 Dip the tops of a large and small ball in icing. Fit a piping bag with a 1 cm (½ in) star nozzle and pipe the reserved cream on top of the large ball. Gently press the small ball on top of the cream, with the icing facing up. Repeat with the other balls.

Chocolate profiteroles

🌀 **MAKES 12**   **306 CALS EACH**

butter for greasing

1 quantity choux pastry (see box, below)

1 egg, beaten

300 ml (½ pint) whipping cream, whipped

WICKED CHOCOLATE ICING

150 g (5 oz) plain chocolate, chopped

150 ml (¼ pint) double cream

1 Butter a baking tray and sprinkle with water. Put 12 tablespoonfuls of choux o the tray and brush with beaten egg. Bake in a preheated oven at 220°C (200°C fan, Gas 7) for 10 minutes, then bake at 190°C (170°C fan, Gas 5) for 20 minutes. Split eac profiterole in half and cool on a rack.

2 Make the wicked chocolate icing: gen melt the chocolate with the double cream in a bowl over a pan of simmering water, stirring until smooth and shiny (take care not to let it get too hot).

3 Sandwich the profiteroles together wit the whipped cream, place on individu plates, and drizzle with the chocolate icin

Basic choux pastry

1 Put 60 g (2 oz) butter, cut into cubes, into a heavy saucepan with 150 ml (¼ pint) water and heat until the butter melts. Bring to a boil.

2 Remove from the heat and add 75 g (2½ oz) sifted plain flour and a pinch of salt, if preferred. Stir vigorously until the mixture forms a soft ball.

3 Leave to cool slightly, then gradually add 2 lightly beaten eggs, beating well between each addition, to form a smooth, shiny paste.

Opposite, clockwise from top left: Co
éclairs, Religieuses, Chocolate profitero

Index

Cook's notes

All the recipes in this book have been carefully tested to ensure that they produce successful results. When selecting a dish, shopping for ingredients, and making a recipe at home, bear in mind the following essential points.

- Use either all metric or all imperial measurements. Metric and imperial measurements are not interchangeable, so never combine the two.
- Tablespoons are 15 ml, and teaspoons are 5 ml. Spoon measurements are always level unless otherwise stated.
- Eggs are medium unless otherwise stated.
- To replace fresh herbs with dried, substitute 1 teaspoon dried herbs for 1 tablespoon chopped fresh herbs.
- Always preheat the oven before the food goes in to ensure successful results. Recipes in this book have been tested (where appropriate) in a preheated oven.
- No two ovens are alike, so temperatures and cooking times may need to be adjusted to suit your oven.
- When a dish is cooked in the oven, always use the middle shelf unless otherwise stated.
- Calorie counts are approximate and given for guidance only.
- Serving suggestions and accompaniments given with the recipes are optional, for guidance only, and are not included in the calorie counts.

Oven temperatures conversion table

Celsius	Fan	Fahrenheit	Gas	Description
110°	90°	225°	¼	Cool
120°	100°	250°	½	Cool
140°	120°	275°	1	Very slow
150°	130°	300°	2	Very slow
160°	140°	325°	3	Slow
180°	160°	350°	4	Moderate
190°	170°	375°	5	Moderate
200°	180°	400°	6	Moderately hot
220°	200°	425°	7	Hot
230°	210°	450°	8	Hot
240°	220°	475°	9	Very hot

Linear measures conversion table

Metric	Imperial
5 mm	¼ in
1 cm	½ in
2.5 cm	1 in
5 cm	2 in
7 cm	3 in
10 cm	4 in
12 cm	5 in
15 cm	6 in
18 cm	7 in
20 cm	8 in
23 cm	9 in
25 cm	10 in
28 cm	11 in
30 cm	12 in

Volume conversion table

Metric	Imperial
125 ml	4 fl oz
150 ml	¼ pint
175 ml	6 fl oz
250 ml	8 fl oz
300 ml	½ pint
350 ml	12 fl oz
400 ml	14 fl oz
450 ml	¾ pint
500 ml	16 fl oz
550 ml	18 fl oz
600 ml	1 pint
750 ml	1¼ pints
900 ml	1½ pints
1 litre	1¾ pints

Weight conversion table

Metric	Imperial
15 g	½ oz
30 g	1 oz
60 g	2 oz
90 g	3 oz
125 g	4 oz
175 g	6 oz
250 g	8 oz
300 g	10 oz
375 g	12 oz
400 g	13 oz
425 g	14 oz
500 g	1 lb
750 g	1½ lb
1 kg	2 lb

Recipe notes

Page	Recipe name	Comments
230	Bobotie serves 6-8	
312	Singapore noodles with pork. Serves 6	
393	Magic lemon pudding. Serves 4	
310	Classic lasagna serves 8	
442	Chocolate and brandy mousse	
443	Zabaglione	
304	Tuna and fennel pasta bake. Serves 6	
297	Tagliatelli with prawns. Serves 4.	
309	Smoked haddock lasagna. Serves 8	
316	Kedgeree Serves 4	
243	Lemon lamb steaks	
179.	Turkey with soured cream + chives. (+ rice) Serves 4	
165.	Sweet and sour chinese chicken. serves 4-6.	
158	Coq au vin serves 4	
132	Haddock with mushrooms + cream serves 4-6.	
125	Koulibiac. serves 8-10	
110	Tiger prawns with tarragon sauce. serves 4	

Acknowledgments

Mary Berry's Complete Cookbook *(2012 edition)*

Author's Acknowledgments

A huge thank you goes to Lucy Young, my assistant of 21 years, for her dedication throughout the updating of this book. Recipes and liaising with the publishers is down to her, so I thank you Lucy, for your work and friendship. Big thanks too to Lucinda Kaizik for testing the new recipes for the book – we discuss, taste, and discuss some more, to make the recipes foolproof. Many thanks also to our wonderful editor Jeni Wright, who is a joy to work with and second to none – she is the best. And to Dawn Henderson and Laura Nickoll at Dorling Kindersley for masterminding the project, to William Shaw for the photography, and Jane Lawrie, Fergal Connolly, Emma Jane Frost, Laura Fyfe, and Vicki Smallwood, the home economists. I am so lucky to work with such a great team.

Publisher's Acknowledgments

The first (1995) edition of this book was created by Carroll & Brown Limited for Dorling Kindersley.
Thanks to the following people for their help:
Editorial consultant Jeni Wright. **Project editor** Vicky Hanson. **Editors** Jo-Anne Cox, Stella Vayne, Anne Crane, Sophie Lankenau, Trish Shine. **Cookery consultants** Valerie Cipollone and Anne Hildyard. **Art editors** Louise Cameron and Gary Edgar-Hyde. **Designers** Alan Watt, Karen Sawyer, Lucy De Rosa. **Photography** David Murray and Jules Selmes, assisted by Nick Allen and Sid Sideris. **Production** Wendy Rogers and Amanda Mackie. **Food preparation** Eric Treuille, Annie Nichols, Cara Hobday, Sandra Baddeley, Elaine Ngan, assisted by Maddalena Bastianelli, Sarah Lowman. **Additional recipes/Contributors** Marlena Spieler, Sue Ashworth, Louise Pickford, Cara Hobday, Norma MacMillan, Anne Gains. **Nutritional consultant** Anne Sheasby

The second (2003) edition of this book was created by Dorling Kindersley.
Thanks to the following people for their help:
Editorial contributor Norma Macmillan. **Editorial assistance** Hugh Thompson. **DK Picture Library** Claire Bowers and Charlotte Oster. **DK India** Dipali Singh (project editor), Kajori Aikat (editor), Romi Chakraborty (project designer), Rashmi Battoo (designer), Narender Kumar, Rajesh Chibber, Nain Singh Rawat (all DTP), Ira Pande (managing editor), Aparna Sharma (managing art editor). **Nutritional consultant** Wendy Doyle. **Index** Helen Smith

This updated (2012) edition of the book was created by Dorling Kindersley.
Thanks to the following people for their help:
Proofreader Helen Armitage
DK India Sumedha Chopra (assistant picture researcher), Pramod Pant (production co-ordinator)

All images © Dorling Kindersley Limited
Discover more at **www.dkimages.com**